THE WORLD
OF THE
OLD TESTAMENT

THE WORLD OF THE OLD TESTAMENT

Bible Handbook, Volume II

General Editor
A. S. VAN DER WOUDE

Contributors
H. A. BRONGERS, H. H. GROSHEIDE, C. HOUTMAN,
M. J. MULDER, B. J. OOSTERHOFF,
J. P. M. VAN DER PLOEG, A. S. VAN DER WOUDE

Translated by
SIERD WOUDSTRA

WILLIAM B. EERDMANS PUBLISHING COMPANY
GRAND RAPIDS, MICHIGAN

Translated from the Dutch edition, *Bijbels Handboek,* Deel IIa:
Het Oude Testament, © Uitgeversmaatschappij J. H. Kok—
Kampen 1982

Library of Congress Cataloging-in-Publication Data

[Het Oude Testament. English]

The World of the Old Testament / general editor, A. S. van der Woude;
contributors, H. A. Brongers . . . [et al.];
translated by Sierd Woudstra.
    p.   cm.   — (Bible handbook: v. 2)
Translation of: Het Oude Testament.
Includes index.
Cloth ISBN 0-8028-2406-4
Paper ISBN 0-8028-0443-8
1. Bible. O.T.—Introductions.
I. Woude, A. S. van der.
II. Brongers, H. A. (Hendrik Antonie), b. 1904.
III. Series: Bijbels handboek. English; v. 2.
      BS1140.2.093   1989
221.6'1—dc19   88-21381
                                CIP

CONTENTS

I. THE HISTORY OF ISRAEL   **1**
by M. J. Mulder and A. S. van der Woude

A. ISRAEL TO THE TIME OF THE BABYLONIAN CAPTIVITY   **2**
   by M. J. Mulder
     1. Preliminary Questions   **2**
     2. The Beginnings of Israel and Its Religion   **7**
        a. The Patriarchal Era   **7**
        b. Exodus and Conquest   **13**
        c. From the Settlement in Canaan to the Origin of the Monarchy   **21**
     3. The Nation and Its Religion during the Monarchical Period   **34**
        a. The Kingship of Saul   **34**
        b. The Kingship of David   **38**
        c. The Kingship of Solomon   **43**
        d. Israel after the Division of the Kingdom   **49**
        e. Judah after the Division of the Kingdom   **59**

Appendix 1: Chronology of Hebrew Kings   **72**

Appendix 2: Chronology of Egyptian, Assyrian, and Babylonian Kings   **75**

B. ISRAEL FROM THE BABYLONIAN CAPTIVITY TO THE RISE OF
ALEXANDER THE GREAT   **77**
   by A. S. van der Woude
     1. Judah under Babylonian Domination   **77**
     2. Judah under Persian Domination   **79**
        a. Return from Captivity and Rebuilding of the Temple   **79**
        b. Judah in the Period between Zerubbabel and Ezra   **84**
        c. Ezra and Nehemiah   **85**
        d. Judah during the Final Century of Persian Domination   **91**

Appendix: Chronology of Neo-Babylonian and Persian Kings   **95**

II. THE LITERATURE OF THE OLD TESTAMENT   **97**
by H. A. Brongers
Introduction   **98**

A. SECULAR POETRY   **100**
     1. The Work Song   **100**
     2. The Harvest Song   **100**

3. The Drinking Song — 100
4. The Marriage and Love Song — 100
5. The Song of the Watchmen — 101
6. The Song of Victory — 102
7. The Lament — 103
   a. The Individual Lament — 103
   b. The Political Lament — 104
8. The Mocking Song — 107

B. RELIGIOUS POETRY — 110

C. POETIC STORIES — 115
1. The Myth — 115
2. The Fairy Tale — 118
3. The Fable — 119
4. The Saga — 119
   a. The Nature Saga — 120
   b. The Tribal and National Saga — 121
   c. The Name Saga — 121
   d. The Hero Saga — 123
5. The Legend — 123
   a. Sanctuary Legends — 123
   b. Legends Connected with Cultic Objects — 124
   c. Legends Connected with Religious Personalities — 126
   d. Prophet Legends — 132
   e. Martyr Legends — 134
6. The Parable — 136
7. The Anecdote — 136
8. The Novelette — 137
   a. The Joseph Story — 137
   b. Ruth, Jonah, and Esther — 138
   c. Judah and Tamar — 138

D. HISTORICAL LITERATURE — 140
1. Historiography — 140
2. Addresses — 142
   a. Joshua's Address at Shechem — 142
   b. Samuel's Farewell Address — 143
   c. Speech of Sennacherib's Messenger — 143
3. Letters — 144

E. PROPHETIC LITERATURE — 145
1. Prophetic Literature outside Israel — 145
   a. The Admonitions of Ipu-Wer — 145
   b. The Prophecy of Nefer-Rohu — 146
   c. The Wen-Amon Story — 146
   d. The Mari Texts — 147
   e. Oracles — 148
2. The Prophetic Literature of Israel — 149
   a. Prophecies — 150

| | b. | Confessions | **153** |
| | c. | Historical Stories about Prophets | **155** |

F. WISDOM LITERATURE — **157**

G. THE LAWS — **159**
1. The Decalogues — **159**
2. The Book of the Covenant — **161**
3. The Priestly Laws — **162**
4. The Holiness Code — **162**
5. The Deuteronomic Code — **162**

III. THE BOOKS OF THE OLD TESTAMENT — **165**
by C. Houtman, H. H. Grosheide, B. J. Oosterhoff, and J. P. M. van der Ploeg

A. THE PENTATEUCH — **165**
by C. Houtman
1. Name, Division, and Content — **166**
2. Hypotheses about the Origin of the Pentateuch — **166**
   a. Moses Is the Author — **166**
   b. Moses Is Not the Author—the Rise of Historical and Literary Criticism — **168**
   c. The Older Documentary, Fragmentary, Supplementary, and Newer Documentary Hypotheses — **170**
   d. The Newer Documentary Hypothesis Defended in a New Form—Kuenen and Wellhausen — **172**
   e. Developments after Wellhausen — **175**
      (1) Form Criticism—Gunkel and Gressmann
      (2) The Newest Documentary Hypothesis—Smend and Eissfeldt
      (3) Critics of Wellhausen
      (4) Tradition Criticism—von Rad, Noth, Pedersen, and Engnell
   f. Recent Developments — **183**
      (1) Alternatives to the Sources Theory
      (2) The Literary-Functional Approach
3. Evaluation — **186**
   a. Does the Pentateuch Contain Material from Moses? — **186**
   b. The Four-Sources Theory Tested — **188**
      (1) The Argument from the Divine Names
      (2) The Argument from Language and Style
      (3) The Appeal to Discrepancies
      (4) The Appeal to Repetitions
      (5) The Dating of the Sources
4. Final Considerations — **198**
   a. Composition, Purpose, Place, and Date of the Pentateuch — **198**
   b. The Pentateuch as Part of a Great Work, Genesis through 2 Kings — **200**

B. THE HISTORICAL BOOKS — **206**
by H. H. Grosheide
1. Introduction — **206**
2. Joshua — **208**

    3. Judges   **211**
    4. Samuel   **213**
    5. Kings   **215**
    6. Chronicles   **219**
    7. Ezra and Nehemiah   **222**

C. THE PROPHETS   **226**
    by B. J. Oosterhoff
    1. Introduction   **226**
    2. The Major Prophets   **229**
        a. Isaiah   **229**
            (1) Person and Time
            (2) The Book of Isaiah
            (3) Isaiah's Preaching
            (4) Deutero-Isaiah
        b. Jeremiah   **236**
            (1) Person and Time
            (2) The Book of Jeremiah
            (3) Jeremiah's Preaching
        c. Ezekiel   **241**
            (1) Person and Time
            (2) The Book of Ezekiel
            (3) Ezekiel's Preaching
    3. The Minor Prophets   **246**
        a. Hosea   **247**
            (1) Person and Time
            (2) The Book of Hosea
            (3) Hosea's Preaching
        b. Joel   **250**
            (1) Person and Time
            (2) The Book of Joel
            (3) Joel's Preaching
        c. Amos   **252**
            (1) Person and Time
            (2) The Book of Amos
            (3) Amos's Preaching
        d. Obadiah   **254**
            (1) Person and Time
            (2) The Book of Obadiah
            (3) Obadiah's Preaching
        e. Jonah   **255**
            (1) Person and Time
            (2) The Book of Jonah
            (3) The Message of the Book of Jonah
        f. Micah   **257**
            (1) Person and Time
            (2) The Book of Micah
            (3) Micah's Preaching
        g. Nahum   **259**

        (1) Person and Time
        (2) The Book of Nahum
        (3) Nahum's Preaching
    h. Habakkuk **261**
        (1) Person and Time
        (2) The Book of Habakkuk
        (3) Habakkuk's Preaching
    i. Zephaniah **263**
        (1) Person and Time
        (2) The Book of Zephaniah
        (3) Zephaniah's Preaching
    j. Haggai **264**
        (1) Person and Time
        (2) The Book of Haggai
        (3) Haggai's Preaching
    k. Zechariah **266**
        (1) Person and Time
        (2) The Book of Zechariah
        (3) Zechariah's Preaching
    l. Malachi **269**
        (1) Person and Time
        (2) The Book of Malachi
        (3) Malachi's Preaching

D. THE WRITINGS **271**
   by J. P. M. van der Ploeg
    1. Psalms **271**
    2. Job **274**
    3. Proverbs **278**
    4. The Five "Scrolls" **281**
      a. Ruth **281**
      b. Canticles **282**
      c. Ecclesiastes **283**
      d. Lamentations **284**
      e. Esther **285**
    5. Daniel **286**
Maps **290**
Index **296**

ABBREVIATIONS

AB	Anchor Bible
ANET	J. B. Pritchard, ed., *Ancient Near Eastern Texts* (Princeton, 1969³)
AOAT	Alter Orient und Altes Testament
ATD	Das Alte Testament Deutsch
BA	*Biblical Archaeologist*
BASOR	*Bulletin of the American Schools of Oriental Research*
BBB	Bonner biblische Beiträge
BHH	B. Reicke and L. Rost, eds., *Biblisch-historisches Handwörterbuch* I-IV (Göttingen, 1962-1979)
Bibl	*Biblica*
BJRL	*Bulletin of the John Rylands Library*
BKAT	Biblischer Kommentar: Altes Testament
BOT	De Boeken van het Oude Testament
BR	*Biblical Research*
BWANT	Beiträge zur Wissenschaft vom Alten und Neuen Testament
BZAW	Beiheft zur Zeitschrift für die alttestamentliche Wissenschaft
CBQ	*Catholic Biblical Quarterly*
COT	Commentaar op het Oude Testament
Cowley	A. E. Cowley, *Aramaic Papyri of the Fifth Century* B.C. (Oxford, 1923; repr. Osnabrück, 1967)
FRLANT	Forschungen zur Religion und Literatur des Alten und Neuen Testaments
GTT	*Gereformeerd Theologisch Tijdschrift*
HAT	Handbuch zum Alten Testament
HKAT	Handkommentar zum Alten Testament
HTR	*Harvard Theological Review*
HUCA	*Hebrew Union College Annual*
ICC	International Critical Commentary
IDB	G. A. Buttrick, et al., eds., *Interpreter's Dictionary of the Bible* I-IV (Nashville, 1962)
IDBS	K. Crim, et al., eds., *Interpreter's Dictionary of the Bible, Supplementary Volume* (Nashville, 1976)
IEJ	*Israel Exploration Journal*
JAOS	*Journal of the American Oriental Society*
JBL	*Journal of Biblical Literature*
JCS	*Journal of Cuneiform Studies*
JEOL	*Jaarbericht Ex Oriente Lux*
JJS	*Journal of Jewish Studies*
JNES	*Journal of Near Eastern Studies*
JPOS	*Journal of the Palestine Oriental Society*
JQR	*Jewish Quarterly Review*

JSJ	*Journal for the Study of Judaism*
JSOT	*Journal for the Study of the Old Testament*
JSS	*Journal of Semitic Studies*
JTS	*Journal of Theological Studies*
KAI	H. Donner and W. Röllig, *Kanaanäische und aramäische Inschriften* I-III (Wiesbaden, 1962-64)
KAT	Kommentar zum Alten Testament
KeH	Kurzgefasstes exegetisches Handbuch zum Alten Testament
KS	*Kleine Schriften*
LXX	Septuagint
MAOG	*Mitteilungen der altorientalischen Gesellschaft*
MDOG	*Mitteilungen der deutschen Orientgesellschaft*
MT	Massoretic text
NICOT	New International Commentary on the Old Testament
NTT	*Nederlands Theologisch Tijdschrift*
OTL	Old Testament Library
OTS	*Oudtestamentische Studiën*
PEQ	*Palestine Exploration Quarterly*
POT	De Prediking van het Oude Testament
RB	*Revue Biblique*
ST	*Studia Theologica*
SVT	Supplement to Vetus Testamentum
TB	Theologische Bücherei
TDNT	G. Kittel and G. Friedrich, eds., *Theological Dictionary of the New Testament* I-X (Grand Rapids, 1964-1976)
TDOT	G. J. Botterweck and H. Ringgren, eds., *Theological Dictionary of the Old Testament* I- (Grand Rapids, 1974-) (English translation of *TWAT*—see below)
TOTC	Tyndale Old Testament Commentaries
TWAT	G. J. Botterweck and H. Ringgren, eds., *Theologisches Wörterbuch zum Alten Testament* I- (Stuttgart, 1970-) (English translation: *TDOT*—see above)
UF	*Ugarit-Forschungen*
VT	*Vetus Testamentum*
WTJ	*Westminster Theological Journal*
WMANT	Wissenschaftliche Monographien zum Alten und Neuen Testament
ZAW	*Zeitschrift für die alttestamentliche Wissenschaft*
ZDMG	*Zeitschrift der deutschen morgenländischen Gesellschaft*
ZDPV	*Zeitschrift des deutschen Palästinavereins*

I

The History of Israel

by M. J. Mulder and A. S. van der Woude

A. Israel to the Time of the Babylonian Captivity

by M. J. Mulder

1. PRELIMINARY QUESTIONS

I feel constrained to mention some of the problems I faced in rewriting a part of "Geschiedenis van Voor-Azië met Egypte en van Israel tot op de inneming van Babel door de Perzen" (History of the Near East and Egypt and of Israel to the capture of Babylon by the Persians), contributed by C. van Gelderen to the first volume of *Bijbelsch Handboek* (Kampen, 1935), for this new handbook. First of all, I have a certain diffidence with respect to my learned predecessor, who in his article provided a masterly exposition of Israel's history that rightly is still being consulted by many today. In addition, one encounters a variety of preliminary questions whenever writing a history of someone or something. One who writes a "history of Israel" must deal with at least one more significant problem: that of the relationship between "secular history" and "salvation history." What stance should the historian take toward this relationship?

One who, with van Gelderen, seeks to build "on the foundation of Holy Scripture" (p. 72) in the writing of Israel's history must seriously consider the consequences of this standpoint for such a description of the history of Israel and its religion. The time that has passed since van Gelderen did his work has seen not only new discoveries, new archeological finds, and further detailed investigations of many aspects of Israel's history; in these decades it has also become clear to conscientious researchers that many so-called historical givens in the Bible ought to be interpreted differently than they often were, especially by those of "orthodox" persuasion. The tension between the biblical account and the findings of modern historians that has existed in the study of Israel's history, especially since Julius Wellhausen and the scholars who followed his thinking, has—on a different level and often in different hues—also made itself felt among those who wish to stand "on the foundation of Holy Scripture" but who nevertheless attempt to describe honestly the course of Israel's history by using the results and methods of modern science.

In this situation a reproduction of Israel's history is often called for that in certain major respects does not seem to agree with the picture presented by the biblical writers. Such topics, to which we return later, include Israel's stay in Egypt, the Exodus and the invasion of Canaan by only a few tribes, and the figure of Moses and his place in the origin of Israel as a nation and as a religious community. Especially where it concerns the description of the earliest period of Israel's history, the historian faces the question of which method to follow. Should the scholar do no more than repeat the theological viewpoints of the many different biblical authors on Israel's oldest history, with the respectable but naive assumption that the Bible is always right, or may one, while utilizing the criteria of modern historiography and considering all sources, whether sacred or secular, construct a history of Israel that in some measure can stand the test of historiographical criticism? Even if in practice the results of the two methods may be similar, the different starting points are clearly important enough to warrant discussion as a "preliminary question." Van Gelderen in his article barely touched on the question; I wish to raise it here explicitly.

The Old Testament is a collection of books, for the most part written in ancient Hebrew, in which a small nation of several centuries B.C. describes its history, especially that of its association with its God. Israel and, later, the Christian Church valued these books collectively as a holy and divine book containing the history of the human race and of God's people from the time of creation. The books of the Old Testament were not an *arbitrary* collection of ancient liturgies, songs, prophecies, chronicles, stories, legends, sagas, and the like but "the Word of God." Through and in the words of this "Word," the voice of God was heard. The content of these books of the Old Testament was therefore "truth," not only formally but also materially, and also, through a blurring of the differences between the two concepts, "what actually happened." The question was not asked, and often could not be asked, how, when, and why the various literary genres arose and whether what presented itself as history was what really happened.

I do not discuss here the philosophical or theological ramifications of this process, nor will I elaborate on the distinction sometimes made between *Historie* and *Geschichte*. These two German terms are used virtually interchangeably. I do, however, wish to point to the consequences that the idea of "the Word of God" has on writing a history of Israel. In its most extreme form in rabbinic Judaism, this idea led to the view that the entire Torah—in fact, the entire Old Testament—was given by God to Moses on Mount Sinai, so that, strictly speaking, there is no "before" and "after" in Israel's history. Adam was singing Psalm 92 in paradise, and all the chronological data of the Old Testament, carefully added together, indicate that the world has been in existence some 5,700 years since its creation! It took the Christian tradition a long time, with great difficulty, often accompanied by misunderstanding and charges of heresy, to disengage itself from these extreme ideas. In fact only a short while ago, in one of the largest Protestant churches in the Netherlands, one could still witness a fierce argument about the historicity of details in the paradise story.

Over against this view, and as a result of historical-critical investigation of the Bible, especially in the nineteenth century but with forerunners as early as the Renaissance humanists and the Reformation, the idea developed that the Old Testa-

ment is a collection of books from a fairly late period in Israel's history, in which only a few poems and the books of some "writing prophets" can be considered part of Israel's oldest literature. Because the documents dealing with Israel's earliest existence were from a much later period and because the literature of later Israel was not intended to be historically informative in the modern sense of the term, it was thought that their historical reliability was not very high, despite an occasional surfacing of old traditions. The primary motivation behind this modern conception of the historical value of the Old Testament data was to distinguish the belief that the biblical books were divinely inspired and therefore reliable (as maintained by virtually all the orthodox) from the idea that the writings constituting the Old Testament were the product strictly of the human spirit, susceptible to investigation and evaluation according to purely scientific norms and methods. With numerous variations and nuances, the discussion of this burning issue continues to the present.

Developments in the knowledge of the ancient Near East in general and the Old Testament in particular have clearly shown, certainly clearer than in 1935, that these positions do not require an either-or answer. One who regards the Old Testament as "the inspired Word of God" need not remove the Old Testament books written in human words and language from ordinary scientific examination. Elsewhere this handbook reveals how the various books of the Bible were composed in different periods by various people with different intentions, in this way becoming that which brings the divine kerygma. But precisely this great diversity in composition and intent demands that the people who want to use these books for something for which they were not primarily written—namely, for a scientific description of the history of the people of Israel—maintain a highly critical attitude toward the subject and toward their own methods. For instance, they must ask whether something they want to use as documentation for the structure they give to history may indeed be used as such. Does a modern author ever use a seemingly historical event as literary dress to communicate more clearly his or her intention to the readers? Furthermore, in noting a fact or drawing a conclusion, has an author been sufficiently critical—as we understand it—of his or her sources? How reliable were the sources? For example, one who, in dealing with Genesis 1, fails to reckon with the intent of this chapter, with its literary structure, and with the time and milieu of origin but accepts the seven days as historical reality comes into conflict not only with geological facts but also with the intention of the chapter within the whole of Genesis. Modern historians would deny themselves the right to isolate from this chapter anything they would regard as historical reality, that is, anything that they could, in a secular manner and against all known geology, assign a place of its own in a history of the world or of Israel.

For the person who is convinced of the divine authority of the Bible, the question arises regarding the extent to which this authority should influence the use of biblical material in preparing a purely historical sketch of the people and the religion of Israel. Are the biblical data (assuming that they are correctly interpreted) of greater value and historically more reliable than data from other sources? What, for example, is the precise relationship between information obtained from archeology and the literary data of the Bible? May one draw on the former to explain the latter or to identify the latter with the former? Has it been demonstrated, for example, that Israel did not take Jericho in the time in which the book of Joshua places this event nor in the manner in which it describes it, simply because the archeological data in Tell es-Sultan do not agree with what are regarded as the biblical indications of it? The answer to this last question is no, because it remains to be demonstrated that the present mound of ruins called Tell es-Sultan is the same place as the one mentioned by the biblical author. In the vicinity of this tell, which was long identified with the Old Testament Jericho, are still other tells that have not been as thoroughly examined as the one mentioned. Another question that remains is whether we may interpret the data in Joshua as exact, historically reliable facts in the modern sense of the term. Often in the past, results of excavations have all too naively been identified with biblical data.

In this brief survey of the history of Israel, I wish to take the biblical data strictly at their face value.

Whether the picture so acquired agrees with what happened in the distant past remains, meanwhile, an open question. Despite all efforts to be as objective as possible in arranging facts and indicating connections, the writing of history remains a very subjective enterprise. Historians attempt to make connections that in reality may never have existed or functioned, or they overlook relationships that were obvious to people living at the time. An additional, complicating factor for the history we attempt to write is the large gaps in our knowledge of important periods in Israel's national existence (notwithstanding the numerous publications in the past and the present that have attempted to deal with such gaps). Israel narrated its own history—not unlike the manner of history writing in vogue in the world of the Near East of that time—in a particular context, namely, praise and faith. One who shares the praise and the faith of Israel but who, at the same time, wants to write a scholarly and responsible essay about Israel's history must seek to be honest toward sources and data, confident (but not with the arrogance of fundamentalism) that the Bible is yet true and will remain true.

From what has been said so far, the reader can correctly infer that in this study I will make critical use, not only of the biblical data, but also of archeological, literary, and other extrabiblical data. Israel's genesis and continuation as a people have indeed carried a great weight of meaning for many, but the fact remains that little of an exact nature about Israel has come down to us from antiquity, because Israel played only a modest role among the peoples living around the Mediterranean. The name Israel is only very rarely found in documents from before the monarchical period, in letters, on steles, and in the literature of the surrounding nations. Even in the monarchical period there are few references. Some historians even doubt that anything can be said with certainty about premonarchical Israel. Do such assertions undervalue or misconstrue the available data?

In my judgment, the data from the Old Testament, though cast in the form of faith testimonies and though they should primarily be valued and interpreted as such, are especially helpful in discovering the outlines of the picture of Israel's origins, however the name Israel may have arisen and should be interpreted. For example, although the name and figure of Moses occur nowhere outside the Old Testament and very little outside the Pentateuch, we cannot therefore regard Moses as someone of dubious historical reality or even as a fictional personality. A person who was of tremendous significance for a particular group of people may have remained a virtual unknown outside that group, perhaps because nations were more willing to keep silent about the disgraceful in their own history than to record the illustrious in the history of others. Particularly the kings of the great powers—Egypt, Assyria, and Babylonia—were accustomed to speak in glowing terms of their triumphs and to gloss over their defeats. Though Israel's record of its own history in the Old Testament is religiously colored, the Israelites were often painfully objective in disclosing their own weaknesses and failures. This openness lends a measure of reliability and practical usefulness to the historical information in the Old Testament. In fact, in my judgment, Israel's record of many significant points in its own history is even more reliable and useful than, for example, the bragging words about Israel by Assyrian kings.

In addition to this principal preliminary question, I mention a few points of lesser importance. First, this survey will not cover the history of the Near East and Egypt, since this topic is treated in volume 1 of this series (*The World of the Bible,* 1986). The world surrounding Israel will be discussed only where it impinges directly on Israel's history. Second, due to practical considerations, this survey extends to and includes the period of Judah's Babylonian captivity. Third, the history of Israel's religion occupies much of our attention in the chapter, also for a practical reason. A historical survey such as follows below does not aim first of all at providing an exact list of dates with facts and data of all sorts about won or lost battles. I intend, rather, to provide a measure of perspective on Israel in the light of its spiritual history. In such a history, socioeconomic, sociological, cultural, and religious factors play a large role. But the religious factors are particularly important because an outline of the history of Israel implies— for the person who believes in the God of Israel— the recognition of a divine secret, which as a guiding and directing power constitutes the back-

ground of that history. From this perspective, ancient Israel recorded its history; guided by that same perspective, we do best not to detach Israel's history from its religious history.

It is impossible and even unnecessary to provide an extensive summary of the histories of Israel that have been written in recent decades. It may be of help to readers, however, if we mention a few recent works that have had an impact on the description of the history of ancient Israel and have left their traces in this survey. The volumes of Rudolf Kittel were long the leading work, because here for the first time archeological material assumed an important role in the writing of history. Martin Noth's pioneering work in the early 1950s, *Geschichte Israels* (first translated in 1958 as *The History of Israel*), marked a change of direction in the methods of writing Israel's history. Noth views the Old Testament as humanly and historically determined, but he does not disparage that which transcends history in the Old Testament, as was occasionally done by scholar from the historical-critical school of the previous century. The focus of Noth's study is the earliest period of Israel's history. Basing his work on the thorough studies of his great teacher Albrecht Alt, he accepts the existence of a sacral league of tribes, or amphictyony, called Israel. By assuming such an amphictyony, one perhaps could shed some light on Israel's prehistory because in this league old traditions lived on, such as the deliverance from Egypt, the covenant at Sinai, and the like. Yet these traditions have little real value for a portrayal of the earliest history of the people of Israel. We shall see that Noth's ideas about the amphictyony have been sharply attacked, but the impulses provided by the studies of Alt and Noth have made their impact felt even outside the study of Israel's history.

Besides these pioneering works, other researchers have published studies about the history of Israel that, though more traditional in outlook, have opened up new perspectives for the quest. I mention here the influence of the work of William Foxwell Albright and scholars from his school such as Cyrus H. Gordon and especially John Bright. The thrust of their work is that great value ought to be attributed to the biblical traditions concerning the earliest era of Israel's national existence and that these traditions ought to be placed in the framework of written and unwritten documents from the world around Israel, such as the Mari Texts, the Nuzi Tablets, the Amarna Letters, the lists of pharaohs, and others. In the work of Bright the formative period of the entity Israel is clearly shifted from the amphictyony—though he too supports this conception—to the period of the Exodus and the entrance into the "Promised Land." In this way the figure of Moses, in Noth virtually no more than a name without a body, becomes a prominent personality. The method of tradition criticism, as it was used by Noth and before him by Hugo Gressmann, seems easily overruled. Siegfried Herrmann contends that it cannot be so easily overruled because the historical assessment of every Old Testament source ought to be preceded by a literary evaluation. In dealing with the problems raised by tradition criticism, Herrmann clearly goes a different way than Noth, as is shown, for instance, by his picture of Moses.

More in line with those who, following Albright and Bright, attach great value to the preliterary traditions of Israel in the context of the results of extrabiblical finds, Roland de Vaux has written a detailed study of Israel's history. (De Vaux actually completed only the first volume, with the second one appearing in part after his untimely death in 1971, the two volumes extending to the period of the judges.) De Vaux himself declares emphatically that, in his history writing, he followed the method of Noth, or what he has called a *voie moyenne* between Bright and Noth.

LITERATURE

Metzger's study provides a useful overview of Israel's history, as does Georg Fohrer, *Geschichte Israels*. Beek's small volume is sensitively written and has gone through several printings in German and English translation. Gunneweg's study is more elaborate. The essays of Otto Eissfeldt in *The Cambridge Ancient History*[3], II/2, and those of Abraham Malamat and Eissfeldt in volumes 2 and 3 of *Fischer Weltgeschichte: Die altorientalischen Reiche* are particularly valuable. The work edited by Hayes and Miller represents an international collaboration in the area of Israel's history. Besides reviewing a vast amount of recent data and the results of historical studies, it also contains exten-

sive bibliographies. The reader will find there background information about the starting points that are determinative for the newer and most recent developments in the historiography concerning Israel.

W. F. Albright, *From the Stone Age to Christianity* (Baltimore, 1946[2]).

———, *Archaeology and the Religion of Israel* (Baltimore, 1953[3]).

A. Alt, *Kleine Schriften zur Geschichte des Volkes Israel* I-III (München, 1953-59).

M. A. Beek, *A Short History of Israel* (London, 1963).

H. H. Ben-Sasson, ed., *A History of the Jewish People* (London, 1976).

J. Bright, *A History of Israel* (Philadelphia, 1981[3]).

F. F. Bruce, *Israel and the Nations* (Grand Rapids, 1969).

H. Cancik, *Grundzüge der hethitischen und alttestamentlichen Geschichtsschreibung* (Wiesbaden, 1976).

G. Cornfield and G. J. Botterweck, DTV-Lexicon, *Die Bibel und ihre Welt* I-VI (München, 1972).

F. M. Cross, *Canaanite Myth and Hebrew Epic* (Cambridge, MA, 1973).

H. Donner and W. Röllig, *Kanaanäische und aramäische Inschriften* I-III (Wiesbaden, 1962-64) (cited as *KAI* with the number of the text).

H. Donner, *Geschichte des Volkes Israel und seiner Nachbarn in Grundzügen, I: Von den Anfängen bis zur Staatenbildungszeit* (Göttingen, 1984).

O. Eissfeldt, "Syrien und Palästina vom Ausgang des 11. bis zum Ausgang des 6. Jahrhunderts v. Chr.," in *Fischer Weltgeschichte: Die altorientalischen Reiche* III (Frankfurt, 1966) 135-219.

———, *Kleine Schriften* I-V (Tübingen, 1962-73).

G. Fohrer, *History of Israelite Religion* (Nashville, 1972).

———, *Geschichte Israels* (Heidelberg, 1977).

K. Galling, ed., *Textbuch zur Geschichte Israels* (Tübingen, 1979[3]).

C. van Gelderen, "Geschiedenis van Voor-Azië met Egypte en van Israel tot op de inneming van Babel door de Perzen," in *Bijbelsch Handboek* I (Kampen, 1935) 69-198.

J. C. L. Gibson, *Textbook of Syrian Semitic Inscriptions, I: Hebrew and Moabite Inscriptions* (Oxford, 1971); *II: Aramaic Inscriptions* (Oxford, 1975); *III: Phoenician Inscriptions* (Oxford, 1982).

C. H. Gordon, *The Ancient Near East* (New York, 1965[3]).

H. Gressmann, *Mose und seine Zeit* (Göttingen, 1913).

———, *Die Anfänge Israels* (Göttingen, 1922[2]).

A. H. J. Gunneweg, *Geschichte Israels bis Bar Kochba* (Stuttgart, 1984[5]).

J. H. Hayes and J. M. Miller, eds., *Israelite and Judaean*

History (Philadelphia, 1977) (indispensable book for background information and comprehensive bibliographies).

S. Herrmann, *A History of Israel in Old Testament Times* (Philadelphia, 1981²) (see the review of the 1st edition by C. H. J. de Geus, *NTT* 30 [1976] 50-70).

H. Jagersma, *A History of Israel in the Old Testament Period* (Philadelphia, 1983).

———, *Van Alexander tot Bar Kochba* (Kampen, 1985).

K. Jeppesen and B. Otzen, eds., *The Productions of Time: Tradition History in Old Testament Scholarship* (Sheffield, 1984).

O. Keel and M. Küchler, *Orte und Landschaften der Bibel: Ein Handbuch und Studien Reiseführer zum Heiligen Land* I-IV (Zürich-Göttingen, 1982ff.).

R. Kittel, *Geschichte des Volkes Israel* I (Stuttgart, 1932⁷); II (Stuttgart, 1925⁷); III (Stuttgart, 1929²).

H.-J. Kraus, *Geschichte der historisch-kritischen Erforschung des Alten Testaments* (Neukirchen-Vluyn, 1969²).

J. K. Kuntz, *The People of Ancient Israel* (New York, 1974).

A. Malamat, "Syrien-Palästina in der zweiten Hälfte des 2. Jahrtausends," in *Fischer Weltgeschichte: Die altorientalischen Reiche* II (Frankfurt, 1965) 177-221.

A. Malamat and I. Eph'al, eds., *The World History of the Jewish People, IV: The Age of the Monarchies: 1: Political History; 2: Culture and Society* (Jerusalem, 1979).

M. Metzger, *Grundriss der Geschichte Israels* (Neukirchen-Vluyn, 1977⁴).

J. M. Miller, *The Old Testament and the Historian* (Philadelphia, 1976).

M. Noth, *The Old Testament World* (London, 1966).

———, *The History of Israel* (New York, 1960²).

———, *Aufsätze zur biblischen Landes- und Altertumskunde* I-II (Neukirchen-Vluyn, 1971).

J. B. Pritchard, ed., *Ancient Near Eastern Texts Relating to the Old Testament* (Princeton, 1969³) (cited as *ANET*).

———, *The Ancient Near East in Pictures* (Princeton, 1969²) (cited as *ANEP,* followed by the number of the picture).

J. Rogerson, *Old Testament Criticism in the Nineteenth Century: England and Germany* (Philadelphia, 1985).

J. Van Seters, *In Search of History: Historiography in the Ancient World and the Origins of Biblical History* (New Haven, 1983).

J. A. Soggin, *Old Testament and Oriental Studies* (Rome, 1975).

———, *Introduction to the Old Testament* (London, 1976).

———, *A History of Israel: From the Beginnings to the Bar Kochba Revolt, A.D. 135* (Philadelphia, 1985).

R. de Vaux, *The Early History of Israel* (Philadelphia, 1978).

J. Wellhausen, *Prolegomena to the History of Israel* (Cleveland, 1965).

———, *Grundrisse zum Alten Testament* (München, 1965).

D. Winton Thomas, ed., *Archeology and Old Testament Study* (Oxford, 1967).

D. J. Wiseman, ed., *Peoples of Old Testament Times* (Oxford, 1973).

See also articles in encyclopedias and other reference works such as *Biblisch-Historisches Handwörterbuch, Cambridge Ancient History, 'Enṣiqlōpedīya Miqrā'ît, The Interpreter's Dictionary of the Bible,* and *The International Standard Bible Encyclopedia* (rev. ed. 1979-1988).

2. THE BEGINNINGS OF ISRAEL AND ITS RELIGION

a. The Patriarchal Era

The origin of the people of Israel and of their name is a matter about which we are completely in the dark. The name Israel is used in the Old Testament in a variety of ways: (1) as another name of the patriarch Jacob (Gen. 32:29 [28]; etc.), (2) as a designation of the league of the twelve tribes after settlement in Canaan, and (3) as a name for the northern kingdom after the division of Solomon's realm. This name acquired, therefore, a personal, a sacral, and a political aspect, which does not facilitate our understanding when it occurs, either in the Old Testament itself or in the writings of modern historians. Unless indicated otherwise, by *Israel* I mean the whole nation before the division and the northern kingdom of the ten tribes after the division of the kingdom.

We also have the term *Hebrew(s),* which in the Old Testament is found especially in the stories about the early beginnings of Israel and once is even attached to the name of Abraham (Gen. 14:13). It became a name of honor for the Jews (see Jdt. 10:12; 4 Macc. 5:2); even today the language of the people is known as Hebrew.

Nevertheless the term does not have enough of an ethnic content to be suitable as a designation for the people of Israel in its early period. The name Hebrew usually stands for someone in the position of a slave, so that it is more a sociological than an ethnic designation (see, e.g., Exod. 2:11; 21:2; Deut. 15:12; Jer. 34:9, 14).

Not until the people of Israel are in Canaan do we have extrabiblical historical and archeological data about them. Even so, scholars are generally agreed that the people, or at least some part of them, must have had a prehistory outside Canaan. This view is in part based on the materials for that history contained in the Old Testament. Reading the book of Genesis, one notices not only that the author seeks to place Israel's history in the context of the history of the whole world (Genesis 1–11) but also that he views Israel as an organic part of all the nations of the world (see the so-called table of nations in ch. 10). In the genealogy in Genesis 10, Israel articulates its own perception of the coherence and of the differences among the many nations. The division of humankind into Semites, Hamites, and Japhethites has for centuries dominated the ethnic distinction of people in Christendom. Racial discrimination on the basis of this Old Testament division, despite the intention of the Old Testament itself, unfortunately still persists in certain parts of the world. One of the many remarkable items in the table of nations is that Canaan, the land in which Israel would live for many years, is regarded as a descendant of Ham, though Israel's ancestors, together with Elamites, Assyrians, Arameans, and others, are included among the Semites. It is clear that this list of nations is not based on strict ethnological or linguistic principles. The "language of Canaan," the precursor of Hebrew, was a Semitic language. Ethnologically it is problematic whether the Assyrians are to be regarded as an Indo-European rather than a Semitic race, even though they spoke a Semitic language.

Whatever the precise situation, Israel's patriarchs are from Semitic stock (see also Gen. 11:10–32) and are therefore not natives of Canaan. One might say that the Semites, as a kind of third power from the east, wedged themselves in between the two great power blocs in the north and the south, the Japhethites and the Hamites (to which also Egypt belonged!). The account of the settlement of Israel's oldest patriarch in the Promised Land might be viewed as an indication of this wedgelike push of the Semites from the east to the west in the second millennium B.C.

Outside the Old Testament we learn something about the situation in the area of Syria and Palestine in the second millennium B.C. from documents, letters, reports, archeological data, and the like coming from various places and times in the Near East. It is assumed from this data that in the Middle Bronze Age (ca. 2200–1550 B.C.) there was a cultural revival in the Near East due to Amorite expansion which expressed itself in a powerful urban civilization. In the first half of the second millennium, a dynasty was established in Babylon, one of whose kings, Hammurabi (often regarded as a contemporary of Abraham on the basis of Genesis 14), has become very familiar, especially because of his law code (see ill. 13). There was a virtually uninterrupted development and flourishing of Canaanite (or Amorite) culture in the Middle Bronze II period (ca. 2000–1550 B.C.).

Data about this period are furnished by the thousands of clay tablets that have been uncovered since the excavations in 1933 and following years in Mari (Tell el-Hariri), a city on the Euphrates in Syria. These tablets cover approximately the period 1765–1694 B.C. They are especially important for the insight they provide into the sociopolitical importance of the nomads. In addition to the Mari correspondence, the recently discovered Ebla library promises to be highly important for a better understanding of this period. Ebla (Tell Mardikh; see ill. 1) is situated about 50 kilometers (30 mi.) south of Aleppo.

Besides the Hittite texts from Boghazköy and the Ugaritic tablets from Ras Shamra, various Egyptian documents from the Eighteenth to the Twentieth Dynasties are important for our understanding of Syria and Palestine in the second millennium. Hieroglyphics on buildings and monuments in Thebes, capital for the pharaohs of the Eighteenth Dynasty, mention campaigns in Syria and Palestine (*ANET*, 232–64). The steles of Seti I and Ramses II at Beth-shean can also be mentioned (*ANET*, 255). There is also the correspondence in Akkadian from the capital of Pharaoh Amenhotep IV (Akhenaten, 1349–

1334), Akhetaten, now called Tell el-Amarna, which is situated on the Nile between Memphis and Thebes. The Amarna Letters, exchanged between Amenhotep III and IV and their vassals in Syria and Palestine, provide a good picture of the sociopolitical situation of that area (*ANET,* 483–90; see ill. 8). The Egyptian execration texts, directed against Egypt's enemies, including those in Syria and Palestine, are a few centuries earlier, as is the Story of Sinuhe, a historical short story recounting the experiences of an Egyptian officer in Syria and Palestine who had fled there (*ANET,* 328–29 and 18-22). In addition, some of the papyrus texts give some idea of the commerce between Egypt and Canaan. From the Nineteenth Dynasty we can mention Papyrus Anastasi III and Anastasi VI. The latter tells of bedouins (the Shosu) arriving from Edom into the Nile Delta searching for pasture (*ANET,* 258–59). Also important is Papyrus Anastasi I (*ANET,* 475–79). For more detailed information about these and similar sources, the reader may refer to what is said elsewhere in this volume on this subject and to the extensive information in Hayes and Miller (see Literature for section 1 above).

Genesis, a book with a literary character and, according to many scholars, composed from sources that are much later than the characters they describe, does not readily provide the modern historian with historical points of contact. The reason is not only that the book contains lively popular tales, is laced with popular etiologies, and is often thematically influenced by certain names but especially that it is concerned with confirming the position of Israel in the Promised Land. Given this emphasis, it is not surprising that— with the exception of the enigmatic fourteenth chapter—there is little in Genesis that offers concrete points of contact with secular world history. Other than its mention of an unidentified pharaoh and a few other items, the book is concerned with justifying Israel's worshiping at and near originally Canaanite shrines such as Shechem, Bethel, and Hebron. Consequently, the reports that the tradition makes about Israel's beginnings are very difficult to verify historically and often impossible to corroborate with data from the surrounding world. An example is the Nuzi Tablets, discovered at the present Yorghan Tepe in Iraq. They show that a married woman who remained childless had a contractual obligation to supply her husband with a substitute. If a son should be born afterward, the slave and her child could not be sent away. This reference supposedly explains Abraham's reluctance to send away Hagar and Ishmael (Gen. 21:10–11). However, because certain practices and customs in the Old Testament are found in many specific periods, such a parallel says little about the historicity of Genesis. The importance of this and similar parallels is often highly exaggerated.

Genesis reports that Abraham, before entering the Promised Land, came from Haran in northwestern Mesopotamia. This city is situated in the area of the upper course of the Balikh, a tributary of the Euphrates, not far from Edessa, the later center of Syrian Christianity. In the Old Testament this area is also called Paddan-Aram (Gen. 25:20; 28:2, 5–7; etc.) or Aram-Naharaim ("Mesopotamia," 24:10; Deut. 23:5 [4]; Ps. 60:2 [superscription]; etc.). Both names contain *Aram,* which has given rise to the conjecture that Abraham and his clan must have been of Aramean descent. Deuteronomy 26:5 might strengthen this conjecture, for there it is said that the Israelites, in bringing the offering of the firstfruits before the altar, had to confess: "A wandering Aramean was my father."

Yet there is another old tradition, according to which Haran was nothing more than a temporary residence on the way to Canaan for Abraham and those with him. In this tradition Ur of the Chaldeans is called the birthplace of Abraham (Gen. 11:28, 31; etc.). It is often assumed that this Ur was the center of ancient Sumer in the south of Mesopotamia that bore the name Ur. Nowadays there is greater caution in making this identification. In the Old Testament, not only is the term *Chaldeans* sometimes a designation for people who elsewhere are called Arameans, but also the reading Ur is not entirely certain. According to the Septuagint, Abraham and his retinue left "*the land of the Chaldeans*" in order to arrive in Haran (v. 28). At any rate, tradition closely connects Abraham with Aram. Later, however, we also find that he had connections with southern parts of the Near East. Genesis 25:1–4, 12–18 offers lists of descendants of Abraham that underline his contact with the Arabian world through Ishmael. It is doubtful, though, that we have here a chronological order (i.e., from Aram to Arabia).

Apart from the question whether the names Abraham, Isaac, and Jacob are names of historical persons who were the forefathers of Israel or whether they actually represent clans, the time periods allotted to the recorded events also offer insuperable difficulties. It is now recognized that many numbers in the Old Testament function as symbols as well as simple indicators of some measurement. Figures such as 3, 5, 7, 12, and 40 play an important role. On that basis the age of the three patriarchs can be explained as follows: Abraham's 175 years $= 7 \times 5^2$, Isaac's 180 years $= 5 \times 6^2$, and Jacob's 147 years $= 3 \times 7^2$. There is here a descending series (7, 5, 3) and an ascending series (5, 6, 7), one starting and the other ending with the number 7. As regards the dating of the patriarchal period, two groups of researchers can be distinguished. One group favors a fairly late dating of the patriarchs, placing them in the Amarna period (14th century B.C.) and pointing out that Moses belonged to the fourth generation after Jacob. The other group dates the patriarchs within the Middle Bronze Age, specifically about 1850 to 1750 B.C.

The setting in which the Old Testament authors have placed the history of the patriarchs shows that there must long have been an awareness of a close interconnection among the Semitic tribes and peoples. It is impossible to trace the sources of that awareness. The various genealogies demonstrate, moreover, the remarkable role of the number 12. In addition to the twelve sons of Jacob, Genesis 36:10–14 mentions the twelve sons of Esau, the brother of Jacob, who must have lived in the south and southeast of Palestine. Nahor, one of the three sons of Terah, had twelve sons, who with their descendants populated northern Syria and upper Mesopotamia. Furthermore, Ishmael, the son of Hagar, Abraham's concubine, had twelve sons, who occupied a large part of the Arabian peninsula. In the northwestern part of this area settled six sons of Keturah, also a wife of Abraham. Finally, mention should be made of Lot, a nephew of Abraham, who was the father of the Ammonites and the Moabites. Perhaps such records indicate that, in a restricted ethnic setting,

the period of the patriarchs must have been relatively family oriented and that, besides Israel, an Aramean clan or collection of clans that initially seemed doomed to failure (Deut. 26:5–9), other clans grew into "nations."

The Israelites used a particular type of narrative for telling their posterity how they became a nation. H. Gunkel called the stories in Genesis "sagas," by which he referred to the ancient mode of orally passing on stories. Particularly striking in these stories is the fact that most of the events in the life of the patriarchs and their families happen in or near familiar shrines. Genesis also emphasizes the wandering existence of the patriarchs. It is possible that the journey narratives are intended to form a link between the narratives of events that happened near shrines.

As shown by T. L. Thompson, the important task now is to trace the function of the patriarchal narratives at the time that they became literature, without overstressing their historicity. Whatever the results of such study, the wandering life of the patriarchs points to an endless search for fertile pasture. The term *transhumance,* referring to the seasonal search for new pasture in winter and summer, is often used in this connection. The term *dimorphic society* has also become popular, referring to a society in which the nomads who wander with their flocks in a particular region provide the food reserves for the people settled in cities or villages in that region. These forms of dimorphic societies existed especially in a strip approximately 30 kilometers (20 mi.) wide between the civilized world and large desert areas. This dimorphic zone, roughly corresponding to the areas that receive about 200 millimeters (8 in.) of rain annually, stretches like a crescent across the Near East, and in Palestine is an area in which the patriarchs often lived.

The abundant material from Mari offers useful analogies for the period of mid-second-millennium Palestine. In general, despite differences in race and language, a society made up of nomads, farmers, and townspeople presented a harmonious picture, which is confirmed by the patriarchal narratives. This newer view differs from older pictures that assume a wavelike inundation of the civilized world by nomads invading or slowly infiltrating from the deserts. A simple opposition of civilized land versus desert is unsatisfactory. Furthermore, archeological discoveries have demonstrated that, in the second millennium B.C. and afterward, the Negeb, for example, must have been much more fertile than at present. For centuries, overgrazing and erosion have had their destructive impact. Genesis 13 describes a discussion between Abraham and Lot about finding the best pastures for their flocks and herds. Lot chooses the now infertile area around the Dead Sea. Abraham, according to chapter 23, bought land near Hebron. Isaac had wells for his cattle in the Negeb, or at least quarreled about them (ch. 26). Though according to some reports Jacob obtained part of his possessions in Upper Mesopotamia, in the Promised Land the boundaries of his territory were still fluid, for example in relation to Esau/Edom. The stories in Genesis localize the patriarchs in the dimorphic zone. The coastal strip was neither then nor later a favorite area for Israel. The fear of coast and sea may have had internal as well as external causes. The latter included the threat of the Sea Peoples, among whom were the Philistines, who for many years would be fierce enemies of Israel.

As already mentioned, many patriarchal stories are localized at family shrines: Shechem (Gen. 12:6; 35:4), Hebron and Mamre (13:18), and Bethel (13:3-4; 31:13). Characteristic of these shrine stories are the patriarchs' experience of an appearance of God that has a deep impact on their later life. These stories speak of "the God of the fathers"—for instance, "the God of my (your) father Abraham" (26:24 [attributed to J]; 28:13; 31:42 [E]), "the God of my father Isaac" (28:13; cf. 31:5, 29), and "the God of my father Nahor" (31:53). Genesis 31:53 shows that such designations of the deity had a special significance: At the making of a covenant between Jacob and his uncle Laban it is said, "The God of Abraham and the God of Nahor, the God of their father, judge between us." In 1929, Alt suggested that these gods were connected not with specific sanctuaries but with certain persons or clans. Alt's analysis of the data about the phrase "God of my [your, etc.] father" showed that these gods at first had no proper names but were associated with the person who experienced the manifestation of the deity for the first time, for example, "the Shield of Abraham"

(15:1), "the Fear of Isaac" (31:42, 53), and "the Mighty One of Jacob" (49:24). This hypothesis, which assumes the historicity of the patriarchs, is based on "gods of the fathers" that are found much later among desert people, such as the Nabateans between the Dead Sea and the Red Sea and the Palmyrenes in the desert between Damascus and the Euphrates. Many desert dwellers worshiped gods that were named after the individuals to whom they appeared for the first time. In a later phase, gods could be combined with each other or associated with certain sanctuaries. Alt distinguishes between the gods of the fathers and deities associated with shrines and other places, the so-called *elim*.

The second striking element in the patriarchal narratives is the name of God. Almost never is he given the name YHWH, the tetragrammaton. Instead, he is called El. It is therefore not without reason that many scholars labeled the patriarchs El worshipers. Genesis 14, a chapter that remains problematic and whose historic framework remains uncertain, recounts the meeting of Abraham with the Canaanite king Melchizedek of Salem, a place often thought to be Jerusalem. The king meets Abraham with bread and wine after Abraham's victory over the combined armies of Amraphel and his allies. Melchizedek is called priest of *el elyon*. The name of this god, also found on some inscriptions elsewhere in the Near East, is possibly a combination of two originally distinct divine names, of which El is Canaanite or generally Semitic. It is not strange for a king of a Canaanite city to worship El. It is unusual, however, for a patriarch to swear emphatically by this God with the words, "I have sworn to YHWH, El Elyon" (v. 22). The worship of El by the patriarchs is mentioned elsewhere in Genesis: *el shadday* in 17:1; *el olam* in 21:33; and *el bethel* in 31:13; 35:7 (see also *el roi* in 16:13).

In Exodus 6:2-3, a passage attributed to P, God says to Moses, "I am YHWH. I appeared to Abraham, to Isaac, and to Jacob, as El Shadday." In 3:13-15, attributed to E, this story is told in somewhat different form. If Israel asks Moses who the god is who sent him, he is to answer, "YHWH, the God of your fathers, the God of Abraham, the God of Isaac, and the God of Jacob, has sent me to you" (v. 15). From this passage it can be inferred that, though according to later tradition YHWH must have been the God of the patriarchs, he was known to them not by this name but by other names. Of these, El was undoubtedly the best known. On the basis of the later faith of Israel, a connection resting on continuity is made between the two divine names. If one could look at this faith from the outside, one would have to say that "the God of the fathers" and YHWH were two unrelated deities who only much later, at the time of Moses, were united. It is sometimes suggested that the worship of El, who in the Ugaritic texts is the older, fatherly but docile, high god, was originally completely like that of YHWH, but this hypothesis is unacceptable. From such a suggestion it would be only a short step to an original Semitic monotheism.

The data in Genesis and elsewhere in the Old Testament, however, are too complicated for such a simplification. It should be noted that the tradition always places the meetings of the patriarchs with El in Palestine, never in Mesopotamia or in the Arabian desert. Also, such designations as Fear of Isaac (or perhaps Kinsman of Israel), Mighty One or Defender of Jacob, and Shield of Abraham are too personal and too closely linked to a particular group to be lumped together. The tradition maintains emphatically and correctly that the fathers worshiped "other gods" (Josh. 24:2, 14–15; cf. Gen. 35:2). In that case, however, it should also be possible to put them in a historical framework. In other words, in their clan the patriarchs must have had greater historical reality than an overly zealous critique sometimes has been willing to grant. Still, there can be differences of opinion about the rise and utilization of a variety of religious ideas in Israel. One theme is the promise of the land to the descendants of Abraham (Genesis 15). Though from the world around Israel examples are known of a deity's promising land and descendants, such examples are not sufficiently cogent to conclude that, historically speaking, the promise to Abraham might not be a later confession in Israel.

It is almost impossible to describe the characteristics of the Israelite cult in the days of the patriarchs. Any fixed shrines with altars must have mainly been places in which one encountered God by a tree or stone (see Gen. 13:18; 14:13; 18:1;

28:11–22; etc.). Possibly those trees and stones had long been Canaanite shrines, as is suggested by the story of Bethel (ch. 28). The patriarchal era offers vague historical contours that are carried forward in the later witnesses of the Old Testament. In these witnesses Abraham is portrayed as the prototype of obedience (ch. 22). Like the whole nation later on, he is called (12:1–3) and elected (15:1–6) by God. His descendants Isaac and Jacob are part of that line. In the biblical tradition they are genealogically closely related, but nowadays it is assumed that at first they were independent tribes and only later joined together. The following example shows the difficulty of the questions that are faced by the historian. The stories about Abraham, though connected with various places, nevertheless cover a large area. The Isaac stories, which in many respects parallel those of Abraham (cf. ch. 26 with 12:10–20; ch. 20; 21:22–34), happen especially at Beer-sheba and the south, or the Negeb. Nevertheless, precisely in the later northern kingdom, Isaac and Beer-sheba enjoy a special reputation (Amos 5:5; 7:9, 16; 8:14; cf. 1 Sam. 8:2). Such verses suggest that groups that once lived around Beer-sheba later moved to the north, taking with them the Isaac traditions.

The stories about Jacob and his son Joseph conclude the history of the patriarchs. Here the historical questions are as different as the question of the precise dating. One Old Testament view of Jacob portrays him as a deceiver (see Gen. 27:36; Jer. 9:3 [4]; Hos. 12:3), and so within the cycle of Jacob narratives his deception of his father, Isaac, and his brother, Esau, is mentioned (Genesis 27). Because of these deceptions Jacob is forced to flee to his uncle Laban in Aram, where, through Rachel and Leah and their maidservants, he becomes twelve tribes. Here, too, the origin of Israel's tribal league is located outside the boundaries of Canaan, namely, in Aram. The journey of Jacob and his people from northern Mesopotamia to Canaan results not only in a covenant between Jacob and Laban but also in a number of Transjordanian tales (Peniel, the struggle between Jacob and God at the Jabbok, where Jacob is called Israel [ch. 32], etc.) that have a remarkable literary structure. From Jacob's stay in Transjordan and the later occupation of this area by the tribes of the firstborn Reuben and of Manasseh and Ephraim (the sons of Joseph), it has sometimes been inferred that there may have been an invasion from the land east of the Jordan to Shechem (33:18–20; 35:2, 4). Particularly Manasseh, who, like Jacob, is connected with the Arameans (see 31:20, 24, 42; Deut. 26:5 [?]; 1 Chr. 7:14), apparently played a role in this movement.

The beautifully told history of Joseph (Genesis 37–50), which is regarded as belonging to the older forms of wisdom literature (von Rad) and also literarily differs from the patriarchal narratives, brings us close to the subject of the next section: Israel's stay in Egypt. In this short story every historically recoverable feature is so artistically covered up that it is impossible to date Joseph or to identify the pharaoh mentioned in the story. The Egyptian character of the Joseph tale is also determined by the aim of the narrator in the Pentateuch to make a great nation of Jacob in Egypt and to connect the patriarchal narratives with the following stories about Moses. Thereby the question how Israel got into Egypt need not be explicitly raised, even though there are stories in and beyond the Pentateuch in which Israel seems to derive its origin not from Egypt but from the wilderness, Kadesh, the Sinai, Transjordan, the Syrian and Arabian desert, or elsewhere in the large area of the ancient Near East. This observation clearly shows the perplexity that is felt by a historiographer of Israel's earliest history. The Old Testament repeatedly uses its own mode of narrative to relate to those living in later times its vision of God's guidance in Israel's earliest history. Meanwhile we encounter obvious difficulty in trying to isolate the genuine historical data from this "salvation history" and to use them in a modern history of Israel.

LITERATURE

W. F. Albright, *Yahweh and the Gods of Canaan* (Garden City, NY, 1969).

A. Alt, *Der Gott der Väter* (Stuttgart, 1929) (cf. the English translation in *Essays on Old Testament History and Religion* [Oxford, 1966], pp. 1-100).

F. M. Cross, *"ēl,"* TDOT I: 242-61.

C. H. J. de Geus, "Nomaden en sedentairen in het oude Midden-Oosten," *Spieghel Historiael* 14 (1979) 11-18.

N. K. Gottwald, "Domain Assumptions and Societal Models in the Study of Pre-Monarchic Israel," SVT 28 (1975) 89-100.

H. Gunkel, *Genesis* (Göttingen, 1963[6]).

D. Irvin, *Mytharion. The Comparison of Tales from the Old Testament and the Ancient Near East* (Neukirchen-Vluyn, 1978).

J.-R. Kupper, ed., *La civilisation de Mari*, XVe Rencontre Assyriologique Internationale (Paris, 1967) (see especially M. B. Rowton, "The Physical Environment and the Problem of the Nomads," pp. 109-21).

J. T. Luke, "Abraham and the Iron Age: Reflections on the New Patriarchal Studies," *JSOT* 4 (1977) 35-47.

A. R. Millard and D. J. Wiseman, eds., *Essays on the Patriarchal Narratives* (Winona Lake, 1983).

M. J. Mulder, *Kanaänitische Goden in het Oude Testament* ('s-Gravenhage, 1965).

————, "Jahwe en El, identiteit of assimilatie?" *Rondom het Woord* 13 (1971) 402-18.

G. Pettinato, "The Royal Archives of Tell Mardikh-Ebla," *BA* 39 (1976) 44-52.

G. von Rad, "The Joseph Narrative and Ancient Wisdom," in *The Problem of the Hexateuch and Other Essays* (New York, 1966), pp. 292-300.

D. B. Redford, *A Study of the Biblical Story of Joseph (Gen. 37–50)* (SVT 20; Leiden, 1970).

H. Ringgren, *Israelitische Religion* (Stuttgart, 1982[2]) (cf. the English translation of the first edition, *Israelite Religion* [Philadelphia, 1966]).

J. Van Seters, *Abraham in History and Tradition* (New Haven, 1975).

W. Thiel, *Die soziale Entwicklung Israels in vorstaatlicher Zeit* (Neukirchen-Vluyn, 1980).

T. L. Thompson, *The Historicity of the Patriarchal Narratives* (BZAW 133; Berlin, 1974).

————, "The Background of the Patriarchs: A Reply to William Dever and Malcolm Clark," *JSOT* 9 (1978) 2-43.

S. M. Warner, "The Patriarchs and Extra-biblical Sources," *JSOT* 2 (1977) 50-61 (with a response by J. M. Miller, pp. 62-66).

b. Exodus and Conquest

Though hotly debated among historians, Israel's exodus from Egypt and conquest of Canaan is nevertheless one of the most important phases of Israel's national existence and is fundamental for the understanding of Old Testament theology.

This theological perspective, however, causes almost insuperable problems for the historiography of Israel. The biblical account suggests simply that all of Israel was in Egypt, was brought out of it, and, after wandering in deserts for forty years, entered Canaan from the southeast and in a few campaigns took possession of the land. Other than the Old Testament accounts, we possess at best only a few intimations about Israel's exodus and conquest. No archeological data confirm or deny the biblical story. As with the stories about the patriarchs, we should remember that the exodus and conquest accounts received their aesthetically beautiful literary shape many centuries after the events themselves, a fact that does not prevent these narratives from containing old and reliable traditions. The various modern historiographies of Israel, however, differ widely in their account of the Exodus and the entrance into Canaan. Is it possible to reach any conclusion from such a tangle of uncertainties?

At the end of the previous section we considered the connection the Joseph tale makes between the patriarchal narratives and the Exodus. The arrival of Jacob and his people in Egypt, where Joseph had risen to viceroy, introduced a relatively peaceful time in the land of Goshen, located in the fertile Nile Delta. A link perhaps exists between the residence of the small livestock keepers and the entering of Semitic sheepherders or bedouins (the Shosu; see *ANET*, 259; Herrmann) or the *habiru*, or Apiru, a socially low class of people in the second millennium in the Near East. The name has often been associated with the word *Hebrews,* but that association is quite uncertain. The Egyptians, though perhaps tolerating these needy immigrants as temporary strangers, would have made it much more difficult for them as permanent residents.

We know that strangers invaded the Delta during the Hyksos period, the time of the "rulers of foreign lands," as the relevant Egyptian word can be translated. But also here we encounter problems because the questions surrounding the Hyksos, the mixed group of Semites, Arians, and Horites, are far from solved. The Hyksos penetrated Egypt about the eighteenth century B.C. and established their capital at Avaris (or at Zoan, or Tanis) in the northeast of the Delta (cf. Num.

13:22; Isa. 19:11, 13; 30:4; Ezek. 30:14; Ps. 78:12, 43). Some have identified this city with the Raamses mentioned in Exodus 1:11; 12:37 (cf. Num. 33:3, 5), a city enlarged by Ramses II after his father, Seti I, had made it his residence, but this identification is not sure. Seti I and Ramses II were rulers in the New Kingdom (19th Dynasty, about 13th century B.C.), much later than the Hyksos, whose rule lasted approximately 1650–1544. Ahmose I (ca. 1554–1529), the first king of the Eighteenth Dynasty, had expelled the Hyksos and captured their capital in the Nile Delta after a long struggle. He pursued them all the way to the south of Palestine. The expulsion of the Hyksos thus occurred long before there could be an exodus of Israel out of Egypt.

Some have tried to date the Exodus by using Old Testament information. According to 1 Kings 6:1, King Solomon began to build the temple in the 480th year of the exodus of Israel out of Egypt. Assuming that the figure 480 is meant to be exact, not symbolic (standing, for example, for the twelve tribes, each of whom had lived without a temple for forty years), one arrives at about 1450 B.C. as the date of the Exodus. The pharaoh who ruled Egypt at the time was Thutmose III (1490–1439), a prince from the Eighteenth Dynasty. We know that this pharaoh waged war against Asiatics and with his armies marched through the coastal regions of Palestine. It is difficult to assume that such a man would have been unable to stop the escape of a group of slaves.

It is likewise impossible to arrive at a satisfactory date for the Exodus by calculating from the date of the presumable occupation of Canaan, especially if the calculations are based on dubious archeological finds that ostensibly indicate that a number of Canaanite cities might have been destroyed in the thirteenth century by invading Israelites. Such a reckoning would point to a pharaoh of the Nineteenth Dynasty as the pharaoh of the Exodus. Although we cannot prove such a hypothesis, this conception apparently receives the support of some Old Testament statements as well as other data. I referred earlier to the building of Raamses, a city that may have been built, together with Pithom (Exod. 1:11), under Pharaoh Ramses II (ca. 1279–1212) by the enslaved Israelites. The so-called Merneptah, or Israel,

Stele provides an interesting extrabiblical insight. Merneptah (see ill. 9), who had succeeded his father, Ramses II, in passing mentions Israel among the cities and tribes he controlled in Palestine: "Israel is destroyed, his descendants are no more . . ." (*ANET,* 378). This comment might imply that about 1220 B.C. there were also Israelites in Palestine, subject to the power of the pharaoh. The stele inscription is peculiar, however, because the term *Israel* is preceded, not by a determinative symbol indicating "lands," but by one meaning "peoples." This brief inscription represents the earliest extrabiblical mention of Israel but is much too vague to allow more specific conclusions about exodus and conquest. In the first place, we do not know how accurate the pharaoh's writers were. Second, one should not simply identify the Israel mentioned on the stele with the Old Testament Israelites. Assuming that Merneptah refers here to the land of Palestine, the name could concern a small group of people that may have belonged to the core of "Israel" but did not participate in the Exodus, or, in case the invasion happened in phases, it may refer to a group that was already settled in the land.

Discarding as too speculative other theories about the Exodus, whereby combinations of biblical data such as Exodus 12:40 (stating that Israel spent 430 years in Egypt), Genesis 15:13 (predicting that Israel would spend 400 years in Egypt), and the date of the founding of Tanis (or Zoan; see Num. 13:22) play a role, I find that the data mentioned above—building of Raamses and Pithom, slave labor of immigrants on behalf of the ruling class in Egypt, and the inscription on the Merneptah Stele—do point to the thirteenth century, in which something like an exodus may have taken place. In the book of Exodus the center and climax of the exodus story is the institution of the Passover (ch. 12). Around it are grouped in a dramatic climax the ten plagues on the Egyptians, culminating in the death of the firstborn and the destruction of the Egyptian army in the "Red Sea." On the other hand, the Passover feast becomes the center of Israel's religious existence as a nation. Certain things are alternately over- or underemphasized to highlight this focus of Israel's history, which makes it difficult for the modern historian to determine the historical sequence of events.

A route of the Exodus is indicated: from Raamses to Succoth (Exod. 12:37) and not "by way of the land of the Philistines" (13:17). The latter was a northern route, the *via maris* ("way of the sea"), running from Raamses, not far from the present El-Qantara, to Gaza. Succoth lies much more to the south. Possibly it is to be identified with the old Tjeku, the present mound of ruins Tell el-Maskhuta, not far from Lake Timsah. The people stopped next, according to v. 20, at Etham on the edge of the wilderness (cf. Num. 33:6–8) and then, according to Exodus 14:1–2, near Pihahiroth, between Migdol and the sea, opposite Baal-Zephon. Some scholars have tried to identify Etham with the fortress *hetem* mentioned in the Egyptian Papyrus Anastasi V (*ANET,* 259). Presumably the word would have been somewhat corrupted in the Israelite tradition. Migdol means "citadel" or "fortress" and also occurs in this papyrus. Yet all these names (even Pihahiroth, which means "mouth of the waterway") are too vague to locate exactly.

We have the best chance with the place-name Baal-Zephon. Probably it represents a Hebrew-Canaanite designation of a shrine of a Canaanite god, also known from Ugaritic texts. This god was worshiped in the Near East and named after the mountain *Spn* near Ugarit (in the Old Testament, *spn* often means "north"). This mountain is known as *Mons Casius* in antiquity, presently the Jebel el-Aqra (1,729 m. or 5,673 ft., 30 km. or 20 mi. north of Ugarit). It is possible that seafarers brought the cult of this deity to other places in the Orient. It is understandable why O. Eissfeldt looked for Baal-Zephon as a shrine on a tongue of land near Lake Sirbon and the Mediterranean Sea (about 10 km. or 6 mi. east of Pelusium). This locale, not one farther south, would then be the place where the miracle of the Red Sea happened that made such a deep impression on Israel. The Old Testament traditions, however, are not in agreement about the location of the Red Sea. On the basis of Exodus 14:2 (P), Eissfeldt thinks of Lake Sirbon, but 13:20–22 (J) seems to suggest the Bitter Lakes or Lake Timsah, and verse 18 (E) even the north end of the present Gulf of Suez (according to others, the Gulf of Aqabah). Some consider "Red Sea" in verse 18 a gloss. Elsewhere in the Old Testament "Red Sea" indeed points in the direction of the

Gulf of Aqabah rather than the Gulf of Suez (e.g., 23:31; Num. 14:25; 21:4; Deut. 1:1, 40; 2:1; Judg. 11:16; 1 Kgs. 9:26; Jer. 49:21).

Such differences do not make it easy to trace the route of Israel's exodus. Some suppose that P indicates the northern route for the exodus of the "Leah tribes" in the wake of the expulsion of the Hyksos and that the southern route is reserved for the "Rachel tribes" under the leadership of Moses. In this view, there was both an expulsion and an exodus, for which the final editor of Exodus left open the geographical setting. Old Testament tradition complicates the entire exodus event even further by its miscellaneous reports. The fragmentary report in 1 Chronicles 7:21–23 of an early exodus of Ephraim, for example, plays a role in the later Jewish targum and midrash tradition and has left its traces elsewhere in the Old Testament (see, e.g., Ps. 78:9–10).

The complexity of the exodus traditions makes it difficult to determine with certainty how many people left Egypt. Exodus 12:37 mentions that 600,000 men left. Adding hundreds of thousands of women and children to this figure, together with the property and livestock, makes an incredibly large company. Such a large group could not have journeyed through the desert for years. As is the case with so many other numbers in the Old Testament, it seems obvious that we must understand this one also in a hyperbolic or symbolic sense. Some have tried to retain the more reasonable figure 600 by reading the word for "thousand" (eleph) here and elsewhere as "tribe" or "family" (see Judg. 6:15; 1 Sam. 10:19; 23:23; Mic. 5:1 [2]; etc.).

In the exodus traditions, Moses acts as the undisputed leader. According to Exodus 2, he is born in a Levite family. Exodus 6:20 and Numbers 26:58–59 identify his parents as Amram and Jochebed. In the story the baby Moses, threatened by the harsh measures of the pharaoh against the Hebrews, is placed in the Nile in a basket coated with tar and pitch. A daughter of the pharaoh finds him there, and she adopts and rears him. This story resembles the legend about the birth of Sargon I of Akkad (ca. 2340–2300 B.C.), founder of the first Semitic dynasty of Babylonia. According to this legend Sargon was the son of a priestess and was also put in a reed basket in a river. There he was found by a man named Akki who had come to draw water, who raised him before he was brought to the court and became ruler (ANET, 119). Following popular etymology, the Old Testament explains the name Moses as meaning "drawn out of the water" (Exod. 2:10; mosheh means "drawn out"), but it can also derive from the Egyptian mesu ("son").

When he grows up, Moses becomes aware that he is a Hebrew, and after a conflict in which he kills a man, he flees to Midian. There he stays with Jethro (Reuel), a Midianite priest, whose daughter he marries. A theophany near Mount Horeb (Sinai) compels him to help his people, who are groaning in slavery. This help becomes effective when he leads Israel out of Egypt after the Egyptians had been struck by ten plagues. Moses leads the people through the sea and the wilderness to Sinai, where a covenant is made between YHWH, "the God of Israel," and the people. Historically and theologically, this covenant enactment was of great significance for the origin of Israel. According to Exodus 19–24 and 32–34 (attributed to a composite JE source), on Mount Sinai Moses receives the Decalogue and the Book of the Covenant. To this account the so-called Priestly Code in chapters 25–31 and 35–40, Leviticus, and Numbers 1–9 adds the giving of the law and numerous cultic regulations. Following this climactic experience at Horeb, Moses leads the people to the borders of the Promised Land at Kadesh. There spies who had been sent out make the people so afraid of the Canaanites that the Israelites rebel, bringing upon themselves the sentence of wandering "forty years" in the wilderness (Numbers 10–36). Finally Moses brings the people to the eastern borders of Canaan but may not enter the land himself (ch. 20). He dies at Mount Nebo, after having admonished the people and having spoken of the great future awaiting them (Deuteronomy 34).

In J and E, Moses occupies a central place—in J predominantly as a shepherd, in E as a miracle-working prophet. In certain premonarchical traditions he clearly occupies an important place. Outside these traditions, however, he is not much mentioned in the Old Testament (Judg. 1:16; 4:11; 18:30; 2 Kgs. 18:4; Hos. 12:14 [13]; Mic. 6:4; Jer. 15:1; and in Deuteronomistic history). In part because of this paucity of other references, the history of Moses has been disputed. On the one hand, some have tried to reduce him to a legendary and historically vague figure, of whom virtually nothing is known with certainty. The traditions concerning Moses indeed have a complex history, which encumbers scientific historical investigation. Furthermore, researchers have found no extrabiblical mention of Moses. Noth, von Rad, and others who separate the exodus tradition from the Sinai tradition contend that only in Canaan did Israel constitute itself as a nation and as a faith community. They thus do not assign a large place to Moses in their portrayal of the history of Israel. On the other hand, scholars such as Albright and Bright believe that the old traditions have at least an initial probability and that Moses must have played an important role in the Exodus as well as at Sinai and in the constitution of the people into a faith community. My own evaluation of Moses lies in between these two conceptions.

As was true for the patriarchal narratives, it is difficult to distill a historical core from the exodus narratives. At the heart of the traditions lies the confession of the later people of Israel that YHWH, the covenant God of Israel, was present when the people left Egypt, journeyed through the wilderness, and entered Canaan and that he used a gifted leader, Moses, to accomplish these feats. Historically this confession is a hypothesis. No less hypothetical, however, is every other construction that is made of the event behind the stories. Noth divides these traditions in the Pentateuch into five themes—exodus from Egypt, entrance into the civilized land of Canaan, promise to the patriarchs, guidance in the wilderness, and revelation at the Sinai—and regards the common features as a redactional attempt to equalize the traditions. Recent historiographies of Israel's most distant past (Siegfried Herrmann) assume that the traditions indicate historical connections that are essentially true. With whatever tradition one wishes to link Moses, it is clear that, in the mind of later Israel, he had a decisive and prophetic role in the formation of the faith in YHWH.

I noted above that, while the patriarchs were familiar with the worship of El, worship of YHWH was explicitly attributed to the period of Moses (though not denying the continuity between the two periods). The Old Testament presents a varied view on the beginning of the YHWH religion. According to J, the worship of YHWH began in the hoary past (Gen. 4:26). In contrast, E connects the origin of Israel's faith in YHWH with the calling of Moses at the burning bush near Mount Horeb (Exodus 3). Here a previously unknown "God of the fathers" appears to Moses under the name YHWH. Here also once and for all the Old Testament explanation of the name YHWH is given: *ehyeh asher ehyeh,* "I am who I am," or "I am because I am" (v. 14). Though this explanation is only one of the many that have been given of the name, it has become the most widely accepted. Attempts to discover the tetragrammaton in the world around Israel have so far had little success. It has been suggested that the name is reflected in the Ugaritic texts that occasionally mention *Yw* or in one of Amenhotep III's lists of foreign nations in the Nubian Soleb. Some have suggested—prematurely, I believe—that the divine name appears in the deciphered but as yet unpublished Ebla texts (Tell Mardikh). A "Kenite hypothesis" has also been suggested, based on the assumption that YHWH was originally the God of the nomadic Midianites or Kenites who lived in the Negeb and in the Sinai peninsula. This hypothesis was first proposed in the nineteenth century and still has its defenders today. I consider this view below.

Regardless of one's conclusion about the origin and significance of the name YHWH, it is remarkable that he distinguishes himself from all other gods in that he is *one.* This characteristic is clearly expressed in the basic confession accepted by later Judaism: "Hear, O Israel, YHWH our God is one YHWH" (Deut. 6:4, called the *shema,* after the opening word). No more than the "gods of the fathers" is he limited to or connected with a particular locality. YHWH is a "jealous" God: he tolerates no other gods besides himself. The discussion about the monotheism of the Mosaic YHWH religion is interesting in this connection. It concerns the question whether the YHWH religion was from the beginning monotheistic. This question is ultimately one of theology or even philosophy, not history. In answer to this question the Old Testament gives at most some hints, but no answer. Israel's religion is based not on abstract theological reflections but on the confession—one that at the same time must have been experientially real for the people—that YHWH, passing by other nations, found his people in "the howling waste of the wilderness" (Deut. 32:10–12) and, as a people elected by him, led them out of the land of Egypt, "the house of bondage" (see Exod. 20:2; Hos. 11:1; etc.). YHWH is Israel's God "from of old." Though other nations also had their gods and could worship them, which Israel never denied (though it was aware of their worship), YHWH was viewed as "the living God" who could give his theophanies even at heathen places.

This superiority of YHWH makes it preferable to speak of "practical monotheism" rather than of "monolatry" or of "henotheism." In the Old Testament, YHWH comes to us as the God who denies the "idols" the powers and authority their devotees ascribe to them. He is the God of nature, but at the same time the God "of heaven and earth." He is powerful to direct and guide the powers in the world and universe. It must have taken Israel centuries to realize fully the significance of this conception of YHWH. Connected with the "making of the covenant" at Sinai is the Decalogue. It prohibited the worship of other gods as well as the fashioning of any image of God. YHWH was nevertheless portrayed anthropomorphically, as early as in Genesis 1:26–27. Astral forms or animallike shapes were foreign to him (see Exodus 32). His humanlike features are expressed in descriptions of anger, hate, care, or joy, without, however, ascribing human weaknesses to him (as is done to the Homeric gods). The fact remains that we encounter problems in analyzing YHWH's being as it is preserved in the Old Testament. (Volz, for example, has described the "demonic" in terms of the image of God.)

This image of YHWH, which contains an undeniable ethical component, raises the question whether the God whom Moses met by the burning bush in Midian and whose name and power he had to proclaim in Egypt is the same as YHWH who so uniquely appears in the later Old Testament writings. This question is inseparably linked to another: Is YHWH originally a—or the—God of the Midianites or of another desert people? A Midianite origin, which G. Fohrer defends, has something in its favor. In Exodus 18:12 we read

that Moses' father-in-law brought sacrifices to elohim and that Aaron and the elders of Israel participated in the meal. This verse and its context lead us to think that Jethro was a worshiper of YHWH, not of El. Furthermore, it is not impossible that, as a Midianite priest (Exod. 3:1), he played a role in passing on the name YHWH. Moreover, another Midianite, Hobab, a brother-in-law of Moses (Num. 10:29; Judg. 4:11) and son of Reuel (see Exod. 2:18), joined Israel. Remarkably, Jethro and Hobab are called not only Midianites (Exod. 3:1; 18:1; Num. 10:29) but also Kenites (Judg. 4:11). Their eponym was Cain. Possibly they were part of the larger whole of the Amalekites (1 Sam. 15:6) but during Saul's kingship joined themselves to Judah. Their territory was especially the Negeb (Josh. 15:56–57; 1 Sam. 27:10; 30:29), though they also settled elsewhere (Judg. 4:17; 5:24). Through Hobab it is possible to link the Kenites with the Midianites.

Now it is assumed that the Kenites were YHWH worshipers, in fact that YHWH originated from this clan of smiths. Though we cannot form a direct link between the Kenites and YHWH, it may be worthwhile, given the continuing interest in the Kenite hypothesis, to indicate how the Kenites and YHWH may be linked. It is said of Cain, the ancestor of the Kenites, that he bore a mark from YHWH (Gen. 4:15). In the days of the later Israelite king Jehu, we meet a certain Jonadab, the son of Rechab, a devoted YHWH worshiper (2 Kgs. 10:15–24; cf. Jeremiah 35). Chronicles, a book that occasionally incorporates old documents, tells moreover that the Rechabites, defenders of YHWH, were of Kenite origin (1 Chr. 2:55). Although this hypothesis is attractive, it does not, of course, solve the problem of the origin of YHWH but only shifts it to the Kenites.

Vriezen and others have pointed out that in old documents YHWH is often associated with the Sinai or with Seir, sometimes as zeh sinay, "that (Lord) of the Sinai" (Judg. 5:5; Ps. 68:9 [8]). Whether, with Noth, von Rad, and others, one detaches the exodus tradition from the Sinai tradition, according to Vriezen two facts seem incontrovertible: (1) Israel received its faith in YHWH in the wilderness and (2) older traditions, whether J or E, report that YHWH is associated with the Sinai. By assuming these two points as definite, we can understand the later bitter struggle between the YHWH faith of the Israelites and the Baal worship of the Canaanites. That struggle would be hard to explain if Israel adopted the faith in YHWH in Canaan. Despite the tremendous pull and influence of the worship of Baal, to which thousands of Israelites eventually succumbed, Israel always retained a core of intense resistance against total syncretism. Here we encounter something unique in Israel's YHWH faith that utterly resists further scrutiny. YHWH's being, for instance, cannot be explained on the basis of identity with El, as Oldenburg contends, though it must be conceded that Yahwism assimilated elements from the patriarchal Father-god type as well as from the El type. It is remarkable that the book of Exodus has virtually no traces of YHWH's struggle against other gods (12:12 is an exception). Later prophets such as Hosea (2:17 [15]; 13:4–5), Amos (2:10–11), and Jeremiah (2:2) characterized Israel's sojourn in the desert as a time of undivided love between the people of Israel and YHWH. According to the Old Testament the struggle against Baal began only at the gates of the Promised Land, in the fields of Moab (note the references to Baal-Peor in Numbers 25 and Hos. 9:10).

I consider here a few aspects of Israel's journey through the wilderness, though little is known about it from secular history. I mentioned above in passing that some scholars have detached the exodus tradition from the Sinai tradition (Noth, von Rad). One argument supporting this view is that, in the Old Testament, the Sinai traditions are embedded in the traditions around Kadesh (Exod. 15:23–18:27 and Num. 10:29–20:22). Especially von Rad here builds on earlier investigations by Wellhausen that were further developed by Gressmann. After the Exodus, the Israelites presumably journeyed directly to Kadesh on the borders of Palestine, where they formed themselves into a closed community and established their religious institutions and customs. From Kadesh the Israelites—or at least a significant group of them, to the extent that they did not yet already live in Canaan—invaded Canaan. Presumably the Sinai tradition was independent of this tradition. There is clearly some ground for this hypothesis. Exodus 15:22 says

that Moses led Israel three days into the wilderness of Shur and that they did not find water there. Israel had also asked the pharaoh for permission to take a three-day journey into the wilderness to sacrifice to God. Such worship would be done at a place that was *qadosh* ("sacred"), which suggests the place Kadesh-barnea, situated near a spring (*en-mishpat*, Gen. 14:7; also *me-meribah*, Num. 27:14).

According to Old Testament data, a journey from Horeb to Kadesh-barnea takes about eleven days (Deut. 1:2). But neither this fact nor any other (cf. Num. 34:4–5; Josh. 15:3; Ezek. 47:19) helps us in locating the precise place of the old shrine. Perhaps the name is preserved in the present Ain Qedeis, about 80 kilometers (50 mi.) south-southwest of Beer-sheba. In Judges 11:16–18, part of Jephthah's message to the Ammonite king, we read that, after Israel had left Egypt, it went to Kadesh and remained there till it journeyed to Moab. Sinai is not mentioned in this brief report. Moreover, in Deuteronomy 1:46 we are informed that Israel stayed in Kadesh for a long time. If this information is combined with Deuteronomy 2:14, Israel's stay in Kadesh covered thirty-eight of the forty years!

These data are not as compelling as they may seem, however. For instance, it is possible to discern a literary dependence of the story of Jephthah on Numbers 20–21. It could also be pointed out that the thirty-eight years mentioned in Deuteronomy 2:14 refer not to the stay in Kadesh itself but to the wanderings between Kadesh and the entrance into Canaan (cf. also v. 1). In its literary setting in the Old Testament, Kadesh definitely follows after the Sinai event. Moreover, it is pure conjecture to link a meeting with Jethro (Exodus 18) or with Hobab (Numbers 10) precisely with Kadesh. We perhaps could see a vague link between Kadesh and some wilderness episodes that are mentioned twice in the Old Testament, such as the manna and the quails (Exodus 16 [J, P]; Numbers 11 [J, E]), the miraculous giving of water at Meribah (Exod. 17:1–7 [J, E]; Num. 20:1–13 [J, P]), and the appointment of judges (Exod. 18:21–26 [E]; Num. 11:16–17 [E]), one before and one after the Sinai event. Furthermore, Kadesh may have played a role in some stories, such as the death of Moses' sister, Miriam

(Num. 20:1), the sending of the twelve spies (chs. 13–14), and the sending of a delegation to Edom (20:14–21). The territory of the Amalekites, whom Israel had to battle soon after the Exodus (Exod. 17:8–16; Num. 14:39–45) and who are again mentioned in the events of Saul (1 Samuel 15; cf. ch. 30), may also be placed in the Negeb in the vicinity of Kadesh. We never find, however, a Sinai tradition that contrasts with a Kadesh tradition. At best one might suppose with de Vaux and Rowley that, before Moses left Egypt with his company, another group had earlier escaped from Egypt and fled by way of the northern route to Kadesh.

Another possibility, which A. S. van der Woude has suggested, is to locate Mount Sinai in the vicinity of Kadesh. It is certainly remarkable that only a Christian tradition locates the mountain of lawgiving in the southern part of the Sinai peninsula near the so-called Moses Mountain. The Old Testament is much more vague in locating this mountain. Sometimes it is called the mountain of God (Exod. 3:1; 4:27; 18:5; 24:13; 1 Kgs. 19:8), which is then identified with Horeb; at other times the name Sinai is used (Exod. 16:1; 19:1–2; Num. 3:4, 14; etc.). The use of these two names for what is apparently the same mountain has been a favorite criterion for source analysis. Presumably E and D prefer Horeb, whereas J and P favor Sinai. In any case, the Old Testament evidence does not compel us to search for this mountain in the south. We might ask whether there are mountains in the vicinity of Kadesh that are comparable to the Jebel Musa (2,285 m. or 7,497 ft.) or the neighboring Jebel Qaterin (2,641 m. or 8,665 ft.), in whose vicinity the monastery of St. Catharines is located. The answer is no, which is not as great a difficulty as it may seem, because it is nowhere said that "the mountain of God" was a very high mountain. (Note that Mount Zion in Palestine was not very high when compared with the Hermon or the highest peaks of the Lebanon.) In principle, then, several mountains in the Negeb—Petra, for instance—might be the place.

It is very well possible that, because of the confused traditions concerning this mountain, the Old Testament authors were not sure of its location. In this respect we should note *Seir*, the third name for the mountain of God. In the Song of Deborah it is said that YHWH went forth from Seir and from the fields of Edom (Judg. 5:4), and in a song of somewhat later date in Deuteronomy 33:2, we find a parallel between Sinai and Seir. Mount Paran (v. 2; Hab. 3:3), mentioned in connection with the Seir (and the Sinai), can be located in the now-familiar Jebel Faran west of the Arabah, the strip between the Dead Sea and the Gulf of Aqabah. In this way the traditions of a mountain of God, which became a center of pre-Canaanite-Israelite religious life, can be placed in an area around Kadesh.

Though a modern historian may rightly view the Exodus and the invasion of Canaan as complex events that have various phases, nevertheless certain aspects of these events are central in the mind of Israel: the theophany at the Sinai; the acceptance of YHWH, the God of the patriarchs, as the God of Israel; the dominating personality of Moses; and the centrality of Kadesh. These traditions cohere and have had a great impact on the religious and social life of later Israel. Because of the close relationship between these traditions, the hypothesis of a dual origin of Israel's YHWH worship (from a group of Israelites living in central Palestine that had received the YHWH worship directly from the Sinai and from another group living in southern Palestine that acquired this worship via Kenites and Midianites) is not very likely, though such a hypothesis might help to explain why later YHWH worship in northern Israel differed from that in the south.

Israel's stay in the desert, which tradition reports as lasting the relatively short time of forty years, is hardly an independent link between exodus and invasion. Many hold that the several desert stories derive from different traditions. One proposal distinguishes between desert traditions stemming from the nomads, such as the miracle of the manna (Exodus 16), the water from the rock (17:1–7), and the feeding by quails (Numbers 11), and traditions arising from southern Palestine tribes, such as the war against Amalek (Exod. 17:8–16), the choice of Hobab to be the guide in the wilderness (Numbers 10), Miriam's leprosy (ch. 12), and the rebellion of Dathan and Abiram (ch. 16). Traditions that are regarded as later are the stories about the bitter water at Marah (Exodus 15), the bronze snake (Numbers

21), the rebellion of the Korahites (ch. 16), and the sin of Moses and Aaron at Kadesh (ch. 20). The theological setting of all these stories and traditions is reflected in the prophetic writings of Hosea, Jeremiah, Ezekiel, and Deutero-Isaiah in the use they make of the wilderness tradition.

LITERATURE

W. Beyerlin, Herkunft und Geschichte der ältesten Sinai-traditionen (Tübingen, 1961).

J. Bright, Early Israel in Recent History Writing (London, 1956).

H. Cazelles, A la recherche de Moïse (Paris, 1979).

G. I. Davies, The Way of the Wilderness. A Geographical Study of the Wilderness Itineraries in the Old Testament (Cambridge, 1979).

J. Day, God's Conflict with the Dragon and the Sea. Echoes of a Canaanite Myth in the Old Testament (Cambridge, 1985).

O. Eissfeldt, Baal Zaphon, Zeus Kasios und der Durchzug der Israeliten durchs Meer (Halle [Saale], 1932).

R. Giveon, Les bédouins Shosou des documents égyptiens (Leiden, 1971).

O. Keel, Monotheismus im Alten Testament und seiner Umwelt (Einsiedeln, 1980).

Caroline J. L. Kloos, Yhwh's Combat with the Sea. A religio-historical investigation into the myth in Psalm xxix and Exodus xx 1-18 (Amsterdam-Leiden, 1986).

D. A. Knight, Rediscovering the Traditions of Israel (Missoula, MT, 1975²).

B. Lang, ed., Der einzige Gott. Die Geburt des biblischen Monotheismus (München, 1981).

M. J. Mulder, Ba'al in het Oude Testament ('s-Gravenhage, 1962).

——, "1 Chronik 7.21b-23 und die rabbinische Tradition," JSJ 6 (1975) 141-66.

E. T. Mullen, The Assembly of the Gods in Canaanite and Early Hebrew Literature (Chico, CA, 1980).

E. W. Nicholson, Exodus and Sinai in History and Tradition (Oxford/Richmond, 1973).

U. Oldenburg, The Conflict between El and Ba'al in Canaanite Religion (Leiden, 1969) (see the review by M. J. Mulder in UF 2 [1970] 359-66).

G. del Olmo Lete, Mitos y Leyendas de Canaan segun la Tradicion de Ugarit (Madrid, 1981) (good bibliographies).

G. von Rad, "The Form-Critical Problem of the Hexateuch," in The Problem of the Hexateuch and Other Essays (New York, 1966), pp. 1-78.

H. H. Rowley, From Joseph to Joshua (London, 1950).

M. B. Rowton, "Dimorphic Structure and the Problem of the 'Apirû-'Ibrîm," JNES 35 (1976) 13-20.

E. P. Uphill, "Pithom and Raamses: Their Location and Significance," JNES 27 (1968) 291-316; 28 (1969) 15-39.

Th. C. Vriezen, The Religion of Ancient Israel (Philadelphia, 1967).

M. Weippert, The Settlement of the Israelite Tribes in Palestine: A Critical Survey of Recent Scholarly Debate (Naperville, 1971).

A. S. van der Woude, Uittocht en Sinaï (Nijkerk, 1960).

c. From the Settlement in Canaan to the Origin of the Monarchy

Old Testament tradition demarcates fairly clearly the period covering the stay in and departure from Egypt of certain Israelite tribes. For the invasion and settlement of Canaan, however, the boundaries between entrance and settlement are very hard to draw. The Old Testament informs us, for example, that the tribes of Reuben, Gad, and half of Manasseh were already allowed to settle in the part of Palestine east of the Jordan River, though it was still necessary to organize an invasion by the other tribes. At closer scrutiny the lines between the journey through the wilderness, invasion, and settlement become so fluid that a modern historian can make only a path of hypotheses through the morass of problems in the hope of gaining somewhat of a solid footing on the other side. De Vaux rightly opened his fascinating essay on the settlement in Canaan with the remark "The problem raised by the settlement of the Israelites in Canaan and the growth of the system of the twelve tribes is the most difficult problem in the whole history of Israel" (p. 475).

The uncertainty of the modern historian is due to the character of the historical books of the Old Testament. In Jewish tradition these books are rightly reckoned among the prophetic books because, like the Pentateuch, they aim first at describing not Israel's secular history but the vision of "men of God" (as the prophets may also be called) on the relationship of YHWH with his people and of the people with its God in the course of history. In the composition of such a history, old traditions, even other books or chronicles, were frequently consulted, as is apparent, for example, from the mention of the Book of Jashar (Josh. 10:13; 2 Sam. 1:18) and of the Chronicles of the Kings of Judah and Israel in later times. But all such references are set in a specific theological framework, perhaps one of explaining how the two small kingdoms of Judah and Israel ended up in captivity. In this history writing, theological considerations, not political or economic motifs, play a primary role. This entire work—whose literary composition is dealt with elsewhere in this handbook—is nowadays subsumed under the term *Deuteronomistic*. It comprises the books of Joshua, Judges, Samuel, and Kings and is known in the Jewish tradition as the Former Prophets.

The stories in Joshua 1–12 create the impression that Israel's invasion and settlement of Palestine was a rather uncomplicated event. These chapters suggest that Israel entered Canaan as a group, that the invasion was accompanied by a display of considerable military power, and that it was accomplished in a relatively short period of time. The second part of the book of Joshua as well as other parts of the Old Testament, however, paints a different picture of the traditions of invasion and settlement. Numbers 13–14, for instance, mention the spying out of the southern part of the Promised Land from Kadesh-barnea, in which Joshua, Moses' successor, and Caleb play a role. Caleb is especially prominent in Judges 1. This remarkable chapter preserves remnants of various invasion traditions that are difficult to harmonize with the unitary picture in Joshua 1–12. Joshua 13–21 also contains a fairly old outline of the various tribes that, in combination with the information in Judges 1, can provide an idea of the situation in Israel before it became one national state. Alt in particular has done pioneering studies in the area of what is called the territorial historical method.

In the modern historiography of Israel one encounters a variety of views on the problem of the entrance into and settlement of Palestine. Scholars such as Alt and Noth regard the entrance as a peaceful infiltration of a group of nomads. During the summer these nomads searched for the green pastures and water found on the outskirts of Canaan. In this way the Israelite nomads pre-sumably practiced transhumance till they settled permanently as farmers in the civilized Canaanite country. Such a peaceful settling naturally required contracts and agreements with the resident population. Joshua 9 records such an agreement between the Canaanites and the newcomers in the form of the story of the Gibeonites' ruse. Here and there such a peaceable penetration may have resulted in servile labor of the indigenous population. Perhaps an example is found in Genesis 49:14–15, which pictures the tribe of Issachar in a state of feudal dependency.

A second view, held by Albright and others, maintains that the invasion of the tribes was a military operation. Here the tribes are usually viewed not as a unity but as separate groups such as the Rachel tribes or the exodus groups. Sometimes it is also assumed that an initially peaceful invasion later turned into bloody clashes, such as the war against the Amorite king Sihon of Heshbon (Num. 21:21–30) and the battles against King Og of Bashan (21:31–22:1).

A third view assumes a slowly evolving process of what might be called a social regrouping of the Israelite tribes already on Palestinian soil. In this hypothesis there was no real invasion, no change in population, but a kind of class struggle, a farmers' revolution against the Canaanite city-states that oppressed the rural population. Mendenhall in particular has promoted this view. Some scholars hold that there was a first phase, in which Canaan was invaded and occupied, followed by a second phase consisting of consolidating the occupied territory and gaining a foothold in the cities. The Old Testament presumably emphasizes the second phase, whereas the first can be reconstructed only from biblical intimations and extrabiblical witnesses.

Albright and others have strongly defended the need to use fully the evidence from archeology to solve the problem of the conquest. Albright has charged the literary-critical and tradition-historical schools, especially those of Alt and Noth, with reckoning too little with the results of archeology in their investigations. For Albright, these results, together with extrabiblical sources that could elucidate the biblical narratives, are part of the external evidence. On the basis of analyses of excavations done in the 1920s and 1930s in

Palestine, in places such as Tell Beit Mirsim (according to Albright, Kiriath-sepher, or Debir), Tell ed-Duweir (Lachish), Betin (Luz, or Bethel), and Tell el-Qedah (Hazor), Albright concludes that, in the thirteenth century B.C., during the transition from the last phase of the Late Bronze Age to the first phase of the Early Iron Age, terrible catastrophes must have taken place in the land. Soon afterward, though under less favorable circumstances, the destroyed cities were rebuilt on the debris and ashes. The destructions during this time must almost certainly be associated with the "conquest of Palestine" by the invading Israelites. In this view of history, identifications of nonliterary finds in debris and ashes with written stories, for instance in Joshua (among others, Josh. 11:10–13, about the fate of Hazor), offered enough external evidence for a reconstruction of the invasion. Yet this view, too, has difficulties. We only mention here the finds at Tell es-Sultan and et-Tell (near Jericho and Ai) that do not agree with the literary data in Joshua 6–8. Without elaborating on these problems, we observe that bringing the archeological evidence into the picture of the invasion could easily lead scholars such as Albright and Wright to the second view above, namely, that Israel conquered Palestine militarily.

What are the fixed points from which we can gain a clear picture of the entrance and settlement by "Israel"? What is the value of the various data? To answer these questions attention must be given to the territorial-historical method that Alt introduced in 1925. This method assumes that the organization and structuring of a territory (Territorialordnung) is everywhere conservative and that even a change in population in a certain area leads only to greater or smaller changes in the details but does not immediately affect the basic structures. Applied to Palestine, this method claims that we can get an idea of the nature of the territorial relationships before the invasion by examining the territorial relationships in this area, mentioned in the sources, after the Israelite conquests. In particular, Egyptian documents and hieroglyphic texts of the period before the (presumable) invasion of Israel can, according to Alt, shed the necessary light on Palestine at the time of the invasion. These documents show that Palestine then had a system of city-states. In sup-

port of this conception Alt appeals first of all to the feudal system of the Hyksos realm and to the Egyptian execration texts of the Twelfth Dynasty. Next, Alt finds the system of city-states even more evident in the documents of the Asiatic campaigns of Pharaoh Thutmose III—in his annals on the stele of Jebel Barkal and in the so-called city lists (see, among others, *ANET*, 234–45, etc.)—and especially in the Akkadian correspondence discovered in the archives of Amarna of Pharaohs Amenhotep III and IV. These letters and copies of letters from the fourteenth century B.C., addressed to or written by city-kings in Syria and Palestine, show clearly that they, while being in some sense subject to the pharaoh, were essentially quite independent of Egyptian authority.

Alt believed that these letters indicated that, in Palestine in the Late Bronze Age, especially the fertile valleys and plains were occupied but the mountains were only sparsely populated and had virtually no cities. Assuming this situation, one might then say that the Israelite tribes were mainly located in the mountains between the Valley of Jezreel and the Jordan Valley and the seacoast. Lists preserved in Joshua 13–19 point indeed in that direction. The list recorded in Judges 1:17–36 is also valuable, since it mentions various places that were *not* immediately captured by the tribes. In this list are found names of cities situated in the Valley of Jezreel (e.g., Megiddo), a fortress such as Beth-shean (see ill. 34), and cities on the coast of the Mediterranean Sea (Dor, Akko, Sidon). The biblical data do not contradict the extrabiblical documents adduced by Alt. Nor do narratives such as that in Joshua 9, the covenant of the Gibeonites with Israel (or perhaps only with Benjamin), and also Genesis 34, which associates Levi and Simeon with Shechem, point directly to military violence. One reason for the Israelites' trying to avoid battle and deciding not to capture the strong Canaanite cities in the plain may have been the use of iron war chariots by the Canaanites. Joshua 17:16–18 gives this reason, stating that the descendants of Joseph made a place to live for their numerous descendants in the forested hill country because the Canaanites of Beth-shean had iron chariots. Iron was also used at an early stage by the Philistines, Israel's later opponents (1 Sam. 13:19–22).

A careful study of the Old Testament data shows that Alt is correct in describing the entrance of the tribes as more a gradual process than a well-organized invasion. Concerning this process we know much more about some tribes than others. Joshua 13–19 describes the boundaries of the tribes, and names of families who constituted tribes are found in Numbers 26:5–65. An old tradition, known to us as the blessing of Jacob, helps further in establishing the character of the tribes and, presented in poetic form, relates the present to events from a distant past (Genesis 49; cf. Deuteronomy 33). This information, as well as stories of the birth of the ancestors of the tribes (Gen. 29:31–30:24), shows that Leah's son Reuben is always mentioned first, followed by the tribes of Simeon, Levi, and Judah. Later, the first three tribes play hardly any role. Reuben is still mentioned in the Song of Deborah (Judg. 5:15–16), but by that time Simeon is already closely linked to Judah (1:3, 17). It is even explicitly stated in Joshua 19:1 that Simeon's inheritance "was in the midst of the inheritance of the tribe of Judah." The Levites also had no territory of their own (see ch. 21) but possessed certain cities. Jacob's blessing speaks rather negatively about Reuben and his brothers Simeon and Levi, their "blessing" consisting in a "being divided" in Jacob and a "being scattered" in Israel (Gen. 49:7). Could this later shifting (Reuben from the center to the east of Palestine, Simeon to the south) and disappearance (Levi) of tribes indicate that at first they did have land in central Palestine (Simeon and Levi in the vicinity of Shechem [ch. 34]) but that later they were pushed out by the invading "brothers" from Rachel's side or assimilated into that tribal organization?

Genesis 29:31–35 and 30:17–20 list Reuben, Simeon, Levi, Judah, Issachar, and Zebulun as the six sons of Leah. This information appears to point to a kind of kinship between these tribes. Judah can be located in the region of Hebron and Bethlehem (Judg. 1:9–18). To it belonged the descendants of Caleb and Othniel (vv. 11–15). Othniel lived in Debir, earlier also called Kiriath-sepher, a place in the vicinity of Hebron that has still not been precisely identified. It is not difficult to identify Judah's geographical boundaries, because they are almost all natural boundaries: the desert to the east and south; in the north a number of Canaanite cities, of which Jebus, Gezer, Aijalon, and Shaalbim (v. 35) were important; and in the west the lower hill country, the Shephelah, with likewise numerous city-states. This delineation of the territory of Judah shows that the Canaanite city-states in the plains and in the hill country constituted a natural obstacle for the settlement of the tribes. In all likelihood they were simply forced to settle in the sparsely populated areas between these cities. This type of settling in a thinly populated and mountainous area may now and then have led to clashes. Some have taken the conflict between Simeon and Levi and Shechem (Genesis 34) to be such a clash. From the Amarna literature we know that a certain Labaya, king of Shechem, engaged in a rather expansionistic policy; also later in Israel's history Shechem gives the impression of being rather independent (see Judges 9). Such facts may indicate that one city-state was more aggressive than another.

On the other hand, less militant invading groups may have tried harder to adapt themselves to the situations in Palestine. Here we may recall Issachar, who in the blessing of Jacob is called "a strong ass" who "saw that a resting place was good, and that the land was pleasant; so he bowed his shoulder to bear, and became a slave at forced labor" (Gen. 49:14–15). The territory of this tribe, bounded in the west by the Valley of Jezreel, in the south by the territory of the city-state of Beth-shean, and in the east by the Jordan Valley, comprised the city of Shunem and the mountain Tabor. From one of the Amarna Letters (ANET, 485), we know that a city-king of Megiddo forced people from Shunem, situated on the other side of the Valley of Jezreel, to perform servile labor as burden bearers. So it is imaginable that the idea arose, reinforced by the tribal blessing for Issachar, whose name is sometimes translated "worker for wages," that this tribe later acquired territory at the price of servile labor. It is likely that this tribe later managed to free itself from its obligations to its taskmasters.

Reconstructing the early history of the other tribes is at least as difficult as it is for Issachar. Tribes such as Asher (in the western hill country in the vicinity of the Phoenician region), Zebulun (on the southern edge of the Galilean mountains), and Naphtali (in eastern Galilee) likely did not play a large role in Israel's early history, though tradition already ascribes to Joshua the capture of the mighty Canaanite city of Hazor, called "the head of all those kingdoms" (Josh. 11:10). This reference suggests the forcing back of the Canaanites for the benefit of the Israelite tribes. Other elements besides confrontation with the Canaanites also played a part in Israel's settlement of Palestine, as is evident from the Old Testament traditions about the tribe of Dan. Especially in recent decades many scholars have suggested that Dan was originally not an Israelite tribe but a clan of the so-called Sea Peoples. Presumably Dan broke away from the Philistines who had settled in the coastal regions of Canaan and journeyed northward to join the tribes of Jacob. This hypothesis is based on several biblical and extrabiblical data.

In the Song of Deborah, Dan is reproachingly asked why he lingered by the ships (Judg. 5:17). It is indeed strange to attribute a fleet to a nomadic tribe in the process of settling. Yadin believes that this reference points to the Sea Peoples. Another remarkable fact is that there are hardly any genealogical lists of Dan. Moreover, some Old Testament passages create the impression that Dan is a tribe that came from outside of Israel. Genesis 49:16 reports that Dan will judge his people "as one of the tribes of Israel," a peculiarity underlined by Judges 18:1, which says that the Danites were seeking an inheritance where they might settle, "for until then no inheritance among the tribes of Israel had fallen to them." Furthermore, Joshua 19:40-48 very closely connects the inheritance of Dan with the territory of the Philistines by the seacoast. From Joshua 19:47 and Judges 18 it appears that Dan, after a great raid through the entire land, found an "inheritance" in the north of Canaan. This raid ended with the capture of the city of Laish, without the neighboring Sidonians coming to the rescue of the city against the invaders. As Yadin has noted, the report in Joshua 19, which still places the inheritance of Dan in the southwest of Canaan, adjoining the land of the Philistines, must hark back to a very old tradition. In the monarchical period, for example, when Dan had for a long time lived in the north, no one would have had any interest in placing this tribe so deep in the south. The problem of a possible link between Philistines and Danites becomes even more interesting through a closer analysis of the stories of the Danite Samson. This cycle of stories points not only to a close relationship between Dan and the Philistines—notwithstanding their frequently bloody clashes—but also to a distance between the Danites and the other Israelite tribes. The report about the strange attitude of the Judeans toward Samson's stay in their territory (Judg. 15:9-13) illustrates this distance.

From extrabiblical sources, researchers refer to Egyptian documents mentioning the Sea Peoples (see ill. 11). In the time of Pharaoh Ramses III (ca. 1185-1155 B.C.), the Sea Peoples included a group called Tjeker (also found in the Wen-Amon Story [*ANET,* 25-29]) that had a center in Dor and lived along the Mediterranean Sea (see *ANET,* 262-63), as well as a group called Denyen. The latter are said to be associated with the Greek Danaoi, whose ancestor Danaos in Greek mythology is related to Egypt: Danaos's father, Belos, was the twin brother of Aegyptos. These Danaoi, or the *D-in-iw-n* of the document of Ramses, are thought to be connected with the Danuna, mentioned in a Phoenician-Hittite bilingual inscription (ca. 720 B.C.) discovered at Karatepe (*ANET,* 499-500; *KAI,* 26). After this identification the step to the "Danites" is obvious, though it should be noted that not all scholars are ready to identify the Danuna mentioned at Karatepe with one of the five Sea Peoples mentioned by Ramses III.

This detailed discussion about the tribe of Dan shows how complicated the formation was of the tribes of Israel on Palestinian soil. The exposition leads naturally to a consideration of Noth's idea of amphictyony, together with the complex of institutions connected with it. This term, mentioned above in section 1, comes from the ancient Greek world, in which it functioned in the Pylaeic-Delphic covenant. According to Wüst, *amphictyony* originally referred to a group of nationally or linguistically diverse people that had come together to form a unity. Only later did the term evolve into a communal name for a sacral league of various groups. Whatever may have been the evolution in Greek of the word *amphictyony,* Noth has applied the term and the accompanying concept to the sacral league of the Israelite tribes. This alliance presumably consisted of twelve tribes who united themselves around a common cultic center. This center was the ark, an object especially important in the early history of Israel in Canaan and kept in a more or less movable sanctuary. According to the amphictyonic hypothesis, regularly for one or two months one of the tribes belonging to the sacral alliance was in charge of the sanctuary and the ark. Another aspect of this tribal alliance, according to Noth, was a regularly recurring renewal of the relationship of the alliance—called Israel—to its covenant God YHWH. This covenant mutually obligated them to keep certain laws (covenant law) and to have or acknowledge certain tribal leaders, the so-called minor judges. Joshua 24 is viewed by Noth and others as a splendid example of the functioning of the amphictyony in Israel. On the "national day of Shechem" described there, the twelve tribes solemnly pledged their bond with YHWH and with each other.

How did Noth, who essentially built on a foundation already laid by Alt, arrive at this theory about the amphictyony? He had observed that the Old Testament consistently speaks of *twelve* tribes of Israel. It mentions only one tradition element, however; there are not twelve traditions about as many tribes, but only one tradition about twelve tribes. In this grouping of twelve the names may change, but the number does not. In the Old Testament this system occurs in two forms, depending on whether Levi is counted as a tribe. Levi and Joseph appear in the first system; in the other, in which Levi is absent, Joseph is split into Manasseh and Ephraim. In the latter system, Gad is moreover included. The first system, considered the oldest, is found in Genesis 49, the other in Numbers 1 and 26. The oldest must precede the formation of Israel as a national state under David. The element uniting the tribes in this alliance was their religion and cult, concentrated at the central shrine in Shechem, which is also the setting for the events narrated in Joshua 24. The occasion for the formation of such an alliance, according to Noth, was the invasion of the Joseph tribes into Canaan. At Shechem they entered into a covenant with an existing six-tribe amphictyony, the Leah group, at which time the God of the

"house of Joseph" became the God of the entire amphictyony.

Since Noth's theory clarifies so well some of the most difficult points in Israel's early history, we may view it as a plausible hypothesis. It explains why the number twelve plays such a significant role in the various tribal lists. Various later phenomena in Israel's history can also be explained on the basis of their presence in an earlier, amphictyonic setting. According to Gunneweg, the entity Israel was determined by this religious background. In its later evolution—and even in modern times—it cannot be totally identified with a nation or with a state, because Israel as a community is at once more and less than these two. When later as a state Israel threatened to become "like the other nations," the prophets called her back from such a course to become "Israel" again. The mysterious element in the name Israel originated at a time when there may well have been an amphictyony.

This hypothesis was refined and elaborated by Noth and other scholars such as Rost, Balscheit, von Rad, and the Albright school. Especially in the 1960s, however, the theory was subjected to fierce criticism, especially by Auerbach, Eissfeldt, Orlinsky, Fohrer, Anderson, and de Vaux. In the first place, the Old Testament contains neither a formal nor a material indication that an amphictyony existed, and it is arbitrary to argue from the existence of a Greek or Italian amphictyony to the presence of a Semitic one. Moreover, the constant change of the central shrine weakens the hypothesis. Not only Shechem but also Bethel, Shiloh, and other places were temporary residences of the ark. Fohrer asked the question why Israel, the name of the tribal alliance, included the divine name El but not YHWH. He also drew attention to the fact that Joshua 24 does not speak of the institution of an amphictyony of twelve tribes; rather, it regards them as already being in existence together. The objection is also raised that the figure 12 need not be a decisive argument for amphictyony. Finally, during the time of the judges, the tribes never displayed the measure of centralization that the idea of an amphictyony presupposes. The union of the tribes of Israel at that time was more an ideal than reality.

Recently de Geus has studied carefully the

tribes of Israel. He too concludes that the term *am-phictyony* is unsuitable as a technical term for designating certain tribal alliances. He also rejects the political function of the amphictyony, which (in contrast to Noth, who favored the idea of a sacral alliance) many have touted. According to de Geus, the amphictyony was an intermediate phase not between *tribe* and nation but between *city* and nation. It has been impossible, however, to find even one amphictyonic institution or office, not to mention a central cult or shrine. Furthermore, the so-called holy wars of YHWH did not proceed from the amphictyony, and the judges, both major and minor, were mainly from the cities and obtained national stature by their achievements. This type of criticism with respect to the amphictyony reflects the ongoing discussion on this subject. Many questions still clamor for answers, such as that concerning the office of the judges and the character of the holy wars. Were the wars in the time of the judges holy wars waged by the amphictyony (von Rad) or "YHWH wars" of certain groups that participated in them (Smend)?

The formation of the people into Israel—the union of groups or tribes that ethnically were perhaps quite diverse into a community around YHWH, his sanctuary, his cult, and his covenant—is a fact that cannot be measured with scientific criteria. This limitation promotes the divergence in viewpoints. Many scholars (e.g., Herrmann) think that Israel resulted from the settling of certain tribes of Aramaic or Canaanite origin in Canaan, while others (e.g., de Geus) defend the idea that Israel was autochthonous in Canaan. This latter conception challenges the assumption that almost all Semitic peoples were nomads or seminomads in early times or that they lived on the fringes of the desert before settling in the civilized world. The social structure of Israelite society offers no warrant for postulating an origin in a nomadic milieu. According to de Geus, such a structure consisted of the following elements: (1) family, (2) clan, and (3) tribe, or nation, of which the first element was exogamous, the last two endogamous. In this relationship the clan was the most significant, based as it was on communal possession of the land. Presumably the political organization was also centered in the clan. Tribes were groups of related clans within a given geographical area. De Geus's idea that the assumption of a conquest of Canaan as a clear historical break is unlikely not only socially and economically but especially on the ground of archeological considerations is interesting. Such evidence would imply that the Israelites have lived much longer in Canaan than is usually assumed. De Geus suggests that there is much in favor of regarding the "Israelites" as the "Amorite population of the central highlands."

Lacking clear archeological evidence to the contrary, we do not need to reject the idea that certain tribes settled in certain geographical areas over a long period of time. The Old Testament tradition seems to point in that direction by its mention of many Canaanite fortresses and cities, especially in the plains of Galilee, Ephraim, and also Judah, that prevented a speedy unification of the tribes that had entered. The initially occupied territory required defense, and so gradually there arose smaller alliances of groups and tribes that later organized themselves into larger units, especially after military successes and under the leadership of powerful, charismatic leaders—the judges. The definitive union of all tribes, however it is spread out or combined in the tradition, was aided by the mystical and intangible, but very real, factor of belief in YHWH, the one God of Israel.

In the matter of the name of Israel's God, it is easier to make hypotheses than to offer sure answers. Israel clearly associated its faith in YHWH with the traditions of the Sinai (see Judg. 5:5; Ps. 68:9 [8]). Already in premonarchical times this faith must have been so deeply rooted in Israel that, in the confrontation with the Canaanite religion, it not only maintained itself but also extended its influence. I have elsewhere dealt extensively with the Canaanite gods and here make only brief remarks. The excavations since 1929 at Ras Shamra, ancient Ugarit on the Syrian coast of the Mediterranean Sea, have especially enabled us to get a better idea of the Canaanite gods. The mythological and epic texts found there show that, in the middle of the second millennium B.C., El as the chief deity had no more than a modest role in the Ugaritic pantheon. There he is a god at rest, flanked by his consort Asherat.

The decisive role in the Ugaritic pantheon is

played by Baal (see ill. 17). In a fierce battle he defeats two formidable opponents: Yam, the god of the sea, also called Shapitu Nahari (Right River), and Mot, the god of the underworld and death and also of the ripening grain and the scorching heat of the sun. Though the texts, because of the condition in which they have been preserved, still present numerous problems and obscurities, Baal clearly was the god of fertility and rain. In his battles and victories he is faithfully supported by his wife and sister, Anat. Baal, also called Hadad, is alternately designated as the son of El and as the son of Dagan (in the Old Testament, Dagon), the god of the harvest. Many believe that Baal's real name was Hadad, which in slightly different forms is also known from Akkadian texts. In any case, the Old Testament has an interest in Baal as a fertility god who presents a strong temptation to Israel. Often it speaks of a conflict between YHWH and Baal, which reaches a climax in the contest at Carmel (1 Kings 18) at the time of King Ahab.

By contrast, the Old Testament does not speak of a conflict between El and YHWH, particularly not in the patriarchal narratives. Though it is not correct to identify YHWH with El (as Oldenburg does), certainly in the patriarchal narratives we do find a measure of assimilation. The "strange gods" who were opposed by YHWH were, according to the Old Testament information, the Baals and the Astartes, the fertility deities. Disregarding Exodus 32, sometimes regarded as a backward projection of the bull worship of Jeroboam I to the early times of Israel, we note that biblical tradition places the first conflict between YHWH and Baal at the borders of the Promised Land, in the fields of Moab, where the people worshiped Baal-Peor (Numbers 25). This Baal, like so many other Baals often differentiated in the Old Testament by place or name, is simply the locally worshiped form of the one Baal. In contrast to the earlier opinion of many scholars, who assumed the presence of numerous local deities connected with mountains, forests, springs, stones, etc., the tendency today is to think of Baal as one god with many local manifestations and cults (cf., e.g., the quite divergent forms of adoration of Mary within Roman Catholicism). We must recognize, though, that there were local cultic differences in the worship of a particular deity; one must be cautious in quickly identifying various gods in places and times that were far apart. Moreover, the Old Testament never encouraged inquiry into the nature of the "strange gods."

The Old Testament refers to a conflict between YHWH and Baal that occurred in the house of the judge Gideon (Judg. 6:25-32). Comparing the account of this confrontation with the one in 1 Kings 18 involving Elijah on Mount Carmel, one soon detects remarkable parallels in the literature. In his historically convincing version of the story, the author of the book of Judges intimates that the intense conflict between YHWH and Baal, though limited in area, had already flared up in Israel's earliest history. Vriezen has pointed out that, spiritually and culturally, the tribes of Israel would never have been able to maintain themselves against the more highly developed Canaanites if their God YHWH had not had a character uniquely his own. Yahwism must have been a spiritual force that was imported into Canaan and, more than the god of the patriarchs or the Canaanite El worship, determined the character of Israel's struggle against its enemies. YHWH must have had an inspiring influence on the young tribes who in Palestine were involved in a battle with the Canaanites. A remarkable poetic reflection of that inspiration is found in the Song of Deborah (Judges 5), a song that "with its impressionism, its lack of logical reflexes, lies deeply rooted in the thought world of ancient Israel with its national-religious vision on life and its emotional piety" (Vriezen).

The description of Israel's earliest history in Canaan often takes insufficient account of the uniting and integrating force the communal faith in YHWH must have had on the various tribes. This faith held by tribes or individuals is an intangible factor in Israel's history, a factor that nevertheless had a decisive influence on the origin and development of the nation. The spiritual power resident in the new groups who started to call themselves "Israel" and who were aglow with Yahwistic ideals gave fresh inspiration to the older as well as the younger tribes. It is speculative, however, to say that the faith in YHWH, radiating from Ephraim as the center of YHWH worship, gradually pushed aside El as the God of Israel. The "wars of YHWH" in the days of the judges that were waged by individual tribes (not by the amphictyony) fail to confirm this notion. Nevertheless, the "holy war," in which YHWH himself acts as a warrior who comes to the aid of his faithful (or initially unfaithful) followers and himself conquers the enemies, remains a remarkable element in the literature of ancient Israel.

We now examine two aspects of Israel's oldest history: the judges and the war against the Canaanites and other tribes who were settled in Palestine. The word *judges* is a translation of the Hebrew *shophetim*. The English word may lead to misunderstanding, since it suggests that these people were especially engaged in administering justice. It is better, with Liedke, to think in terms of people who act to restore a broken society, those who preserve or restore the *shalom* within a smaller or larger community. The judges were thus rulers, often acting on behalf of the elders of a city or small community, who had acquired their position because of special ability or charisma.

Linguistically related to the Hebrew word and also related to the Old Testament judges in function are the *Sufeten,* the highest officials in the Punic society of Carthage and its daughter cities. The latter were elected in pairs for one year, largely on the basis of prestige and wealth. As presidents they convened the council of elders and the popular gathering, administered justice, and with the council handled foreign affairs. Documents found at Mari near the Euphrates refer to the related word *shapitu.* Though geographically as well as chronologically these documents are closer to Israel, the term here is likely only a Canaanite loanword, applied to a political and social situation that differed substantially from the one in Israel.

In contrast to judges in the societies around them, Israel's judges were charismatic leaders (here we follow M. Weber). In the Old Testament, especially in times of distress, we witness the emergence of deliverers who came from various places and whose authority was not hereditary. They and their tribesmen perceived that they were called by YHWH to provide leadership and deliverance. The "major judges," Othniel, Ehud, Gideon, Deborah (the only woman among them), Jephthah, and Samson, clearly exemplify these

characteristics. Besides them we find the "minor judges," men to whom few or no heroic deeds are ascribed and of whom very little is known (Judg. 10:1–5; 12:7–15), although occasionally a biblical tradition briefly lifts the veil hanging over these men in the book of Judges. So we know from Numbers 32:41 (see also 1 Chr. 2:22) that Jair (Judg. 10:3–4) made conquests in the north of the territory east of the Jordan. The difference between the major and minor judges is mainly literary. In reality the two groups likely differed little in calling and deeds.

As city or tribal leaders, the judges occupy a position between the great leaders Moses and Joshua before them and Saul, the first king, after them. Many have also regarded Joshua from the tribe of Ephraim as a charismatic leader. It is notable that Joshua and several judges came from the territory of central Palestine. Ehud was from Benjamin (Judg. 3:15) and courageously defeated the Moabite king Eglon. Gideon, from Ophra in Manasseh (6:11), defeated the Midianites in a one-sided but decisive battle. Jephthah was a Gileadite (11:1), a group perceived as runaway Ephraimites (12:4). Deborah came from the hill country of Ephraim between Ramah and Bethel (4:5), though her faithful helper Barak hailed from Naphtali (v. 6).

Deborah and her song deserve a bit closer attention in this overview. The battle of Deborah and Barak against Jabin, the king of Hazor, has come to us in two versions, one prose (Judges 4), the other poetic (ch. 5). But Jabin and Hazor are mentioned also in Joshua 11:1–15, where it is reported that Joshua defeated a coalition organized by Jabin of Hazor and razed his city. These different reports pose difficult historical and chronological problems to the investigator, and various solutions have been proposed. The most plausible solution appears to be to assume that the different traditions (Joshua 11; Judges 4 and 5) refer to the same event but that, as it was handed down, changes in names and situations crept in. The important point in the story, however, is the alliance between Deborah and the tribes of Ephraim, Benjamin, and the men of Machir on the one hand, and Barak and the tribes of Naphtali and Zebulun on the other. In the book of Judges this battle alliance marks a climax in the union of tribes that are predominantly in central Palestine with some northern tribes to create a fairly firm tribal league. It is remarkable that such tribes as Reuben, Gilead, and Asher (Judg. 5:16–17) did not yet join this league, Dan remained with the ships, and Judah was conspicuous by its absence. This ancient tradition also teaches us something about the military tactics of the Israelites, who were inexperienced and poorly equipped, compared with the Canaanites. As the mustering point for the battle, they selected Mount Tabor, strategically located in the plain of Jezreel and very difficult for the Canaanite war chariots to climb. Israel began the battle in the rainy season, when the plain is turned into a morass and less passable for war chariots. According to the narratives Jabin's armies perished in the brook Kishon, and General Sisera had to flee on foot, finally to be killed by a woman.

Beyond question, the victory of Joshua/Deborah/Barak strengthened Israel's position in the Valley of Jezreel and in central Palestine at the expense of the Canaanites. In Malamat's view, the weakening of Canaanite power and the reduction or disappearance of Egyptian influence in Palestine resulted in various nomadic tribes' entering Palestine from the desert and ravaging it. Perhaps the raid of the Midianites at the time of Gideon may be regarded as an example (Judges 6–8). The surprise attack on the inhabited land in the period of harvest to carry off the grain seems to point in that direction. (According to tradition, the Midianites used camels, thus further confusing the Israelites.) The farmers in the plain, led by Gideon from Ophra, an as yet unidentified place in Manasseh, countered the attack. Isaiah 9:3 (4) and 10:26 report the deep impression the victory of Gideon's small army over the Midianites in the northern spur of the plain of Jezreel (near Endor, according to Ps. 83:11 [10] must have made on contemporaries and on later generations.

After Gideon's victory over the Midianites in Cisjordan, in which he defeated Zebah and Zalmunna (Judges 8; cf. Ps. 83:12 [11]), the elders offered him a kind of hereditary kingship, which Gideon declined (Judg. 8:23). The tradition tells us that his son Abimelech, who from his mother's side had close connections with Shechem, took cruel advantage of this offer. He killed his brothers

who could thwart him, while he himself became king in Shechem, supported by the population of the city (ch. 9). This kingship, however, did not bring him happiness. A quarrel arose between him and the citizens of Shechem, the city was burned, and Abimelech was finally killed near the city of Thebez as the war spread through central Palestine (vv. 50–57; see also 2 Sam. 11:21). It was still the time of the judges; there was yet no king in Israel.

The traditions in the book of Judges make it clear who the enemies were whom Israel had to fight. Some of these enemies are present through virtually the whole history of Israel, and others opposed Israel only at the beginning of its settlement in Canaan. The Midianites are mentioned in the time of the patriarchs (see Gen. 25:4; 37:28, 36), Moses had a confrontation with them (Exod. 2:15–17; cf. 18:1–12, etc.), but they disappear from Israel's history after the major battle against the army of Gideon, likely because they withdrew for good to their pastures in the vicinity of the Gulf of Aqabah.

The Moabites exercised an influence on Israel over a much longer period. According to Genesis 19:30–37, they were related to Israel, and it is possible that, as *sht (Shutu),* they are found in Egyptian execration texts from the nineteenth century B.C. They inhabited the high fertile plateaus east of the Dead Sea, where the grain would grow even when the land west of the Jordan was afflicted by drought and famine (cf. Ruth 1:1). Attempts by the Moabites to expand their territory to the north across the Arnon (Deut. 2:9–10) or to the west across the Jordan to Jericho (Judg. 3:12–30) were soon foiled, particularly by the daring act of the judge Ehud. The course of Israel's later history shows continued tension with the Moabites. The children of an Israelite and a Moabite were not allowed in Israel until the tenth generation. Saul and David often had to make war on the Moabites. I discuss later the well-known Mesha Stone, which also tells of this period. Many prophecies of doom against the Moabites found their way into Israel's literature (e.g., Isaiah 15; Jeremiah 48; Ezek. 25:8–11; Amos 2:1–3).

The Ammonites, who lived north of the Moabites, were probably of Aramaic stock. Settling in the twelfth century in Transjordan by the Jabbok, they likely pushed out such tribes as the Rephaites, or Zamzummites (Deut. 2:20). The present-day Amman, capital of Jordan, preserves both the location and name of the ancient Ammonite capital, Rabbath-ammon (or Rabbah). The relationships between the Ammonites and Israel were quite similar to those of the Moabites and Israel. Like the Moabites, the Ammonites were related to Israel (Gen. 19:30–38) and also fought with Israel. In the time of the judges Ammon allied itself with Moab (Judg. 3:13), and Jephthah ultimately dealt them a resounding defeat (10:6–12:4). Under Saul (1 Sam. 11:1–11) and David (2 Sam. 10:1–14; 12:26–31), they raised their head again. We read later of further battles between Israel and the Ammonites (2 Chr. 20:1–30; cf. 26:8; 27:5). Though the Ammonites, like the Moabites and Israelites, were subdued by the Assyrians, they managed to attack Israel as late as the Babylonian period (2 Kgs. 24:2; Jer. 40:14; 49:1–2). Even 1 Maccabees 5:6–8 mentions a battle between Ammonites and Judeans. It is not surprising that several prophets addressed their prophecies of doom also against this nation (e.g., Jer. 9:25; 49:1–6; Ezek. 21:33–37 [28–32]; 25:1–7). Though extant inscriptions do not reveal as much about the Ammonites as the Mesha Stone does about the Moabites, in recent decades there have been some significant Ammonite finds, including a well-preserved, inscribed bronze flask discovered in 1972 at Tell Siran. Not only do such finds show that the Ammonite language is closely related to Moabite and Hebrew (Canaanite), but an inscription also mentions two kings of the Amorites named Amminadab, a name that, though in a different context, is also found in the Old Testament.

The Old Testament often includes among the indigenous population of Canaan at the time of Israel's entry a number of ethnic groups that are known in the rabbinic tradition as "the seven peoples" and that had to be exterminated. In the Old Testament traditions the number and names of these nations vary. Genesis 15:19–21 lists as many as ten: Kenites, Kenizzites, Kadmonites, Hittites, Perizzites, Rephaites, Amorites, Canaanites, Girgashites, and Jebusites. The location of these peoples covers a huge area, from the Euphrates to the Egyptian border. More often, a smaller number of people in a less extensive area is mentioned. So Exodus 3:8, 17, and other passages speak of the Canaanites, Hittites, Amorites, Perizzites, Hivites, and Jebusites. In Deuteronomy 7:1, the "seven nations" are explicitly mentioned: Hittites, Girgashites, Amorites, Canaanites, Perizzites, Hivites, and Jebusites (cf., e.g., Josh. 3:10). Some of these groups are fairly familiar to us, while others are little more than names. The Jebusites were the Canaanite inhabitants of Jebus, often identified with Jerusalem (see, e.g., Judg. 19:10), though some scholars disagree. The biblical tradition suggests that they were a separate people (cf. Gen. 10:16 and 1 Chr. 1:14). Genesis 15:21 links the Canaanites and Amorites; and Numbers 13:29, the Hittites and Amorites with the Jebusites. On the basis of the (possibly) Jebusite names recorded in the Old Testament, it would seem that Melchizedek (Gen. 14:18–20) is an Aramaic name, and Araunah (2 Sam. 24:16–25; 1 Chr. 21:15–30), Hittite. This information suggests that "Canaanite" is more of a collective name for all the ethnic groups inhabiting the land before and during Israel's entry.

As regards their language, culture, and history, the Hittites of the Old Testament are fairly familiar to us in their setting in the history of the ancient Near East (see the information on the Hittites in *The World of the Bible*). The meaning of the Old Testament term *Hittite,* however, is determined by the connotation this word acquired in later Mesopotamian literature. Many Akkadian authors regarded Hatti-land as the territory along the Mediterranean seacoast, from Egypt following Canaan and Phoenicia to the Gulf of Iskenderun. The word *Hittite* thus has a wider connotation than "belonging to the actual realm of the Hittites."

Equally vague is the group of people designated as Amorites. In early cuneiform literature the term *amurru,* "west," occurs as a designation of nomads in the desert northeast of Palmyra. Very early the Amorites formed what could be called dynasties. The nearly legendary king Hammurabi of Babylon (once considered a contemporary of Abraham) belonged to one such dynasty. Living in western Mesopotamia, the Amorites were also found around Aleppo and in other regions of Syria and Palestine. The Old Testament records that there were Amorites in pre-Israelite Palestine on both sides of the Jordan and even in the Negeb (Num. 21:21–35; Deut. 2:26–3:11; Josh. 10:1–5; cf. Gen. 14:7). On closer scrutiny of the terms *Amorites* and *Canaanites* in the Old Testament, one discovers that it is difficult to find criteria for differentiating between the two groups, even though many solutions to the problem have been proposed. In the list of nations in Genesis 10, the Amorites belong to the Canaanites, not to the Semites, as we understand the term. This classification may seem surprising, since we know, from remnants of their language, preserved especially in personal names, that the Amorites must have spoken a dialect related to Hebrew. As is commonly known, however, affinity in language does not guarantee a tribal or racial relationship. Genesis 10, we should note, has a religious tenor, not primarily one that is historical or ethnological.

The Old Testament mentions many other nations and tribes from the earliest period of Israel's history, of which we consider further only the Edomites and the Philistines. According to the biblical tradition, the Edomites were a "brother nation" of Israel and first drove out the Horites, sometimes regarded as the Hurrites mentioned in Mesopotamian sources, before settling in the area of the brook Zered (Deut. 2:12–22; cf. Gen. 14:6 and 36:20–21). According to ancient Egyptian reports dating from about 1300–1200 B.C. (see *ANET,* 259 [Aduma], 262 [Seir]), the region they inhabited must have extended from the Dead Sea to the Red Sea or the Gulf of Aqabah. The Edomite genealogies in the Old Testament (Gen. 36:1–5, 9–19) include several Arabic nomadic tribes, but Genesis 36:6–8, 19, 43, in contrast, strongly emphasizes the link between the Edomites and Esau, Jacob's twin brother in the patriarchal narratives. The Edomites became an organized state ruled over by kings before the Israelites did (vv. 31–39; cf. 1 Chr. 1:43–54).

As with other neighboring countries, Israel's relationship with Edom was generally stormy. Much of the fighting over the years may have been due both to the important north-south trade routes that cut through Edom's territory and to its mineral deposits (see Num. 20:14–21). In their days, Saul (1 Sam. 14:47) and David (2 Sam. 8:13) had to do battle with the Edomites. David reduced

them to a state of dependence whereby they were allowed to keep their own kings (2 Kgs. 3:9; cf. Gen. 36:31), but under Solomon this arrangement led to an abortive revolt (1 Kgs. 11:14–22). Later the Edomites succeeded in regaining a measure of independence (see 2 Kgs. 8:20–22; 14:7, 22; 16:6) until the Assyrians again subdued them. When the Babylonians under Nebuchadrezzar pressed in on Judah, the Edomites were not lax in venting their hostility on Israel (cf., e.g., Isa. 34:5–17; 63:1–6; Ezek. 25:12–14; 35:10; 36:5). Though in the centuries before and after our era, the Nabateans, an Arabic nomadic tribe that used Aramaic as their written language, lived in the territory of the ancient Edomites, the name Idumean has continued. (Herod, who murdered the children of Bethlehem, was an Idumean!)

More so than all the above-mentioned nations on Palestinian soil, the Philistines were the dangerous and persistent enemies of Israel. Their origin, appearance, culture, and weaponry all seem to be non-Semitic, perhaps Indo-Germanic. They are included among the Sea Peoples, who are associated with the Doric migrations at the end of the Minoan-Mycenean cultural era. About 1200 B.C. the Sea Peoples were more successful in attacking the Hittite kingdom than that of the Egyptians. Several pharaohs mention their battles with these Sea Peoples. Ramses III, for example, lists the Philistines, the Tjeker, the Shekelesh, the Weshesh, and the Denyen, whom we discussed above in connection with the tribe of Dan (see *ANET,* 262). Ranging far, the Philistines in the last half of the second millennium B.C. also occupied the coastal strip of Canaan and in many respects became assimilated with the Canaanites. In the south of the coastal plain, they formed a confederation of five cities: Ashdod, Ashkelon, Ekron, Gath, and Gaza. The biblical tradition specifies their origin as Caphtor (Deut. 2:23; Jer. 47:4; Amos 9:7), which has been identified with Crete. This identification, however, is questionable. The Philistines are indeed mentioned at the time of the patriarchs (Gen. 26:1–16), but this reference is almost certainly an anachronism (cf. also 21:34; Exod. 13:17, and other references), underscoring the literary character of the patriarchal narratives.

The Old Testament tradition makes it clear that the Philistines, after whom Palestine is still named, employed different military tactics than the Canaanites did. The Philistines were skilled in metalworking and enjoyed a kind of blacksmith monopoly (1 Sam. 13:19–22). As is also indicated by archeological finds, at the beginning of the Iron Age they tried to expand their power in Canaan. The result was a clash with the Israelites. (The battle of the judge Samson against the Philistines is nowadays sometimes interpreted as an internal tribal war that had come into the open, as I have previously mentioned [see Judges 13–16 and 18]). In section 3, I consider in more detail the battles in the monarchical era between Philistines and Israelites. The two peoples were not always hostile to each other. The Philistines did not practice circumcision, as was common in Israel (14:3; 15:18; 1 Sam. 17:26; 18:25), but perhaps they were part of the bodyguard of King David, composed of the Kerethites and Pelethites (2 Sam. 8:18; 15:18; 20:7, 23; etc.). It is thought that the Kerethites were Cretans and the Pelethites, Philistines.

The Philistines must have quickly assimilated the culture, religion, and language of the Canaanites, though some Philistine words seem to have been preserved in the Old Testament. For example, *seranim,* used as a title of the rulers of the Philistine pentapolis, is supposedly connected with the Greek *tyrannos* (Josh. 13:3; Judg. 3:3; 16:5, 8, 18, 23, 27, 30; etc.). The names of the Philistine gods mentioned in the Old Testament are apparently of Canaanite origin. Dagon (see 1 Samuel 5), Astarte, and Baal-Zebub (2 Kings 1; likely an Old Testament corruption of Zebul-Baal) are widely known names of Canaanite deities. In later times we also meet names such as Marna ("our Lord") and Derketo (Atargatis). The portrayal of Dagon as half-human and half-fish, occasionally still seen in older pictures, rests on an erroneous interpretation of the available data. Many of the personal Philistine names that have come to us are Semitic in character, except perhaps that of Achish, the king of Gath (see 1 Sam. 21:10); Ikausu, the king of Ekron (*ANET,* 291, 294); and the familiar Goliath (1 Sam. 17:4).

I mention finally some of the gods of the nations surrounding Israel. From the Old Testament and also from the Mesha Stone we know that Chemosh was the god of the Moabites (see Num. 21:29; Jer.

48:7, 46; see also 1 Kgs. 11:7, 33; 2 Kgs. 23:13). The Edomites worshiped the god Qaush, who in the Old Testament is mentioned only in combination with a few names and who, according to Vriezen, must have been a god of war and of stormy weather. By contrast, the god of the Ammonites, Milcom, is somewhat better known (1 Kgs. 11:5, 7, 33; 2 Kgs. 23:13). It is an open question whether there is a connection between this god and Moloch, who is also mentioned in the Old Testament and to whom child sacrifices were brought. In any case, *mlk,* "king," was commonly used as a predicate of many gods that were worshiped in Canaan (e.g., in Ugarit).

LITERATURE

A. G. Auld, "Judges 1 and History: A Reconsideration," *VT* 25 (1975) 261-85.

J. R. Bartlett, "Sihon and Og, Kings of the Amorites," *VT* 20 (1970) 257-77.

———, "The Rise and Fall of the Kingdom of Edom," *PEQ* 104 (1972) 26-37.

C. F. Burney, *Israel's Settlement in Canaan. The Biblical Tradition and its Historical Background* (London, 1921³).

J. A. Callaway, "New Evidence on the Conquest of 'Ai,'" *JBL* 87 (1968) 312-20.

A. Caquot and M. Sznycer, "Textes ougaritiques," in *Les religions du Proche-Orient asiatique* (Paris, 1970), pp. 351-458.

C. H. J. de Geus, *The Tribes of Israel* (Assen/Amsterdam, 1976) (provides an overview of the pros and cons of the amphictyony hypothesis; see the review by M. J. Mulder, *Studia Rosenthaliana* 11 [1977] 234ff.).

N. K. Gottwald, *The Tribes of Yahweh: A Sociology of the Religion of Liberated Israel, 1250-1050 B.C.E.* (New York, 1979).

B. Halpern, "Gibeon: Israelite Diplomacy in the Conquest Era," *CBQ* 37 (1975) 303-16.

A. J. Hauser, "Israel's Conquest of Palestine: A Peasants' Rebellion?" *JSOT* 7 (1978) 2-19 (with a discussion of the problem by T. L. Thompson, G. E. Mendenhall, and N. K. Gottwald, pp. 20-52).

———, "The Revolutionary Origins of Ancient Israel: A Response to Gottwald," *JSOT* 8 (1978) 46-49.

A. H. Jones, *Bronze Age Civilisation: The Philistines and the Danites* (Washington, 1975).

G. H. Jones, "'Holy War' or 'Yahweh War'?" *VT* 25 (1975) 642-58.

D. Livingston, "Location of Biblical Bethel and Ai Reconsidered," *WTJ* 33 (1970/1) 20-41 (see *WTJ* 34 [1971/2] 39-50).

A. Malamat, "The Danite Migration and the Pan-Israelite Exodus-Conquest: A Biblical Narrative Pattern," *Bibl* 51 (1970) 1-16.

————, *Early Israelite Warfare and the Conquest of Canaan* (Oxford, 1978).

A. D. H. Mayes, *Israel in the Period of the Judges* (London, 1974).

B. Mazar, "The Sanctuary of Arad and the Family of Hobab the Kenite," *JNES* 24 (1965) 297-303.

J. L. McKenzie, *The World of the Judges* (Englewood Cliffs/London, 1966).

G. E. Mendenhall, "The Hebrew Conquest of Palestine," *BA* 25 (1962) 66-87.

————, *The Tenth Generation* (Baltimore, 1973).

J. M. Miller, "Jebus and Jerusalem: A Case of Mistaken Identity," *ZDPV* 90 (1974) 115-27.

S. Mowinckel, *Tetrateuch-Pentateuch-Hexateuch. Die Bericht über die Landnahme in den drei altisraelitischen Geschichtswerken* (Berlin, 1964).

J. Muilenburg, "The Birth of Benjamin," *JBL* 75 (1956) 194-201.

E. Nielsen, *Shechem: A Traditio-Historical Investigation* (Copenhagen, 1959²).

M. Noth, *Das System der zwölf Stämme Israels* (Stuttgart, 1930).

M. Ottosson, *Gilead, Tradition and History* (Lund, 1969).

G. von Rad, *Der Heilige Krieg im alten Israel* (Göttingen, 1969⁵).

W. Richter, *Traditionsgeschichtliche Untersuchungen zum Richterbuch* (Bonn, 1966²).

J. Van Seters, "The Terms 'Amorite' and 'Hittite' in the Old Testament," *VT* 22 (1972) 64-81.

R. Smend, *Yahweh War and Tribal Confederation* (Nashville, 1970).

A. Sumner, "Israel's Encounters with Edom, Moab, Ammon, Sihon and Og," *VT* 18 (1968) 216-28.

R. de Vaux, *The Early History of Israel* (Philadelphia, 1978).

Th. C. Vriezen, "The Edomitic Deity Qaus," *OTS* 14 (1965) 330-53.

M. Weber, *Gesammelte Aufsätze zur Religionssoziologie* III (Tübingen, 1923²).

M. Weinfeld, "The Period of the Conquest and of the Judges as Seen by the Earlier and the Later Sources," *VT* 17 (1967) 93-113.

M. Weippert, "'Heiliger Krieg' in Israel und Assyrien," *ZAW* 84 (1972) 460-93.

G. E. Wright, *Biblical Archaeology* (Philadelphia, 1962²).

————, "Fresh Evidence for the Philistine Story," *BA* 29 (1966) 70-86.

F. R. Wüst, "Amphiktyonie, Eidgenossenschaft, Symmachie," *Historia. Zeitschrift für alte Geschichte* 3 (1954/55) 129-53.

Y. Yadin, "'And Dan, why did he remain in Ships,'" in J. G. P. Best and Y. Yadin, *The Arrival of the Greeks* (Amsterdam, 1973), pp. 55-74.

---

3. THE NATION AND ITS RELIGION DURING THE MONARCHICAL PERIOD

a. The Kingship of Saul

In terms of both length of time and coverage in Old Testament literature, Saul's kingship was brief. The writing about Saul's kingship is a part of the work of the (fictional) author often called the Deuteronomist, who in broad lines is responsible for the Former Prophets. This writer lived and wrote probably during the time of the Captivity, utilizing old archives, documents, stories, and traditions. Writing with a special purpose in mind, he presented a selective picture of King Saul and his time. Such a record presents the same difficulties as encountered elsewhere for the modern historian who seeks to construct a historically objective picture of Saul and his period.

Saul is important in the Old Testament tradition because, with his rule, the monarchy became a fixed part of Israel. According to that same tradition, before Saul there had been only one genuine, though failed, kingship in a mixed Israelite situation—the kingship of Abimelech (Judg. 8:31–9:57), the son of the judge Gideon. The latter had turned down this dignity, saying, "I will not rule over you, and my son will not rule over you; YHWH will rule over you" (8:23). These words embody the vision that would later be regularly employed, especially by the prophets, to evaluate the monarchy: YHWH is and remains the real king in Israel. Despite all the similarities between the kingship in Israel and that of the surrounding nations, this view of YHWH as king remains the principal difference. The collapse of the monarchy at the beginning of the Babylonian captivity did not in principle seriously affect Israel (Judah). The event was viewed rather as a divine judgment over a failed earthly kingship (see, e.g., Isa. 40:2).

Politically, the primary cause of the monarchy in Israel was apparently the military and economic pressure exerted by the Philistines on the tribes that were beginning to form a unity. According to a biblical report, the first large-scale confrontation with the Philistines involved "the ark of the covenant" (1 Sam. 4:3–7:1). In this account, a young prophet and judge named Samuel was serving at the central shrine at Shiloh in the south of Ephraim. He was not yet, however, actively involved in the war. At Aphek, possibly Tell el-Muhmar in the western part of the mountains of Ephraim, the Israelites were defeated. (Which "Israelites" they were is not exactly clear.) Later, the sanctuary at Shiloh was apparently destroyed (see Jer. 7:12, 14; 26:6, 9), which, some scholars maintain, archeological finds have demonstrated. The ark was carried off to Philistine territory, but after many wanderings returned to Kiriath-jearim on Israelite soil, from where finally in David's time it was brought to "the city of David" (see 1 Sam. 6:21; 7:1; Ps. 132:6; cf. 1 Chr. 13:5–6; 2 Chr. 1:4). Meanwhile the Philistines tried to gain control over the Israelites. They occupied strategically situated points, such as Gebah (1 Sam. 13:3), Ziklag (27:5), and Bethlehem (2 Sam. 23:14), and they organized raids through the land (1 Sam. 13:5–6). Because of their skill in working with iron, they exercised great power over Israel. Perhaps this fact explains the opposition in Israel to the use of the new weapon, iron, as is shown by the objection against the use of an iron razor (Num. 6:5).

The critical situation in which the Israelite tribes found themselves understandably fueled the desire for "a king to govern us like all the nations" (1 Sam. 8:5). These words were addressed to Samuel, who was judge in Mizpah as the successor of weak Eli, under whom the ark temporarily went to the land of the Philistines. The little that the tradition reports about Samuel indicates that he too had to oppose the Philistines (7:10–14) and that he judged the people of Israel at various places (Bethel, Gilgal, Mizpah, and Ramah). The text conveys the impression that the people sought the monarchy partially because they wanted continuity in leadership and the formation of a powerful military apparatus to oppose the Philistines. For the tradition mentions emphatically that Samuel's sons did not measure up to the high standard of their father. In 1 Samuel 7–12, the institution of the monarchy is recounted in a literary setting in which regularly different motifs are used to give relief to the choice of Saul as king: in chapters 9–10 the story of the lost donkeys, in 10:17–24 a kind of supernatural guidance, and in chapter 11 a campaign against the Ammonite Nahash and his army at the instigation of the inhabitants of Jabesh in Gilead. Though the historicity of all these motifs and reports is sometimes challenged, it is quite possible that especially the campaign against the Ammonites may have provoked Philistine activities against Saul, because in the campaign Saul and his army entered Philistine territory to free Jabesh.

A study of the reports about the beginning of Saul's kingship shows that the new and old forms of government, the kingship and the judgeship, displayed an essential similarity and that there was a gradual transition from the one office to the other. Although Ishida has emphasized "dynastic succession" as one of the characteristics of kingship in Israel, the insight of Alt and others who hold to a "charismatic" kingship is still valid. For Saul, even as many judges before him, is presented as a charismatic upon whom, now and then, "the spirit came in power." Saul was a tall man physically, and also in his spiritual qualities he must have been above his people. In addition, his family enjoyed a measure of prestige and possessed some means. Above all, he was a man of courage and character. In the literary tradition of the Old Testament, he is pictured as a man who at the end of his life was maniacally depressed, mentally unstable, and often tragically clashing with his best friends, all of which may perhaps be due to the author's dislike for Saul and partiality to David.

Besides the hereditary character of the kingship, other aspects of the monarchy became visible during Saul's reign, though certain institutions became more prominent under Saul's successors. For example, Saul started levying taxes, which some people naturally opposed (1 Sam. 10:27; cf. 11:12–13). 1 Samuel 10:25

mentions the "rights and duties of the kingship" and a book in which Samuel recorded them. The implication of these and similar reports is that Saul was not just a local tribal chief but actually a king who ruled over a larger and more heterogeneous territory. Chapter 11 even speaks of "all of Israel" when Saul goes to battle against the Ammonites. It is furthermore remarkable that the people had a voice in Saul's appointment as king. Apparently the various tribes came to an agreement about the person to be so named. Saul's kingship clearly must have been more than that of a ruler over a petty Canaanite city-state. On the other hand, one should not entertain grand ideas about an "Israelite state" or a tribal confederacy headed by a hereditary king.

According to 1 Samuel 13:1, Saul reigned only two years, but this text seems to be corrupt. Much about Saul's life and reign remains vague in the often-romanticized literature. For example, we do not know how old Saul was when he became king or where he was actually appointed king. According to chapter 11, Samuel called the people to Gilgal, where, after the destruction of the shrine at Shiloh, there must have been a shrine that was suitable for the anointing of a king. The place lay at the border of Ephraim and Benjamin, Saul's own tribe. The shrine of Gilgal must have been particularly important for the tribes living in central Palestine because it was outside the sphere of direct Philistine influence. The crowning of Saul at this place by the people is to be seen as a politically significant event for his rule.

In 1 Samuel 13 we read about the defense against the Philistines; three thousand men were chosen, of whom two thousand remained with Saul in Michmash and in the mountains at Bethel, while the rest, under the command of Saul's son Jonathan, were stationed at Gibeah in Benjamin. At the same time, Abner, a cousin of Saul, was appointed as commander. Later, David must also have belonged to this staff of generals (see 20:25). The battle against the Philistines, who numerically and qualitatively were greatly superior to the Israelites, is fascinatingly recounted, embellished with the literary features later narrators loved to add to increase the glory of their ancestors. The fact remains that Saul and his army obtained a sensational victory. The triumph over the Philis-

tines was, however, still far from definite. Gibeah was freed from the Philistines and likely made into Saul's residence, the Philistines were routed till past Beth-horon toward Aijalon in the direction of the Philistine Ekron, but the victory was not fully exploited (14:46), and thus the threat remained.

Saul also had to fight on other fronts. A brief report (1 Sam. 14:47–48) mentions his successes against Moabites, Ammonites, and Edomites in Transjordan. He also took action against nomads and small Aramean tribes. One of these groups, living for the most part in the steppe and desert, was the Amalekites in the south of Palestine. As early as in Exodus 17:8–16 they are pictured as fierce enemies of Israel, who only recently had escaped from Egyptian slavery (see also Deut. 25:17–19). According to other reports, they attacked Israel in the time of the judges, together with other desert people (Judg. 3:13; 6:3; 7:12). Saul managed to defeat them roundly. In the account of Saul's battle with the Amalekites, it is noteworthy that Saul apparently acted more humanely than Samuel, who with his own hands killed King Agag, who at first had been spared. Only under David did the Amalekites seem to have been completely destroyed (1 Sam. 27:8; 30:1–2); at least in Israel's narratives we hear nothing more about them (cf. also 1 Chr. 4:42–43 with Deut. 25:17–19 and Num. 24:20). Perhaps the remnants of their people were assimilated into Israel or other nations.

Disregarding for a moment the battles Saul fought, we note that little is known about his reign that is out of the ordinary. 1 Samuel 28:9 confirms the impression gained elsewhere that Saul was active in purifying the YHWH worship by banning mediums and spiritists from the land. The context of this story and also other reports make it clear that, in his zeal for YHWH, Saul did not always act according to the norms of later orthodoxy. In 13:7–14, Saul's acting as a priest is censured, and in the account of the battle against the Amalekites, his transgression of the law of the ban is rebuked (15:10–29). These misdeeds supposedly threatened his hereditary kingship. Even if these reports are regarded as an interpretation of Saul's reign from a much later period, the YHWH cult was clearly in a stage of growth and consolidation. There was, as we have noted, not yet one central

YHWH sanctuary. Furthermore, the Philistines' capture and retention of the ark was not regarded as a final defeat. The "high places," which at a later date were criticized, were legitimate cultic sites, despite the obvious reminders of the Canaanite fertility cult (cf. 9:12–25; 2 Chr. 1:3–4). In Saul's time we hear virtually nothing of the worship of Canaanite gods such as Baal and others. From his days some personal names contained the name Baal, including Eshbaal (1 Chr. 8:33; 9:39), or Ishbosheth (2 Sam. 2:8, 10, 12; etc.); and Meribbaal (1 Chr. 8:34; 9:40), or Mephibosheth (2 Sam. 4:4; 9:6–13; etc.).

As already noted, the Old Testament tradition mentions Saul's personal conflicts with prominent persons, of whom Samuel and David are the best known. This tradition blames Saul's attitude primarily on his mental instability. Yet it is possible that internal political complications also influenced his attitude. In the conflict with Samuel one gets the strong impression that Saul overstepped the boundary between his prerogatives and those of Samuel. This conflict led to the secret anointing of a young shepherd from Bethlehem as king (1 Sam. 16:1–13). This act symbolized the goal of some in Israel to promote David at the expense of the house of Saul. As scholars have often pointed out, the roots of the rift into north and south after Solomon's death go much further back into history. As long as a common need forced the tribes together, Saul and his house were a more or less acceptable monarchy for all of Israel. But as soon as the external pressure disappeared, underlying tribal differences resurfaced.

The tradition informs us of meetings between Saul and David on several occasions, which for the most part are negative for Saul and positive for David, but the Old Testament narrator is able to tell the gradual worsening of the relationship in a fascinating manner. In 1 Samuel 16:14–23, David is still pictured as Saul's favored musician, and in the next chapter as a young hero who defeats a Philistine giant while Saul watches passively. Finally, the women sing, "Saul has slain his thousands, and David his ten thousands" (18:7), and Saul can no longer avoid giving his daughter in marriage to David (v. 25). Gradually the biblical narrator builds up the tension between Saul and David, in favor of David and at the cost of Saul.

David is active on the borders of Judah in Philistine territory, but Saul puts his hands on the priestly helpers of David and his men (22:11–19). One priest, Abiathar, escapes Saul's massacre of the priests of Nob, and so he is able to make David the center of the cult and priesthood.

In this dramatized tradition of Saul's conflict with David, David has two things in his favor: his great popularity among the southern tribes and his prominent position among the priestly caste, two points that also play a role in other traditions about David in the Old Testament. David's power in the south was secured by his marriages to women from prominent clans (1 Sam. 25:42–43) and also by receiving Ziklag as a kind of fief by the Philistine Achish from Gath. The tradition concerning the latter event has even been preserved in two versions (21:10–15; 27:2–12). The report is significant because it points to the moment when the Philistines thought the time was ripe for launching a massive attack on Israel: in the south there was a kind of civil war against the people from the north under Saul, while the troops under David's command seemed to have been willing even to take the side of the "uncircumcised" against their own "brothers."

The Philistines' strategy in attack was based on the above-mentioned inner weakness of Israel. The Philistines marched straight to the north and avoided engaging Saul's main army in the central Ephraim mountains. By encamping at Beth-shean, they cut the country in two and blocked Transjordanian troops from coming to Saul's rescue. With their chariots they controlled the plain of Jezreel and avoided battle in the more difficult mountains. Saul was thus unable to resist the Philistines in the plain and pulled back to Gilboa (1 Samuel 29–31). Here on the mountains Israel's brave first king died in battle together with his three noble sons, of whom Jonathan has received almost proverbial fame. As a sign of their victory the Philistines hung the bodies of Saul and his men upon the walls of Beth-shean, from which they were taken down by the people of Jabesh, who remembered their previous deliverance by Saul.

The period of Saul's reign poses many unanswered questions for the modern historian. For example, to what extent was Saul really "king" over the tribes that called themselves Israel? The various traditions create the impression that many decisive political, military, and religious events in his life happened in the area of the later kingdom of the "ten tribes." In 2 Samuel 2:8–11, Saul's general Abner has one of Saul's sons, Eshbaal (Ishbosheth), crowned king in the Transjordanian Mahanaim. In this connection a list of names is mentioned: Gilead, Asher, Jezreel, Ephraim, Benjamin, and "all of Israel," this last designation being simply a summary of and explanation for the preceding names. It is interesting, however, that Judah is here identified explicitly as following David as king. However vague the boundaries may have been of Saul's "kingdom" (note here Herrmann's contrast between nation-state and territory-state), Judah was not part of it.

LITERATURE

B. C. Birch, "The Development of the Tradition on the Anointing of Saul in 1 Sam. 9.1–10.16," *JBL* 90 (1971) 55-68.

———, *The Rise of the Israelite Monarchy: The Growth and Development of 1 Samuel 7–15* (Missoula, MT, 1976).

J. Blenkinsopp, "Did Saul Make Gibeon his Capital?" *VT* 24 (1974) 1-7.

H. J. Boecker, *Die Beurteilung der Anfänge des Königtums in den deuteronomistischen Abschnitten des 1. Samuelbuches* (Neukirchen-Vluyn, 1969).

H. Cazelles, "Déborah (Judg. V 14), Amaleq et Mākîr," *VT* 24 (1974) 235-38.

R. E. Clements, "The Deuteronomistic Interpretation of the Founding of the Monarchy in I Sam. viii," *VT* 24 (1974) 398-410.

W. Dietrich, *Israel und Kanaan. Vom Ringen zweier Gesellschaftssysteme* (Stuttgart, 1979).

V. Fritz, "Die Deutungen des Königtums Sauls in den Überlieferungen von seiner Entstehung I Sam 9–11," *ZAW* 88 (1976) 346-62.

J. H. Grønbaek, *Die Geschichte vom Aufstieg Davids (1 Sam. 15–2 Sam. 5). Tradition und Komposition* (Copenhagen, 1971).

T. Ishida, *The Royal Dynasties in Ancient Israel* (Berlin, 1977).

F. Langlamet, "Les récits de l'institution de la royauté (I Sam. vii-xii): De Wellhausen aux travaux récents," *RB* 77 (1970) 161-200.

J. M. Miller, "Saul's Rise to Power: Some Observations concerning 1 Sam. 9.1–10.16; 10.26–11.15 and 13.2–14.46," *CBQ* 36 (1974) 157-74.

———, "Geba/Gibeah of Benjamin," *VT* 25 (1975) 145-66.

M. J. Mulder, "Un euphémisme dans 2 Sam. xii 14?" *VT* 18 (1968) 108-14.

J. R. Vannoy, *Covenant Renewal at Gilgal. A Study of I Samuel 11:14–12:25* (Cherry Hill, NJ, 1977).

T. Veijola, *Die ewige Dynastie* (Helsinki, 1975).

b. The Kingship of David

When David, after Saul's death, was called to the kingship by the men of Judah, Israel found itself in a desperate situation. The Philistines threatened to dominate the Israelite tribes. In such a situation the tribes, who felt themselves linked to Saul and his kingship and who perhaps would have preferred a scion from the house of Saul whom they could in some way hold accountable for the losses suffered against the Philistines, wanted someone who could effectively lead the nation, regardless of his tribal connection. It took much pain and difficulty, however, before the tribes united under the leadership of one man.

At first, Eshbaal, and even more Abner, former commander of Saul's army, became to Saul's house symbols of hope and encouragement for the future. The new king Eshbaal initially set up his residence in Mahanaim (sometimes identified with Tell Hegag in Transjordan), and Abner led a small army to the Gibeon region. There Abner clashed with a group of men led by Joab, the notorious commander of David's army, and in the process unintentionally killed Asahel, a brother of Joab (2 Sam. 2:12–3:1). Though the two sides soon made peace with each other after this brief "brotherly quarrel," the consequences of this conflict became painfully evident in the course of Israel's history. After some time, perhaps because he was dissatisfied with the weak leadership of King Eshbaal, Abner openly indicated his ambition for a position of rulership in Israel by taking Rizpah, one of Saul's concubines. Eshbaal immediately saw through this act and rebuked Abner. Thereupon Abner deserted Eshbaal and sought contact with David, who was residing in Hebron. The talks were successful, and David and Abner struck an agreement. On the way home, however,

Abner was slain by Joab, who had looked for an opportunity to avenge his brother Asahel. Eshbaal, never a courageous man, even while Abner still lived (see 3:11), was seized with fear. Assassins from his own army killed him (ch. 4), which opened the way for David to become king over all of Israel. We focus now on the life of the man who, religiously speaking, is called the greatest king of Israel.

On the assumption that the figures mentioned in the Old Testament are historically correct and not intended merely symbolically, David must have been about thirty years old when he became king (2 Sam. 5:4) and must have reigned about forty years. It is assumed that David was born about 1030 B.C. He was the youngest son of Jesse (1 Sam. 16:11; 17:12; Ruth 4:17, 22; 1 Chr. 2:15). The Old Testament literary tradition portrays his youth as idyllic and romantic; he is pictured as a shepherd, singer, and musician who unexpectedly enters the court and life of Saul. Apart from the question of the historical reliability of this presentation, the arrival of the Judean David need not imply that all of Judah had joined Saul. It was relatively easy then to transfer to a more or less foreign military service (recall Abner!).

The Old Testament reports about David indicate that very early he must have become a more or less legendary figure in Israelite literature and culture. The accounts about David seem to blend imagination and reality, from which a modern historian finds it difficult if not impossible to extract "solid facts." Even David's own name is problematic. Was *David* actually a proper name? This question was asked seriously when cuneiform texts discovered at Mari on the Euphrates, dating from the seventeenth century B.C., yielded a word that was read *dawidum* and translated "chief." Scholars now know that the word is a variant of *dabdu,* "defeat," but the example illustrates the problems that can be raised by the far-from-common name David in the Hebrew texts.

Old Testament writers have pictured David from different angles, which have proven difficult to harmonize. The author of Chronicles, who devoted no less than nineteen of the sixty-five chapters to David (1 Chronicles 11–29), attributes more virtues to him than his Deuteronomistic colleague in 1–2 Samuel. The Chronicler omits several unfavorable stories about David, both from his private life (David's affair with Bathsheba and the murder of her husband, Uriah, told in 2 Samuel 11) and from his public life (David's conflict with Eshbaal before becoming king over "all Israel," as described in 2 Samuel 2–4). The writer of Chronicles is particularly interested in David as a man who organized the priests and Levites and who was divinely charged to make preparations for building the temple (see 1 Chr. 28:19; 2 Chr. 29:25). The Deuteronomistic author also attempts to link the building of the temple with David and to emphasize the exclusiveness of Jerusalem as the city of the worship of YHWH. In the author's history of David, 2 Samuel 7 occupies a central position; this chapter states in capsule form the role of David in the life of Israel. As in an epic poem, the Deuteronomist tells in masterful literary fashion the two theologically informed aspects of "David blessed" and "David cursed" (chs. 10–24). These sections represent "the facts" about David's kingship.

Stripped of romanticism and legendary accretions, David appears to have been a man who was interested in more than war, heroes, and women. He personally combined bravery, desire for power, charm, and, in particular, artistic talent—David the musician, poet, and builder is portrayed as a promoter of culture. The tradition mentions not only his laments for Saul and Jonathan (2 Sam. 1:19–27) and Abner (3:33–34) but also a large number of psalms. It is not too bold to say that David and his son Solomon initiated a kind of literary and cultural renaissance in Israel. The international contacts that each established also point in that direction. David maintained friendly relations with the Phoenicians of Tyre and Sidon, who were regarded as culturally highly gifted and civilized (5:11; 1 Chr. 14:1). As the traders of the ancient Orient, the Phoenicians since time immemorial maintained contacts with culturally advanced Egypt and also with the Greek world. As far as the Strait of Gibraltar (or, according to some, the Canary Islands!), the Phoenicians controlled trade and contributed to the development of science and culture in the Mediterranean world. They developed the writing system from which our own alphabet eventually emerged and were renowned for their skills in architecture and shipbuilding, from all of which David and Solomon profited.

Notwithstanding this positive evaluation, we stand at the beginning of a spiritual crisis that would later deeply affect Israel as "the people of YHWH"—which prominent religious leaders insisted that Israel exclusively become. The cultural policies of David and Solomon posed a radical threat to this exclusivism. Saul, despite his kingship and personal qualities, had essentially remained a culturally isolated gentleman farmer. He hardly needed a residence, and his foreign policy was limited to fighting Israel's immediate enemies. David introduced the friendship with Phoenician and Canaanite culture, aided by a great measure of linguistic affinity. Elements thus penetrated Israelite society that later almost completely destroyed Israel. As long as the golden age continued under the powerful rule of a Yahwistic king, the consequences remained limited—in fact, developments could be favorably interpreted within the religious perspective. David's policy, like that of great kings of any time, aimed at promoting the unity of his people through unity of language, unity in laws, and unity in religion. David's concern was the worship of YHWH, the God of the *twelve* tribes of Israel. Solomon continued this course of David, which to some extent was "pleasing to YHWH" (note, however, the criticism of Solomon's polygamous practices). Later, less-powerful kings threatened the worship of YHWH through their support of Baal worship. David's cultural policies were one of the factors that later contributed to this evil.

Returning to David's kingship, we note that, after the death of Eshbaal, the northern tribes sought to join the king of Judah, who resided in Hebron, so that they might find protection and strength against the menacing Philistines. Such a union constituted a threat to the Philistines, who could tolerate two small weak states in the hill country surrounding them more easily than they could one united kingdom. But David, at one time a vassal of the Philistines and acquainted as none other with their strategy and tactics, recognized the Philistine menace and took timely action. To strengthen his own position in the now-united north and south, he needed a central government in a neutral location. Hebron, where he had

reigned for the first seven years, was unsuitable as the capital. Between Judah and the northern realm there was a strip of territory inhabited by the Canaanite Jebusites. The capture of this territory would do two things for David: (1) eliminate a wedge of Canaanite power between the recently united areas, a wedge that constituted a serious threat to the preservation of the union, and (2) create a neutral area for northerners and southerners in which a capital could be built. David had Jebus captured by his fearless chief commander, Joab (2 Sam. 5:6–10; 1 Chr. 11:4–9). The Philistines, becoming aware of David's intentions, launched an attack. Again it was aimed at that part of the united kingdom that seemed to them the weakest: the Valley of Rephaim, not far from Jerusalem, the new capital. But here as well as a little later the Philistines were dealt a terrible defeat by David. With his small, well-trained army David pursued them all the way to their own territory. The former vassal of the Philistines had now reversed the roles (2 Sam. 5:17–25; 1 Chr. 14:8–17).

David's victory over the Philistines freed his hands to turn Jerusalem into the political and especially the religious center of his newly united kingdom. In contrast to Shiloh, Shechem, and other places that had shrines for YHWH, Jerusalem was religiously neutral. As we noted earlier, the El cult in Jerusalem likely had a long history (see Genesis 14), and there no doubt were Canaanite shrines in or near Jerusalem. In the opinion of many scholars, the later cult of YHWH in Israel assimilated much from the Jerusalem El cult and incorporated it into the so-called Zion theology. The Old Testament tradition tells us that David took the ark, which was stationed in Kiriath-jearim after its Philistine adventures, and brought it to Jerusalem (2 Samuel 6; cf. 1 Chronicles 13 and chs. 15–16). This move initiated not only centralization of the cult but also a close tie between kingship and sanctuary. In the tradition David became the "chosen king" of YHWH, an election that also applied to his dynasty (see 2 Samuel 7). We may assume that the ark was placed where a sanctuary had earlier stood that belonged to Araunah, a Hittite. For David, ruling over this area, the ark became a royal sacred object, even as the king himself had become a divine instrument. David's son Solomon extended these features by building the temple adjacent to his palace.

A consequence of this royal sanctuary, already established in principle by David in Jerusalem, was his organization of a priestly caste that was essentially a staff of royal servants (2 Sam. 8:15–18; 1 Chr. 18:14–17). Though the classes and divisions of Levites, priests, singers, and others attributed to David in 1 Chronicles 23–24 are often regarded as a later idealization of David's concern with cult and religion, at the historical core is the king's objective to further the unity of his kingdom. It can no longer be determined to what extent in his cultic reforms David adopted existing Jerusalemic regulations and used people who formerly served in the cult. Tradition shows that the Israelite priest Abiathar was from the family of Ithamar (cf. Exod. 6:23) and was the only one to escape Saul's massacre of the priests of Nob. He took the side of David (see 1 Sam. 22:20–23; 23:6–9; 30:7; 2 Sam. 8:17; 1 Chr. 18:16; 24:6) and for a while shared the priesthood with Zadok (2 Sam. 15:24–36; 17:15; 19:11; 20:25). Abiathar had to retire in favor of Zadok and his family, who were regarded as belonging to the pre-Davidic cultic personnel of Jerusalem, or Jebus (1 Kgs. 1:7, 19, 25; 2:22, 26–27).

David's foreign policy was marked by positive and negative contacts with many nations. Though in the Old Testament writings these contacts are presented as military confrontations, economic motifs were undoubtedly also involved. Sometimes the mention of a war serves only as a setting for an altogether different story. The subjection of the Ammonites (2 Sam. 10:6–11; 12:26–31), for example, provides the background for the story of David's murder of Uriah and his taking of Uriah's wife, Bathsheba. The war against the Arameans, who had founded several small city-states north of Israel, involved not only a confrontation with linguistically related brother nations but also an expansion of David's influence in the direction of the wood and mineral treasures in Lebanon. 2 Samuel 8:6 states that even Damascus was controlled by David. Such military operations became possible because the Assyrian king Ashurrabi II (ca. 1012–972) was so preoccupied by Arameans who lived still further to the north that he had no time for military expeditions to the south. The Assyrians did succeed in driving away the Arameans on the Euphrates, but under Hadadezer of Soba some small Aramean kingdoms united and in turn were subdued by David. In his conquest David carried off a large quantity of bronze (v. 8), which brings out the economic aspect of the invasion.

Further scrutinizing David's military activities, we notice that, at least in our thinking, he was not soft on his enemies. For instance, he slaughtered two-thirds of the Moabite army in a manner that, though perhaps original, was nevertheless gruesome (2 Sam. 8:2). Edom was treated in similar fashion; for six months David gave Joab freedom to murder and plunder, in an effort to exterminate the entire male population (vv. 13–14; 1 Kgs. 11:15–17). It is not surprising that the Edomites always remained bitter enemies of Israel. For David, sovereignty over Edom was economically important. It gave him access to the Gulf of Aqabah and control over the ore mines in the south of the Negeb. So David, through military successes, bloody excesses, shrewd diplomacy (e.g., with Tyre and Sidon), and many marriages with women from prominent families, built a sizable kingdom between Egypt and Assyria, the two moderately strong world powers. Israel, not without sacrifice, had become a medium-sized power. As Gunneweg has observed, Israel revered David as "God's anointed" and "father of the fatherland," perhaps more from human appreciation than from a sense of his divine uniqueness. In typical Israelite fashion, however, the Deuteronomistic version in particular candidly displays the darker sides of David's life and refuses to cover up the essential inner division of the realm.

The Old Testament tradition tells of two revolts during David's reign that demonstrated the inner disharmony of the realm and nearly destroyed it. The first was instigated by David's son Absalom, an offspring from David's marriage to an Aramean princess (2 Sam. 3:3). Absalom had kingly ambitions at an early age and was infatuated with himself (18:18). Harboring some grievances against his father, he cunningly exploited the dissatisfaction of the people (chs. 13–14). After he had ingratiated himself with many of the people, he tried to seize the kingship over Israel in Hebron, where earlier his father had been anointed king over Judah (ch. 15). At first his design seemed to succeed: David fled from Jerusalem, and Absalom made his entrance there. Following oriental custom, he consolidated his coup by publicly taking possession of his father's harem. He lacked the necessary experience, however, to exploit his situation fully. Ignoring the wise counsel of Ahithophel, former adviser to his father, and listening to Hushai, an undercover friend of David, he assembled a large army to fight David's guerrilla forces in Transjordan. This decision led to his downfall. Joab's army won the day for David in the forests, and Absalom was slain by Joab's own hand. David regained his sovereignty over "all the tribes of Israel" and returned in triumph to Jerusalem. Faced with the need of regaining the confidence of Judah, his own tribe, David appointed the Judean Amasa to succeed Joab as commander of the armed forces, despite Amasa's earlier appointment by Absalom as commander of the Judeans (17:25; 19:14). The rivalry between Judah and the tribes of Israel is emphasized by the report that the two groups clashed in their asseverations about loyalty to the king (19:42–43).

The smoldering fire of the deep-seated discord burst into flame again at the revolt of Sheba (2 Samuel 20). As a Benjamite, he made himself the spokesperson for northern Israelite interests. This revolt, too, was repressed; one of the casualties was the new commander, Amasa, who fell victim to Joab's jealousy and was slain by the old commander himself. As often happens in civil wars, personal motifs became intertwined with the political issues. Even so, Joab's animosity was not entirely of a personal nature, since Amasa had supported the revolt of Absalom. At Abel Bethmaacah, a city in the far north of the country, Sheba was killed on the advice of a woman. The north-south polarity had again been reduced to that of a fire smoldering underground. David could continue upbuilding the kingdom, doing everything in his power to promote unity in the realm. He thus had to stop potential enemies from rising up against him, which is evident from his policy toward the Gibeonites. This group demanded revenge on the descendants of Saul (21:1–14). Some of these descendants were clearly subject to David, as is shown in chapter 9, which tells that Mephibosheth, a son of Jonathan, came "to

David's court"—that is, under the immediate supervision of David. David allowed the Gibeonites a free hand with respect to Saul's descendants, of which they took cruel advantage. It speaks well for the objectivity of the writer that he did not condone this horrendous behavior on the part of David, even as it speaks well for David that he openly revised his actions.

One of the measures ordered by David for the strengthening of the realm was a census (2 Samuel 24; 1 Chronicles 21). He wanted to learn the number of available soldiers and laborers in the kingdom and also to set up an efficient system of taxation. This census was opposed by the populace and, in the accounts in the books of Kings and Chronicles, was attended by drought and contagious diseases that threatened to afflict the whole land. A third element in this census story is David's sacrifice on "the threshing floor of Araunah" (2 Sam. 24:18–25), the site of the later temple of Solomon, north of Jerusalem. The Mari Texts, from the first half of the second millennium B.C., show that it was customary in such a census to bring purification offerings as a kind of head tax, a custom perhaps also referred to elsewhere in the Old Testament (Exod. 30:11–16). It is uncertain, however, whether this explanation can be applied to the literary account that we have of this event in David's life. It seems more likely that the sacrifice story here aims to prepare the reader for the later building of the temple by Solomon. In any case, the census itself yielded a great number of men: 800,000 in Israel and 500,000 in Judah. These figures, however, are either exaggerated or based on a wrong understanding of the word translated "thousand" (*eleph*). Sometimes it is preferable to translate this term "contingent" or "part of a tribe" (cf., e.g., Judg. 6:15). Questions remain, however (cf. 1 Chr. 21:5 with 2 Sam. 24:9).

In the reports in 2 Samuel 24:21–24, the explicit statement that David bought the cultic site of Araunah implies that the future temple would become a royal sanctuary (cf. also 2 Chr. 3:1). This decision, too, was a link in the chain of astute political measures that David had to forge for the sake of a strong central government. His measures established specific policies that could be utilized by competent successors. But who would become that successor? At the end of his life, David had difficulty deciding which of his sons should take his place, and factions involving some of the princes threatened to deal a heavy blow to the unity of the country. According to 1 Kings 1, Adonijah regarded himself as the crown prince. Supported by Joab and by Abiathar the priest, he prepared to take over the reins of government from the aged king. Unlike Absalom's revolt, Adonijah's plotting to seize the throne should be regarded not as a direct revolt but as an example of the ancient oriental idea that a sick or aged and powerless king constituted a threat to the well-being of a country and people (see the example in the Keret Text, discovered at Ugarit). The Canaanite substructure of this story illustrates the ever-present influence of the Canaanite religion in Israel, which not even Joab and Abiathar could escape.

But Solomon had also gathered a group of trusted people around him, including Bathsheba his mother, Nathan the court prophet, Zadok the priest, and Benaiah the commander of the bodyguard. Was their conduct perhaps influenced more by Yahwistic ideals than by Canaanite religion? In any case, the unauthorized enthronement feasts by Adonijah and his followers were thwarted by the royal proclamation that Solomon was to be David's successor. The authority of the aged king guaranteed that the people accepted Solomon and rejected Adonijah. The unity of the two kingdoms was temporarily saved. Under peaceful conditions the stage was set for continued working on a Davidic ideal: a golden age of one people under a king of one house, with one language and one religion. Many a prophet and poet would later idealize this vision.

LITERATURE

A. Carlson and H. Ringgren, *"dāvidh," TDOT* III: 157-69.

R. A. Carlson, *David, the Chosen King: A Traditio-Historical Approach to the Second Book of Samuel* (Stockholm, 1964).

W. Dietrich, *Prophetie und Geschichte* (Göttingen, 1972).

J. W. Flanagan, "Court History or Succession Document? A Study of 2 Samuel 9–20 and 1 Kings 1–2," *JBL* 91 (1972) 172-81.

D. M. Gunn, "David and the Gift of the Kingdom (2 Sam. 2–4, 9–20, 1 Kgs. 1–2)," *Semeia* 3 (1975) 14-45.

———, "Traditional Composition in the 'Succession Narrative,'" *VT* 26 (1976) 214-29.

T. N. D. Mettinger, *Solomonic State Officials* (Lund, 1971).

M. J. Mulder, "Versuch zur Deutung von *sokènèt* in 1 Kön. I 2, 4," *VT* 22 (1972) 43-54.

R. Rendtorff, "Beobachtungen zur altisraelitischen Geschichtsschreibung anhand der Geschichte vom Aufstieg Davids," in H. W. Wolff, ed., *Probleme Biblischer Theologie* (Festschrift G. von Rad; München, 1971), pp. 428-39.

K.-D. Schunck, "Juda und Jerusalem in vor- und frühisraelitischer Zeit," in K.-H. Bernhardt, ed., *Schalom* (Festschrift A. Jepsen; Berlin, 1971), pp. 50-57.

E. A. Speiser, "Census and Ritual Expiation in Mari and Israel," *BASOR* 149 (1958) 17-25.

A. Weiser, "Die Legitimation des Königs David," *VT* 16 (1966) 325-54.

R. N. Whybray, *The Succession Narrative: A Study of II Sam. 9–20 and I Kings 1 and 2* (London, 1968).

E. Würthwein, *Die Erzählung von der Thronfolge Davids—theologische oder politische Geschichtsschreibung?* (Zürich, 1974).

---

c. The Kingship of Solomon

Before reviewing the period of Solomon's kingship, we must look more carefully at *chronology,* an aspect of Israel's history that we have so far not considered. Before David's kingship, dates are necessarily very vague. But also for his reign and that of his successors, we cannot construct a totally satisfactory chronology. If David was born about 1030 B.C., then about 960 he died and was succeeded by Solomon, who perhaps ruled as coregent with his father for one or more years after the abortive grasp for power by his half-brother Adonijah. According to the tradition Solomon, like David, reigned forty years (1 Kgs. 11:42; 2 Chr. 9:30). He thus died about 920, after which the break in the realm occurred. Careful calculations, however, based on the length of reign of Solomon's successors in Judah and Israel, indicate that these dates cannot be right. Constructing a chronology of the divided kingdom has occasioned considerable controversy and produced a diversity of often highly ingenious solutions. After the death of Solomon the books of Kings present an uninterrupted sequence of the dates of the accession and death of each Judean and Israelite king, which give the impression of having been derived from official annals in the royal archives. In addition it is occasionally possible to correlate the fixed Assyrian chronology (for which, see *The World of the Bible*) with certain biblical events. It would therefore seem that we should be able to construct a totally coherent chronology. For several reasons, such is unfortunately not the case.

In Kings the beginning or concluding dates of a king's reign in one kingdom are stated in terms of the regnal year of the ruler from the other kingdom. Furthermore, the dates pertaining to the reign of a particular king are in turn expressed in terms of the beginning of his own reign. For the monarchical period the first such reference is in 1 Kings 6:37–38, where it is stated that the foundation of the temple was laid in the fourth year of Solomon and that it was completed in his eleventh year. Yet occasionally in Kings these relational dates, whether referring specifically to the realms of Judah and Israel or to events in the world around, cause considerable difficulty. The problem in establishing the absolute chronology of the separate kings is even greater because of the uncertainty whether the reign of kings was computed with a "predating" or a "postdating" system and whether, within the northern or southern kingdom or both, one dating system replaced the other over a period of time.

In Egypt and Assyria a reckoning in terms of regnal years was not something new, and it seems plausible that Judah and Israel may have adopted this system. In the predating method, the last year of a king's reign is counted both in the old king's total and as the first year of the new king. In postdating, a new king's reign is counted only from the first new-year festival after the death of the old king. Another question concerns the start of the new year: was it in Tishri (Sept./Oct.) or in Nisan (Mar./Apr.)? Or did Judah begin in Tishri and Israel in Nisan? Or were different systems followed at different times? Whichever calendar was used, scholars must make a number of unprovable hypotheses and must also contend with the possibility of errors in the figures reported in the

tradition. As an example of the latter, consider 2 Kings 15:27, which reports Pekah's reign of twenty years in Israel. This figure must be wrong, but the corrections proposed by researchers vary widely, from two to twelve years. Yet the text here is not corrupt. Was there perhaps an originally lower figure that was made larger? If so, why? Some have suggested that several years of coregency may have been included. Such a "solution," however, only complicates the problem.

There are some indications that, under Assyrian-Babylonian influence, Nisan was later regarded as the first month of the new year in both kingdoms and that Judah followed a postdating system of computation, perhaps indicated by the phrase "in the beginning of the reign of . . ." (Jer. 26:1; 27:1; 49:34; etc.). 1 Kings 15:1 and 9 indicate that Judah also employed the predating method. These verses mention Abijam, who became king over Judah in the eighteenth year of Jeroboam I, and Asa, who became king in the twentieth year of that same king. Yet verse 2 states that Abijam reigned *three* (not two) years. We do not know when the shift was made from one system to the other. According to Thiele, Israel used the predating system from Jeroboam I to Jehoahaz and the postdating system from Joash to Hoshea. According to others (Begrich, Jepsen), the Assyrian system of postdating was in vogue in Israel, adopted with the coming of Tiglath-pileser of Assyria, so that in the fixation of a year two successive years can be indicated (e.g., 853/852). A third group of scholars (Andersen, Herrmann) believes that both kingdoms used the same method of computation continuously during their entire existence, with the calendar year always beginning in Tishri and with coregencies and rival kings not being included in the official regnal years of the kings.

A variety of extrabiblical data aid in constructing a chronology that is somewhat reliable. Josephus mentions certain numbers, some of which may need correction. More important are the aforementioned absolute data furnished, for example, by various Assyrian and Babylonian chronicles or recorded in the astronomical *Canon of Ptolemy*. Records of solar and lunar eclipses can on occasion provide useful points of reference for chronology. Some of the reasonably certain fixed dates that have been obtained in this way are the first capture of Jerusalem by Nebuchadrezzar and the end of the three-month reign of Jehoiachin on 16 March 597 B.C., the battle at Qarqar involving Ahab in 853, Jehu's payment of tribute to Shalmaneser III in 841, and the payment of tribute by (presumably) Joash to Adad-nirari III in 802 (according to a stele discovered in 1967 at Tell ar-Rima in Iraq). These few specific references, however, do not allow us to solve all the problems of biblical chronology.

On the basis of these considerations for determining the regnal period of the Judean and Israelite kings, we know that Solomon's forty-year reign must have ended about 930 B.C. The number 40 is often used as a round number in the Bible, however, which suggests that its use here may be symbolic. In any case, Solomon's kingship, like that of his father, was very important for the nation and the people. To some extent it was a time of peace, a quality perhaps reflected in Solomon's throne name (shalom, "peace"; cf. Jedidiah, his name at birth [2 Sam. 12:24–25]).

In the formation of the later tradition and legends around the figure of Solomon, the idea of a realm of peace played an important role. But the section in the Old Testament that narrates Solomon's history also shows that Solomon had to wage few wars (1 Kings 3–11; 2 Chronicles 1–9 is a kind of excerpt of those chapters). Unlike the accounts of David's climb to power, success, and last days, this section about Solomon reads more like a chronicle and is more statistical in nature. Its author must have consulted a number of archival documents and other reports to record a variety of often only partially lucid data about the construction projects and governmental and political activities of the king. Here and there this account is interspersed with an anecdote from the life of Solomon, of which the historical value is hard to appraise. The literary information about Solomon's activities is religiously slanted, more so in Chronicles than in Kings.

One of Solomon's deeds as king was to execute Adonijah and Adonijah's political friends Joab and Abiathar (1 Kgs. 2:13–24; 28–34). We should note that Adonijah had done enough to make Solomon distrust him by asking for the beautiful young woman of his father's old age to be his wife.

Shimei, a possible claimaint to the throne from Saul's house, was also put to death (vv. 8, 36–46). This bloody start of Solomon's era makes us aware that, during his kingship, not everything proceeded as peacefully as later traditions imply. His fairly extensive building activities, the reorganization of the country into governmental districts (favoring Judah), and other measures create the suspicion that, for many people in the land, especially "Israelites" and "Canaanites," it was not always a golden age. We perceive this attitude when the people (especially "Israel") later asked Solomon's son Rehoboam to lighten the yoke his father had imposed on them (12:4). For many people Solomon's reign was an oppressive era, and only a later retouching of this period was able to make it a golden time.

The Old Testament tells us less about Solomon than about his father, David. It is hard to say whether he was a greater genius than his father. The text gives much attention to his building activities (which concerned primarily his court), the court cult, and defense. These activities may suggest that the king had a great interest in culture. The impression rather seems to be that Solomon, benefiting from the politically favorable circumstances, made splendid use of the means that his surroundings, far and near, offered him to enhance his own reputation. His numerous marriages, too, consolidated his stature as a mighty monarch. The Solomon cycle in Kings even opens with the announcement that the king allied himself by marriage with the house of the pharaoh (1 Kgs. 3:1), an act that yielded him Gezer (9:16). Pharaoh's daughter was held in particularly high regard—he even built a separate palace for her (7:8)—but Moabite, Ammonite, Edomite, Sidonian, and Hittite women also enjoyed his favors and lived at his court (11:1–3). He furthered the political peace with his neighbors especially through commerce, though armed skirmishes were not entirely unavoidable. In 11:14, 21–22, 25, an Edomite called Hadad is mentioned as an enemy, and in vv. 23–25, an Aramean from Damascus. With such adversaries Solomon must have had mainly border skirmishes, because these enemies were not nearly as powerful as Solomon's important friends Egypt and Phoenicia.

Especially his friendship with Hiram of Tyre is

told in great detail (1 Kgs. 5:15–32 [1–18]). For the construction of his palace and the temple (see ill. 29 and 30), Solomon had at his disposal the ample wood, metal, and stone resources of the Tyrian hinterland, the Lebanon. He could also avail himself of Tyrian skills. In chapters 6–8, these building activities are described in the context of the overall purpose of the book of Kings. These chapters give considerable and often detailed attention to the building and arrangement of the temple, whereas the building of the palace, which took all of thirteen years, is mentioned only in passing as a brief report sandwiched between the building of the temple and its arrangement. Phoenician and Canaanite influence on the architectural design and construction of these magnificent buildings is clearly confirmed by the Old Testament tradition. Solomon indeed had to pay a high price for this friendly help. According to 9:11–14, some twenty cities in Galilee were given as compensation for Hiram's services, who, however, was not pleased with them.

Solomon's building activities likely had two important consequences: (1) an efficient organization for mustering workers and collecting money for the building of palace and sanctuary, and (2) the building of a useful network of roads and trade connections. For the latter, some information is provided in 1 Kings 9:26–28; 10:11, 22, where it is reported that the king of Tyre helped Solomon with the equipping and manning of a large commercial fleet that sailed from the harbor of Ezion-geber at the Gulf of Aqabah. These ships brought back gold, precious wood, silver, ivory, and—if we understand the meaning of the Hebrew words— even monkeys and peacocks. In this connection the somewhat mysterious and as yet unidentified Ophir (see ill. 32) is also mentioned. On the boundaries of the Arabah, not far from the Gulf of Aqabah, there must have been copper and iron mines that were also exploited in Solomon's time, about which the Old Testament is silent. Solomon engaged in an interesting trade in horses and chariots (10:28–29), a kind of intermediary trading in which the horses came from Mizraim. Possibly this name refers not to Egypt but to a territory that, with Kue, constituted a region in Asia Minor near the Taurus mountains.

The visit of the "queen of Sheba," if the story is historical, was connected with Solomon's extensive commercial relations (1 Kgs. 10:1–13). In the cycles of sagas and legends of the Middle East, this story has become one of the most widespread and inspiring, climaxing in the chief work in Ethiopian literature, the Kebra nagast (Praise of the kings). The historical core of this story is the relationship between Israel and southern Arabia. Ophir, occurring in this incident, has been thought to be located in this latter area. In Saba in southern Arabia, where inscriptions from the ninth century B.C. have been found, no names of queens from ancient times have been discovered.

Besides mentioning Solomon's trade, the tradition likewise describes the internal organization of his realm. 1 Kings 4:7–19, which follows an enumeration of some high officials, including Adoniram, who earlier served under David (see 2 Sam. 20:24), lists twelve district governors. Each of these districts had to supply provisions for the king and the royal household for one month every year. Closer study of this list as well as of the information in 1 Kings 4:27 (cf. 9:20–23) shows the remarkable fact that regularly "all Israel" and the non-Israelite population are mentioned, but Judah is left out. Herrmann, for example, has interpreted this omission as indicating the still-latent breach in the kingdom united by David and Solomon. (For a different view, see Albright.) It does not seem likely, however, that the burdens were distributed too unequally between north and south. A sensible ruler such as Solomon—the tradition credits him with exceptional wisdom (see 3:9, 12, 28; 5:9–14 [4:29–34]; etc.)—was undoubtedly aware of the advantages of spreading power and burdens over all segments of his people. With hindsight, however, we see that the period of Solomon's reign clearly must have helped Judah more than it did the north.

Solomon apparently organized his kingdom according to a foreign model. The list in 1 Kings 4 (see map I.B) shows that, in organizing originally Canaanite territories, he followed the traditional Old Testament tribal divisions only partially. His organization of the cult also manifested foreign influence. Solomon consolidated his father's choice of Jerusalem as metropolis of his kingdom and as religious center. On a rocky hill north of the "city of David," he built his palace and the temple, which overlooked the surroundings like an eagle's nest. This temple was a royal sanctuary in which priests functioned as royal officials, whose livelihood was provided by the king himself. Jerusalem and the cult of YHWH established there were like an exclave in the united kingdom. Both had a great influence not only on the political but especially on the religious shaping and developing of Israel. The foundation of the temple involved in particular a change in the religious tradition of the YHWH-worshiping tribes, though at first it must have hardly affected the function of the local shrines scattered throughout the land, since Solomon himself initially emphasized the importance of these sacred places. Here we could mention Gibeon, "the great [i.e., most important] high place" (1 Kgs. 3:4–5), where Solomon went at the inauguration of his kingship. Also in the sequel of the narratives about Solomon, nothing is said about the abolition of such local shrines.

In Jerusalem, however, a cultic tradition began to develop that was specifically neither Judean nor Israelite (and for that reason basically acceptable to both groups) but that did include pre-Israelite cultic traditions. With the temple mount in Jerusalem, or Mount Zion, Solomon aimed at the union of all groups in his kingdom around "the dwelling place of YHWH." Such an emphasis was bound to have a leveling influence on Judeans, Israelites, and Canaanites alike. This kind of policy well suited kings whose domain included large minority groups. Naturally it entailed dangers for the special character of YHWH, "the God of Israel," concern for which is seen in the the the so-called Deuteronomistic evaluation by the author or redactor of the histories of Solomon. Positively, such concern can be seen in the prayer attributed to Solomon at the dedication of the temple (1 Kgs. 8:22–53); negatively, in the condemnation of Solomon's extreme tolerance of foreign gods (11:1–13). Israel must remain the people of YHWH and must serve him, rather than first of all a king, as God. This God cannot be contained in a house made with hands, nor can he remain in the background as some divine manifestation subject to the power of the king. With this outlook, the writer opposes any kingly ideology informed by an Egyptian or Akkadian model and

reveals his perspective on the history of Solomon and all succeeding kings.

The Old Testament tradition is silent about Canaanite Baal worship for the period of David and Solomon. In part this fact may mean that these kings strongly promoted the centralization of the cult of YHWH. In part it may also indicate that these kings practiced great tolerance toward those who wanted to serve their own gods but who were not missionary-minded about them. It is commonly assumed, for example, that elements from the El cult at Jerusalem were assimilated into the YHWH cult, without either party resisting it or regarding it as harmful for its own cult. Reading between the lines, one also gets the impression that Solomon and his highest officials were so preoccupied with all kinds of mundane affairs that religious matters, despite their importance, took a back seat.

The Old Testament tries to show Solomon's versatility in several ways (see 1 Kgs. 5:1–14 [4:21–34]). There is likely considerable exaggeration here, coming from a later generation who were living in difficult times and who looked back nostalgically to those days. Nevertheless, the listing of Solomon's material and spiritual riches undeniably contains a core of historical truth. The tradition pictures him as the versatile poet of thousands of proverbs and songs; he sang about the trees of the Lebanon and about the hyssop growing out of the walls. Later tradition attributed to him such books as Canticles and Ecclesiastes, and also Psalms 72 and 127 (see also 1 Kgs. 11:41). From a still later time are the "Wisdom of Solomon" and a collection of eighteen "Psalms of Solomon" preserved in Greek, to which can be added the "Odes of Solomon," handed down in Syriac but originally written in Greek. It is interesting that this tradition also compares Solomon's wisdom with that of the Egyptians and of wise men of other nations, some of whom are mentioned by name (5:10–11 [4:30–31]). Alt has rightly compared the wisdom of Solomon with the encyclopedic studies popular in his time, paying special attention to the Onomasticon of Amenemope (ca. 1100 B.C.) and to the wisdom of the Sumerians, expressing itself in the series *HAR-ra* (= *hubullu;* middle of 2nd millennium B.C.). Undoubtedly Solomon wanted to promote literature and science in his kingdom, as other nations around him had done in their heyday. The flourishing of a nation's politics, economy, architecture, and other areas often goes hand in hand with that of growth in literature and art. In the eyes of the modern historian, Solomon's era may have been anything but golden (the signs of decay are too clearly noticeable for that!), but it certainly represented a splendid period in the history of Israel.

This cultural flowering was aided by an era of political and military tranquility. The Assyrians under Tiglath-pileser II had not yet threatened the peace in Palestine, the Egyptians governed by the weak rulers of the Twenty-first (Tanite) Dynasty were preoccupied with internal problems, and the Phoenicians were interested more in a neighbor who was a friendly trading partner than in one who threatened their prosperity. Since Solomon in this time of relative political and military equilibrium did not neglect the defense of his kingdom, against either attacks from without or rebellion from within (to which, cities such as Megiddo [see ill. 28], Hazor [see ill. 31 and 33], Gezer, and Beth-horon bear archeological witness), he had all the more opportunity to promote the security and grandeur of his dynasty. It should not be forgotten, however, that the Solomonic enlightenment and artistry were probably limited to his court and to Jerusalem (see 1 Kgs. 10:16–27). Solomon may have made silver as common in Jerusalem as stones and cedar as plentiful as the sycamore of the Shephelah (v. 27), yet one may rightly question whether the majority of the ordinary people in the land shared in this prosperity. 1 Kings 11:26 indicates that the king, in addition to having enemies at the borders, also had enemies within his own kingdom. One of these rivals was the Ephraimite Jeroboam, the son of Nebat, who escaped from Solomon and was granted asylum at the Egyptian court (v. 40). This episode leads us directly to the next phase in Israel's history.

LITERATURE

Y. Aharoni, "Arad: Its Inscriptions and Temple," *BA* 31 (1968) 2-32.

G. W. Ahlström, *Royal Administration and National Religion in Ancient Palestine* (Leiden, 1982).

W. F. Albright, "The Administrative Divisions of Israel and Judah," *JPOS* 5 (1925) 17-54.

K. T. Andersen, "Die Chronologie der Könige von Israel und Juda," *ST* 23 (1969) 69-114.

J. Begrich, *Die Chronologie der Könige von Israel und Juda* (Tübingen, 1929).

F. C. Fensham, "The treaty between the Israelites and Tyrians," *SVT* 17 (1969) 71-87.

J. Finegan, *Handbook of Biblical Chronology* (Princeton, 1964).

V. Fritz, *Tempel und Zelt. Studien zum Tempelbau in Israel und zu dem Zeltheiligtum der Priesterschrift* (Neukirchen-Vluyn, 1977).

P. Garelli, "Nouveau coup d'oeil sur Muṣur," in *Hommages à André Dupont-Sommer* (Paris, 1971), pp. 37-48.

C. E. Hauer, Jr., "Who was Zadok," *JBL* 82 (1963) 89-94.

E. W. Heaton, *Solomon's New Men: The Emergence of Ancient Israel as a National State* (London, 1974).

S. W. Horn, "Who was Solomon's Egyptian Father in Law?" *BR* 12 (1967) 3-7.

A. Jepsen and F. R. Hanhart, *Untersuchungen zur israelitisch-jüdischen Chronologie* (Berlin, 1964).

A. Jepsen, "Noch einmal zur israelitisch-jüdischen Chronologie," *VT* 18 (1968) 31-46.

――――, "Zeitrechnung," *BHH* III: 2211-14.

A. Kuschke, "Der Tempel Salomos und der 'syrische Tempeltypus,'" in F. Maass, ed., *Das ferne und das nahe Wort* (Festschrift L. Rost; Berlin, 1967), pp. 124-32.

B. Mazar, "The Aramaean Empire and its Relations with Israel," *BA* 25 (1962) 97-120.

M. J. Mulder, "Einige Bemerkungen zur Beschreibung des Libanonwaldhauses in I Reg 7, 2f.," *ZAW* 88 (1976) 99-105.

A. F. Rainey, "Compulsory Labour Gangs in Ancient Israel," *IEJ* 20 (1970) 191-202.

D. B. Redford, "Studies in Relations between Palestine and Egypt during the First Millennium B.C.: I. The Taxation System of Solomon," in J. W. Wevers and D. B. Redford, eds., *Studies on the Ancient Palestinian World* (Festschrift F. V. Winnett; Toronto, 1972), pp. 141-56.

――――, "Studies in Relations between Palestine and Egypt during the First Millennium B.C.: II. The Twenty-second Dynasty," *JAOS* 93 (1973) 3-17.

E. I. J. Rosenthal, "Some Aspects of the Hebrew Monarchy," *JJS* 9 (1958) 1-18.

K. Rupprecht, *Der Tempel von Jerusalem. Gründung Salomos oder jebusitisches Erbe?* (Berlin, 1977).

H. Tadmor, "Assyria and the West: The Ninth Century and Its Aftermath," in H. Goedicke and J. J. M. Roberts, eds., *Unity and Diversity* (Baltimore, 1975), pp. 36-48.

———, "Chronologia," *'Enṣiqlōpedīya Miqrā'īt* IV: 249-310.

E. R. Thiele, *The Mysterious Numbers of the Hebrew Kings* (Grand Rapids, 1965²).

E. Ullendorff, *Ethiopia and the Bible* (London, 1968).

G. E. Wright, "The Provinces of Solomon," *Eretz-Israel* 8 (1967) 58-68.

d. Israel after the Division of the Kingdom

Methodological objections can be raised against the heading of this section, because I did not specifically discuss the schism in my treatment of Solomon. Practically, however, the division of the kingdom after Solomon's death was an event whose roots go back to the Davidic and Solomonic kingdom, even before the period of great prosperity. Another objection that might be raised against the method followed in this section is that a separate treatment of the history of Israel and Judah divides what for the author of the book of Kings remains a unity, albeit a damaged unity. This objection, too, is met by the design of this essay. First, I attempt to describe diachronically a history that in the books of Kings and Chronicles is recounted more or less synchronically. Second, the author of the book of Kings, though regularly referring to chronicles, annals, and other sources, did not intend to write isolated biographies of the kings. Rather, he wanted to use a theological-literary form to write the history of all Judean and Israelite kings in its totality as a complex of guilt that was shared by kings and people and that led to the Captivity. Keeping in mind this objective, the author made selections from annals and prophetic legends. Sometimes he utilized stories that are of little value for the history; sometimes also he omitted historically significant facts for Judah and Israel, as is occasionally evident from extrabiblical finds.

Narratives about prophets are frequently used to connect the elements in the books of Kings (see, e.g., 1 Kgs. 12:22–24; chs. 17–19 and 21; 22:5–28; etc.), which explains why the Jewish organization of the Old Testament includes the books of Kings among the "Prophets." Even in the prologue to the division after Solomon's death, at the mention of Jeroboam's rebellion, there is a prophetic narrative. The prophet is Ahijah, who plays a role also later in Kings (14:1–18). In a symbolic way he predicted to Jeroboam the schism in the Davidic kingdom. His prediction was based on the old division of twelve tribes (11:29–39), an ideal that helps determine the framework for the books of Kings (see, e.g., 18:30–31).

Solomon's son Rehoboam, forty-one years old at the time of his accession (1 Kgs. 14:21), was a son of the Ammonite Naamah. It is striking that the author almost always mentions the name of the mother of the new king. History also demonstrates that especially the queen-mother, who could play a role in the monarchical structure of the government, was not content to be lost in the anonymity of a royal harem. In his accession, Rehoboam apparently faced no challengers. The Judeans no doubt accepted him right away. For the other tribes his kingship was not a matter of course, however. Their initial hesitation was due not first of all to personal reasons but to the fact that he was a Judean, a southerner; in the north, people were not inclined to view the kingship as bound by heredity to one tribe. Furthermore, the time seemed ripe for insisting that the new king do something about improving social conditions, because the northern tribes in particular, as well as the original Canaanite population, which Solomon had quietly incorporated with the Israelites, had legitimate concerns.

At Shechem (see ill. 16), a historic city for national gatherings (see, e.g., Joshua 24), Rehoboam sought to be acclaimed king. At that point the conflict erupted and quickly led to the schism in the personal union of the two parts of the kingdom (1 Kgs. 12:1–16). Jeroboam, who earlier under Solomon had fomented rebellion, played a large role in this conflict. Rehoboam's director of forced labor was killed, and Rehoboam himself barely escaped with his life (v. 18). Against his will and following the prophetic message of Shemaiah (vv. 22–24), Rehoboam had to content himself with Judah and—according to tradition—Benjamin. The role of Benjamin in this account is rather uncertain, however, because the prophetic message of Ahijah mentions only one tribe (11:36). At any rate, the breach between Rehoboam and Jeroboam was total, and the state of war between the two kings lasted throughout their lifetimes (14:30). Possibly the tribal territory of Benjamin was also disputed in this war.

Meanwhile the "ten tribes" in Shechem, at the direction of Ahijah, had acclaimed Jeroboam as king (1 Kgs. 12:20). In contrast to the kingship in the southern kingdom, which retained the Davidic dynasty, the kingship in the northern kingdom is sometimes called charismatic. This designation is due to the example of Saul, because, except in the case of interim kings who ruled only briefly, the holding of the royal office was sanctioned by a direction from YHWH and the acclamation of the people. A king on the Israelite throne could never be entirely certain whether YHWH, in secret, had not already designated a new king who would wipe out his generation. These ideas have been developed by Alt, who calls this period in Israel's history the stage of the "revolutions willed by God." Following Alt, it is usually assumed that the monarchy in Israel had a character different from that in Judah. Lately, however, Ishida and others have raised objections to Alt's theory.

An important decision faced by Jeroboam when he became king was the choice of a place of residence. It is not surprising that Shechem, centrally located and with a respectable cultic tradition, became the first residence of the new king (1 Kgs. 12:25). He fortified the city, and also Peniel in Transjordan (probably Tell ed-Dahab esh-Sherqi). Tirzah was a third key city, which especially later, under his successors, played an important role as a residence (14:17; see also 15:21, 33). This city is located on the Wadi Fara, an important river for traffic. Such decisions showed that Jeroboam recognized the threats against him and was determined to prepare himself militarily. The first threat, of course, was Judah. Jeroboam was at war with the Judean king Abijah (15:7; 2 Chronicles 13), to whom he was forced to relinquish some important southern cities, including Bethel.

Egypt constituted a second threat. The books of Kings mention only a campaign of "Shishak" against Jerusalem, which happened in the fifth year of Rehoboam, on which occasion the temple treasures were plundered (1 Kgs. 14:25–26; 2 Chr. 12:9). Shoshenq I, however, the founder of the Twenty-second Dynasty (of the Bubastides; see *ANET*, 242–43, 263–64), in a "Palestine list" on a wall of the Amun temple in Karnak mentions Gibeon, Beth-horon, Aijalon, and even Taanach, Shunem, Beth-shean, Rehob, and Mahanaim, cities that must have belonged to Israel. There is perhaps a connection between Jeroboam's changes in residence and these Egyptian campaigns. Yet one should be cautious and not give greater credence to the "Palestine lists" of Shoshenq than to the silence about this Egyptian campaign in Jeroboam's history. At that time the Egyptian army had no more strength than it had generally in the second half of the second millennium B.C. Moreover, this campaign may have had no lasting results. It has been plausibly suggested that the pharaoh may have exploited the brotherly quarrel between Judah and Israel in order to regain some of Egypt's lost influence along the Palestinian coastal area. This action by the Egyptian pharaoh does not display much affection on his part toward his erstwhile protégé, but perhaps Jeroboam during his stay in Egypt did not do much to hide his ambitious character.

Jeroboam's ambition is demonstrated by the measures he took regarding the cult. In order to put a stop to the many pilgrimages from the north to the royal sanctuary in Jerusalem, a custom that had arisen under David and spread under Solomon, and thus to avert the danger of a renewed allegiance to Judah, Jeroboam took a step that was at once daring as well as politically and cultically significant, an action that for a long time to come set the course of the development of the YHWH cult in Israel. He had national shrines built in Dan in the north and Bethel in the south. In them he placed images of young bulls, symbols reminiscent of the Canaanite fertility cult and undoubtedly linked to old cultic traditions of Israel at Dan and Bethel (see 1 Kgs. 12:27–32). It is striking that, according to the Deuteronomistic editor of this passage, Jeroboam connected these images with the Exodus (v. 28). Back in Exodus 32, the people of Israel are denounced for a similar calf worship. Many consider this chapter to be a projection to the time of the desert of the cultic practices at the shrines of Dan and Bethel. Certainly not only Deuteronomists in later times felt that such calf worship conflicted with the essence of the cult of YHWH; this worship itself was also opposed to the worship of YHWH as Israel had adopted it at an early period in its history.

The question remains why Jeroboam chose these bull images, even if he may have regarded them as theomorphic forms of an invisible deity. A plausible answer is that Jeroboam, in trying to combine the worship of YHWH and Baal, devised a cultic object that was acceptable to the Canaanite part of his people. To achieve his objective he abolished the service of the Levites (1 Kgs. 12:31) and introduced another calendar for the feast days (v. 32). As might have been expected in such a case of cultic reform, traditional Yahwists fiercely opposed this reorganization of the "royal sanctuaries" (cf. also Amos 7:13). David and Solomon, however, had also freely organized cult and temple service as suited their political aspirations. Politically considered, therefore, Jeroboam's reorganization of the religious service was no more laudable or censurable than theirs. From the religious or theological standpoint, however—the vision of the writer or editor of Kings—Jeroboam's deeds served as an ominous refrain in Israel's history: "the sins of Jeroboam, the son of Nebat, who made Israel to sin," a sin that became the prime reason for Israel's downfall (see 1 Kgs. 13:34).

The Old Testament tradition says little more about Jeroboam I ("I" to distinguish him from his namesake in the first half of the 8th century B.C.). We may assume that he was an effective ruler with strong personality traits. The same can hardly be said of his successors. After the twenty-two-year reign of Jeroboam, his son Nadab was briefly king. 1 Kings 15:25–31 reports that, during the assault on the Philistine city Gibbethon, Nadab was killed by Baasha, who was from the tribe of Issachar. This Gibbethon is situated about 4 kilometers (2 mi.) west of Gezer and the same distance east of Ekron (perhaps the present Tell el-Melat). The precise reason for Baasha's rebellion is unknown. Some have suggested that he may have been displeased with the military and political failures of Jeroboam I. In any case, Nadab was the first of eight kings of Israel who were assassinated. Among Israelite kings, only Jeroboam I and the later kings Omri and Jehu were able to establish

a dynasty that ruled for as many as two generations. Often Israel's kings were acclaimed by a word from a prophet, just as their end was often foretold by a similar prophetic word. In the case of the house of Jeroboam, we read of such a prediction in 14:10 by the mouth of Ahijah, a prophet from Shiloh (see 15:29); in the case of Baasha, by the mouth of the prophet Jehu, the son of Hanani, who earlier had announced that Baasha would be king (16:1–4). In the Old Testament tradition of the description of kings, there is an alternating pattern of peaceful and violent succession, caused primarily by the unstable character of the northern kingdom.

The few data at our disposal indicate that at first Israel's foreign policy was oriented more toward safeguarding its own borders against attacks from its next-door neighbors Judah and Aram-Damascus than toward arming itself against the more distant great powers that would later play a role in its history. About Baasha's long reign of twenty-four years (1 Kgs. 15:33) we know that he was at war with his Judean counterpart Asa, who also reigned for many years (witness his battle for Ramah [vv. 16–22]), and that he made Tirzah, one of the cities fortified by Jeroboam I, his residence. Baasha died a natural death and was succeeded by his son Elah (16:8–14). Not long after he became king, Elah and his family were murdered by Zimri, a rebellious officer, following a drinking bout in Tirzah in the home of Elah's chief officer, Arza. Zimri did not survive his deed very long, however. Seven days afterward (v. 15), Omri was proclaimed king by the army, which was again battling the Philistines at Gibbethon. He marched to Tirzah, where a hopeless Zimri set fire to his own palace and perished in the flames. Omri's difficulties were not yet over, however, for part of the people wanted to make Tibni king (vv. 21–22). A civil war, likely only of minor proportions, turned out to Omri's advantage. Tibni died and Omri assumed the throne. He reigned for twelve years, the first six in Tirzah. During Omri's dynasty, which lasted over thirty years, Israel achieved a level of political power that it had not enjoyed for years.

The Old Testament says very little about Omri. Some have suggested that he may have been a foreigner, for his name and his son Ahab's name may be of Arabian origin (but cf. Noth). It would be going too far, however, to derive conclusions concerning the religious conduct of Omri and his dynasty from this fact alone. We know that foreigners in ancient Israel commonly served in the army (e.g., Uriah the Hittite, the Cushite messenger in 2 Sam. 18:21-32). 1 Kings 16:24 mentions that Omri bought a hill from a certain Shemer for two silver talents and that he named it Samaria, which he made his residence (see ill. 40). Geographically Samaria is more central and faces the west more directly than Tirzah does. Omri's choice of Samaria can be associated with his expansionist policy toward the seacoast. Politically the establishment of a residence on neutral territory was a calculated gesture of reconciliation to both the Israelite and the Canaanite segments of the population. Omri's purchase of a piece of land on which to establish his residence resembles David's purchase of the threshing floor of Araunah (2 Samuel 24). Alt believes that Omri was intentionally copying David's policy, with the difference that David turned a Canaanite city (Jebus), once situated in tribally neutral territory, into the capital of the united kingdom of Judah and Israel, whereas Omri picked an undeveloped piece of land, a strategically situated mountain, for the building of the residence of his kingdom, in which Israelites and Canaanites had to live together.

Extrabiblical data suggest that, as a politician and soldier, Omri was greater than portrayed in the Old Testament tradition. An inscription from the Assyrian Shalmaneser III (858-824 B.C.) calls Jehu "son of Omri" (see *ANET,* 284-85; *ANEP,* 351-55), and inscriptions from Tiglath-pileser III (745-727) and Sargon II (722-705) call Israel "land of Omri" (*ANET,* 284-85). Though Jehu was of course not in the line of Omri, the fact that the name and fame of King Omri could reach as far as the court of the Assyrian ruler witnesses to his renown and the respect he enjoyed. His fame is even clearer from the well-known Moabite, or Mesha, Stone (*ANET,* 320-21). According to 2 Kings 3:4-5, Mesha, king of Moab, rebelled against Israel after the death of Omri's son Ahab. On this well-preserved inscription, discovered in 1868 in the area of ancient Moab, Mesha tells that the Israelite king Omri humiliated Moab for many years "because Chemosh [the Moabite deity] was angry

with his land." He further recounts that Omri's son planned to do the same and that Omri and his son occupied "the land of Medeba" for forty (!) years. Reading such a report one can properly ask, If Omri could thus control a relatively unimportant and quite inaccessible territory on the other side of the Jordan, how much more may he have been able to do in other important areas, for instance on the borders with Judah and Aram?

The author of Kings evaluates Omri religiously, concluding that he was worse than all his predecessors (1 Kgs. 16:25). Omri initiated a policy of toleration whereby the Canaanite religion was introduced into Israel and ultimately acquired the upper hand at the court. Due to Ahab's marriage with a Phoenician princess (a political marriage engineered by Omri?), the Canaanite cult was given a powerful impulse, even extending into Judah, where, according to the word of the prophet Micah, the people "kept the statutes of Omri" and did "all the works of the house of Ahab" (Mic. 6:16). We may characterize Omri, then, as politically famous but religiously notorious.

After Omri's twelve-year reign, his son Ahab became king. He ruled for twenty-two years over Israel, having Samaria as his residence (1 Kgs. 16:29-30). The author of Kings devotes more attention to Ahab than to Omri, again from a definite theological perspective and in the context of the Elijah-Elisha stories that uniquely color this part of the book. We learn little more of his political significance than we do of Omri's. Ahab married Jezebel, a daughter of Ethbaal of Tyre (v. 31), or, as the Old Testament calls the Phoenicians, the Sidonians (see Josephus, *Antiquities* 8.324). Before discussing the Baal cult promoted by his wife, I will now consider Ahab's political actions. The information on the Moabite Stone is confirmed by 2 Kings 1:1; for a long time Ahab maintained a tight rein on Moab. It is not surprising that, after his marriage to Jezebel, he kept the peace with the Phoenicians. It is notable that, assisted by a marriage arrangement, he established good relations with his southern neighbor, Judah: a daughter of Omri, Athaliah, likely a sister of Ahab (8:26), married Jehoram of Judah. This event marked the end of the prolonged border skirmishes between the two states and the beginning of political and military cooperation against

1. *A storeroom in the archives of the royal palace at Ebla (Tell Mardikh). Excavations in 1964 found clay tablets such as these where they had fallen off their shelves centuries before (ca. 2500 B.C.; see p. 8). (Photo archive Kok, Kampen)*

2. *The "Peace Panel" from Ur (25th century B.C.). A procession of burden-bearers (bottom), animals being led (middle) for use in a banquet (top). A mosaic of shells, lapis lazuli, and red limestone. (Trustees of the British Museum)*

3. *An earthenware cultic object from Ashdod: a mother goddess depicted as a bed (about 17 cm. [7 in.] high; 12th century B.C.). The form demonstrates Mycenean influence on Egyptian culture. (Israel Museum, Jerusalem)*

4. *A praying Egyptian (a priest or a high official). From a papyrus of the Book of the Dead of Hunefer (19th Dynasty, New Kingdom, ca. 1300 B.C.). (Trustees of the British Museum)*

5. *Negro slaves and Egyptian slave drivers. A relief from the tomb of Haremheb, ca. 14th century B.C. (Museo Civico, Bologna)*

6. *Agricultural labor depicted in scenes from Egyptian tomb paintings. (Royal Ontario Museum, Toronto)*

7. *Brickmakers depicted in a facsimile of an Egyptian tomb painting of the Eighteenth Dynasty. (The Metropolitan Museum of Art)*

8. *Amarna Tablet 325 (see p. 9). The governor of Ashkelon tells the Egyptian ruler that he is fulfilling his duties by guarding the cities and sending provisions and tribute. (Trustees of the British Museum)*

9. *A granite statue of Merneptah (see pp. 14-15). (Cairo Museum; photo courtesy of The Metropolitan Museum of Art)*

10. *The wilderness of Midian. (A. D. Baly)*

11. *A maritime battle between Egypt and the Sea Peoples at the time of Ramses III. The drawing is reconstructed from reliefs at Medinet Habu* (see p. 25). *(Biàlik Institute, Jerusalem)*

12. *The desert of Sinai after winter rains. (W. Braun)*

13. *A stele of black diorite inscribed with the laws of Hammurabi, king of Babylon in the Amorite Dynasty (ca. 1700 B.C.). On many points his laws resemble those of ancient Israel. (Musée du Louvre, Paris)*

14. *Fragment (25 cm. [10 in.] high) of a Babylonian clay tablet; a copy of the Atra-hasis Epic (see p. 117), in which the creation of the first people is told. They are created because the gods are tired of working the land and want people to do it for them (ca. 1650 B.C.). (Trustees of the British Museum)*

15. *Jebel Musa, traditionally identified with Mt. Sinai. (W. Braun)*

16. *The city of Shechem in Samaria, situated between Mount Ebal (right) and Mount Gerizim (left). The modern city of Nablus, home of the remnant of the Samaritans, is in the foreground. (Dr. E. Noort, 't Harde, the Netherlands)*

17. *Bas-relief of the storm god Baal swinging his club (see p. 28). Standing before the god is the miniature figure of the prince of Ugarit. Stele from Ras Shamra (ca. 1600 B.C.). (Musée du Louvre, Paris)*

18. *A sacred pillar in the forecourt of the temple of Shechem (ca. 1450-1150 B.C.). (Joint Expedition to Shechem, photo L. C. Ellenberger)*

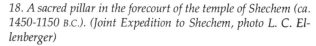

19. Stelae from a Canaanite temple at Hazor (1500-1200 B.C.). (Israel Museum, Jerusalem)

20. Ruins of three Canaanite temples at Tell Kittan in the Jordan Valley. (Israel Department of Antiquities and Museums)

common threats—the Arameans and later the Assyrians.

The situation with respect to the Arameans who lived in and around Damascus is not altogether clear, despite the fairly detailed information about them in 1 Kings 20 and 22. Chapter 20 reports that Benhadad at first successfully attacked Israel as far as Samaria but that later he was forced to withdraw. Apart from the possibility that 1 Kings 20 belongs to a later context of Ahab's reign, it likely concerns here Benhadad II, king of Aram. Benhadad I, the son of Tabrimmon, who is mentioned on the so-called Melqart Stele (*ANET,* 655), must have ruled at the time of Asa of Judah and Baasha of Israel (see 1 Kgs. 15:18–20; 2 Chr. 16:2–4). The name Benhadad perhaps means generally "king of Aram," which would explain why the so-called monolith inscription of Shalmaneser II of Assyria, which describes the campaign in the sixth year of this king (853 B.C.) against Arameans and Israelites, refers to the king of Damascus as Adad-idri. In this connection, too, Ahab of Israel is mentioned (see *ANET,* 278–79). Shalmaneser claims that at Qarqar he dealt the allied nations, including Phoenicians, Ammonites, and even Arabs, a stunning defeat. It is not unlikely that, at approximately the time of Ahab's death, Arameans and Israelites were allies. The battles with the Arameans, not only the battle at Aphek and its consequences described in 1 Kings 20:23–30, but also the skirmishes with the Arameans around Ramoth in Gilead narrated in chapter 22, against which Ahab and the Judean king Jehoshaphat went to battle, must have taken place either before that time or have been an incidental episode, in view of dating problems with Ahab's death. (Was he killed in the battle against the Arameans, or did he die a natural death?)

It should not be overlooked that also later the Arameans fought with Israel (2 Kgs. 6:8–25; 9:14–15). When Israel and Aram were not united by the common threat of the Assyrians, it seems that they were always feuding about something, as Israel and Judah used to do. In general we could say that, in his foreign policy, Ahab continued and consolidated the policies of Omri and that, for the greatest part of his rule, Israel was at the height of its power. These political successes, even as in Solomon's time, are confirmed by certain cultural and architectural monuments. 1 Kings 22:39 mentions briefly that he fortified many cities and even had an ivory palace built. From the Old Testament we know also that Ahab had a residence in Jezreel with a considerable estate (18:45–46; 21:1). Archeological data demonstrate the extent of the building activities of the Omrides in Samaria.

All these good qualities and activities of Ahab disappear in the Old Testament tradition behind his religious and cultic wickedness. The Old Testament in fact speaks more about the house of Ahab and his evil than about the house of Omri. At this time Ahab's great antagonist Elijah appears on the scene. This prophet dominates in the Elijah-Elisha cycle (1 Kings 17–19; 21; 2 Kings 1–8; 13), reaching his apex in the confrontation on Mount Carmel (1 Kings 18). Historically, nothing can be ascertained with certainty about the person and work of Elijah or about the important contest on Mount Carmel. The story simply says that Elijah ordered King Ahab, at the end of a period of drought that had struck the land due to Ahab's wickedness, to assemble the people on Mount Carmel (near modern Haifa) for a definite decision who would be God in Israel: YHWH, the covenant God of Israel; or Baal, the god of fertility, surrounded by a pantheon in which Astarte occupied a chief place and by a host of priests whom Jezebel had augmented with priests from Tyre.

Was this Baal a local deity worshiped on Mount Carmel? Was he the Tyrian Melqart? Or was he the central Baal, possibly Baal-Shamem ("Lord of Heaven")? Each of these answers has its defenders, especially the view that we have here a Tyrian Baal, imported by Jezebel. In answering such questions, we must remember that the story itself is molded by literary perspectives, with the result that we have little hard evidence for answering questions concerning historical and geographical details and cultic backgrounds. Yet it is not unlikely that Mount Carmel, where, long before and long after, local deities were worshiped and where also YHWH must have had a place of worship (see 1 Kgs. 18:30, with the altar dating from the time of David or Solomon?), functioned as a meeting place of Phoenician and Canaanite Baal worshipers and Israelite YHWH worshipers. Where a

YHWH altar once stood, the Baal cult was practiced in Ahab's time.

Who was the "Lord of Carmel" and so in the final analysis "the Lord of Israel"? The decision turned out in favor of YHWH, the God of Israel, which ended Ahab's policy of putting the worship of Baal and the worship of YHWH on a par. This change explains Jezebel's fierce pursuit of Elijah (1 Kings 19). In this conflict we should regard Jezebel and her Phoenician followers as worshipers of the universal Baal, not just of Melqart, a Tyrian Baal. The writer of Kings wants to show that, although in the days of the Omrides the Baal cult had a chance to dominate in Israel as never before or later, YHWH and his worship were nonetheless victorious, though just barely (according to v. 18, only seven thousand had not bowed their knees to Baal). From this perspective lonely Elijah receives his orders: he must anoint Hazael king over Damascus, Jehu king over Israel, and Elisha to succeed himself as prophet. These three men, each in his own way, would clinch the ultimate victory of YHWH and his worship that had begun at Carmel (vv. 15-18).

Ahab openly served Baal. For him he erected an altar and sanctuary. He also served YHWH. He accepted the advice of various YHWH prophets (1 Kgs. 20:13-14, 22, 28; 22:6-8, etc.) and gave names to his children that included YHWH as the theophoric element (Ahaziah, Jehoram). Occasionally he also tried to effect social changes, which were opposed, however, by those affected by them. I refer here to the story of the vineyard of Naboth (ch. 21), a story that has evoked some juridical questions. In this incident Naboth, on the basis of ancient Israelite law, defended his ancestral property against the demands of the king, who sullenly acknowledged Naboth's rights. Jezebel, however, acting upon the laws in vogue in her country, got Naboth's land for Ahab. Such episodes (cf. ch. 19) portray Jezebel as a powerful defender of her own faith and that of the Canaanites, making her a feared opponent of the worshipers of YHWH. One also gets the impression that, because of her tactless and fanatic actions, she often did more harm than good to the cause of Baal and of the Canaanites. In contrast, Ahab followed a more balanced policy.

We noted above that our source appears to present two versions of Ahab's death: a natural death ("Ahab slept with his fathers" [1 Kgs. 22:40]) and a violent death in the battle of Judah and Israel against the Arameans at Ramoth in Gilead (vv. 29-37; cf. 21:19 and 2 Kgs. 9:36-37). In either case, with Ahab's death the Omri dynasty had passed its zenith. Ahaziah, Ahab's son, became king for two years in Samaria. The Old Testament reports about him only his sickness, his consultation of Baal-Zebub, the god of Ekron, and the prediction of his death by Elijah (2 Kings 1). He also proposed to Jehoshaphat of Judah that men from the two nations form a common crew to sail for gold to the mysterious land of Ophir (1 Kgs. 22:50 [49]).

Because Ahaziah was childless, Joram, another son of Ahab, became king over Israel. The Deuteronomistic evaluation of Joram, who is said to have reigned twelve years, is fairly favorable (2 Kgs. 3:2), for he removed the pillars of Baal erected by his father. This action perhaps indicates that the Israelites who favored YHWH became more influential. We also know that, together with his Judean colleague Jehoshaphat and his Edomite colleague, Joram attacked Mesha of Moab, who had revolted. Initially this common attack seems to have been successful. When the coalition had come to the gates of Kir-hareseth, however, Mesha offered his oldest son as a sacrifice on the city wall. This act seems to have turned the fortunes of Moab, inducing the coalition to raise the siege. Perhaps Mesha refers to the departures of the allies when, in the so-called Mesha Stone (see ill. 41), he mentions the "downfall of Israel." Although 2 Kings 3:27b is problematic, Israel's hegemony over Moab, which had to pay a heavy tribute to Israel (v. 4), had clearly come to an end. Not only was Israel threatened in the south, but in the north it found it increasingly hard to maintain its defenses. Again with a Judean colleague, this time King Ahaziah, grandson of Jehoshaphat and son of the unfortunate Judean king Jehoram and Athaliah, a daughter of King Ahab, Joram set out against Hazael, whom Elisha had anointed king over Aram-Damascus (8:7-15). The objective was to retake Ramoth-gilead (v. 28). On this campaign Joram was wounded, after which he was carried to his residence at Jezreel. Here, while Ahaziah of Judah was visiting him, fate struck him and the entire Omri dynasty.

At that time Jehu, who had been anointed king over Israel by a messenger of Elisha (2 Kings 9), undertook a coup d'état. This Jehu ben Jehoshaphat ben Nimshi was commander over the army at Ramoth. Marching to Jezreel, he killed Joram and, later near Megiddo, the fleeing King Ahaziah. Next he slaughtered Jezebel the queen-mother and the entire Omri dynasty. The people now accepted Jehu as king; he established a dynasty that would stay in power the longest in Israel. The tradition pays detailed attention to the extermination of the Baal cult in Samaria. This bloody action was approved by the rigidly conservative Rechabites and their leader Jonadab, apparently zealous worshipers of YHWH (see Jer. 35).

In addition to Ahab's descendants, several relatives of the Judean king Ahaziah were killed by Jehu (2 Kgs. 10:12–17). This bloody reorganization, which on the whole was endorsed by Yahwistic circles (cf., however, Hos. 1:4), did not have favorable consequences for Israel's foreign policy. We read in 2 Kings 10:32–33 that all of the territory east of the Jordan was lost to Israel (cf. Amos 1:3). Much of that loss was due to Hazael (see ill. 43), the king of Damascus, who had come to the throne by murdering Benhadad II (2 Kgs. 8:7–15) and whom Shalmaneser III called "a son of nobody" (*ANET*, 280). Benhadad had effectively united many of the small Aramean kingdoms in the Syrian territory and made Damascus the center of a militarily well-organized realm that increasingly controlled the trade routes in the Near East. The language of this kingdom spread enormously, so much so that centuries later it became not only the language of diplomacy but also the vernacular in large areas of the Near East. A powerful Aramean state on the northern boundary of Israel not only constituted a buffer against the campaigns of the booty-hungry Assyrians but also threatened Israel's own safety, as noted above in the history of Ahab. Under the leadership of the Aramean king, Ahab joined a coalition with many other armies in a battle against the Assyrian juggernaut at Qarqar on the Orontes. Besides such uniting against their common enemy Assyria, Israel and Aram never made a real alliance.

Hazael took advantage of a breathing spell in Assyria's expansionistic policy to enlarge and fortify his territory. Not only did he capture from Israel all of Transjordan, he also established an outpost on the Euphrates directed against Assyria. Nor did Judah escape Hazael's grip (2 Kgs. 12:18–19 [17–18]). The Judean king Joash was forced to pay a heavy tribute. Shalmaneser III mentions Hazael a few times in the description of his campaigns against the west (see *ANET*, 280–81). Though he brags about the defeats he dealt Hazael's "enormous" army, Shalmaneser was apparently less successful against Hazael's forces than against Jehu, whom he always calls the son of Omri (*Ia-u-a mar Humri*) and whom some scholars recently have tried to identify with the later king Joram. Shalmaneser claims to have received tribute from Jehu, a famous portrayal of which has been preserved on the so-called black obelisk of Shalmaneser III (see *ANEP*, 351–55; see also ill. 48). Jehu's payment of tribute likely took place about 841.

Not much more can be said about the twenty-eight regnal years of Jehu. Under his son and successor Jehoahaz, who reigned seventeen years, the dominance of Aram-Damascus, already evident during Jehu's days, continues (2 Kgs. 13:22). At that time Hazael's previously mentioned campaign against Judah must have occurred. Verse 5 speaks of a mysterious "deliverer" whom the Lord gave to the Israelites in their straitened circumstances, whose identification has so far proved impossible. Jehoahaz died around the turn of the century and was succeeded by his son Jehoash, who ruled 798–783 B.C. He achieved some successes in the war against Aram-Damascus, recapturing from Benhadad (who had succeeded his father, Hazael) some of the cities that Hazael had taken from Jehoahaz (v. 25). Connected with this recapture is the story of Elisha, who on his deathbed announced that Jehoash would be victorious over Aram (vv. 14–19). Jehoash's successes were not limited to Aram. At Beth-shemesh he routed the Judeans, a victory that even allowed him to invade Jerusalem and loot the temple treasures (14:8–14). According to the report in Kings, the hostilities were provoked by the Judean king Amaziah. We also read that the Moabites regularly raided Israel (13:20). Surveying the period of Jehoash's reign, one gets the impression that he began his reign with the country desolate, strapped and starved by the

Arameans and menaced by the immediate neighbors Judah and Moab. He was able to withstand this crisis situation during his life and even to repel his enemies, which indicates a strong rule. When at his death he hands the reigns of government to his son and successor Jeroboam—called Jeroboam II to distinguish him from the first king of Israel—the country can look forward to a final period of greatness.

Jeroboam II is said to have ruled for forty-one years, a very long period for an Israelite king. His was also a relatively happy time for Israel, coming before the disastrous campaigns of the Assyrian king Tiglath-pileser III (see ill. 52). Jeroboam II and his father were little troubled by the Assyrians. Adad-nirari III (810–783 B.C.) did report campaigns to Damascus and Palestine (ANET, 281–83), but his successes were apparently limited to seizing some booty. Because of the weakened condition of the Aramean kingdom, not only did Jeroboam manage to maintain the equilibrium between Israel and Aram that his father had previously restored, he also acquired superiority. The tradition reports that Jeroboam recovered the territory of Israel "from the entrance of Hamath as far as the Sea of the Arabah" (2 Kgs. 14:25). This description is more an idealistic picture of a Davidic kingdom than it is reality, even if we do not associate Hamath with the northern state situated on the Orontes.

The authors of the Old Testament books typically say less about political affairs than about the religious and social conditions in Israel. About the latter we are fairly well informed by the book of Amos. Amos was a prophet from Judah who prophesied in the northern kingdom. In no uncertain terms he denounced the social ills rampant in Samaria and Israel. Luxurious wealth on the part of some was matched by the extreme poverty of, and discrimination against, the lower classes. Moreover, in the eyes of the faithful worshipers of YHWH and the Judeans, the religious situation in Israel, particularly in the cultic center of Bethel, was horrible. Amos 7:10–13 reports that Amos was told to stay away from Bethel on account of his severe prophecies against Jeroboam and the people. His younger contemporary Hosea perhaps also denounced Jeroboam's religious and social policies. (Hos. 1:1, however, which was added

later, does not prove conclusively that Hosea was already active during Jeroboam's reign; cf. v. 4.) At any rate, this period of Israel demonstrates that political and economic prosperity was not necessarily accompanied by social and religious well-being.

Zechariah succeeded his father Jeroboam, but was assassinated after only six months on the throne, thus ending Jehu's dynasty. The murderer, Shallum, was himself assassinated a month later by Menahem, likely an army officer, who led his army from Tirzah to Samaria, where he assumed power. He wielded power for ten years (ca. 750–740). His kingship was marked by Assyria's mounting influence on Israel's internal affairs. Tiglath-pileser III (see illustration in ANEP, 445) had come to power, and he in turn—at quite a price (2 Kgs. 15:19–20)—supported Menahem's shaky throne. It is possible that the ostraca discovered in Samaria are from this period. They are letters accompanying supplies of oil and wine and may indicate the demands of the Assyrians, which the king in turn had to exact from the people. Tiglath-pileser himself, who enjoyed military successes everywhere and who is referred to in the Old Testament by his Babylonian throne-name Pul, also mentions Menahem's tributary status, together with that of others, including Rezin of Damascus (v. 37; 16:5–9; Isa. 7:1–9; 8:6; 9:10) and Hiram of Tyre (see ANET, 283, though there are synchronistic problems). Menahem was far from soft, as is shown in 2 Kings 15:16. The ripping open of pregnant women is a cruelty he may have learned from his Assyrian masters.

Pekahiah, Menahem's son, was king after the death of his father for only a short period before he was assassinated by his chief army officer, Pekah, son of Remaliah (see Isa. 7:5, 9). Pekah, who according to 2 Kings 15:27 ruled in Samaria for twenty years (there is, however, uncertainty about the length of his reign), joined the anti-Assyrian coalition under the leadership of the above-mentioned Rezin of Damascus. Meanwhile Tiglath-pileser III steadily expanded his power. In 738 and 734 he must have undertaken campaigns into Palestine, going as far as the "brook of Egypt," or Wadi el-Arish. Presumably in those campaigns he also crossed the territory of Judah and Israel. A certain Hanun, prince of Gaza, fled before him to Egypt (*ANET,* 283). This campaign apparently did not seriously weaken Israel, for the following year Damascus, allied with Israel and a few other small kingdoms, tried to form a coalition to which Judah under King Ahaz also was invited. When he refused to join, the coalition tried to force him. The war that ensued is known as the Syro-Ephraimite war (see also Isa. 7:1–17 and Hos. 5:8–6:6). Despite his slim chances for success, Ahaz managed to hold his own in this war (cf. Isa. 7:6, which refers to the son of Tabeel, whom the invaders planned to put on Ahaz's throne). He bought his independence by appealing for help to Tiglath-pileser (2 Kgs. 16:8). With the gold Ahaz possessed he bought the help of the powerful Assyrian, who promptly attacked Damascus, killed Rezin, and deported the population.

Israel also was not spared (2 Kgs. 15:29). Several cities and areas were occupied by the Assyrians, and the population was deported. Tiglath-pileser III writes about the conquests in his annals, in which he also mentions the fall of Pekah and the enthronement of Hoshea, the last king of Israel (*ANET,* 283–84). In Kings these events are reported in a familiar manner: "Then Hoshea the son of Elah made a conspiracy against Pekah the son of Remaliah, and struck him down, and slew him, and reigned in his stead . . ." (v. 30). After his kingdom had been reduced to a torso, Hoshea became a vassal king of the Assyrian ruler and was forced to pay a heavy tribute as the price for his "independence." The rest of the once great and important kingdom of Israel became an Assyrian province.

Damascus fell to the Assyrians in 732 B.C. Other states also were either made subject directly to Tiglath-pileser or paid tribute, including the land of the Philistines, Moab, and Edom. The book of 2 Kings reports that Edom regained control of the city of Elath on the Gulf of Aqabah after it had been captured by Rezin of Damascus (16:6), an action that the Assyrian king must have known about. At the time of his death in 727 B.C., Tiglath-pileser had built an empire whose power reached far and wide. Hoshea soon felt it. Under Shalmaneser V (727–722), Hoshea tried not only to escape his tributary status to the Assyrians but also to form a coalition of revolters against Assyria. In this connection So, "king of Egypt," is mentioned (17:4).

Some scholars think that this name refers not to an Egyptian king but to an Egyptian city (Sais) in the Delta. On the basis of the inscriptions of Sargon II, Borger has identified So with *Re-e tar-ta-nu Mu-su-ri,* an otherwise unknown commander. Goedicke thinks of So as Tefnakht, the founder of the Twenty-fourth Dynasty in Sais. He and his son Bochchoris ruled in the Delta between approximately 740 and 715 B.C., until the Ethiopians put an end to their dynasty. Hoshea perhaps appealed to Tefnakht for help, without result.

Shalmaneser, hearing of the revolt of his Israelite vassal, promptly took action. He invaded Israel and for three years laid siege to Samaria. In 722/721, shortly before Shalmaneser's death, the city fell. Around 720, Sargon II, his successor, decided to put an end to the regularly recurring revolts in Samaria (see *ANET,* 284–85). He recaptured the city and deported the remaining population to Calah (Kalhu), the Habur River area, and some cities in Media. At the same time the Assyrians repopulated the formerly Israelite territory with people deported from Babylon, Cuthah, Avva, and some other cities (2 Kgs. 17:24). According to a figure from Sargon II, 27,290 inhabitants were deported from Samaria. Leaving aside the question whether this figure is precise, we can see that a considerable segment of the Israelite population—especially the poorer ones—must have been left behind. For a long time to come this remnant may have kept alive the hope for the restoration of Israel. The ten northern tribes did not just disappear; on the contrary, with the immigrants they constituted a mixed people, the Samaritans, who were later despised by the Judeans on account of their deviant religious views (see vv. 27–34). Samaria and Galilee thus had their own development. For the time being Judah was able to resist the power of Assyria and later that of Babylonia, as we shall see in the following section.

For the writer of 2 Kings 17, the fall of Israel was due to its "sins": Baal worship, nature worship, and practicing the customs of the Canaanite peoples. It is undeniable that Jeroboam I erected the bull images in order to couple Yahwism and Baalism (or the religion of the Canaanite population generally) and thus integrate the Canaanite population into the state of Israel. Israelite kings followed this policy until the end of the nation. The success of this policy varied, with Yahwism and Baalism alternately becoming dominant. Though separate religions are never easy to integrate, even in antiquity, and though Yahwism, nourished by ancient traditions, did not cease to condemn the religious situation in the northern realm, it nevertheless was infected by Baalism. As a result a YHWH-Baal syncretism could develop, as mentioned especially in the book of Hosea. It is thus not surprising that the Old Testament frequently describes YHWH and his service using terms that are derived from Canaanite religion.

From the course of Israel's history it is also apparent how great an impact the monarchy had on Israel's religious development. Jeroboam I, Ahab, and Jehu are the three clearest examples. The writer of Israel's history could not resist projecting back to the time of Saul his theological objections against the monarchy as such (cf. 1 Sam. 8:6–22). The more the desert time was idealized (cf. the Rechabites in Jeremiah 35) and the stronger the confession of the unique nature of YHWH's kingship by prophets and faithful followers of YHWH, the greater was their sense of failure about the Israelite monarchy. The fall of the kingdom of Israel, however painful, thus became an event from which a new Israel would someday arise like a phoenix from its ashes.

LITERATURE

M. Aberbach and L. Smolar, "Jeroboam's Rise to Power," *JBL* 88 (1969) 69-72.

M. C. Astour, "841 B.C.: The First Assyrian Invasion of Israel," *JAOS* 91 (1971) 383-89.

S. R. Bin-Nun, "Formulas from Royal Records of Israel and Judah," *VT* 18 (1968) 414-32.

G. Buccellati, *Cities and Nations of Ancient Syria: An Essay on Political Institutions with Special Reference to the Israelite Kingdoms* (Rome, 1967).

H. Donner, *Israel unter den Völkern* (Leiden, 1964).

———, "Der Feind aus dem Norden: Topographische und archäologische Erwägungen zu Jes. 10, 27b-34," *ZDPV* 84 (1968) 46-54.

———, "Adadnirari III. und die Vasallen des Westens," in A. Kuschke and E. Kutsch, eds., *Archäologie und Altes Testament* (Festschrift Kurt Galling; Tübingen, 1970), pp. 49-59.

———, "'Hier sind deine Götter, Israel!'" in H. Gese and H. P. Rüger, eds., *Wort und Geschichte* (Festschrift Karl Elliger; AOAT 18; Neukirchen-Vluyn, 1973), pp. 45-50.

M. Elat, "The Campaigns of Shalmaneser III against Aram and Israel," *IEJ* 25 (1975) 25-35.

D. G. Evans, "Rehoboam's Advisers at Shechem, and Political Institutions in Israel and Sumer," *JNES* 25 (1966) 273-79.

H. L. Ginsberg, "The Omrid-Davidid Alliance and its consequences," *Fourth World Congress of Jewish Studies* (Jerusalem, 1967) I: 91-93.

H. Goedicke, "The End of 'So, King of Egypt,'" *BASOR* 171 (1963) 64-66.

D. C. Greenwood, "On the Jewish Hope for a Restored Northern Kingdom," *ZAW* 88 (1976) 376-85.

M. Haran, "The Rise and Decline of the Empire of Jeroboam ben Joash," *VT* 17 (1967) 266-97.

T. Ishida, "The House of Ahab," *IEJ* 25 (1975) 135ff.

K. A. Kitchen, *The Third Intermediate Period in Egypt (1100-650 BC)* (Warminster, 1973).

R. W. Klein, "Jeroboam's Rise to Power," *JBL* 89 (1970) 217-18.

L. D. Levine, "Menahem and Tiglath-Pileser: A New Synchronism," *BASOR* 206 (1972) 40ff.

A. Malamat, "Origins of Statecraft in the Israelite Monarchy," *BA* 28 (1965) 34-65.

A. R. Millard and H. Tadmor, "Adad-Nirari III in Syria: Another Stele Fragment and the Dates of his Campaigns," *Iraq* 35 (1973) 57-64.

J. M. Miller, "The Elisha Cycle and the Accounts of the Omride Wars," *JBL* 85 (1966) 441-54.

———, "The Fall of the House of Ahab," *VT* 17 (1967) 307-24.

———, "The Rest of the Acts of Jehoahaz (I Kings 20; 22.1-38)," *ZAW* 80 (1968) 337-42.

———, "The Moabite Stone as a Memorial Stela," *PEQ* 106 (1974) 9-18.

S. Moscati, *L'Epigrafia Ebraica Antica 1935-1950* (Rome, 1951).

M. J. Mulder, "karmel," *TWAT* IV: 340-51.

———, *De naam van de afwezige god op de Karmel* (Leiden, 1979).

B. D. Napier, "The Omrides of Jezreel," *VT* 9 (1959) 366-78.

A. Negev, ed., *Archaeological Encyclopedia of the Holy Land* (Jerusalem, 1972).

M. Noth, *Die israelitischen Personennamen im Rahmen der gemeinsemitischen Namengebung* (Stuttgart, 1928).

B. Oded, "The Historical Background of the Syro-Ephraimite War Reconsidered," *CBQ* 34 (1972) 153-65.

——, "The Phoenician Cities and the Assyrian Empire in the Time of Tiglath-pileser III," *ZDPV* 90 (1974) 38-49.

S. Page, "A Stela of Adad-Nirari III and Nergal-ereš from Tell al Rimah," *Iraq* 30 (1968) 139-53.

O. H. Steck, *Überlieferung und Zeitgeschichte in den Elia-Erzählungen* (Neukirchen-Vluyn, 1968).

M. E. W. Thompson, *Situation and Theology: Old Testament Interpretations of the Syro-Ephraimite War* (Sheffield, 1982).

T. C. G. Thornton, "Charismatic Kingship in Israel and Judah," *JTS* 14 (1963) 1-11.

S. Timm, *Die Dynastie Omri: Quellen und Untersuchungen zur Geschichte Israels im 9. Jahrhundert vor Christus* (Göttingen, 1982).

e. Judah after the Division of the Kingdom

In the preceding section we of necessity touched on the history of Judah in connection with that of Israel. We noted also the unique character of the monarchy in Israel compared with that in Judah. In Judah there was an uninterrupted line of Davidic kings, though there were moments in its history when the continued existence of the dynasty hung by a single thread. As above, we refer to the sparse information available from extra-biblical information but primarily to the book of Kings and the later, frequently midrashlike additions from Chronicles as well as random information in the prophetic writings. Elsewhere in this handbook the character of Chronicles and its view of Judah and the Davidic dynasty are discussed. We may assume that the sources used for Chronicles, insofar as they do not run parallel with those of Kings or use Kings directly, must have been the same as that of Kings. The Chronicler, however, presented the history of Judah from a very specific point of view, in terms of which we can explain the stories found only in Chronicles as well as certain changes in the information contained in Kings.

2 Chronicles 11:5–23 records some details about Rehoboam's kingship that are not found in Kings. It reports that Jerusalem became or remained his residence, which is not surprising. It is certainly interesting, however, that several cities are mentioned that Rehoboam had fortified.

Besides familiar places such as Bethlehem, Tekoa, Lachish, Gath, and Hebron, less familiar places are mentioned. From this section we get a good idea of the size of the Judean territory. Evidently neither the coastline nor the deep south lay within the area defended by these Judean cities, though territory outside this region may de facto have belonged to Judah. It may be assumed, however, that after the period of David and Solomon, Egyptians as well as Philistines took control of former Judean territory. In the preceding section we considered the hostilities between Judah and Egypt, which reached their climax in the fifth year of Rehoboam in the campaign of Shishak (Shoshenq) against Jerusalem. 1 Chronicles 12 expands the sparse information in 1 Kings 14. First, there is an exaggerated account of the military manpower available to the Egyptians. Second, the writer has the prophet Shemaiah give a religious interpretation of the Egyptian invasion. Even as in the work of the Deuteronomist historians, in Chronicles the good and bad fortunes in Israel's and Judah's history are evaluated in terms of religious norms and merits. The observation in 2 Chronicles 12:12 that, in spite of everything, "conditions were good in Judah" may be regarded as characteristic for the story about Rehoboam and all of the history of Judah.

A cause for concern, certainly in the first phase of the history of Judah, was its northern border. For several reasons, the breach between Judah and Israel was difficult to heal. It is not surprising that the data in Kings and Chronicles in their own manner stress the cultic innovations of Israel's king Jeroboam. Without these religious measures, Jerusalem as the central sanctuary not only would have retained a dangerous attraction to many in northern Israel but also would have diverted many priests and Levites to the south (see 2 Chr. 11:13–17). It is not hard to see why a historian writing in much later times presented matters in this light. It is obvious that Jerusalem, as the capital of Judah and situated close to the border of Israel, was threatened especially from the north. Judah gained an advantage when the tribe of Benjamin joined the southern kingdom, creating a small but important area in the north that offered protection to Judah and to Jerusalem in particular. The need for this buffer zone against Israel is evident not only from the laconic note that, in the forty-one years of Rehoboam's reign, there was continual warfare between the two kingdoms all the time that he was king simultaneous with Jeroboam I (1 Kgs. 14:30; 2 Chr. 12:15) but also from the sequel as surveyed in the previous section. Rehoboam's son and successor, Abijah, who became king of Judah in the eighteenth regnal year of Jeroboam, continued the war with Israel begun by his father. As brief as the account in Kings is about Abijah, so detailed is the account in 2 Chronicles (13:1–14:1) about his war against Israel. This latter account, with obvious homiletic and exhortative intent, shows that Judah, despite the power of Israel and its own difficult situation, was able to maintain itself. It even captured some cities, including Bethel.

The tense and often confused situation on Judah's northern boundary is not clear. Periods of relative quiet (see, e.g., 2 Chr. 14:1) alternated with periods of war. After Abijah's brief reign (given as three years), Asa ruled for forty-one years and died about 873 B.C. Kings who were contemporary with him in Israel were Jeroboam and his successors and even Omri and Ahab. Asa and Baasha, who was king over Israel for twenty-four years, were contemporaries and enemies. Baasha seems to have started the hostilities by using Ramah, located only 10 kilometers (6 mi.) north of Jerusalem, as a checkpoint from which to control the traffic to and from the capital—certainly not an attractive situation for Judah! But Asa found an effective solution. At a high price, paid from the temple treasury (which was at the same time the national treasury), Asa persuaded Benhadad I of Damascus to attack Baasha from the north. This war on two fronts forced Baasha to relinquish his grip on Ramah. Judah seized the fortifications Israel had constructed in Ramah and used them to build up Geba and Mizpah. The latter places were in the vicinity of Ramah (likely Deba and Tell en-Nasbe) and were important for Judah's control of the road to Israel.

About Asa's long reign 2 Chronicles relates only a few details. An elaborate account is given of Asa's actions against the illegitimate cult in the land and at the court (ch. 15). Maacah, the queen-mother (or mother [v. 16], or grandmother [1 Kgs. 15:2]), was removed from her official position as "ruler" (*gebirah*) because she possessed an Asherah image, likely a carved tree symbolizing fertility. This report, occurring both in 1 Kings (15:13) and in 2 Chronicles (15:16), along with other comments about the cult, indicates that Judah was by no means free from Canaanite religion. On the political front mention is made of a raid of "Zerah the Cushite" (14:8–14 [9–15]), who invaded as far as Mareshah, a city in the lower hill country, between the coast and the Judean hill country (see also 11:8). Asa stopped him at Mareshah and then forced him back to Gerar, between Gaza and Beer-sheba. Asa's effective counteraction was no doubt due partially to the large military fortifications he had constructed in peacetime (14:5–7 [6–8]). We are not yet able to identify Zerah the Cushite. Scholars have abandoned the earlier identification with Osorkon I, the son of Pharaoh Shoshenq, because the former was of Libyan not Cushite or Ethiopian background. Moreover, Cush is more likely connected with the north Arabian region Cushan than with southern Egypt.

The story as a whole offers few points of historical contact. That fact, however, represents no reason to ignore this remarkable history, as Herrmann and others have done. This story perhaps provides a unique insight into the nature of the Judean fortifications under Asa, namely, the consolidation of the southern part of his land through the construction of a strong defense line and the driving back of nomads who, with good or bad intentions, tried to enter his territory via the desert or steppe. For Asa to provide security and safety to the inhabitants of his country, especially those who lived near open deserts and steppes, must have promoted prosperity. Even though the writers of Kings and Chronicles do not as a rule evaluate history socioeconomically, such considerations perhaps contributed to the relatively favorable appraisal of the era of Asa. When Asa fell ill toward the end of his life, his bad spirit seems to have prevailed over his wise statecraft (2 Chr. 16:10–12), bringing his rule into disrepute among the prophets—who were fairly active during his reign—and among the people. The passing observation in verse 10 indicates the presence of a spirit of resistance among the people, either against his foreign policy or—more likely—

against domestic measures in the areas of economy, religion, and defense.

The coming to the throne of Jehoshaphat, who was a contemporary of the Omride dynasty in Israel, introduced a change in the relationship between the two kingdoms. The kings of Judah and Israel, instead of fighting each other, now became friends and allies and even established family ties through the marriage of their children. In part this reconciliation can be attributed to the emergence of common enemies, the Arameans being the nearest, and the Assyrians the most powerful. In part also the change reflects the eagerness of Jehoshaphat to share in the rise and future possibilities of his northern neighbor. Jehoshaphat thus soon became involved, together with King Ahaziah, in the ill-fated venture of outfitting and sending ships from Ezion-geber to bring gold from Ophir (1 Kgs. 22:49 [48]; cf. 2 Chr. 20:36).

Despite these aspects of Jehoshaphat's reign, which are questionable also in the eyes of the authors of Kings and Chronicles, the latter in particular appraises him positively on account of his positive attitude toward the service of YHWH, his judicial reform (2 Chr. 19:4-11), and his good sense and fortune in domestic and foreign policy. As mentioned above, he allied himself with Ahab against Aram-Damascus. His successes against other neighboring nations are pictured hyperbolically in 17:10-11: Philistines and Arabians became tributary to him, and with the wealth so received, he strengthened his territory. The total picture recalls the Solomonic kingdom of peace. Jehoshaphat's fortunes continued in his battle against Moabites and Ammonites described in chapter 20. According to this account, Jehoshaphat had only to gather the booty, because the Moabites and Ammonites had slaughtered each other. However we may assess this account, the story does add to the conception of Jehoshaphat's reign as a golden age, an aspect that was apparently very important to the Chronicler. In presenting this picture, he also intimates something that is not immediately apparent in Kings, namely, that this period must also have been a prosperous one for Israel. Both kingdoms shared not only the misery but also the grandeur. The former, however, would not be long in coming, for Jehoshaphat's son Jehoram married a daughter of the infamous King Ahab.

Soon after Jehoshaphat's death and Jehoram's accession, the influence of the Omride religious policy, which so far had been visible only in Judah's political and economic life, also made its impact felt in religious and cultic affairs. 2 Chronicles 21:2-4 mentions as a particular example of Jehoram's depravity the fact that, at the beginning of his kingship, he murdered all his brothers, possibly at the instigation of his wife Athaliah, against whom suspicions may have arisen at the court. The king was not fortunate in his foreign policy, for the Edomites revolted and freed themselves from Judah's yoke (2 Kgs. 8:20-22; 2 Chr. 21:8-10). In a clearly related setback, Judah (and Israel) lost the sea harbor Ezion-geber, and the safety of Judah's southern border was seriously threatened. The result of such losses was not only that a city such as Libnah in the Shephelah managed to free itself, a city with a large contingent of Canaanites (cf. Josh. 10:29-30; 12:15; 15:42) and likely long annexed to Judah, but also that the Philistines and the Arabians, old enemies of Judah whose power should not be overestimated, dared to attack. Chronicles even mentions their taking captive the royal family.

The Chronicler, because of the perspective from which he writes, perhaps presents too desolate a picture. He describes vividly the seriousness of the king's sickness, of which he was to die, and reports the people's utter lack of sympathy for Jehoram. In the judgment of the writer, who even adduced a posthumous letter of Elijah, the root cause of Jehoram's affliction was Ahab's wickedness. The analysis could hardly be more negative. Although we might dispute this account historically in some respects, it is obvious that the religious policy in the north, based on tolerance and syncretism, was extremely perilous to the worship of YHWH. This religious attitude had found entrance especially among the higher echelons of officials and merchants who had become well organized under Jehoram's predecessor, Jehoshaphat. One might in fact blame Jehoram's character on his wife Athaliah and his father Jehoshaphat!

The close ties with Israel continued during the very brief reign of Ahaziah (note the difference in synchronism between 2 Kgs. 8:25 and 9:29 and the difference in age between 8:26 and 2 Chr. 22:2). He actively showed his ties with the

Israelite king Joram, the son of Ahab, who fought the Arameans at Ramoth-gilead. When Joram was wounded, Ahaziah visited him in Jezreel. That visit became his downfall, for Jehu had seized power and had taken an oath to exterminate not only the Israelite branch of Omri's house but also the Judean side (cf. the different versions of the death of Ahaziah in 2 Kgs. 9:14–29 and 2 Chr. 22:6–9).

Murder and bloodshed remained for some time to come a regular feature of Judah's history. Athaliah, informed of the death of her son, seized power and immediately tried to secure her shaky position as Israelite-Phoenician princess by killing all of the Davidic family who had remained alive from a similar purge that her husband, Jehoram, had earlier perpetrated. Only the lad Joash escaped this bloodbath, being rescued by Jehoram's daughter Jehosheba, wife of the priest Jehoiada. She was able to hide Joash in the temple for about six years.

Meanwhile Athaliah ruled in Judah. We do not know much about her reign, but no doubt she effectively supported the policy of the Omrides and encouraged Canaanite Baal worship in Judah. Her devotion is evident from a reference to a temple of Baal in Jerusalem, complete with priests and altars (2 Kgs. 11:18; 2 Chr. 23:17). This royal promotion of Baal worship at the expense of the worship of YHWH, coupled with the suspicion that many leaders must have had about a national policy that was strongly oriented toward Israel and Phoenicia, no doubt explains the success of the plot among army officers and other prominent people led by the priest Jehoiada, the guardian of the secretly hidden Joash. Both Kings and Chronicles give a detailed account of this revolution. One of the results, of course, has been that Athaliah's actions are recorded from a negative perspective and stand as a black page in Israel's history.

After Athaliah had been put to death and the people's wrath vented on her supporters and on the Baal worship, and after the seven-year-old Joash had been acclaimed and accepted as king, the problem of the actual exercise of power had to be faced. Jehoiada, the man behind the conspiracy, functioned as an active regent and had little difficulty in carrying out his policies. He par-

ticularly aimed at the domestic religious situation and, as one might expect from a priest, strengthened the role of the temple and of the service of YHWH. In view of the central position of the temple as royal sanctuary, it is not surprising that Joash, when he became older, actively supported this policy. In a literal sense it put money into the till (he had placed a chest in the temple). This material focus on the temple apparently included some compulsion of the people on the part of the leaders. For after the death of Jehoiada (2 Chr. 24:15 says that he died at the age of 130!), Joash soon received a request for tolerance toward those of different beliefs in his kingdom, and also for relief from the heavy burdens, to which Joash was sympathetic.

Joash's easements evoked the displeasure of the faithful YHWH worshipers. The prophet Zechariah, who rebuked Joash's tolerance, was even stoned at the king's command. Only 2 Chronicles mentions this fact (24:20–22; cf. Matt. 23:35 and parallels), adding as a special detail that Zechariah was a son of Joash's guardian, Jehoiada. Could such mention indicate that the priests felt threatened after Jehoiada's death? With the outbreak of a war, Judah seems to have experienced difficult times economically. Hazael from the Aramean Damascus had attacked the Philistine Gath, a remarkable move because it involved his crossing Judean territory. The Arameans dared to do so because they considered Judah weak militarily and also because they had strengthened their position in Transjordan against Israel (2 Kgs. 13:3–7). Possibly Aram wanted to use Philistia as a bridgehead from which to conquer Judah and Jerusalem. Joash diverted the threat by sending some of the temple treasures to Hazael, which represented a heavy drain on Judah, for it was not rich as it once was. The nation became so discontented with its desolate situation that people turned against Joash. He was assassinated by a few courtiers (note the different versions of this event in 2 Kgs. 12:21–22 [20–21] and 2 Chr. 24:25–26). Thus ended sadly a forty-year reign about which remarkably little information has been preserved.

Joash was succeeded by his twenty-five-year-old son, Amaziah, whose rule coincided with that of Jehoash and Jeroboam II of Israel. Amaziah is said to have reigned twenty-nine years, but very few details about him have been preserved. According to 2 Kings 14:5, he took revenge on the assassins of his father, but—following a rule formulated in Deuteronomy 24:16—he spared their children. According to the standards of that time, his revenge was not harsh or unusual. It is not clear whether Amaziah's leniency was due to a certain mildness in his character or to political considerations. In his foreign policy the king was more forceful and fortunate than his predecessors. One reason for Amaziah's success was a decline in the strength of the Arameans. Ben-hadad III had suffered severe defeats against the invading Assyrians, opening up opportunities for Judah on which Amaziah capitalized. Militarily he turned against Edom, which under Jehoshaphat or Jehoram had revolted. He took Sela (Bosra? Petra?), whose population he cruelly killed by throwing them down a cliff (2 Chr. 25:12). The subjection of the Edomites provided open access to the Gulf of Aqabah and thus a trade route to the south.

Amaziah was less fortunate in a brief but disastrous war against his northern neighbor Israel. The cause of this war is not certain; probably more was involved than Amaziah's somewhat naive challenge to the Israelite king (2 Kgs. 14:8; 2 Chr. 25:17). The Chronicler has King Jehoash of Israel reply in a fable about plants, one that resembles Jotham's parable in Judges 9. Israel prevails in the ensuing war with Judah; Amaziah is defeated at Beth-shemesh and taken captive. Jehoash even enters Jerusalem and partially dismantles the city walls, after which he returns to Samaria, loaded with booty. Though the vague data at our disposal indicate that, after this debacle against Israel, Amaziah remained king for another fifteen years (see 2 Kgs. 14:17), he apparently was relieved of his power, and in Jerusalem a conspiracy was formed against him. Perhaps such political defeat explains his fleeing to Lachish, from where he may have plotted to regain the power taken from him. He was killed, however, though still given a burial in Jerusalem.

Amaziah's son Uzziah—in Kings also called Azariah (cf. also Isa. 1:1; 6:1; 7:1; etc.)—was only sixteen when he became king. He ruled for fifty-two years, longer than any other king in Judah ex-cept Manasseh. Some of these years perhaps were regent years: at the beginning of his reign when his father, Amaziah, was exiled, and at the end when his son Jotham became regent after Uzziah contracted "leprosy." When Uzziah ascended the throne, Jeroboam II was king in Israel. Uzziah's death likely happened in the time of Pekah. His regnal period may be characterized as a relatively prosperous one for Judah. As it does for other Judean kings, 2 Kings provides only brief details about the life and work of Uzziah. Chronicles is more detailed. One report found in both books is Uzziah's strengthening of Elath on the Gulf of Aqabah and his annexation in Judah of the harbor area and surrounding territory (2 Kgs. 14:22; 2 Chr. 26:2). Some have felt that certain archeological finds indicate traces of Judean influence in this area, for instance, a seal with the name Jotham. Uzziah also strengthened or extended Judah's power in other parts of his kingdom. 2 Chronicles 26:6–8 lists victories over the Philistines, the Arabs, and the Meunites. Even the Ammonites, who were generally in Israel's sphere of influence in Transjordan or who maintained a measure of independence, became tributary. Uzziah's renown also spread to Egypt.

The military successes, made possible by the relative weakness of his oppone _s, large and small, resulted in various improvements, including fortresses constructed in the deserts and water cisterns made for the large herds of cattle. It is striking that Uzziah's agrarian interest is specifically mentioned in 2 Chronicles 26:10. He also promoted new initiatives in other areas. He had ingenious weaponry designed and placed in Jerusalem. The impression is inescapable that Uzziah's time was another golden age in Judah's history. Less pleasant events also occurred. A terrible earthquake caused terror and destruction (Amos 1:1; Zech. 14:5). Some scholars have thought that Uzziah was tributary to Assyria, on the strength of a reference to a King Azriyau of Yadiya (Yaudi) in an Assyrian text that mentions the campaign of Tiglath-pileser III in 738 B.C. (*ANET,* 282–83). The king referred to here, however, is one from the northern Syrian region Yadiya that we know from an inscription of the kings of Samal (Zenjirli). Not being certain about the year in which Uzziah died, we may take the mention of his name in that time as doubtful. In matters of religion, the tradition calls Uzziah a good king, though his attitude toward the priests in Jerusalem indicates that he wanted to make the weight of his position as king felt. His arrogant conduct is said to be the cause of his leprosy. After he had fully experienced the miserable fate of lepers and had died a lonely death, he was buried not in but near the royal tombs (2 Chr. 26:23; cf. Josephus, *Antiquities* 9.227, which reports Uzziah's burial "only in his gardens").

Meanwhile his son Jotham, who for several years had acted as a regent for his father, carried forward the favorable political course followed by Uzziah. He subdued the Ammonites and forced them to pay tribute (2 Chr. 27:5). He also engaged in building activities in Jerusalem (2 Kgs. 15:35; 2 Chr. 27:3) and in Judea (v. 4). It is usually assumed that Uzziah was living throughout all of Jotham's reign as well as at the beginning of the reign of his grandson Ahaz.

Ahaz's rule coincided with the last few decades of the northern kingdom of Israel. We have seen that Judah experienced an enormous rise in prosperity, power, and prestige under Uzziah and that he must have reigned over a sizable territory. Although Judah was small, it was a power to be reckoned with and regarded as a desirable ally. Meanwhile the threat of Assyria in the north grew much more ominous. I have already described how the warlike Tiglath-pileser extended his military campaigns deep into the south and how Israel together with Aram-Damascus and some other small nations tried to form a coalition against the Assyrians. This attempt led to the Syro-Ephraimite war, which was very hard on Judah. The tradition reports this event in 2 Kings 16, 2 Chronicles 28, and Isaiah 7. In this war a great deal of territory that had been conquered and later fortified apparently fell to the Arameans and their allies, including Elath on the Gulf of Aqabah (2 Kgs. 16:6). Chronicles mentions even deportations to Damascus and Israelite massacres in Judah at the instigation of King Pekah.

Though Isaiah, who had been called to be a prophet in the year of Uzziah's death (Isa. 6:1), tried to encourage Ahaz, the king had greater confidence in his own limited ideas than in the prophetic oracle (ch. 7). He appealed to Tiglath-pileser for help against the coalition, paying for it with the treasures of the temple. Tiglath-pileser immediately saw his chance. He captured Damascus, restrained Israel and the other members of the coalition, but at the same time made Ahaz his vassal. Judah's king appeared before the great Assyrian ruler in Damascus, whither he had been summoned, and there humbly awaited his orders. Ahaz submitted to the point of formally accepting the religion and cultic practices of the Assyrians. He had a copy made of an altar (likely Assyrian) he had seen in Damascus and placed it in the temple in Jerusalem, while removing Solomon's brass altar from its former place. It is not surprising that the religious turnabout of Ahaz, whose faith in YHWH was not the strongest anyway, is negatively judged by the authors of Kings and Chronicles. Ahaz's syncretism—a form of primitive tolerance—also is evident in the worship of Baal and his bringing of child sacrifices.

The author of Chronicles reports, contrary to the record in Kings, that Ahaz was not buried in the royal tombs (cf. 2 Kgs. 16:20 with 2 Chr. 28:27). Particularly the Chronicler is highly negative in his final judgment of Ahaz. This negative judgment agrees completely with the picture Isaiah presents of him and is based on two considerations: (1) Ahaz's disastrous pro-Assyria policy, which led only to dependence on that great empire and which, after a period of relative prosperity, quickly impoverished Judah, and (2) Ahaz's tolerant syncretism, which left him religiously no better than his hostile Israelite colleague.

In this troublesome setting, Ahaz's son Hezekiah became king. According to the synchronistic reports in 2 Kings (18:1), Hezekiah began to rule in the third year of Israel's last king, Hoshea, so that he may have been king from 725/724 to 697/696. In the beginning of his rule he thus witnessed the demise of Israel, together with some small cities and nations that had opposed Assyria. But the fall of these independent nations did not guarantee a time of peace. On the contrary, there regularly were revolts somewhere among these former petty nations, which the Assyrian armies under Shalmaneser III, Sargon II, and Sennacherib quickly quelled. Like his father, Hezekiah sided with the Assyrian rulers and was initially able to stay out of these conspiracies. For instance,

Hezekiah is not mentioned as a revolting rebel in inscriptions of Sargon's campaigns to the west and south (*ANET*, 285). The situation must have changed when Ashdod, in about 712 B.C., organized several territories from Philistia and elsewhere against Assyria (see *ANET*, 287). These groups all hoped that Egypt would be a powerful ally against Assyria. (Since 715, the Ethiopian dynasty, which included Pharaoh Shabako, had been in power; cf. Isaiah 18 and 20.) Egypt's help, however, never materialized, and the only consequence of the revolt was Assyria's gaining even more territory.

After Sargon II died in 705 B.C. and Sennacherib had succeeded him in confused political circumstances, the west again raised the cry for freedom from the Assyrian yoke. Hezekiah may have been one of the instigators. The Old Testament as well as the annals of Sennacherib reports in detail the confrontation of the parties. The Assyrian ruler says on the famous Sennacherib prism (see *ANET*, 287-88; ill. 47) that, on his third campaign (in 701 B.C.), he marched to the land of the Hatti (the region of Syria and Palestine) and there besieged and took a large number of cities. "The ministers, dignitaries and the people of Ekron, who had put Padi, their ruler, who by oath was bound to Assyria, in iron chains and hostilely delivered up to Hezekiah—, on account of this wicked deed fear had struck their hearts and they appealed to the princes of Egypt and the king of Meluhha (Ethiopia), an innumerable army" (2.73-81). Sennacherib next recounts a battle in the vicinity of Elteqe (cf. Josh. 19:44; 21:23, *hirbet el muqanna* [?]), in which the Egyptians and all their helpers were defeated. Ekron and other cities were taken and Padi was freed from Jerusalem, but Sennacherib fails to mention the capture of Jerusalem, though Hezekiah had to cede much territory and pay a heavy tribute to the Assyrian.

In outline, this account matches fairly well the reports in 2 Kings 18:13-19:37; Isaiah 36-37; and 2 Chronicles 32:1-22. In the details, however, there is considerable variation, as there is among the different biblical accounts themselves. In a way, 2 Kings 18:14-16 agrees the most with Sennacherib's account, but it has no parallels in Isaiah or Chronicles. On the other hand, 18:13 and 18:17-19:9a relates the story to the moment when Sennacherib withdrew from Jerusalem, hearing a rumor of the approach of Egyptian armies under the command of General Taharqa, while 19:9b-37 reports that Sennacherib was forced to retreat because "an angel of YHWH" slew 185,000 men, likely through a contagious disease. Herodotus's *Histories* (2.141) contain a parallel, reporting that Pharaoh Seti had only a weak army with which to battle Sennacherib, "the king of the Arabians [!] and of the Assyrians." Encouraged by a god in a dream, the Egyptian king with an assortment of people marched against Sennacherib to Pelusium on the Egyptian border. During the night thousands of field mice appeared and ate the quivers and bows of the Assyrians, so that the next day they suffered a terrible defeat. The question is whether all these versions, so diverse in substance and in literary form, refer to the same event or whether Sennacherib besieged Jerusalem more than once.

According to older calculations, Taharqa was about fifteen years old in 701 B.C.; more recent analysis, however, indicates that he was over twenty. Old Testament synchronisms add to the problem. According to 2 Kings 18:13, Sennacherib attacked Palestine in the fourteenth year of Hezekiah's reign, though Hezekiah already became king over Judah in the third year of Hoshea (v. 1; cf. the added difficulty that, according to v. 10, Samaria was captured in the sixth year of Hezekiah). In any case, Taharqa, who had an Ethiopian background, must have been pharaoh over Egypt from 688 to 664 B.C. It is of course possible that Shabako could have entrusted him with the command of the army at an early age. Some have suggested that there was a second campaign against Hezekiah not recorded in Sennacherib's annals, a hypothesis that seems less likely than the view that Taharqa led the army at an early age.

We can assume that Hezekiah's position, which was still strong before Sennacherib's attack on Palestine, must have been severely weakened after the retreat of the Assyrian king, even though Sennacherib's contention that the Philistine rulers controlled the land is highly exaggerated. The political power left to Hezekiah is evident not only from 2 Kings 18:8, which mentions his victory over the Philistines "as far as Gaza," but also from

20:12–20 (cf. Isaiah 39), which describes his friendly diplomatic initiatives with Merodak-Baladan (Mardukapaliddina) of Babylon. Like Hezekiah, Merodak-Baladan was a vassal of Assyria. With Elamite help, he was able to maintain himself on Babylon's throne for a while, meanwhile constantly searching for allies in his struggle against Assyria. It is not fully clear whether Hezekiah received his Babylonian colleague (against whom he had wisely been warned by the prophet Isaiah) after Sennacherib's campaign or whether this initiative represented part of Hezekiah's engineering of the rebellion before Sennacherib's campaign.

Hezekiah is also said to have been active in other areas, such as that of the cult. Thus it is recorded that he removed Nehushtan, the "bronze snake" said to have been made by Moses (Num. 21:4–9), together with the "high places" and the cultic objects dedicated to Baal and Asherah (2 Kgs. 18:4). The Deuteronomistic author also emphasizes Hezekiah's promotion of the service of YHWH and stresses Hezekiah's unique religious contribution to Judah: "there was none like him among all the kings of Judah after him, nor among those who were before him. For he held fast to YHWH" (vv. 5–6). Hezekiah's piety, related in detail in Isaiah 36–39, demonstrates this trust. The Chronicler supplements this report with a sketch of Hezekiah's purification of the temple, his lead in celebrating the Passover, and his role in other temple activities (2 Chronicles 29–31). The account reaches a climax in the portrayal of the almost legendary prosperity of the king (32:27–33). The attention given to him by the Chronicler demonstrates the tremendous significance that future generations attributed to Hezekiah's cult-reforming activities. This picture may contain a measure of exaggeration, yet the fact remains that, despite Assyria's threat, such things were possible in Hezekiah's time. Another indication of Hezekiah's activities is the tunnel he built that brought water from the Gihon Spring into the city proper. The Siloam inscription recording the excavation of this tunnel may well be the permanent witness to this feat (see 2 Kgs. 20:20; 2 Chr. 32:30; ANET, 321; ill. 45).

Hezekiah's cultic reforms, highly praised by the writer of Chronicles, were rather short-lived.

Under Hezekiah's son Manasseh, who assumed the crown at age twelve upon Hezekiah's death and who, according to Kings and Chronicles, occupied Judah's throne for fifty-five years, many reforms apparently passed into oblivion, and the foreign cult was ardently promoted (2 Kgs. 21:1–18; 2 Chr. 33:1–20). This foreign religion was predominantly of Canaanite character and involved child sacrifice, divination, augury, magic, and the worship of the heavenly bodies. This cultic about-face by Manasseh was possibly due to strong Assyrian influence (v. 11). The stories about Manasseh's Assyrian exile and his conversion give the impression of being legendary. Chronicles goes into greater detail than does Kings in describing the building and fortification activities carried out by Manasseh in and around Jerusalem. The latter were likely associated with the campaigns of the Assyrian king Esarhaddon (681–669 B.C.) against Egypt. His annals mention a Manasseh (ANET, 291) as one of the vassals who contributed toward the Assyrian campaigns. (Manasseh appears also in the annals of Esarhaddon's successor, Ashurbanipal [669–ca. 630 B.C.; see ANET, 294].) In the Assyrians' eyes, a strong buffer zone between north and south was welcome.

Some have attempted to provide a historical context for Manasseh's captivity by pointing, for example, to his possible participation in the revolt of Shamashshumukin of Babylon against Ashurbanipal. Assyria's clemency toward Manasseh could in that case be explained by Assyria's expansionistic designs toward Egypt. Furthermore, Ashurbanipal was less a man of war and conquests than a man of culture and letters, as the discovery of a magnificent library for posterity in Nineveh has demonstrated. On the other hand, Manasseh must have experienced firsthand the rapid decline in Assyria's power. Even with such warlike rulers as Sennacherib and Esarhaddon, it soon became a relatively weak state, hardly capable of quelling internal division and rebellion. The Old Testament says little about this period of the seventh century.

The reign of Manasseh's son Amon was too brief to accomplish anything of significance (2 Kgs. 21:19–26; 2 Chr. 33:21–25). He continued the policies of his father, particularly those of Manasseh's earlier years. For reasons unknown to us, a plot was made against him to which he fell victim. "The people of the land" made his son Josiah king at the age of eight. Favored by the international climate, tiny Judah under Josiah once more acquired a measure of independence vaguely reminiscent of the golden age of David or of Solomon (2 Kgs. 22:1–23:30; 2 Chronicles 34–35).

The changes that took place during Josiah's reign (640–609 B.C.) in the nations surrounding Judah had a decisive impact on the deterioration and eventual collapse of the Assyrian empire in 608 (four years after the destruction of Nineveh) and the rise of the neo-Babylonian, or Chaldean, empire under Nabopolassar, who had ruled since 626. Egypt experienced a revival under the Twenty-sixth, or Saite, Dynasty; such pharaohs as Psammetichus I (664–610) and Neco II (609–594) made their power felt inside and outside Egypt's border. Farther away from Judah's territory, but ultimately of equal political and military significance, were the rise of the kingdom of the Medes and Persians and the raids of the Scythians. In this movement of nations Josiah in Judah was able to chart an independent course and to do what seemed most advantageous for his country. His tragic death in the battle against the Egyptians under Pharaoh Neco occurred as the result of a wrong decision on his part. At home, Josiah was able to expand Judah's territory considerably. 2 Kings 23:15, 19–20 (2 Chr. 34:6–7) and archeological data give evidence that he subdued and annexed large parts of the former northern Israelite country. According to Alt, Joshua 15, 18, and 19 divide the tribal areas into districts that were current at the time of Josiah. Archeological discoveries such as ostraca from *Mesad Hashavyahu* (near Jabne-Jam), fortifications at Engedi on the Dead Sea and Arad in the Negeb, and excavated parts of old Jerusalem point to the powerful position of King Josiah.

Also of great significance was Josiah's cultic reform, sparked by, or perhaps resulting in, the discovery of "the book of the law." There are still many unresolved questions in connection with this incident. 2 Chronicles 34:3 reports that Josiah, in the eighth year of his reign, began to worship "the God of David his father." In the twelfth year he began to purify Judah and Jerusalem from idols, efforts that are described in considerable detail by the authors of Kings and Chronicles. As is so often the case, each book has its own emphasis. They agree in placing the beginning of the restoration of the temple in Jerusalem in the eighteenth year of Josiah (2 Kgs. 22:3; 2 Chr. 34:8). On other points they vary because the author of Kings views Josiah's reform, which was started as a consequence of the discovery of the book, as an interrelated whole, whereas the Chronicler sees it happening step by step as part of a national revival that accompanied Judah's increasing independence of the surrounding nations.

The removal of all sorts of specific Babylonian and Assyrian practices, such as the astral cult (2 Kgs. 23:5, 11–12), and the use of *kemarim* (a denigrating word for "priests"; cf. Akkadian *kumru[m]*) indicate Josiah's liberation from Assyrian pressure. The discovery of the book of the law, often assumed to be Deuteronomy or a very old form of it, was of revolutionary importance for the king and his people. We cannot deal here with the questions that arise in respect to this remarkable find. We should note that Josiah, after reading the scroll and having consulted with the high priest Hilkiah, the prophetess Huldah, and some other officials, and being sensitive to the threats contained in the "book of the covenant" (22:11, 13, 16), had a covenant made between YHWH and the people (23:1– 3; 2 Chr. 34:29–31) and had the Passover celebrated "for the first time" since the days of the judges (2 Kgs. 23:22; according to 2 Chr. 35:18, since the time of the prophet Samuel). The description of this Passover celebration contains definite similarities with the directions given in Deuteronomy 16:5–6.

Josiah, more than any other king before him, promoted the centralization of the YHWH cult in Jerusalem (2 Kgs. 23:8; cf. Deut. 12:13–14). From Jeremiah 22:15–16 ("he judged the cause of the poor and needy"), it can be inferred that Josiah's reforms were not restricted to the cult and the worship of YHWH in the temple but also extended to social reforms. Recalling all such reform measures, as well as the expansion of his kingdom, we are not surprised that Josiah was viewed in every way as a David redivivus. According to the tradition, David too had attempted to combine the north and the south in his kingdom around the one cult, even though from the outset his attempts were thwarted. Alt, followed by others, has suggested that Deuteronomy preserved traditions of the northern state of Israel and that, after the fall of Samaria, the book as a kind of ideal program miraculously surfaced in the Jerusalem temple. It thus provided the impetus for Josiah's reformation, restoration, and especially the centralization of the cult and the kingdom. In this way Josiah became the defender of the traditions of both kingdoms; in particular, the ancient northern traditions also became of paramount significance for Judah. This fact would become important for the subsequent course of Israel's history, though not immediately.

The course of Josiah's reign shows that his opportunities for reform and expansion were brought to a halt when the superpowers made their presence felt. In 612 B.C. Nineveh was captured and destroyed by the combined armies of the Babylonians and the Medes (see ill. 53). Egypt tried to help the mortally weakened Assyria and at the same time assert its claims to power in Mesopotamia. After the fall of Nineveh the last Assyrian king, Ashuruballit II, made Haran his residence, but that city too was lost in 610. Supported by Neco, Ashuruballit tried to restrain the Babylonians. We cannot be sure whether Josiah refused the violation of his territory by Egypt or whether, driven by his anti-Assyrian sentiments and in league with Babylon, he felt obligated to attack the Egyptian army. At any rate, Josiah took his stand at Megiddo to block Pharaoh Neco and was killed in battle (cf. 2 Kgs. 22:20). He was buried in Jerusalem. 2 Chronicles 35:25 adds that Jeremiah composed a lament on the death of the king. The author of Kings eulogizes him with the words "Before him there was no king like him, who turned to YHWH with all his heart and with all his soul and with all his might, according to all the law of Moses; nor did any like him arise after him" (2 Kgs. 23:25). May we hear in these words the appreciation of the Deuteronomist for the ruler who tried to give the book of the law a dominant place in Israel?

With the sudden and tragic death of Josiah, Judah's preexilic history enters its final phase. These last years are marked by confusion, degeneration, dominance by strangers, and violence. Politically as well as religiously, soon little was left of the revived ideal of a large Israelite kingdom. As happened with the young Josiah (2 Kgs. 21:24), "the people of the land" acted, this time making Jehoahaz king in his father's stead (23:30; 2 Chr. 36:1). Jeremiah (22:11) calls him "Shallum," probably his given name. (Especially for Jehoahaz and his successors, it is apparent that throne-names differed from personal names.) Jehoahaz was king for only three months. On account of his anti-Egyptian politics, and because of Egypt's control of Syria and Palestine after the collapse of the Assyrian empire and before the coming of the neo-Babylonian empire, Pharaoh Neco summoned Jehoahaz to Riblah (in Syria, in the land of Hamath), where the pharaoh still had his headquarters after his war against the Babylonians. Jehoahaz was later deported to Egypt, where he died, lamented by Jeremiah (vv. 10–12).

Judah was laid under heavy tribute and forced to accept a new king, Jehoahaz's brother Eliakim, whom Pharaoh Neco gave the throne-name Jehoiakim. Using a system of head taxes, in which each person had to contribute according to ability, a method earlier used by the Israelite king Menahem (cf. 2 Kgs. 15:20 with 23:35), the new ruler tried to meet the obligations imposed upon him by the pharaoh. Egypt's dominance in Syria and Palestine did not last very long. After having had mixed success in previous battles with the Egyptians, the Babylonians dealt them a stunning defeat in 605 B.C. at Carchemish, on the upper course of the Euphrates. We have a good picture of this battle—mentioned in Jeremiah 46:2 and recorded in detail by Josephus (*Antiquities* 10.84ff.)—through the publication in 1956 of the cuneiform Babylonian Chronicle. Though Nabopolassar, the founder of the neo-Babylonian empire and a successful general, was still alive, he was apparently not healthy and strong enough (see *Antiquities* 10.221) to participate actively in the battles against Egypt. Prince Nebuchadrezzar was the commander in chief of the army that subdued the Egyptians, and he took full advantage of Babylon's superiority. He marched to the south and laid siege to Jerusalem (cf. also Dan. 1:1–2). Nebuchadrezzar also pursued the Egyptian troops to their own country, from which they for the present ventured no military attacks (2 Kgs. 24:7; cf.

KAI, no. 266, a papyrus fragment discovered at Saqqara). In the same year that Syria and Palestine fell to Nebuchadrezzar, his father, Nabopolassar, died after a reign of twenty-one years (626–605 B.C.), which compelled Nebuchadrezzar to return to Babylon to take the throne.

Thus began the long kingship (605–562 B.C.) of an energetic ruler who became of great importance to the fate of Judah. In the year of his crowning he returned to "Hatti," as Syria and Palestine are called in Assyrian and Babylonian documents, to establish there the power and control of Babylon (cf. the prophecy of Jer. 25:1–14). With some exceptions, such campaigns became an annual event. The explosive situation in Syria and Palestine indeed demanded a strong display of power. Already in the first year of his monarchy, in 604 B.C. in the month Kislev (December), Nebuchadrezzar had to send an army to Ashdod. He took the city, razed it to the ground, and deported the population. It is very possible that, during the same expedition, Jehoiakim was made a vassal of Nebuchadrezzar (a state of subjection that lasted three years, assuming that 2 Kgs. 24:1 refers to this event). Supporting this hypothesis, the Babylonian Chronicle records that three years later Nebuchadrezzar had little success with his invasion of Egypt, which is possibly connected with Jehoiakim's rebellion. This subjection to Nebuchadrezzar at first created a state of emergency in Judah, to which the time of fasting in the fifth year of Jehoiakim corresponds (Jer. 36:9). The biblical and Babylonian data seem to agree quite well. Also from this period is Jeremiah's somewhat unfavorable judgment of Egypt, "the beautiful heifer" (46:13–26).

A few years later Nebuchadrezzar was defeated by Egypt, and in his fifth year he remained in his land to recover from the wounds. In December 599 we find him warring against the Arabians living in Palestine (see Jer. 49:28–33). In this way he secured the eastern and southern desert areas against attack. In the meantime he also mustered troops for attacking the areas that had not yet been fully subdued (cf. 2 Kgs. 24:2, which mentions Chaldean, Moabite, and Ammonite raiders). This fact can be related to the inscriptions found at Arad that report Edomite activities in the Negeb. A year later, in the seventh year of Nebuchadrezzar, in the month Kislev (December 598), the Babylonian ruler attacked Jerusalem. He laid siege to the city of Judah, and on the second of Adar (about March 16, 597), he captured Jerusalem and took the king captive. According to the Babylonian Chronicle he "appointed a king after his heart, received heavy tribute from him, and sent him to Babylon." There is some discrepancy in the Old Testament about these happenings in the beginning of 597 (cf. 2 Kgs. 24:6–12 with 2 Chr. 36:6–10; Dan. 1:1–2). Likely it was not Jehoiakim but his son Jehoiachin, an eighteen-year-old who ruled only three months, who was taken captive by Nebuchadrezzar. It appears likely that Jehoiakim died (or was assassinated?) during the siege of Jerusalem. His reign will forever remain one of the black pages in Judah's history because he followed in the footsteps of his grandfather Manasseh and apparently maintained his power in Judah only through injustice and the shedding of innocent blood (cf. also Jer. 22:13–19). He was given "the burial of an ass" (v. 19).

Though Nebuchadrezzar's campaign in the spring of 597 was directed not only against Jehoiachin, he clearly wanted a more agreeable king on the Jerusalem throne. Jehoiachin, whom he carried into exile together with a number of other important people (Jer. 52:28; see also 2 Kgs. 24:12–16; 2 Chr. 36:10), was apparently not reliable in Neuchadrezzar's eyes. This unfortunate king had to spend the rest of his life in Babylon. Babylonian food lists mention that daily he was given a set ration of food (*ANET*, 308). Finally, in the thirty-seventh year of his captivity, he was released by the son of Nebuchadrezzar (2 Kgs. 25:27–28; Jer. 52:31–34) and given a place at the Babylonian court. None of his children would succeed him on the Judean throne (see Jer. 22:30). Nebuchadrezzar appointed Zedekiah in his place, who became the last Davidic king before the Captivity (see ill. 54).

Before his elevation to the throne Zedekiah was called Mattaniah (2 Kgs. 24:17). He was an uncle of Jehoiachin, hence a son of Josiah (perhaps the word *brother* in 2 Chr. 36:10 means no more than "related to"). We have an incomplete picture of his rule. At first he undoubtedly showed a measure of loyalty toward his Babylonian lord and master. The relative quiet at the beginning of his reign can thus easily have drawn Babylonian attention to Elam (cf. Jer. 49:34–39), which Nebuchadrezzar attacked in 596 B.C. Soon, however, Zedekiah began to display anti-Babylonian sentiments. In 595/594 there was a revolt in Babylon itself, and according to the Babylonian Chronicle, in the course of 594 the Babylonian troops were mustered for a campaign to Palestine. The Babylonian documents unfortunately break off at this point. Data from Jeremiah 27 and 28, however, indicate that in Jerusalem, supported by Tyre, Sidon, and other areas (27:3), there was an anti-Babylonian mood. Such developments may have stimulated Pharaoh Psammetichus II (594–588) even more; perhaps about 592 B.C. this pharaoh made a more or less successful raid on Palestine.

One can only guess at Zedekiah's conduct during this turmoil. In the literature he manifests a weak personality. On the one hand, he wanted to listen to the counsel of Jeremiah; on the other hand, ostrichlike, he tried to ignore the unvarnished and strong language of the prophet (Jeremiah 37–38). The cultic and religious practices in Jerusalem, from the Deuteronomistic perspective still very good under Josiah, now became totally syncretistic (see, e.g., Ezekiel 8). In the eyes of prophets such as Jeremiah and Ezekiel, but likely no less in the opinion of the commoner in Jerusalem, Zedekiah's course was heading toward disaster. "False prophets," such as Hananiah the son of Azzur from Gibeon, tried to make the king and people believe that the power of Babylon and its king would soon be broken. But reality was different (Jeremiah 28); Jeremiah, not Hananiah, was right. Continually urging surrender to Babylon, Jeremiah thereby ran the risk of being regarded as a collaborator. It is not clear whether a journey of Zedekiah in the fourth year of his reign, mentioned in Jeremiah 51:59 (cf. 29:3) but not further known, belongs to this setting. Possibly under the guise of promoting peace, he quietly prepared for war against Babylon.

Such preparations, however, did not escape the attention of Nebuchadrezzar. In the ninth year of Zedekiah's reign, on the tenth day of the tenth month—so 2 Kings 25:1 (see also Jer. 39:1; 52:4; Ezek. 24:1–2)—the king of Babylon marched with his army against Judah and its capital. This action began probably in the spring of 588 B.C.

and was the beginning of a long siege, the misery of which is pictured in 2 Kings 25 and parallel passages. The so-called Lachish Letters (*ANET,* 321–22; *ANEP,* 279; *KAI,* 192–99; ill. 46) shed some light on the situation in rural Judah. These ostraca concern letters that apparently were sent to the commander of Lachish. One of the letters reports that the troops in the field have only the signal fires of Lachish left to go by, because Azekah no longer answers. Azekah had probably already fallen to the Babylonians (cf. Jer. 34:7, which mentions these cities as the last two remaining). Another letter is interesting because it complains about people who assumed a defeatist attitude in the war against Babylon. The charge agrees with 38:4, even in some of the exact words. A further significant item in these letters is the report of a high-ranking Judean officer who was sent to Egypt. The purpose of his journey is not stated, but his mandate can be connected with 37:5, which states that the Egyptians had marched out against the Babylonian troops who were besieging Jerusalem. Is the reference here to Pharaoh Apries (588–568), in Jeremiah 44:30 also called Hophra? And does Ezekiel in his prophecies (29:1–12; 30:20–26) refer to this unappreciated Egyptian help? Despite fierce opposition by king and people, Ezekiel and Jeremiah saw only wisdom in capitulating to Babylon. This conviction is movingly symbolized by Jeremiah's purchase of a field near beleaguered Jerusalem (Jer. 32).

After carrying no less than 832 deserters into exile in the preceding siege (Jer. 52:29), the Babylonian armies managed to breach the wall of Jerusalem (2 Kgs. 25:4; Jer. 39:2–4; 52:6–7; Ezekiel 12), likely in the summer of 586 B.C.—the precise date 587 or 586 is disputed. Soon the city capitulated. Under the supervision of a high officer of Nebuchadrezzar, the temple and palace were plundered (2 Kgs. 25:8–9). The city of Jerusalem was leveled, and many people, particularly the notables, were carried into exile. Only the poorest and those most needed for the economy were left behind. Zedekiah and his retinue tried to escape but were captured at Jericho. Judah's last king was taken to Riblah in the plain north of the Lebanon. After his sons had been slain before his eyes, the Babylonians blinded him. In brass chains Zedekiah was dragged off to Babylon, which he likely never left.

However significant the Babylonian captivity may have seemed to the later history of Israel, we should not overlook the fact that only a small number of people, albeit an influential minority, were carried off to Babylon and that also on Judean soil a part of Israelite history continued. Jeremiah 52:28–30 (cf. 2 Kgs. 24:16; 25:19) lists the following numbers of deportees: in the seventh year of Nebuchadrezzar, 3,023 Judeans; in the eighteenth year (587/586), 832; and in the twenty-third year, 745 more under army commander Nebuzaradan. (Since these figures are quite small, we may take them as reliable.) These various deportations perhaps coincide with rebellions against Babylonian authority. Babylon's deportation policy was much less disruptive than that of the Assyrians. The exiles apparently stayed together. Nowhere is it mentioned that strangers immigrated into Judah or that it became a Babylonian province. In 2 Kings 25:22–24 and Jeremiah 40:5–6, it is reported that the Babylonians appointed Gedaliah, the son of Ahikam, as governor of the remaining Judeans. He resided in the Benjamite Mizpah, to which he invited the other Judeans in order to stimulate them to put forth all their efforts to cultivate the land and also to urge them to submit to the Babylonians.

At the instigation of the Ammonite king Baalis, however, a certain Ishmael—a man of royal blood—plotted Gedaliah's assassination. He and many Judeans and Babylonians with him were murdered (Jer. 41:3). On the day after Gedaliah's assassination, yet another eighty people, coming from the former northern kingdom and on the way to "the house of YHWH," were attacked, and seventy of them were killed by Ishmael (vv. 4–8). The ten escaped only because they were able to point out a hidden food supply. This revolt of Ishmael, however, accomplished little. In an attempt to reach the Ammonite border, he was stopped by a group of men led by Johanan, the son of Kareah. Though Ishmael was able to escape with some of his followers, most of them walked away from him. Johanan, likely with good reason, feared reprisals from the Babylonians and, though opposed by Jeremiah (ch. 42), decided to flee to Egypt. Jeremiah and his scribe, Baruch, were carried off

to Tahpanhes, a boundary fortress in the eastern Nile Delta (43:7). Nothing is known of the fate of these refugees.

This part of the history of Israel ends in a chaotic period in which all hope for any restoration had disappeared. Besides the deportees, many others left the Promised Land for other reasons. Politically, religiously, and economically, Judah and Israel were devastated areas. No longer was there a strong king, a selfless leader, or an inspiring prophet. It seemed as if the only hope for a better future lay with life in Babylon, where at first the exiles disconsolately hung their harps on the willows. There was perhaps also some hope left in Palestine, if we can associate such chapters as Ezekiel 34–37 or Jeremiah 31–32 with the immovable faith of the nameless people who kept hoping for the restoration of Jerusalem and who prophetically saw "a new covenant" beckoning as the climax of a new freedom.

LITERATURE

P. R. Ackroyd, *Exile and Restoration: A Study of Hebrew Thought of the Sixth Century B.C.* (Philadelphia, 1972²).

Y. Aharoni, *Arad Inscriptions* (Jerusalem, 1975 [Hebrew]).

N. Avigad, "Excavations in the Jewish Quarter of the Old City of Jerusalem 1971," *IEJ* 22 (1972) 193-200.

M. Broshi, "The Expansion of Jerusalem in the Reigns of Hezekiah and Manasseh," *IEJ* 24 (1974) 21-26.

H. Cazelles, "Sophonie, Jérémie, et les Scythes en Palestine," *RB* 74 (1967) 24-44.

B. S. Childs, *Isaiah and the Assyrian Crisis* (London, 1967).

W. E. Claburn, "The Fiscal Basis of Josiah's Reform," *JBL* 92 (1973) 11-22.

M. Cogan, *Imperialism and Religion: Assyria, Judah and Israel in the Eighth and Seventh Centuries B.C.E.* (Missoula, MT, 1974).

F. M. Cross, "A Reconstruction of the Judean Restoration," *JBL* 94 (1975) 4-18.

K. S. Freedy and D. B. Redford, "The Dates in Ezekiel in Relation to Biblical, Babylonian and Egyptian Sources," *JAOS* 90 (1970) 462-85.

S. B. Frost, "The Death of Josiah: A Conspiracy of Silence," *JBL* 87 (1968) 369-82.

S. H. Horn, "Did Sennacherib Campaign Once or

Twice Against Hezekiah?" *Andrews University Seminary Studies* 4 (1966) 1-28.

M. Kochavi, *Judea, Samaria and the Golan* (Jerusalem, 1972).

H. D. Lance, "The Royal Stamps and the Kingdom of Josiah," *HTR* 64 (1971) 315-32.

G. Larsson, "When did the Babylonian Captivity Begin?" *JTS* 18 (1967) 417-23.

A. Lemaire, *Inscriptions Hébraïques, I: Les Ostraca* (Paris, 1977).

————, "'MMŠT-Amwas, vers la solution d'une enigme de l'épigraphie Hébraïque," *RB* 92 (1975) 15-23.

C. Levin, *Der Sturz der Königin Atalja: Ein Kapitel zur Geschichte Judas im 9. Jahrhundert v. Chr.* (Stuttgart, 1982).

D. D. Luckenbill, *The Annals of Sennacherib* (Chicago, 1924).

A. Malamat, "The Last Kings of Judah and the Fall of Jerusalem," *IEJ* 18 (1968) 137-56.

————, "Josiah's Bid for Armageddon," *Journal of the Ancient Near Eastern Society of Columbia University* 5 (1973) 267-78.

————, "The Twilight of Judah: in the Egyptian-Babylonian Maelstrom," *SVT* 28 (1975) 123-45.

J. McKay, *Religion in Judah under the Assyrians 732-609 BC* (London, 1973).

J. M. Miller, "The Korahites in Southern Judah," *CBQ* 32 (1970) 58-68.

J. M. Myers, "Edom and Judah in the Sixth-Fifth Centuries BC," in H. Goedicke, ed., *Near Eastern Studies in Honor of W. F. Albright* (Baltimore, 1971), pp. 377-92.

N. Na'aman, "Sennacherib's 'Letter to God' on his Campaign to Judah," *BASOR* 214 (1974) 25-39.

J. M. Newsome, "Towards a New Understanding of the Chronicler and His Purpose," *JBL* 94 (1975) 201-17.

E. W. Nicholson, "The Meaning of the Expression 'm h'rs in the Old Testament," *JSS* 10 (1965) 59-66.

E. Nielsen, "Political Conditions and Cultural Developments in Israel and Judah During the Reign of Manasseh," *Fourth World Congress of Jewish Studies* (Jerusalem, 1967), I: 103-06.

B. Oded, "Observations on Methods of Assyrian Rule in Transjordania after the Palestinian Campaign of Tiglath-Pileser III," *JNES* 29 (1970) 177-86.

————, *Mass Deportations and Deportees in the Neo-Assyrian Empire* (Wiesbaden, 1979).

H. W. F. Saggs, *The Greatness that was Babylon* (London/New York, 1962).

E. J. Smit, *Die ondergang van die ryk van Juda* (Groningen, 1965).

J. A. Soggin, "Der judäische 'Am-Ha'areṣ und das Königtum in Juda," *VT* 13 (1963) 187-95.

H. Spieckermann, *Juda unter Assur in der Sargonidenzeit* (Göttingen, 1982).

E. Stern, "Israel at the Close of the Period of the Monarchy: An Archaeological Survey," *BA* 38 (1975) 26-54.

H. Tadmor, "Philistia under Assyrian Rule," *BA* 29 (1966) 86-102.

S. Talmon, "The Judean 'am ha'areṣ in Historical Perspective," *Fourth World Congress of Jewish Studies* (Jerusalem, 1967), I: 71-76.

E. Thiele, *The Mysterious Numbers of the Hebrew Kings* (Grand Rapids, 1965²).

M. Weinfeld, "The Worship of Molech and the Queen of Heaven and its Background," *UF* 4 (1972) 133-54.

D. J. Wiseman, *Chronicles of Chaldaean Kings (626-556 B.C.) in the British Museum* (London, 1961).

Y. Yadin, "Beer-sheba: The High Place Destroyed by King Josiah," *BASOR* 222 (1976) 5-18.

APPENDIX 1

Chronology of Hebrew Kings

Given the uncertainties mentioned above in section 3.c concerning the dates of the kings of Judah and Israel, I attempt here no original chronology. This appendix simply lists a number of recent chronologies side by side. For older systems of dating, see E. R. Thiele, *The Mysterious Numbers of the Hebrew Kings* (Grand Rapids, 1965²), pp. 254-55; and H. Tadmor, "Chronologia" (see literature for section 3.c), which contains fourteen chronologies devised between 1884 and 1961, in parallel columns. For this appendix, I have used the numbers of Tadmor ("Chronologia," 301-

302), Jepsen (*BHH*, III: 2213; 1968), Bright (1981), Gunneweg (1984), and Herrmann (1981). Dates begin with the divided kingdoms of Judah and Israel. The preceding regnal periods of David and Solomon are generally regarded as totaling eighty years and must have extended from about 1005 to 927/926 B.C. Not much can be said with certainty about the dates of Saul's reign or the period before him. After the various chronologies, I list the synchronistic dates of both kingdoms, based on data in the books of Kings and Chronicles.

REIGNS OF JUDAH'S KINGS

	Tadmor	Jepsen	Bright	Gunneweg	Herrmann
Rehoboam	928–911	926–910	922–915	926–909	932/31–916/15
Abijam	911–908	910–908	915–913	909–908/07	916/15–914/13
Asa	908–867	908–868	913–873	908/07–868/67	914/13–874/73
Jehoshaphat	867–846	868–847	873–849	868/67–851/50	874/73–850/49
Jehoram	846–843	(852)847–845	849–843	850–845	850/49–843/42
Ahaziah	843–842	845	843/42		843/42–842/41
Athaliah	842–836	845–840	842–837	845/44–840/39	842/41–837/36
Joash	836–798	840–801	837–800	840/39–801/00	836/35–797/96
Amaziah	798–769	801–773	800–783	801/00–787/86	797/96–769/68
Uzziah (Azariah)	769–733	787–736	783–742	787/86–736	769/68–741/40
Jotham	758–743	756–741	742–735	756–741	741/40–734/33
Ahaz	743–727	741–725	735–715	742/41–726/25	734/33–715/14
Hezekiah	727–698	725–697	715–687/86	725/24–697/96	715/14–697/96
Manasseh	698–642	696–642	687/86–642	696/95–642/41	697/96–642/41
Amon	641–640	641–640	642–640	641/40–640/39	642/41–640/39
Josiah	639–609	639–609	640–609	639/38–609	640/39–609/08
Jehoahaz	609	609	609	608	609/08
Jehoiakim	608–598	608–598	609–598	608/07–598/97	609/08–598/97
Jehoiachin	597	598	598/97		598/97
Zedekiah	595–586	597–587	597–587	597/96–586	598/97–587/86

REIGNS OF ISRAEL'S KINGS

	Tadmor	Jepsen	Bright	Gunneweg	Herrmann
Jeroboam I	928–907	927–907	922–901	929–906	932/31–911/10
Nadab	907–906	907–906	901–900	906–905	911/10–910/09
Baasha	906–883	906–883	900–877	905–882	910/09–887/86
Elah	883–882	883–882	877–876	882–881	887/86–886/85
Zimri	882		876	881	886/85
Omri	882–871	(882)878–871	876–869	881–870	886/85–875/74
Ahab	871–852	871–852	869–850	870–851	875/74–854/53
Ahaziah	852/51–851/50	852–851	850–849	851–850	854/53–853/52
Jehoram	851/50–842	851–845	849–843/42	850–845	853/52–842/41
Jehu	842/814	845–818	843/42–815	845–817	842/41–815/14
Jehoahaz	814–800	818–802	815–802	817–801	815/14–799/98
Joash	800–784	802–787	802–786	801–786	799/98–784/83
Jeroboam II	784–748	787–747	786–746	786–746	784/83–753/52
Zechariah	748–747		746–745	746	753/52–752/51
Shallum	748–747		745	746	752/51–751/50
Menahem	747/46–737/36	747–738	745–737	746–736?	751/50–742/41
Pekahiah	737–735	737–736	737–736	736–734	742/41–741/40
Pekah	735/34–733/32	735–732	736–732	734–732	741/40–730/29
Hoshea	733/32–724/23	731–723	732–724	732–723	730/29–722/21

SYNCHRONISTIC DATES
ACCORDING TO THE BOOKS OF KINGS AND CHRONICLES

Judah

	Synchronistic dates	length of reign	age at accession	compare
Rehoboam		17 yrs.	41 yrs.	1 Kgs. 14:21/2 Chr. 12:13
Abijam	18th yr. of Jeroboam	3 yrs.		1 Kgs. 15:1, 2/2 Chr. 13:1, 2
Asa	20th yr. of Jeroboam	41 yrs.		1 Kgs. 15:9, 10
Jehoshaphat	4th yr. of Ahab	25 yrs.	35 yrs.	1 Kgs. 22:41/2 Chr. 20:31
Jehoram	5th yr. of Jehoram	8 yrs.	32 yrs.	2 Kgs. 18:16/2 Chr. 21:5, 20
Ahaziah	11th yr. of Jehoram	1 yr.	42 yrs.	2 Kgs. 9:29/2 Chr. 22:2
	12th yr. of Jehoram		22 yrs.	2 Kgs. 8:25
Athaliah		6 yrs.?		2 Kgs. 11
Jehoash	7th yr. of Jehu	40 yrs.	7 yrs.	2 Kgs. 11:21; 12:1/2 Chr. 24:1
Amaziah	2nd yr. of Jehoash	29 yrs.	25 yrs.	2 Kgs. 14:1/2 Chr. 25:1
Azariah (Uzziah)	27th yr. of Jeroboam	52 yrs.	16 yrs.	2 Kgs. 15:1, 2/2 Chr. 26:1, 3
Jotham	2nd yr. of Pekah	16 yrs.	25 yrs.	2 Kgs. 15:32/2 Chr. 27:1, 8
Ahaz	17th yr. of Pekah	16 yrs.	20 yrs.	2 Kgs. 16:1, 2/2 Chr. 28:1
Hezekiah	3rd yr. of Hoshea	29 yrs.	25 yrs.	2 Kgs. 18:1, 2/2 Chr. 29:1
Manasseh		55 yrs.	12 yrs.	2 Kgs. 21:1/2 Chr. 33:1
Amon		2 yrs.	22 yrs.	2 Kgs. 21:19/2 Chr. 33:21
Josiah		31 yrs.	8 yrs.	2 Kgs. 22:1/2 Chr. 34:1
Jehoahaz		3 months	23 yrs.	2 Kgs. 23:31/2 Chr. 36:1
Jehoiakim (Eliakim)		11 yrs.	25 yrs.	2 Kgs. 23:36/2 Chr. 36:5
Jehoiachin		3 months (+10 days?)	18 yrs.	2 Kgs. 24:8/2 Chr. 36:9
Zedekiah		11 yrs.	21 yrs.	2 Kgs. 24:18/2 Chr. 36:11

Israel

	synchronistic dates	length of reign	compare
Jeroboam		22 yrs.	1 Kgs. 14:20
Nadab	2nd yr. of Asa	2 yrs.	1 Kgs. 15:25
Baasha	3rd yr. of Asa	24 yrs.	1 Kgs. 15:33 (cf. 2 Chr. 16)
Elah	26th yr. of Asa	2 yrs.	1 Kgs. 16:8
Zimri	27th yr. of Asa	7 days	1 Kgs. 16:10, 15
Omri	31st yr. of Asa	12 yrs.	1 Kgs. 16:23
Ahab	38th yr. of Asa	22 yrs.	1 Kgs. 16:29
Ahaziah	17th yr. of Jehoshaphat	2 yrs.	1 Kgs. 22:52
Jehoram	18th yr. of Jehoshaphat	12 yrs.	2 Kgs. 3:1 (cf. 2 Kgs. 1:17: 2nd yr. of Jehoram)
Jehu		28 yrs.	2 Kgs. 10:36
Jehoahaz	23rd yr. of Joash	17 yrs.	2 Kgs. 13:1
Joash	37th yr. of Joash	16 yrs.	2 Kgs. 13:10
Jeroboam II	15th yr. of Amaziah	41 yrs.	2 Kgs. 14:23
Zechariah	38th yr. of Azariah	6 months	2 Kgs. 15:8
Shallum	39th yr. of Azariah	1 month	2 Kgs. 15:13
Menahem	39th yr. of Azariah	10 yrs.	2 Kgs. 15:17
Pekahiah	50th yr. of Azariah	2 yrs.	2 Kgs. 15:23
Pekah	52nd yr. of Azariah	20 yrs.	2 Kgs. 15:27
Hoshea	12th yr. of Ahaz	9 yrs.	2 Kgs. 17:1
	20th yr. of Jotham		2 Kgs. 15:30

APPENDIX 2

Chronology of Egyptian, Assyrian, and Babylonian Kings

This appendix lists the regnal periods of the rulers of Egypt and of the Assyrians and Babylonians as these individuals were roughly contemporary with Judah and Israel. For more elaborate details, see *The World of the Bible,* chapter 5, section A, "History of the Ancient Near East to the Time of Alexander the Great."

SOME REGNAL PERIODS AND OTHER DATES FROM THE HISTORY OF EGYPT AND ASSYRIA-BABYLONIA RELEVANT TO ISRAEL AND JUDAH

Egypt

(according to data from J. von Beckerath, *Abriss der Geschichte des alten Ägypten* [München, 1971])

ca. 1554/51–1305	**18th Dynasty**
1403–1365	Amenophis (Amenhotep) III
1365–1349/47	Amenophis (Amenhotep) IV (Ikhnaton/Akhenaten)
ca. 1305–1196	**19th Dynasty**
1303–1290	Sethos (Seti) I
1290–1224	Ramses II
1224–1214	Merneptah
ca. 1196–1080	**20th Dynasty**
ca. 1080–946	**21st Dynasty**
979–960	Siamun (Neterkheperre). Possibly a daughter of this pharaoh married King Solomon
ca. 946–720	**22nd Dynasty**
946–925	Shoshenq (Shishak) I. About 927 undertook a campaign into Palestine
ca. 792–720	**23rd Dynasty**
ca. 740–712	**24th Dynasty (in Sais)**
ca. 745–655	**25th Dynasty (Cushite dynasty)**
713–698	Shabako
698–690	Shebitku
690–664	Taharqa. Raids of the Assyrians on Egypt
ca. 664–525	**26th Dynasty**
664–610	Psammetichus I
610–595	Neco (Necho). In 609 and 608 he marches to the Euphrates, in which campaign he defeats King Josiah at Megiddo. In 605 at Carchemish he is defeated by Nebuchadrezzar II
595–598	Psammetichus II
589–570/68	Apries. In vain he tries to relieve Jerusalem beleaguered by Nebuchadrezzar II

Assyria-Babylonia

(according to data from the *Chronological Chart* in D. J. Wiseman, ed., *Peoples of Old Testament Times*, [Oxford, 1973], pp. 358–59)

1605–1150	**Kassite Period**
1157–1025	**Second Dynasty of Isin**
1116–1110	Tiglath-pileser I
911–612	**Neo-Assyrian Period**
911–891	Adad-nirari II
890–884	Tukulti-Ninurta II
883–859	Ashurnasirpal II
859–824	Shalmaneser III
823–810	Shamshi-Adad V
810–782	Adad-nirari III
781–772	Shalmaneser IV
771–754	Ashurdan III
753–746	Ashur-nirari V
745–727	Tiglath-pileser III
727–722	Shalmaneser V. Samaria falls in 722 (end of Israel)
722–705	Sargon II
722–711	Mardukapaliddina (Merodak-Baladan, king of Babylon, with whom Hezekiah made an alliance)
705–681	Sennacherib
681–669	Esarhaddon
669–625	Ashurbanipal
625–621	Ashuretililani
621–612	Sinsharishkun. In 612 Nineveh falls into the hands of the Babylonians
625–539	**Neo-Babylonian Period**
625–605	Nabopolassar
605–562	Nebuchadnezzar II. He captures Jerusalem and deports Judeans
562–560	Amel-Marduk (Awil-Marduk)
560–556	Neriglissar
556–539	Nabonidus (In 539 Babel falls into the hands of Cyrus, marking the beginning of Persian rule over Mesopotamia)

B. Israel from the Babylonian Captivity to the Rise of Alexander the Great

by A. S. van der Woude

1. JUDAH UNDER BABYLONIAN DOMINATION

We have only limited data concerning the history and religion of the Jews who, after the fall of Jerusalem, remained in Palestine under Babylonian domination. Except for the murder of Gedaliah and the mercy shown to Jehoiachin by the Babylonian king Evil-merodach, 2 Kings says nothing about this period. The writer of Chronicles so completely identifies the community of Yahweh with the exiles deported to Babylon that he pays no attention to the situation in Judah. He is convinced that the land was desolate for seventy years (see Jer. 25:11; 29:10) in order to make up for all the neglected sabbatical years (2 Chr. 36:20–21; cf. Lev. 25:1–7; 26:34–35, 43). We thus have to use indirect data in order to obtain an idea of this period. Such information appears in Lamentations, Jeremiah (esp. chs. 37–44 and 52), the so-called Deutero-Isaiah (Isaiah 40–55) and Trito-Isaiah (chs. 56–66), and a number of psalms (including 74 and 79).

The fall of Jerusalem must have made an indelible impression on the exiles and those left behind. The belief in the inviolability of Mount Zion, which used to be proclaimed with great zeal (see, e.g., Mic. 4:11–13; Jer. 7:4), had been completely dashed by the destruction of city and temple. The expectations of a new future linked to the house of David, based on the prophecy of Nathan (2 Samuel 7), had not come true as had been hoped. Instead the country had been devastated, and the society shattered. The book of Lamentations and collective laments such as Psalms 74 and 79 picture the gloom and dismay of the people left behind in the land. The reactions to the ignominious end of national independence and the sufferings that had to be endured ranged from penitence and consciousness of guilt to bitterness and arrogance. The final editor of the Deuteronomistic history depicts Israel's history as the story of a people elected by Yahweh; they spurned his grace and as a result lost the land he had given them. The book of Lamentations and the psalms of lament from that time refer to transgressions of the will of Yahweh that had resulted in the catastrophe. Others felt that blind fate had struck: "The fathers have eaten sour grapes, and the children's teeth are set on edge" (Jer. 31:29; see also Ezek. 18:2). In the hearing of Jeremiah, the Jews that had fled to Egypt complain that the abolition of the worship of the "queen of heaven" (Astarte or, better, Ishtar) was the cause of the great calamity and that therefore they refused to listen to a prophet of Yahweh (Jer. 44:15–19). Finally, those left behind in Palestine, appealing to the promise of land made to Abraham, regarded the fact that they had not been carried off into captivity as proof that from now on the land was solely theirs (Ezek. 33:24).

It causes no surprise that, in a time of spiritual and material disarray, many looked for help and comfort not to Yahweh but to the idols. Trito-Isaiah indicates that heathen cults again gained ground during the time of the Babylonian domination. Isaiah 57 relates how numerous people abandoned themselves to the Canaanite fertility rites. And in Isaiah 65:3–5, 11, we read about sacrifices on the heights, consultation of the dead, eating of unclean foods, and worship of Gad and Meni, the gods of fortune. Gad is a Syrian god whose name occurs in such place-names as Baal-Gad (Josh. 11:17) and Migdal-Gad (15:37) and also in Phoenician, Nabatean, and Palmyrene personal names (cf. also the old Israelite names Gad, Gaddiel, Azgad, etc.). Meni is connected with Manat, one of the three goddesses of the pre-Islam Arabs. Possibly behind both names there are Canaanite gods. The extent to which pagan religion and syncretistic forms of Yahweh worship must have been commonplace in those days is also shown by Ezekiel 33:25 and the seventh night vision of Zechariah, in which it is announced that wickedness will be removed from the land and transported to Babylon (Zech. 5:5–11).

From the above we see that the suggestion of the Chronicler that the land was desolate for seventy years was theologically motivated; according to him the future expectations of the people of Yahweh lay exclusively with the exiles in Babylon. The view that the spiritual focal point of Israel at the time of the Babylonian captivity did not lie in Palestine returns implicitly in the book of Ezra, and many commentators, on the basis of the messages of Deutero-Isaiah and Ezekiel, have adopted this point of view. Taking exception, Noth has emphatically defended the idea that the spiritual center of Israel's community remained in Palestine, even after the fall of Jerusalem.

Despite the impression created by 2 Kings 25 and especially by the writer of Chronicles that the land was almost totally depopulated, the figures mentioned in Jeremiah 52:28–30 indicate that, after the deportation of 3,023 Judeans in 597 B.C., at the fall of Jerusalem in 586 only 832 were deported and in 582 once again only 745 more. Though the exiles included mostly the leading civil officials, military people, and artisans, their number is still too small to allow us to speak of any resulting drastic effect on the population of Judah. This conclusion agrees with the fact that the Babylonians apparently did not resettle strangers in Judah, unlike the repopulation of the Samaritan territory commanded by the Assyrian kings Sargon II (2 Kgs. 17:24) and Esarhaddon (Ezra 4:2). Though a number of Jews, of their own accord, fled to Egypt after the murder of Gedaliah,

taking Jeremiah with them (2 Kgs. 25:26; Jer. 41:16–43:7), many other Jews returned to their villages and cities after having hid themselves after the events in 586 (Jer. 40:7–9) or after having fled to neighboring countries (vv. 11–12). Though the Babylonian troops had ravaged Jerusalem and many Judean cities, these centers did not remain uninhabited afterward (see v. 10). Despite the social revolution created by the donation of the royal domains and expropriated lands of the exiles to the "poorest of the land" (2 Kgs. 25:12), the large majority of the Judeans did not leave their country.

Just as we cannot speak of a massive depopulation of Judah after the catastrophe of 586 B.C., so we cannot deny that the spiritual history of Jerusalem and Judah continued after the fall of Jerusalem. Judah remained a spiritually significant center for Israel even during the Babylonian domination, which we can infer from the Deuteronomistic history (likely extending from Genesis to 2 Kings). This record must have been composed during the Babylonian rule, because the concluding verses of the document mention the favorable treatment accorded Jehoiachin. The final Deuteronomistic editor apparently lived not in Babylon but in Judah. Also, the Deuteronomistic editing of parts of the book of Jeremiah is better placed in Judah than in the land of captivity. Furthermore, prophetic writings perhaps either were written in this period in Judah (e.g., Obadiah) or received their final form there (e.g., Zephaniah, Habakkuk). In any case, many people at this time listened again to the words of the prophets who had announced to the people the divine judgment upon their sins and thus recognized these prophets as proclaimers of the will and the work of Yahweh.

At least in part, public worship seems to have continued. Collective laments such as Psalms 74 and 79 were likely recited in the court of the temple. The same may be true of the so-called Lamentations of Jeremiah. Remarkable in this connection is the information in Jeremiah 41:4–5 that, at the time of Gedaliah, eighty men from northern Israel went to Jerusalem to offer food offerings and incense in the house of Yahweh.

These bits and pieces of information demonstrate that Judah at the time of the Babylonian domination was not the spiritual and religious wasteland many have thought it was. Not only did Ezekiel and Deutero-Isaiah in the land of captivity inspire new hope in the hearts of the dispersed community of Israel, but also in Judah itself voices were heard that called for a new reflection on the history of Yahweh with his people, voices that promised a glorious future if the people would repent. If Beuken's suggestion is correct (as it seems) that the prophet Haggai himself had not gone into captivity, there was also a significant voice from within the population left in Judah that contributed to the restoration of the community.

For the time of the Babylonian domination, we possess no direct information about the administrative structure of Judah, except that, shortly after the fall of Jerusalem, the king of Babylon appointed Gedaliah over "the people who remained in the land of Judah, whom Nebuchadnezzar king of Babylon had left" (2 Kgs. 25:22; cf. Jer. 40:7). The tradition does not state or imply that Gedaliah was subject to the governor of Samaria. To the contrary, his appointment by Nebuchadrezzar creates the impression that Judah was turned into a Babylonian province. Alt has suggested that, after the murder of Gedaliah, the area was administratively added to Samaria, a view that I find questionable. The appointment of Sheshbazzar and Zerubbabel as governors of Judah suggests that Judah was an independent province in the early Persian period and thus also under the Babylonians. See further under section 2.a.

The province of Judah was considerably smaller than the earlier independent kingdom of Judah. The southern boundary ran from east to west from a point just north of Engedi past the area south of Beth-zur to the vicinity of Keilah, then turned north toward Emmaus east of the Valley of Aijalon. The northern boundary ran north of Mizpah. The most western territory of the original kingdom was added to Ashdod, while the southern parts of Judah had since 597 been conquered by the Edomites (unless Nebuchadrezzar gave this area to the Edomites to show his thankfulness for their support in his war against Judah and Jerusalem).

LITERATURE

P. R. Ackroyd, *Exile and Restoration* (Philadelphia, 1972[2]).

————, *Israel under Babylon and Persia* (London, 1970).

————, "The Temple Vessels—A Continuity Theme," *SVT* 23 (1972) 166-81.

A. Alt, "Die Rolle Samarias bei der Entstehung des Judentums," in *Festschrift O. Procksch zum 60. Geburtstag* (Leipzig, 1934) 5-28 (= *KS* II [München, 1953] 316-37).

N. Avigad, "Seals of Exile," *IEJ* 15 (1965) 222-30.

W. A. M. Beuken, *Haggai-Sacharja 1–8* (Assen, 1967).

C. H. J. de Geus, "Idumaea," *JEOL* 26 (1979-1980) 53-74.

J. H. Hayes and J. Maxwell Miller, eds., *Israelite and Judaean History* (Philadelphia, 1977), pp. 476-538.

E. Janssen, *Juda in der Exilszeit* (FRLANT 69; Göttingen, 1956).

Y. Kaufmann, *The Babylonian Captivity and Deutero-Isaiah* (New York, 1970).

A. Kuschke, ed., *Verbannung und Heimkehr. Beiträge zur Geschichte und Theologie Israels im 6. und 5. Jahrhundert v. Chr.* (Festschrift W. Rudolph; Tübingen, 1961).

M. Noth, *The History of Israel* (New York, 1960[2]).

M. Smith, *Palestinian Parties and Politics that Shaped the Old Testament* (New York, 1971).

E. F. Weidner, "Jojachin, König von Juda, in babylonischen Keilschrifttexten," in *Mélanges . . . René Dussaud* II (Paris, 1939) 923-35.

C. F. Whitley, *The Exilic Age* (London, 1957).

D. Winton Thomas, "The Sixth Century B.C.: A Creative Epoch in the History of Israel," *JSS* 6 (1961) 33-46.

See further section I.A above by Dr. M. J. Mulder, which gives an overview of the history of Israel, and the commentaries on Deutero-Isaiah and Ezekiel listed in section III.C.2 below.

2. JUDAH UNDER PERSIAN DOMINATION

a. Return from Captivity and Rebuilding of the Temple

After the nobility of Media and Persia proclaimed Cyrus king and after he had built a vast empire through the conquest of territory in eastern Iran and Asia Minor (see *The World of the Bible*, pp. 316–17), the end of the Neo-Babylonian empire, which had increasingly disintegrated after the death of Nebuchadrezzar, seemed imminent. It is therefore not surprising that the exiles, who regarded Babylon as a foreign and unclean land (Ps. 137:4; cf. Ezek. 4:13), recognized in Cyrus the coming liberator. Deutero-Isaiah became the spokesperson of these people by proclaiming Cyrus as a tool in the hands of Yahweh, even as his anointed, or messiah (Isa. 45:1–7). Through his prediction of the fall of Babylon (ch. 47) and the people's imminent deliverance and glorious return to Jerusalem and Judah, which would be rebuilt and restored, this prophet gave new hope to the exiles who doubted the power of Yahweh and his involvement in their plight and also aroused high expectations that they would soon return to the land of their fathers and have a great future ahead of them. Ezekiel, through his prophecies concerning Israel's purification and restoration (see Ezek. 20:33–44; chs. 34 and 36–37) and especially through his vision of a new temple and a new land (chs. 40–48), had also encouraged the people in exile, exhorting them to trust in Yahweh and to look forward to a future that Yahweh would bring.

On the one hand, the Persian takeover of power in Syria and Palestine (possibly even before the fall of Babylon in 539 B.C.) did not deeply affect the people who had remained in Judah; it was simply an exchange of one overlord for another. On the other hand, the change in power opened up new perspectives not only for them but also for the exiles in Babylon. These new possibilities arose from the policy of the Persian government toward conquered peoples in its vast realm, a policy based more on self-interest than on kindness. Cyrus and his successors not only respected the religious beliefs and customs of their subjects but also were prepared to support the local cult, if necessary with funds from the royal treasury, and wherever needed or desired were willing to restore a particular cult. They broke with the Assyrian and Babylonian policy of mass deportations, instead allowing exiles to return to their homelands. The so-called Cyrus Cylinder (*ANET*, 315–16) provides an impressive testimony to this policy, by which the Persian rulers tried to win the

favor of their subjects. Referring to the kindness shown toward Babylon, the cylinder reads, "From . . . to Ashur and Susa, Agade, Ashnunnak, Zamban, Meturnu, Deri, with the territory of the land of Gutium, the cities on the other side of the Tigris, the sanctuaries of which have been ruins for a long time, the gods that dwelt in them, I brought back to their places . . . all their inhabitants I collected and restored them to their dwelling places."

Cyrus's son and successor Cambyses (530–522 B.C.), who incurred the anger of many on account of his atrocities during his campaign against Egypt, as a rule respected the religious beliefs and customs of those whom he subdued (he did, however, raze some Egyptian temples). At the instigation of Udjahorresne, his Egyptian chamberlain and head of his palace, and after having proclaimed himself king in Sais in accordance with Egyptian ritual, Cambyses cleansed the temple of the goddess Neith, made temple property available, and reintroduced the old feasts. Cambyses' successor, Darius I (522–486), continued the policy of his predecessors. A significant piece of evidence is his decree addressed to the Persian official Gadatas in western Asia Minor, which has been preserved in Greek on an inscription from the Roman period. In this inscription Darius speaks of his favorable attitude toward the gods, one characterizing his predecessors, and he threatens Gadatas with his anger if he does not immediately stop violating the ancient privileges of the "holy gardeners of Apollo." Among the documents discovered at Elephantine is the so-called Passover Papyrus (Cowley, no. 30) from the fifth year of the reign of Darius II (423–404), which mentions a letter from the Persian court concerning the Passover celebration in the Jewish colony at Elephantine in southern Egypt. This papyrus is unfortunately very fragmented and contains no indication why the Persian ruler considered it necessary to interfere in the affairs of the Jewish community at Elephantine, though we may assume that also in this case complaints about prevalent evils had reached the court.

In view of such data there is no good reason to doubt the historicity of the decree of Cyrus in which he ordered the rebuilding of the temple in Jerusalem and the return of the temple utensils that had been confiscated and carried to Babylon by Nebuchadrezzar. We possess a memorandum of the royal decree in Aramaic, the official language of the Persian court, in a letter from Darius I to the satrap of the territory "Beyond the River," or Syria and Palestine (Ezra 6:3–5). According to the scroll stored in the royal archives, Cyrus commanded not only that the temple be rebuilt as a "place where sacrifices are offered" and that specific measurements be followed in the construction of the sanctuary but also that the costs were to be borne by the royal treasury. In addition to the memorandum, the composer of the books of Ezra and Nehemiah preserved Cyrus's proclamation in Hebrew (Ezra 1:2–4), the historical reliability of which is often disputed. According to the information in these verses, Cyrus not only mandated the rebuilding of the temple but also allowed the captives in Babylon to return to Jerusalem and Judah and urged those who remained behind in Babylon to give financial support. Though the author of Ezra and Nehemiah clearly reproduced Cyrus's decree in his own words, there are no compelling reasons to doubt the accuracy of his report.

We know further from the Cyrus Cylinder that the king permitted other captives to return to their homelands. In the case of the Jews, we do not know who made Cyrus aware of the situation in Jerusalem and Judah and of the temple utensils confiscated by Nebuchadrezzar. The measures taken by the new ruler mentioned in Ezra, however, agree very well with Cyrus's policy, for he wanted to have a well-organized bureaucracy in order to keep a firm grip on the reins of government, yet at the same time allowing his subjects a great measure of freedom. It was consistent with this policy to grant self-government, under a representative of the people themselves, to a province that formed part of a larger satrapy. Cyrus thus appointed as governor, or *peha*, over Judah a certain Sheshbazzar, who, despite his Babylonian name, was certainly of Jewish blood (though it is unlikely that he should be identified with Shenazzar, mentioned in 1 Chronicles 3:18, a son of Jehoiachin). Following Alt, many scholars doubt that Sheshbazzar occupied the office of governor, asserting that he was something like a royal commissary. This view is based on the fact that not until the fifth century under Nehemiah did Judah

receive the status of a semi-independent province. The district earlier was presumably part of the province of Samaria.

More than likely, however, Judah was a province right from the beginning of the Persian period, a conclusion supported by the fact that, already in Ezra 2:1 and 5:8, Judah is called a *medinah*, a governmental unit with its own jurisdiction. Ezra 2:63, in connection with Sheshbazzar (or Zerubbabel?), uses the term *tirshata*, "excellency," a Persian honorary title later used to designate the governor Nehemiah (Neh. 8:9). Furthermore, Nehemiah speaks of governors who were before him (5:15), meaning Judean rather than Samaritan governors. Finally, clay seals and jar stamps from the final decades of the sixth and fifth centuries, published in 1976 by Avigad, appear to confirm Judah's status as an independent province from the beginning of the Persian era. These records mention the official name for Judah as a separate province with its own administration (*yehud;* cf. *yehud medinta* [Ezra 5:8]) and also list the names of three persons who are designated *phw,* "governor": Elnathan, Yehezer, and Achzai. Apparently they were governors of Judah in the time between Zerubbabel and Nehemiah. Their Hebrew names argue for the fact that, also in that period, governors of Jewish blood were appointed by the Persian government to rule over Judah. The size of the territory for which they were responsible must have been the same as in the Babylonian period.

After he had been given the temple utensils, Sheshbazzar undertook the rebuilding of the temple (Ezra 5:16). Under his leadership not only was the altar of burnt offerings restored, but also the foundations of the temple were laid. The writer of Ezra and Nehemiah mentions these activities in detail in Ezra 3, attributing them, however, to Jeshua, the son of Jozadak (the high priest known as Joshua in the books of Haggai and Zechariah), and Zerubbabel, who succeeded Sheshbazzar as governor. Because it is unlikely that both Joshua and Zerubbabel returned to Judah already at the beginning of Persian rule and because identifying Sheshbazzar with Zerubbabel (as sometimes proposed) is unacceptable, the obvious conclusion is that the writer of Ezra 3 has historically telescoped into one the rule of

Sheshbazzar and Zerubbabel. In any case, an official letter that Tattenai, the satrap of the district Beyond the River, sent to Darius I about twenty years later mentions only the laying of the foundations of the temple by Sheshbazzar (5:16).

The work of restoring the temple soon had to be stopped, however. The author of Ezra attributes the cessation of the work (which lasted to 520 B.C.) to "the adversaries of Judah and Benjamin," who are further described as people deported to the district of Samaria by the Assyrian king Esarhaddon, who ruled from 681 to 669 B.C. (4:1–3; see also Isa. 7:8b). After these people were refused permission to participate in the rebuilding of the temple, they resorted to intrigue to frustrate further work on the sanctuary (Ezra 4:3–5). The people of Judah indeed became discouraged (v. 4), which we may assume was because of outside influences and also because of the poor social and economic conditions in the province. Harvest failures (Hag. 1:6, 9–11; 2:17; Zech. 1:12; 8:10), inflation (Hag. 1:6), danger (Zech. 8:10), oppression of the poor caused by rank self-interest (Isa. 58:3–10; 59:1–8), religious syncretism and idolatry (Isa. 57:3–10; 65:1–7, 11; 66:3, 17; Ezek. 33:25), and conflicts about property rights (Zech. 5:3–4; cf. Ezek. 33:24) created the conditions for passivity, disappointment, and dejection. There was a sharp contrast between everyday reality and the high expectations that had been inspired by Ezekiel and Deutero-Isaiah. In addition to these conditions, the belief that the temple would be rebuilt only in the messianic age (which had not yet come, see Ezek. 37:24–28) and that the sacrificial service could effect blessings (cf. Hag. 2:15) must have given rise to the thinking that the time for rebuilding the temple of Yahweh had not yet come (1:2).

The prophet Haggai saw more clearly than anyone else in his time that the national and religious identity of the community of Yahweh was at stake as long as they were without a temple as the spiritual rallying point. On the basis of the preexilic prophecies of salvation, he was convinced that the promised salvation would become a reality only if Yahweh would again live in the midst of his people and from his sanctuary would manifest his glory (Hag. 1:8; cf. Zech. 1:16–17; 8:1–8, 11–15).

Despite initial opposition (Hag. 1:2), Haggai, Zerubbabel, Joshua, and other leading figures convinced the people of the need for rebuilding and finishing the temple. This work was begun on 18 December 520 B.C. (Hag. 1:15; 2:18). Soon afterward Zechariah also threw his support to Haggai (Zech. 1:1–6). For good reasons Haggai directed himself first of all to Zerubbabel, who had succeeded Sheshbazzar as governor, to take the initiative for rebuilding the temple. In the ancient east the building of a temple was a government concern, and it could not be done without permission from the political authorities. Hence Zerubbabel could be called the builder (4:9–10).

Apparently during this time some Samaritans, fearful of the religious and political competition from a rebuilt temple (especially considering the former position of Jerusalem and its temple), tried to frustrate the labor at the sanctuary. They must have been the people who contacted Tattenai, the satrap of the district Beyond the River, inducing him to go to Jerusalem to learn who was rebuilding the temple and why (Ezra 5:3–5). After his talk with the "elders of the Jews," who appealed to Cyrus's decree authorizing their work on the sanctuary, he seems initially to have been satisfied. At least he issued no temporary restraining order (v. 5) but instead asked King Darius for clarification and confirmation of the explanation the Jewish rulers had given him. The correspondence between Tattenai and the Persian king is preserved in Ezra 5:7–6:12. Darius's reply agreed with Cyrus's original decree, which removed any external obstacles toward the rebuilding of the sanctuary.

It is often thought that the troubles in connection with the accession to the throne of Darius I, who after the death of Cambyses (522 B.C.) was able to seize power in the Persian empire, gave the Judeans new hope that history would take a significant turn and that it provided the impetus for the prophetic ministry of Haggai and Zechariah. On closer investigation this view is hardly tenable. Though demonstrating distinctive emphases and ministering in new circumstances, Haggai revives a long-standing theology of the temple. At the time of his ministry in 520 B.C., the Persian realm had been brought under control by Darius (cf. also Zech. 1:11). The starting point of Haggai's preaching was not the contemporary international situation but the curse that he saw resting on the land on account of the people's neglect and lethargy in rebuilding the destroyed temple (Hag. 1:4–11). Only after the restoration of the temple and the return of Yahweh to his dwelling did the prophet expect a cosmic revolution (1:8; 2:6–9, 22–23). The belief of the people that the time had not yet come for the temple of Yahweh to be rebuilt (1:2) does not suggest that the Judean community in 520 was marked by great eschatological and messianic expectations. On the contrary, these expectations were aroused by the preaching of Haggai and Zechariah.

There is also a considerable difference in the future expectations of both prophets. After the revolutionary change in the world, Haggai envisions Zerubbabel, a descendant of David and the grandson of King Jehoiachin (1 Chr. 3:18–19), as the ruler of the messianic era elected by Yahweh (Hag. 2:23). Zechariah, however, expected that high priest and king would be side by side as equal partners (Zech. 4:14; 6:13). Many scholars suggest that special circumstances caused Zechariah to revise his expectation of the future. Whereas first he would have been convinced that Zerubbabel would complete the building of the temple (4:9), later he is silent about him and instead announces the coming of a "Branch" who would finish the rebuilding of the sanctuary (3:8; 6:12–13). The prophet would have been forced to change expectations of the future regarding Zerubbabel (and Joshua) first of all because Zerubbabel is supposed to have disappeared from the stage during the construction of the temple. Likewise based on conjecture is the hypothesis that Zerubbabel was relieved of his post or died before the completion of the temple. But Zechariah 4:9 in fact suggests that Zerubbabel completed the construction of the temple. Nor does Zechariah 6:13 disagree with this, for it speaks of the future messianic king who would turn Zerubbabel's humble construction (*bayit*) into a palace-like temple (*hekal*). The two "anointed ones" of 4:14 do not refer to the high priest Joshua and the governor Zerubbabel, but to the high priest and the king of the future messianic era. Zechariah's expectation was aimed right from the beginning at the latter two.

The religious and historical significance of the ministry of Haggai and Zechariah can hardly be overestimated. In difficult circumstances that threatened the identity of the Jews, they encouraged the people and evoked fresh hope for the future. Moreover, by their immovable faith in Yahweh and his power, they provided the Jews with a spiritual focal point that bound together not only the inhabitants of the province of Judah but also those living in the Dispersion, a focal point that proved to be of tremendous significance in the coming centuries for the spiritual unity of the Jews.

LITERATURE

P. R. Ackroyd, *Exile and Restoration* (Philadelphia, 1972[2]).

———, *Israel under Babylon and Persia* (London, 1970).

———, "Archaeology, Politics and Religion in the Persian Period," *The Iliff Review* 39 (1982) 5-24.

———, "Historical Problems of the Early Achaemenian Period," *Orient* 20 (1984) 1-15.

A. Alt, "Die Rolle Samarias bei der Entstehung des Judentums," in *Festschrift Otto Procksch* (Leipzig, 1934) (= *KS* II [München, 1953] 316-37).

N. Avigad, *Bullae and Seals from a Post-Exilic Judean Archive* (Jerusalem, 1976).

W. A. M. Beuken, *Haggai-Sacharja 1–8* (Assen, 1967).

K. M. Beyse, *Serubbabel und die Königserwartungen der Propheten Haggai und Sacharja* (Stuttgart, 1972).

E. J. Bickermann, "The Edict of Cyrus in Ezra 1," *JBL* 65 (1964) 249-75.

S. A. Cook, "The Age of Zerubbabel," in H. H. Rowley, ed., *Studies in Old Testament Prophecy* (Festschrift T. H. Robinson; Edinburgh, 1950), pp. 19-36.

A. E. Cowley, *Aramaic Papyri of the Fifth Century BC* (London, 1923; Osnabrück, 1967[2]).

W. D. Davies and L. Finkelstein, eds., *The Cambridge History of Judaism, I: Introduction; The Persian Period* (Cambridge, 1984).

K. Galling, *Studien zur Geschichte Israels im persischen Zeitalter* (Tübingen, 1964).

A. Gelston, "The Foundations of the Second Temple," *VT* 16 (1966) 232-35.

W. T. In der Smitten, "Historische Probleme zum Kyrosedikt und zum Jerusalemer Tempelbau von 515," *Persica* 6 (1974) 167-78.

B. Kanael, "Ancient Jewish Coins and Their Historical Importance," *BA* 26 (1963) 38-62.

A. Kuhrt, "The Cyrus Cylinder and Achaemenid Imperial Policy," *JSOT* 25 (1983) 83-97.

E. Meyer, *Die Entstehung des Judentums* (Halle, 1896).

J. M. Myers, *The World of the Restoration* (Englewood Cliffs, 1968).

A. T. Olmstead, *History of the Persian Empire* (Chicago/London, 1948).

A. F. Rainey, "The Satrapy 'Beyond the River,'" *Australian Journal of Biblical Archaeology* 1 (1969) 51-78.

L. Rost, "Erwägungen zum Kyroserlass," in A. Kuschke, ed., *Verbannung und Heimkehr* (Festschrift W. Rudolph; Tübingen, 1961), pp. 301-7.

J. W. Rothstein, *Juden und Samaritaner* (BWANT 3; Leipzig, 1908).

G. Sauer, "Serubbabel in der Sicht Haggais und Sacharjas," in F. Maass, ed., *Das ferne und nahe Wort* (Festschrift L. Rost; BZAW 105; Berlin, 1967), pp. 199-207.

E. Sellin, *Serubbabel. Ein Beitrag zur Geschichte der messianischen Erwartung und der Entstehung des Judentums* (Leipzig, 1898).

————, *Studien zur Entstehungsgeschichte der jüdischen Gemeinde nach dem babylonischen Exil* I-II (Leipzig, 1900-1901).

E. Stern, "The Province of Yehud: The Vision and the Reality," *The Jerusalem Cathedra* 1 (1981) 9-21.

See also section I.A above by Dr. M. J. Mulder, which gives an overview of the history of Israel, and the commentaries on Haggai and Zechariah listed below in section III.C.3.

---

b. Judah in the Period between Zerubbabel and Ezra

We know very little about the Judeans during the final decades of the sixth century and the first half of the fifth century B.C. In spite of the restoration of the temple, the age of bliss predicted by Ezekiel, Deutero-Isaiah, Trito-Isaiah, Haggai, and Zechariah had not materialized. The prophet Malachi, who was active in Judah about 480 B.C., depicts the Jewish community as suffering divisive contrasts and abuses. Through exploitation of day laborers and the impoverished, the elite were enriching themselves (Mal. 3:5). This upper class also sought to strengthen their socioeconomic position through marriages to foreign women (2:10–16). The mounting contrast between rich and poor led to a crisis in the faith community (see Neh. 5:1–5), while the mixed marriages constituted a serious threat to its identity (see 13:23–27). An additional factor was a priesthood that, likely appealing to the poor economic conditions, was satisfied with a profaned cult, thus making a mockery of the sacrificial service (Mal. 1:6–10). Heavy taxes (Neh. 5:15) and natural catastrophes (Mal. 3:11) made life almost unbearable, especially for the less privileged. Religious duties were performed only partially or not at all (3:6–10). Because the full tithes were not being paid, many of the Levites felt compelled to leave the service of the temple and to return to working their own fields (Neh. 13:10). Many did not keep the sabbath (Isa. 58:13; Neh. 13:15–18). Under these circumstances, many doubted Yahweh's saving interest in them and felt that it was useless to serve faithfully the God of Israel (Mal. 1:2–3; 3:14).

The small Jewish community not only suffered internal disruptions but also was threatened by the hostility of its neighbors. Ezra 4:6 contains a puzzling reference to a complaint about the Judeans by the Samaritans, sent to the Persian court during the first year of the reign of Xerxes I (485–465 B.C.). On the ground of this passage and several others, Morgenstern has hypothesized that in 485 Jerusalem was destroyed by the neighboring nations with the support of a Persian army, that the temple was burned down, and that a large part of the population was killed or sold into slavery. Some scholars have seen confirmation of this view in the destruction that, according to archeological data, many cities suffered in Palestine during the fifth century. The weaknesses of his hypothesis are that the passages quoted by Morgenstern allow different, if not better, explanations and that it requires the assumption that, between 485 and the arrival of Nehemiah, there was a new building of the temple. If there had indeed been such a construction, we might have expected some reference to it in the books of Ezra and Nehemiah. These books, however, record no such construction.

According to Ezra 4:8–23, during the reign of Artaxerxes I (465–424 B.C.) an attempt was made to restore the walls of Jerusalem. The undertaking was frustrated through the interference of the Samaritan governor Rehum and his men, who had addressed a letter to the king. Possibly the exiles who had returned to Jerusalem with Ezra in 458 (cf. 4:12 and 7:1–10) were the ones who had provided the impetus for rebuilding the walls of the city.

The little we know about the fortunes of the Jewish community in Judah and Jerusalem during the first half of the fifth century B.C. is nevertheless enough to make us aware that there was a need for a wholesale reorganization and restoration if religion and society in Judah were not to disintegrate totally. Ezra and Nehemiah were the leaders who took the necessary measures, without which Palestinian Jewry likely would not have weathered the crisis of the first half of the fifth century.

LITERATURE

T. Chary, *Les prophètes et le culte à partir de l'exil* (Tournai, 1955).

F. M. Cross, "A Reconstruction of the Judean Restoration," *JBL* 94 (1975) 4-18 [= *Interpretation* 29 (1975) 187-203].

J. Morgenstern, "Jerusalem—485 BC," *HUCA* 27 (1956) 101-79; 28 (1957) 15-47; 31 (1960) 1-29.

J. M. Myers, *The World of the Restoration* (Englewood Cliffs, 1968).

See also section I.A above by Dr. M. J. Mulder, which gives an overview of the history of Israel, and the commentaries on Malachi listed in section III.C.3 below.

c. Ezra and Nehemiah

In attempting to write a critical description of the period of Ezra and Nehemiah and the significance of both for the restoration of the Jewish community in Jerusalem and Judah, one is faced with formidable problems. Here we do not need to answer the question whether the books of Ezra and Nehemiah are to be regarded as part of the history that includes 1–2 Chronicles. In recent decades, Japhet, Williamson, and others have denied a direct relationship between Ezra and Nehemiah and the books of Chronicles. In my judgment, the decisive question for evaluating the available data concerns the composition of Ezra and Nehemiah.

The author of these books clearly made use of letters (see Ezra 4:8–22; 5:6–17; 6:3–12; 7:11–26) and lists (see ch. 2; 8:1–14; 10:18–44; Neh. 7:4–73; 10:1–27; 11:3–36; 12:1–26) but especially had access to the memoirs of Ezra (Ezra 7–10) and Nehemiah (Nehemiah 1–7; 12:27–43; 13:4–31). Though it is impossible here to discuss in detail the complicated literary-critical problems of both books, I mention the important points in understanding the composition of Ezra and Nehemiah. The history of Ezra is described in Ezra 7–10 and in Nehemiah 8. This last chapter must literarily and chronologically be placed after Ezra 8. Ezra and his people left Babylon in the *first* month of the seventh year of King Artaxerxes and arrived in Jerusalem in the *fifth* month (Ezra 7:8–9; cf. 8:31), and the *seventh* month mentioned in Nehemiah 8:1 seems to refer to the same year. Later, Ezra 10:9 mentions the *ninth* month. Nehemiah 9–10, then, despite appearances to the contrary, is not the direct sequel of Nehemiah 8 but a separate tradition about a covenant made at the time of Nehemiah. The data in the memoirs of Nehemiah are not always presented in chronological order. Nehemiah 5:10, for example, seems to suggest that Nehemiah's measures on behalf of the poor did not happen during the building of the walls. Also, the repopulation of Jerusalem (ch. 11) occurred presumably after, not before, the dedication of the wall (12:27–43). The same can be said about the making of the covenant related in chapters 9 and 10, which likely did not happen until after 433 B.C.

Inseparably connected with the literary-critical questions raised by the books of Ezra and Nehemiah is one of the most difficult problems in the study of the Old Testament: the chronological sequence of the ministry of Ezra and Nehemiah in Jerusalem. In Ezra 7:7 we read that Ezra went up from Babylon to Jerusalem in the seventh year of Artaxerxes. In Nehemiah 2:1–6 it is reported that, in the twentieth year of Artaxerxes, Nehemiah addressed the king with the request to be sent to Jerusalem to rebuild the city walls. We can hardly doubt that the writer of Ezra and Nehemiah had the same Artaxerxes in mind. It is possible, however, that, in using the documents available to him, the writer confused one King Artaxerxes with another. We know of three Persian kings by that name: Artaxerxes I Longimanus (465–424), Artaxerxes II Mnemon (404–359), and Artaxerxes III Ochus (359–338). Because Nehemiah speaks of the thirty-second year of Artachsasta, that is, Artaxerxes (5:14; 13:6), he—and, as generally thought, also Ezra—cannot have meant the last-mentioned king. It is also undisputed that Artaxerxes II cannot have been the Artachsasta of Nehemiah. According to one of the Elephantine Papyri (Cowley, no. 30), Johanan was priest in Jerusalem in 408 B.C. Nehemiah, however, mentions Johanan's grandfather Eliashib as high priest (3:1). According to the same papyrus Sanballat, the governor of Samaria, had grown sons in 408, but already at the time of Nehemiah he was an influential man (2:19). Therefore there can be no doubt that the Artachsasta who gave permission to Nehemiah to go to Jerusalem was Artaxerxes I and that consequently in 445, or the twentieth year of Artachsasta (v. 1), Nehemiah left the royal residence.

There is a difference of opinion about the identification of the Artachsasta of Ezra. After Hoonacker in 1890 resolutely decided in favor of Artaxerxes II and accordingly dated the arrival of Ezra and his people in Jerusalem in 397 B.C., or the seventh year of Artachsasta (Ezra 7:7), many scholars, though not without hesitation, have adopted this position. To be able to maintain that Ezra and Nehemiah were contemporaries, as is assumed by Nehemiah 8:9 and 12:36, others have proposed to emend "the seventh year" in Ezra 7:7 to "the thirty-seventh year," which would mean that Ezra left for Jerusalem in 428.

I do not discuss here in detail all the arguments that have been advanced against a dating of Ezra's ministry in 458 B.C. under Artaxerxes I. For an exhaustive discussion of the problem and a defense of the traditional view that places the arrival of Ezra before that of Nehemiah, the reader may refer to the commentary by H. H. Grosheide on the book of Ezra. Because I also reject a dating of Ezra's ministry in 397, I briefly review the main arguments adduced in favor of Ezra's arrival at the time of Artaxerxes II. At his arrival, it has been pointed out, Ezra found a heavily populated Jerusalem, surrounded by a wall (Ezra 9:9), whereas Nehemiah rebuilt the wall (Nehemiah 1–6) and took measures for the repopulation of the city (7:4–5; 11:1–2). Ezra 9:9, however, mentions a "wall in *Judea* and Jerusalem," which cannot

refer to a city wall, while Ezra 10 speaks of a meeting of the people in Jerusalem, without saying anything about the number of people in the city. Nehemiah forbade parents to let their children marry strangers (Neh. 13:23–27), but Ezra was much more drastic in his measures, demanding the divorce of foreign women (Ezra 10). Strict measures do not always follow upon less strict, however. The reverse can also be the case, especially if the strict measures prove to be ineffective. Ezra 10:6 mentions a stay of Ezra at the residence of Jehohanan, the son of Eliashib. Nehemiah 12:10–11, 22 mentions Jonathan (which we may take as a clerical error for Jehohanan) as grandson of the high priest Eliashib. Because Jehohanan was high priest in Jerusalem about 400, the argument goes, Ezra would have arrived in the city about that time, not fifty years earlier. (Even apart from the question, however, whether "Jehohanan the son of Eliashib" in Ezra 10:6 refers to a *grandson* instead of a *son,* it cannot be demonstrated that Eliashib in this passage refers to the high priest. It was such a common name in those days [see Ezra 10:24, 27, 36; Neh. 13:4] that nothing requires that conclusion.)

Because changing "the seventh year" to "the thirty-seventh year" in Ezra 7:7 seems arbitrary, and because in my judgment there are no compelling arguments for a stay of Ezra in Jerusalem during the reign of Artaxerxes II, I agree with the view that the writer of Ezra and Nehemiah had only one Artaxerxes/Artachsasta in mind. I feel confident in this position because, in my opinion, a dating of Ezra before Nehemiah agrees with the historical data available to us. It is not impossible that Ezra was still in Jerusalem when the wall restored under Nehemiah was dedicated (Neh. 12:36). In contrast to this text, the phrase "Nehemiah, who was the governor" in Nehemiah 8:9 is to be regarded as a later and historically inaccurate addition to the Ezra stories.

One year after Artaxerxes I had ascended the throne in 465 B.C., Persian rule in Egypt was in serious jeopardy. A certain Inaros, son of Psammetichus, revolted (Thucydides, I, 104ff.) and appealed to the Athenian fleet for help. The successful Inaros took the Delta and defeated the army of the Persian satrap Achaemenes. Not until about 455 was the Persian satrap of Syria, Megabyzus, able to quell the revolt of Inaros. Under these circumstances it was natural that the attention of Artaxerxes was drawn to Judah and similar areas that constituted an outpost on the way to rebellious Egypt. It must have been very important for the king to have a well-ordered and politically reliable province in that part of Palestine.

For that reason Ezra, coming with the request "to make inquiries about Judah and Jerusalem" according to the law of his God (Ezra 7:14) and asking to be allowed to take appropriate governmental-juridical measures (vv. 25–26), might expect a favorable response from Artaxerxes. Ezra was not only a priest whose family tree could be traced back to Aaron (vv. 1–5) but also "the scribe of the law of the God of heaven" (v. 12), an official for Jewish affairs at the chancellery of the royal residence. The task with which Ezra was charged shows remarkable similarities to the steps undertaken by the Persian government in Egypt, which, in the so-called demotic chronicle, codified the local laws and used them to organize the government.

Armed with a royal letter, a royal subsidy for the use of the cult in Jerusalem, and gifts collected by the Jews in Babylon, Ezra was able to accept his special mandate. He secured the right to obtain funds from the royal treasury, while the treasurers in the satrapy Beyond the River were ordered to provide all necessary assistance. The cultic personnel in Jerusalem were exempted from taxation, and Ezra was authorized to appoint judges and officials to promote and maintain the law of God as the law of the king. These steps are reported in an official letter from Artaxerxes I, preserved in Ezra 7:12–26, whose authenticity seems beyond doubt.

With specific permission from the king, Ezra on his journey to Jerusalem was accompanied by a caravan of exiles who, including wives and children, must have numbered about five thousand (Ezra 8:1–14). In view of the unrest in Egypt and the western Semitic districts, an augmentation of the population of Judah with law-abiding Babylonian Jews must have been welcome to Artaxerxes. The caravan gathered by the canal of Ahava (vv. 15, 21, 31), a place unknown to us but presumably in the vicinity of Babylon. Because there were no Levites among the returnees, Ezra

at the last moment tried to enlist some to emigrate back to the Promised Land. He managed to persuade 38 Levites and 220 temple servants to return with him to Jerusalem (vv. 15–20). Ezra refused to request a detachment of soldiers to accompany him (vv. 21–23), and after fasting and praying for Yahweh's protection against the perils of the journey, the expedition took to the road on the twelfth day of the first month of the year 458 B.C. (v. 31). Four and a half months later, having escaped attack from soldiers or robbers, the caravan arrived safely in Jerusalem, where the treasures brought along were given to the temple authorities and a sin offering and burnt offerings were brought to the God of Israel (vv. 31–35).

Aided by the authority he received from the king, Ezra in a short time must have been able to assure himself of the cooperation of the local authorities. Two months after his arrival in Jerusalem, a popular gathering was held at the square before the Water Gate in Jerusalem (Nehemiah 8). The gathering was carefully prepared: a wooden pulpit was ready (v. 4) and Ezra was requested to bring "the book of the law of Moses which the Lord had given to Israel" (v. 1). Translating into Aramaic and interpreting while reading, Ezra read from this law, one of the first instances of paraphrasing a normative text (for which later the term *targum* was used). Apparently thinking of the later synagogal custom of paraphrasing the text of the Hebrew Bible in Aramaic, the author of this passage introduces Levites and others as assisting Ezra with the instruction, a piece of information that does not quite fit the setting of Ezra's ministry. The people were so deeply impressed by Ezra's word that they had to be exhorted to be joyful instead of grieving (vv. 9–12). The next day Ezra had a discussion with the heads of the families, the priests, and the Levites, which ensued in a new celebration of the Feast of Tabernacles (vv. 14–19), during which instruction in the law of God was again given.

Alarmed by numerous reports of marriages with foreign women, especially by upper-class Jews wishing to strengthen their own economic and social position, Ezra called a gathering of "all the men of Judah and Benjamin" on the twentieth day of the ninth month (19 December 458) in Jerusalem (Ezra 10:9). At this meeting he ordered them to divorce their foreign wives. For the first time now we hear of opposition to Ezra's actions. Not only was a commission appointed to discuss the matter of the dissolution of the marriages (v. 14), but there was also a voice of open protest against the measure demanded by Ezra (v. 15). Except for the names mentioned in verses 18–19, the list of the men involved, preserved in Ezra 10:18–44, does not tell us whether the divorces were actually carried out. The fact that there is an abrupt break in the data about Ezra in the book named after him suggests that his zeal for the dissolution of the marriages with foreign women became his downfall. Ezra was perhaps right in his judgment that the mixed marriages threatened the integrity of the community and constituted a real danger to the spiritual restoration he envisioned. He may also have thought that the measures he took were implied in the mandate he received from Artaxerxes. Nevertheless, for these decisions Ezra did not have the king's specific permission, and by acting as he did, he interfered in the lives of the spiritual leaders in Jerusalem, the very people whose help he needed. Ezra was a government official and priest, but not a natural statesman. Nor did he possess political power to carry out his ideas. For that function, another person was necessary—Nehemiah.

Ezra 4:8–23 intimates that in other respects as well Ezra was not able to realize his ideas. The letters mentioned in this passage report that an attempt was made at the time of Artaxerxes I to rebuild the wall of Jerusalem. The initiative for this effort came in all likelihood from the exiles who had returned to Palestine with Ezra and specifically from Ezra himself. Persian officials in Samaria managed to raise suspicions about the work with the king, however, which led the weak and hesitating monarch to order a stop to the work until he ordered its continuation (v. 21). If Ezra was indeed involved in the activities at the wall, Artaxerxes's prohibition must have weakened his position even more.

One gets the impression that the work of Ezra was in more than one respect taken over by Nehemiah. This statesman, who knew his limits and acted cautiously, had more success than the "scribe of the God of heaven." As the cupbearer of King Artaxerxes, Nehemiah had obtained a high position at the court and enjoyed immediate access to the king. A delegation from Jerusalem, to which his brother Hanani also belonged (Neh. 7:2), had reported to him the "great trouble and shame" endured by the people in Jerusalem and Judah and had notified him of the violent destruction of the wall of Jerusalem (1:3). This event apparently refers to the military action taken by the Samaritans against the restoration, mentioned in Ezra 4:23. The complaint of Hanani and his men cannot refer to the destruction of Jerusalem by the troops of Nebuchadrezzar 140 years earlier. Depressed by the reports about Jerusalem and Judah, Nehemiah felt the urge to do something for his people. He obtained permission from Artaxerxes to rebuild the wall of Jerusalem. After the completion of that task, the king expected him back at the court in Susa (Neh. 2:6). Nehemiah was thus not governor from the very outset. Shortly after his arrival in Jerusalem, however, he apparently was called to this office (cf. 5:14) and, contrary to the original intention, must have stayed in Jerusalem after the rebuilding of the wall, although about 433 B.C. he spent some time at the royal court (13:6–7).

Artaxerxes provided Nehemiah with the things he needed most to carry out his mandate: a military detachment to protect him on the way (Neh. 2:9), letters of recommendation for the governors of the satrapy Beyond the River, and a letter for Asaph, the supervisor of the royal domains (or "keeper of the king's forest"), containing the order to provide Nehemiah with the timber needed for the restoration of the fortress of the city, the gates, and the building of a house for himself (v. 8).

Aware of the internal and external threats, Nehemiah after his arrival in Jerusalem thoroughly and cautiously prepared for rebuilding the wall. During a nighttime tour he inspected the wall that had never been completely leveled since the Babylonians had done their destructive work in 586 B.C. There were nevertheless huge gaps in the wall, and in places it had been completely torn down; at other places the ruins made it impassable for a beast of burden (Neh. 2:14). Aided by the royal decree, Nehemiah in a short time was able to obtain the cooperation of the local officials (vv. 16–18), with the result that the rebuilding of the wall could quickly begin. To speed the work and complete it successfully, Nehemiah used laborers from the whole province, having different groups work simultaneously at various places (ch. 3). Nehemiah saw the work completed in the exceptionally short period of fifty-two days (6:15), although it faced serious challenge. Though at first Sanballat, the governor of Samaria (see the Elephantine Papyri [Cowley, no. 30]), and the Ammonite Tobiah had mocked the undertaking, confident that it would fail (2:19; 4:1–3), they soon changed their thinking when they saw the speedy and successful rebuilding. By intrigues and military buildup, for which they also secured the support of the Arabs in the south and the people of Ashdod in the west, they continued to try to stop the work (4:7–8).

In contrast to their success a few years previously (Ezra 4:23), this time the enemies of the Jews could not get the support of Artaxerxes, who himself had ordered Nehemiah to rebuild the wall of Jerusalem. In view of the close ties many Samaritans had with Jerusalem on account of the temple (according to an Elephantine Papyrus, the sons of Sanballat had Yahwistic names [Cowley, no. 30.29]) as well as the family relationship with the priesthood there (see Neh. 13:4, 28; cf. also 6:17–19), drastic improvements in the capital of the province of Judah were bound to draw their attention, for political as well as personal reasons. Samaritan Jews, however, informed Nehemiah in time of the plans of Sanballat and his men, enabling Nehemiah to arm the workers and to post guards at night, thus preparing himself for a possible military raid (4:12–23). His enemies were thus forced to resort to diplomatic means to accomplish their aim. A repeated request from Sanballat and his men to have talks was resolutely turned down by Nehemiah (6:1–9). Some Jerusalemites also conspired with Sanballat to capture and kill Nehemiah (vv. 10–13). They were unsuccessful, but it was another indication of the grave dangers from within and without. In fact, after the restoration of the gates, Nehemiah at first opened them only during the day (7:1–3). With great ceremony, the Jews celebrated the completion of the rebuilding (12:27–43).

As a statesman and capable administrator who was devoted to Yahweh, Nehemiah was wise enough to realize that the reconstruction of the wall of Jerusalem was only the beginning of the complete restoration of the community. Many other reforms and changes were necessary in order to bring about and ensure the spiritual unity and identity of the community. Jerusalem was sparsely populated and would have no real future unless it once again had a sizable population. Nehemiah therefore had one-tenth of the population of the province move into the city (Neh. 7:4–5; 11:1–24). By inducing the well-to-do to cancel the debts of those who had been forced to sell their fields or sell themselves into slavery, Nehemiah ended the sharp social and economic contrasts that had arisen between rich and poor and that had been aggravated by the oppressions of the ruling elite (5:1–5, 14–15). Nehemiah was fully aware that a rebellion on the part of a discontented proletariat could undo his work. By voluntarily relinquishing the normal income of a governor and by contenting himself with receiving the necessary means in goods, he himself set an inspiring example for a just reform of society (vv. 14–18).

After Nehemiah returned briefly to the royal court in about 433 B.C., he apparently continued his reforms in the second period of his rule as governor. During his absence the priest Eliashib, who was in charge of the temple storerooms, had again established closer ties with the neighboring provinces. He was also a blood relative of the Ammonite Tobiah, whom he had provided with a large room in the temple, which was formerly used for cultic purposes (Neh. 13:4–5). In Nehemiah's judgment, this policy of rapprochement with the neighboring peoples constituted the major threat to the identity of the community of Judah and Jerusalem. Therefore after his return from Babylon all his measures were designed at keeping the community separate. Not only did he expel the son-in-law of Sanballat (v. 28) and return the room in the temple given to Tobiah to its original use (vv. 6–9), he also took resolute measures against the threat that mixed marriages posed to the identity of the people. As a statesman who was sensitive to his limitations, he did not, unlike Ezra, order the dissolution of existing marriages, but he did have the parents take a solemn oath that they would not let their children marry foreigners (vv. 23–27). For the sake of the cult, which, despite the preaching of Malachi, showed grave weaknesses and lack of zeal, Nehemiah ordered the people to bring the tithes regularly (vv. 10–13) as well as wood for the altars (v. 31). In accordance with the strict celebration of the sabbath by the Babylonian exiles, Nehemiah prohibited work on that day and took action to eliminate the extensive trading that was being practiced on the sabbath (vv. 15–22).

These obligations imposed on the people by Nehemiah are recorded in the report of the covenant that Nehemiah, according to chapters 9–10, made with the chiefs, the Levites, and the priests. As it stands, however, the information provided in these chapters comes after the section of the history of Ezra that relates Ezra's reading of the law that he had brought with him (Nehemiah 8). Chapters 9–10, however, are a document that has no literary connection with the preceding chapter; the writer of Ezra and Nehemiah must have received it as an independent unit. That he put it after chapter 8, even though the making of the covenant between Nehemiah and the leaders of the people apparently occurred during the second period of Nehemiah's rule as governor to ensure the effectiveness of his measures, does suggest a material connection between the law of Ezra and the making of the covenant. In this covenant Nehemiah and the leaders entered into "a curse and an oath to walk in God's law which was given through Moses the servant of God" (10:29). Is this law to which Nehemiah and the leaders bound themselves the same as the law brought by Ezra from Babylon? If so, then also in this case Nehemiah would have continued the work of his predecessor.

There are many differences of opinion about the substance of the law of Ezra. Kellermann and others believe that Deuteronomy is meant. Some take it to be the so-called Priestly Code (P), while still others suggest the entire Pentateuch. Considering the narrative character of large sections from Genesis to Deuteronomy and the many chapters relating to priestly ritual, we see that the entire Pentateuch can hardly have functioned as the basic law for the people. Nevertheless the law of Ezra must in large part have been based on regulations in the Pentateuch, an indication of which is its designation as "the law of Moses" (Neh. 8:1;

cf. 10:29). With C. Houtman, I tend to regard the law of Ezra as a separate law code that could constitutionally function as "the law of the king" (Ezra 7:26). Supporting this conception is also the fact that providing wood for the altar is nowhere prescribed in the Pentateuch. According to Nehemiah 10:34, however, the law to which Nehemiah and the leaders bound themselves included this regulation. In this view, the law of Ezra was a law code that primarily contained statutes from the Pentateuch, similar to the temple scroll from Cave 11 from Qumran, which is likewise regarded as a law given by Yahweh to Moses.

If this conjecture is correct, the law of Ezra suggests that the Pentateuch was already closed before 458 B.C. (The note in Neh. 8:18 that, in accordance with the ordinance, the Feast of Tabernacles was concluded with a festive gathering agrees with Lev. 23:36, which belongs to the Priestly Code, regarded as the youngest source of the Pentateuch, and not with Deut. 16:13–15.) Now, however, a law code based on the Pentateuch became constitutional law and thus constitutive for ordering the whole of society in the province of Judah. Such a step enabled later generations to appeal to the tradition of the fathers as containing legally valid privileges not only in religious matters but also in civil and political affairs.

The work of Ezra and Nehemiah made a crucial contribution toward ensuring that the community in Jerusalem and Judah would maintain its own identity. Under the circumstances this objective required an isolation from the surrounding peoples, notwithstanding historical and religious ties, as with Samaria and the districts in Transjordan. The separatism to which Ezra and Nehemiah felt themselves compelled, encouraged by the political tensions between Samaria and Judah that surfaced in the fifth century, eventually resulted in a religious schism between Samaritans and Jews. We should, however, regard this separation as a gradual development and not as resulting from a single event (for instance, from the building of the temple on Mount Gerizim in Hellenistic times). Until the breach became definite there remained, at least in the Persian era, close marriage ties between the Samaritan elite and leading Jewish circles (see Josephus, *Antiquities* 12.302–303, 312).

Ezra and Nehemiah belonged to the Babylonian exiles. Another consequence of their activities in Judah must have been the strengthening of the religious ties between those living in dispersion in Mesopotamia and the community in Judah.

LITERATURE

M. Avi-Yonah, "The Walls of Nehemiah—A Minimalist View," *IEJ* 4 (1954) 239-48.

J. Bright, "The Date of Ezra's Mission to Jerusalem," in M. Haran, ed., *Yehezkel Kaufmann Jubilee Volume* (Jerusalem, 1960), pp. 79-87.

A. E. Cowley, *Aramaic Papyri of the Fifth Century BC* (London, 1923; Osnabrück, 1967²).

F. M. Cross, "A Reconstruction of the Judean Restoration," *JBL* 94 (1975) 4-18 (= *Interpretation* 29 [1975] 187-203).

J. A. Emerton, "Did Ezra Go to Jerusalem in 428 BC?" *JTS* 17 (1966) 1-19.

H. H. Grosheide, *Ezra-Nehemia* I (Kampen, 1963).

A. van Hoonacker, "Néhémie et Esdras, une nouvelle hypothèse sur la chronologie de l'époque de la restauration," *Le Muséon* 9 (1890) 151-84, 317-51, 389-401.

C. Houtman, "Ezra and the Law," *OTS* 21 (1981) 91-115.

W. Th. In der Smitten, *Esra: Quellen, Überlieferung und Geschichte* (Assen, 1973).

———, "Erwägungen zu Nehemias Davidizität," *JSJ* 5 (1974) 41-48.

S. Japhet, "The Supposed Common Authorship of Chronicles and Ezra-Nehemiah Investigated Anew," *VT* 18 (1968) 330-71.

U. Kellermann, *Nehemia: Quellen, Überlieferung und Geschichte* (BZAW 102; Berlin, 1967).

———, "Erwägungen zum Problem der Esradatierung," *ZAW* 80 (1968) 55-87.

———, "Erwägungen zum Esragesetz," *ZAW* 80 (1968) 373-85.

K. Koch, "Ezra and the Origins of Judaism," *JSS* 19 (1974) 173-97.

B. Mazar, "The Tobiads," *IEJ* 7 (1957) 137-45, 229-38.

E. Meyer, *Die Entstehung des Judentums* (Halle, 1896).

S. Mowinckel, *Studien zu dem Buche Ezra-Nehemia* I-III (Oslo, 1964-65).

J. M. Myers, *The World of the Restoration* (Englewood Cliffs, 1968).

———, *Ezra, Nehemiah* (AB; Garden City, NY, 1965).

G. von Rad, "Die Nehemia-Denkschrift," *ZAW* 76 (1964) 176-87.

H. H. Rowley, "The Chronological Order of Ezra and Nehemiah," in D. S. Löwinger and J. Somogyi, eds., *Ignace Goldziher Memorial Volume* I (Budapest, 1948) 117-49 (= *The Servant of the Lord* [London, 1965], pp. 135-68).

———, "Nehemiah's Mission and its Background," *BJRL* 37 (1954-55) 528-61 (= *Men of God* [London, 1963], pp. 211-45).

W. Rudolph, *Esra und Nehemia* (HAT I/20; Tübingen, 1949).

H. H. Schaeder, *Iranische Beiträge* I (Halle, 1930) 197-296.

———, *Esra der Schreiber* (Tübingen, 1930).

M. Smith, *Palestinian Parties and Politics that Shaped the Old Testament* (New York, 1971).

E. Stern, *The Material Culture of the Land of the Bible in the Persian Period* (Warminster, 1982).

H. G. M. Williamson, *Israel in the Book of Chronicles* (Cambridge, 1977).

See also section I.A above by Dr. M. J. Mulder, which gives an overview of the history of Israel, and the commentaries on Ezra and Nehemiah listed in section III.B.3 below.

---

d. Judah during the Final Century of Persian Domination

R. Kittel in his famed *Geschichte des Volkes Israel* called the final century of Persian hegemony over Judah "a time of silence." We indeed have very little information available to us that describes this age. The Old Testament says hardly anything about this period in Israel's history, except perhaps for some indirect information in a number of books or parts of writings that may have been produced in the course of the fourth century B.C., for example, Joel, Jonah, Job, 1–2 Chronicles, Ezra and Nehemiah, Zechariah 12–14, and Isaiah 24–27, the so-called Isaiah apocalypse. Disregarding the dating problems, which in many cases have no satisfactory solution, we note that these parts of Scripture either offer no direct data for the era in question or are so susceptible to different interpretations that historical conclusions drawn from them remain highly tentative. We are sure that the fifth and especially the fourth centuries produced literature, though we often are not certain which of the preserved writings are from this period. In other words, for even the sketchiest description of happenings in Judah in this period, we are dependent primarily on extrabiblical sources. Such documents include the Elephantine Papyri, the Samaria Papyri, and the *Jewish Antiquities* of Flavius Josephus.

The Elephantine Papyri were discovered in the late nineteenth century and in later digs at Elephantine (Egyptian Yeb), an island in the Nile opposite Aswan (see ill. 61). They provide a picture of religious and daily life of a Jewish colony established there, consisting primarily of military personnel. This colony must have been established by a pharaoh as early as the seventh or sixth century B.C., with a view to the defense of the southern border of Egypt. The colony possessed not only a synagogue but also a temple, where sacrifices were brought to Yahu (Yahweh). The papyri, written in Aramaic and dating from the period between 494 and 399, consist primarily of letters, requests, official government documents, name lists, and marriage, purchase, and rental contracts. They offer a picture of the administrative policies of the Persian government and the private laws of the Jewish colonists. They also indicate, however, that the Yahweh religion there was highly syncretistic. Other gods besides Yahu were worshiped, including Eshem-Bethel, Herem-Bethel, and Anat-Bethel.

The famed Passover Papyrus (Cowley, no. 21) from the year 418 B.C. indicates that, by royal decree (cf. Ezra 7:12–26), the Jewish garrison was commanded to celebrate the Feast of Unleavened Bread in accordance with the regulations of Exodus 12:15–20, part of the Priestly Code. The letter suggests that the royal chancellery possessed up-to-date information about Jewish religious laws and customs and thus throws a welcome light on what we are told concerning the mission of Ezra. The residents of Elephantine were associated with the worshipers of Yahweh in Palestine, which is evident from copies of another letter that the high priest of the Yahu temple sent in 408 B.C. to Bagoas, the governor of Judah (Cowley, nos. 30–31). In this letter it is reported that, three years previously, during the absence of the satrap Arsames (cf. Neh. 13:6), the Egyptian priests of the ram-god Khnum together with the governor Vidranga had razed the temple of Yahu and robbed

it of its treasures. Reference is made to another letter, copies of which were sent to Bagoas, the high priest Johanan and his colleagues, and Ostanes and the other members of the Jewish "nobility," a letter to which no reply was received. Bagoas is asked to take steps that will lead to the rebuilding of the temple and the resumption of the sacrificial service. Finally it is reported that contact concerning this matter has also been made with Delaiah and Shelemaiah, the sons of Sanballat, the governor of Samaria. Another papyrus, in the form of a memorandum, contains the combined answer of Bagoas and Delaiah, in which the restoration of the temple and the bringing of sacrifices is recommended to Arsames (Cowley, no. 32).

This correspondence indicates how, toward the end of the fifth century B.C., Jewish and Samaritan groups were prepared to act together in religious matters. The colonists of Elephantine apparently also assumed that Yahweh was honored as God in both provinces, though apparently they tried to play one group against the other by sending a petition both to Jerusalem and to Samaria. It is remarkable in this correspondence that, in the memorandum of Bagoas and Delaiah, not a word is said about the high priest Johanan, who earlier was involved in this matter. It is possible that, after the activities of Ezra and Nehemiah, he did not recognize the temple and sacrificial cult at Elephantine; it is also possible that Bagoas deliberately excluded him.

If Bagoas may be identified with Bagoses, mentioned by Josephus in his *Antiquities* (11.297ff.), the relationship between the governor and the high priest must have been strained. Josephus records that Bagoses was a friend of Jesus/Joshua, the brother of Johanan. The governor promised the high priesthood to Joshua, which led to such a vehement quarrel between the two brothers in the temple that Johanan killed Joshua. Outraged by this deed, Bagoses committed the sacrilegious act of entering the sanctuary. He ordered that fifty drachma be paid for every sacrificial lamb, a punishment he continued for seven years (till the death of Johanan?).

The information about Judah in the fourth century B.C. provided by Josephus has received new light from the Samaria Papyri, discovered in 1962 by bedouins at Wadi ed-Daliyeh, about 15 kilometers (10 mi.) north of Jericho. The documents are from the period 375 and 335 B.C. and at one time belonged to people who, before Alexander the Great destroyed Samaria, had fled the city and sought escape in a cave in the wadi. There they were later discovered by the Macedonians, who killed them by suffocation by lighting a large fire at the entrance to the cave. The papyri, dealing entirely with juridical and administrative matters, offer information about the governors who ruled Samaria during the fourth century. As a result we now know that Delaiah, the son of Nehemiah's adversary Sanballat, was succeeded by his son Sanballat II. After him both his sons Jeshua and Hananiah ruled. From a carefully dated papyrus it can be determined that the latter was governor in 354. Likely he was succeeded by Sanballat III; though not mentioned in the papyri, he seems to be the one who, according to Josephus (*Antiquities* 11.302), was appointed governor over Samaria by Darius III Codomannus (336–330).

Presumably this Sanballat gave his daughter Nikaso in marriage to Manasseh, the brother of the high priest Jaddua. Josephus's report that Jaddua succeeded Johanan as high priest is true in the sense that Johanan, who was high priest about 400 B.C., indeed passed on the high-priestly office to his son Jaddua. This Jaddua, however, cannot be identified with the brother of Manasseh who lived at the time of Darius III. Josephus not only confused the governor Bagoas with a general of Artaxerxes III, who ruled from 359 to 338 B.C. (see *Antiquities* 11.300), he also seems to have identified the successor of the high priest Johanan with a later high priest Jaddua who is not further known to us. The information Josephus presents about Manasseh may indeed be correct, but at present we cannot confirm its reliability. Josephus relates that, because of Manasseh's marriage to a foreign woman, the elders of Jerusalem refused to give him permission "to share in the high priesthood" (*Antiquities* 11.306). They requested that he either divorce Nikaso or else not approach the altar. Because his brother also took the side of the elders, Manasseh departed to Sanballat, his father-in-law. Sanballat offered Manasseh the job of high priest in a Yahweh temple that Sanballat would build on Mount Gerizim if Manasseh would remain married

to his daughter. According to Josephus, Darius III indeed permitted Sanballat to build the sanctuary.

Numerous priests and laymen who likewise had married foreign women viewed the attitude of the elders as a threat to their own position and joined Manasseh. Sanballat received them with open arms and gave them much money and other presents. After the victory of Alexander the Great over Darius III in the battle at Issus (333 B.C.) and at the time of the siege of Tyre and Gaza, Sanballat apparently took the side of Alexander, from whom he received permission to construct another temple on Mount Gerizim. The temple was presumably built and Manasseh installed in the high-priestly office in the new sanctuary. Digging at Tell er-Ras, the northernmost point of the Gerizim, and examining the remains of the temple erected for Zeus Hypsistos during the reign of Emperor Hadrian (A.D. 117–38), R. J. Bull identified the remnants of building complex B and of an altar with the Samaritan temple. The pottery found there is, however, not older than the third century B.C.

Apart from the Elephantine Papyri, we possess no primary data concerning contacts of the community in Jerusalem and Judah with the Jewish Diaspora, which geographically had not remained limited to Mesopotamia and Egypt. The examples of Ezra and Nehemiah tell us that Jews in the Persian empire could rise to high posts (see also the book of Esther). After Ezra we hear of no large groups of exiles who returned to the Promised Land. By means of its sacred writings, preservation of the rite of circumcision, and strict observance of the Sabbath, the Jewish community in Babylon managed to maintain its own identity in the land of captivity. As they increased in prosperity and improved their social position, the desire to return to Palestine, where they faced an uncertain future, decreased. In Babylon the Jews enjoyed freedom of religion, were able to maintain their traditional customs, and could buy property (Jer. 29:5) and even slaves (Ezra 2:65). The Murashu Documents from the fifth century B.C., clay tablets from the archive of a trading business discovered at Nippur, show that the Jews managed to acquire prestigious social positions in everyday life. The names of the sons of Murashu mentioned in this archive point to a Jewish business that included the buying of land.

LITERATURE

On the Elephantine Papyri:

A. E. Cowley, *Aramaic Papyri of the Fifth Century BC* (London, 1923; Osnabrück, 1967[2]).

G. R. Driver, *Aramaic Documents of the Fifth Century BC* (London, 1954).

P. Grelot, *Documents araméens d'Egypte* (Paris, 1972).

———, "Etudes sur le 'Papyrus Pascal' d'Éléphantiné," *VT* 4 (1954) 349-84.

———, "Le Papyrus Pascal d'Éléphantiné et le problème du Pentateuque," *VT* 5 (1955) 250-65.

———, "Le Papyrus Pascal d'Éléphantiné. Essai de Restauration," *VT* 17 (1967) 201-7.

E. Kraeling, *The Brooklyn Museum Aramaic Papyri: New Documents of the Fifth Century BC from the Jewish Colony of Elephantine* (New Haven/London, 1953).

Y. Muffs, *Studies in the Aramaic Legal Documents of Elephantine* (Leiden, 1969).

B. Porten, *Archives from Elephantine: The Life of an Ancient Jewish Military Colony* (Los Angeles/London, 1968).

A. Vincent, *La religion des judéo-araméens d'Éléphantiné* (Paris, 1937).

On the Murashu Documents:

G. Cardascia, *Les archives des Murašū: Une famille d'hommes d'affaires babyloniens à l'époque perse (455-403 av. J.-C.)* (Paris, 1951).

A. T. Clay, *Business Documents of the Murashū Sons of Nippur Dated in the Reign of Darius II (424-404 BC)* (Philadelphia, 1904).

———, *Business Documents of the Murashū Sons of Nippur Dated in the Reign of Darius II* (Philadelphia, 1912).

M. D. Coogan, "Life in the Diaspora: Jews at Nippur in the Fifth Century BC," *BA* 37 (1974) 6-12.

———, "Patterns in Jewish Personal Names in the Babylonian Diaspora," *JSJ* 4 (1973) 183-91.

———, *West Semitic Personal Names in the Murašû Documents* (Missoula, MT, 1976).

H. V. Hilprecht and A. T. Clay, *Business Documents of Murashū Sons of Nippur Dated in the Reign of Artaxerxes I (464-424 BC)* (Philadelphia, 1898).

On the Samaria Papyri:

F. M. Cross, "The Discovery of the Samaria Papyri," *BA* 26 (1963) 110-21.

P. W. and N. Lapp, "Discoveries in Wadi ed-Daliyeh," *Annual of the American Schools of Oriental Research* 41 (Missoula, MT, 1976).

On the Samaritans:

R. J. Bull, "The Excavations of Tell er-Ras on Mt. Gerizim," *BA* 31 (1968) 58-72.

R. J. Coggins, *Samaritans and Jews: The Origins of Samaritanism Reconsidered* (Oxford, 1975).

F. M. Cross, "Aspects of Samaritan Jewish History in Late Persian and Hellenistic Times," *HTR* 59 (1966) 201-11.

H. G. Kippenberg, *Garizim und Synagoge: Traditionsgeschichtliche Untersuchungen zur samaritanischen Religion der aramäischen Periode* (Berlin/New York, 1971), pp. 33-171.

R. Marcus, "Josephus on the Samaritan Schism," *Josephus* VI (Loeb Classical Library; London, 1937) 498-511.

J. D. Purvis, *The Samaritan Pentateuch and the Origin of the Samaritan Sect* (Cambridge, MA, 1968).

H. H. Rowley, "Sanballat and the Samaritan Temple," *BJRL* 38 (1955-56) 166-98 (= *Men of God* [London, 1963], pp. 246-76).

———, "The Samaritan Schism in Legend and History," in B. W. Anderson and W. Harrelson, eds., *Israel's Prophetic Heritage* (Festschrift J. Muilenburg; New York/London, 1962), pp. 208-22.

G. E. Wright, *Shechem* (New York, 1965), pp. 170-84.

Other Literature:

K. Galling, *Studien zur Geschichte Israels im persischen Zeitalter* (Tübingen, 1964).

R. Kittel, *Geschichte des Volkes Israel* I (Stuttgart, 1932[7]); II (Stuttgart, 1925[7]); III (Stuttgart, 1929[2]).

L. Y. Rahmani, "Silver Coins of the Fourth Century BC from Tel Gamma," *IEJ* 21 (1971) 158-60.

C. G. Tulland, "Josephus, Antiquities, Book XI, Corrections or Confirmation of Biblical Post-Exilic Records," *Andrews University Seminary Studies* 4 (1966) 176-92.

See also section I.A above by Dr. M. J. Mulder, which gives an overview of the history of Israel.

APPENDIX

Chronology of Neo-Babylonian Kings		Chronology of Persian Kings	
		ca. 560–530	Cyrus
605/04–562	Nebuchadnezzar II	530–522	Cambyses
562–560	Amel-Marduk	522–486	Darius I Hystaspes
	(Ewil-Merodak)	485–465	Xerxes I
560–556	Neriglissar	465–424	Artaxerxes I Longimanus
556	Labasji-Marduk	423	Xerxes II
555–539	Nabonidus	423–404	Darius II Nothus
		404–358	Artaxerxes II Mnemon
		358–337	Artaxerxes III Ochus
		337–336	Arses
		336–330	Darius III Codomannus

II

The Literature of the Old Testament

by H. A. Brongers

Introduction

In this part, I will consider the Old Testament from a literary standpoint. Though the thirty-nine books that together constitute the Old Testament are virtually all religious in content, it can hardly be denied that they are also literary products, conceived and constructed according to rules that are also followed in the writing of secular literature. In the books of the Old Testament we meet a great number of literary genres that are also familiar to us from other literature everywhere else in the world. It should be worthwhile to examine these genres more closely and to ask, for example, To what extent are they Israel's own literary possession? And what use did Israel make of foreign material (e.g., myths), and how did it make such forms serve the needs of its religious message?

Some introductory remarks are in order. Though it would be somewhat of an exaggeration to say that the present Old Testament, literarily speaking, is no more than a torso, the fact remains that Israel originally possessed more literature than is contained in the Old Testament. The so-called historical books repeatedly refer to sources that the author used: the Book of the Kings of Judah and Israel (2 Chr. 25:26), the Book of the Chronicles of the Kings of Judah (2 Kgs. 16:19), the Book of the Chronicles of the Kings of Israel (15:26, 31), the Book of the Acts of Solomon (1 Kgs. 11:41). These books were presumably annals kept at the courts, in which the events and deeds of the kings were faithfully recorded. The authors of Kings and Chronicles derived from these annals only what they felt was necessary for their story. Anyone wanting more detailed information about the life and deeds of a particular king could consult these official sources. Such sources, then, must have

been freely available. Unfortunately, nothing has been preserved of these writings.

That these sources often contained elaborate information is shown by a reference in 2 Chronicles 33:18-19: "Now the rest of the acts of Manasseh, and his prayer to his God, and the words of the seers who spoke to him in the name of Yahweh the God of Israel, behold, they are in the Chronicles of the Kings of Israel. And his prayer, and how God received his entreaty, and all his sin and his faithlessness, and the sites on which he built high places and set up the Asherim and the images, before he humbled himself, behold, they are written in the Chronicles of the Seers."

This last reference shows that, not only were there carefully kept, up-to-date annals, but biographies of prophets and seers were also in circulation, of which none has survived. The Old Testament mentions the chronicles of Samuel the seer, of Nathan the prophet, and of Gad the seer (1 Chr. 29:29); the prophecy of Ahijah the Shilonite; and the visions of Iddo the seer (2 Chr. 9:29). In addition, the chronicles of Shemaiah the prophet and of Iddo the Seer are mentioned (12:15). Somewhat comparable are the Elijah and Elisha stories, to which I return later.

There were also such books as the Book of Jashar (Josh. 10:13; 2 Sam. 1:18) and the Book of the Wars of Yahweh (Num. 21:14). Though our knowledge of these books is extremely limited, from the fact that only poetry is cited, it may be inferred that these collections described the great deeds of Yahweh in poetic form. Rather aptly, T. Vriezen compares the first-mentioned book with *Valerius's Gedenckclanck* (Vriezen and van der Woude, *Literatuur*). We could reasonably assume that there were other such works in addition to these mentioned. In the heyday of the Solomonic renaissance, for instance, more such works must have been produced than those we know of now. Finally it may be assumed that the great cultic centers such as Jerusalem, Bethel, and Dan provided a powerful stimulus toward the production of literature, particularly that of a religious character. This brief sketch is sufficient to indicate that Israel's literature must have been considerably more extensive than we might be led to think on the basis of what has been preserved in the Old Testament.

The question why none of these writings has survived is not easily answered. We know, however, that the formation of the canon has had a great and selective influence. Writings that were included in the canon were assured of continued existence. They were regularly copied for cultic use and carefully protected. Writings not part of this protective environment were apparently not able to keep up the struggle for survival for very long and quietly disappeared.

Though literary historians generally assume that prose is a more recent form of literature than poetry, this generalization can hardly be maintained in regard to Israel, where in antiquity both forms are found side by side. There is, for instance, no reason to assume that Judges 4, which offers a prose account of the battle against the Canaanites at Taanach, is more recent than the Song of Deborah in chapter 5, which describes the same event in poetry. Nevertheless, following accepted custom, I begin this survey of Israel's literature with the poetic genres. In the interest of a clear outline, I deal separately with secular and religious poetry, although recognizing that writers in ancient Israel did not maintain a rigid distinction between these two categories.

A. Secular Poetry

I follow here the division of Eissfeldt, who includes in secular poetry the work song, the harvest song, the drinking song, the marriage and love song, and the song of the watchmen.

1. THE WORK SONG

Songs could be heard in Israel on all kinds of occasions. Most kinds of work, such as the threshing of grain and the treading of grapes, were accompanied by the rhythmic singing of brief songs. Unfortunately none of this simple poetry has been preserved. Though not a work song in the strict sense of the word, the famed Song of the Well (Num. 21:17–18) should be mentioned here. This song, not uniquely Israelite (the genre is also known in ancient Arabia), was sung in order to make a dry well yield water again:

> Spring up, O well!—Sing to it!—
> the well which the princes dug,
> which the nobles of the people delved,
> with the scepter and with their staves.

2. THE HARVEST SONG

The harvest song is of course only a particular instance of the work song. Though also in this case no complete songs have survived, it is abundantly clear from such passages as Judges 9:27; 21:21 and Isaiah 16:10 that, especially during the grape harvest, there was a lot of singing. The vineyard, in fact, was the most prominent place for rejoicing. The threat of the prophet Amos (5:17) that, on the Day of Yahweh, there would be only wailing in the vineyards must therefore have hit the people hard. Such lamenting was the last thing one expected to hear in a vineyard!

The "joy at the harvest" mentioned in Isaiah 9:2 (3) must be associated with the barley and wheat harvest. In rejoicing at the bringing in of the harvest, Israel resembles peoples around the world.

3. THE DRINKING SONG

Like its neighbors, Israel had its drinking feasts and bacchanalia. The prophet Isaiah denounces those who, even early in the morning, reach for strong drink and who stay up till late at night to sing their drinking songs to the accompaniment of harp, tambourine, and flute (Isa. 5:11–12). In similar manner previously, Amos had announced the coming judgment to the rich who were feasting in Samaria (Amos 6:6–7). Only one of these drinking songs has been preserved in the Old Testament:

> Let us eat and drink,
> for tomorrow we die.
>
> (Isa. 22:13)

4. THE MARRIAGE AND LOVE SONG

Fortunately, more marriage and love songs have been preserved. In Israel there was a lot of singing at wedding parties, which used to last at least seven days (Gen. 29:27; Judg. 14:12) and were characterized by much tumult and noise. We are fortunate that a great many of these wedding songs have been preserved in the Canticles. They were sung in honor of bride and bridegroom. In some songs the bridegroom extols the beauty and charm of his wife-to-be, in other songs the bride sings of her husband-to-be. These oriental wedding and love songs contained language that was very vivid and flowery and often frankly sensuous. Yet Vriezen is right when he says that the collection in the Canticles, compared with much else in ancient Eastern literature, is overall as chaste and virtuous as it is honest and warm. A few passages demonstrate these qualities. Chapter 4 contains the song in which the bridegroom praises the beauty of the bride:

1. Behold, you are beautiful, my love,
      behold, you are beautiful!
   Your eyes are doves
      behind your veil.
   Your hair is like a flock of goats,
      moving down the slopes of Gilead.
2. Your teeth are like a flock of shorn ewes
      that have come up from the washing,
   all of which bear twins,
      and not one among them is bereaved.
3. Your lips are like a scarlet thread,
      and your mouth is lovely.
   Your cheeks are like halves of a pomegranate
      behind your veil.
4. Your neck is like the tower of David,
      built for an arsenal,
   whereon hang a thousand bucklers,
      all of them shields of warriors.
5. Your two breasts are like two fawns,
      twins of a gazelle,
      that feed among the lilies. . . .

7. You are all fair, my love,
      there is no flaw in you. . . .

9. You have ravished my heart, my sister,
      my bride,
   you have ravished my heart with a glance
      of your eyes,
   with one jewel of your necklace.
10. How sweet is your love, my sister, my bride!
      how much better is your love than wine,
   and the fragrance of your oils than any
      spice!

As the counterpart to these verses, the song of the bride praises the bridegroom (5:10–16):

10. My beloved is all radiant and ruddy,
      distinguished among ten thousand.
11. His head is the finest gold;
      his locks are wavy,
      black as a raven.
12. His eyes are like doves
      beside springs of water,

bathed in milk,
   fitly set.
13. His cheeks are like beds of spices,
      yielding fragrance.
   His lips are lilies,
      distilling liquid myrrh.
14. His arms are rounded gold,
      set with jewels.
   His body is ivory work,
      encrusted with sapphires.
15. His legs are alabaster columns,
      set upon bases of gold.
   His appearance is like Lebanon,
      choice as the cedars.
16. His speech is most sweet,
      and he is altogether desirable.
   This is my beloved and this is my friend,
      O daughters of Jerusalem.

Even though King Solomon himself is mentioned as the author, this collection of wedding and love songs would obviously never have been deemed worthy of a place in the canon if it had not first been interpreted allegorically. The rabbis indeed interpreted the Canticles as a spiritual song celebrating the love of Yahweh for his people. Later the Christian Church saw in it a reflection of the love of Christ for his church.

The songs brought together in Canticles are from different periods and exhibit a great similarity with comparable songs in Egypt and Babylonia. The background of the book can perhaps be better understood if it is compared with the Palestinian and Syrian love songs and wedding customs that were carefully examined by J. G. Wetzstein, who, for many years in the middle of the nineteenth century, was consul of Prussia in Damascus. Wetzstein noted, "The day before the wedding the bride dances a sword dance to the accompaniment of a song that is sung by those around her in which her jewels and personal charm are praised (*wasf*). In the week following the bridal night, the young couple are honored as king and queen. An elevation placed on the threshing floor serves as a throne" (Wetzstein, "Die syrische Dreschtafel," *Zeitschrift für Ethnologie* 5 [1873] 270–302). The German Old Testament scholar Karl Budde deserves the honor of having drawn the proper conclusions from these observations for better understanding the Canticles.

5. THE SONG OF THE WATCHMEN

In a country such as Israel, which, on account of its geographical location, was often threatened, constant vigilance was necessary. For this reason the Old Testament frequently mentions watchmen, individuals who were posted on elevated positions to sound an immediate alarm in case of invasion by enemies. We may assume that these watchmen, in order to pass the time while they were doing their routine work, tried to cheer each other with songs. It is just as likely that some of these songs may have had a more sober undertone. In Psalm 130, for example, Israel is exhorted to wait for the Lord "more than watchmen for the morning." Eissfeldt may be right when he conjectures that the songs of these watchmen also expressed their desire for the end of the long night. A counterpart to such a tone would be a passage such as Isaiah 52:8–9, through which Israel, by means of a prophecy of blessing, this time is made aware of a joyful message the watchmen are bringing:

Hark, your watchmen lift up their voice,
    together they sing for joy;
for eye to eye they see
    the return of Yahweh to Zion.
Break forth together into singing,
    you waste places of Jerusalem;
for Yahweh has comforted his people,
    he has redeemed Jerusalem.

Secular poetry also includes songs that have a meaning that is deeper than the affairs of everyday life, contents that are more or less ideological. Within this kind I include here the song of victory, the lament, and the mocking song.

6. THE SONG OF VICTORY

I alluded above to the Song of Deborah in Judges 5, one of the most beautiful songs of victory. This song describes a great triumph of the Israelites over the Canaanites in the vicinity of Taanach. The poem is so vivid and dramatic and possesses such a simple beauty that it conveys the impression of having been composed immediately after the battle, when events were still fresh in people's minds. As is customary in this genre, the poem begins by singing the praises of Yahweh, from whom alone the victory has come (vv. 2–5). It con-

tinues with a description of the distressing situation before the battle (6–8) and then exhorts various people to participate in the battle (9–12). Next the mobilization of the tribes is described (13–18), followed by the course of the battle (19–22) and the ruse of Jael (23–27). The poem ends with a kind of gleeful mocking of the despair of Sisera's mother, who looks in vain for the return home of her son (28–31).

Although thankful for the victory, the poet was also annoyed over the laxity of certain tribes who failed to heed the call to give help and who left the hard work to others:

15. Among the clans of Reuben
        there were great searchings of heart.
16. Why did you tarry among the sheepfolds,
        to hear the piping for the flocks? . . .
17. Gilead stayed beyond the Jordan;
        and Dan, why did he abide with the ships?
    Asher sat still at the coast of the sea,
        settling down by his landings.

It is remarkable that songs of victory are so often put into the mouths of women. The Song of Deborah is of course the great example. But in Exodus 15:21 we read that, after the Egyptians had perished in the Red Sea, Miriam took a timbrel and, together with the women who were with her, sang antiphonally:

Sing to Yahweh, for he has triumphed
    gloriously;
the horse and his rider he has thrown into
    the sea.

In Judges 11:34, the daughter of Jephthah came out with timbrels and dancing to meet her father after he returned home from his victory over the Ammonites. A song of victory doubtless was sung on that occasion, but unfortunately we have no written record of the song. It was women also, from "all the cities of Israel" (1 Sam. 18:6), who, again with singing and dancing, terribly upset and angered Saul. After his victory over the Philistines, they sang the refrain (v. 7):

Saul has slain his thousands,
and David his ten thousands.

I could also mention the Song of Hannah (1 Sam. 2:1–10) and the fact that women played a large and vocal role at weddings and funerals.

Psalm 18 is a song attributed to David. According to the superscription, he composed this psalm "on the day when Yahweh delivered him from the hand of all his enemies, and from the hand of Saul." In verses 38–43 (37–42) the following song of victory is put on his lips:

38. I pursued my enemies and overtook them;
    and did not turn back till they were
    consumed.
39. I thrust them through, so that they were not
    able to rise;
    they fell under my feet.
40. For thou didst gird me with strength for the
    battle;
    thou didst make my assailants sink
    under me.
41. Thou didst make my enemies turn their
    backs to me,
    and those who hated me I destroyed.
42. They cried for help, but there was none
    to save,
    they cried to Yahweh, but he did not
    answer them.
43. I beat them fine as dust before the wind;
    I cast them out like the mire of the streets.

7. THE LAMENT

At the outset a distinction should be made between the individual lament and the communal lament, the latter category including, for example, the so-called prophetic lament. Common to all these laments is the *qinah* rhythm: the lines are divided into two half-lines, of which the first contains three beats and the second two, giving the form its peculiar, somber tone. Characteristic of the funeral dirge is furthermore the repetition of the shout *ek* or *ekah*, "Alas!"

a. The Individual Lament

Impressive examples of a personal funeral dirge are David's lamentation over Saul and Jonathan (2 Sam. 1:19–27) and the lament David uttered over Abner at his funeral in Hebron (3:33–34). As a rule, the individual as well as the communal lament is found in a political context. David's elegy for Saul and Jonathan is more obviously personal than political, although his lament for Abner, while expressing his deep personal grief over Abner's death, also was evidently intended to remove any thought in people's minds that David was in some way responsible for his murder.

The high literary qualities of David's lament over Saul and Jonathan have often been mentioned. Together with the Song of Deborah, this elegy must be regarded as Israel's most important literary product. Such a high poetic level is not attained overnight and without effort by any people; a lengthy history must have preceded it. I am inclined to agree with Eissfeldt that its beginnings may go back to the pre-Canaanite Hebrews, that is, the Israelite tribes who were already settled in the land of Palestine before the conquest. Though the translation of a poem never measures up to the original and only suggests the texture, it is appropriate to give here David's famous lament in 2 Samuel 1.

19. Thy glory, O Israel, is slain upon thy
    high places!
    How are the mighty fallen!
20. Tell it not in Gath,
    publish it not in the streets of Ashkelon;
    lest the daughters of the Philistines rejoice,
    lest the daughters of the uncircumcised
    exult.
21. Ye mountains of Gilboa,
    let there be no dew or rain upon you,
    nor upsurging of the deep!
    For there the shield of the mighty was defiled,
    the shield of Saul, not anointed with oil.
22. From the blood of the slain,
    from the fat of the mighty,
    the bow of Jonathan turned not back,
    and the sword of Saul returned not empty.
23. Saul and Jonathan, beloved and lovely!
    In life and in death they were not divided;
    they were swifter than eagles,
    they were stronger than lions.
24. Ye daughters of Israel, weep over Saul,
    who clothed you daintily in scarlet,
    who put ornaments of gold upon your
    apparel.
25. How are the mighty fallen
    in the midst of the battle!
    Jonathan lies slain upon thy high places.
26. I am distressed for you, my brother
    Jonathan;
    very pleasant have you been to me;
    your love to me was wonderful,
    passing the love of women.

27. How are the mighty fallen,
and the weapons of war perished!

b. The Political Lament

In form and content the political funeral dirge shows great similarity with the individual lament. Illustrative are the so-called Lamentations of Jeremiah, which sing about the downfall of the city of Jerusalem in 586 B.C. Here also we encounter the familiar cry *ekah,* as well as the poignant contrast between past and present conditions. Chapter 1 begins:

1. How lonely sits the city
that was full of people!
How like a widow has she become,
she that was great among the nations!
She that was a princess among the cities
has become a vassal.

The lament here is for the city of Jerusalem, destroyed by violence of weapons and deserted by her inhabitants. The contrast between former glory and present desolation is further developed in chapter 4:

2. The precious sons of Zion,
worth their weight in fine gold,
how they are reckoned as earthen pots,
the work of a potter's hands!

5. Those who feasted on dainties
perish in the streets;
those who were brought up in purple
lie on ash heaps.

7. Her princes were purer than snow,
whiter than milk;
their bodies were more ruddy than coral,
the beauty of their form was like sapphire.

Whereas with the Lamentations we may assume that the poet sings about an event in the past, namely the destruction of Jerusalem, in the so-called prophetic laments the situation is as a rule quite different. Here laments are composed over rulers, cities, and countries, even though situations and living conditions are still perfectly normal and nothing seems to indicate a threatening future. For such poetry, scholars use the term *prophetic perfect,* which refers to the description of something that is expected to happen in the fu-

ture (e.g., the defeat of a country or the fall of a city) in terminology that evokes the impression that these calamities have already taken place. A good example of such a prophetic perfect is Amos 5:2:

Fallen, no more to rise,
is the virgin Israel;
forsaken on her land,
with none to raise her up.

When Amos took up this qinah over Israel, the land under Jeroboam II was enjoying a period of unprecedented prosperity; nothing indicated that it would soon end. Only to Amos had it been revealed that the catastrophe was imminent.

It is interesting to note the variety in the imagery used in the qinahs. In Lamentations 1:1 Jerusalem is compared to a widow, a woman bereft of husband and children. Here in Amos 5:2 Israel is a *betulah,* a young woman still at the beginning of her life. The terrifying character of the imagery may be sensed as we recall that an untimely death in Old Testament Israel was experienced as deeply painful and almost too much to bear. The death of a young woman, whose sun had set while it was still day (Jer. 15:9), seemed unbearable. On the other hand, one could accept the passing of someone who was old and full of days, for such a death belonged to the inevitable things in life.

Another example of a prophetic perfect occurs in Jeremiah 9:20–21 (21–22), in which the prophet urges the inhabitants of Jerusalem to teach each other:

20. For death has come up into our windows,
it has entered our palaces,
cutting off the children from the streets
and the young men from the squares.
21. Speak, "Thus says Yahweh:
'The dead bodies of men shall fall
like dung upon the open field,
like sheaves after the reaper,
and none shall gather them.'"

It is virtually certain that death here refers to pestilence. Like a person, it entered the house through the window. This lament is usually associated with a passage in the Ugaritic Baal epic, in which Baal expresses his fear that Mot, or Death, may sneak in through a window and kill him and his family (see A. Pohl, "Miszellen. 3. Jer. 9,20," *Bibl* 22 [1941] 36–37). A. van Selms (*Jeremia* I [POT; Nijkerk, 1972] 154) disputes this view, however, arguing that the passage is not about the intruding of Mot but about the daughters who break out of the house and are in danger of being caught by the god Yammu. Such political laments are perhaps intended as a threat, as a final call to the people to repent of the error of their way.

Ezekiel 19 contains a qinah about the rulers of Israel. As a lament it is unusual because it deals exclusively with an event that happened in the past. From the literary-critical perspective it is problematic, for it seems to consist of two parts. In the first part (vv. 2–9) the imagery is derived from the animal world; in the second (10–14), from the plant world. I quote from only the beginning of both parts:

2. What a lioness was your mother
     among lions!
   She couched in the midst of young lions,
     rearing her whelps.
3. And she brought up one of her whelps;
     he became a young lion,
   and he learned to catch prey;
     he devoured men.
4. The nations sounded an alarm against him;
     he was taken in their pit;
   and they brought him with hooks
     to the land of Egypt.

10. Your mother was like a vine in a vineyard
      transplanted by the water,
    fruitful and full of branches
      by reason of abundant water.
11. Its strongest stem became
      a ruler's scepter;
    it towered aloft
      among the thick boughs;
    it was seen in its height
      with the mass of its branches.
12. But the vine was plucked up in fury,
      cast down to the ground.

Unlike Zimmerli (*Ezekiel* I [Hermeneia; Philadelphia, 1979] 392), who regards verses 2–9 as the original poem and verses 10–14 as later additions to it, I believe that we have here two independent poems that later were combined by an editor, a process often noticed in the Psalter. In both poems

the subject is the same. The first sings about the sad fate of one of Judah's kings, using the imagery of a dangerous young lion who is finally caught in a pit; the second poem is about another Judean king who is compared to a fruitful and sprouting vine, which fails to bear fruit, however, because it is uprooted by enemies before it can produce.

Opinions differ as to the historical interpretation of these two laments. The original hearers will have had little difficulty understanding the imagery, but we can only guess at the meaning. It is generally assumed that the mother in verses 2 and 10 refers to the Davidic royal house. The young lion of verse 4 is identified with King Jehoahaz of Judah, whom Pharaoh Neco deported to Egypt in 609 B.C., where he also died (2 Kgs. 23:31–33; Jer. 22:10–12). The identification of the vine in verse 10 is more difficult. Here it is not certain whether Jehoiakim or Zedekiah is meant. It is interesting to note that some of the figures used are also found outside Israel. The image of the pit (v. 4), derived from the lion hunt, is found in the Gilgamesh Epic (1.109, 136), and that of the net (v. 8) in *Enuma elish* (4.41, 95), the Babylonian creation story.

The political laments so far discussed deal with the fall of the kingdom of Judah or the destruction of Jerusalem. In laments in Ezekiel, the object is more typically a foreign power or ruler. Consider the lament over Tyre in Ezekiel 27:3b–10, 26–36. The unity of this poem is interrupted by an extensive prose section (vv. 11–25) that continues and completes the description of the beautiful ship in verses 3b–10, symbolizing the city of Tyre. In the known world, Tyre was one of the most powerful trading cities, making it natural to express her power and glory in the image of a splendidly rigged merchant vessel:

3. O Tyre, you have said,
     "I am perfect in beauty."
4. Your borders are in the heart of the seas;
     your builders made perfect your beauty.
5. They made all your planks
     of fir trees from Senir;
   they took a cedar from Lebanon
     to make a mast for you.
6. Of oaks of Bashan
     they made your oars;
   They made your deck of pines

from the coasts of Cyprus,
   inlaid with ivory
7. Of fine embroidered linen from Egypt
   was your sail,
      serving as your ensign;
   blue and purple from the coasts of Elisha
   was your awning.
8. The inhabitants of Sidon and Arvad
      were your rowers;
   skilled men of Zemer were in you,
      they were your pilots.
9. The elders of Gebal and her skilled men
         were in you,
      caulking your seams;
   all the ships of the sea with their mariners
      were in you,
   to barter for your wares.
10. [Men of] Persia and Lud and Put
      were in your army as your men of war;
   they hung the shield and helmet in you;
      they gave you splendor.

This first part of the lament represents the first component of the contrasting scheme, stating how things were in the past, Tyre at the zenith of her glory. The second part (Ezek. 27:26–36) describes the shipwreck—in other words, the downfall of the city. I quote below only five verses from this part:

28. At the sound of the cry of your pilots
      the countryside shakes,
29. and down from their ships
      come all that handle the oar.
   The mariners and all the pilots of the sea
      stand on the shore
30. and wail aloud over you,
      and cry bitterly.
   They cast dust on their heads
      and wallow in ashes;
31. they make themselves bald for you,
      and gird themselves with sackcloth. . . .
32. In their wailing they raise a lamentation
      for you,
      and lament over you:
   "Who was ever destroyed like Tyre
      in the midst of the sea?"

It is not easy to determine the historical context of this lament. We do know that Nebuchadrezzar beleaguered Tyre for not less than thirteen years (585–572 B.C.), but nothing is known at that time concerning its capture, much less its destruction.

The capture of the city did not happen until the time of Alexander the Great, who managed to take it after a siege of seven months. That gives the pictured fall of the hated city (cf. Joel 4:4–8 [3:4–8]; Amos 1:9–10; Isaiah 23; Ezekiel 26–28; Zech. 9:3–5) the character of a prophetic perfect or, more informally, of wishful thinking. In Ezekiel 28:11–19 the object of the lament is the king of Tyre, whom the prophet regards as the personification of the city of Tyre. Though being similar to the previous lament in having the familiar contrast between past and present and in describing the reaction of the surrounding nations to the calamity, this lament shows in addition a mythological coloring:

12. You were the signet of perfection,
      full of wisdom
      and perfect in beauty.
13. You were in Eden, the garden of God;
      every precious stone was your covering,
   carnelian, topaz, and jasper. . . .
14. With an anointed guardian cherub I placed
      you;
   you were on the holy mountain of God;
   in the midst of the stones of fire you
      walked. . . .

Zimmerli (*Ezekiel* II [Hermeneia; Philadelphia, 1983] 258) correctly observes that, on account of this mythological choice of words, the poem is far removed from the traditional, individual lament. It soon begins to resemble the prophetic threat of judgment.

17. Your heart was proud because of your
         beauty;
      you corrupted your wisdom for the sake
         of your splendor.
   I cast you to the ground;
      I exposed you before kings,
      to feast their eyes on you.
18. By the multitude of your iniquities,
      in the unrighteousness of your trade
      you profaned your sanctuaries;
   so I brought forth fire from the midst of you;
      it consumed you,
   and I turned you to ashes upon the earth
      in the sight of all who saw you.

Political laments as a rule deal with hostile foreign nations. In the world of that time they were a familiar genre. Their primary significance, however, was political, not literary. Ezekiel 32 contains a clear example of the use of lament as a political weapon. Verse 16 instructs, "This is a lamentation which shall be chanted; the daughters of the nations shall chant it; over Egypt, and over all her multitude, shall they chant it, says the Lord GOD." The spoken word as well as the sung word possessed an almost magical power. A lament or a mocking song was an excellent means of boosting one's own morale and of breaking that of the enemy.

Ezekiel 32:2–15 is a lament over the pharaoh of Egypt. It is open question, however, to what extent the entire pericope may be regarded as a qinah. Some limit the lament to verse 2 and regard the rest as an expansion in prose, while others include only verses 2–8. The translation of the Dutch Bible Society is one of the few that print the whole pericope in metric form. In favor of this translation, verse 16 identifies the entire pericope as a qinah. It is conceivable, however, that the original lament has been enlarged by adding a prose section.

We should regard the pericope as a counterpart of Ezekiel 29:3–6, which clearly possesses the meter of a qinah:

3. Behold, I am against you,
    Pharaoh king of Egypt,
   the great dragon that lies
    in the midst of his streams,
   that says, "My Nile is my own;
    I made it."
4. I will put hooks in your jaws
    and make the fish of your streams stick to
     your scales;
   and I will draw you up out of the midst of
    your streams,
    with all the fish of your streams
    which stick to your scales.
5. And I will cast you forth into the wilderness,
    you and all the fish of your streams;
   you shall fall upon the open field,
    and not be gathered and buried.
   To the beasts of the earth and to the birds of
    the air
    I have given you as food.
6. Then all the inhabitants of Egypt shall know
    that I am Yahweh.

Even as in Ezekiel 32:2, the king of Egypt is pictured here in the image of a great dragon, or mon-

ster, residing in the streams of the Nile, where it considers itself master over all. By this dragon the crocodile must be meant. A hymn to Thutmose III reads, "I showed them your majesty as a crocodile, the terrible ruler over the water, the unapproachable." Yahweh, however, will soon obliterate this creature, almost certainly a reference to Pharaoh Hophra (588–568 B.C.). The monster, lifted out of its element and cast down on the land, will die a wretched death and become a prey to the vultures.

8. THE MOCKING SONG

Though political and religious mocking songs are not totally different categories, for practical reasons it is desirable to distinguish between them. The political mocking song is sometimes incorporated into a victory song, as in the conclusion of the Song of Deborah in Judges 5, in which the poet mocks the mother of Sisera as she anxiously awaits the homecoming of her son.

28. Out of the window she peered,
     the mother of Sisera gazed through the
      lattice:
    "Why is his chariot so long in coming?
     Why tarry the hoofbeats of his chariots?"
29. Her wisest ladies make answer,
     nay, she gives answer to herself,
30. "Are they not finding and dividing the
      spoil?—
     A maiden or two for every man;
    spoil of dyed stuffs for Sisera,
     spoil of dyed stuffs embroidered,
     two pieces of dyed work embroidered for
      my neck as spoil?"

Isaiah 14:4–21, generally regarded as the most powerful mocking song preserved in the Old Testament, has a more independent status. It is a song of tremendous expression, occasionally having a satirical character. G. B. Gray (ICC) divides it into five strophes: verses 4b–8, 9–11, 12–15, 16–20a, and 20b–21. The poem expresses joy at the fall of a tyrant who for years cruelly and brutally terrorized the world. It is difficult, however, to identify this tyrant. Though verse 4a relates the song to Babylon, nothing in the contents of the song itself supports such a reference. The descriptions are so general that it is equally possible to think of an Assyrian king. Thus P. Rost (*MAOG* 4 [1928–29] 175–79) proposed the last Assyrian king, Ashuruballit II, and A. Parrot (*Nineveh and the Old Testament* [London, 1955], pp. 49–51) proposed Sargon II. Because the poem lacks any indication of time, it is difficult to make a decision.

Both verse 4b and verse 12 begin with *ek*, "how," again an indication that there is no clear-cut formal distinction between a mocking song and a lament, or funeral dirge. In this mocking song, too, the contrast between past and present predominates. The song opens with a sigh of relief that the reign of terror has come to an end:

4. How the oppressor has ceased,
  the insolent fury ceased!
5. Yahweh has broken the staff of the wicked,
  the scepter of rulers,
6. that smote the peoples in wrath
  with unceasing blows,
  that ruled the nations in anger
  with unrelenting persecution.
7. The whole earth is at rest and quiet;
  they break forth into singing.
8. The cypresses rejoice at you,
  the cedars of Lebanon, saying,
  "Since you were laid low,
  no hewer comes up against us."

Arriving in the realm of the dead, the tyrant causes great amazement and consternation among the rulers already there. "How is it possible," they ask, "that you also have become like us and that the worms make ready to eat you?" (see vv. 9–11). These rulers now are not afraid to attack him with bitter mockery:

12. How you are fallen from heaven,
  O Day Star, son of Dawn!
  How you are cut down to the ground,
  you who laid the nations low!
13. You said in your heart,
  "I will ascend to heaven;
  above the stars of God
  I will set my throne on high;
  I will sit on the mount of assembly
  in the far north;
14. I will ascend above the heights of the clouds,
  I will make myself like the Most High."
15. But you are brought down to Sheol,
  to the depths of the Pit.
16. Those who see you will stare at you,

and ponder over you:
  "Is this the man who made the earth tremble
  who shook kingdoms,
17. who made the world like a desert
  and overthrew its cities. . . ?"

Everyone in the realm of the dead agrees that it was right that this enemy of humankind was not given an honorable burial:

18. All the kings of the nations lie in glory,
  each in his own tomb;
19. but you are cast out, away from your
    sepulchre,
  like a loathed untimely birth [like a
    loathsome branch?],
  clothed with the slain, those pierced by the
    sword,
  who go down to the stones of the Pit,
  like a dead body trodden under foot.
20. You will not be joined with them in burial,
  because you have destroyed your land,
  you have slain your people.
  May the descendants of evildoers
  nevermore be named!
21. Prepare slaughter for his sons
  because of the guilt of their fathers,
  lest they rise and possess the earth,
  and fill the face of the world with cities.

The target of the religious mocking song is usually the impotence of foreign gods. Such a song seldom stands by itself but is generally embedded in an address to another nation. The song typically contrasts the power and omnipotence of Yahweh, the Creator of heaven and earth, with the impotence and insignificance of the foreign gods, whose inability to do either good or evil means that one does not have to be afraid of them. This genre is predominantly found in prophetic literature, though occasionally also in the Psalms (e.g., 135:15–18).

A good example of the religious mocking song is found in Jeremiah 10:1–16, a pericope, incidentally, that most modern expositors believe is not from Jeremiah. The mocking song is embedded in a passage in which the author tries to convince his readers how absurd it is to fear the images of foreign gods. Although this warning may seem strange to us, the fact that the prophets regularly return to this theme proves that, for many people in those days, such fear was a terrible reality. According to the prophet, however, such fear is entirely unfounded. For what do these images amount to?

3. The customs [i.e., idols] of the peoples are false.
   A tree from the forest is cut down,
       and worked with an axe by the hands of a craftsman.
4. Men deck it with silver and gold;
       they fasten it with hammer and nails
       so that it cannot move.
5. Their idols are like scarecrows in a cucumber field,
       and they cannot speak;
   they have to be carried,
       for they cannot walk.
   Be not afraid of them,
       for they cannot do evil,
       neither is it in them to do good.

B. Religious Poetry

The religious mocking song constitutes a good transition to the much broader genre of religious poetry, to which especially the Psalms belong. It is important to note that the Old Testament includes more psalms than just the 150 in the Psalter, such as Hezekiah's "writing" (Isa. 38:10–20), Hannah's song (1 Sam. 2:1–10), Jonah's prayer (Jonah 2:3–10 [2–9]), Habakkuk's prayer (Hab. 3:2–19), and the song of praise in Isaiah 12. Psalm 18 appears in 2 Samuel 22, and Psalm 105 is found in 1 Chronicles 16. Quotations from a psalm are found in Amos 4:13; 5:8–9; and 9:6. It seems likely that all these psalms were originally independent of the Psalter and were used by a writer or editor as best seemed to fit the context. Thus the editor of the book of Isaiah regarded the psalm now found in Isaiah 12 as a solemn conclusion to chapters 1–11. The psalms cited here from 1 Samuel and Jonah also illustrate the closing function of the psalm.

In its present form the book of Psalms is a collection of five originally separate books of religious songs. These five books (calling to mind the five books of Moses) comprise Psalms 2–41, 42–72, 73–89, 90–106, and 107–50. The First Psalm was later added as an introduction to the entire collection, while Psalm 150 constitutes an eloquent conclusion. The individual books end with doxologies.

Behind this more or less formal division, however, one can observe many subgroupings that were later included in these five books. I mention here only the songs of Korah (Psalms 42–49; 84–85; 87–88); those of Asaph (50; 73–83); the songs of ascent, or pilgrim songs (120–34); and the Hallelujah psalms (104–106; 111–17; 135–36; 146–50).

Modern research, to which especially the name of Hermann Gunkel is connected, has categorized the psalms according to contents and distinguishes no less than twelve groups (Gunkel and Begrich, *Einleitung*):

1. Hymns (33, 65, 67–68, 96, 100, 103–105, 117, 145–50)
2. Songs praising Yahweh's kingship (47, 93, 96–99)
3. Royal psalms (2, 18, 20–21, 45, 72, 110, 132)
4. Laments of the people (44, 74, 79–80, 83)
5. Individual laments (3, 6, 13, 22, 38, 39, 42–43, 51, 61, 63, 86, 102, 130, 140–43)
6. Psalms of blessing and cursing (1, 28, 34, 137)
7. Pilgrimage songs (84, 120–34)
8. Songs of victory (18, 46, 66, 76)
9. Individual songs of thanksgiving (9, 18, 32, 107, 116)
10. Songs of thanks by Israel (67, 124, 135)
11. Historical psalms (78, 95 [end], 105–106, 114)
12. Praises of the law (19 [end], 119)

Though this division has proven its value as a working hypothesis, other analyses are possible. Many psalms have a mixed character and could just as well be categorized differently. Psalm 105, for example, is mentioned above in groups 1 and 11 (hymns and historical psalms). Furthermore, some psalms are composed of more than one song (19, 24, and 27).

Particularly in the twentieth century the Psalms have received diligent and intensive study. This research has yielded much information about Israel's treasure of psalmody. Though scholars have demonstrated formal similarities especially between the psalms of lament and Sumerian and Babylonian psalms and the Ugaritic myths, the Psalter must nevertheless be regarded as an independent entity. "Observing the rigid composition of the Babylonian psalms and comparing it with the free composition of the Hebrew psalms, it must be acknowledged that Hebrew psalmody went entirely its own way" (Vriezen and van der Woude, *Literatuur,* p. 263). In content, though, Hebrew religious poems often show great similarity to the comparable poetry of other nations. Note three examples that appear in Falkenstein and von Soden (*Hymnen und Gebete,* pp. 269, 272, 247).

Compare the following psalm of lament of King Ashurbanipal (see ill. 60) with many individual biblical psalms of lament:

To God and men, dead and living, I did good.
Why [nevertheless] do I suffer illness, deep
  grief, loss of strength, and misfortune?
In the land discord remains, in the house
  there continually are sharp quarrels.
Constantly I am confronted with revolt and
  rebellious language.
Deep anxiety and physical suffering have
  bent my posture;
  With complaints of pain I fill all my days.
On the [feast] day of the city god, on the
  feast of the month I am sad:
  death holds me in its grip, I am in great
  need.
With pain in my heart and continually
  moaning I spend my days.
  It has made me so tired: "O God, give [all
  this] to those who do not fear God; show
  me, however, your light!"
How long, O God, will you do this to me?
  I am treated as one who does not fear god
  and goddess!

No less illustrative is the following fragment of an Akkadian prayer for forgiveness of sins:

Who can maintain that he has never sinned
  against his God,
  who has always obeyed the command?
All mankind knows what sin is!
I, your servant, have repeatedly sinned in
  many ways. . . .
  Repeatedly I spoke lies, did not take
  seriously my sin.
  Evil-filled words were always on my lips;
  you know all that!

My God, who created me, whatever was
  abominable I took to myself,
  walked in places where people may
  not walk,
  always did wrong things.
Upon your large possessions I cast my eyes,
  your precious silver I desired.
I lifted up my hand, knocked over what had
  not fallen;
  though unclean, I always went into your
  temple.
What was most repulsive to you, I regularly
  did;
  everything that displeases you I rashly
  ignored. . . .
Angered in my heart, I scoffed at your
  divinity;
  again and again committed conscious and
  unconscious sin;
  went everywhere my own way and so fell
  prey to sin.
My God, your heart . . . ; may it find rest!
The goddess who was angry, may she be fully
  satisfied!
Be done with your wrath, which was so
  great; be reconciled to me.
However numerous my sins, forgive my
  transgression;
  though my iniquities may be seven in
  number, may your heart find rest
  [concerning me]!
Though my wrongs be ever so numerous,
  be all the more gracious!

The affinity between Hebrew psalms and Sumerian and Babylonian psalms is clearest in the genre of the psalms of lament. Hymns, for example, show much less similarity. Compare the following hymn of King Ashurbanipal to the sungod Shamash with any hymn from the Psalter:

[. . . rays] of radiance of the great gods, light
  of the earth, illuminator of the world,
[Shamash,] highly exalted judge, creator of
  all that is below and above!
[Like] a clay tablet you by your light survey
  all lands together;
make [for him who] does not tire seeing the
  sacrifices,
each day anew the decisions of the dwellers
  in heaven and on earth.
[As soon as by] your [rising] the fire glow
  lights up,

the stars in the firmament all day long do not
send forth their light;
[in the firmament] you alone [then] shine in
all your glory,
none among the gods can be compared with
you.
With your father, Sin, you take counsel and
you give your order.
Without your foreknowledge Anu and Enlil
do not take counsel together.
Ea, about whom is the decision, in the depths
of the water looks up to your eyes;
the ears of all the gods are directed toward
your brilliant rising.
The conjurers heap up the incense, bring
pure sacrifices of bread, and [kneel]
before you that you may pass by with the
evil omens;
these observing the sacrifices [pray] that you
will make their hands suitable for
handling whatever the observance of the
sacrifice has brought to light.
[Him,] your [servant] Ashurbanipal, whose
royal regiment you have commanded by
a sacrifice observance, who [observes]
your radiant divine [light]
and beautifully gives shape to everything
your divinity is entitled to,
who [praises] your [illustrious deeds],
glorifies your greatness before the people
here and everywhere.
[Look to him in your faithfulness,] pronounce
his judgment, make a favorable
arrangement for him,
[give life] to him, in order that, guided by
your radiant light, he may go his way in
prosperity and in justice may [always]
guard the subjects you will give him!
[Because he has built your sanctuary] and let
you live therein with joy, may his heart
always rejoice, his heart be happy, [and
he] be satisfied through life!
[A future ruler, who] will sing this [song for]
Shamash and [thereby] pronounce the
name of Ashurbanipal,
may all the days of his life in joy and
gladness be concerned about the subjects
of Enlil!
[One . . .] who memorizes this passage [and]
praises the judge of the gods, Shamash,
may he be held in honor by his [god];
may what he says be agreeable to the
people.

Whoever [however] suppresses this song and
does not praise Shamash, the light of the
great gods, and also substitutes the name
of Ashurbanipal for that of another king,
may his music on stringed instruments
not be pleasing to people;
his song of praise be like the prick of a thorn!

This poem clearly has a hybrid character. It is a
song of praise to the sun-god Shamash, whose
power and greatness are highly extolled. The end
of the hymn, however, leaves no doubt that the
royal singer expects the recitation of this song not
only to honor Shamash but also to increase his
personal well-being. The biblical hymns, in contrast, solely concern the praise of the greatness
and glory of the God of Israel and typically do not
even mention the personal interests of the poet.

The superscriptions of the Psalms have thus far
resisted satisfactory scholarly analysis. B. D. Eerdmans thought they could be explained on the basis
of the contents of the psalm. He proposed, for example, that *al mut-laben* in Psalm 9 should not be
translated "according to 'The Death of the Son'"
but "at the death of N. N., by the son" (*The Hebrew Book of Psalms* [OTS 4; Leiden, 1947],
p. 118). The superscription would thus indicate
that the psalm was to be recited at the death of a
father. It is clear that certain psalms were indeed
composed for specific occasions. Psalm 102, for
example, is identified as "a prayer of one afflicted,
when he is faint and pours out his complaint
before Yahweh." This psalm could thus be uttered
as a ritual prayer by anyone in difficulties.

Another difficulty is the dating of the Psalms.
The superscriptions suggesting a specific occasion
for the composition of particular psalms are from
much later times and have no historical value.
Only the postexilic psalms 126 and 137 indicate
clearly the historical setting of their composition.
The bulk of the psalms are timeless: they may be
old or recent. Many questions still await an answer, for instance, the connection of the Psalms
with the cult. Since, after the Exile, the Psalter
served as the songbook for temple worship, some
scholars have suggested that the Psalms were
composed specifically for use in public worship.
From the fact that Psalms 38 and 70 have the
heading "for the memorial offering," and Psalm
100 "for the thank offering," however, it cannot

be deduced with certainty that these psalms were actually composed for the sake of the cult. Such headings demonstrate only that they were later considered suitable for the stated purpose. The grounds of this decision are not now clear to us. In suggesting that the contents of these psalms do not necessarily point in the direction of the cult, we are in danger of reading the Psalter through Western spectacles. We must now leave these informal observations and continue our investigation of the literary genre.

Here we consider Hebrew poetry more generally. Its most striking characteristic is the parallelism of the parts of the verse, a feature also found in the literature of Egypt, Ugarit, and Babylon. This stylistic phenomenon was first discussed by Robert Lowth in his book *De Sacra Poesi Hebraeorum* (1753). Three or four types of parallelism are usually distinguished: synonymous (or repeating), antithetical (or opposing), synthetic (or supplementary), and climactic (or step).

In synonymous parallelism, a verse consists of two lines, each of which expresses the same thought in about the same words:

Have mercy on me, O God, according to thy
  steadfast love;
  according to thy abundant mercy blot out
  my transgressions.
Wash me thoroughly from my iniquity,
  and cleanse me from my sin!
For I know my transgressions,
  and my sin is ever before me.

(Ps. 51:3–5 [1–3])

Other examples are Psalms 2:1–3; 36:6, 9–13 (5, 8–12); 103:8–10; 114.

In the second type of parallelism, the lines state a particular thought in positive and then negative form:

Better is a little that the righteous has
  than the abundance of many wicked.
For the arms of the wicked shall be broken;
  but Yahweh upholds the righteous.

(Ps. 37:16–17)

See also Psalms 1:6; 7:10 (9); 20:9 (8); 27:10; 32:10.

In the third type, the second line of the verse supplements the first:

When Yahweh restored the fortunes of Zion,
  we were like those who dream.

(Ps. 126:1)

See also Psalm 23; 25:6, 8, 10–12, 15–17; 51:16–17 (14–15).

In the fourth kind of poetic parallelism, the second line repeats a word from the first line:

Ascribe to Yahweh, O heavenly beings,
  ascribe to Yahweh glory and strength.

(Ps. 29:1)

Yahweh reigns; he is robed in majesty;
  Yahweh is robed, he is girded with strength.
Yea, the world is established; it shall never be
  moved.

(Ps. 93:1)

Synonymous parallelism is by far the most common type in the Psalter. In such parallelism we should not put the greatest emphasis on mere repetition but should note instead a progression in thought, for which the apt term *thought rhyme* has been coined. Because of their interest in matching thoughts, the Jews apparently felt no need to rhyme words.

Genuine composition of strophes, in the sense of a carefully constructed rhythmic unit, is likewise not found in Hebrew poetry. Vriezen finds a clear strophic form in certain psalms, for example, Psalms 42 and 43. According to van der Ploeg (*Psalmen* [BOT; Roermond, 1971], p. 27), however, such supposed structure is not original. The phenomenon can be explained by seeing it as an attempt on the part of the psalmist to stretch the parts of the verse out to two (and sometimes more) verses. Only seldom is such a form consistently and convincingly carried through in an entire poem.

Much study and discussion have gone into the question whether Hebrew poetry has meter. Many scholars answer this question negatively, though making an exception for the obvious qinah, or lament, meter. Sievers and Hölscher in particular have argued for a fixed metric scheme in Hebrew poetry, a conclusion that only a few researchers share. Van der Ploeg has forcefully argued against this hypothesis, pointing out that European scholars have failed to see that the ancient poetry of Israel was not recited in a manner familiar to us.

> This recitation, or performance, was always melodious, with modulations (think for example of the old Gregorian chant), not bound to melodies with fixed measure and length. In the composition and singing of the Psalms there was thus no need of a meter. In singing the stress was, however, put on significant words. The nature of the Hebrew language (many words of approximately the same length) and the desire to give the two parts of a verse the same length (except the above mentioned lament rhythm) had as its consequence that the number of words, or the number of words with stress, became about the same in the two parts of the verse. This has nothing to do with "meter," and therefore it is absent from Hebrew poetry. (*Psalmen,* p. 26)

Vriezen and van der Woude's judgment is quite similar. They tentatively conclude that,

> in the case of Eastern poetry, particularly Hebrew poetry, it is not so much the measure but the rhythm that is essential. The poetry is governed not by short and long syllables that alternate according to a specific sequence but by a specific rhythm, an alternation of stressed and unstressed syllables. The length of the syllables has no immediate effect on it, nor does the number of unstressed syllables before or after the one with stress. The important matter is a certain relationship of the number of stressed syllables. The relationship—that is the difficult point—is not always constant. Not only are there a variety of relationships in the various poems (that would be understandable, and one might therefore speak of various measures), but also within a specific poem there are often various relationships. It appears that Hebrew poetry was not rigidly determined by this numerical relationship and exhibits no more than a free rhythmic movement. (*Literatuur,* p. 58)

C. Poetic Stories

Though virtually all the literary genres that are found in Israel are also represented in Ugarit, Egypt, and Mesopotamia, one type that is found in other nations is missing in Israel: the epic. Such an omission is perhaps not surprising. An epic narrates the deeds of one or more heroes, as in the Babylonian Gilgamesh Epic, for example, which is a straightforward hero tale. But though Israel had its heroes too—we have only to think of such men as Gideon, Jephthah, David, and Jonathan—it is not their exploits that are sung as much as it is the praises of Yahweh, who enabled them to win the victory. In Israel the primary concern is always the glorification of God, in light of which the individual must draw back. Believers are continually exhorted to praise *Yahweh* and to sing a new song to *him,* "for he has done marvelous things! His right hand and his holy arm have given him victory" (Ps. 98:1). Such a theocentric climate left no room for a flourishing epic.

On the other hand, we must not conclude that nations outside Israel possessed no awareness that, in the final analysis, great human achievements could be accomplished only with the help and assistance of the deity. In the Assyrian decorative inscriptions the king repeatedly had his court poet emphasize the fact that he went to battle trusting only in the help and support of Ashur or Ishtar and that victory was achieved only because the enemy became confused and unable to offer resistance because of the fearful light radiated by these gods. Once this truth had been conceded, however, enough room was left for emphasizing the personal heroism displayed by the king in the battle. The contrast with Israel is evident. For the Jews, victories and deliverances are

exclusively due to the action and intervention of the God of Israel.

After this understandably brief discussion of the epic literary genre in Israel, we turn to several other genres, discussed here under the heading "Poetic Stories." I consider in order the myth, the fairy tale, the fable, the saga, the legend, the parable, the anecdote, and the novelette.

1. THE MYTH

The situation in Israel in regard to the myth is similar to that described concerning the epic. A myth is a story that happens in the world of the gods. In view of Israel's monotheistic faith, which lies at the basis of all its stories, we might well expect not to find a fully developed myth. Israel, after all, has only one God—Yahweh, the God of the fathers. On the other hand, Israel did not live on an isolated island. It was surrounded by people who had a rich mythology. Much of this literature must have been known in Israel, and there are abundant indications that Israel's poets and prophets made extensive use—albeit a critical use—of foreign mythological material in preparing their own messages. Though we do find some purely illustrative use of mythology in the Old Testament, in general the authors' purpose was apologetic in nature. In many cases a historicizing process also took place.

Much of the material available to us betrays acquaintance with foreign creation myths. Mention first should be made of the Babylonian creation epic *Enuma elish* ("When above"). In this poem the creation of heaven and earth was preceded by a gigantic battle between the (masculine) god

Marduk and the (feminine) monster of the chaos Tiamat.

> They entered the arena against each other, Tiamat
> and the wisest of the gods, Marduk.
> They advanced for battle, got ready for the fight.
> The Lord spread his net and enveloped her.
> The hurricane, which was following him, he unleashed;
> Tiamat opened her mouth to devour him,
> but he made the hurricane enter it so that she could no more close her lips.
> The furious winds took possession of her body;
> her heart was paralyzed, she opened wide her mouth.
> He shot the arrow, tore apart her body;
> he pierced her bowels, cut her heart in pieces.
> After he had subdued her, he extinguished her life,
> cast away her corpse and stood on top of it.

The poem records in passing that the fate of Tiamat's helpers was no better, after which it continues:

> [Then] he returned to Tiamat, whom he had defeated.
> The Lord stood on Tiamat's legs;
> with his merciless weapon he cleaved her skull,
> cut the arteries of her blood and had the north wind bring her to a secret place.
> Then the Lord rested to consider the corpse
> and how he might divide the torso to make something artistic out of it.
> He split her like a shellfish into two parts;
> the first half he set apart, from which he made the firmament.
> He made a bar, posted guards in front of it
> and ordered them to make sure the waters could not escape.

Elsewhere in the poem Tiamat is called the Mother of the Deep, a designation of the primeval waters. In this view creation is actually nothing but the victory over the chaotic powers that threaten the life of gods and people. Certain poetic passages indicate that Israel was familiar with these ideas. The Hebrew word for "primeval waters" is *tehom,* related to the Babylonian *tia-*

mat. In biblical passages the chaos waters are also personified. We read, for example, in Psalm 104:

> 6. Thou didst cover [the earth] with Tehom ["the deep"] as with a garment;
> the waters stood above the mountains.
> 7. At thy rebuke they fled;
> at the sound of thy thunder they took to flight.
> 8. The mountains rose, the valleys sank down to the place which thou didst appoint for them.
> 9. Thou didst set a bound which they should not pass,
> so that they might not again cover the earth.

The enclosing of the primeval waters, alluded to in verse 9 above, was a familiar motif in the mythology of the entire ancient Near East. It is not surprising that we can still detect traces of it in biblical passages (e.g., Jer. 5:22; Job 26:10; 38:10-11).

As personified chaotic power, Tehom is also mentioned in the familiar theophany in Habakkuk 3:

> 10. The mountains saw thee, and writhed;
> the raging waters swept on;
> Tehom ["the deep"] gave forth its voice,
> it lifted its hands on high.

In this passage the personification of Tehom as a man is remarkable and is difficult to explain. Such personification is perhaps related to the fact that the theophany in its present form has the traits of a thunder theophany. "He is the God who manifests himself in the thunderstorm (Isa. 19:1; Ps. 18:12 [11]; 104:3), before whom the heaven darkens itself, so that only the brilliance of the lightning, catapulted like arrows or spears, cleaves the dark (Ps. 18:15 [14]; 77:18 [17]); he calls forth the cloudburst and makes the earth quake (cf. Judg. 5:4-5)" (T. H. Robinson and F. Horst, *Die zwölf kleinen Propheten* [HAT; Tübingen, 1938], p. 181).

Such names as Yam (Sea), Tannin, Rahab, Leviathan, and Nahash (Serpent) also suggest a connection with Canaanite and Babylonian myths. In Job 38 Yahweh asks Job:

> 8. Who shut in the sea with doors,
> when it burst forth from the womb;

9. when I made clouds its garment,
    and thick darkness its swaddling band,
10. and prescribed bounds for it,
    and set bars and doors,
11. and said, "Thus far shall you come, and no
    farther,
    and here shall your proud waves be
    stayed"?

The motif of power restrained is also found in Job 7:12, where Yam is, however, parallel with Tannin.

In the passing of time all these chaos myths were demythologized and historicized. Rahab and Tannin thus became figurative names for Egypt (Isa. 30:7; 51:9–10). In the latter passage the drying up of the Red Sea is interpreted as Yahweh's victory over Rahab/Tannin, which in this passage still refer to the chaotic powers:

Awake, awake, put on strength,
  O arm of Yahweh;
awake, as in days of old,
  the generations of long ago.
Was it not thou that didst cut Rahab in pieces,
  that didst pierce Tannin ["the dragon"]?
Was it not thou that didst dry up the sea,
  the waters of Tehom ["the great deep"];
that didst make the depths of the sea a way
  for the redeemed to pass over?

Here the myth is historicized, and the mention of Rahab and Tannin serves only to induce Yahweh to manifest his power again, as he did earlier when he fought these monsters of the chaos.

Another interesting example of demythologization is found in Psalm 104:26, where Leviathan (liwyatan) has completely lost his original mythological terror (cf. Isa. 27:1; Ps. 74:14), has been reduced to the size of a great fish, and functions only as a plaything for Yahweh. Amos 9:2–4, which speaks of the Serpent (nahash) on the bottom of the sea, perhaps preserves the memory of a Babylonian myth of the great serpent, of which only a fragment has survived (see H. A. Brongers, *Die Scheppingstradities bij de Profeten* [Amsterdam, 1945], p. 181).

Besides such creation myths, of which remnants are preserved in the prophetic and poetic literature, the Old Testament contains traces of several other kinds of myths. In the taunt of the king of Babylon, preserved in Isaiah 14, the king is compared with Helel, the morning star, who announces the dawn (v. 12). The aspirations of the king were as great as the aspirations of that planet, who desired to rise above the clouds and make himself equal to the Most High (elyon). For that brazenness Helel was severely punished by being cast out of heaven by Elyon. Here the prophetic poet has clearly incorporated this fragment of an ancient myth into his mocking song.

A similar use of myth occurs in Ezekiel 28:12–19. There the king of Tyre is described as a cherub, formerly residing on the mountain of the gods but now banned from it, apparently also as punishment for his brazen behavior. Reminiscences of old myths are also found in the paradise story in Genesis 2, with its two trees that can impart divine knowledge and eternal life, and in 5:24, where it is said that Enoch did not see death because God took him. This latter story exhibits unmistakable affinity with a passage in the deluge story on the eleventh tablet of the Gilgamesh Epic, where it is said that, after the flood, the Babylonian king Utnapishtim was brought to the island of the saved and thus rescued from the power of death (de Liagre Böhl, *Gilgamesjepos,* p. 96).

In recent years much has been written about the literary background of the biblical story of the Flood. It used to be thought that this background was especially the Babylonian deluge story on the above-mentioned eleventh tablet of the Gilgamesh Epic. Nowadays scholars are more inclined to associate the Genesis story with the Atra-hasis Epic (see ill. 14), which has been studied especially by W. G. Lambert and A. R. Millard. The Atra-hasis Epic may be regarded as a more recent and more detailed version of the flood story in the Gilgamesh Epic, and it also offers much more. The story runs about parallel with the stories in Genesis 2–9. It begins with the Creation, explaining that people are needed to serve the gods and to provide them with all they need. When more and more people are born, however, the noise level on earth is increased and Enlil becomes enraged. After some failed attempts to decimate humanity, he finally resorts to drowning them in a flood. Just as in the biblical story, so here only one person is saved from the destruction—Atra-hasis.

Lambert and Millard have demonstrated in their interesting studies that this ancient story has repeatedly been reworked; proof is found in the many editions of the text. Though the biblical writer must have been acquainted with the Atrahasis Epic, in its present form his flood story stands closer to the Babylonian version of the Gilgamesh Epic, with its many similarities and differences. He made drastic changes in the story, including the elimination of all evidence of polytheism and the attribution of an ethical cause to the catastrophe.

Finally there is the remarkable story of the marriage of the sons of God with the daughters of men in Genesis 6:1–4, perhaps the most mythological pericope in the entire Old Testament. Procksch called it a *rissiger erratischer Block* ("cracked, stray boulder") that, due to its non-Israelite content, is entirely out of keeping with the prehistory (*Die Genesis übersetzt und erklärt* [KAT; Leipzig, 1913], p. 57). Of this myth, too, which has been reworked by the biblical writer, we have only a fragment. Apparently it was a so-called etiological myth, a story that seeks to explain the origin of "the mighty men that were of old, the men of renown." It thus concerns heroes and later was perhaps extended to include people of unusual stature, whom others could not believe were the product of a normal union and who were therefore assumed to have issued from a union of divine beings with ordinary, mortal women. The Israelites, themselves short in stature, looked up with awe to much taller people, as for example the inhabitants of Hebron and vicinity at the time of the conquest of the land, whom they therefore called giants (Num. 13:33; Deut. 2:10–11).

As the myth now lies before us, it seems to try to explain two phenomena: the origin of the mythical heroes, the men of renown in hoary antiquity, and the presence on earth of unusually tall people. The story is fragmentary, of course, and leaves a confused impression. At all costs the biblical writer wanted to include the myth in his account, while on the other hand he urgently needed a suitable introduction to the story of the Flood that he wanted to tell next. The result was that the author had the myth provide the reason for the Deluge—namely, the wickedness of humankind. Moreover, he wanted to explain why the human life span was limited. As a punishment for human sin, the maximum age was set at 120 years. In the present con-

text the transgression can refer only to the illicit sexual relations between the daughters of men and the sons of God. We may wonder, however, whether the women could be blamed for this transgression. How could they have resisted the violence of the sons of God? Furthermore, in the flood story, the cause of the catastrophe is the universal wickedness of humankind (Gen. 6:5), not just the sins of some of the women. The transition to the story of the Flood is thus not very smooth.

2. THE FAIRY TALE

Hempel correctly characterizes the fairy tale as "the most original story form, the magic faith prevailing at a certain time, deeply rooted in those far off days, when man did not yet see a cleft between himself and the animal, but perceived himself with his mind, will, and ability in such a story" (*Literatur,* p. 87). In fairy tales as well, Israel shared in the experience of nations around the world, for the Old Testament contains many examples of this genre. A particularly fascinating category is the fairy tales in which an animal, often presented as being able to speak, is set in a certain relationship to humans. In the Old Testament fairy tales the animals have primarily a serving function: the big fish who swallows Jonah so that he will not drown (Jonah 2:1, 11 [1:17; 2:10]), the donkey who protects Balaam from mortal danger (Num. 22:21–34), the cows hitched to the cart carrying the ark who bring their guides straight to Beth-shemesh (1 Sam. 6:7–12), and the ravens who feed the prophet Elijah (1 Kgs. 17:6). Only in the story of the serpent in paradise who tempts Eve to become disobedient to God is the animal a power hostile to human beings (Gen. 3:1–15).

Other kinds of fairy tales could also be mentioned. The magic fairy tale, for example, is illustrated by the stories of Aaron's rod that changed into a serpent (Exod. 7:8–12) and the mantle with which Elisha parted the water of the Jordan (2 Kgs. 2:8). Examples of the good-luck fairy tale include the story of the younger brother who, contrary to all expectations, bypassed all his older brothers and was called to be king (1 Sam. 16:11–12) and the no less surprising experience of Saul, who, searching for lost donkeys, finds instead a kingdom (9:1–10:1). Finally, we have the wish fairy tale: the flour in the pot was not used up, and the oil in the jar did not run dry (1 Kgs. 17:14).

Closer investigation of the Old Testament shows that, even as with the myth, there is nowhere a fully developed fairy tale; at best, there are fairy tale *motifs*. More important, these motifs are auxiliary and have no independent significance. They serve the proclamation and are only a part of the story that tells Yahweh's way with his people. In this redemptive-historical narrative the fairy tale serves an illustrative function. It would have been impossible for the Old Testament to give it an autonomous setting.

3. THE FABLE

Closely related to the fairy tale is the fable. Though Egypt and Mesopotamia offer many examples of fables involving animals, the two fables found in the Old Testament deal with plants: the tree fable in Judges 9 and the fable of the thistle and the cedar in 2 Kings 14. Again, they are told not for any independent literary significance but because of their place in a historical context in which they serve a secondary function.

In Judges 9 the historical context is the dispute concerning the kingship of Abimelech in Shechem. Having assassinated his brothers, whom he presumed to be potential rivals, and believing that he had a firm grip on the throne, Abimelech suddenly saw himself threatened by his youngest brother, Jotham, who had escaped the bloodbath and wisely had hidden himself for a while. Jotham naturally was not at all pleased with the violence done by his brother, but he was unable to do anything about Abimelech's seizure of power. Instead he acted indirectly, by telling a fable from which the Shechemites would have to draw their own conclusions. By means of that strategy he tried to undermine Abimelech's position and depict his kingship as illusory. The fable starts with the announcement that, at a certain time, the trees agreed to anoint a king over them. After the olive tree, the fig tree, and the vine had in turn declined the honor, nothing remained but to offer the kingship to the thornbush. The thornbush accepted, but only after stipulating certain conditions. The

moral of the fable is clear: Abimelech was not the most qualified king, and not much good could be expected from him. Of all the available options, the Shechemites picked the worst. For reasons that are not clear to us, Jotham nevertheless saw a bright aspect in the choice of the Shechemites. He could interpret it as an attempt to do something in return to Jerubbaal and his house for something they had done for the Shechemites. The choice of Abimelech would then be an expression of thanks to their father for the fact that he had once delivered the Shechemites from the power of the Midianites.

2 Kings 14:9 records the fable of the thistle and the cedar. Here the historical context is the reckless challenge of the king of Judah, Amaziah, to do battle with Jehoash, his colleague in Israel. Jehoash, aware of his own power, saw Amaziah's challenge as little more than suicidal. He did not answer Amaziah directly, however, but tried to warn him in a roundabout way by telling a fable. On an ill-fated day, a thistle in Lebanon forgot his humble status in the plant world and boldly proposed to the cedar in Lebanon that the cedar's daughter marry the son of the thistle. Here, too, the story is left unfinished. For instance, we are not told what the answer of the cedar was. We do learn that the thistle, apparently as punishment for his megalomania, was trampled by the animals. It cannot have been difficult for Amaziah to discover the moral of the parable. How did he dare to risk small and weak Judah in a confrontation with powerful Israel? The advice given him by Jehoash is entirely to the point: stay home and recall the glorious memories of Judah's defeat of the Edomites.

4. THE SAGA

The saga is intermediate between the fairy tale and the myth. According to van Dale, it differs from the fairy tale by being restricted to a specific time and place, and from the myth by not serving as the vehicle for religious ideas or moral truths. Van Dale characterizes the saga as a transmitted and romantic popular story, the poetic reworking of a historical event. Closer scrutiny of the Old Testament sagas shows that this characterization is incomplete. It omits completely the didactic function of the saga, which in the Old Testament is very important. The biblical writers used the saga to teach or explain something, such as a name or the origin of a custom or institution. For this reason virtually all sagas in the Old Testament can be characterized as etiologies or etymologies. The widely diverse sagas in the Old Testament can be classified as nature sagas, tribal and national sagas, name sagas, and hero sagas.

a. The Nature Saga

A particularly fine example of a nature saga appears in Genesis 19, which contains the story of Sodom and Gomorrah. Viewing the area around the southern shore of the Dead Sea, visitors must have asked themselves the cause of its barrenness and desolation. The saga answers with the story that this area, once dotted with flourishing cities, was at one time a very fertile region. The immorality of the inhabitants, however, had evoked the anger of Yahweh, which led to the end of these cities: "Then Yahweh rained on Sodom and Gomorrah brimstone and fire from Yahweh out of heaven; and he overthrew those cities, and all the valley, and all the inhabitants of the cities, and what grew on the ground" (vv. 24–25). This story is thus an etiological saga.

But the story also aims to explain a few other curiosities. In the middle of a completely uninhabited area lay the city of Zoar, which had been spared from the catastrophe. To answer people's questions why Zoar escaped, the saga explains that Yahweh had spared the city to give Lot a place of escape. The saga also explains the remarkable fact that, in this salt-rich area, there was a pillar with an obviously human shape. This pillar was the wife of Lot, who had looked back during her flight. Such an element doubtless illustrates the didactic character of this saga. One who runs for his life must forget what lies behind (Phil. 3:13) and look only to the future. Otherwise one gets set in his ways and, like Lot's wife, changes into a pillar of salt.

Another nature saga is the story of the serpent in Genesis 3:13–15. The serpent has long been the most intriguing animal to humankind. How, for example, could one explain that, whereas other animals use legs for locomotion, the serpent crawls on its belly and eats dust? Why do humans instinctively try to kill a serpent that crosses their path? The saga answers that God has designed it that way, punishing the serpent for having seduced the first human beings to disobey God.

Many scholars have thought that this verse implies that the serpent originally had legs. Josephus held this view, and it is also found in the *Targum Yerushalmi*. According to van Selms, however, the writer was not interested in this question. In the serpent's crawling on its belly, he perceived one of the aspects of the curse on the serpent, and he did not ask himself what the serpent may have looked like before the curse. "Crawling on one's belly is the ultimate humiliation that can be inflicted upon defeated enemies: a continuous prostration. The same thing is indicated by eating dust. In Babylonian the same expression means to be humiliated (cf. also Ps. 72:9; Isa. 49:23). In the Babylonian epic *Ishtar's Descent into the Underworld*, dust is the food of the dead. The serpent, the animal of life with the Canaanites, is condemned to be the food of the dead" (van Selms, *Genesis* I [POT; Nijkerk, 1967] 71).

In my judgment this interpretation underestimates the etiological motif. The writer wanted to explain the strange fact that the serpent is the only animal that crawls with its belly on the ground. The one conception, however, does not necessarily exclude the other. Both represent an aspect of the truth. Though von Rad is fully aware of this etiological aspect, he also believes that the author had more in mind. According to von Rad the verse has a spiritual background, and in order to make this specific, the narrator used a language that was designed to make spiritual realities visible by means of an illustration. In the story the serpent not only is a biological phenomenon but also the evil that has become incarnate, evil that is inexplicably present in this world and that is bent on destroying human beings. For the serpent is an animal that possesses all kinds of uncanny qualities with which it seeks to rival humankind. It was not the writer's primary intention to make vivid the enigmatic relationship of the serpent to humankind and so of humankind to evil. And as regards the enmity between the serpent and human beings, one should have no illusions about it: "Wherever man and serpent meet, the meeting always involves life and death. . . . It is a struggle of the species ('between your seed and her seed'), and as such there is no foreseeable hope that a victory can be won by any kind of heroism. Just that is real doom" (von Rad, *Genesis* [OTL; Philadelphia, 1972²], p. 93).

b. The Tribal and National Saga

Tribal and national sagas aim to explain the relationship between, and the origin of, various peoples or the existence of various customs with certain peoples. So in Genesis 25:19–26 the relationship between Edom and Israel is traced to the fact that Rebecca, Isaac's wife who was regarded as barren, gave birth to twin boys, who, according to a divine revelation, would become the ancestors of two nations:

23. Two nations are in your womb,
    and two peoples, born of you, shall be
       divided;
   the one shall be stronger than the other,
    the elder shall serve the younger.

Here an actual, historical situation—Israel, though the younger of the twins, was indeed always more important than Edom—is thus explained with a reference to a divine revelation given to Rebecca even before the birth of the twins.

In the saga describing the origin of the Moabites and the Ammonites (Gen. 19:30–38), one can still detect the contempt Israel always had for these peoples. Though distantly related to each other, Israel's descent was honorable, whereas the birth of Moab and Ammon was due to incest. Their mothers were daughters of Lot, who seduced their father after having made him drunk with wine. Israel thus regarded the Moabites and Ammonites as bastards who had no part in the cultic community and who were not allowed in the temple (see Deut. 23:3–6 and Neh. 13:1–3, which, however, gives a different reason for the exclusion).

This saga indicates Israel's unflattering view of two of her neighbors. The Moabites and Ammonites, not surprisingly, viewed their own origin in a much more positive light. Some scholars hold that this saga was originally not Israelite but Moabite and Ammonite and that it glorified the origin of these nations. In such a form nothing was said about the incestuous character of the descent! All the emphasis was placed instead on the heroic deed of these women and on the purity of the descent. The sons can be proud that they are not from strange seed, but from father and daughter (H. Gunkel, *Genesis übersetzt und erklärt* [HKAT; Göttingen, 1966⁷], p. 218)!

Other contemporary customs are explained by sagas. The fact that the members of the desert tribe of the Kenites, with whom the Israelites from of old had maintained relations (Num. 10:29–32; Judg. 1:16; 1 Sam. 15:6), had a peculiar way of tattooing themselves intrigued everyone who met them. That custom demanded an explanation, which is given in Genesis 4. After he had murdered Abel, Cain—regarded by the Kenites as their ancestor—was condemned by Yahweh to be a fugitive and a wanderer on the earth. To protect him against revenge Yahweh put a mark on him. We do not know the place or shape of this sign, but according to some, it had religious significance and expressed a great devotion to Yahweh. The relevant element of this conjecture is that the Kenites, even as the Rechabites who were related to them (2 Kgs. 10:15–24; Jeremiah 35; 1 Chr. 2:55), had indeed the reputation of being strongly devoted to Yahweh.

Also explained in a saga is the taboo against eating the *nervus ischiadicus* (or, according to van Selms [*Genesis*, II, 142], the *sartorius*). This sinew or tendon is not eaten by the Israelites because, according to Genesis 32:32, Jacob was touched there by his opponent while he wrestled with him at night by the Jabbok, as a result of which he was compelled to leave the field as a cripple. This restriction is not mentioned in the list of food taboos in the book of Leviticus, but it does appear in the Mishna tract *Hullin* 7. Besides noting that the location of this tendon or sinew suggests a sexual taboo, we cannot recover the real background of this restriction. The history of religion has many examples of such food taboos.

c. The Name Saga

Name sagas occur frequently in the Old Testament, in particular in the book of Genesis. Forty sagas relating to names of persons and forty relating to place-names have been counted there. They are as a rule etiological or etymological in nature and thus pertain to the derivation of names. The majority provide an explanation for names that have been in existence for some time (note the common phrase "to this day").

Consider first some explanations of place-names. The well Esek (Gen. 26:20), for example, is connected with a quarrel between the herdsmen of Gerar and the servants of Isaac regarding the ownership of a well that Isaac's men had discovered. The Hebrew verb for quarrel is *hitasseq.*

The amount of leeway possible in explaining a place-name is seen in the three etiologies the Old Testament gives for the city Beer-sheba. In Genesis 21:31 the name is associated with seven *(sheba)* lambs that Abraham gave to Abimelech to secure his rights of ownership on a well he had dug and also with the oath that both men had sworn *(nishba,* "swear") to seal the treaty they had made. Genesis 26:32–33 also mentions the digging of a well, this time by Isaac. He called this well Shibah *(sheba),* a word meaning "abundance," perhaps going back to the name of a goddess Sheba: "therefore the name of the city is Beer-sheba to this day" (v. 33).

Judges 15:9–19 preserves the story of how Ramath-lehi got its name. At a place that already had the name Lehi, Samson killed no less than a thousand Philistines with a fresh jawbone of a donkey. He gave poetic expression to this heroic deed in the paean:

With a donkey's jawbone
  I have made donkeys of them,
With a donkey's jawbone
  I have killed a thousand men.

(v. 16 NIV)

When he had finished speaking, he threw away the jawbone and called that place Ramath-lehi, that is, the Throwing Away of the Donkey's Jawbone.

The explanation of the place-name Perez-uzzah is found in 2 Samuel 6:8. It is part of the story that details the carrying of the ark from Baalah of Judah to Jerusalem. In the vicinity of the threshing floor of Nacon, something terrible happened. The oxen pulling the cart on which the ark was placed stumbled, and for a moment it looked as if the ark might fall off the wagon. One of the guides, a certain Uzzah, steadied the ark with his hand. Yahweh, however, was not pleased with what he did; Uzzah, however well intentioned, had transgressed the holy law that forbade touching the ark (Num. 4:15) and had to pay for it with his life. He dropped dead on the spot by the ark. Then the story continues: "David was angry because Yahweh had broken forth *(paras peres)* upon Uzzah; and that place is called Perez-uzzah, to this day."

Genesis 31:45–53 tells why a particular heap of stones in the land got its Hebrew name Galeed and its Aramaic name Jegar Sahadutha. This heap of stones had been erected by Jacob and Laban as a witness *(ed)* to a covenant they had made with each other. *Gal* is the Hebrew word for heap of stones, and *yegar* the Aramaic equivalent. Remarkably, at the end of the story the name Mizpah (guardpost) is also given for the heap. Laban is reported to have said, "Yahweh watch between you and me, when we are absent one from the other."

Explanations of personal names are also often transmitted in the form of a saga. A good example is Genesis 17:5. Though the name Abraham is only a dialectical variant of Abram, the author associates the formation of the longer name with a promise from God to make the patriarch a father *(ab)* of a multitude *(hamon)* of nations. This passage once again highlights the great importance that was attached to being able to recover the meaning of a name and the liberties that could be taken in the analysis. In this particular instance, for example, the element *ra* in the name is completely ignored! The whole episode gives the impression of having little to do with the patriarch's story as such. The name change is out of keeping with the long tradition that such a change marks the inception of a new calling or responsibility (cf. the change in the New Testament from Simon to Peter). Here there is no new situation; on several earlier occasions Yahweh had already revealed himself to Abram and given him a similar promise (Gen. 12:1–3; 15:1).

In Genesis 17:15 the wife of the patriarch also receives a different name: she will no longer be called Sarai but Sarah. Actually nothing changes.

The name Sarai is only an older variant of Sarah. Perhaps for this reason the name change could not be incorporated into a story, as was done in the case of her husband. In other patriarchal narratives the names of Ishmael, Isaac, Jacob/Israel, and the twelve sons of Jacob are the subjects of name sagas.

Another name saga occurs in Judges 6:32, which explains the origin of Gideon's name Jerubbaal: "Therefore on that day he was called Jerubbaal, that is to say, 'Let Baal contend against him,' because he pulled down his altar." The context of the verse is the story of a Baal sanctuary (a rival to a Yahweh sanctuary located in Ophrah) that was destroyed and leveled by Gideon the son of Joash. The people living there were highly displeased with this deed and demanded that Joash hand over his son to them so that they might put him to death for this sacrilege. But Joash, apparently all too happy with the elimination of the rival shrine, refused to heed this demand and suggested instead that they leave the vengeance up to Baal himself. Gideon's new name is associated with the verb *rib* ("contend"). Many, however, dispute the correctness of this association. Even as with the name Jeroboam, the verbal component may relate to the verb *rabab* ("be numerous, be great"). Instead of "let Baal contend against him," then, we would have to translate, "let Baal manifest that he is great (manifest himself as Lord)." If this latter idea is right, this passage, in which Jerubbaal is connected with the verb *rib,* would present an interesting popular etymology, one of many in the Old Testament.

d. The Hero Saga

Israel is unique in the ancient East in not developing the hero saga. We search in vain in the Old Testament for descriptions of heroic efforts on the battlefield such as are found in the *Iliad* or in the Gilgamesh Epic, which exuberantly sing the praises of the hero's victory. As mentioned above, Israel attributed its victories to its God and jealously guarded against giving praise to human beings that was due only to him. The Old Testament provides many examples. How could Joshua after his victory at Gibeon conquer all of Canaan? Because Yahweh, the God of Israel, fought for Israel (Josh. 10:42). When Gideon wanted to fight the Midianites with a huge army, he was told, "The people with you are too many for me to give the Midianites into their hand, lest Israel vaunt themselves against me, saying, 'My own hand has delivered me'" (Judg. 7:2). After two reductions in his army, Gideon prepared to attack the Midianites with only three hundred men. The report of the murder of Sisera by Jael, the wife of the Kenite Heber, ends with: "So on that day God subdued Jabin the king of Canaan" (4:23). Even before the battle began, the victory was already sure; the leader of Israel was assured by God: "See, I have given into your hand . . ." (Josh. 6:2; 8:1, 18; Judg. 7:15; 11:32; 1 Sam. 14:6).

It is obvious that this climate, which resounds with the *Soli Deo gloria* after every victory, leaves little room for praising human achievements. Sometimes the word *hero* is accorded to courageous men, as in David's lament over Saul and Jonathan (2 Sam. 1:17-27), which is about as far as the Old Testament goes in honoring individuals. Because of its theocentric outlook, Israel never had a fully developed panegyric.

5. THE LEGEND

The boundaries between the saga and the legend are generally fluid. Like the sagas, many legends are etiological in character, designed to explain an institution or a remarkable fact. They can be divided into categories, based on the topic of the legend: a sanctuary, a cultic object, a religious person, a prophet, or a martyr.

a. Sanctuary Legends

Long before Israel's conquest of Canaan, the land must have been dotted with sacred places. Every human settlement of some importance had its own sanctuary, many of which were simply taken over from the original owners by the newcomers after they had been settled in that area for some time or were altered so that they could use the shrines for their own worship. Most of them never enjoyed more than local fame, and their names have passed into oblivion. Others, however, grew into important cultic centers, each organizing great feasts and drawing visitors from far and near. For a long time Bethel was one of these quasi-national religious shrines. Any holy place of significance had its own *hieros logos,* or legend recounting the history of its origin and growth and explaining the reason for its sanctity. The *hieros logos* of Bethel is recorded in Genesis 28:10–22.

The story tells that the patriarch Jacob, journeying from Beer-sheba to Haran, stops for the night at an unidentified place. The area was regarded as uninhabited, because the traveler is compelled to spend the night in the open air. He finds one of the many stones lying around to use as a pillow. During the night Jacob receives the dream from which the story would later get its name. In the dream he sees a ladder, its top reaching to heaven, and angels ascending and descending on it. On top of the ladder stood Yahweh himself, who revealed himself by saying to the dreamer:

> I am Yahweh, the God of Abraham your father and the God of Isaac; the land on which you lie I will give to you and to your descendants; and your descendants shall be like the dust of the earth, and you shall spread abroad to the west and to the east and to the north and to the south; and by you and your descendants shall all the families of the earth be blessed. Behold, I am with you and will keep you wherever you go, and will bring you back to this land; for I will not leave you until I have done that of which I have spoken to you. (Gen. 28:13–15)

Awaking in the morning, Jacob realizes the significance of this nocturnal revelation: "'Surely Yahweh is in this place; and I did not know it.' And he was afraid, and said, 'How awesome is this place! This is none other than the house of God *(beth elohim),* and this is the gate of heaven'" (vv. 16–17). Believing that the holiness of this place should be marked for all time, Jacob makes a pillar of the stone on which he had slept by pouring oil on it and also names the place *beth-el* ("house of God").

This story links the holiness of the place Bethel with an epiphany of Yahweh in which the patriarch received certain promises. In reality we have here the Israelite version of Bethel's *hieros logos.* Behind this story can still be detected the traces of the Canaanite legend, in which the revealing God was not Yahweh but El and in which the holiness of the stone anointed with oil was central.

The name Bethel can be linked with El, but not possibly with Yahweh. Therefore verse 17 says correctly that the place is *beth-elohim,* and not—as required by the context—*beth-yahweh.* According to von Rad (*Genesis,* p. 286), in pre-Israelite times a god named Bethel was worshiped at this place, a god with which centuries later Israel was still familiar (Jer. 48:13). Recall also the names of deities in Elephantine associated with Bethel, such as Eshem-Bethel, Anat-Bethel, and Herem-Bethel.

Unfortunately few of the *hieroi logoi* have been preserved. It is virtually certain that the story of Gideon's calling in Judges 6 still contains the *hieros logos* of a Yahweh sanctuary in Ophrah. Even as in Genesis 28, here too the founding of a sanctuary was due to an epiphany. Having survived the encounter with the angel of Yahweh unharmed, Gideon decides to build an altar at the place and names it "Yahweh is *shalom*" ("peace"). The author adds the assurance that to this day it stands in Ophrah of the Abiezrites. Also in this instance it is not a matter of an entirely new sanctuary. The epiphany happened at a place that had been known as sacred for many years, namely under the holy tree in Ophrah, a tree belonging to Gideon's father Joash (v. 11). The name of the altar, moreover, was not intended to guarantee the people living there that they would be free from war but only to keep alive the memory of the fact that Gideon, after his encounter with the angel of Yahweh, had been greeted by Yahweh with the words "peace be to you" (*shalom leka;* v. 23)!

The *hieros logos* of Israel's youngest sanctuary, the temple in Jerusalem, is preserved in only a very fragmentary form. The foundation of the temple goes back to the building of an altar to Yahweh on the threshing floor of Araunah the Jebusite, which was intended to stop a plague David had brought upon himself and his people as punishment for the census he had conducted (2 Sam. 24:18–25).

b. Legends Connected with Cultic Objects

In ancient Israel every sanctuary possessed one or more cultic symbols that served a particular function in the worship or that were kept for reasons of piety. A good example is the Nehushtan mentioned in 2 Kings 18:4. This cultic object had been stored in the temple at Jerusalem for centuries but fell victim to the reform of King Hezekiah. By happy circumstance the *hieros logos* of this Nehushtan has been preserved. The word contains the noun *nahash* ("serpent"), which reminds us of the etiological story in Numbers 21:6–9. According to that account, the Israelites at one point on their journey through the wilderness complained bitterly to God and to Moses about their lack of food and water. In judgment, Yahweh sent poisonous snakes among the people, and many Israelites died. Confessing their sin, the people asked Moses to pray to Yahweh for relief. The answer came in Yahweh's direction to Moses: "Make a fiery serpent, and set it on a pole; and every one who is bitten, when he sees it, shall live" (v. 8). Moses made a bronze snake, and the people were spared further destruction. The snake in this story functions as a healing animal, a capacity for which it was known throughout the ancient world. In the story in Numbers there is no worship of the bronze snake. But such was the case with the Nehushtan in the story of 2 Kings 18, which induced Hezekiah to destroy it as part of his cultic reform.

Many legends are associated with the history of the temple ark, a sacred object that was far more renowned than the Nehushtan (see H. A. Brongers, "Einige Aspekte der gegenwärtigen Lage der Lade-Forschung," *NTT* 25 [1971] 6–27). Scholars are sharply divided as to the origin and purpose of this object, which is variously described and which later received its fixed place in the Most Holy Place in the Jerusalem temple. Here we are most interested in the legends associated with it. Yet in order to understand something of the message conveyed by these legends, we must make some decision regarding the many interpretations that have been put forward through the centuries. In its original form the ark must have been a simple wooden box, provided with carrying poles so that it could be transported by appointed priests. The familiar ark proverb in Numbers 10:34–36 and also the reference in 1 Samuel 4:4 indicate that the ark was regarded as a self-representation of Yahweh and that the holy object, if necessary, could be carried into battle as a good-luck charm.

The ark was thus an unusually holy object that, under certain circumstances, could bring death and destruction (see 2 Sam. 6:7). A good example of its inherent power is the story in 1 Samuel 5. The Israelites had been soundly defeated by the Philistines near Aphek, and the ark, which the Israelites had brought into battle as a last resort, had been carried off as a trophy by the victors. The Philistines put the sacred box in the temple of Dagon in Ashdod, beside the image of Dagon. The next day not only was the image of Dagon lying in pieces on the floor of the temple, but Ashdod and the surrounding territory were struck by a plague. The inhabitants of Ashdod discerned a connection between this calamity and the presence of the ark in their town, and they sent the ark on to Gath. The people of Gath suffered the same calamity, and they in turn forwarded the ark to Ekron. The Ekronites, however, did not wait for trouble to strike but took counsel how they could return the dangerous object to Israel as quickly as possible. This incident may be regarded as the first ark legend.

The second legend details how the ark left the territory of the Philistines and returned into the possession of the Israelites. Advised by priests and diviners, the Philistines prepared a new cart to transport the ark. In order to avert the anger of the God of Israel in the future, five gold tumors and five gold rats (according to the number of the Philistine rulers) were placed in a box beside the ark as a guilt offering. Then two cows that had calved and had never been yoked were hitched to the cart, after the Philistines had first taken the calves back to the barn. There was no driver, which would allow the cows to go wherever they wanted. The Philistines prepared this test in order to find out who was responsible for the calamities. If the cows pulled the cart toward Beth-shemesh in Israel, then they would know that Israel's God brought this great affliction upon them. If the cows went the other way, they would know that his hand had not been upon them but that everything had happened by chance. The cows started pulling and, without turning to the left or the right, went straight to Beth-shemesh in Israelite territory. There the people were harvesting their wheat and with great rejoicing welcomed the ark. Out of gratitude for its return, they sacrificed the cows as a burnt offering to Yahweh, using the wood of the cart for the fire. The ark meanwhile was given a temporary place on the large rock which "to this day" can still be seen in the field of Joshua of Beth-shemesh.

Still a third ark legend is connected with the name Perez-uzzah, as discussed above in section 4.c. It is important to notice that these ark legends were not included in the historical narrative on account of their own literary qualities, however significant we may consider them to be. We do not have belles lettres here but, as in the historicized myth, a particular form of proclamation. The content of this proclamation is the power and greatness of Yahweh, who does not leave his offended honor unavenged but who continually takes up the cause of his people Israel and puts their enemies to shame. Within this proclamation, legend has a strictly auxiliary function.

c. Legends Connected with Religious Personalities

The life history of famous historical personalities is often surrounded by legends. Biographies of religious figures likewise often have various stories linked with them, which have little or no connection with historical reality. Though these people are in themselves important and impressive, their admirers have nevertheless often believed that something should be added to their fame.

The birth accounts of great religious personalities are often accompanied by a legend. Consider first the story of Moses' birth. Exodus 2 contains the account of the miraculous rescue of Moses when his life was threatened as an infant. His mother had placed him in a wicker basket among the reeds along the bank of the Nile, hoping that a passerby would find him. The child was discovered by an Egyptian princess as she was going to bathe with her attendants. Though fully aware that the child was Hebrew and thus, by order of her father, had to be killed together with all the other Hebrew baby boys, the princess miraculously decided to take care of the abandoned infant. After the child was nursed by his own mother for the usual time, he was adopted by the princess and given the name Moses. Although he would have received an Egyptian name such as Thut-

mose or Ahmose, popular Hebrew etymology derived his name from the Hebrew verb *masha*, "draw out," and interprets his name as "the one drawn out of the water."

Scholars have long known that the account of Moses' birth contains many features that are also part of the birth legends of other great historical personalities. (For comparative material, see A. Jeremias, *The Old Testament in the Light of the Ancient East* [London/New York, 1911], II: 93–96; H. Gressmann, *Mose und seine Zeit* [Göttingen, 1913], pp. 7ff.) I mention here only Sargon of Akkad, who, in the second half of the third millennium B.C., wielded the scepter in the north of Babylonia (H. Gressmann, *Altorientalische Texte zum Alten Testament* [Berlin/Leipzig, 1926²], pp. 234ff.), and Cyrus, king of the Persians (Herodotus, I, 100ff.). It is interesting that the Cyrus legend also contains the motif of a ruler who seeks to kill a child whom he suspects of being a future antagonist. As in the Moses story, this child miraculously escapes from death, later becomes king himself, and finally defeats the ruler who years ago tried to kill him. It would seem obvious that these foreign stories were also known in Israel and made their imprint on the birth history of Moses.

Miraculous birth stories in the Old Testament are also found in connection with Isaac, Samson, Samuel, and Jeremiah. A frequently recurring motif is the initial barrenness of the mother and the promise of a man of God, assuring her in the name of Yahweh that her barrenness will soon come to an end and that she will bear a son who will be given an important task by Yahweh. Samson, for example, would be a Nazirite, would be set apart to God from birth, and would begin the deliverance of Israel from the hands of the Philistines (Judg. 13:5).

Hannah, one of the wives of Elkanah, was also childless for many years. Her more fortunate rival, Peninnah, had children and kept provoking Hannah. Finally, at her wit's end, Hannah poured out her anguish to Eli the priest, in Shiloh. From him she heard that Yahweh would be mindful of her misery and would give her what she had asked of him. After a year a son indeed was born, whom she named Samuel, meaning, according to popular etymology, "asked from the Lord." Like the mother of Samson, Hannah gave her son as a Nazirite to Yahweh (1 Samuel 1).

In the case of Jeremiah there is no birth legend as such. Here the promise that the child was destined by Yahweh for something great was given before his birth. For at his calling the prophet is told:

Before I formed you in the womb I knew [elected] you,
and before you were born I consecrated you;
I appointed you a prophet to the nations.

(Jer. 1:5)

As A. Weiser (*Das Buch des Propheten Jeremia* [ATD; Göttingen, 1952], p. 11) has correctly noted, the theological relevance of this divine promise lies in the fact that Jeremiah must hear from God that his own abilities mean nothing; Jeremiah does not belong to himself but is a creature formed by God, even predestined by God to what he will become. "The idea of election is here in its personal form (cf. Isa. 49:1, 5) elaborated to the idea of predestination" (cf. Judg. 13:5; Ps. 139:16). Many centuries later the apostle Paul also applied the idea of election before birth to himself (Gal. 1:15).

In legends involving the actions of religious personalities, the story of Moses is again striking. In the account of the Exodus, the interest in Moses' staff is remarkable. Already at his calling (Exodus 3), when he receives the charge to lead the Israelites out of Egypt and when he tells Yahweh that he fears that the Israelites will not believe his message that the God of Abraham, Isaac, and Jacob has appeared to him, the question is heard: "What is that in your hand?" Moses replies, "A staff." Yahweh orders Moses to throw it on the ground, where it immediately changes into a serpent. In panic Moses runs away from it. He is, however, ordered to come back and take the serpent by the tail, "and it became a rod in his hand" (4:4). This legend describes one of a great many miraculous signs in the Old Testament, which are intended to confirm a divine mandate or promise.

The staff also plays an important role in the account of the ten plagues preceding the flight from Egypt. In Exodus 7:20 Yahweh orders Moses to strike the water of the Nile, which is thereby turned into blood (= 1st plague). In 9:23 Moses must stretch out his staff toward the sky, after which Yahweh sends thunder and hail and brings fire down upon the earth (= 7th plague). Finally, according to 10:13, Moses must stretch out his staff over the land of Egypt, after which Yahweh makes an east wind blow across the land, carrying with it a large swarm of locusts (= 8th plague).

The chief moment of the history of the Exodus is the passing through the Red Sea. This travel is made possible because Moses, at Yahweh's command, divides the waters of the Red Sea with his staff (Exod. 14:16). During the journey through the desert there is one more staff miracle. When the people are in danger of perishing with thirst, Moses strikes the rock at Horeb with his staff, so that water gushes out (17:6; Num. 20:11).

Not many legends have been preserved in the account of the entrance into the Promised Land. Though the tradition of the capture of Jericho contains legendary features (Josh. 5:13– 6:27), they are not related to Joshua, the commander of the Israelite troops. In this entire episode Joshua and his men are hardly more than observers. The author took great pains to impress upon the minds of his readers that the fall of the city was purely Yahweh's work. In that respect the story is no different from the stories around Moses, discussed above. In addition, Moses did nothing more than carry out orders given him by Yahweh. In this way the Old Testament removes all occasion for the glorification of persons. Only Yahweh is Israel's Savior and Deliverer. Although he regularly made use of people in his dealings with the people of Israel, such human involvement, according to this line of thinking, should be regarded as a special favor on his part.

A similar legend involving Joshua is the story of the sun's standing still over Gibeon (Josh. 10:12). Joshua had asked that the sun would not continue its course so that he might avail himself of a longer day to avenge himself on his enemies (v. 13). According to verse 14, "There has been no day like it before or since, when Yahweh hearkened to the voice of a man; for Yahweh fought for Israel." H. Hertzberg is therefore correct in saying that the courage of Joshua and his men "required basically nothing else than the obedience of faith" (*Die*

Bücher Josua, Richter, Ruth [ATD 9; Göttingen, 1953], p. 73).

In the list of the so-called major judges, Samson is not only the last but also the most remarkable. In his actions he differs from all his predecessors not only in always carrying out his mission but also in demonstrating great physical strength that enables him to perform solitary feats. Unlike the other judges, he does not lead an army that has been recruited from one or more tribes, but he acts entirely on his own. Instead of being interested in enhancing his own reputation, Samson, as a Nazirite, is aware of being no more than an instrument in the hands of Yahweh. For it was expected of him that he would begin the deliverance of Israel from the power of the Philistines (Judg. 13:5). Many miraculous stories were obviously in circulation about this remarkable personality, which are intended to highlight either his ingenuity or his tremendous physical strength. Judges 15:4–5 contains a fascinating illustration of the former. To do great harm to the Philistines, he thinks of a trick that at the same time demonstrates his sense of humor. Catching three hundred foxes, he ties them tail to tail in pairs and fastens a torch to every pair of tails. Then he lights the torches and lets the foxes loose in the standing grain of the Philistines, which sets fire both to the shocks and to the standing grain and the olive groves.

The legendary character of this popular story can hardly be doubted. Such things simply do not happen in ordinary life. Nevertheless, the original, less-critical listeners to this story must have enjoyed it. The trick their hero Samson played on the Philistines can only have added to their feelings of superiority over the despised uncircumcised Philistines.

The next chapter then gives some examples of Samson's incredible physical strength. The first is his feat in the Philistine city of Gath, where the hero had gone into the very den of a lion. His hiding place in one of the rooms near the city gate is soon discovered. Because Samson had gone there to sleep, his pursuers think it better to wait till daybreak. Samson, however, does not wait for things to happen. Getting up in the middle of the night and taking hold of the doors and posts of the city gates, he tears them loose, bar and all, lifts them to his shoulders, and carries them to the top of the hill that faces Hebron (Judg. 16:3).

In the sequel three more episodes are told that illustrate Samson's physical prowess. Three times the Philistines try to overpower the strong man by tying him up: first by means of seven fresh thongs (Judg. 16:4–9), then with new ropes that had never been used (vv. 10–12), and finally by weaving the seven braids of his hair into the fabric on the loom and tightening it with a pin (vv. 13–14). Samson is roused each time by the shout "the Philistines are upon you, Samson!" and has no difficulty whatever in breaking the thongs and ropes like a thread and tearing loose the weaver's pin, the loom, and the web. It is obvious that these also are legendary popular tales. The legendary character is made even more explicit by the repeated use of the number seven—the holy number, the number of completeness.

Samson's final tour de force leads to his death. Having succumbed to the tears of his lover Delilah, who finally succeeded in discovering the secret of his great strength, Samson falls into the hands of the Philistines. They incarcerate him in Gaza, gouge out his eyes, bind him with two bronze shackles, and force him to grind grain at the mill in the prison. "But the hair of his head began to grow again after it had been shaved" (Judg. 16:22). This bit of information is obviously intended as the introduction to the story of his final feat of strength, to which he also falls victim himself. At a feast in honor of the god Dagon, the Philistines get him out of prison and force him to entertain them. So that everyone can see him, they position Samson between the two pillars of the building. When the feast is in full swing, Samson prays to Yahweh, "O Lord Yahweh, remember me, I pray thee, and strengthen me, I pray thee, only this once, O God, that I may be avenged upon the Philistines for one of my two eyes" (v. 28). Then he reaches toward the two central pillars on which the building rested, bracing himself against them. Pushing with all his might, he causes the building to collapse on the rulers and people in it. The writer concludes the story with the information that this last feat of Samson killed more than he had killed in all his previous exploits (v. 30). Here, too, the legendary nature of the story is clear. For example, how could three thousand people not only find a place on a flat roof but also, while up there, have a view of Samson's antics as he stood between the two pillars?

It is surprising that the life of such an important man as Samuel, who for many years made his impact felt on Israel as seer and judge and even as a kind of uncrowned king, is virtually without legendary additions. All we have is an incident recorded in 1 Samuel 12. Samuel stands before the people, giving a farewell address in which he recounts the events that have happened since the days of Moses and Aaron. He points out that, after the worship of the Baals and the Ashtoreths, Israel's greatest sin was that of asking for a king. But now that they have a king, Samuel expects that they will faithfully serve Yahweh and no longer rebel against him. If not, Yahweh will be against them as he was against their fathers. This admonition itself is not forceful enough; it cries out for confirmation by a mighty sign, which brings us to the legend. "Stand still," says Samuel to the people, "and see this great thing, which Yahweh will do before your eyes. Is it not wheat harvest today? I will call upon Yahweh, that he may send thunder and rain; and you shall know and see that your wickedness is great, which you have done in the sight of Yahweh, in asking for yourselves a king" (vv. 16–17). Samuel then calls upon Yahweh, and that same day Yahweh sends thunder and rain. The people stand in awe of Yahweh and Samuel, and they all say, "Pray for your servants to Yahweh your God, that we may not die; for we have added to all our sins this evil, to ask for ourselves a king" (v. 19). The wheat harvest in Israel was normally in May, when the season of thunder and rain was over. The fact that, suddenly at this time of the year, there was such bad weather in answer to Samuel's prayer to Yahweh was thus understandably taken as a fearful miracle.

Prayers for a natural miracle are also found in Joshua 10:12–14 and 1 Kings 18:36–39. Though the answer to these prayers served in the first place to honor God himself, nevertheless, according to the writer of the stories, a little of that honor may go to the man at whose intercession the miracle happened.

Most legends of this type were told in connection with the prophets Elijah and Elisha. These legends are so numerous that scholars have divided them into cycles, so that we now commonly speak of the Elijah cycle and the Elisha cycle. Whether there actually were such cycles, of which the authors of Kings were able to avail themselves, or whether these stories were originally independent and unconnected and only much later incorporated by a redactor into the historical narrative is a literary-critical problem for which no satisfactory solution has yet been found.

There can be no doubt that, in their time (9th century B.C.), Elijah and Elisha were impressive personalities who on many occasions determined the course of events in Israel and who awed people by their power and influence. Though we know more about Elisha than about Elijah, the latter must nevertheless be regarded as the more important personality. It is remarkable that he picked a man like Elisha to succeed him, considering how different the two men were. Elijah is a typical loner who, in carrying out the divine mandate, goes his own way and seldom mixes with people. As a person he is hard to grasp, and there is an aura about him of an almost supernatural secrecy. Today he is here, and tomorrow he suddenly shows up at a totally different place. Nothing is said in the record about his background. The writer knows him only as Elijah the Tishbite, and without a formal introduction mentions him for the first time in a conflict with King Ahab of Israel. After monitoring Ahab throughout his rule, Elijah continues his watchdog role with the royal court through his contacts with Ahab's son Ahaziah (2 Kings 1).

A man like Elisha is seemingly much more accessible to us. He regularly mixes with the people and therefore seems to be much closer to them. His ministry is far less shrouded in supernatural secrecy. His contacts with ordinary people are much more frequent than those of his great predecessor, Elijah, and numerous stories show that he was highly popular, a reputation Elijah never enjoyed.

Elijah's first public act was in connection with a lengthy period of draught that struck the land of Israel during the reign of King Ahab. "Now Elijah the Tishbite, of Tishbe in Gilead, said to Ahab, 'As Yahweh the God of Israel lives, before whom I stand, there shall be neither dew nor rain these years, except by my word'" (1 Kgs. 17:1). In order to protect Elijah from the consequences of this drought, Yahweh orders him to the brook Cherith, from which for the time being he can quench his thirst. The legendary aspect of the story begins with Yahweh's ordering the ravens to provide the man of God with food. In the morning as well as in the evening these birds will bring him bread and meat.

It has always been regarded as strange that ravens provided Elijah with food. Not only are they voracious animals, they were also regarded as unclean (Lev. 11:15; Deut. 14:14). It has therefore been proposed to emend *orebim* ("ravens") to *arabim* ("Arabs") or to think of a tribe of the Orebites, presumably settled in this region—a tribe, however, that is nowhere else mentioned in the Old Testament. All these rationalizations are, however, to be rejected, since it is clearly the intent of the author to write something miraculous.

Elijah's stay with the widow of Zarephath (1 Kgs. 17:7-24) is the logical continuation of this story. It is fascinating to observe that the miracle is not enlarged to the extent that Yahweh continues to keep enough water in the brook. On the contrary, after a while the water dries up, forcing the prophet to look for another place to stay. Yahweh orders him to go to the Phoenician Zarephath, situated 13 kilometers (8 mi.) south of Sidon, nowadays known as *ras sarafand,* but in the Septuagint and the New Testament (Luke 4:26) as Sarepta. Yahweh orders a widow living there to provide Elijah with food and drink (1 Kgs. 17:9). In Phoenicia, however, food has also become scarce because of the protracted drought. When he asks this woman for a piece of bread, the man of God is told that all that she has left in the house is a handful of flour in a jar and a little oil in a jug. At this point, too, this story takes on a legendary character. Elijah assures the woman that she can go ahead and make something for him, because the flour in the pot will not be used up and the oil in the jar will not run out until the day Yahweh will send rain on the earth. How the prophet imagines this supply to continue is not explained. The woman must unconditionally believe the word of Yahweh, the God of Israel. The character of the story does not allow for a rational explanation. Fichtner rightly points out that

we should not try to weigh every word in this story that so obviously contains miraculous features. All it intends to show is that Yahweh, the God of Israel, keeps his prophet alive in a time of great drought and likewise surrounds with his faithfulness those who make his care possible by their willingness to sacrifice (*Das erste Buch von den Königen* [Botschaft des Alten Testaments; Stuttgart, 1964], p. 257).

The next story, that of the raising from the dead of the son of the widow (1 Kgs. 17:17-24), is the last instance in which Elijah performs a miracle in a nonpolitical context. The accounts that follow, preserved in 18:20-46 and in 2 Kings 1:1-14, can be fully understood only in their political framework. My interest here, however, is the legendary features in these traditions. Immediately striking is the large role that fire plays in these stories. Consider first the story in 2 Kings 1.

Ahaziah, who had succeeded his father as king over Israel, is seriously injured in a fall in his house in Samaria. Wondering fearfully whether he will recover, Ahaziah sends messengers to obtain an oracle. Instead of taking the obvious step of asking Yahweh for an oracle, Ahaziah sends his messengers to Baal-Zebub, the god of the Philistine city Ekron, who at the time was widely known as a healing god. But even before the messengers of Ahaziah are able to consult the oracle, they are suddenly confronted with Elijah. The prophet has been ordered by Yahweh to meet them and to ask them if they are going to the heathen god Baal-Zebub because there is no God in Israel whom they can consult. The messengers have no answer. Then Elijah orders them to go home and to report to the king that Yahweh—not Baal-Zebub—has said that he will not leave the bed on which he is lying but will surely die. When this report reaches the king, he is furious and sends a captain with fifty soldiers to take Elijah prisoner. The captain commands Elijah to come with him, but Elijah responds, "If I am a man of God *(ish elohim),* let fire *(esh)* come down from heaven and consume you and your fifty" (2 Kgs. 1:10). Immediately fire comes down and the company is destroyed. A second group of fifty sent by the king to Elijah meets with the same fate. A third group of fifty stays alive only after the commanding officer has begged for his life and that of his men.

The legendary character of the story should be obvious even from the threefold repetition, typical of such stories. Even more telling is the fact that the heart of the story consists of a play on the words *ish* and *esh*. Such plays on words were favorite ploys, not only in story literature but also in prophetic literature (see, e.g., *qayis*, "summer," and *qes*, "end," in Amos 8:2; *shaqed*, "almond tree," and *shoqed*, "watching," in Jer. 1:11–12). The story is clearly intended to be a hagiology designed to portray the tremendous power of Elijah as a man of God, including his ability to order fire from heaven at will, apparently even without praying to Yahweh for it.

The second story in which fire plays a large role has as its context Elijah's contest with the Baal prophets at Mount Carmel (1 Kgs. 18:20–46). Like the account of Joshua 24—but involving a much more dramatic incident—this story belongs to the genre that deals with the theme of decision. Here again Elijah is fully in charge and determines the course of events. Nowhere do we read that Yahweh had ordered the man of God to go to Carmel. At the climax, fire from heaven comes in response to Elijah's prayer to God (1 Kgs. 18:37–38). This story as well contains several legendary features, designed to make the miracle even more impressive. The wood on which the bull is to be sacrificed is first to be drenched three times (note the repetition!) with water (vv. 33–34). The fire from heaven consumes not only the sacrifice and the wood but also the stones with which the altar had been built and the soil on which it was placed (v. 38).

I mention finally the story of Elijah's flight to Horeb (1 Kgs. 19:1–18). Some may wish to interpret the entire story as a legend. The account contains at least some legendary features. After having lain down under a broom tree, the man of God is awakened by an angel who orders him to get up and eat some food. Then suddenly there is in the barren desert a cake of bread baked over hot coals and a jar of water (v. 6). Though the meal is not exactly sumptuous, it enables Elijah to complete the journey of forty days and forty nights to Horeb (v. 8).

Turning to Elijah's successor, we note that Elisha is often mentioned as the head of dervishlike, ecstatic prophets who lived in communes in or around holy places such as Bethel and Gilgal. The many stories about miracles or wonders that are now part of the Elisha cycle must have come from such groups. Such is the case with the story of the widow's jar of oil (2 Kgs. 4:1–7), the raising of the son of the Shunammite (vv. 8–37), and the anointing of Hazael and Jehu (8:7–15; 9:1–13). It is generally assumed that these incidents are counterparts to the corresponding Elijah stories. Here and in stories such as the death in the pot (4:38–41), the feeding of a hundred prophets in Gilgal (vv. 42–44), the healing of the well water in Jericho (2:19–22), and the floating ax in the Jordan (6:1–7), Elisha acts solely as a miracle worker who provides help in every precarious situation and who is always available to people in need.

I should point out, however, that some interpreters reject anything miraculous in these incidents, seeing them rather as typical examples of Elisha's great wisdom and common sense. From experience Elisha knew something of the purifying power of salt, which could make foul well water drinkable again, and he knew how flour could neutralize a poisonous plant. In the case of the floating ax in the Jordan, we are to think of imitative magic. The iron was to be thought of as floating, even as wood floats on water. These interpretations are theologically quite irrelevant, unless one attempts to find relevance in the fact that all these things happened in the communes of the so-called sons of the prophets.

Unmistakably legendary, however, is the story of the miracle-working bones of Elisha (2 Kgs. 13:20–21). It is clearly hagiological, intended to show that, even after his death, Elisha could still perform miracles. Once while some Israelites were burying a man, they were surprised by a group of Moabite raiders. Wanting to flee as fast as they could, but not wanting to leave the body unburied, they quickly removed the stone from Elisha's tomb, which happened to be nearby, and put the body beside the bones of the prophet. As soon as the body touched Elisha's bones, the corpse came back to life, and the man stood up on his feet.

Just like Elijah, Elisha did not restrict his activities to his own, limited environment. He also played a significant political role in the life of his own country and beyond its borders. He had a hand in more than one coup d'état (2 Kgs. 8:7–15; 9:1–15). In this connection it is worthwhile to point out that Elisha's significance as a religious personality stands out much more clearly in the accounts that deal with his political activities than in the so-called miraculous narratives. For in the political accounts we see Elisha as a man who gave his utmost for the defense of the worship of Yahweh, in a time when the faith of the fathers was everywhere threatened by a steadily encroaching syncretism.

Legendary features also appear in the political narratives. In the story of Joram's campaign against Moab (2 Kings 3), the water that had flowed from the direction of Edom had, at Elisha's command, collected in the ditches. The sun's shining on this water made it red in appearance (but did it really seem like blood in the eyes of the Moabites?). For the Moabites the matter was entirely clear: "The kings have surely fought together, and slain one another" (v. 23).

In the war against Aram (2 Kgs. 6:8–23), Elisha helps the king of Israel to gain the victory by asking Yahweh to strike the enemy with blindness, a prayer that is promptly answered. The man of God then leads the blind soldiers to Samaria. Here Elisha prays again to Yahweh, asking him to restore their sight. When this prayer is heard they discover too late that they are inside the capital of the enemy!

In the matter of prophetic symbolism, 2 Kings 13:14–21 gives another good example of imitative magic. Just before he dies, Elisha orders King Jehoash, who has come to console him, to get a bow and some arrows. Then Elisha has Jehoash open the east window of the sickroom and shoot one of the arrows. Elisha announces that the arrow was Yahweh's arrow of victory over Aram, which will be completely destroyed at Aphek. Then the king must take the remaining arrows in his hand and strike the ground with them. He does so three times and then stops, angering and infuriating the man of God, who tells him that he should have struck the ground five or six times—then he would have eliminated Aram completely. Now, however, he will defeat it only three times.

One of the characteristics of a legendary story is its use of hyperbole, a feature that we find also in the Elisha narratives. When such an important

person as the commander of the king of Aram goes to Elisha for healing, he is well aware that such a request ought to be accompanied by a great gift. So Naaman takes no less than ten talents of silver, six thousand shekels of gold, and ten sets of colored clothing with him as a gift for Elisha when he goes to visit him in Samaria (2 Kgs. 5:5). When King Benhadad of Aram lies on his deathbed and sends his courtier Hazael for an oracle from Elisha, who happened to be in Damascus at the time, this mission, too, is accompanied by a truly royal gift: forty camel-loads of the finest wares of Damascus (8:9). The round figure 40 is a favorite hyperbole in the Old Testament.

d. Prophet Legends

Besides the legends that are part of the Elijah and Elisha cycles, the first book of Kings contains yet another two, more or less independent legends about prophets. The first (1 Kings 13) contains the theme of the disobedient prophet who does not strictly observe the terms of his mission (cf. the stories of Balaam and Jonah). It gives the story of an unnamed man of God from Judah, whom Yahweh sends to Bethel to denounce Jeroboam of Israel for usurping a cultic prerogative. Jeroboam has built an altar in Bethel and is ready to put fire to the sacrifice on it. At the command of Yahweh, the man of God addresses this altar with the words: "O altar, altar, thus says Yahweh: 'Behold, a son shall be born to the house of David, Josiah by name; and he shall sacrifice upon you the priests of the high places who burn incense upon you, and men's bones shall be burned upon you'" (v. 2). Infuriated by these words, the king stretches out his hand against the man of God and orders his men to seize him. But the hand he stretches out stiffens, so that he cannot pull it back. Now the king is on the defensive, for he is forced to ask the prophet to intercede with Yahweh to restore the use of his arm. This prayer is heard, and out of gratitude the king offers the man of God a gift. This gift is resolutely refused, as is the invitation to go with the king to his palace to be entertained there. Taking a different route home, the man of God begins his journey back to Judah.

This story could have suitably ended at this

point. There is, however, a sequel that we should regard as the actual prophet story (1 Kgs. 13:11–32), for here the author deals with his real theme—the disobedient prophet. This second part is introduced with the information that there is an old prophet living in Bethel, whose sons have witnessed the event related in verses 1–10 and report it to their father. As soon as the father learns the direction the man of God is taking, he saddles his donkey and goes after him. He finds him resting under an oak tree. Even as the king had done, so also the old prophet invites the man of God to go home with him and have a meal together. This time, too, the man of God declines the invitation, saying, "It was said to me by the word of Yahweh, 'You shall neither eat bread nor drink water there, nor return by the way that you came'" (v. 17). The old prophet, however, persists and tells the man of God that he too is a prophet and that he has been told by an angel of Yahweh to bring the man of God back to his house to eat with him. The man of God relents and goes with the old prophet to his house. He soon has ample cause to regret his decision.

While they are sitting at the table, the word of Yahweh comes to the old man, and he cries out in judgment against the man of God who has come from Judah: "Thus says Yahweh, 'Because you have disobeyed the word of Yahweh, and have not kept the commandment which Yahweh your God commanded you, but have come back, and have eaten bread and drunk water in the place of which he said to you, "Eat no bread, and drink no water"; your body shall not come to the tomb of your fathers'" (1 Kgs. 13:21–22). The man of God then leaves the house of his host. On the road a lion meets him and kills him. The lion does not devour him, however, nor does it harm his donkey. His body remains lying on the road and is found by some passersby, who report what has happened to the inhabitants of Bethel. When the old prophet hears of it he again orders his donkey saddled and immediately goes to the place where it happened. Arriving there, he lays the dead body on the donkey and brings it back to Bethel. After the funeral he instructs his sons to bury him in the grave of this man of God.

This story, embellished with all sorts of miraculous details by later generations, raises many questions. As I have noted, the central feature is the disobedience of the prophet, who is punished by Yahweh with death. The objectionable element in the story is that Yahweh, in order to test the obedience of his servant, uses means that in our opinion are dubious. For the old prophet uses a lie to seduce the man of God to be disobedient to Yahweh. This act must have aroused the indignation of an early editor, who added to verse 18 the explicit comment that the old prophet was lying. To be sure, later we see that lying words were not unusual in the mouth of Yahweh's prophets (1 Kgs. 22:20–22), but in this story we have problems with it. The author apparently does not intend to put all the stress on this detail in the story. His main concern is to show that a man of God, or prophet, must unconditionally obey Yahweh in everything and may not alter his course, even if some other prophet gives him an apparent counterorder.

The story contains salient features. Remarkable, for example, is the anonymity of the chief actors. The personal names mentioned (e.g., Josiah and Jeroboam, in 1 Kgs. 13:2, 4) are clearly secondary. Later generations were not content with this anonymity. For instance, Josephus calls the man of God from Judah "Yadon" (*Antiquities* 8.9.1), sometimes connected with the name Iddo in 2 Chronicles 13:22. The reference to the old age of the prophet living in Bethel (1 Kgs. 13:11) serves to indicate that he was a man of authority, someone who was not to be easily refused. This detail certainly heightens the dramatic effect. For however difficult it may have been for the man of God to turn down the invitation of this venerable person, he nevertheless should have done so. Finally, as mentioned above, the lion's behavior was most miraculous. After killing the man of God, the beast ignored the donkey, the passersby, and finally the old prophet as he brought back the body. Such details give the story its legendary coloring. Some of these details are to be regarded as later elaborations.

The second, more or less independent prophet story has as its context the plan of King Ahab of Israel to capture the fortress Ramoth in Gilead, assisted by King Jehoshaphat of Judah. Benhadad of Syria, after his defeat by the king of Israel (1 Kings 20), had to cede this city to Ahab but was dragging his feet in handing it over. Before going to battle, Ahab, as was customary before any rather important military expedition, seeks the counsel of the four hundred court prophets. Their oracle is unanimously favorable, so that nothing seems to stand in the way of going ahead. The unanimity of the counsel of these prophets, however, creates suspicions in the mind of Jehoshaphat. He insists on asking the advice of an independent prophet of Yahweh, someone not belonging to the collective prophets of Ahab. Ahab has no choice but to give in. He mentions Micaiah son of Imlah, even though this man did not have his sympathy because Micaiah never prophesied anything good about him. An official is sent to bring Micaiah, who is told that the court prophets have already been consulted and that they are unanimous in their favorable advice to the king. The messenger suggests that Micaiah go along with what they have said. Micaiah, however, indignantly rejects this proposal and declares that he will prophesy only what Yahweh will tell him.

The story gives the impression that Micaiah saw Ahab's mission as hopeless. Yet to Ahab's request for advice, Micaiah gives an encouraging answer: "Go up and triumph; Yahweh will give it into the hand of the king" (1 Kgs. 22:15). Ahab, however, senses that Micaiah is not honestly speaking his mind, and he insists that the prophet give him a true oracle from the Lord. Micaiah complies, this time saying, "I saw all Israel scattered upon the mountains, as sheep that have no shepherd; and Yahweh said, 'These have no master; let each return to his home in peace'" (v. 17). This prophecy should have been enough for Ahab to abandon his plan. There was, however, also the counsel of the four hundred court prophets who had advised positively. How could they also believe that they were proclaiming Yahweh's will? In the story Micaiah explains what had happened. Micaiah had received a vision in which the will of Yahweh had been revealed to him:

> I saw Yahweh sitting on his throne, and all the host of heaven standing beside him on his right hand and on his left; and Yahweh said, "Who will entice Ahab, that he may go up and fall at Ramoth-gilead?" And one said one thing, and another said another. Then a spirit came forward and stood before Yahweh, saying, "I will

entice him." And Yahweh said to him, "By what means?" And he said, "I will go forth, and will be a lying spirit in the mouth of all his prophets." And he said, "You are to entice him, and you shall succeed; go forth and do so." (vv. 19–22)

Micaiah then tells Ahab directly that his four hundred prophets are inspired by a lying spirit and that Yahweh has indeed decreed disaster over him. Disregarding this message, Ahab attacks Ramoth-gilead and is fatally wounded.

The historical context of the story is more or less incidental. The focus is not the death of the northern Israelite king in battle at Ramoth-gilead but the problem of true and false prophecy. The issue raised here was one that engaged minds and hearts in Israel for centuries. This story is therefore properly categorized under the rubric *prophet legend*. The tradition seeks to make clear that false prophecy does not lie outside Yahweh's sovereignty and that, in some cases, it is even used by him for the proclamation of his word.

e. Martyr Legends

Martyr legends occur in the Old Testament only in the book of Daniel. As is well known, martyrology is not the only distinctive feature of the youngest book in the Old Testament. The other is apocalyptic, concretized in the visions of Daniel in which the rule of God in world history and the imminent arrival of the messianic realm are made visible to the believers. This book was a source of genuine comfort and inspiration to Judas Maccabeus and his people at the time of the Maccabean war (167–164 B.C.).

The context of the first of the two martyr stories (Daniel 3) is the order of Nebuchadrezzar that everyone must kneel down before and worship the golden image he had set up in the plain of Dura. Anyone defying the order would be thrown into the fiery furnace. Three Judean young men, Shadrach, Meshach, and Abednego, who were educated at the Babylonian court to serve in the palace of the king and who were taught the language and literature of the Chaldeans (1:4), refused to obey the order. The king was promptly informed of this disobedience. Asked whether they still intended to resist, the young men answered confidently, "O Nebuchadnezzar, we have no need to answer you in this matter. If it be so, our God whom we serve is able to deliver us from the burning fiery furnace; and he will deliver us out of your hand, O king. But if not, be it known to you, O king, that we will not serve your gods or worship the golden image which you have set up" (3:16–18). The king predictably reacted in rage and ordered that the young men be bound and thrown into the oven, after first heating it seven times hotter than usual.

But what happened? The only ones who were killed by the fire were the men who had tied them and thrown them into the furnace. The young men remained unharmed, because God had sent a protecting angel. Then to his surprise the king saw not three but four men walking unharmed in the fire. When they left the furnace, the fire had not harmed their bodies, their hair had not been singed, their robes were not scorched, and there was not even the smell of fire on them. The king was instantly converted, professing his faith in the God of Shadrach, Meshach, and Abednego, who had so miraculously rescued his servants from death. Furthermore, the king ordered that anyone, of whatever nation or language, who said anything against the God of Shadrach, Meshach, and Abednego be cut into pieces and his house be turned into a pile of rubble, because no other god could save like theirs did (Dan. 3:29).

The time and locale of the second martyr legend is altogether different, namely the time of Darius the Mede, a ruler now known also from secular history. According to Daniel 6:29 (28), Cyrus the Persian was his successor. Cyrus died in 530 B.C. in the battle against the Massagetes at the Jaxartes. According to chapter 6, Daniel was one of the three administrators whom Darius had appointed over the three provinces of his mighty realm. Here the story shows some similarity with the history of Joseph, who likewise as a Hebrew had achieved a high position in a foreign land. Like Joseph, Daniel gets into difficulties. Because of his exceptional personal capabilities, he incurs the jealousy of the two other administrators and the 120 satraps, who try to bring about his downfall in any way possible. Nothing succeeds, and so they arrive at the conclusion that only in connection with the service of his God will they find any basis for charges against Daniel. At this point there is an obvious association with the story in 3:1–30, where religion was also the point at issue. They managed to have a royal decree issued in which it was stipulated that anyone who prayed to any god or man during the next thirty days, except to the king, would be thrown into the lions' den. Daniel, then, was easily caught in the act of praying to the God of Israel. Though the king left no stone unturned in trying to save Daniel, he could not legally get around the demands of his administrators and satraps. So Daniel was thrown into the lions' den. A stone was placed over the mouth of the den and was then sealed with the signet ring of the king so that Daniel could not escape his punishment (Dan. 6:18 [17]).

The next morning at the crack of dawn, the king hurried to the lions' den to find out what had become of Daniel. There, to his astonishment, he heard that Daniel's God had sent an angel (cf. the story of the fiery furnace in Daniel 3!) who had shut the mouths of the lions so that they had been unable to hurt Daniel. Overjoyed that everything had turned out as it did, the king ordered Daniel to be pulled out of the den. Then Darius had all those who had plotted Daniel's death, together with their wives and children, thrown to the lions. Before they reached the bottom of the den, the lions overpowered them, crushing all their bones. The end of the story exceeds even that of chapter 3. Instead of merely making it illegal to say anything against the God of the Jews, Darius decreed that all peoples, nations, and languages everywhere must fear and reverence the God of Daniel:

> For he is the living God,
>   enduring for ever;
> his kingdom shall never be destroyed,
>   and his dominion shall be to the end.
> He delivers and rescues,
>   he works signs and wonders
>   in heaven and on earth,
> he who has saved Daniel
>   from the power of the lions.
>
>   (Dan. 6:27–28 [26–27])

6. THE PARABLE

As a literary genre the parable is not well represented in the Old Testament. The three examples are the fable of Jotham (Judg. 9:8–15), the rich man and the ewe lamb (2 Sam. 12:1–4), and the song of the vineyard (Isa. 5:1–2). Like the other literary genres discussed above, parables serve the overall proclamation and do not exist for their own sake. They are fictitious stories that sharply criticize the actions of the listeners and that are intended to bring them to their senses. In the Old Testament the parable thus functions as a poetically formulated complaint. In the fable of Jotham, discussed above in section 3, this purpose is obvious. In the story the trees went out to anoint a king for themselves and, after unsuccessfully approaching the highly qualified olive tree, fig tree, and vine, had to be content with the thornbush. The residents of Shechem must immediately have realized that this story was meant to express Jotham's displeasure over their decision to offer the kingship to Abimelech.

The criticism by the prophet Nathan of David's adultery with Bathsheba is also told in an indirect way. Nathan did not openly denounce the king but couched his rebuke in a fictitious story, trusting that David would still sense his meaning. Nathan, however, succeeded only in making the king very indignant about the deed of the rich man who had dared to take the poor man's only possession, his ewe lamb. Nathan was forced to interpret his parable to David, telling him directly, "You are the man!" (2 Sam. 12:7). This incident indicates that in practice not every paraenetic parable accomplished its goal.

The final parable is the song of the vineyard, earlier discussed in another context. The parable takes up only two verses (Isa. 5:1–2) and here is in the form of a love song, almost certainly being recited as such at the Feast of Tabernacles. We may assume that the prophet put his parable in the form of a song primarily so that he might be assured of a large audience. A song, certainly a love song, always attracts attention. This parable also is exhortative in intention. Even without the explanation added later, the meaning of the parable is obvious. Here the inhabitants of Jerusalem are told that in every respect they have failed their

God and disappointed his expectations. They were the vineyard on a fertile hillside to which God had done everything possible, expecting that it would produce a rich yield. But at harvest time there were only bad grapes, not good ones. The content of this denouncement is easily guessed. The good grapes represent good government and proper justice, the bad grapes stand for a government of bloodshed and perversion of justice (v. 8). Following the parable itself, Yahweh issues a call to enter into judgment with him (vv. 3–4) and announces that he will destroy them (vv. 5–6).

7. THE ANECDOTE

According to *Webster's,* an anecdote is a short narrative of an interesting, amusing, or curious incident, often biographical and generally characterized by human interest. Some of the short stories preserved in the Old Testament fit such a definition quite well. Comical aspects are found, for example, in the story of Balaam and the talking donkey (Num. 22:22–35) and in the account of Samson and the three hundred foxes (Judg. 15:1–7). In general, however, the short stories preserved in the Old Testament deal with more serious topics. Often they concern murder and killing, in the context of Israel's wars with foreign enemies. Such is the setting, for example, of the story of the judge Ehud, who craftily kills Eglon, the king of Moab. Ehud enters Eglon's quarters under pretense of having a secret message for him and then plunges a sword into the belly of the unsuspecting king (3:15–30).

To the same genre belongs the story of Jael, the wife of Heber the Kenite. In a friendly manner she invites Sisera, commander of Jabin's army, who was fleeing from the battle, into her tent. There, after he has fallen asleep from exhaustion, she takes his life by driving a tent peg into his temple (Judg. 4:17–22).

The tradition in Judges 9:50–55 is likewise an illustration of a bloody war. Abimelech had succeeded in besieging and capturing the town of Thebez. Inside the city, however, stood a tower that held out for a long time. Eventually Abimelech got close enough to try to set it on fire. At that dramatic moment a woman dropped an upper millstone on Abimelech's head, crushing his skull.

Not wanting it to be said that a woman had killed him, Abimelech hurriedly called for his armor-bearer and persuaded him to finish the job.

The story of Jonathan's victory over the Philistines is somewhat longer (1 Sam. 13:23–14:15), but it still has the marks of an anecdote. Jonathan suggests to his armor-bearer that together they try to sneak up on a carefully selected Philistine outpost and, if possible, take it by surprise. Jonathan encourages himself and his armor-bearer by saying that Yahweh can save just as easily by using a few as by using many (14:6). The armor-bearer agrees to the plan, and together they approach the Philistine outpost. Jonathan outlines his strategy as follows: "We will cross over to the men, and we will show ourselves to them. If they say to us, 'Wait until we come to you,' then we will stand still in our place, and we will not go up to them. But if they say, 'Come up to us,' then we will go up; for Yahweh has given them into our hand. And this shall be the sign to us" (vv. 8–10). The latter response occurs as the Philistines shout to the men to come up. Waiting for the right moment to take the enemy by surprise, the two of them attack and kill no less than twenty Philistines (v. 14). The anecdote ends with the report that this heroic act resulted in panic within the enemy camp and among all the people—even the earth quaked (v. 15).

8. THE NOVELETTE

The dictionary defines a novelette as a long short story. Hempel believes that this genre represents "Israel's most valuable literary advance." He characterizes the novelette as follows: "It is a form that is constructed upon a certain motif, either an original one or one that is ancient and perhaps common to many other cultures, and that uses suspense and denouement, progression and delay. Whether the style is abbreviated or elaborate, the work manifests such a unity that every segment is meaningful only as a part of the whole. Both materially and artistically, the novelette follows the rules for the popular tale" (*Literatur,* p. 93). The Joseph story (Genesis 37–50); the books of Ruth, Jonah, and Esther; and the story of Judah and Tamar (Genesis 38) all indeed fit this definition.

a. The Joseph Story

With its more than four hundred verses, the Joseph story is the most elaborate novelette in the Old Testament. Because of its outstanding literary qualities it has also become the most widely known outside Israel. It was, for instance, incorporated into the Koran, with new details added to it. The same thing happened to the story in the Jewish midrashim (such as *Bereshit Rabba*) and in Old Syrian religious literature. The story even made its way to Java, with still further embellishments. Hermann Gunkel believed that the Joseph history was a "wreath of sagas," that is, a collection of originally independent fictitious stories, beautifully fashioned into a unity by the author. Nowadays it is thought that it was a single story that grew as it was told and retold, though incorporating a variety of motifs from foreign soil, notably Egypt. From the start, however, the Joseph history has been an independent story.

Unlike what one might expect, the history of Jacob's most-beloved son shows no affinity with the patriarchal stories in the early part of the book of Genesis. In his essay "The Joseph Narrative and Ancient Wisdom," von Rad enumerates some salient differences. The Abraham, Isaac, and Jacob stories are always connected with a place and with the cult practiced there. Moreover, they are linked to each other by the theme of the promises of land and descendants to the patriarchs. The Joseph history, however, is thoroughly novelette in style and totally without specific local references. In its literary form, the Joseph history goes far beyond the ancient sagas. In this respect the story is much closer to the history of David's rule (2 Samuel 6 to 1 Kings 2). Literarily and historically it is hardly possible to place the Joseph story before the early monarchical period. During this period interest in the patriarchal traditions decreases, while at the same time there is an entirely new spiritual development for which we could best use the term *enlightenment*. The people demonstrated a great interest in what was strange and unknown, including broadening their perspective beyond the borders of Israel. No other story, for example, reports so elaborately about Egyptian customs and usages as the Joseph history.

In this early monarchical period we are also

confronted with a specific interest in what von Rad calls "the anthropological," that is, "a concentration upon the phenomenon of man in the broadest sense, his potentialities and his limitations, his psychological complexity and profundity" (p. 293). In addition, the awareness arose that this human situation could and must be formed and developed, which required specific educational objectives. The ancient wisdom of Israel knew this objective and strongly propagated it.

In this context von Rad suggests that there were close relations between this ancient Israelite wisdom tradition and the Joseph history. Joseph exemplifies the ancient wisdom ideal of the perfectly educated young man, as this model is not only vividly set forth in the biblical book of Proverbs but also expounded by the Egyptian wisdom teacher Amenemope. To cite von Rad (pp. 295–96) once again,

> In his relationship with his brothers, Joseph is the very pattern of the man who can "keep silence", as described in Egyptian wisdom-lore. He is the "prudent man who conceals his knowledge" (Prov. 12:23), and who "restrains his lips" (Prov. 10:19). Above all, the "patient man" does not give way to his passions, and the writer intends us to be amazed at the extraordinary control which Joseph is able to exercise over his emotions. It must not be forgotten that this prohibition of any display of emotion ran counter to the whole instinct of the ancient Hebrew.

In the novelette Joseph's wisdom reveals itself in many ways. Not only is he able to interpret the dreams of the butler and the baker and afterward that of the pharaoh himself (Gen. 40:1–41:45), he also knows the steps to take to avert the famine that threatens Egypt. The secret of all these successes was the fact that Yahweh was with him (39:21). Therefore in this history one should pay attention not only to the wisdom element but also to the theological aspect. Though the name of God is seldom mentioned, the author leaves no doubt that Yahweh alone determines the course of events and is in full control. The truth of the saying "Man proposes, but God disposes" is nowhere made as evident as in this history. "It was not you who sent me here," says Joseph to his brothers, "but God; and he has made me a father to

Pharaoh, and lord of all his house and ruler over all the land of Egypt" (45:8). God's providence is, however, most impressively expressed in the final words of Joseph to his brothers: "Fear not. . . . You meant evil against me; but God meant it for good, to bring it about that many people should be kept alive, as they are today" (50:19–20).

b. Ruth, Jonah, and Esther

The little book of Ruth, which Goethe called an idyll in his *Noten und Abhandlungen zu besserem Verständnis des west-östlichen Divans* (1819), has all the marks of the novelette and is rightly regarded as one of the best-told stories in the Old Testament. The book causes some problems, however, for which no final solution has yet been found (see P. Humbert, "Art et leçon de l'histoire de Ruth," in *Opuscules d'un Hébraïsant* [Neuchâtel, 1958]). The book of Jonah is a good example of didactic literature. Esther is a well-written novel that in its style and in many other respects reminds us of the Joseph history (see S. Talmon, "'Wisdom' in the Book of Esther," *VT* 13 [1963] 419–55). For more detailed discussion of these three books, see the respective discussions in part 3 below.

c. Judah and Tamar

The novelette regarding Judah and Tamar, which so remarkably interrupts the Joseph history, literarily is not a product of art for art's sake. Instead, it presents the reader with a question: can Tamar be blamed for what she did or not? The author himself clearly took the side of Tamar, yet he must have been aware that he had not said the final word in the matter.

At the outset we must realize that it is absolutely impossible as well as irrelevant to the problem to judge Tamar's deed in terms of our Western view of marriage and marital laws. We are confronted with a cultural pattern that is totally foreign to us, one that can be understood only from within its own context. The problem at issue in Genesis 38 hinges on the institution of so-called levirate marriage. This form of marriage is spelled out in Deuteronomy 25:5–10. Its major stipulation is that, in case a man dies without offspring, his brother must marry the widow. The first-born child from this union will be regarded as the child of the deceased brother so that "his name may not be blotted out of Israel" (v. 6). Ignoring here the many implications of this type of marriage, we shall consider only the complicated situation in Genesis 38.

Tamar is married to Er, the oldest son of Judah. The union, however, is short-lived. Er seems to have incurred the displeasure of Yahweh, who punishes him with death. It now falls to his brother Onan to perform the levirate duties for his sister-in-law. He fails in this duty, however, for whenever he lies with her he practices coitus interruptus. As punishment for this lovelessness Yahweh kills him too. Judah now advises his daughter-in-law to return to her father's house and to wait there till his youngest son, Shelah, has grown up and is ready for marriage. In reality, however, Judah has no intention of having Shelah marry Tamar. He suspects that Tamar is a man-killer and fears that this marriage might also cost the life of his youngest son.

Tamar, however, is determined at all cost to succeed in her objective of having a son and resorts to guile. Hearing that her father-in-law plans to go to Timnah, she puts on the disguise of a prostitute and sits along the road that Judah will travel on his way to Timnah. Judah is interested in Tamar and agrees to give her a young goat in return for her services to him. As a pledge from him,

however, she demands the seal that he wears on a gold or silver cord around his neck and also his staff, the sign of his position as head of a clan.

The encounter results in Tamar's becoming pregnant. She removes her veil and puts on her widow's clothes again. Meanwhile Judah sends a friend to the place where he met Tamar to give her the young goat they had agreed upon. The man fails to find her there, however, and unsuccessfully searches the area for her. After about three months Judah is informed that his daughter-in-law is pregnant and therefore obviously guilty of prostitution. Furious, he commands that she be brought out and burned to death in punishment. Then Tamar plays her trump card. She sends the message to Judah, "I am pregnant by the man who owns these. . . . See if you recognize whose seal and cord and staff these are" (Gen. 38:25 NIV). Judah can hardly deny that these objects indeed belong to him. He is honest enough to admit that Tamar is right with respect to him, because he had not given his son Shelah to her. The story ends with Tamar's giving birth to twins and with their names being given an etiological explanation.

In this story, one of the many in which a woman plays the key role, Tamar is depicted as a person of great moral courage, one who is prepared to go to any length to obtain what she is entitled to. The manner in which her heroic deed is described makes this story one of the literary high points in the Old Testament.

D. Historical Literature

1. HISTORIOGRAPHY

The general aim of modern historiography, according to the ideal of the great historiographer Leopold von Ranke, is to record events of the past for the future and to do so as objectively as possible. Ideally only "the way it actually happened" is what should be recorded. In Israel this type of approach to the past is not found. There the writing of history also served the ends of politics and religion, and such an unbiased view and evaluation of the past was never cultivated. Like all other literature in Israel so far discussed, historical writing was used to serve the proclamation, an orientation that implies a critical stance toward the material that is recorded. This character of Israel's historiography is particularly evident in the marvelous account of David's rule in 2 Samuel 9–20 and 1 Kings 1–2, chapters that contain a defense and glorification of the Davidic dynasty.

Every historiography, whatever its guiding motif, depends on reports whose objective truth is beyond dispute. In this connection we can think of the court annals, good examples of which are contained in 2 Samuel 8 and in 1 Kings 9:10–28 and chapter 16, and also of official documents, such as the lists of important functionaries and officials in the courts of David and Solomon (2 Sam. 8:16–18; 23:8–39; 1 Kgs. 4:1–19; etc.). The authors of the books of Kings and Chronicles made use of these annals. Finally, for everything relating to the cult, they could draw material from the temple chronicle (1 Kings 6–8; Nehemiah 8; 10–12; see also 2 Kings 22–23). For the description of the later monarchical period, the so-called diaries of the kings of Judah and Israel, known by such titles as the Book of the Kings of Judah and Israel (2 Chr.

25:26) and the Book of the Chronicles of the Kings of Judah (2 Kgs. 16:19), must have been important, though unfortunately they have been lost.

It has sometimes been asserted that Israel was the first country in the ancient world to engage seriously in genuine history writing. The element of truth in this view is that Israel indeed attempted to link historical facts together in a meaningful pattern and to look at the course of history from a particular viewpoint—wherever necessary, also critically. Other countries had indeed nothing comparable, at least not on the scale found in Israel. In this respect we think of victory reports of Egyptian kings on steles and temple walls (Thutmose III, Amenhotep II, Merneptah), of Hittite royal inscriptions (Shuppiluliumash, Hattushilish), of Canaanite and Syrian royal inscriptions (Mesha Stone), and of the decorative inscriptions of Assyrian kings (one of many examples is the hexagonal clay prism of Sennacherib). One important difference between Israelite and non-Israelite historiography is that the former was practiced in a much more independent manner. In other nations, historiography was a function strictly of court biographers, whose only task was to present their employers in as favorable a light as possible. In Assyria this arrangement led to pure self-glorification of the monarch by letting him speak in the first-person singular in his victory reports.

In Israel, however, the king is spoken of in the third person. This approach leaves the author much more freedom and gives him room for a critical evaluation where he feels such is necessary. Remarkable, too, is what one might call the democratic character of Israel's historiography. The books of Kings not only provide biographies of the kings of Judah and Israel but also pay a great deal of attention to men of God and prophets who were often critically involved in the actions of the kings. More to the point, we could say that all of Israel's historiography is imbued by the spirit and viewpoint of the prophets.

The first piece of genuine history writing is the history of David's family and of his succession to the throne. This literary masterpiece initiates Israel's history writing. Scholars differ, however, as to where they place the beginning of this history. The tradition of the succession to the throne is found in 1 Kings 1 and 2, but it clearly has had a long prehistory. In my judgment, 2 Samuel 9–20 is within the scope of this history (following Noth, von Rad, Rost, and the majority of others), but on purely literary grounds Eissfeldt believes that it is 2 Samuel 13–20 (*Introduction*, p. 137).

Every commentary rightly praises the literary beauty of this piece of history writing. It displays a beautiful composition and psychological depth, and the question is asked how this literary masterpiece could have been produced at the very beginning of the monarchical period. Here, too, one should point to the impulses that came from the so-called Solomonic renaissance, which had a stimulating influence on so many areas of Israel's spiritual life.

Vriezen rightly characterizes the work as a "spiritually noble piece of dynastic history, being intermediate between a biography and an epic poem in prose, even though according to form it is not an epic." It displays a clear national and political aim: to provide a moral-religious base for the recognition of the kingship of David and his son Solomon.

So far there is no unanimity about who wrote this history. It is obvious that the writer must have been very close to the court and have personally witnessed many of the events he described or have had reliable informants who provided him with all the desired details. For many years it was thought that Abiathar was the author. He seemed to fit best the criteria for authorship just mentioned. Closer scrutiny shows that this hypothesis is not very plausible. As someone who was opposed to Solomon's accession, he could not very well be regarded as an advocate of Solomon's kingship. Vriezen's suggestion that the author may have been Zabud, son of Nathan, called a priest in 1 Kings 4:5, where he is also said to be the "king's friend," deserves consideration. Of this Zabud it is known at least that he was a personal confidant of Solomon (Vriezen and van der Woude, *Literatuur*, p. 40).

The history of Solomon's disputed succession to the throne is told in two chapters (1 Kings 1–2). There were no obvious reasons why Solomon, the son of Bathsheba, should succeed his father. It happened because of a palace plot concocted mainly by the priest Zadok, the prophet Nathan, Bathsheba, and the royal bodyguard. Solomon's opponent was the handsome Adonijah, the son of Haggith, who was born after Absalom and to whom, according to 1:24 and 2:15, the kingship had been promised. His collaborators were the general Joab and the priest Abiathar. The author leaves no doubt that, from the outset, Adonijah's chances were not good. Against such powerful adversaries as Nathan and Zadok, who moreover could count on the support of the queen, Joab and Abiathar were at a great disadvantage. Therefore the writer characterizes Adonijah's grasp for power as a fit of exuberant boldness (1:5) that was bound to fail. The author's sympathies are clearly with Solomon, whose elevation to the throne he sees as being totally in agreement with the will of Yahweh (2 Sam. 12:25; 1 Kgs. 2:24). Adonijah's grasp for the throne indeed failed; he escaped death for the moment only because after the debacle he sought refuge in the sanctuary (1:53). When some time later he was careless enough to ask for Abishag to be his wife, an act that Solomon could only interpret as another covert attempt to seize power, his fate was soon decided (2:25). After another two personal enemies of his father, the general Joab and Shimei, the Benjamite from Bahurim (vv. 34, 46), had been liquidated, the writer at the end of his story could note with relief that the kingdom was firmly established in Solomon's hands (v. 46).

As I have previously noted, the succession to the throne was preceded by a long series of events. A superficial reading might create the impression that these accounts are only remotely connected with the main story. Appearance is deceptive, however, for on closer scrutiny it becomes clear that, for an exact evaluation of the main story, none of the preceding traditions is dispensable.

Most of the chief actors who play in these traditions return in the main story. Two units of unequal length in 2 Samuel 9–20 should clearly be regarded as literary peaks: the history of David's adultery with Bathsheba (chs. 11–12) and the story of Absalom's attempt to seize power (chs. 15–20). Between these two segments we also find, however, other jewels of the art of storytelling, such as the story of the rape of Tamar (13:1–22), the death of Amnon and the flight of Absalom (vv. 23–39), and the return of Absalom (ch. 14).

Finally, mention should be made of a number of other stories of historical content that have been preserved in the books of Kings and that are likewise remarkable on account of their high literary qualities: the schism in the realm in the opening days of Rehoboam's reign (1 Kgs. 12:1–24), Ahab's war against Ramoth-gilead (22:1–38), the murder of Joram and Ahaziah (2 Kgs. 9:16–29), the death of Jezebel (vv. 30–37), and the threat against Jerusalem by Sennacherib (18:13–37).

For completeness, I mention also the large historical works that elucidate the entire history of Judah and Israel: the so-called Deuteronomistic history (the books from Deuteronomy to 2 Kings) and the two books of Chronicles (see Noth, *Studien;* K. Roubos, *I Kronieken* [POT; Nijkerk, 1969]). They offer a view of history from a specific theological perspective, whose author or authors were not interested in an elegant literary style.

2. ADDRESSES

Addresses and letters constitute a rather significant element in the historical literature. Although there are some exceptions, both forms are specifically literary in character. That is, the biblical authors have not reproduced the literal text of what a speaker or writer said in the given situation but have presented their own version of it, much as Greek and Roman historiographers summarized what in their judgment their heroes would have said or written in the given situation. From the addresses in the Old Testament I select the three most important examples: Joshua's address at the covenant renewal at Shechem (Josh. 24:1–27), Samuel's farewell address (1 Samuel 12), and the address of Sennacherib's

messenger to the inhabitants of Jerusalem (2 Kgs. 18:19–25, 28–35).

a. Joshua's Address at Shechem

I ignore here the literary question whether the order of Joshua 23 and 24 should not be reversed, since chapter 23 contains the farewell address of the leader and would seem to follow the events recorded in chapter 24 (H. W. Hertzberg, *Die Bücher Josua, Richter, Ruth* [ATD 9; Göttingen, 1953], p. 132). In brief the contents of 24:1–27 are as follows: In the first part of this speech, which follows the familiar Deuteronomistic scheme (cf. the first chapters of Deuteronomy), Joshua presents a summary of Yahweh's dealings thus far with his people. He had led the fathers Abraham, Isaac, and Jacob from the land beyond the Euphrates to the land of Canaan. From there Jacob and his sons had gone to Egypt. Mistreated by the Egyptians, they had fled into the wilderness and, after having wandered there for some years, had returned to Canaan. Before reentering Canaan, they had been successful in Transjordan in battle against the Amorites and the Ammonites, who had refused them passage through their territory. They had but recently crossed the Jordan and arrived at Jericho and, after fierce battles with the Amorites, Perizzites, Canaanites, Hittites, Girgashites, Hivites, and Jebusites, had secured for themselves fixed places of residence in the land of Canaan. In this way Israel, according to the divine plan, had reached the end of its wanderings, for there it would always live. This brief historical survey in Joshua's address gives the impression of being a summary of the much more detailed resume in Deuteronomy 1–3 and is therefore likely from the same author.

But now the moment had also come to thank and honor Yahweh, who had so greatly prospered them. Israel is expected to do so with a heart that is totally loyal and dedicated to Yahweh. Therefore Joshua exhorts them to put away all the gods their fathers served beyond the river and the gods of the Amorites they themselves had worshiped and from now on to serve only Yahweh. After the people have expressed their willingness, Joshua makes a covenant with them and draws up for them statutes and ordinances at Shechem.

b. Samuel's Farewell Address

Like his great predecessor Joshua, Samuel gave a farewell address at the end of his rule (1 Samuel 12). The contents of both speeches were of course determined by the circumstances. Joshua's speech was actually little more than a detailed challenge to the people to remain faithful to Yahweh, who had done so many good things for them in bringing them into the good land of Canaan. In Samuel's day the situation was altogether different. For instance, during his rule Samuel had regularly been confronted with the request for a king. Not surprisingly, in his farewell address he brought up this question again in detail. Like Joshua's address, Samuel's speech included a detailed historical look backward. The most important difference between the two addresses, however, is that Samuel, at the beginning of his address, asked a kind of formal discharge from his rule: "Whose ox have I taken? Or whose ass have I taken? Or whom have I defrauded? Whom have I oppressed? Or from whose hand have I taken a bribe to blind my eyes with it?" (v. 3). The answer of the people is as we might have expected: "You have not defrauded us or taken anything from any man's hand" (v. 5). Yahweh is then invoked as witness to the declaration, and Samuel can regard himself as being fully discharged (12:1-25).

In the Old Testament the chief elements in the farewell address are a retrospective look at God's intervention in the life of the speakers or that of their people, guidelines for the future, an exhortation to the hearers to lead an exemplary life (often with a reference to the example of the life of the speakers themselves), and a final farewell with a blessing, prayer, or wish for prosperity for the future. Besides the two addresses discussed here, the Old Testament contains the farewell address of Jacob (Gen. 47:29–50:14), Moses' final song of praise and blessing (Deuteronomy 31–33), and David's final words to Solomon (1 Kgs. 2:1-9). The farewell address is a literary genre that was also used by classical authors, who wrote the words of Patroclus (Homer, *Iliad* 16.85ff.), Socrates (Plato, *Apology* 39 c and *Phaedo* 85 b), Cambyses (Herodotus 3.65), and Cyrus (Xenophon, *Cyropaedia* 8.7). (See A. van den Born, ed., *Bijbels Woordenboek* [Roermond, 1966-1969[3]], p. 30.)

c. Speech of Sennacherib's Messenger

The Assyrian king Sennacherib (705–681) has assembled his troops before Jerusalem but has not yet decided to assault the city. First he will attempt to persuade Hezekiah to surrender the city to him without bloodshed. With that objective in mind he sends a delegation from Lachish to Jerusalem, consisting of the supreme commander (*tartannu*), the chief officer (*rab saris*), and the field commander (*rab shaqu*). These high officials meet with a Judean delegation consisting of the palace administrator Eliakim, the scribe Shebna, and the recorder Joab at the aqueduct of the Upper Pool (2 Kgs. 18:17–18).

The *tartannu* opens the talks. It soon becomes clear that the Assyrian is interested only in a monologue and that there will not be any real talks. His speech is aimed at driving a wedge between the people and the king of Judah, in the hope of undermining the moral strength of each. First, talking over the heads of the Judean delegation, he tells Hezekiah that it is useless to rely on Egyptian support. Egypt is nothing but a cracked reed of a staff, one that pierces the hand of anyone who leans on it. It makes no sense either to depend on Yahweh, for he is the one who has told Sennacherib to come and attack Judah (2 Kgs. 18:25). After thus having minimized all help Judah might expect from the outside, the chief commander continues to ridicule the weakness of the Judean forces; even if he would give the Judeans two thousand horses, they could not find the riders to put on them.

The language in which the Assyrian spoke was Judean. The commander, of course, intends not only the Judean authorities but also the ordinary people to understand him. Eliakim and his men, however, request that the Assyrian speak in Aramaic, the language of diplomats and the better educated. The Assyrian, however, has no intention of giving up the favorable position afforded him by his knowledge of Judean. Therefore he now directly addresses the Judeans sitting on the city wall. They should no longer trust in Hezekiah, for he cannot do anything for them. However, if they surrender to Sennacherib, they will not lack a thing. People would eat from their own vine and fig tree and would drink from their own cistern. Even if the people would have to be deported to Assyria, they would suffer no calamity, for there they would find plenty of grain and new wine, a land of bread, vineyards, olive trees, oil, and honey—in other words, a land in no way different from Judah. Hezekiah, however, has ordered his people to listen to the Assyrian in silence and not to respond in any way whatever to his words. The order is obeyed by the people as well as by the delegation, who bring back to Hezekiah a report of the meeting.

It is not difficult to determine that also here we have a speech drafted by the author himself. For he puts typically Judean arguments and figurative language into the mouth of the Assyrian, and even goes so far as to have him speak Judean. So the argument of 2 Kings 18:25 is directly based on Isaiah 10:5, where Assyria is called the rod of Yahweh's anger. The characterization of Egypt as a "broken reed of a staff" is based on a Judean expression (Ezek. 29:6), as is the term "vine and fig tree" (1 Kgs. 5:5 [4:25]; Mic. 4:4; Joel 1:7, 12; Ps. 105:33). So also verse 32 expresses the author's perspective. The Assyrian doubtless knew from his own observation how altogether different Judah and Assyria were. For example, the growing of olive trees, common in Palestine, was totally impossible in the Assyrian climate (H. A. Brongers, *II Koningen* [POT; Nijkerk, 1970], p. 187).

3. LETTERS

The genre of letters is remarkably well represented in the Old Testament. With the exception of the private letter that King David sent to his chief commander Joab in connection with Uriah (2 Sam.11:14–15), all letters that we have are official in character. I list them here in chronological order:

1. Queen Jezebel to the elders and nobles in Israel (1 Kgs. 21:9–10)
2. The king of Aram to the king of Israel (2 Kgs. 5:6)
3. Jehu to the rulers of Israel (2 Kgs. 10:2–3, 6)
4. King Sennacherib to King Hezekiah (Isa. 37:10–13)
5. Jeremiah to the exiles in Babylon (Jer. 29:4–23)
6. People from the territory Beyond the River to Artaxerxes, in which they try to blacken the Judeans in the eyes of the ruler (Ezra 4:9–16)

All these letters have their function in the history told by the writer and give the impression of having been drafted by the writer himself. I would make an exception for Jeremiah's letter to the exiles in Babylon, since there is no reason to assume that this letter was not written by the prophet himself, or at least not dictated to his secretary Baruch. In general these letters are all literary forms that have their own function in the story and that, in the judgment of the authors, could very well have been written in the particular form given by the people involved. For that reason the beginning and the ending of these letters are always missing and only the matter at issue is mentioned, introduced by the customary *weattah,* "to the point" (H. A. Brongers, "Bemerkungen zum Gebrauch des adverbialen *wᵉ'attāh* im Alten Testament," *VT* 15 [1965] 289–99).

E. Prophetic Literature

1. PROPHETIC LITERATURE OUTSIDE ISRAEL

As I have noted above, throughout its history Israel never in any respect led an insular existence, devoid of contact with its neighboring countries. One of the consequences of this contact was that, not only materially but also religiously, Israel had much in common with its neighbors. In religious matters, for example, we have long known that Israel was not unique in having prophets. Through archeological finds in recent decades, our knowledge in this area has greatly increased, and we have learned that the remarkable phenomenon of prophecy was also present, in one form or another, throughout virtually all of the ancient East. I comment first on three examples of prophecy from Egypt.

a. The Admonitions of Ipu-Wer

The manuscript containing the admonitions of Ipu-Wer dates from the New Kingdom, from the time of the Nineteenth or Twentieth Dynasty (ca. 1345–1085 B.C.), but the original is much older (*ANET*, 441ff.; H. O. Lange, "Prophezeiungen eines ägyptischen Weisen aus dem Papyrus I, 344 in Leiden," in *Sitzungsberichte der Preussischen Akademie der Wissenschaften* [1903], pp. 585, 601–10; A. H. Gardiner, *The Admonitions of an Egyptian Sage from a Hieratic Papyrus in Leiden* [Leipzig, 1909]). It is generally assumed that the conditions described in this text refer to the rule of Pepi II, one of the pharaohs of the Sixth Dynasty (ca. 2350–2150), who, according to the tradition, ruled ninety years.

The text, unfortunately not fully preserved, contains the words of a wise man, a certain Ipu-Wer, with which he addresses the king. According to the text, at that time Egypt experienced a period of total chaos—politically, socially, and economically. The royal court, however, shows total unconcern about it. The pharaoh leads his own life, disregarding completely the bitter misery of his subjects. Like an Old Testament prophet, Ipu-Wer appears on the scene and points out the king's duties. In vivid language Ipu-Wer depicts the misery that holds land and people in its grip:

Every man sees in his son an enemy. . . .

The Nile has overflowed, but no one starts plowing; everyone says, "We do not know what is going to happen in the land. . . ."

Poor people now possess great wealth. Whoever could not make even a pair of sandals for himself now wallows in luxury. Nobles lament, but the poor rejoice. Laughter has stopped. Lamentations are heard throughout the land, mixed with weeping. . . .

The children of the nobles are dashed against the wall [cf. Ps. 137:9!]. Children, fervently prayed for, now lie in the open field. . . .

So the lament goes on and on. The king remains unimpressed, however, which induces Ipu-Wer to denounce him in harsh words.

For our purposes here, it is important that this passage apparently deals with an ideal king. We are not sure, however, whether it deals with a past or a future king. Grammatically the tense is quite uncertain. If the subject matter is assumed to be a future king, we indeed have a prophecy here. We would then translate the relevant lines, "And it will happen that he will give refreshing to the heart. The people will say: he is the shepherd of all people. There is no evil in his heart. May his flocks be small, since every day he is concerned about them."

b. The Prophecy of Nefer-Rohu

The copies of this text date from the period of the Eighteenth and Nineteenth Dynasties (ca. 1570–1200; W. Golénischeff, *Les Papyrus hiératiques no. 1115, 1116 A et 1116 B de l'Ermitage Impérial à St. Petersbourg* [1913]; Erman, *Literatur,* pp. 174–85). It tells about King Snofru of the Fourth Dynasty (ca. 2600), who, apparently in a moment of boredom, expressed the wish that a search be made throughout the land for someone who could entertain the king with an interesting story. The king is put in touch with a certain Nefer-Rohu, a lecturer-priest serving Bastet, the cat goddess of Bubastis in the eastern half of the Delta. The storyteller asks the king whether he prefers a tale from the past or one about the future. The king opts for the latter, and Nefer-Rohu begins. His story has considerable similarity with that of Ipu-Wer, discussed above.

In this story, too, a somber picture is drawn of the desolate condition of the country and of the total disintegration ravaging it. This time, however, we are told something about the cause of the misery. Asiatics have invaded the land and brought it to the brink of collapse. This detail seems to indicate that we have here a prediction after the fact. We are told how the land has been turned upside down and how things happen that have never happened before. "I will show you," says the priest, "that the son is a foe and the brother an enemy and that a man will kill his own father." Apparently the occupation by the Asiatics also resulted in the complete disintegration of the families. The situation is so deplorable that even the rivers of Egypt have run dry and the sun shines only one hour a day. No one knows when it is noon, for there is no shadow. Here also we witness a complete revolution in social relations, as is common in such situations. "He who used to be without any importance is now a powerful man. People greet [respectfully] him who [formerly] had to greet himself." So the picture of the deplorable situation in Egypt continues for a while, until we suddenly read:

But there will come a king from the south—Ameni, the triumphant, is his name. He is the son of a woman from the land of Nubia; he is born in Upper Egypt. He will take the [white] crown; he will wear the red crown; he will unite the two mighty ones [Upper and Lower Egypt]. He will slay the Asiatics by the sword and deliver the Libyans to the flame. The wall of the ruler will be built and the Asiatics will no longer be permitted to enter Egypt to ask for water as before to let their animals drink.

We get the impression that the text refers to the time between the Old Kingdom and the Middle Kingdom (11th–13th Dynasties, or 2100–1800 B.C.). The king who brings restoration is Amenemhet I, the founder of the Twelfth Dynasty. In our text he is called Ameni, a name more often used for Amenemhet.

The text claims, however, to be from the time of Snofru, which would imply that it was no less than seven hundred years old. Though scholars today agree that this age is incorrect, opinions differ about the actual time of composition. It is generally assumed that we have here a prediction after the event. Hugo Gressmann has correctly noted: "One could chance upon the idea of representing present situations as if they had been foretold in the past only if one were already familiar with true predictions of a political nature. From that perspective one dared from the copy to reason back to the original and to make use of these secondary sources for the historical reconstruction of the lost primary sources" (*Der Messias* [Göttingen, 1929], p. 432).

c. The Wen-Amon Story

The final Egyptian document to be discussed is especially significant in illustrating so-called ecstatic prophecy, one of the oldest forms of prophecy, also found in the Old Testament as early as the days of Samuel (*ANET,* 25–29; Erman, *Literatur,* pp. 174–85). This report is written on a papyrus discovered in 1899 by the Russian W. Golénischeff and later published by him (*Recueil de Travaux . . .* 21 [1899] 74–102). The papyrus dates from approximately 1090 B.C. Written in the first person singular, it is the travel report of a certain Wen-Amon, a high official who was sent on a journey by the high priest of Amon to buy cedar wood for the restoration of the royal boat of Amon-Re. The destination of the journey was Byblos, the harbor on the Phoenician coast, from which the wood that was cut in the Lebanon was usually shipped to other countries. To protect his mission the high priest of Thebes gave Wen-Amon an image of the god Amon-Re. The undertaking, however, did not have the expected favorable results.

At this time Egypt experienced a period of political weakness, as a result of which Egyptians traveling abroad were often looked upon with contempt. Wen-Amon had such a reception in Byblos, for as soon as he got there the king of Byblos told him to leave the city as quickly as possible. The shipping trade between Byblos and Egypt had shrunk to a fraction of what it used to be, and it therefore took Wen-Amon no less than a month to find a ship that could return him to his own country. During that time the following happened:

While he [the king of Byblos] made sacrifices to his gods, the god [i.e., the Baal of Byblos] seized an old [?] man from his old [?] people [or of his squires] and drove him to a frenzy and said to him: "Bring here the image [of Amon that Wen-Amon had with him]! Bring the messenger who is carrying him. Amon is the one who sent him; he is the one who made him come." While the frenzied person was raving during the night, . . . the harbormaster came to me and said, "Thus says the king: remain until morning!"

Ecstatic prophecy is an international religious phenomenon. For Israel we only have to recall the pericopes 1 Samuel 10:1–12 (note the question "Is Saul also among the prophets?") and 19:20–24 (where the saying occurs in another context).

d. The Mari Texts

The discovery of the so-called Mari Texts has tremendously enriched our knowledge of extrabiblical prophecy in Mesopotamia. Excavations at Tell el-Hariri on the Euphrates in 1933 yielded great treasures and were therefore continued in subsequent years. In several seasons of digging the tremendous palace of King Zimri-Lim of Mari was uncovered. One of the major finds was the state

archives, consisting of no less than twenty thousand clay tablets. This mighty palace with its three hundred rooms, which during the tourist season drew visitors from far and near, was destroyed by Zimri-Lim's great rival, Hammurabi of Babylon, who was afraid that his realm might be eclipsed by the increasingly more powerful kingdom of Mari.

Included in the contents of this state archives were some fifty letters that provide important information for our knowledge of extrabiblical prophecy. The first text is a report of the governor of Mari, a certain Itur-asdu, directed to his king, who is on a military campaign somewhere abroad. Itur-asdu writes as follows:

On the day on which I sent this letter to my master, Malik-Dagan, a man from Shakka came to me and informed me of the following: "In my dream I and a man with me from the district of Sagaratum in the upper district wanted to go to Mari. In my vision I entered Terqa. As soon as I had entered, I stepped into the temple of Dagan and prostrated myself before Dagan. While I lay kneeled, Dagan opened his mouth and spoke thus to me: 'Have the kings of the Benjamites and their men made peace with the men of Zimri-Lim who had advanced?' I [said], 'They have not made peace.' When I was at the point of going outside, he said to me, 'Why are there no envoys from Zimri-Lim with me, and why does he not give a complete report to me? Otherwise long ago I would have given the kings of the Benjamites into the hands of Zimri-Lim. Now go. I send you. Thus you shall say to Zimri-Lim: "Send your envoys to me and give me a complete report. Then will I also put the Benjamites in a fish basket and bring them before you."'" This is what the man saw in his dream, and he related it to me. Now I have written it to my lord. May my lord make a decision regarding this dream. Moreover, if it pleases my lord, may my lord make a complete report to Dagan, and may the envoys of my lord be continually on the way to Dagan. The man who told me this dream will bring an animal sacrifice to Dagan; therefore I have not sent him. And because he is a speedy messenger [?], he did not bring along the lock of his hair nor the hem of his garment [meaning of these last words is uncertain]. (Ellermeier, *Prophetie,* pp. 25ff.)

The following document is a letter from Kibri-

Dagan, governor of Zimri-Lim in Terqa, where, as was evident from the previous letter, there was a temple of Dagan. The contents are as follows:

> To my lord, speak: thus says Kibri-Dagan, your servant: Dagan and Ikrub-El are in good health. The city of Terqa and the province are doing well. To the point: On the day in which I had this letter brought to my lord, the muhhum of Dagan came and spoke a word to me, as follows: "The god has sent me. Write quickly to the king that sacrifices for the dead may be brought to the spirit of the dead of Jachdun-Lim." This is what that muhhum said to me and thus I have written to my lord. My lord may do what pleases him! (Ellermeier, *Prophetie*, p. 35)

The Mari Texts repeatedly mention the activity of a *muhhum* (Herrmann, *Heilserwartungen*, p. 47; F. M. Th. de Liagre Böhl, "Prophetentum und stellvertretendes Leiden in Assyrien und Israel," in *Opera Minora* [Groningen, 1953], pp. 63–80). He appears as the messenger of the deity, whose will, perhaps revealed in a state of frenzy, he reveals to the king. The identity of this speaker is not clear. Some are inclined to think of an official functionary, for instance a cultic prophet. In the first letter, however, the *muhhum* seems to be a man of humble origins, who does not seem to have been connected with a temple and who is simply introduced as "a man from Shakka." Though receiving the divine message in the temple, he says specifically that it happened in a dream.

We should note here some common features in these reports. First, in all these passages the ones who act do so without having been asked and present messages that are not pleasing to the recipients. Second, the deity is always introduced as speaking. Finally, it is noteworthy that the bearers of the revelation never enter into direct contact with the king but always deliver their message via some kind of functionary. That person passes the message on to the king in very polite terms, leaving it up to the king to respond as he wishes.

These passages exhibit formal similarities and differences with Old Testament prophecies. As is true in the Old Testament, individuals in the Mari Texts, regardless of their social group, deliver messages to the king that are unasked and unpleasant and yet that have divine authority. In these texts the spokesperson says, "Thus you shall say to Zimri-Lim"; in Jeremiah 1:7 Yahweh says to his prophet, "To all to whom I send you you shall go, and whatever I command you you shall speak."

A difference, however, is that in Mari these messengers never have direct contact with the king but always seek contact with one of his high authorities. It is striking, too, that these messengers are not always convinced of the importance of the message, yet they do not wish to run the risk that later they may be called to account if it should turn out that the message was indeed important. Hence the stereotype ending: I leave it up to the king to respond as he wishes.

The material comparison is more difficult. On the surface there is considerable difference between what the Old Testament prophets pass on as divine revelation and what the Mari spokespersons deliver. In Mari the topics concern merely the failure to bring prescribed sacrifices for the dead and whether or not to build a gate. Yet caution is needed here, for we know nothing of the background. What we may regard as insignificant may for these people have been a matter of life and death. Moreover, in the first letter discussed, it concerns the intervention of the deity in a political and military conflict, a situation with which we are also familiar from the Old Testament. Though many questions still await an answer, it is clear that, in the study of prophecy in the Old Testament, the Mari Texts cannot be ignored.

e. Oracles

Long before the discoveries in Mari, a number of texts had become known that likewise deal with communications from gods to earthly mortals, whether or not through an intermediary. In Mesopotamia this person was in most cases not a prophet but a priest, more specifically, a *baru* priest, that is, a seer or a viewer, to some extent comparable to the Old Testament *roeh* (1 Sam. 9:9). Regularly on the eve of an important undertaking such as a battle, these *baru* priests were consulted, and they exercised great political influence. The following is an interesting example of this last aspect. We know that the accession to the throne of Esarhaddon (681–669 B.C.) was accom-

21. *An ewer from Lachish (ca. 13th century B.C.). (Israel Department of Antiquities and Museums)*

22. *A Philistine painted jug and cup. (University Museum, University of Pennsylvania, neg. #70492)*

23. *An ivory plaque depicting the prince of Megiddo receiving tribute and prisoners (14th to 12th centuries B.C.). (Oriental Institute, University of Chicago)*

24. Excavations in 1982 at Ophel in Jerusalem, south of the temple square. Depicted is a tower from the time of the Hasmoneans. (Dr. E. Noort, 't Harde, the Netherlands)

25. Fortifications from the time of Saul at Tell el-Ful. (photo P. W. Lapp, courtesy of Nancy L. Lapp)

26. View of Mount Ophel (earlier called the Millo?) and, to the north (on the right in the photo), the temple mount in Jerusalem. The city of David was located on the southern part of Ophel. In 1961 Kathleen Kenyon uncovered on Ophel remnants of the defense wall of the old fortress of Jebus from the time of David's capture of the city. In the area north of this fortress wall, between the wall and the temple, Solomon built his palaces (the "House of Pharaoh's daughter," the "Forest of Lebanon," his own palaces, and the stables; see 1 Kings 7). (Photo archive Kok, Kampen)

27. A tunnel cut out of solid limestone, part of the water system of Gibeon (12th–11th centuries B.C.). (University Museum, University of Pennsylvania, neg. #10090)

28. The city-mound and ruins of Megiddo. (W. Braun)

29. *The laver in Solomon's temple. (based on a re-construction by P. L. Garber)*

30. *A drawing of Solomon's temple in Jerusalem following the reconstruction of T. A. Busink. (Nederlands Instituut voor het Nabije Oosten, Leiden)*

31. *A Solomonic gate and wall at Hazor. (L. T. Geraty)*

32. *A potsherd from Tell el-Qasileh with an inscription mentioning "gold of Ophir." (Israel Department of Antiquities and Museums)*

33. *Hazor, one of the cities expanded and fortified by Solomon (1 Kgs. 9:15; see p. 48). In this aerial photograph of the excavations, the fortress is on the hill in the middle, and the entrance gate constructed by Solomon is in the foreground. Behind the gate is the colonnade of a large storehouse from a later time (ca. 850 B.C., built by Ahab). The buildings in the background are from more recent times, when Hazor was a residence for governors appointed by foreign rulers. (Dr. E. Noort, 't Harde, the Netherlands)*

34. *Tell Beth-shean with the excavated remnants of the city of Beth-shean, which was at the time of Solomon a Philistine city situated like a wedge entirely in Israelite territory. (Dr. E. Noort, 't Harde, the Netherlands)*

35. A scarab seal made of crystal, 15 x 13 mm. (0.6 x 0.5 in.), and the impression made from it, with a Hebrew inscription reading "Nehemiah, son of Micaiah" (ca. 550 B.C.). (Trustees of the British Museum)

36. Hadad, the Syrian god of thunder and storm. Here he is depicted standing on a bull calf, holding in his hands the attributes of his divine power: pronged lightning, sword, and quiver. A basalt stele, about 135 cm. (53 in.) high, from Arslan Tash, Syria (ca. 750 B.C.). (Musée du Louvre, Paris)

37. An Assyrian cylinder seal and the impression made with it: Ishtar, the goddess of love and war, on a lion. From Nineveh (Küyünjik; ca. 650 B.C.). Hundreds of such seals from Babylonia and Assyria have been preserved. (Trustees of the British Museum)

38. *Weights from Nimrud (8th century* B.C.*), some with inscriptions in Aramaic and Assyrian cuneiform mentioning the reigning monarch and the weight (from one-fourth talent [= 15 minas] to 3 shekels). (Trustees of the British Museum)*

39. *Weapons from Palestine: a thirteenth-century* B.C. *axehead in the form of a hand, daggers, spearheads, and arrowheads. (Israel Department of Antiquities and Museums)*

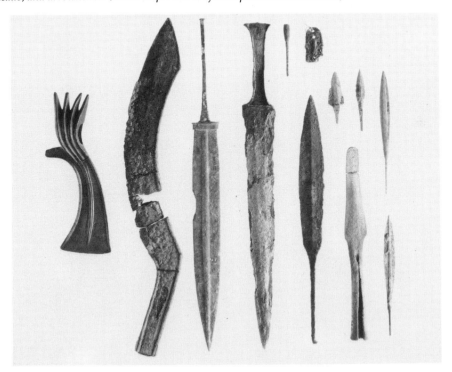

40. The wall of Omri's palace at Samaria (see p. 52). (J. C. Trever)

41. The Mesha Stone (see p. 54). (Oriental Institute, University of Chicago)

42. One of the numerous ivories from Samaria, this one showing most clearly the Egyptian artistic and religious influence felt in the capital of Israel. (Israel Department of Antiquities and Museums, photo H. Burber)

panied by great disturbances. Sennacherib had designated Esarhaddon as his successor, though he was not the oldest son (cf. Solomon's being selected over Adonijah), which seems to have been the reason why the other two sons murdered Sennacherib (see 2 Kgs. 19:37; Isa. 37:38). (See *ANET*, 289; R. Campbell Thompson, *The Prisms of Esarhaddon and of Ashurbanipal* [London, 1931].) In the disturbances that followed, the *baru* priests played a large role. One group of them stood on the side of Esarhaddon and gave oracles that were favorable to him, while another group stood on the side of his opponents. A prophetess of the first group addressed Esarhaddon himself with the following passages: "There I will conquer the enemies of the king. I grant the throne to no one else but the king."

Oracles, asked or unasked for, given by priests, priestesses, or laypeople, played an important role in Babylon as a vehicle of revelation. They could be couched in words such as the following:

Oracle of the woman Rimute-allate in the city of Darahuya, which lies in the midst of the mountains: Fear not, Esarhaddon! I, the god Bel, speak to you. . . . Sixty mighty gods are with me to protect you. Sin stands on your right hand, Shamash on your left. Fix your gaze on me! I am Ishtar of Arbela; I grant you Ashur's favor. When you were still young, I was supporting you. Fear not, praise me! Where is the enemy [which I have not defeated]? The future will be like the past. (*ANET*, 450)

Passages with a clearly predictive content often take the form of a dream oracle. In the following dream, King Ashurbanipal (669–ca. 630 B.C.), the king to whom we owe the important library, is the central figure:

The goddess Ishtar heard my anxious sighs. "Fear not," she said and gave confidence to my heart. "Because you have lifted up your hands in prayer [and] your eyes are filled with tears, I am gracious to you." In the night in which I appeared before her, a seer lay himself down to sleep and received a dream. When he awoke, Ishtar had given him a nighttime vision. He reported to me as follows: "Ishtar of Arbela came to me. Quivers with arrows hung on her right and left side. She had a bow in the one hand and a sharp sword in the other, ready for battle.

You stood right in front of her, and she spoke to you like your mother who bore you. Ishtar addressed you—she who is exalted among the gods—and gave you the following intructions: 'You shall fully carry out my orders. In whatever direction your face turns, I shall go before you.' You said, however, 'Wherever you go, let me follow you, O goddess of goddesses!' She spoke to you as follows: 'You must remain here, here where the house of Nabu is. Eat food, drink wine, provide music, praise my holiness, while I go to do the work that will fulfill your wish. Your face [need] not be pale, you need not tire your feet, nor consume your strength in the battle [cf. Exod. 14:14, 25; Josh. 10:14!].' She embraced you in her living bosom and protected you completely with it. Before her burned a fire. To defeat [your] enemies [she will] stand [on your] side. Against Teumman, the king of Elam, with whom she is angry, she has turned her face."

Predictions presented without an intermediate dream or vision are rare, although a few have survived. With this kind of passage, however, it is always difficult to determine whether the message is a genuine prediction or a "prediction" after the fact. I mention here one example:

A prince will arise and rule for thirteen years. There will be a revolt of Elam against Akkad. Akkad's property will be plundered. [Elam] will destroy the temples of the great gods; the downfall of Akkad is fully determined. Revolution, chaos, and catastrophes will strike the land. A tyrant, son of a nobody [i.e., a usurper], whose origin is unknown, will arise. As a king he will ascend the throne, he will fight his masters with weapons. In the ravines of Tupliash half of the troops of Akkad will fall. They will cover the valleys and the hills. The people of the land will have great scarcity. (*ANET*, 451)

2. THE PROPHETIC LITERATURE OF ISRAEL

Considering prophetic literature in Israel, we note first that most of it is anonymous. Though some of the prophets may perhaps have recorded some of their own pronouncements (Isa. 8:16; 30:8; Jer. 36:2; Hab. 2:2), in most cases we owe the written record of their prophecies either to the good offices of a secretary (e.g., Jeremiah's Baruch) or to the devotion of their pupils who wanted to preserve the words of the honored master for the future.

Classical prophecy in Israel, by which I mean the prophecy of the so-called writing prophets and which I regard as beginning with Amos, covers little more than a few centuries. Not only is it the most developed in the ancient East, it also has a unique character. It displays only a limited number of formal similarities with prophecies in the surrounding nations. A major difference between Israelite and non-Israelite prophecy is that the former manifests a compelling ethical-religious message that demands being heard and taken seriously. Sometimes this message is directed to the government (i.e., the king and the princes), at other times to all the people. Both audiences are expected to be guided in all their actions by the divine law. Another difference is that prophecy in Israel has a universal character. It is addressed not only to the country and people of Israel but also to Israel's neighbors, a point to which I return later.

Though the prophetic writings of Israel use all available literary genres, we can distinguish naturally between the prophecies, the confessions, and historical narratives about a prophet.

a. Prophecies

In the nature of the case, prophecies are found in every prophetic book, very often in a poetic form, but occasionally also in prose. Their contents can be highly diverse, but here we may distinguish predictions, penitential sermons, and indictments. All aspects of the prediction can be categorized as being announcements of either blessings or woe. The most familiar *predictions of blessings,* here cited only by their opening words, are found in the following passages:

Hosea: *2:16–25 (14–23)* Therefore, behold, I will allure her; *11:8–11* How can I give you up, O Ephraim? *14:6–9 (5–8)* I will be as the dew to Israel; he shall blossom as the lily, he shall strike root as the Lebanon.

Amos: *9:11–15* In that day I will raise up the booth of David that is fallen.

Isaiah: *2:2–5* It shall come to pass in the latter days that the mountain of the house of Yahweh shall be established as the highest of the mountains (cf. Mic. 4:1–5); *9:1–6 (2–7)* The people who walked in darkness have seen a great light; *11:1–10* There shall come forth a shoot from the stump of Jesse; *32:1–8* Behold, a king will reign in righteousness; *ch. 35* The wilderness and the dry land shall be glad.

Jeremiah: *23:5–8* Behold, the days are coming, says Yahweh, when I will raise up for David a righteous Branch; *30:3–24* For behold, the days are coming, says Yahweh, when I will restore the fortunes of my people, Israel and Judah; *32:36–44* Now therefore thus says Yahweh, the God of Israel, concerning this city; *ch. 33* The word of Yahweh came to Jeremiah a second time.

Micah: *2:12–13* I will surely gather all of you, O Jacob; *5:1–4 (2–5)* But you, O Bethlehem Ephrathah, who are little to be among the clans of Judah, from you shall come forth for me one who is to be ruler in Israel.

Isaiah: *41:8–20* But you, Israel, my servant, Jacob, whom I have chosen; *42:8–17* I am Yahweh, that is my name; my glory I give to no other; *44:1–5* But now hear, O Jacob my servant, Israel whom I have chosen; *51:17–23* Rouse yourself, rouse yourself, stand up, O Jerusalem; *ch. 54* Sing, O barren one, who did not bear; *ch. 60* Arise, shine; for your light has come; *ch. 61* The spirit of Adonai Yahweh is upon me, because Yahweh has anointed me; *ch. 62* For Zion's sake I will not keep silent.

Joel: *2:18–32* Then Yahweh became jealous for his land, and had pity on his people.

Ezekiel: *34:11–31* For thus says Adonai Yahweh: Behold, I, I myself will search for my sheep; *ch. 36* And you, son of man, prophesy to the mountains of Israel and say . . . ; *37:1–14* The hand of Yahweh was upon me, and he brought me out by the Spirit.

Zechariah: *8:3–23* Thus says Yahweh: I will return to Zion, and will dwell in the midst of Jerusalem; *9:9–13* Rejoice greatly, O daughter of Zion.

Though we might not expect the prophets to predict blessings for people that were hostile to

Israel, a few are nevertheless found in some younger writings:

Isaiah: *19:23–25* In that day Israel will be the third with Egypt and Assyria, a blessing in the midst of the earth, whom Yahweh of hosts has blessed, saying, "Blessed be Egypt my people, and Assyria the work of my hands, and Israel my heritage"; *25:6–12* On this mountain Yahweh of hosts will make for all peoples a feast of fat things, a feast of wine on the lees, of fat things full of marrow, of wine on the lees well refined.

Zephaniah: *3:9* Yea, at that time I will change the speech of the peoples to a pure speech, that all of them may call on the name of Yahweh and serve him with one accord.

All these predictions of blessings are addressed collectively to a people—in the first place to Judah and Israel, but also occasionally to Egypt and Assyria. On rare occasions, we also find predictions of blessings addressed to individuals.

Isaiah: *45:1–8* (Yahweh's promise to Cyrus, whom Yahweh calls his anointed) I will go before you and level the mountains, I will break in pieces the doors of bronze and cut asunder the bars of iron.

Jeremiah: *23:5–8* (promise of Yahweh concerning the accession to the throne of a new king from the house of David, who is called the righteous Branch and in v. 6 is given the name Yahweh Sidqenu [Zedekiah?]) He shall deal wisely, and shall execute justice and righteousness in the land; *39:15–18* (promise of blessing to the Ethiopian Ebed-melech, out of gratitude and as a reward for his rescuing Jeremiah from the pit into which some evil inhabitants of Jerusalem, with Zedekiah's approval, had thrown him) I will surely save you, and you shall not fall by the sword; but you shall have your life as a prize of war.

Haggai: *2:21–24* (promise to Zerubbabel, the governor of Judah) On that day, says Yahweh of hosts, I will take you, O Zerubbabel, my servant, the son of Shealtiel, says Yahweh, and make you like a signet ring; for I have chosen you, says Yahweh of hosts.

The contents of the predictions of blessings are in most cases general in character, such as the promise of the return of the earlier prosperity (Isaiah 60; 62; Jer. 33:6–26; Ezekiel 34–37; Joel 2:23–27), but in some cases the prediction is more concrete. The following list illustrates the specific prophecies:

- Restoration of the paradisiacal peace (Isa. 11:6–10)
- Creation of a new heaven and a new earth (Isa. 65:17)
- Birth of the Messiah (Isa. 9:1–6 [2–7]; 11:1–10)
- Restoration of the Davidic dynasty (Amos 9:11–12; Jer. 23:5–8; Zech. 9:9–10)
- Return from captivity (Isa. 43:5–7; Jer. 30:3; 32:37; Mic. 2:12–13; Zech. 8:4–8)
- Restoration of temple worship (Zech. 8:1–3)

Besides the promises of blessing, the Old Testament contains many *predictions of woe.* Such prophecies are frequently introduced with the so-called messenger formula, "Thus says Yahweh," or with the admonition, "Hear the word of Yahweh," or with the pronouncement, "Behold, the days are coming." These prophecies also can be divided into those that are against the nation of Israel, those against individuals, and those against Israel's enemies. We consider first some of the predictions of woe to the land and people of Israel that occur in the various Old Testament prophetic writings:

Hosea: *5:9* Ephraim shall become a desolation in the day of punishment; *8:14* Israel has forgotten his Maker, and built palaces; and Judah has multiplied fortified cities; but I will send a fire upon his cities, and it shall devour his strongholds.

Amos: *2:4–5* Thus says Yahweh: "For three transgressions of Judah, and for four . . . I will send a fire upon Judah, and it shall devour the strongholds of Jerusalem"; *3:1–2* Hear this word that Yahweh has spoken against you, O people of Israel, against the whole family which I brought up out of the land of Egypt: "You only have I known of all the families of the earth; therefore I will punish you for all your iniquities"; *4:1–3* Hear this word, you cows of Bashan . . . Adonai Yahweh has sworn by his holiness that, behold, the days are coming upon you, when they shall take you away with hooks, even the last of you with fishhooks; *7:1–3* (1st vision of judgment: threat

THE LITERATURE OF THE OLD TESTAMENT

of a locust plague); *7:4–6* (2nd vision) A judgment by fire, and it devoured the great deep and was eating up the land; *7:7–9* (3rd vision) A plumb line in the midst of my people Israel . . . ; the high places of Isaac shall be made desolate, and the sanctuaries of Israel shall be laid waste; *8:1–3* (4th vision) A basket of summer [ripe] fruit . . . the end has come upon my people Israel; I will never again pass by them; *9:1–6* (5th vision, the decisive judgment) Not one of them shall flee away, not one of them shall escape.

Joel: *1:2–2:11* (a locust plague announces the Day of Yahweh).

Isaiah: *1:24* Ah [woe!], I will vent my wrath on my enemies, and avenge myself on my foes; *5:8–24* (a sixfold woe).

Micah: *1:6* I will make Samaria a heap in the open country, a place for planting; *2:1–5* Woe to those who devise wickedness.

Jeremiah: *1:13–16* (vision of the boiling cauldron) Out of the north evil shall break forth upon all the inhabitants of the land; *4:5–6:30* (the calamity from the north) A lion has gone up from his thicket, a destroyer of nations has set out; he has gone forth from his place to make your land a waste; *7:29–8:3* (the Valley of Slaughter) Cut off your hair and cast it away; raise a lamentation on the bare heights, for Yahweh has rejected and forsaken the generation of his wrath.

Ezekiel: *4:1–5:17* (the siege of Jerusalem); *6:3–7* Thus says Adonai Yahweh to the mountains and the hills, to the ravines and the valleys: Behold, I, even I, will bring a sword upon you, and I will destroy your high places; *ch. 7* An end! The end has come upon the four corners of the land; *chs. 9–10* (the judgment upon the inhabitants of Jerusalem); *12:1–20* (the Captivity predicted); *ch. 16; 21:1–27; ch. 22; 24:1–14* (judgments against Jerusalem).

In a few cases, individuals are addressed directly with a prediction of woe:

Jeremiah: *22:10–12* In the place where they have carried [Shallum] captive, there shall he die; *22:13–19* With the burial of an ass [Jehoiakim] shall be buried, dragged and cast forth beyond the gates of Jerusalem; *22:20–30* (Jehoiachin will

also end his life in captivity); *24:8–10; 38:23* (Zedekiah) shall be seized by the king of Babylon.

Ezekiel: *17:19–24* Thus says Adonai Yahweh: . . . I will spread my net over [Zedekiah], and he shall be taken in my snare, and I will bring him to Babylon.

We have seen examples of predictions of woe upon the land and people of Israel. No less numerous are such predictions concerning hostile neighbors. I list here alphabetically the various peoples addressed by the Old Testament prophets.

- Ammon (Amos 1:13–15; Jer. 49:1–6; Ezek. 21:33–37 [28–32]; 25:1–7)
- Arabia (Isa. 21:13–17; Jer. 49:28–33)
- Assyria (Isa. 14:24–27; Ezekiel 31)
- Babylon (Isaiah 13; 21:1–10; Jeremiah 50–51)
- Chaldea (Habakkuk 2)
- Damascus (Amos 1:1–6; Isaiah 17; Jer. 49:23–27)
- Edom (Amos 1:11–12; Isa. 21:11–12; Jer. 49:7–22; Obadiah; Ezek. 25:12–14; ch. 35)
- Egypt (Isaiah 19; Jer. 46:2–28; Ezekiel 29–30)
- Egypt and Ethiopia (Isaiah 20)
- Elam (Jer. 49:34–39)
- Ethiopia (Isaiah 18)
- Gog (Ezek. 39:1–16)
- Moab (Amos 2:1–3; Isaiah 15–16; Jeremiah 48; Ezek. 25:8–11)
- Nineveh (Nahum 2–3)
- Philistia (Amos 1:6–8; Joel 3:4–8; Isa. 14:28–32; Jeremiah 47; Ezek. 25:15–17)
- Sidon (Ezek. 28:20–26)
- Tyre (Amos 1:9–10; Ezek. 26:1–28:19)
- Tyre and Sidon (Isaiah 23; Joel 4:1–8 [3:1–8])

As with prophecies of blessings, so also in predictions of woe the contents may be either general or more specific. Natural catastrophes are prominent and include earthquakes (Amos 8:8), locust plagues (Amos 7:1–3; Joel), prolonged droughts (Amos 4:7–8; Jer. 14:1–6), and resultant famine (Amos 4:6). In its wake follow crop diseases such as blight and mildew (v. 9) and epidemic diseases such as the plague (v. 10; Jer. 14:12). A second category consists of wars and, in their wake, military occupation (Isa. 5:26–30; 7:18–19; Jer. 1:13–15; 4:5–6; 10:22), decimation of the population (Amos 5:3), and exile (4:3; 5:27; 6:7; Jer. 9:16; Ezek. 12:1-20). Finally there is the threat of depopulation of the land due to a low birth rate (Hos. 8:10).

Occasionally predictions of calamity enumerate several catastrophes in a stock phrase. The book of Jeremiah in particular exhibits such a tendency, as the writer frequently refers to sword, hunger, and the plague (Jer. 14:12; 21:7, 9; 24:10; 27:8, 13; 29:17–18; 32:24, 36; 34:17; 38:2; 42:17, 22; 44:13; see also Ezek. 12:16; 14:21), or just sword and hunger (Jer. 5:12; 14:13, 15, 18; 18:21). Jeremiah also frequently mentions threat by sword (4:10; 5:17; 6:25; 9:15 [16]; 11:22; 12:12; 19:7; 20:4; 25:16, 27, 29; 31:2; 33:4; 42:16; 44:28; 46:10, 14, 16; 47:6; 48:2; 50:35–37).

All prophets have their own preference. For example, the prophet Amos frequently refers to the threat by fire (1:4, 7, 10, 12, 14; 2:2, 5), while the prophet Joel typically mentions the threat of the Day of Yahweh that is to come (1:15; 2:1–2, 11; 3:4 [2:31]; 4:14 [3:14]).

Predictions of calamity are often preceded by a sermon of penitence, as a rule consisting of rebukes and indictments. Although it would carry us too far afield to discuss them all, I mention the following interesting examples of reproaches:

Hosea: *8:4* They made kings, but not through me. They set up princes, but without my knowledge. With their silver and gold they made idols for their own destruction; *9:10* Like grapes in the wilderness, I found Israel. Like the first fruit on the fig tree, in its first season, I saw your fathers. But they came to Baal-peor, and consecrated themselves to Baal.

Amos: *4:6–13* (a detailed rebuke of Israel's unrepentance; neither famine, prolonged drought, harvest failure, locust plague, pestilence, or earthquake has been able to bring Israel to its senses and to repentance).

Jeremiah: *2:31* You, O generation, heed the word of Yahweh. Have I been a wilderness to Israel, or a land of thick darkness? Why then do my people say, "We are free, we will come no more to thee"?

Though the boundary between rebuke and indictment is not rigid, the following pericopes seem to illustrate indictments rather clearly.

Amos: *5:12* For I know how many are your trans-gressions, and how great are your sins—you who afflict the righteous, who take a bribe, and turn aside the needy in the gate.

Hosea: *10:13* You have plowed iniquity, you have reaped injustice, you have eaten the fruit of lies. Because you have trusted in your chariots and in the multitude of your warriors; *12:1–2 [11:12–12:1]* Ephraim has encompassed me with lies, and the house of Israel with deceit. . . . Ephraim herds the wind, and pursues the east wind all day long; they multiply falsehood and violence; they make a bargain with Assyria, and oil is carried to Egypt.

Jeremiah: *2:13* They have forsaken me, the fountain of living waters, and hewed out cisterns for themselves, broken cisterns, that can hold no water; *2:18* Now what do you gain by going to Egypt, to drink the waters of the Nile? Or what do you gain by going to Assyria, to drink the waters of the Euphrates? *2:29* Why do you complain against me? You have all rebelled against me.

Micah: *3:9–11* Hear this, you heads of the house of Jacob and rulers of the house of Israel, who abhor justice and pervert all equity, who build Zion with blood and Jerusalem with wrong. Its heads give judgment for a bribe, its priests teach for hire, its prophets divine for money; yet they lean upon Yahweh and say, "Is not Yahweh in the midst of us? No evil shall come upon us."

b. Confessions

In the prophetic literature, *confession* refers to biographical statements made by prophets concerning the circumstances under which they were called to their task by Yahweh and the cares that befell them as they carried out their mandate. As could be expected, these first-person comments are highly colored emotionally; men are revealing both their person and their special office. The most important of the so-called writing prophets—Hosea, Amos, Isaiah, Jeremiah, and Ezekiel—have all given us a history of their call.

The call of the prophet Hosea seems to have coincided with the mandate Yahweh gave him to marry a woman of impure morals, a certain Gomer, the daughter of Diblaim. This marriage, described in the third person in chapters 1 and 3, must be regarded as a symbolic act, intended to open the eyes of the Israelites to their terrible unfaithfulness to Yahweh.

We learn a few details about Amos's call in connection with his dispute with Amaziah, the priest of Bethel, who told him to speak no more in the national shrine and warned him to go back to Judah as quickly as possible. That would be a better place for him to eat bread and prophesy (7:12–13)! This advice indicated that Amaziah saw Amos only as a man who dabbled in religion, one of many who were then trying to make a living by proclaiming supposedly divine revelations to a gullible people. Amos repudiated this charge indignantly. He had nothing to do with these professional prophets. As a farmer and grower of sycamore-fig trees, Amos was a man of some means and did not have to make a living from giving spiritual messages, as Amaziah thought he did. Yahweh, however, had called him away from the sheep and had said to him, "Go, prophesy to my people Israel" (v. 15).

Isaiah 6 describes the call of the prophet Isaiah. Unlike Hosea and Amos, Isaiah received his call by means of a vision. This revelation, which came to him in the year that King Uzziah died (ca. 738 B.C.), had transported him to the temple, where he had seen Yahweh seated on a very high throne, surrounded by a retinue of seraphim. Seeing the Most Holy One, Isaiah became aware of his sinfulness: "Woe is me! For I am lost; for I am a man of unclean lips, and I dwell in the midst of a people of unclean lips" (v. 5). Then one of the seraphim flew to Isaiah, carrying a live coal that he had taken with tongs from the altar. With it the angel touched his mouth and said, "Behold, this has touched your lips; your guilt is taken away, and your sin is forgiven" (v. 7). Then followed immediately the mandate to the prophetic office: "Go, and say to this people: 'Hear and hear, but do not understand; see and see, but do not perceive'" (v. 9).

The most remarkable history of a call, however, is that of the prophet Jeremiah (1:4–19). His call is unusual because Yahweh had destined him to be a prophet even before he was born (v. 5). Jeremiah nevertheless viewed this predestination as a call, which is demonstrated by his initial opposition to it: "Ah, Adonai Yahweh! Behold, I do not know how to speak, for I am only a youth" (v. 6). Yahweh immediately replied, however, "Do not say, 'I am only a youth'; for to all to whom I send you you shall go, and whatever I command you you shall speak. Be not afraid of them, for I am with you to deliver you, says Yahweh" (vv. 7–8). Thereupon Yahweh touched the mouth of the young man with his hand and said, "Behold, I have put my words in your mouth. See, I have set you this day over nations and over kingdoms, to pluck up and to break down, to destroy and to overthrow, to build and to plant" (vv. 9–10).

In Ezekiel's call to be a prophet, visions also played an important part: "In the thirtieth year, in the fourth month, on the fifth of the month, as I was among the exiles by the river Chebar, the heavens were opened, and I saw visions of God" (1:1). This happening is to be dated in the year 593 B.C. In one of these visions Ezekiel received his call to be a prophet: "'Son of man, stand upon your feet, and I will speak with you.' And when he spoke to me, the Spirit entered into me and set me upon my feet; and I heard him speaking to me" (2:1). The first task assigned to him was to go to the Israelites living in exile in Tel-abib, by the river Chebar, and to warn them of the punishments they could receive for their rebellious attitude against Yahweh (2:5; 3:18). Besides the pericope in 1:1–3:15, some are inclined to view 3:22–27 as yet another calling vision. In my judgment, however, this latter pericope relates merely a second appearance to Ezekiel, like so many others he received later.

Another aspect of the confessions involves the often moving laments that the prophets utter concerning the troubles and difficulties that they so often face in discharging their responsibilities. These laments come especially from the prophet Jeremiah. The hostile atmosphere that surrounded him every day, the frequent plots and schemes against him by his enemies, the calumnies that he had to cope with, and the constant threats on his life—all these things at times became too much for him. Then he poured out his heart in words such as the following: "My grief is beyond healing, my heart is sick within me" (Jer. 8:18); "O that my head were waters, and my eyes a fountain of tears" (8:23 [9:1]); "Woe to me because of my hurt! My wound is grievous" (10:19). The pressure could become so intense that, like

Job, Jeremiah cursed the day of his birth: "Woe is me, my mother, that you bore me, a man of strife and contention to the whole land!" (15:10).

At a certain moment, however, he realized that human beings were not able to decide their own fate: "I know, O Yahweh, that the way of man is not in himself, that it is not in man who walks to direct his steps" (Jer. 10:23). Jeremiah found that one was too powerful for him: "O Yahweh, thou hast deceived [*or* persuaded] me, and I was deceived [persuaded]; thou art stronger than I, and thou hast prevailed" (20:7).

c. Historical Stories about Prophets

The textbook example of this genre is the small book of Jonah, which in its entirety is a story about a prophet (see further the discussion of Jonah in part III below). Of the so-called classical prophets, reports of a biographical nature have been preserved about Amos, Hosea, Isaiah, Jeremiah, Ezekiel, and Haggai. The biographical pericope Amos 7:10–17 has already been considered in the previous section and requires no further discussion here.

Hosea's prophetic labors start with his obedience to Yahweh's command to marry an immoral woman and to have children by her. The purpose of the command is to show Israel symbolically the immensity of its sin when it rejected Yahweh and instead took Baal as its husband. The pericope 1:2–2:3 (1:2–2:1), written in the third person singular and introduced with "Yahweh said to Hosea, 'Go, take to yourself a wife of harlotry,'" may have been written by a disciple of the prophet.

Biographical details about the prophet Isaiah are found in chapters 36–39, taken over from 2 Kings 18–20. Of these chapters, 36–37 describe the siege of Jerusalem by the Assyrian king Sennacherib. The prophet is first mentioned in 37:2, where he is met by a delegation sent by King Hezekiah and asked to pray to Yahweh on behalf of "the remnant that is left." In reply to this request, Isaiah sends the delegation back to Hezekiah with the promise that Yahweh will not permit Sennacherib to succeed in his schemes: "Behold, I will put a spirit in him, so that he shall hear a rumor, and return to his own land; and I will make him fall by the sword in his own land" (v. 7).

The second appearance of the prophet is in connection with his second prediction of Jerusalem's deliverance (Isa. 37:21–35). Hezekiah received a letter from the envoys of Sennacherib and, after having read it, took it to the temple. There he spread it out before the face of Yahweh and fervently pleaded with God to save him from the power of this oppressor. In one way or another Isaiah heard of this prayer and, through the mediation of a third person, gave the message to the king that Yahweh had noticed Hezekiah's prayer as well as Sennacherib's blasphemy against the Holy One of Israel. "Therefore thus says Yahweh concerning the king of Assyria: He shall not come into this city, or shoot an arrow there, or come before it with a shield, or cast up a siege mound against it. By the way that he came, by the same he shall return, and he shall not come into this city, says Yahweh" (vv. 33–34).

Isaiah's third appearance is mentioned at the end of the prayer of thanks Hezekiah recited after he had been healed from his sickness. In addition to his fervent prayer to Yahweh, the king also owed his recovery to the advice of Isaiah, who had said, "Let them take a cake of figs, and apply it to the boil, that he may recover" (Isa. 38:21).

The fourth and final contact with Hezekiah happened after the visit of a delegation from Babylon who, on behalf of Merodak-Baladan, had come to congratulate the king on his recovery (Isaiah 39). On that occasion Hezekiah showed them his storehouse with the treasures in it: the silver and the gold, the spices and the precious oil, his entire armory, and everything else found among his treasures. There was nothing in his palace and in his whole kingdom that Hezekiah did not show them. For this highly censurable naïveté the king is called to account by Isaiah in these words: "Hear the word of Yahweh of hosts: Behold, the days are coming, when all that is in your house, and that which your fathers have stored up till this day, shall be carried to Babylon. . . . And some of your own sons, who are born to you, shall be taken away; and they shall be eunuchs in the palace of the king of Babylon" (vv. 5–7). Hezekiah, apparently content that he would not witness any of this disruption, reacted rather indifferently to this threat, saying only, "The word of Yahweh which you have spoken is good" (v. 8).

All the biographical details about the prophet Jeremiah refer to dramatic events during the final years of Judah's national existence (chs. 36–45). This long pericope begins with King Jehoiakim's burning the scroll that Baruch had written and Yahweh's commanding Jeremiah to have a new scroll made. Then 37:1–10 narrates how King Zedekiah, who has recently come to the throne, sends a few dignitaries to Jeremiah with the request that he intercede with Yahweh on behalf of him and his people, in light of the needs caused by the Chaldeans' siege of Jerusalem. Yahweh's answer, however, is disappointing. Zedekiah is told that the Chaldeans will not move away from the city. At that point, however, hearing a rumor that an Egyptian army is coming to deliver the city, the Chaldeans do break up the siege and move away. Jeremiah now prepares to go to the land of Benjamin to handle a certain business matter. The captain of the guard, who suspects Jeremiah of deserting to the Chaldeans, stops him at the Benjamin Gate and, after an interrogation, hands him over to the rulers. They give him a beating and then imprison him in the house of the scribe Jonathan, which they had made into a prison (vv. 11–16). Jeremiah does not remain long there, however. At his request to Zedekiah, who under no circumstance wants to lose contact with the prophet, Jeremiah is placed in the courtyard of the guard, where he is given a daily portion of bread until all the bread in the city is gone (v. 21).

From the court of the guard the prophet continues to speak to all the people: "Thus says Yahweh, He who stays in this city shall die by the sword, by famine, and by pestilence; but he who goes out to the Chaldeans shall live; he shall have his life as a prize of war, and live" (Jer. 38:2). The rulers are furious about this defeatist preaching and, with Zedekiah's consent, have Jeremiah thrown into the muddy cistern of the courtyard of the guard. Then, however, an official of Zedekiah, an Ethiopian by the name of Ebed-melech, becomes concerned about him and is able to persuade the king to have Jeremiah pulled out of the

cistern again and returned to the courtyard of the guard (vv. 4–13). Afterward a second secret conversation occurs between the king and the prophet. In view of the hopeless situation, the prophet can only advise the king to surrender unconditionally to the Chaldeans. Only by so doing is there a chance that Zedekiah's life may be spared and that the city will not be burned with fire. The king does not come to a decision, however, and the conversation ends inconclusively (vv. 14–28).

The next chapter tells the story of the capture of Jerusalem by King Nebuchadrezzar (Jer. 39:1–14). The Babylonians took Jeremiah out of the dungeon and turned him over to the custody of Gedaliah, the son of Ahikam, who gave him back his freedom. While still in prison the word of Yahweh had come to him concerning the Ethiopian Ebed-melech, who had rescued him from the cistern. He was told that Yahweh would protect him from the war and preserve his life: "You shall not fall by the sword; but you shall have your life as a prize of war, because you have put your trust in me, says Yahweh" (v. 18).

Chapters 40–45 describe the dramatic events that happened to Jeremiah after the fall of Jerusalem. Shortly after his appointment as governor, Gedaliah, who had taken pity on the prophet, was assassinated by a fanatic. Fearful of reprisals, a great part of the population fled to Egypt, though Jeremiah had pleaded with them to remain in their own land and not to be afraid of what might come. He himself was compelled to join the fugitives in their flight to Egypt. The town of Tahpanhes was their first place of stay (43:7). Here Jeremiah continued his prophetic activities for a while among the fugitives, but then his story suddenly ends.

Other than the personal report about Ezekiel in 1:1–3, which gives the exact date and place of his call, very few biographical details have survived about the life of the prophet Ezekiel. Finally, a similarly dated report tells about the mandate to the prophet Haggai. He was commanded to tell the governor Zerubbabel, the high priest Joshua, and the remnant of the people not to lose heart in the work of rebuilding the temple (Hag. 2:2–9).

F. Wisdom Literature

Besides prophets and priests, Israel also had its wise men. We do well here to speak of wise men, not philosophers, because in Israel wisdom was never practiced for its own sake and never developed into a general system of philosophical concepts and ideas. The wisdom literature that we meet in Israel and also in the neighboring nations is of a pragmatic and empirical character, a knowledge that was constructed out of the experience of many centuries (von Rad, *Wisdom*). Wisdom was thus concerned not with a cerebral pursuit of truth in a metaphysical sense but with the study of practical and experiential wisdom and its formulation in maxims and aphorisms, whose number could always be expanded (i.e., the so-called proverbial wisdom). As regards Israel, this wisdom is primarily recorded in the book of Proverbs, but we also possess interesting collections from Egypt, Mesopotamia, and Syria (B. Gemser, *Sprüche Salomos* [HAT I/16; Tübingen, 1963²]). The pursuit of this empirical wisdom was an international concern. It served also the extremely practical goal of training the youth.

In Egypt most collections of proverbs bear the title "teaching, instruction, admonitions of N.N." The following are the most important Egyptian collections:

1. Teaching of Ptahhotep, vizier of King Issi. This collection, dated by some approximately 2675 B.C. and by others about 2870, has come to us in older and in more recent versions (Erman, *Literatur,* pp. 86–98; *ANET,* 412–14).
2. Instruction of Ka-gemmi, dating from the end of the Third Dynasty (about 2700 B.C.; Erman, pp. 99–100).
3. Teaching for King Merikare of the Tenth Dy-

nasty (2070–2041 B.C.; Erman, pp. 109–19; *ANET,* 414–18).
4. Teaching of King Amenemhet I (1991–1962 B.C.), known only from copies from the period of the New Kingdom (ca. 1580–1085 B.C.; Erman, pp. 106–109; *ANET,* 418–19).
5. Instruction of Duauf, poorly preserved in school exercises from the period of the Nineteenth Dynasty (about 1300 B.C.; Erman, pp. 100–105).

All these didactic collections contain commandments, prohibitions, counsel, and admonition to youth as a kind of vade mecum for life. This instruction was aimed at elite youth who desired to be trained for careers as officials or for functions at the court. The profession of scribe was highly respected in Egypt, and many desired to be trained for this work.

Collections of proverbs from a later time are directed much more to the average person. Included in such documents are especially:

6. The wisdom teaching of Ani, a didactic papyrus from the Eighteenth Dynasty (1580–1314 B.C.; *ANET,* 420–21; E. Suys, *La Sagesse d'Ani* [Rome, 1935]).
7. Teaching of Amenemope (see ill. 62), a document from the Twenty-second Dynasty (950–730 B.C.). Albright, however, dates this period between 1150 and 1000 B.C. (*ANET,* 421; A. Erman, "Eine ägyptische Quelle der 'Sprüche Salomos,'" *Sitzungsberichte der Preussischen Akademie der Wissenschaften* [1924], pp. 86–93).
8. The Insinger Papyrus, dating from the late Persian or early Ptolemaic era. This document is also known as "the demotic wisdom book"

(A. Volten, *Das demotische Weisheitsbuch* [Copenhagen, 1941]).

9. Instruction of Onchsheshonqy (B. Gemser, "The Instructions of Onchsheshonqy and Biblical Wisdom Literature," SVT 7 [1960] 102–28) or Anchsheshonq (B. H. Stricker, "De wijsheid van Anchsjesjonq," *Oudheidkundige Mededelingen uit het Rijksmuseum van Oudheden te Leiden* 39 [1958] 11–33), a papyrus likely dating from the last century before our era.

Especially these late collections must be deemed important for a comparison with the biblical book of Proverbs. Particularly the small collection Proverbs 22:17–23:11 exhibits great affinity with the Teaching of Amenemope.

From Mesopotamia we have likewise received many documents with proverbs, for the most part in the form of copies from the library of King Ashurbanipal (669–ca. 630 B.C.). Most items are bilingual, written in Sumerian and Semitic (Lambert, *Wisdom;* S. Langdon, *Wisdom;* Brongers, *Literatur*). In the Sumerian period large collections of proverbs were made, of which we currently possess some seven hundred tablets. While Egyptian proverbs and maxims are strongly didactic in orientation, in Mesopotamia the emphasis is much more on the various aspects of ordinary daily life. In this respect these latter collections are similar to the biblical book of Proverbs.

Finally, from a later period (5th century B.C.), we have the wisdom book of Ahiqar, written in Aramaic and discovered at Elephantine. Ahiqar, according to the biography that comes before his proverbs, occupied an important office at the Assyrian court in the seventh century. This book, too, exhibits affinity with some parts of the book of Proverbs (P. Grelot, "Les proverbes araméens d'Ahiqar," *RB* 68 [1961] 178–94; Cowley, *Papyri*).

The biblical *hokmah,* or wisdom, literature includes the books of Proverbs, Ecclesiastes, and Job. The book of Proverbs offers a conglomeration of originally independent collections of proverbs.

A striking feature in many proverbs is the formal use of parallelism (Lowth, *Sacred Poetry*), while in 30:15–33 the conjoining of many unrelated proverbs is notable (A. Bea, "Der Zahlenspruch im Hebräischen und Ugaritischen," *Bibl* 21 [1940] 196–98).

Opinions differ whether Ecclesiastes is to be regarded as a philosophical treatise. As Vriezen noted, the fact that the book is devoid of deductive or inductive reasoning argues against this view. The writer states basic convictions rather than logically developing his ideas. At best he writes a book about the art of living, though in that respect his book does occupy a unique position in the wisdom literature known to us from Egypt, Babylonia, and Greece (T. Vriezen, "Prediker en de achtergrond van zijn wijsheid," *NTT* 1 [1946-1947] 3–14, 65–84).

The book of Job, rightly regarded as a literary climax in the Old Testament and as a masterpiece in world literature, deals with the righteousness of God in his dealings with human beings and the world. Its theme reminds us of the Babylonian document *Ludlul bel nemeqi* ("I will praise the lord of wisdom"), in which a righteous person expresses his grief about the inexplicable and unjust suffering he experiences. In the end, however, he is delivered by the god Marduk (Brongers, *Literatur,* pp. 132–35). In this connection the so-called Babylonian Theodicy should also be mentioned, which contains a dialogue between a believer and a doubter as well as the following lamentation, which expresses the impenetrability of God's ways:

> The heart of God is unfathomable like the
>   interior of heaven;
> his wisdom is impenetrable and unintelligible
>   to man.

(J. J. Stamm, "Die Theodizee in Babylon und Israel," *JEOL* 9 [1944] 99–107)

Part III below contains further discussion of these three biblical books.

G. The Laws

Though it is arguable whether laws are to be regarded as a literary genre, the Old Testament does integrally incorporate two bodies of law (two decalogues) into its historical narrative. It may thus be appropriate in this literary survey to give some detailed attention to the laws. In the Old Testament we can distinguish the following units: the Decalogues, the Book of the Covenant, the Priestly laws (Leviticus and random juridical passages in Exodus and Numbers), the Holiness Code (Leviticus 17–27), and the Deuteronomic Code (Deuteronomy 12–26).

1. THE DECALOGUES

The so-called ethical Decalogue has come to us in two versions (Exod. 20:1–17; Deut. 5:6–21). In their present form, neither version is likely original. Scholarly opinion differs regarding its age as well as its formulation. The original form of the ethical Decalogue may have been the following:

1. I, Yahweh, am your God. You shall have no other gods besides me.
2. You shall not make a graven image.
3. You shall not take the name of Yahweh your God in vain.
4. Remember the sabbath as a holy day.
5. Honor your father and your mother.
6. You shall not murder.
7. You shall not commit adultery.
8. You shall not steal.
9. You shall not bear false witness against your neighbor.
10. You shall not desire the house of your neighbor.

Some passages were later expanded, in most cases because of development in theological ideas. It is interesting, for example, to note the great difference in the sabbath commandment in the two versions. The Decalogue in Exodus 20 turns it into a kind of creation ordinance: even as Yahweh did his creative work in six days and rested on the seventh day, so man, after working for six days, must rest one day. By contrast, Deuteronomy 5 motivates the sabbath commandment by referring to the stay in Egypt, where Israel lived in slavery for many years and from which it was at last rescued by Yahweh's mighty arm. Here the motivation is social as well as religious: one who has been a slave himself will not easily deprive his workers of the seventh day as a day of rest. The difference in motivation is a clear indication that the fourth commandment must originally have been much briefer. It also shows that such texts were subject to change and not, as used to be thought, regarded as sacrosanct.

I consider briefly the contents of these commandments. As regards the first commandment, there is no reason to interpret it monotheistically. The existence of other gods is neither denied nor questioned—but Israel may not worship them. For that reason it is better to think here of monolatry rather than monotheism. The second commandment, which is likely of relatively recent date, can be regarded as the complement of the first. For it refers to the making of images not only of Yahweh but also of other gods. The third commandment opposes the use of the name of Yahweh for magical purposes. For the ancients a name contained mysterious powers. People who knew the name of a god and pronounced it thereby acquired a kind of power, enabling them to avail themselves of the power of the deity who bore that name. The

Israelites are to protect themselves against such a misuse of the holy name. The sabbath commandment, formally speaking, stands on the dividing line between the commandments relating to Yahweh and those that concern relationships among people. In the fifth commandment it is noteworthy that children are commanded not to love their parents but to honor them. As long as one lives, one is responsible for one's parents. Therefore it may be assumed that this commandment refers to aged parents, people no longer able to make their own living and now dependent on their children. Age must be respected: "Rise in the presence of the aged, show respect for the elderly" (Lev. 19:32 NIV). In showing such respect it is best to start with one's parents.

Contrary to what is often thought, the sixth commandment does not refer to the safeguarding of life in general. It is still a big step from this prohibition to Albert Schweitzer's "respect for life." The meaning is that an Israelite may not treacherously murder a member of his people. Hence in the original the verb *rasah*, "murder, slay," is used, not the more neutral *qatal*, "kill." The seventh commandment does not refer to the breaking of one's own marriage but to that of one's fellow human being. The interests of the woman are not in view here, for this commandment appears in a male-dominated society, with no idea of emancipation. The prohibition is aimed at the man, who is told not to start a love relationship with the wife of a member of his people and so violate the property rights of this neighbor. Compare in this connection Leviticus 20:10 and Deuteronomy 22:22, which require the death penalty for both the man and the woman. The eighth commandment aims at securing personal property. Later elaboration of this commandment included the wife among the property to be safeguarded. The ninth commandment deals with the administration of justice, the proper exercise of which stands or falls with reliable witnesses. The meaning of the tenth commandment remains a matter of dispute. Perhaps much is to be said for the idea of Eerdmans, who thinks of the need to protect someone's property during an absence. He refers appropriately to Exodus 34:24, where God says that he will take care that the men can safely leave their house to make a pilgrimage, because in their absence "no one will covet their land."

The ethical Decalogue can rightly be called Israel's constitution. In lucidly formulated commandments and prohibitions, numbering no more than the fingers of the two hands, the foundation is laid here for a society in which God receives the honor due to him and the interests of people are safeguarded. Scholars are still far from agreed about the age of this Decalogue. In my judgment its present form seems definitely no older than the beginning of the seventh century B.C., the time that is usually regarded as the period of the so-called Deuteronomistic reform. If we assume, however, that originally these commandments were much briefer in form, then the tenth commandment prevents us from thinking of the time of Moses.

The so-called cultic Decalogue (Exod. 34:10–28), regarded by some as even older than the ethical Decalogue, is materially quite similar to the latter. An important difference is that the cultic Decalogue, as the term implies, is concerned not with relationships among people but with those between individuals and their God. Disregarding later additions, the original form may perhaps be reconstructed as follows.

1. Behold, I am making a covenant. Obey what I command you today: be careful not to worship another god.
2. Do not make cast idols.
3. The first offspring of every womb belongs to me.
4. No one is to appear before me empty-handed.
5. Six days you shall labor, but on the seventh day you shall rest.
6. Three times a year you shall appear before the face of Yahweh.
7. You shall not offer the blood of a sacrifice to me with anything containing yeast.
8. The sacrifice from the Passover may not be left until the morning.
9. You shall bring the best of the firstfruits of your ground to the house of Yahweh, your God.
10. You shall not boil a young goat in its mother's milk.

The ninth commandment gives us some idea about the dating of this Decalogue. It speaks of the firstfruits of the ground, which suggests the time when Israel was permanently settled in the land of Canaan and was engaged in agriculture. The second part of the commandment assumes the existence of the temple or some other fixed sanctuary. In Exodus 20:23–26; 23:12–19, the cultic Decalogue is found in still another context, namely as introduction and conclusion to the Book of the Covenant.

2. THE BOOK OF THE COVENANT

This term commonly designates a collection of laws that are found in written form in Exodus 20:22–23:19, with an appendix in 23:20–33. The name suggests that these laws were promulgated in the context of the enactment of the covenant, described in chapter 24. In fact, however, the words from chapter 20 lie at the basis of this making of the covenant. In the original the collection is called *mishpatim,* "legal customs." For here we have not a lawbook but a book that describes customary or common law, in which casuistic law is predominant. The common laws are as a rule introduced with the conditional *ki,* "when," which states the general case, after which special circumstances are summarized in a clause with the much weaker *im,* "if." A good example of this formulation is 21:2–6.

When *(ki)* you buy a Hebrew slave, he shall serve six years, and in the seventh year he shall go free without paying anything. If *(im)* he came alone, he alone shall go free; if he was married, his wife shall go free with him; if his master gave him a wife and she bore him sons and daughters, the woman with the children shall remain the possession of her master and the slave alone shall go free. If, however, the servant declares that he loves his master and his wife and children and that he does not want to go free, then his master must take him to Elohim. The master shall take him to the door or the doorpost and shall pierce his ear with an awl, and he will be his master's servant forever. (The meaning of "take to Elohim" is not clear. It may refer to the temple or the local sanctuary, but it may also be a reference to house gods.) The regular formulation of such a common law we would call civil law. This juridical formulation is found throughout the ancient East in the formulation of laws (e.g., the Code of Hammurabi, Hittite Laws, Middle Assyrian Laws).

I survey here some of the other stipulations in the Book of the Covenant. The lawbook begins with some prescriptions relative to public worship (Exod. 20:22–26). Altars were preferably to be made of earth. Stone altars must be made of unhewn stones and, like the earthen altars, may not have steps. The pericope 21:12–36 is a collection of prescriptions that aim at safeguarding the life of fellow human beings. Deliberate killing was punishable by death, but for a man who accidentally caused the death of his neighbor, the possibility was created to save his life by seeking refuge in the sanctuary. Exodus 21:37–22:16 (22:1–17) contains prescriptions regarding the property of the neighbor. From verses 15–16 (16–17) it can be inferred that children were regarded as being someone's property. Verses 17–19 (18–20) address the sins of magic, sodomy, and idolatry. Throughout the Near East, women in particular engaged in black magic. Magic was regarded as a kind of religious high treason, because it undermined the foundations of true religion and did great harm to the spiritual health of the people. Sodomy, or sexual relations with animals, was quite common in the ancient East, especially among the Canaanites, the Hittites, and the Egyptians (Lev. 18:23). The practice has its roots in religion and was basically regarded as a religious, not a sexual, sin. The idolater was put under the ban, which meant that, together with his wife, children, and everything else he possessed, he was declared to be the property of Yahweh. In practice this decree meant that he and his whole family were put to death and all his possessions were burned.

Exodus 22:20–26 (21–27) gives regulations for the socially vulnerable—the alien, the widow, the orphan, and the poor. The demand to show love toward one's neighbor is here, too, anchored in religion. Yahweh is concerned about the oppressed (v. 26 [27]). Interest may not be asked of a member of the people, and a garment taken in pledge must be returned before the evening. Verses 28–30 (29–31) again deal with the cultic sphere. They contain regulations concerning the bringing of sacred gifts, as well as the prohibition against eating the meat of animals that have been torn by wild beasts. In the same breath the sacrifice of the firstborn son is demanded. This requirement indicates that in ancient times the Israelites also were familiar with child sacrifice. Exodus 13:11–13, however, shows that provision very early was made for redemption, that is, for substituting something else for the son.

The passage Exodus 23:1–19 has a special character. The laws here are admonitions rather than commandments that have sanctions. Verse 8 illustrates the paraenetic rather than the juridical character of these verses. The admonition there not to take a bribe is validated and underscored by a proverb, something that would be strange in a law corpus. The pericope 23:10–19, which concludes the actual Book of the Covenant, again deals with a variety of cultic regulations. Verses 10 and 11 speak about the sabbatical year. For six years the ground may be tilled, but in the seventh year the land must remain unplowed and unused. Here the purely agricultural necessity of giving the land rest from time to time is embedded in the religiously based motif of the sabbath commandment. Every year there are three feasts: the Feast of Unleavened Bread, the Feast of the Firstfruits, and the Feast of Ingathering, called the Feast of Tabernacles in Deuteronomy. All three are typically agricultural feasts with a strong religious coloring: during these feasts the men must appear before the face of Yahweh (v. 17). The prohibition here against boiling a young goat in its mother's milk must be very old and no doubt goes back to animistic ideas. The boiling of a young animal in the milk of its mother was viewed as contrary to nature and supposedly resulted in the permanent barrenness of the mother animal.

The socioeconomic background of the Book of the Covenant reflects the situation in the later period of the judges. The Israelites have left behind the stage in which they were seminomads. They are now a settled people of farmers with fields, vineyards, and olive orchards. Economically the families are independent, owning their own land and living from what they have grown themselves. The economic relations are still simple and uncomplicated, and there are not yet large landowners. There are two classes, the free and the slave, but the latter are virtually all those who have sold themselves into slavery and who are members of the people themselves.

In regard to the cult, the Book of the Covenant does not yet know of the national sanctuary in Jerusalem. Sacrifices are still made in the open field, which presupposes a plurality of sanctuaries.

3. THE PRIESTLY LAWS

The book of Leviticus contains an extensive collection of cultic laws pertaining to the arrangement of the sanctuary and the sacrifices (especially chs. 1–7). Laws about what is clean and what is unclean, including which animals may or may not be eaten, are found in chapters 11–15. Chapter 16 gives rules and regulations for celebrating the Day of Atonement.

4. THE HOLINESS CODE

This body of laws in Leviticus 17–27 derives its generally accepted name from the familiar addition to some articles: "You shall be holy, for I, Yahweh your God, am holy" (19:2; 20:7–8, 26; 21:8; etc.). It seems likely that we have here a program of reform in the spirit of Deuteronomy. We could point, for example, to chapters 18 and 26 and to the commandment to make sacrifices in one place (ch. 17). The influence of prophetic preaching is very obvious. In general, this collection best reproduces the contents of Yahwistic religion and cultic institutions. The appendix (ch. 27) deals with the value and payment of vows, redemption of the firstborn, things devoted to the Lord, and the tithes.

The laws in Numbers, which deal with a variety of issues (e.g., uncleanness, adultery, food offerings, rights of inheritance of daughters), are generally regarded as of more recent origin. Behind some of these regulations, however, there are many older stipulations.

5. THE DEUTERONOMIC CODE

In the year 622 B.C., while the temple in Jerusalem was being restored, a lawbook was found that induced King Josiah to institute a thorough reform of Israelite life and religion. Scholars widely agree that this lawbook (or at least part of it) underlies the present book of Deuteronomy. The name Deuteronomy is usually translated "repetition of the law." A better view of the book regards it as reform legislation, as a renewal of the law. The law of Moses had been given for all times, but every age required a fresh interpretation of it. The Deuteronomic Code (chs. 12–26) aims to be a new interpretation of the Book of the Covenant, adjusted to the needs of the present time. It turned out to be a magnificent piece of work. In practice it amounted to a drastic reform that covered doctrine and practical living. The prophetic-priestly groups, who were responsible for this book and who managed to get the support of King Josiah for their ideas, believed that there could be an efficient purging of religious life only by restricting the bringing of sacrifices to Jerusalem (ch. 12). The intent was to make the temple in Jerusalem the sole legitimate sanctuary and to declare all rural shrines illegitimate. It was hoped that this measure would eliminate syncretism. We may well ask, however, what this large-scale reform program ultimately amounted to. In the ancient East there were many such attempts, but it cannot be shown that they were ever really effective. Life everywhere is stronger than a superimposed doctrine. A king may dictate that, from now on, sacrifices may be brought only to Jerusalem, but it does not seem likely that a farmer in Galilee would pay much attention to such a decree.

Like other bodies of law in the ancient East, Deuteronomy is preceded by a prologue (chs. 1–11) and concludes with an epilogue (chs. 27–34). The intent appears to have been to give the code the kind of historical setting that would create the impression that it had been promulgated by Moses himself. The actual code is found in chapters 12–26. Chapter 12 deals with the centralization of worship. Chapter 13 contains regulations against the threat of idolatry. Chapter 14 forbids a number of mourning customs of foreign origin, presents a summary of clean and unclean animals, and finally regulates the paying of tithes. Chapter 15:1–11 contains regulations concerning the sabbatical year, while verses 12–18 deal with the freeing of slaves and verses 19–23 contain the law concerning the firstborn. Chapter 16 opens with some rules for the celebration of the three major feasts and ends with stipulations for the administration of justice. Chapter 17 has three divisions: verses 2–7 deal with the punishment of idolatry, verses 8–13 concern the highest law court, while verses 14–20 contain the so-called royal law.

Chapter 18 deals again with the cult. Verses 1–8 regulate the income of priests and Levites, and verses 9–22 concern fortune-telling and false prophecy. Chapter 19 speaks first about the law of the cities of refuge and next about theft of land and false witness. Chapter 20 presents a great number of laws pertaining to warfare.

Chapter 21 gives rules on how to handle certain situations, for instance, an unsolved murder. The pericope 21:10–14, which apparently has become dislocated (it seems to fit much better among the laws concerning wars in the previous chapter), gives regulations on how to deal with a captive woman. Then follows a law concerning the right of the firstborn, following which verses 18–21 tell how to deal with a rebellious son. The chapter concludes with laws concerning the burial of a member of the people who was executed. Chapter 22 provides rules for a great variety of situations, such as lost animals, tranvestism, and protection of birds. Verses 13–30 bring together a number of laws pertaining to marriage. Chapter 23 determines who may enter the congregation of Yahweh and gives regulations concerning sanitary conditions in the camp. The following verses require merciful treatment of a fugitive slave, condemn sacred prostitution, forbid charging interest to a member of the people, insist that vows to Yahweh be kept, and regulate the taking of a neighbor's grapes and grain. Chapter 24 deals first of all with divorce, next with protection of the neighbor, and finally with showing mercy. Chapter 25 also deals with widely divergent subjects, including unnecessary cruelty, levirate marriage, proper modesty, and honesty in weights and measures. The final chapter deals with the offering of the firstfruits (26:1–11) and the giving of the tithes (vv. 12–15).

A special characteristic of Deuteronomy is its humanity. Social legislation has a dominant place in it (ch. 15; 22:1–4; 23:20–21 [19–20]; 24:6–7). The influence of the preaching of the prophets and the salutary impact of the instruction of the wisdom teachers is readily apparent.

LITERATURE

A. Alt, "Die Ursprünge des israelitischen Rechts," *KS* I (München, 1953) 278-332.

R. Alter, *The Art of Biblical Narrative* (New York, 1981).

B. W. Anderson and W. Harrelson, eds., *Israel's Prophetic Heritage* (Festschrift J. Muilenburg; New York, 1962).

W. Baumgartner, "Vom hebräischen Erzählungsstil," in H. Schmidt, ed., *Eucharisterion: Studien zur Religion und Literatur des Alten und Neuen Testaments* (Festschrift H. Gunkel; FRLANT 19; Göttingen, 1923), I: 145-57.

J. A. Bewer, *The Literature of the Old Testament* (New York, 1949[8]).

H. A. Brongers, *De literatuur der Babyloniërs en Assyriërs* (Den Haag, 1951).

————, *Oud-oosters en bijbels recht* (Nijkerk, 1960).

————, *De Jozefsgeschiedenis bij Joden, Christenen en Mohammedanen* (Nijkerk, 1962).

L. Bronner, *The Stories of Elijah and Elisha* (Leiden, 1968).

B. S. Childs, *Introduction to the Old Testament as Scripture* (Philadelphia, 1979).

G. W. Coats, ed., *Saga, Legend, Tales, Novella, Fable. Narrative Forms in Old Testament Literature* (JSOT Supplement Series 35; Sheffield, 1985).

F. M. Cross, Jr., *Canaanite Myth and Hebrew Epic* (Cambridge, MA, 1973).

J. J. A. van Dijk, *La sagesse suméro-accadienne* (Leiden, 1953).

O. Eissfeldt, *The Old Testament: An Introduction* (New York, 1965).

P. Ellermeier, *Prophetie in Mari und Israel* (Herzberg, 1968).

A. Erman, *Literatur der Ägypter* (Leipzig, 1923).

A. Falkenstein and W. von Soden, *Sumerische und Akkadische Hymnen und Gebete* (Zürich, 1953).

G. Fohrer, *Einleitung in das Alte Testament* (Heidelberg, 1979[12]).

————, *Elia* (Zürich, 1968[2]).

G. Gerleman, "The Song of Deborah in the Light of Stylistics," *VT* 1 (1951) 168-80.

C. H. Gordon, *Ugaritic Literature* (Rome, 1949).

H. Gunkel and J. Begrich, *Einleitung in die Psalmen* (Göttingen, 1966[2]).

J. Hempel, *Die althebräische Literatur und ihr hellenistisch-jüdisches Nachleben* (Potsdam, 1930).

S. Herrmann, *Die prophetischen Heilserwartungen im Alten Testament* (Stuttgart, 1965).

S. N. Kramer, *Mythologies of the Ancient World* (New York, 1961).

H.-J. Kraus, *Die Psalmen* (BKAT XV; Neukirchen, 1960).

J. L. Kugel, *The Idea of Biblical Poetry* (New Haven, 1981).

W. G. Lambert, *Babylonian Wisdom Literature* (Oxford, 1960).

W. G. Lambert and A. R. Millard, *Atraḫasis. The Babylonian Story of the Flood* (Oxford, 1969).

S. Langdon, *Babylonian Wisdom* (London, 1923).

F. M. Th. de Liagre Böhl, "Bijbelse en babylonische dichtkunst," *JEOL* 15 (1957-58) 133-53.

————, *Het Gilgamesjepos* (Amsterdam, 1958[3]).

J. Lindblom, *Prophecy in Ancient Israel* (Philadelphia, 1963).

R. Lowth, *Lectures on the Sacred Poetry of the Hebrews* (London, 1847).

B. Meissner, *Babylonien und Assyrien* (Heidelberg, 1920/25).

M. Noth, *The History of Israel* (New York, 1960[2]).

————, *Überlieferungsgeschichtliche Studien—Die sammelnden und bearbeitenden Geschichtswerke im Alten Testament* (Tübingen, 1957[2]).

————, "The Laws in the Pentateuch," in *The Laws in the Pentateuch and Other Studies* (London, 1966), pp. 1-107.

M. O'Connor, *Hebrew Verse Structure* (Winona Lake, 1980).

J. L. Palache, *Het karakter van het Oudtestamentisch verhaal* (Amsterdam, 1925).

D. Patrick, *Old Testament Law* (Atlanta, 1985).

J. B. Pritchard, ed., *Ancient Near Eastern Texts Relating to the Old Testament* (Princeton, 1969[3]).

G. von Rad, "The Joseph Narrative and Ancient Wisdom," in *The Problem of the Hexateuch and Other Essays* (New York, 1966), pp. 292-300.

R. Rendtorff, *Die Gesetze der Priesterschrift* (Göttingen, 1954).

H. H. Rowley, *Moses and the Decalogue* (Manchester, 1951).

R. Smend, *Die Entstehung des Alten Testaments* (Stuttgart, 1981[2]).

J. A. Soggin, *Introduction to the Old Testament* (Philadelphia, 1976).

R. Sonsino, *Motive Clauses in Hebrew Law. Biblical Forms and Near Eastern Parallels* (Chico, CA, 1980).

Th. C. Vriezen and A. S. van der Woude, *De literatuur van Oud-Israël* (Wassenaar, 1980[6]).

W. G. E. Watson, *Classical Hebrew Poetry. A Guide to its Techniques* (JSOT Supplement Series 26; Sheffield, 1984).

C. Westermann, *The Basic Forms of Prophetic Speech* (Philadelphia, 1967).

————, *Praise and Lament in the Psalms* (Atlanta, 1981[2]).

III

The Books of the Old Testament

by C. Houtman, H. H. Grosheide, B. J. Oosterhoff, and J. P. M. van der Ploeg

A. The Pentateuch

by C. Houtman

1. NAME, DIVISION, AND CONTENT

The term *Pentateuch,* which via Latin goes back to Greek, means "book in five parts" and as such is used for the first five books of the Old Testament. So far as is known, the word was first used with this meaning in the second century A.D. The division of the content into five books is known from the first century A.D. but is likely older. Though the division is probably secondary, it is nevertheless natural, since each of the books is a more or less distinct unit. (Besides the designation Pentateuch, Old Testament scholarship uses the term *Tetrateuch* [fourfold book] for Genesis through Numbers, and the term *Hexateuch* [sixfold book] for Genesis through Joshua.)

The names of the five books current in the Christian tradition—Genesis, Exodus, Leviticus, Numbers, and Deuteronomy—are from the Vulgate and, except for Numbers (a translation of *Arithmoi*), are derived from a transliteration of the Greek names in the Septuagint. These names are based on the contents of the books: Genesis is so called because it describes the *origin* of the world; Exodus deals with the *exodus* of Israel out of Egypt; Leviticus gets its name from the laws pertaining to the *Levitical* cult and priesthood; Numbers gives surveys of the *countings* of the people (see chs. 1 and 26); and Deuteronomy records the *second giving of the law* mentioned in the earlier books.

In the Jewish tradition the first five books are designated with the word *torah,* which in the Septuagint and the New Testament is reproduced by the Greek *nomos,* usually translated "law." Torah, however, contains especially the notion of direction or instruction. In the Jewish tradition the individual books are designated with words derived from the first line of the books: *bereshit* ("in the beginning"; Genesis), *weelleh shemot* ("and these are the names"; Exodus), *wayyiqra* ("and he called"; Leviticus), *bammidbar* ("in the wilderness") or *wayyedabber* ("and he spoke"; Numbers), and *elleh haddebarim* ("these are the words") or *debarim* ("words"; Deuteronomy).

The content of the Pentateuch can be divided into two parts: first, a description of the prehistory of the people of Israel. This record is given in the book of Genesis, which begins by recounting the creation and the history of the world and humankind (chs. 1–11) and then continues by narrating events in the life of the patriarchs of Israel (chs. 12–50). Second, the Pentateuch describes the history of Israel to the arrival of the people at the borders of Canaan. This account is given in Exodus through Deuteronomy and can be divided into the following episodes: (1) Israel's sojourn in Egypt, the Exodus, and the arrival at Sinai (Exod. 1:1–19:2); (2) Israel's stay at Sinai (Exod. 19:3 through Num. 10:10), including several collections of law; (3) the journey to Transjordan (Num. 10:11–36:13); and (4) the final days of Moses, during which Moses, in lengthy admonishing addresses, bids farewell to the people and gives Israel laws for its life in Canaan (Deuteronomy).

2. HYPOTHESES ABOUT THE ORIGIN OF THE PENTATEUCH

a. Moses Is the Author

For centuries "official" Judaism and "official" Christianity have regarded Moses as the writer of the entire Pentateuch. The reader should realize, however, that this view did not arise as a result of historical research into the question of the origin of these books. Rather, by presenting Moses, the confidant of God, as the writer of the Pentateuch, this position attempted to stress the divine origin and thus the authority of the Pentateuch. There was hardly any concern about questions involving the origin of these writings. The focus of interest in the Pentateuch was doctrinal and practical.

Other groups (usually called heretics) in the first centuries after Christ had a similar interest. With them, however, the study of the five books led to the conclusion that the Pentateuch in its present form could not in its totality be regarded as the work of Moses. For example, in the Pseudo-Clementines, Jewish-Christian writings that also show gnostic traits, the idea is found that through the centuries the words of Moses became overgrown by devil-inspired lies as well as by human additions, including some from Moses himself (e.g., the sacrificial laws). In that way many offensive elements found their way into the Pentateuch, such as the anthropomorphic descriptions of God and the description of Adam as transgressor, of Noah as a drunk, of Abraham and Jacob as polygamists, of Moses as a murderer, etc. Here and in other documents from heretical circles, dogmatic and ethical objections against the content of the Pentateuch are raised as reasons for refusing to regard the whole Pentateuch in its present form as the Word of God. According to such groups, a variety of voices was heard in these books; the result was a loosening of the tie between Moses and the Pentateuch in its present form.

The Pseudo-Clementines, then, view the Pentateuch as the result of a process of corruption. By way of further insight, these documents also point to the long and checkered history of the Pentateuch in Israel and to its destruction during the Captivity. Such data and others indicate that the experiences of the people of Israel apparently created doubt regarding the reliability of the transmission of the Pentateuch, or at least occasioned the question how it could be possible that the Pentateuch, despite its long history, might be regarded as the infallible Word of God. It is likely that several church fathers, also in order to an-

swer this question adequately, accepted the following approximate picture, derived from 4 Ezra 14:14–48, concerning its origin: during the Babylonian captivity the holy writings of Israel were lost through fire; in answer to Ezra's prayer, God equipped him for forty days to dictate the lost books (and a great number of apocalyptic writings not meant for public use) to five scribes. The church fathers did not intend to deny the Mosaic authorship of the Pentateuch but rather to secure the authority and infallibility of the Old Testament as the Word of God.

Though for many centuries the Mosaic authorship of the Pentateuch was in general not a point of discussion in Jewish and Christian circles, gradually the awareness arose that the Pentateuch contained additions to the work of Moses—not everything in it could be from his hand. The above-mentioned Pseudo-Clementines even contain the remark that Moses had not been active as an author but had given orders that his words were to be passed on orally. An argument adduced against the authorship of Moses is that he could not possibly have written the account of his own death (Deut. 34:5–8). Here the Pseudo-Clementines raise an issue that, as other data indicate, has been an age-old question with respect to the Mosaic authorship of the Pentateuch. The radical conclusion that, since Moses could not have been the writer of the end of Deuteronomy, he wrote none of the Pentateuch, was not drawn again until the sixteenth century. Then Andreas Bodenstein, better known as Karlstadt, made this proposal in his *De canonicis Scripturis libellus* (1520); his assertion, however, found no acceptance. Before Karlstadt, less radical proposals for solving the problem had been made. Two Jewish authors from the first century A.D., Philo of Alexandria (*De vita Mosis* 2.291) and Flavius Josephus (*Antiquities* 4.326), maintained that Moses himself, by virtue of his prophetic gifts, recorded his own death! By contrast, the Talmud (*Baba Bathra* 14b) contains the apparently more rational idea that Joshua wrote the ending of Deuteronomy.

Throughout the centuries Deuteronomy 34:5–8 played a role in discussions concerning the authorship of the Pentateuch. In the course of time, other parts whose contents could hardly be from the time of Moses were added to this passage. The twelfth-century Jewish exegete Ibn Ezra indirectly alluded to a number of such passages. In his commentary on Deuteronomy, in addition to pointing to the account of Moses' death, Ibn Ezra drew attention to the fact that the reference to Transjordan in 1:1 ("on the other side of the Jordan") presupposes that the writer lived in Cisjordan, where Moses never was. He also points out that 3:11 gives the impression of having been written after Moses' death (cf. 2 Sam. 12:30) and that "Moses wrote" in Deuteronomy 31:9 presupposes someone other than Moses as the writer. Before Ibn Ezra it had already been pointed out that Genesis 36:31–39 assumes familiarity with the institute of the monarchy in Israel, and Jerome (*De perpetua virginitate* [Migne, *PL* 23.190]) had already pointed out that "until this day" in Genesis 35:4 (LXX) and in Deuteronomy 34:5–6 suggests that these verses were written in the period after Moses. In the Middle Ages and following centuries, other passages were added to the list, such as Genesis 12:6; 14:14 (cf. Judg. 18:29); 23:2 (cf. Josh. 14:14–15); Exodus 16:35; Numbers 12:3; Deuteronomy 2:12; 3:14. We should note here that the critical voices raised over the centuries may have been more numerous than the available data seem to suggest. We must remember that the church, after it had suppressed the heretical movements, was eager to see the heresies pass into oblivion and was ready to persecute anyone who expressed oneself critically. In Judaism the fear of excommunication from the synagogue restrained many an author from making overly audacious statements.

The presence of such passages did not at first lead to doubts about the Mosaic authorship of the Pentateuch. Many scholars even denied emphatically that these verses could be used as arguments against overall Mosaic authorship of the Pentateuch. Following Philo and Josephus, some pointed to the fact that Moses was also a prophet, an argument heard until the eighteenth century. It was assumed that this observation was sufficient to explain a problem such as Genesis 36:31–39, in which Edomite kings from the time of Israel's monarchy are mentioned by name. In contrast, a number of scholars from the Middle Ages and the sixteenth century, and likely also Jerome, argued for a role for Ezra and/or Joshua and

Eleazar in the Mosaic work. The idea that the Pentateuch, except for a certain number of minor corrections, is essentially the product of Moses gained wide acceptance in the seventeenth and eighteenth centuries. To the present day it is advocated by orthodox Protestant authors such as Young and Möller and also by orthodox Jewish authors such as Segal. Other conservative Protestant scholars such as Aalders and Harrison do not wish to regard Moses as the author of the Pentateuch but believe that the documents from which it was compiled in the time after Moses were in the main Mosaic material and received their present shape in or before the early monarchical period. Before the rise of a more liberal climate in Roman Catholic biblical studies in the wake of the encyclical *Divino afflante Spiritu* (1943) and the letter of the papal Bible commission to Cardinal Suhard (1948), similar conservative ideas with respect to the origin of the Pentateuch were also current in Roman Catholic biblical scholarship.

b. Moses Is Not the Author—the Rise of Historical and Literary Criticism

In the seventeenth century under the influence of a growing rationalism, some great thinkers questioned and attacked the traditional idea of Mosaic authorship of the Pentateuch. One of their arguments was the presence of passages that cannot be from Moses, such as those discussed in the preceding section. But these writers went further. In their study of the Pentateuch they noted historical inaccuracies, inconsistencies, the presence of remarkable repetitions, and variations in style. In an attempt to answer the question of the age and authorship of the Pentateuch, they wanted to be unbiased, guided only by the data in the writings themselves, and thus they did not accept the traditional view concerning Mosaic authorship. The fact that certain parts contained no elements that argued against Mosaic authorship was not accepted as an argument for their authenticity. Using this methodology did not lead them to deny every Mosaic contribution to the Pentateuch (unlike the practice in later historical criticism, they accepted the reliability of passages such as Exod. 17:14; 24:4; Num. 33:2; Deut. 31:9), but they did affirm that the origin of the Pentateuch was much more complex than traditionally thought. On account of their approach these scholars may be regarded as the fathers of historical and literary criticism.

One philosopher who expressed this kind of criticism was the English Deist Thomas Hobbes in his *Leviathan* (1651). Another was the French Protestant Isaac de la Peyrère in his *Praeadamitae* (1655). De la Peyrère attempted to reconcile scriptural data with the new scientific insights regarding the age and size of the world by maintaining on the basis of scriptural data that there were also people before Adam. In his judgment much in Scripture remained inexplicable if one did not adopt such a theory, such as the fact that Scripture speaks twice about the creation of human beings, first in Genesis 1 (the creation of the pre-Adamites) and then in Genesis 2 (the creation of the Adamites). Considering the obscurity, the confusion, the unfinished and distorted stories, and the contradictions in the Pentateuch, de la Peyrère contended that these books must be the work of more than one author. In his opinion, Scripture is far from clear and reliable. It is up to reason and faith to distinguish between the voice of God and the hands of men.

The considerations of Hobbes and de la Peyrère are fragmentary, incomplete, and systematically imprecise. In the seventeenth century more detailed critical viewpoints were published by the Jew Baruch Spinoza, the French Roman Catholic Richard Simon, and the Remonstrant Jean Le Clerc. In his discussions of the Pentateuch in his *Tractatus Theologico-Politicus* (1670), Spinoza built on what was said by Ibn Ezra (see previous section) and proposed that all the books from Genesis through 2 Kings are a comprehensive work, composed by Ezra, who made use of documents from various sources. He pointed to the heterogeneous character of the material and to the haphazard arrangement. He noted, for example, that the phrase "at that time" in Genesis 38:1 cannot refer to what precedes, because the events described in this chapter cannot possibly have happened in the twenty-two years that, according to Genesis, lay between the selling of Joseph into Egypt and the arrival of Jacob and his sons in that country.

In his *Histoire critique du Vieux Testament*

(1678), some of the arguments Simon used against Mosaic authorship were the presence of striking repetitions (e.g., in the account of the Flood), which could hardly be from Moses, and the different styles. He explained the heterogeneous character of the material and its haphazard arrangement with the following theory: Until the time of Ezra there existed in Israel the institution of public scribes, people resembling archivists, who were in charge of the official records and who recorded the history of the people. Moses and these public scribes, whom one should view as inspired persons, wrote on small scrolls or loose sheets. In the course of time the material became disorganized. Moreover, it should be borne in mind that, for the most part, the books of the Bible contain only excerpts from the documents of Israel. With his theory Simon aimed to show that the Pentateuch is the result of a long process of compilation. On the one hand he sought to offer an acceptable explanation for the problems in the text of the Pentateuch (repetitions, variations in style, faulty sequence); on the other hand he wanted to show that the phenomena observed do not violate the authority of Scripture, because through the centuries inspired persons, who may be regarded as belonging to the prophets, have worked on the Pentateuch, so that alterations and additions are just as authoritative as the original parts. As an aside, it may be pointed out that Simon's idea of inspiration still persists today. For instance, the conservative Protestant Old Testament scholar Noordtzij suggests that the laws of Moses were in the course of time supplemented by specially qualified persons.

Simon's views were challenged by Le Clerc, who wrote a book in the form of a series of letters entitled *Sentimens de quelques théologiens de Hollande sur "l'Histoire critique du Vieux Testament" composée par le P. Richard Simon de l'Oratoire* (1685). Despite his criticism of Simon, Le Clerc's view on the Pentateuch did not differ substantially from Simon's. He rejected Simon's theory of the public scribes and of the small scrolls, maintaining that private documents constituted the sources of the Pentateuch. Like Simon he believed that the Pentateuch was the result of a long process of compilation, and he regarded it as plausible that the priest who was deported from

Samaria and later sent back by the king of Assyria and who then settled in Bethel (2 Kgs. 17:27–28) was responsible for the present form of the Pentateuch.

The views just presented elicited fierce opposition in the seventeenth and eighteenth centuries but, at least in the more official literature, had little influence. The few critical voices that were heard in the more official literature after Le Clerc offered few new ideas. We should not forget, however, that radical rationalistic criticism was then widely propagated among freethinkers of English and French Deists through correspondence and pamphlets, a criticism that went much further than merely calling into question the Mosaic authorship of the Pentateuch. Only in the second half of the eighteenth century were books published that attributed only part of the Pentateuch to Moses. At that time also the well-known German rationalist Hermann Samuel Reimarus set forth his ideas about the Bible in his *Apologie oder Schutzschrift für die vernünftigen Verehrer Gottes*. His conception of the making of the Pentateuch was similar to Spinoza's and contained no significant new idea.

The French rationalist Voltaire also expressed himself critically about the Mosaic authorship of the Pentateuch. He did so in incidental remarks about the difficulty of writing a five-volume work—the Pentateuch—in the desert at a time when wood and stone were used as writing materials. He made some sketchy suggestions about the origin of the Pentateuch, including the idea that, hundreds of years after Moses, some Levites wrote down the fables. For the enlightened minds of that time, the question of the authorship of the Pentateuch gradually lost its interest and relevance. Beginning in the second half of the eighteenth century, however, the discipline of biblical studies developed more carefully defined and initially also more conservative theories with respect to the origin of the Pentateuch than those that were proposed in the seventeenth century. We now consider these more recent proposals.

c. The Older Documentary, Fragmentary, Supplementary, and Newer Documentary Hypotheses

Above it was noted that, in the seventeenth and eighteenth centuries, the Mosaic authorship of the Pentateuch was widely accepted. Some scholars strongly defended this position against critical voices. Others, though not expressing themselves critically, did not feel the need to defend the traditional view. One of the questions occupying both opponents and proponents of the Mosaic authorship was how Moses could have written the history before his time, as narrated in Genesis. A variety of answers was given: Moses was able to do it because of his prophetic gifts and by special revelation from God; Moses recorded the oral tradition of his ancestors that reached back to Adam; Moses made use of written documents. The views of the French doctor Jean Astruc, an advocate of this third position, are even today regularly referred to because they provided the impetus for the development of the so-called four-document theory, a theory regarding the origin of the Pentateuch that is still very important in biblical studies. Therefore we need to spend some time reviewing this hypothesis.

In his *Conjectures sur les mémoires originaux dont il paraît que Moïse s'est servi pour composer le livre de la Genèse* (1753), Astruc sought to refute the criticism of Hobbes, de la Peyrère, Spinoza, and Le Clerc and to demonstrate that the blemishes, contradictions, and inaccuracies they had observed in the chronology need not lead to a denial of Mosaic authorship. Astruc did not deny that the text of Genesis was marked by flaws and the like. According to him, however, there is a good explanation for them. He opined that Moses wrote a kind of tetrapla, compiling in four columns the sources of the history before his time (a kind of synopsis such as the Gospels provide). Later copiers combined them into a continuous story and are responsible for the disorder typical of the present book of Genesis. By reconstructing Moses' writing in this way, Astruc indeed managed to solve some of the chronological problems in Genesis.

Astruc based his theory on the presence of striking duplications and on the use of the two divine names. He pointed out that there are two creation narratives (Genesis 1 and 2) and that the story of the Flood contains many repetitions (chs. 6–8). He also pointed out that sometimes, in a long chapter (e.g., ch. 1), the divine name Elohim is used, and then later, also in a long section (e.g., chs. 2–4), only the name Jehovah (the so-called tetragrammaton *yhwh,* nowadays usually designated as Yahweh). From this fact he concluded that Moses had at his disposal two documents, one regularly using the divine name Elohim and the other characterized by the use of the divine name Jehovah. He believed he found support for his thesis in the fact that, after Exodus 1–2, the use of the divine name no longer provides a basis for the differentiation of sources, for beginning with chapter 3, Moses describes his own time and no longer employs documents. The Elohim and the Jehovah sources, each entered in a separate column, are by far the most important for Astruc. The rest of the material, only a small quantity, which in his judgment may have come from diverse documents, he compiled in two other columns.

Astruc's work initially received little attention. His proposal, known as the *older documentary hypothesis,* became more widely known as a result of the work of the German biblical scholar Johann Gottfried Eichhorn. We do not know whether Eichhorn was familiar with Astruc's *Conjectures* or whether he arrived independently at a similar theory. At any rate, his thoughts have their own character. In his *Einleitung in das Alte Testament* (1780–83; 1823–24⁴), he defended a more refined documentary hypothesis with respect to Genesis and Exodus 1–2. Besides drawing attention to the presence of duplications and the alterations in the divine names, he referred to other literary features, variations in style, and typical elements in the contents. At least in the fourth edition of his *Einleitung,* Eichhorn exhibited reserve regarding the question whether Moses was responsible for the definitive form of Genesis. On the whole, however, he had little difficulty assigning significant parts of the Pentateuch to Moses. According to him the content of the Pentateuch was from Moses himself and from some of his contemporaries, and these books received their present form in the time between Joshua and Samuel.

Though in this respect he was close to the traditional views, he was less concerned about the historicity of what was narrated.

The documentary hypothesis did not gain universal acceptance. Other theories regarding the origin of the Pentateuch enjoyed a greater interest in the first half of the nineteenth century. One such view was the *fragmentary hypothesis.* In his *The Holy Bible,* I (1792) and *Critical Remarks on the Holy Scriptures,* I (1800), Alexander Geddes, a Scottish Roman Catholic priest, contended that the Pentateuch is composed of larger and smaller fragments that are independent of one another and often contradict each other, and that they were pieced together by a redactor who likely lived at the time of Solomon. Geddes's ideas were elaborated and given more exposure by the German scholar Johann Severin Vater in his *Commentar über den Pentateuch* (1802–1805). The significance of the work of Vater was that, unlike Astruc and Eichhorn, he not only concerned himself with Genesis but also carefully analyzed the other books of the Pentateuch. Particularly because of the presence of much legal material, it is very difficult to distinguish continuous documents in these books. It is thus not strange that Vater's research of these books led him to reject the documentary hypothesis. To some extent his standpoint can be characterized as a return to the critical conceptions of the seventeenth century. One should, however, guard against posing too great a distance between Vater's thesis and the documentary hypothesis. Besides his two main sources, Astruc acknowledged the existence of a number of fragments in Genesis and made the observation that the Elohim and the Jehovah documents themselves perhaps each go back to various documents. On the other hand, Vater sought to explain the remarkable use of the divine names in Genesis by conceiving of an Elohistic and a Jehovistic circle as sources of groups of fragments.

In Germany the publication of Vater's studies heralded a period of intensive reflection on the questions concerning the origin and composition of the Pentateuch. For most scholars the discussion about the fragmentary hypothesis led neither to a consensus nor to outright rejection but to a diversity of standpoints that cannot be simplistically subsumed under one term. During this period, a number of other positions were widely held. Besides an orthodox group of biblical scholars who defended the Mosaic authorship of the Pentateuch and a moderately critical group who accepted the presence of substantial Mosaic parts in the Pentateuch, a number of scholars held views that were marked by extreme historical criticism. They regarded much of what is narrated in the Old Testament as historically unreliable and denied that Moses had any part in the making of the Pentateuch. Wilhelm Martin Leberecht De Wette, for example, in his *Beiträge zur Einleitung in das Alte Testament* (1806–1807), denied that Moses was the author of the laws in the Pentateuch. He maintained that the Mosaic legislation developed gradually. Others even denied that Moses was literate, contending that the Pentateuch obtained its present form only after the Exile.

Characteristic of this period, several scholars more than once changed their viewpoint over the years. So De Wette, who at first defended a form of the fragmentary hypothesis, later accepted the *supplementary hypothesis* as promoted in the 1830s by many scholars. This hypothesis assumes the existence of a basic Elohistic document, comprising continuous parts in the books Genesis through Joshua but not including Deuteronomy, a document characterized by the use of the divine name Elohim. This document was then presumably supplemented by a Jehovist, a writer using the divine name Jehovah (and also Elohim). Presumably Deuteronomy, which, since the publication of De Wette's *Dissertatio Critica* (1805) and *Beiträge,* was regarded by many scholars as the lawbook discovered under Josiah in 622/621 (2 Kings 22–23) and considered to be the most recent part of the Pentateuch (see further under section 3 below), was included in this document. By way of elucidation we should point out that, when the idea that the entire Pentateuch was from Moses and/or his contemporaries was discarded, it was no longer natural in the search for the sources of the Pentateuch to limit oneself to Genesis and the beginning of Exodus. The question could now be asked whether possible sources in Genesis might also extend to other parts of the Pentateuch.

The supplementary hypothesis evoked criticism on a number of points. Critics contended, for example, that certain parts of the Pentateuch so clearly had their own identity that it was impossible to regard them either as part of the "basic document" or as part of the Jehovistic additions. This criticism led Hermann Hupfeld, a hundred years after Astruc, to a position that is usually called the *newer documentary hypothesis,* and its relative simplicity ultimately discredited the supplementary hypothesis. In his *Die Quellen der Genesis und die Art ihrer Zusammensetzung von neuem untersucht* (1853), Hupfeld advocated the following theory: Genesis through Joshua contains three continuous sources—the oldest, an Elohistic writing, contains a continuous narrative from the Creation to the partition of the land in the book of Joshua; a more recent Elohistic writing, containing the history of Israel from the time of the patriarchs; and a Jehovistic writing that is still more recent and starts with an account of the Creation but that otherwise is quite similar to the second Elohistic writing. These documents were combined by a redactor. Next to these sources Deuteronomy was recognized as having an independent origin. In this way the theory that the Pentateuch is composed of four sources took shape, one that continues to play a significant role.

d. The Newer Documentary Hypothesis Defended in a New Form— Kuenen and Wellhausen

In the second half of the nineteenth century, the view that the Pentateuch is composed of four sources became increasingly popular. At the end of the century it was accepted by the majority of Old Testament scholars. The popularity of the four-sources theory is connected with the names of the Dutch Abraham Kuenen and in particular the German Julius Wellhausen. In the nineteenth century they were able to combine into a grand conception the insights that scholars such as De Wette, J. F. L. George, J. K. W. Vatke, G. H. A. Ewald, H. Hupfeld, J. W. Colenso, E. Reuss, and K. H. Graf had gained in the areas of literary and historical criticism and the history of the religion of Israel. In this view the idea concerning how the Old Testament had come into being seemed to offer a convincing basis for a magnificent picture of the manner in which the religion of Israel might gradually have evolved. As we shall see, Kuenen's and Wellhausen's views of the origin of the Pentateuch played an important role in their overall theory.

Before describing broadly the viewpoint of these scholars, we should consider some of the individual details. The work of Kuenen and Wellhausen was preceded by a long preparatory process, for the outlines of their conception were evident earlier in the nineteenth century. As early as the first half of the nineteenth century, some scholars had proposed that large sections of the laws in Exodus through Numbers were from the postexilic period and were thus more recent than Deuteronomy, Josiah's lawbook. Such sections were regarded as representing a phase in the development of Israel's religion following upon Deuteronomy and as younger than the prophets. Another issue, already alluded to by earlier scholars, concerned the historical unreliability of Chronicles. Research had shown that its presentation of the law of Moses as having existed in ancient times was untenable. Scholars also found that the other historical writings—with the exception of the late books of Ezra and Nehemiah—likewise did not presuppose the existence of Mosaic legislation. It was concluded that much of the Mosaic material is unknown in the older historical books and that nothing of this legislation demands exclusive validity for itself. The acquaintance with Deuteronomy found in Joshua through 2 Kings was attributed to a Deuteronomic editing of these books following the reform of Josiah.

As long as the supplementary hypothesis was popular, these observations could not gain a full hearing. Deuteronomy was regarded as the youngest document in the Pentateuch, and there was little desire to lift the laws out of the "basic document" and date them as a separate entity after the Exile. At the same time the supplementary hypothesis, with its extensive basic document with varying content and with its idea of the Jehovistic supplementer, whose work on many points showed affinity with the material of the basic document, made it impossible to assign a post-Deuteronomic dating to its central document. Moreover, on account of its precise recording of detailed data (recall, for example, the summaries of the ages in the genealogies in Genesis), the basic document was regarded as old and authentic.

The documentary hypothesis of Hupfeld, by contrast, left room to accommodate the above-mentioned observations. In this hypothesis, the so-called basic document was divided into two Elohistic documents, of which the one exhibited affinity with the Jehovist, but not the other. Hupfeld regarded the bulk of the laws in Exodus through Numbers (laws that some scholars dated as postexilic) as belonging to the latter, the older and first Elohist. Because Hupfeld had given an independent position to this first Elohist vis-à-vis (1) the Jehovistic elements and (2) the Elohistic passages in the basic document of the supplementary hypothesis that are related to the Jehovistic elements, both of which lend an archaic character to the text, it was possible to assign a later date to the laws and the narratives in which they are embedded. Such a possibility became even more real when it was suggested that, historically speaking, the more authentically the passages present themselves, the less reliable they are, implying that passages presented as authentic are therefore of more recent date.

Conditions were thus created for the basis of Kuenen's and Wellhausen's conceptions: the law (also the Psalms) in the Old Testament is more recent than the prophets. To establish this position it was necessary only to change the sequence of Hupfeld's sources, which indeed happened. Using the currently accepted terms and abbreviations for the sources, we note that Hupfeld proposed the following order: P (Priestly Code, the first Elohist, the oldest source), E (the second Elohist), J (Yahwist [= older "Jehovist"]), D (Deuteronomy, the lawbook of Josiah; for a characterization of all the sources, see section 3.b below). The order now is changed to J, E, D, P—the oldest document becomes the youngest. This order makes clear why the late books of Chronicles, Ezra, and Nehemiah show a familiarity with the Mosaic legislation and why the early books Joshua through 2 Kings seem familiar only with Deuteronomy. The bulk of Mosaic legislation did not take shape until the Exile and later. We now must further describe and elucidate these major points in the views of Kuenen and Wellhausen.

A careful consideration of the questions concerning the origin of the Pentateuch and detailed investigation over many years led Kuenen to present the following picture of the origin of the Hexateuch (with others, Kuenen assumed a close connection between the Pentateuch and the book of Joshua), as described in the second edition of his *Historisch-Critisch Onderzoek* (Amsterdam, 1885): The Hexateuch consists of three clearly distinguishable components—JE, D, P—that were recorded in that order. The prophetic parts JE, so called on account of their affinity in some respects with the prophets of the eighth and seventh centuries B.C., are composed of a Yahwistic document (produced in southern Israel in the ninth century or the first years of the eighth century) and an Elohistic document (produced in northern Israel ca. 750 B.C.). After a Judaic editing at the end of the seventh or the beginning of the sixth century, these two sources were combined by a redactor R, usually designated Jehovist. In the Exile JE was combined with D. The priestly parts were collected and edited either in Babylon before 458 B.C. (the year of Ezra's return) or in Jerusalem between 458 and 444. At the end of that century, then, the editing of the Hexateuch took place, and reworking of the text continued until the third century.

The linchpin of this view of the origin of the Hexateuch is the dating of Deuteronomy in 622/21 (the period of Josiah's reform). This theory determines which parts of the Hexateuch are younger and which are older, on the basis of their relation to Deuteronomy. I illustrate this type of reasoning by giving a brief description of some important features of Wellhausen's *Prolegomena zur Geschichte Israels* (Berlin, 1905[6]; the 1st ed. appeared under a different title in 1878; the English translation is *Prolegomena to the History of Ancient Israel*), a book that has had a great influence. I intend to show that the sequence and dating of the sources is not an insignificant matter but has far-reaching consequences for our understanding of the development of Israel's religion. As we shall see, the picture presented by Wellhausen is altogether different from that presented by the Old Testament itself.

Characteristic of Wellhausen's conception are his ideas about the development of the cult in Israel, which I outline as follows:

JE + the older layer of Judges through Kings

1. There are many holy places.
2. Ordinary people are allowed to bring sacrifices.
3. The feasts are nomadic agricultural feasts.

D + the more recent layer of Judges through Kings

1. There must be only one sanctuary.
2. Only priests/Levites (the two are not distinguished) may bring sacrifices.
3. The agricultural feasts also commemorate historical events.

P + Ezra-Nehemiah and Chronicles

1. There is in fact one sanctuary.
2. The duties of priests and Levites are carefully defined; only priests may sacrifice, and there is an elaborate priestly hierarchy.
3. The feasts are exclusively to commemorate great events in history.

The above outline shows how, according to Wellhausen, each of the literary layers of the Hexateuch represents a certain phase in Israel's cultural history, phases that can also be traced in the other historical writings of the Old Testament. In that way they offer a basis for reconstructing the history of the religion of Israel. The supposition that Deuteronomy is the lawbook of Josiah (2 Kings 22–23), written and discovered in 622/621 B.C., is the critical point of the entire conception. Starting from this assumption, Wellhausen asserted that the requirement in Deuteronomy 12 that Israel could have only one sanctuary was formulated for the first time at the time of Josiah. It then follows that those parts of the Old Testament whose writers were apparently not aware of that requirement—the JE parts in the Hexateuch and the older layer in Judges through Kings—must be older than Deuteronomy and represent an earlier stage of Israel's religion. The JE law, for example, allows more than one sanctuary (Exod. 20:24), and the patriarchs sacrifice in various localities in the land.

Those parts (the P layer, Ezra-Nehemiah, and Chronicles), however, that assume the existence of the one sanctuary are presumed to be younger and to represent a phase in Israel's religion that follows upon Deuteronomy. They present a picture that in no way does justice to the historical reality. The Priestly writers have projected their ideal image of the cult of Israel back into the time of the desert. The one sanctuary of P, the tabernacle, is a fiction, based on the temple at Jerusalem. Wellhausen presented a similar picture for the sacrifices and the cult personnel: in ancient times (before the proclamation of Deuteronomy), sacrificing was not solely the privilege of the priests; Deuteronomy deprives laypeople of the right to sacrifice and permits them only the ordinary slaughtering of their animals (ch. 12); P offers very detailed prescriptions for the sacrifices. In ancient times the rich had professional priests, and everyone was free to become a priest; Deuteronomy permits only the descendants of Levi to become priests but shows no acquaintance yet with the difference between priest and Levite (ch. 18) nor with the office of the high priest; Ezekiel created the difference between priest and Levite (Ezek. 44:6–16) and laid the basis for the detailed priestly hierarchy as this took shape in P; only the descendants of Aaron, the priests, are entitled to bring sacrifices. Deuteronomy is always the transition phase in a certain development. This fact is also very clear as regards the feasts: in Deuteronomy (e.g., ch. 26) the feasts are related to agriculture (JE), but also to history (P).

From the above it is obvious that Wellhausen discerned a process in the history of Israel's religion that was characterized by centralization, ritualization, and historicizing of the cult. If read according to the sequence of their origin, the documents of the Old Testament demonstrated, in his judgment, the correctness of this picture. Additionally we should note that, according to Wellhausen, the prophets before Jeremiah evidence no acquaintance with Deuteronomy. To some extent they are to be regarded as men who prepared the way for Deuteronomy. Wellhausen thus views the religion of ancient Israel as a religion of nomads and farmers, one marked by freedom, naturalness, and spontaneity. This early form, however, through the emergence of the law at the time of Josiah (a process in which the religion of the prophets also made its influence felt), evolved

into the priestly and law religion of Judaism, which was altogether the opposite of the religion of ancient Israel.

Opponents of Wellhausen have often seized upon this picture of the development of Israel's religion to charge him with having been too deeply under the influence of Hegel. Certainly in his view of the gradual evolution of Israel's religion, Wellhausen was a child of his time.

After the publication of his *Prolegomena* many Old Testament scholars agreed that his views were correct. His presentation seemed to answer satisfactorily all the questions.

e. Developments after Wellhausen

Old Testament scholarship after 1900 witnessed a number of changes, particularly because scholars began to pay attention to the results of excavations in Egypt and Mesopotamia. Wellhausen and his school focused their study especially on the current Old Testament text and followed a predominantly literary-critical approach. They tried to detect every flaw in the text. Their scrutiny was virtually limited, however, to internal study of the literature of the Old Testament, which means that, according to present insights, they were quite one-sided. In addition, when Wellhausen first presented his ideas, scholars knew of hardly any other approach. There were scarcely any other data available and little willingness to use what was known. Historicism prevailed, and those studying the Old Testament were interested in reconstructing the religion of Israel with the aid of datable, written sources. Those sources were found in the Old Testament. The evolution of Israel's religion was regarded as an immanent process that happened without outside influences; Israel was viewed as a people leading an isolated existence, uninfluenced by events in the world at large such as in the deltas of the Nile and Euphrates. It was thought that foreign influences on Israel's religion did not make an impact until the Babylonian captivity.

The results of excavations from the middle of the nineteenth century in Mesopotamia and Egypt changed such a conception. These results became more widely known in the 1880s, but not until the second decade of the twentieth century did the majority of Old Testament scholars grasp the significance of these findings. Study of these discoveries showed that it was untenable to view Israel's religion as having evolved in a short time from a low level to the level of the prophets. Slowly the awareness emerged that, before Israel appeared on the world scene, there was already advanced civilization in the ancient Near East. It became evident that there was a lively cultural exchange among the different nations and that Israel was intimately linked with the culture and history of the world of that time. The discovery of a Babylonian story of creation and a Babylonian account of a flood, which showed surprising similarities with the biblical accounts, and the discovery of laws of the Babylonian king Hammurabi, which in many points resemble the laws of Moses, made a deep impression. Excavations carried out in the twentieth century in such places as Nuzi, Ugarit, and Ebla gave further evidence of the ties between Israel and the world of the ancient Near East.

The results of the excavations induced some scholars to attach a greater value to the biblical tradition. Though they were of a critical bent of mind, some researchers argued for the presence of Mosaic elements in the Pentateuch. Conservative authors in particular (see, e.g., K. A. Kitchen, *Ancient Orient and Old Testament* [London, 1966], and Harrison) have consistently used the new data that became available through the opening up of the ancient Near East to advocate the reliability of the biblical tradition and the involvement of Moses in the origin of the Pentateuch. In general, however, Old Testament scholarship has demonstrated a much more nuanced assessment of the value of the data that have become available through the excavations. One of the more generally accepted views is that Israel came in contact with the culture of the ancient Near East only after its settlement in Canaan, through the culture of that land. Furthermore, the observation that there are many ancient presentations in the Pentateuch did not necessarily prompt scholars to accept the idea that, literarily speaking, these parts are early. Rather, the idea gained currency that younger texts could contain old material, a possibility also recognized by Kuenen and Wellhausen but now clearly supported by the newer

data. The discovery of the Babylonian story of creation *Enuma elish,* for example, showed that the roots of Genesis 1 must reach far back into antiquity. We first consider, however, how the developments after 1900 resulted in a diversity of viewpoints in Old Testament scholarship relative to questions concerning the origin and composition of the Pentateuch.

(1) FORM CRITICISM— GUNKEL AND GRESSMANN

In the first place the work of Hermann Gunkel and Hugo Gressmann should be mentioned. Stimulated by the unlocking of the literature of the ancient Near East and highly interested in the origin and history of the religious ideas of Israel, these German scholars were not satisfied with studying the literature of the Old Testament in its present form, but they endeavored to describe its history from its very beginnings. In order to discover the roots of the religious ideas and how they had evolved, it was not enough to ascertain with the literary critics how a particular piece of literature was composed or who were its authors. It was especially necessary to inquire about the background of the texts and the religious ideas of the authors, to search for the origin (*Sitz im Leben*) of the forms and genres (*Gattungen*) that were used, and to trace the origin of the motifs and themes in the documents (*Stoffgeschichte*). It is thus necessary to go back into history to the era of oral transmission, the stage at which the religious ideas of the people are encountered and their real life is found.

Gunkel assumed that in ancient times literature was not produced by important persons who singly or together composed it. Literature was regarded as being the concern of the people, who had their own *Gattungen,* or modes of expression with particular formal and material characteristics, each of which belonged to a particular situation in the life of the people. Examples would be girls who met the victorious army with a song on their lips, the wailing woman who sang the funeral dirge by the bier of the dead, or the priest who gave his instructions near the sanctuary. In that way, it was thought, it was possible to penetrate to the source of the literature. This interest in literary forms and their origin has become known as *Gattungsforschung* and *Formgeschichte* and has become an integral aspect of Old Testament studies. Here we can only outline the role this approach has had in the examination of the Pentateuch.

For that purpose we refer to the introduction to Gunkel's commentary on Genesis (1901; Göttingen, 1910³). In this introduction Gunkel characterizes Genesis as a collection of brief and separate sagas, and he further describes the characteristics of the various stories. He distinguishes, for example, two main groups, the *Ursagen* (Genesis 1–11) and the *Vätersagen* (chs. 12–50), and he discusses the etiological character of many sagas. In his opinion, for example, chapter 1 answers the question how heaven and earth came into being and why the sabbath is celebrated. Chapter 28 answers the question why Bethel is a holy place, why the sacred stone there is anointed, and why tithes are brought there. Each of the sagas in Genesis is assumed to have its own prehistory, and each contains material of diverse nature and origin. In the form in which they appear in Genesis, they have for the most part the character of popular tales that initially were orally passed on by special storytellers. In the preliterary period several separate sagas were collected and joined together, which schools of collectors eventually wrote down.

At this point Gunkel sees a connection with the documentary hypothesis. He wants to regard the Yahwistic and the Elohistic elements of the documentary hypothesis as the result of the activities over many years of such schools of collectors. Gunkel tentatively dates J in the ninth century B.C. and E in the first half of the eighth century. He assumes that the two collections were put together in the late days of Judah. As regards P (who is a real author) and the final editing of the Pentateuch, Gunkel adopts the standpoint customary since Wellhausen. On that issue and others, Gunkel followed traditional paths. His great interest in the small units, the separate stories, and the resultant characterization of the Yahwistic and Elohistic work as the result of bringing the stories together, however, implied a significant change in respect to the Wellhausenian standpoint. For Wellhausen was of the opinion that J and E were individual authors, each with his own distinct personal character, and that their work reflected the religious ideas of their spiritual fathers and/or their days. By contrast, Gunkel held that the documents of the Yahwist and the Elohist contained a mix of old and young material, and that J and E, though they put their stamp on the material, primarily served as editors of the material and transmitted it as faithfully as possible. Consequently it would be wrong to attribute the ideas in J and E to these redactors themselves. It should be obvious that, in Gunkel's conception of the layers J and E, their dating and their mutual demarcation become problematic. It can even be said that Gunkel's approach, whose starting point is the recognizability of the separate sagas, leads, if consistently pursued, to a fragmentary hypothesis.

Similar reflections to those by Gunkel are found in Gressmann's *Mose und seine Zeit: Ein Kommentar zu den Mose-Sagen* (Göttingen, 1913) with regard to the Pentateuchal narratives on Moses. Gunkel wrote about the composition of the Pentateuch as a whole in the introduction to *Die Schriften des Alten Testaments,* I/1 (Göttingen, 1921²). Entirely in the spirit of his introduction on Genesis, Gunkel characterizes the Pentateuch as *ein Sammelwerk,* "a collection."

(2) THE NEWEST DOCUMENTARY HYPOTHESIS—SMEND AND EISSFELDT

I have described above how the standpoint of Gunkel and Gressmann, though they continued to hold to the newer documentary hypothesis, as a whole implied a radical revision of the Wellhausenian conception. Similar changes can be observed in other authors. Though professing their agreement with Wellhausen, their views amounted to more or less radical changes, generally more in the nature of continued literary-critical investigations.

Though Kuenen and Wellhausen were generally agreed about the division of the Hexateuch into the four sources, there was uncertainty in places. Consequently for the younger members of their school there remained enough work to continue the literary-critical investigation. A subject that in particular had aroused the interest of Kuenen's and Wellhausen's followers was the question of the composition of the sources. The masters themselves had already called attention to the complex nature of the sources, in particular of P. Building on the observations of Kuenen and Wellhausen, the followers now tried, through minutely detailed investigation, to map out the complex character of the sources—the additions to each one, the various editors, and so forth. The various elements were designated by sigla such as J, J¹, J², J³, P, Pᵍ, Pʰ, Pˢ, P¹, P², and P³ (numbers indicating the first or subsequent layer of additions, letters standing for *Grundschrift* ["oldest document"], holiness law, supplement, and similar distinctions) and were often distinguished in print by using different type styles or different colors. Note, for example, the commentaries published around the turn of the century and also later. These scholars were confident that they could determine the source of each part of a verse. The increasingly refined and artificial investigation resulted in exceedingly atomistic analyses. Literary criticism was pursued for its own sake, no longer with the aim of reconstructing the history of Israel's religion, and became a sterile concern that demonstrated only the cleverness and subjectivity of those who practiced it.

This interest in the origin and the composition of the sources caused a shift in scholarly assessment. The respective sources could no longer be viewed as more or less homogeneous documents, each the work of one author who had a specific intent, but they were to be regarded as documents that came into being gradually, in a complicated manner, in contexts that had their own characteristics. This view implies, however, an undermining of the documentary hypothesis. For the further analysis of the sources presumed that the documentary hypothesis was correct and that the sources possessed a high degree of homogeneity. Closer scrutiny, however, brought out the heterogeneity, and so the question could be asked whether the kind of analyses found in Wellhausen's school, assuming an unfamiliarity with the documentary hypothesis, might not rather have led to a form of fragmentary hypothesis.

These developments evoked various reactions. In the first place, as a reaction against the disintegration of the sources in the school of Wellhausen, some advocated a documentary hypothesis in a new and stricter form, which is sometimes called *the newest documentary hypothesis*. Elaborated by Rudolf Smend in *Die Erzählung des Hexa-*

teuch auf ihre Quellen untersucht (Berlin, 1912), since 1922 it has found a strong advocate in Otto Eissfeldt. According to Eissfeldt, the Hexateuch is composed of five layers, which he designates with the sigla L, J, E, D, P. L is a designation for *Laienquelle*, "lay-source," the oldest layer, produced at the time of David or Solomon, a layer reflecting a nomadic ideal of life and containing a protest against Canaanite influences in Israel. Much of the content of L is material that the newer documentary hypothesis attributed to J; to a lesser extent it contains material from the other layers, notably E. Eissfeldt regards the writers of the sources as real authors, whose work is recognizable, though (here the influence of Gunkel and Gressmann is noticeable) it is not completely homogeneous and betrays the incorporation of older material. Like others, Eissfeldt assumes that the sources of the Hexateuch underlie additional books (in his opinion, J and E continue through Kings).

Reacting to the disintegration of the sources in Wellhausen's theory, other scholars proposed restricting, not expanding, the number of primary sources. The interest in the preliterary phases of the transmission, encouraged by the studies of Gunkel and Gressmann, prompted several scholars to propose a different explanation of the phenomena in the texts (such as discrepancies and variations in style and word usage) that critics had used as a basis for radically splitting up the sources. These students suggested that such features had their origin in natural blending in the preliterary phase. The notion is even defended that there are no compelling arguments to regard E as an independent source. In any case, E was presumably no more than the redactor of a Yahwistic document. This idea was defended by P. Volz and W. Rudolph in *Der Elohist als Erzähler: Ein Irrweg der Pentateuchkritik?* (Giessen, 1933) and by W. Rudolph in *Der "Elohist" von Exodus bis Josua* (Giessen, 1938). Later it found defenders, among others, in Vriezen and Mowinckel. Volz and Vriezen go as far as to deny that P is a separate source and see him as editor of the material in JED. These authors thus support to a greater (Volz, Vriezen) or lesser (Rudolph, Mowinckel) extent a form of supplementary hypothesis. Vriezen, moreover, exhibits a tendency toward a fragmentary hypothesis. Following J. Hempel

(*Die althebräische Literatur und ihr hellenistisch-jüdisches Nachleben* [Wildpark-Potsdam, 1930]), Vriezen believes that the Yahwistic document is composed of three complexes, each deriving from a different author: J¹ (Genesis 12ff.), J² (chs. 37–50), and J³ (chs. 2–11). He thus arrives at the following picture of the origin of the Pentateuch: J¹ is supplemented with J², E and J³ become JE, JE fuses with D, and then P-elements are added.

(3) CRITICS OF WELLHAUSEN

So far in our outline of the developments in Pentateuch research after Wellhausen, we have limited our attention to the ideas of those Old Testament scholars who were not particularly unsympathetic to the Wellhausenian conception but believed that, to a greater or lesser degree, it required only revision. Before describing how the contribution of Gunkel and Gressmann has resulted in newer, more detailed conceptions with respect to the origin of the Pentateuch, I wish to say a few things about other, less sympathetic reactions to Wellhausen's ideas. These reactions in many cases were connected in some way with the developments after Wellhausen that I described in the preceding sections.

To the present day, the newer documentary hypothesis has been attacked by conservative Protestant writers. Reactions have varied from a defense of the Mosaic authorship of the Pentateuch (e.g., Young, Möller) to opposition to Wellhausen's specific categorization and dating, even while openly admitting that the Pentateuch comprises several documents, that additions were made to it in the course of history, and that its production extended beyond the lifetime of one man (e.g., Noordtzij).

In Roman Catholic biblical studies the reactions varied. There was opposition, but around the turn of the last century a number of noted scholars accepted the main lines of Wellhausen's literary criticism. They objected, however, to Wellhausen's historical criticism. They were willing to consider the Pentateuch Mosaic, but only in the sense that certain constitutive components derived from Moses. However, the decree *De Mosaica Authentia Pentateuchi* of the papal Bible committee of 1906 left no room to detract from Mosaic authorship. It allowed only for the possibility that Moses used sources and that the text might contain glosses and additions. After a more liberal climate had arisen in the church by the end of the 1940s, the development before 1906 was resumed and the theory of sources has gained new influence. Its acceptance is accompanied by a positive attitude toward the historical reliability of the biblical tradition (for which the results of excavations play a role) and the assertion that the beginning of the Pentateuch dates back to the time of Moses. His spirit and work are regarded as dominating the Pentateuch (see, e.g., de Vaux and Cazelles).

Jewish biblical scholars have also been divided in their reactions to the Wellhausenian conception. Prior to Wellhausen some Jewish scholars propounded somewhat similar ideas, but there has also been a variety of criticism. Besides protagonists of Mosaic authorship (e.g., Segal), some scholars who do not hold that position nevertheless have tried to show the untenability of the arguments advanced in support of the documentary hypothesis. Without denying that the Pentateuch contains a variety of material, they defend the proposition that unity and coherence are characteristic of its composition (e.g., B. Jacob, *Das erste Buch der Genesis übersetzt und erklärt* [Berlin, 1934]; U. Cassuto, *The Documentary Hypothesis* [Jerusalem, 1961]). Other Jewish authors (e.g., Weinfeld), while accepting the newer documentary hypothesis, dispute the Wellhausenian sequence of sources. These writers follow Y. Kaufmann (see, e.g., his "Probleme der israelitisch-jüdischen Religionsgeschichte," *ZAW* 48 [1930] 23–43; 51 [1933] 35–47; see also *The Religion of Israel* [Chicago, 1960]), who had argued in great detail against the propositions that P reflected the situation in Judah after the Exile, that P presupposed the existence of D, and that the prophets came before the law. They regard D, the lawbook of Josiah, as the youngest part of the Pentateuch and thus adopt a pre-Wellhausenian standpoint in respect to the origin of the Pentateuch. This position implies a view of the history of the religion of Israel different from the one in vogue since Wellhausen.

Besides these critics of Wellhausen, I mention, finally, some other critics not related to a particular school. In his *Alttestamentliche Studien*, I–IV (Giessen, 1908–12), the Dutch B. D. Eerdmans subjected the documentary hypothesis to a detailed critique, pointing out weaknesses in it. He himself defended a kind of crystallization hypothesis, according to which the Pentateuch is the result of collecting materials; over the centuries smaller and larger traditions were joined together, edited, and augmented. His views, which reflect the influence of the excavations in Mesopotamia (repeatedly he argues for the antiquity of certain passages), suffer considerably from the intermeshing of his literary analyses with his religio-historical hypothesis that Israel long had a polytheistic religion.

Two British scholars, E. Robertson (*The Old Testament Problem* [Manchester, 1950], a collection of his articles since 1936) and R. Brinker (*The Influence of Sanctuaries in Early Israel* [Manchester, 1946]), have attempted to offer a complete alternative to the conception of Wellhausen. To mention only a few points, they regard the various sanctuaries of Israel after it had settled in Canaan as localities where the various parts of the Pentateuch were transmitted, and they view Deuteronomy as the work of Samuel, who wanted to centralize the cult. They thus argue for the antiquity of the Pentateuch. While their critique of Wellhausen's views contains several valuable elements, their own views are, however, highly speculative.

(4) TRADITION CRITICISM—VON RAD, NOTH, PEDERSEN, AND ENGNELL

The popularity of the so-called form-critical approach to the Old Testament introduced by Gunkel and Gressmann resulted in a renewed interest in questions concerning the origin of the Pentateuch. Gunkel and Gressmann had intended their method as an approach that would deal with the origin and growth of all the literature in the Old Testament. In their publications, however, their interest was clearly the earliest phases of the transmission. Inspired by their work, other scholars directed their attention to the process of transmitting material in the other phases. In respect to the Pentateuch they researched how the smaller units underwent change in their shape and content through the centuries, how they obtained their place in the Pentateuch as it is extant today, and so on. Though the terms are not always

used with the same meaning, this approach has been called the *überlieferungsgeschichtliche* (tradition-historical or tradition-critical) method. The questions mentioned here elicited attention from two directions.

First, consider Gerhard von Rad and Martin Noth. Both were influenced by the ideas of their teacher, Albrecht Alt. In *Das formgeschichtliche Problem des Hexateuch* (Stuttgart, 1938; English translation: "The Form-Critical Problem of the Hexateuch," in *The Problem of the Hexateuch and Other Essays* [London/New York, 1966], pp. 1–78), von Rad discusses the problem of the origin of the Hexateuch in its present form. He observes that the scheme governing the entire Pentateuch (history of the patriarchs, sojourn in Egypt, journey through the desert, entrance into the Promised Land) occurs in more or less summary form in a number of passages in the Hexateuch (Deut. 6:20–24; 26:5–9; Josh. 24:2–13). In his judgment these passages are based upon an ancient cultic creed containing a scheme of salvation history that had already become canonical ("the small historical credo"), which presumably had its *Sitz im Leben* in the cult at Gilgal. The credo lacks a description of the Sinai event as described in Exodus 19–24 and 32–34. From this omission von Rad concludes that these parts represent a separate tradition complex whose roots are found in the cult at Shechem. He assumes that there was a gradual growth of the tradition complexes, but he does not view the origin of the Hexateuch as a gradual process. In his view, the Yahwist, living in the time of David and Solomon, augmented the canonical scheme of the history of salvation, which itself was already a Hexateuch in a nutshell, with material of greatly diverse origin. The Yahwist is responsible for the incorporation *(Einbau)* of the Sinai tradition, for the elaboration *(Ausbau)* of the patriarchal history, and for the prologue *(Vorbau)* of primordial history (Genesis 2–11). So he fitted the diverse material into the theme of the conquest that governs the scheme of salvation history. The incorporation of this diverse material into the canonical scheme gives it a new dimension and alters its character. The addition of the sources E and P to J did not alter the picture created by the Yahwist.

Von Rad views the origin of the Pentateuch as

very complex. He particularly directs his interest and attention, however, to the final stage of the various traditions in the sources of the Hexateuch and to the meaning that the traditions acquired in the hands of the authors of the sources, in particular, J. He never did research the coherence of the text of the Hexateuch in its present form, though he expressed the desirability of doing so in the foreword of his commentary to Genesis (in the series *ATD*, 1964[7]; not in the English translation). It should be added, however, that von Rad did think the Hexateuch bore the stamp of the Yahwist. J made the confession of the conquest, once the property of only a few tribes, the confession of all the tribes. His belief that David was the one who carried out the divine will and had completed the conquest and that God continued to deal with his people on that basis pervades the entire Pentateuch.

In his *Überlieferungsgeschichtliche Studien* (Halle/Saale, 1943; partial English translation: *The Deuteronomistic History* [JSOT Supplement Series 15; Sheffield, 1981]), Noth rejects the idea of the existence of a Hexateuch and defends the idea that Deuteronomy is the beginning of a large Deuteronomic work of history, spanning from Deuteronomy through Kings, which was created in the middle of the sixth century by an individual author who availed himself of diverse sources. In brief, Noth disagrees that the sources J, E, and P extend through Joshua. He finds them only in Genesis through Numbers (the Tetrateuch). He discusses their origin in his *Überlieferungsgeschichte des Pentateuch* (Stuttgart, 1948). Noth observes that J and E have many common traits, which he assumes is due to the fact that both go back to a common source G (for *Grundlage*, or "common basic work"). He notes further that the subject of the Pentateuch is the twelve tribes of Israel. In his opinion this presentation assumes the existence of a tribal confederation. In an earlier publication *Das System der zwölf Stämme Israels* (Stuttgart, 1930), Noth defended its origin in the time of the judges through the union of the tribes. In this study Noth employed the term *amphictyony* for this tribal confederation, by which he meant a loose association of tribes, having certain things in common, including a common central shrine and common laws.

Noth connects his thesis of the amphictyony and the origin of the Pentateuch as follows: through the formation of the amphictyony the traditions of the tribes became blended; experiences and traditions of individual tribes became the property of the entire amphictyony, which led to the picture that is found in the Pentateuch. This process continued until the rise of the monarchy, by which time G had taken shape, a source that includes the main themes of the Pentateuch. According to Noth the five themes rooted in the cult are, in order of their age: the exodus out of Egypt, the entrance into Palestine, the promise to the fathers, the journey through the desert, and the revelation at Sinai. Originally the themes were unconnected, and each had its own history. The oldest is the original confession of Israel and is the crystallization point of the traditions. Each of the themes contained very little narrative and attracted a great deal of material of diverse provenance. The history of the plagues in Egypt and the celebration of the Passover represent some of the augmentations, but so also does everything that is told about Moses himself. His name does not occur in the core of any of the themes. Originally independent traditions, such as the accounts of the patriarchs, became fused, resulting in the picture of a family relationship. Gradually the themes are linked and blended together, such as that of the person of Moses, who began to play an important role in all the themes. This process happened likely in the preliterary phase of the tradition. Each of the individual authors J, E, and P passed the material on with their own accents. Their work lies at the basis of the Pentateuch, giving it the character of a collection.

This sketch of the labors of von Rad and Noth shows that their approach and understanding contain both similarities and differences. Both maintain the now standard theory that the Pentateuch is composed of sources. In contrast to von Rad, however, Noth rejects the classical conception that the sources continue through Joshua, an idea that is basic to von Rad's understanding, in which the conquest plays such an important role. Von Rad assumes the existence of two tradition complexes that underlie the Pentateuch, whereas Noth assumes the existence of five cores. Moreover, Noth attributes much less importance to J than von Rad does. According to von Rad, J heavily influenced the transmitted material, and in distinction from Noth, von Rad sees him as dominant relative to the other sources. Noth is particularly interested in a careful tracing of the preliterary traditions, whereas von Rad's interest concerns the theological ideas of the traditions in their final phase. Finally I note that Noth's and von Rad's views on the origin of the Pentateuch interrelate with their view of the earliest history of Israel. They see a great difference between the actual course of that history and Israel's picture of it in its traditions. One can speak of a historical Israel only after the tribes have united in the times of the judges. The picture presented by Israel itself results from the blending of the traditions by the tribes participating in the tribal league. The actual prehistory, however, was a great deal more complex. For example, not all of Israel was in Egypt; the tradition of the invasion actually goes back to a peaceful infiltration of the civilized land by groups of seminomads.

Besides von Rad and Noth, some Scandinavian scholars have focused on tradition criticism, emphasizing that the Pentateuch is the result of a complex tradition process and in some cases drawing conclusions that differ from those of the two Germans. In various publications, Johannes Pedersen has charged that literary critics have taken an overly Western approach to the literature of the Old Testament and have shown a lack of insight into the culture and mentality of ancient Israel ("Die Auffassung vom Alten Testament," *ZAW* 49 [1931] 161–81; "Passahfest und Passahlegende," *ZAW* 52 [1934] 161–75; *Israel, Its Life and Culture,* I–IV [London/Copenhagen, 1926–40]). He further has opposed the schematic conception of the evolution of the religion of Israel by Wellhausen and his school. With the literary critics he acknowledges the presence of contradictions and problems in the texts, but unlike them he maintains that these features are due to alterations and additions made in the course of the tradition process.

Gradually Pedersen distanced himself from the sources theory. Initially, however, he maintained this theory in its broad lines, though in his opinion J and E could not be distinguished from each other, while JE, D, and P are to be regarded as designations of collections that received their present shape only in the postexilic period and consequently are both preexilic and postexilic. The collections cannot be chronologically ordered in the way Wellhausen arranged the sources. They reflect for the most part the ideas of groups that existed side by side and so give a picture of the multiformity of Israelite culture. Pedersen characterizes the idea of the centralization of the cult in Deuteronomy, which plays a crucial role in Wellhausen's conception, as an ideal that was maintained in certain circles but was not recognized in other groups. It should be clear from this summary that Pedersen wants to repudiate the simplistic picture of the development of Israel's religion that views it as a progressive development in which radically different movements follow upon each other. He is, however, willing to concede that certain developments within certain groups may have had a polarizing influence on each other.

Similar ideas have been defended by the Swede Ivan Engnell, the founder and head of the so-called Uppsala School (see, e.g., the first part of his *Introduction to the Old Testament* [1945; Swedish]; *A Rigid Scrutiny* [Nashville, 1969; some encyclopedia articles translated into English]). Engnell was influenced on the one hand by Pedersen and on the other by the Swedish orientalist H. S. Nyberg, who defended the proposition that the Old Testament was originally transmitted orally and written down only by the postexilic Jewish community. Nyberg does not deny that the art of writing was known in antiquity or that traditions were written down before the Exile. In his opinion, however, written texts were at that time regarded as supporting the oral tradition. The latter was normative. In brief, the source of the material in the Old Testament was not the prophets and poets who were also active as writers; rather, centers of transmission passed on the material through the centuries.

Nyberg's view, which is accompanied by emphasis on the reliability of the oral tradition, confidence in the Massoretic text, and an aversion to literary criticism, is shared by Engnell. He sharply attacks the documentary hypothesis. According to him the idea of a book composed from documents by redactors is an irrelevant Western idea, evidencing a lack of knowledge of the cultural conditions in the ancient Near East. For example, the literary critics fail to see that repetitions do not point to separate sources but are due to the oral tradition. Engnell himself develops the following theory: Genesis through Kings consists of two sizable works, a P-work and a D-work, each having its own character. The P-work, comprising Genesis through Numbers, which likely concluded with the death of Moses, comes from the P-circle and, in the process of transmission, included a great variety of material (e.g., JE). The final version is from Jerusalem, from the time of Ezra and Nehemiah, but the roots go back to Hebron and Kadesh-barnea. The D-work comprises Deuteronomy through Kings and received its definitive form at approximately the same time as the P-work.

The idea that the material of the Old Testament was primarily orally transmitted until the time of the Captivity has been hotly contested but today no longer has its defenders. It has made Old Testament scholars more aware, however, that transmission is a living reality and that, besides the written transmission, there was also oral tradition (see, e.g., the work of Mowinckel). As regards the Pentateuch, this insight has induced certain authors, while maintaining the major aspects of the sources theory, to attribute to the sources the character of tradition currents (e.g., Bentzen; de Vaux). They do not feel the need to split up the sources into literary layers. They regard the flaws and difficulties in the source as belonging to the oral-transmission phase of the material. Despite Engnell's critique, however, he manages only to cast the documentary hypothesis in a different form, now with elements of the supplementary hypothesis. Finally, we should note that the thesis of the high reliability and normativity of oral tradition is without proof. Likewise misleading is the impression sometimes given that written tradition is by definition more reliable than oral tradition.

f. Recent Developments

The foregoing has shown that Pentateuchal studies accelerated after Wellhausen. There has been much criticism of Wellhausen's conception, yet even in their differing positions, many critics have been deeply influenced by Wellhausen. The work of this scholar is here to stay. Conceptions developed after Wellhausen, such as the five-sources theory and the notion that E is not to be regarded as an independent source, have met with scant approval. For many scholars the main lines of Wellhausen's conception are still the most satisfactory answer to the questions concerning the origin of the Pentateuch. The simplicity of the four-sources theory presently enjoys the preference of many writers (e.g., Kaiser, Soggin, Westermann). Generally speaking, however, it must be said that the diversity in opinions that was so characteristic of Pentateuchal studies after Wellhausen continues until the present. The diversity, in fact, seems to be increasing. New conceptions and new approaches demand a place beside the established standpoints and methodologies.

(1) ALTERNATIVES TO THE SOURCES THEORY

Today there is no lack of effort to improve the four-sources theory by those who follow the approach of literary criticism. Other scholars use the same methodology to subject the sources theory to radical critique. Presently their work is very much in the center of attention. In his book *Abraham in History and Tradition* (New Haven/London, 1975), J. Van Seters, on the basis of a study of the Abraham narratives in the light of archeological data, has drawn the conclusion that the historical, social, and political situations of the middle of the first millennium before Christ constitute the background of what is said about the patriarchs. Literary analysis of the texts, which led him to critique the four-sources theory and the work of Gunkel, Alt, Noth, and von Rad, confirmed his conclusion. For Van Seters, there is no reason to assume a lengthy and complex history in which the texts came into existence: J is to be dated in the Exile, and P afterward.

Van Seters is highly critical of the view, particularly advocated by W. F. Albright and his school and accepted by many, that the results of the excavations in Mari, Nuzi, and other places show convincingly that the patriarchal narratives reflect the cultural and historical situations of the ancient Near East of the second millennium. Approximately at the same time and independently of Van Seters, T. L. Thompson criticized the standpoint of Albright and his followers. In *Historicity of the Patriarchal Narratives* (Berlin/New York, 1974), Thompson agrees with the usual dating of J and assumes that J's narratives about the patriarchs are to be read against the background of the tenth or ninth century B.C. In a later publication he is critical of Van Seters and very hesitant about the possibility of dating ("A New Attempt to Date the Patriarchal Narratives," *JAOS* 98 [1978] 76–84). Criticism of the standpoint of Albright and his followers may be justified. They often all too easily and prematurely made a connection between the results of the excavations and the biblical data. Reserve is also necessary, however, in approaching Van Seters's standpoint.

In a study entitled *Der sogenannte Jahwist: Beobachtungen und Fragen zur Pentateuchforschung* (Zurich, 1976), H. H. Schmid defends the thesis that the parts of the Pentateuch attributed to J and, since von Rad, usually dated in the time of Solomon on account of their affinity with the Deuteronomistic literature must have originated approximately the same time, that is, in a later period. Schmid employs a series of arguments, such as the use of language and style, and points out that all sorts of problems inherent in an early dating disappear if a later dating is assumed. Such a late dating obviously has consequences for the history of Israel's religion: the picture of the tribal league in the premonarchical period is a later construction, the large-scale Canaanization of Israel's religion happened during Solomon's reign, and the process of being freed from it was still in full swing in the time of the Exile. Like Van Seters, Schmid believes that the promises to the patriarchs, including the assurance of a great nation and a great country, fit the time of the Exile, the time of the expectation of a new future.

A radical attack on the sources theory was made by R. Rendtorff in *Das überlieferungsgeschichtlichte Problem des Pentateuch* (Berlin/New York, 1977). In his opinion it was wrong to retain the sources theory after the rise of the form-critical and tradition-historical approach. According to Rendtorff, a consistent tradition-historical approach leads to the conclusion that the Pentateuch (ignoring Deuteronomy and the laws) consists of a number of independent, finished units without solid cross-connections: the history of origins

(Genesis 1–11), the history of the patriarchs (chs. 12–50), the stories about Moses and the Exodus (Exodus 1–14), the record of the revelation at Sinai (chs. 19–24; 32–34), the stories of the sojourn in the desert (chs. 16–18; Num. 11:1–20:13), and the stories about the conquest and taking possession of the land (Num. 20:14–end). It is impossible to trace specific lines running through the units, and consequently the sources theory is a fiction. Rendtorff emphatically denies the existence of J. The units are connected by only a few editorial remarks, which were made by P (to be regarded as a working document, not as an independent source) and also by Deuteronomistic circles. Rendtorff suspects that particularly the latter had a significant part in the origin of the Pentateuch as a whole.

Critique of the sources theory, but with entirely different results, was also offered by S. Tengström in *Die Hexateucherzählung: Eine literaturgeschichtliche Studie* (Lund, 1976). In contrast to Rendtorff, Tengström points to the coherence and continuity in the Hexateuch and thus arrives at a kind of supplementary theory: a coherent, epic narrative forms the basis of the Hexateuch. This work recounts the story of the patriarchs, Israel's exodus out of Egypt, the sojourn in the wilderness, and the conquest of Canaan. Presumably this epic work originated in or near Shechem before the establishment of the monarchy, possibly in the first half of the eleventh century. According to Tengström, this basic narrative was augmented in many different ways. Particularly significant was the activity of Deuteronomistic authors. Supposedly they wrote Deuteronomy and also the historical sequel up through 2 Kings 25. In addition, Tengström sees a contribution of Priestly authors. See also his *Die Toledotformel und die literarische Struktur der priesterlichen Erweiterungsschicht im Pentateuch* (Lund, 1982).

Some comments about these newer publications are in order. These studies criticize the documentary hypothesis. However, they deal very little with the arguments on which this hypothesis is based, so that many questions remain unanswered. For example, the authors who favor a late dating of J ignore the crucial point of Wellhausen's chronology of the sources: JE does not know of the centralization of the cult and hence is older than D. Recent criticism has thus been highly fragmentary, coming from standpoints that seem undeveloped so far. They hardly deal, for example, with the consequences of literary analysis for the picture of the religion of Israel. A new, comprehensive conception is not offered, or else is alluded to only vaguely. A great many elements and conclusions of the newer studies are not really new. In a variety of forms and in new frameworks, older ideas are defended that earlier were unable to obtain significant acceptance. A late dating of all parts of the Pentateuch, for example, has been advocated before, as has the idea (presently defended by various writers) that P is not a continuous source but the work of a redactor. With his rejection of the tribal league, Schmid goes back to the time before Noth. With their idea that the patriarchal narratives tell us only about the time and the ideas of the writers, Van Seters, Thompson, and Schmid return to the standpoint of Wellhausen.

(2) THE LITERARY-FUNCTIONAL APPROACH

The description of the above-mentioned newer studies has shown that there continues to be great interest in the questions concerning the origin of the Pentateuch. In addition to attention to the origin of the Pentateuch, there is nowadays, however, a growing interest in the questions concerning the form and the function (the *Sitz im Buche* and the *Sitz in der Literatur*) of the present Pentateuchal texts, particularly the narrative sections. Without denying the legitimacy of the historical (diachronic) approach to the literature, which focuses on questions concerning the origin of the texts, their *Sitz im Leben,* and their dating, many Old Testament scholars argue that the interpretation of the texts themselves ought to be the focus (the synchronic approach). These writers are under the influence both of Jewish scholars, of whom particularly Martin Buber should be mentioned, and of the so-called autonomy movement in the study of literature. It is argued that the meaning is to be found in the texts themselves and not outside them. These scholars attempt to do justice to the texts and to bring out their meaning by focusing on the structure, word usage, and rhythm of the texts themselves. It is held that

structure and style are not just ornamental to the texts but are crucial for interpretation. This method, then, which is variously designated as a stylistic and structural approach or rhetorical criticism, I would characterize as literary-functional.

In the Netherlands, parts of Genesis have been analyzed in this manner by K. A. Deurloo in *Kain en Abel: Onderzoek naar exegetische methode inzake een "kleine literaire eenheid" in de Tenakh* (Amsterdam, 1967) and by J. P. Fokkelman in *Narrative Art in Genesis: Specimens of Stylistic and Structural Analysis* (Assen/Amsterdam, 1975). The former represents the so-called Amsterdam school, a group of theologians whose base is the University of Amsterdam but who as such are not a homogeneous group. Inspired by his teacher M. A. Beek, Deurloo takes a critical stand with respect to the historical-critical approach to the Old Testament. From the Jewish scholar J. L. Palache, Deurloo adopted the idea that the Old Testament demonstrates a midrash style and that the narrative parts are the result of a very free tradition. Deurloo is skeptical about the possibility of reconstructing the historical origin of the texts and about the historical content of the narratives. In addition to these influences, one can also notice the influence on Deurloo of the theologians K. H. Miskotte and F. H. Breukelman, whose appreciation and understanding of the writings of the Old Testament fit in very well with the ahistorical approach to the Old Testament inspired by the autonomy movements in literary science.

In the Netherlands the use of the literary-functional approach is often accompanied by criticism of the results of the traditional methods and, at least in practice, by abandonment of these methods. Elsewhere, however, the literary-functional approach is presented as a method that does justice to a neglected aspect of the study of the Old Testament. See, for example, J. Muilenburg, "Form Criticism and Beyond," *JBL* 88 (1969) 1–18, who argues in favor of "rhetorical criticism." In this same spirit are two studies that do not dispute the results of literary criticism but that point out the careful composition of the deluge narrative: B. W. Anderson, "From Analysis to Synthesis: The Interpretation of Genesis 1–11," *JBL* 97 (1978) 23–39; G. J. Wenham, "The Coherence of the Flood Narrative," *VT* 28 (1978) 336–48. Literary criticism shows a tendency to focus on the redactional activity that gave the text of the Pentateuch its present form. The significance of this form has often been downplayed by adherents of the documentary hypothesis. The importance of explaining the text in its present form has been stressed, among others, by B. S. Childs, *The Book of Exodus* (Philadelphia, 1974), and D. J. A. Clines, *The Theme of the Pentateuch* (Sheffield, 1978). Specimens of literary analysis of Pentateuchal narratives are presented among others by R. Alter, *The Art of Biblical Narrative* (London/Sydney, 1981), and M. Sternberg, *The Poetics of Biblical Narrative: Ideological Literature and the Drama of Reading* (Bloomington, 1985).

This last point requires some cautionary comments. The growing interest in the text as it lies before us is to be applauded. There is a place for a reaction to the atomistic approach that often predominated in Old Testament studies. We should not, however, allow this reaction to lead to a new one-sided approach, one in which, for example, it is assumed that, as linguistic works of art, the narrative parts of the Pentateuch can be regarded as similar to the products of European literature. This position would in a sense be a return to a precritical approach, in which the unity of the text was assumed a priori. The literary-critical approach (which has its origin in a careful reading of the texts themselves!) and the form-critical method may contribute to make clear that the Pentateuch is a work of art of a different kind: the ordering and combination of diverse material has creatively produced an integral piece of work. Only a mutually correcting combination of the various approaches can lead to a balanced approach that will allow the texts to speak their own language.

Finally, I mention that the influence of linguistics sometimes plays a role in the growing interest in the present form of texts. In the science of linguistics, Ferdinand de Saussure developed the structuralist approach to language in which language is regarded as a sign system. Via application of structuralism in cultural anthropology (C. Lévi-Strauss) and in the science of literature (A. J. Greimas), at the end of the sixties and in the seventies it also begins to play a role in biblical studies. Attention is being drawn to the fact that the texts of the Bible are not a conglomerate of loose units but constitute a sign system in which the parts are related to each other. (With respect to the Pentateuch, see, e.g., R. Barthes, "La lutte avec l'ange: Analyse textuelle de Genèse 32.23–33," in R. Barthes et al., eds., *Analyse structurale et exégèse biblique* [Neuchâtel, 1971], pp. 27–39; cf. W. Roth, "Structural Interpretations of 'Jacob at the Jabbok' [Genesis 32:22–32]," *BR* 22 [1977] 51–62; G. Rouiller, "Le sacrifice d'Isaac," in F. Bovon and G. Rouiller, eds., *Exegesis: Problèmes de méthode et exercises de lecture* [Paris/Neuchâtel, 1975], pp. 274–90). To understand structuralism properly, it should be kept in mind that the concern is not to describe the *single* meaning of a story but to indicate the semantic possibilities inherent in a text. The structuralist is interested in the deep structure of the story—in its systematics, grammar, and syntax. In the great diversity in the stories, structuralism looks for a similar basic pattern and is more interested in the constant elements in the stories than in their special ones. The ever-present danger, of course, is that of overlooking the particular details of the texts.

3. EVALUATION

a. Does the Pentateuch Contain Material from Moses?

The notion that, except for some additions, Moses is the author of the Pentateuch (see section 2.a above) lacks cogency. The phenomena pointed out by literary criticism, such as stylistic variation, discrepancies, and contradictions, make Mosaic authorship untenable. The argument that Moses was a great man who could use various literary styles and who availed himself of older sources, even buttressed with the fact that classical writers such as Xenophon and Caesar also wrote about themselves in the third person, lacks cogency in light of the conclusions of literary criticism. The notion that Moses is the chief author of the Pentateuch is supported only by tradition, not by the Old Testament itself. Some data in the Pentateuch connect Moses with literary activity (Exod. 17:14; 24:4, 7; 34:27; Num. 33:2; Deut. 31:9, 24), but they do not permit us to say that Moses was greatly involved in recording the events in the life of Israel and its forefathers. Moreover, the rest of the Old Testament contains no data that would support such a supposition. In the New Testament the name of Moses is variously connected with the Pentateuch (e.g., Mark 7:10; 12:26; Luke 24:27, 44; John 1:45). From such references one can infer only the type of thinking about the authorship of the Pentateuch that was current at the time of Jesus and the apostles.

There seem to be more arguments in favor of the idea that the Pentateuch, particularly the legal sections, contains a great deal of Mosaic material. For the laws are regularly introduced with formulas such as "Yahweh said to Moses" (Exod. 20:22; Lev. 1:1; etc.) and, according to the description in the Pentateuch, were given in the concrete historical situations before the conquest. Their local and temporal background appears to be the residence in Egypt and the sojourn in the desert. For example, it is virtually certain that the materials used for the making of the tabernacle, such as the acacia wood and the *tahash* skins (Exod. 25:5; etc.), came from Egypt and the Sinai peninsula. Furthermore, various laws were manifestly promulgated in the desert (e.g., Lev. 16:10, 21–22; Num. 5:17; 18:28), while others have their origin in an event during the journey through the wilderness (e.g., Lev. 24:15–16, 23; cf. vv. 10–12; Num. 15:35; cf. v. 32).

Other data, however, have led the majority of Old Testament scholars to deny the possibility of extensive Mosaic material in the Pentateuch. They point out that, for the most part, the laws refer to life in a civilized land: mention is made of houses (Exod. 20:17), cities (Lev. 14:40), agricultural feasts (Exod. 23:14–19), and the monarchy (Deut. 17:14–20). They believe that at least the bulk of the laws arose after Israel's settlement in Canaan. Others counter by saying that Moses gave many laws with a view to the future settlement in Canaan. It is also pointed out that excavations have shown that, in the ancient Near East, there were extensive written collections of laws as early as the second millennium. Furthermore, Moses was an erudite man (Exod. 2:10; Acts 7:22), who, through his Mesopotamian ancestors, may be regarded as having been familiar with the laws of the ancient Near East. Finally, it is sometimes assumed that, ever since its time in Goshen, Israel

constituted a community that had its own laws and that, during its long stay in Kadesh-barnea (Num. 13:26; 20:14; Deut. 1:19–20, 46; 2:14), was engaged in agriculture. It is thus not surprising to find agricultural prescriptions and the like in the Mosaic laws. However, many Old Testament scholars are not receptive to such argumentation, because in their opinion neither the Old Testament picture of Moses nor that of the history of Israel is historically reliable (see section 2.e.[4] above).

If the bulk of the laws in the Pentateuch are not from Moses, then we must regard as a later development the textual account that the laws were given by Yahweh to Moses in the wilderness. This view leads to the notion that later writers introduced laws, framed in their time, and inserted words such as "Yahweh spoke to Moses." That way of writing is called pseudepigraphy. The term is used to designate a custom, widespread in antiquity and the Middle Ages, whereby writers deliberately present their words as the words of an important person in antiquity, with the intention that their writing will be regarded as the work of that ancient person and as such will become influential. Pseudepigraphy typically involves the attempt to make a very authentic impression, carefully anchoring one's writing in the time of the earlier "writer."

The problem of pseudepigraphy also plays an important role in connection with Deuteronomy. This book is cast in the form of a farewell address of Moses, and as such it creates the impression of being fully authentic (see, e.g., Deut. 5:2–3; 6:18–19; 9:1–6). To the present day, therefore, many of conservative persuasion hold that it is very unlikely that Deuteronomy is an address put into the mouth of Moses. Critics, on the other hand, from the beginning of the nineteenth century have argued that Deuteronomy, because it makes such an authentic impression, is manifestly a work of pseudepigraphy.

Besides these two options, however, there is still a third and better alternative. While it is quite possible that the Pentateuch contains old traditions and laws that go back to Moses, to a greater or lesser extent the Pentateuch also contains additions, elaborations, and emendations made by groups who regarded themselves as the heirs of

Moses. Standing in the Mosaic tradition and living in changing times, they aimed at giving answers to timely questions and at formulating new norms and yet felt fully justified in presenting their material as the work of Moses. The similarities and differences that are found at certain points in the various legal collections in the Pentateuch are evidence that, over the centuries, the laws have been altered and updated. Recall, for example, the differences in the Decalogue in Exodus 20 and in Deuteronomy 5.

It is, however, difficult to determine to what extent the laws indeed hark back to the time of Moses. This difficulty is particularly due to the effective pseudepigraphy of the groups that have transmitted the Mosaic legacy. Their effort makes it virtually impossible to date the laws and to differentiate between Mosaic and non-Mosaic material. As noted above, other factors also have a decisive input, such as the admittedly subjective consideration that certain things could have happened in the wilderness and others could not. Another significant factor is the writer's standpoint relative to the reliability of the historical data in the Pentateuch. The above considerations lead us to the conclusion that, though we must admit the possibility that Mosaic material is present in the Pentateuch, there are no compelling arguments that the Pentateuch is primarily a compilation of Mosaic material.

b. The Four-Sources Theory Tested

In the historical survey above we noted that, in the judgment of many scholars, the four-sources theory still provides the most satisfactory answer to the question concerning the origin of the Pentateuch and that, at least in its main outlines, the theory is correct. For that reason it deserves some additional attention. I do not further consider other theories, such as the fragmentary and supplementary hypotheses defended in the previous century, because in their original form they are currently without advocates. For the sake of clarity I repeat here that, according to the four-sources theory, the Pentateuch/Hexateuch is composed of three more or less independent documents or parts of documents that to a great extent deal with the same events, that arose in dif-

ferent periods, and that in any case were written by people with diverse interests. The basis of this theory was the discovery that the Pentateuch throughout manifests three layers, each with its peculiar language and style and theological viewpoint. Alongside these three strands, Deuteronomy was regarded as an independent source. The sources can be characterized as follows:

J = *Yahwist.* His work starts with Genesis 2:4b. He writes as if the divine name was already known from primitive times (4:26). His simple narrative style is highly praised. A typical feature is the anthropomorphic depiction of God (2:7–8, 22; 3:8–9, 21; 7:16; etc.). Included in J are, among others, the following sections: Genesis 2:4b–4:26; 6:1–8; 9:18–27; 10:8–19, 21, 25–30; 11:1–9, 28–30; 12:1–4a, 6–20; etc.

E = *Elohist.* His hand is discovered for the first time in the history of the patriarchs (Genesis 15 or 20). E links the divine name Yahweh with the revelation to Moses. His style of writing too, though to a lesser extent, is considered true-to-life. Distinctive features of E include his treatment of divine revelation as involving not a direct encounter with God but an angel from heaven (21:17; cf. 16:7 [J]) or a dream (20:3) and his favorable portrayal of the conduct of the patriarchs (e.g., 20:12; 21:11–14; cf. 12:10–20; 16:6 [J]). In addition, E's vocabulary differs from that of J. So he uses the name Horeb (Exod. 3:1; 17:6; 33:6) for Sinai (J). The E portions include Genesis 20:1–8; 21:8–34; 22:1–19; etc.

P = *Priestly Code.* P begins at Genesis 1 and, in the main, contains stipulations with respect to the cult and the priesthood (Exodus 25–31; Leviticus; large sections of Numbers) and also some narrative parts. The latter, however, also manifest the interest in the cult: the creation story culminates in the sabbath (Gen. 2:2–3); the prohibition against eating blood is given in the context of the story of the Flood (9:4); etc. Unless his cultic interest leads him to be more detailed, P restricts himself to brief historical notations (see 19:29; 31:18b; 33:18b; 36:6–8). He makes no mention of sacrifices before the time of Moses. It was not until Moses' time that the legitimate sacrificial cult was instituted. In his writing he demonstrates scholarly interest, offering genealogies (ch. 5; 11:10–32), lists (Numbers 1–3), and chronological notations (Gen. 7:11; 8:13; 17:24), and he also manifests an eye for details (6:14–17; Exodus 25–31). His style is dry and characterized by stereotype formulations and repetitions (Genesis 1; 5). With few exceptions (e.g., ch. 23), the lively descriptions of J and E are altogether absent. The people mentioned are not people of flesh and blood. P's concern is not people, but God—that is, the laws and regulations God has given to people. P also has his own vocabulary. He employs the divine name Yahweh after Exodus 6. P includes, among others, Genesis 1:1–2:4a; 5:1–27, 30–32; 9:1–17, 28–29; 11:10–27, 31–32; 12:4b–5; 17; 23; 25:7–10.

Ideas concerning the extent, origin, and dating of J, E, and P continue to be varied. The classical theory detected the three sources through Joshua. Since Noth (see section 2.e.[4] above), there is a tendency to extend J, E, and P only to Deuteronomy. Eissfeldt and others find J and E from Genesis through Kings. In general there is greater certainty about the P sections. Researchers emphasize, however, their heterogeneous character, stressing the fact that P contains material from various times and sources. As regards the distribution of the narrative material over the various sources, there is a measure of unanimity with respect to Genesis, but not to the other books. A number of passages (e.g., Genesis 14), it is assumed, possess no points of reference that allow us to attribute them to a particular source. Presently it is generally assumed that J was composed in southern Israel and E in northern Israel. J is usually dated in the tenth century B.C., and E in the second half of the eighth century. Viewpoints on these questions, however, remain diverse. Some scholars, for example, have argued that E came before J. It is customary now to consider P postexilic, while acknowledging that it contains much old material. There have always been some voices, however, that consider P preexilic. Most scholars think that P composed in Babylon, but some would locate him in Jerusalem.

D = *Deuteronomy* (or *Ur-Deuteronomy*). As noted above, according to the adherents of the sources theory, Deuteronomy, or at least the bulk of it (chs. 12–26, possibly with introduction and conclusion), is the lawbook found in the temple at the time of Josiah that provided the impetus for Josiah's reform in 622/621 (2 Kings 22–23). The idea that Deuteronomy (not, as was usually assumed, the whole Pentateuch) is the lawbook of Josiah is found already in some of the church fathers. They did not, however, question Mosaic authorship, regarding the lawbook as having actually been rediscovered. When, however, following De Wette's suggestion (see section 2.c), the idea gained currency that the lawbook of Josiah (i.e., Deuteronomy) was a previously unknown lawbook, it was coupled with the idea that Deuteronomy was the product of a pious fraud: namely, that a small group of people at the court, including Hilkiah and Shaphan, wrote Deuteronomy to bring about a reformation. Some more moderate scholars weakened this bold assertion, saying instead that the book dated from the time of Hezekiah or Manasseh, a viewpoint that can still be found today, one that offers the possibility of regarding Deuteronomy as truly rediscovered. In all cases, however, it is assumed that Deuteronomy was for the first time proclaimed as law under Josiah.

In defense of considering Deuteronomy a separate document, it is pointed out that the book has its own unique paraenetic style and word usage. Some typical elements in it are the expressions "with all your heart and with all your soul" (e.g., 4:29) and "by a mighty hand and an outstretched arm" (e.g., v. 34) and the verbs *love* (e.g., v. 37a; 5:10) and *fear* (e.g., 4:10). Though at first Deuteronomy was largely regarded as a unity, the consistent application of the literary-critical approach in the school of Wellhausen led to the view that it also had different layers and that its origin could best be explained by means of documentary and supplementary hypotheses. In reaching these conclusions, scholars noted in particular the remarkable phenomenon in Deuteronomy that the people of Israel are alternately addressed in the second person singular and in the second person plural. Such explanations, however, have never found general acceptance. Many today, though, agree that Deuteronomy is the product of a complex transmission process and contains much old material. It is even thought that its roots go back to the time of Moses. Such an appreciation for Deuteronomy is to a significant extent due to form-critical and tradition-historical research.

Following a form-critical and tradition-historical approach, Gerhard von Rad (see 2.e.[4]), without denying that Deuteronomy is the law-book of Josiah, concluded in his *Deuteronomium Studien* (Göttingen, 1947; English translation: *Studies in Deuteronomy* [London/Chicago, 1953]) that Deuteronomy was the result of a long and complex development and the product of a reform movement whose advocates, Levites living everywhere in the land, go back to the amphictyonic traditions that originated in northern Israel. (A characteristic feature of Deuteronomy is the large place given to the Levites and to the proclamation and the interpretation of the laws in it.) The supposition that Deuteronomy is of northern Israelite origin and from Levitical circles has also been accepted and defended by other Old Testament scholars. In support of this idea it is sometimes pointed out that there seems to be an affinity between Deuteronomy on the one hand and the northern Israelite E and Hosea on the other hand. Some even theorize that E is from proto-Deuteronomic circles, whose labors were continued in the circles that produced Deuteronomy. This supposition represents a considerable shift away from the standpoint defended in the school of Wellhausen—namely, that Deuteronomy arose in Jerusalem in priestly and prophetic circles. It should also be noted that, because of the supposition that Deuteronomy harks back to the traditions of the amphictyony, the requirement of a centralized cult (Deuteronomy 12) has become less unrealistic for many scholars, in view of the fact that the amphictyony was familiar with a central sanctuary (while not proscribing coexistent local shrines).

An entirely new idea concerning the origin of Deuteronomy has been defended by Weinfeld. He proposes the view that the book was composed in the circles of writers and wise men at the court of Hezekiah and Josiah and that it received its final shape in the second half of the seventh century B.C. These circles of writers were also the ones who were responsible for the production of the corpus of Deuteronomistic history. Weinfeld partially bases his thesis on similarities in structure and terminology between Deuteronomy and ancient Near Eastern treaties (the court scribes may be assumed to have been familiar with such treaties)

and on affinities that Deuteronomy shows with wisdom literature.

In order to appraise more closely the validity of the four-sources theory, I examine here in more detail the specific arguments adduced.

(1) THE ARGUMENT FROM THE DIVINE NAMES

Ever since Astruc (see section 2.c), the alternation of the divine names Elohim and Yahweh in Genesis and in Exodus 1–2 has been the basis for the theories concerning the origin of this part of the Pentateuch. Not everyone has agreed, however, that such an alternation of the divine names was a sufficient argument for a documentary hypothesis. It has been pointed out, for example, that the names differ in content: Elohim is God as Creator, and Yahweh is God in his relation to Israel. Presumably the names were deliberately selected in view of their content and also from a desire for variation and a pleasing style. There are indeed passages in which these suggestions offer a satisfactory explanation for the variation. In other instances such is not the case (cf., e.g., Genesis 20 with ch. 26). There are, however, some elements that render the argument from the divine names at least problematic: J, too, can use Elohim (e.g., 3:1–5; 4:25; 16:13), the dual name Yahweh Elohim in chapters 2–3 (J) is remarkable, Yahweh occurs also in parts attributed to P and E before Exodus 3 and 6 (Gen. 17:1; 20:18; 22:14–16; 28:21), not all passages contain a divine name (e.g., chs. 23; 34; 36–37; 47), and the argument makes it possible to distinguish layers only up to Exodus 3.

This last observation brings us to another point. The sources theory presupposes that contradictory traditions with respect to the age of the divine name Yahweh have been brought together in the Pentateuch. According to J the name was already in use in ancient times (Gen. 4:26). E (Exod. 3:13–15) and P (6:2–3), in contrast, supposedly believed that the name had not been revealed until it was given to Moses. More than once it has been contended that such a conclusion cannot be drawn from these two passages in Exodus 3 and 6. "What is his name?" in 3:13 is then interpreted as asking for the *meaning* of the (already known) name Yahweh. Exodus 6:2–3 is understood to mean that, although the name Yahweh was known to the patriarchs, its deeper content—God is the God who will fulfill his promises—had remained concealed from the patriarchs.

Exodus 3:13–15, however, is a problematic passage. According to verse 14, the revealed name is Ehyeh ("I am"); verse 15 calls the God of the fathers simply Yahweh. The passage evidently is playing on the name Yahweh. It is questionable that it intends to say that the name was first revealed to Moses. More transparent, at least on the surface, is 6:2–3. Here it is apparently said that the name Yahweh was not yet known to the patriarchs. But that fact does not mean that the existence of a source P has been determined. The most that can be supposed is that there is a relation between Exodus 6:2–3 and other passages with "God the Almighty" (Gen. 17:1; 28:3; 35:11; 43:14; 48:3). Other arguments are needed to make it plausible that there is such a relation and that a connection between these and other passages may be assumed.

Also significant is the fact that, after the name change from Abram to Abraham and from Sarai to Sarah in Genesis 17, all the sources consistently employ the names Abraham and Sarah. A similar adaptation is not found in connection with the divine names. Apparently the editors of the Pentateuch did not feel that there were discrepancies with respect to the use of the divine names and apparently they understood Exodus 6:2–3 differently than did later critical scholarship. Relative to the question of the divine names, it is also important that J has people use the divine name Yahweh before Genesis 4:26 as well (e.g., in v. 1). It can be asked whether this fact conflicts with the principle of the sources theory that, according to J, the cult of Yahweh began with Enosh. The question can be asked whether the emphasis in 4:26 is not much rather on the *calling upon* than upon the name Yahweh, so that the text refers to the beginning of public worship and not to the first use of the name Yahweh.

(2) THE ARGUMENT FROM LANGUAGE AND STYLE

The descriptions of the sources theory in older handbooks often contain lengthy summaries of the word usage of J, E, D, and P, a practice that has provoked much criticism. It has been pointed out that the presence of synonyms need not indicate an intermeshing of various sources but may be due solely to the desire for stylistic variation. It has been emphasized that style is very much dependent on the subject matter under discussion. For example, when J presents a genealogy, his style is dry (e.g., Gen. 4:17–18), or when P is narrating, his style is lively (e.g., ch. 23).

Currently the adherents of the sources theory are more restrained in their use of the arguments of language and style, which is related to the change in appraisal of the character of the sources. Wellhausen and his followers viewed the sources as the labor of authors who each put their own stamp on their work. The studies of Gunkel and Gressmann (see 2.e.[1]) have shown that old traditions have been incorporated in the sources. The usual assumption is that the hand of the writer/redactor has nevertheless remained recognizable in the sources. It is obvious, however, that it will remain difficult to determine at which points one encounters the language and style of the writer/redactor and at which points the style of the original documents (the *Vorlagen*). Illustrative of such complexity is the analysis of anthropomorphic descriptions. These elements are normally regarded as typical of J, ye in the opinion of Westermann (p. 775; see lit.), for example, they belong to the material of J but are not characteristic of him.

Another ever-present danger is that of circular reasoning. The question may be asked whether the sources provide the arguments for the theory or whether the arguments produce the sources. The fact that P to a large extent has material that is of a consistent character might be an argument in favor of the sources theory. In my judgment, however, the very complex character of P, also acknowledged by the adherents of the sources theory, renders it doubtful that P can really be regarded as a source, as a work with a clear intent of its own.

The above is not intended to intimate that word usage and style can in no way be used to discern certain connections. Frequently they make it likely that certain passages are from the same writer. It is thus natural to assume that the passages that speak of human beings as bearing the image of God are from the same writer(s) (Gen. 1:26–27; 5:1–2; 9:6). As should be obvious, however, several factors also make it doubtful whether one can use the argument of word usage and style to discern specific lines that run through the Pentateuch.

(3) THE APPEAL TO DISCREPANCIES

It is difficult to devise a theory that can account for all the discrepancies in the Pentateuch. For example, J presumably presents the relationship between God and humankind as a personal relationship in which God reveals himself through direct contact (e.g., Genesis 18). In contrast, P supposedly assumes a great distance between God and individuals, presenting God as the Transcendent One. In P there are hardly any theophanies, and God reveals himself through the "glory of Yahweh" (e.g., Exod. 16:10). It is pointed out that P has a colorless and abstract way to indicate the appearance of God (Gen. 17:1; 35:9). J and E indeed contain detailed descriptions of theophanies (15:17–18; ch. 18). But J (12:7; 26:2, 24) and E (35:1) also have the "colorless" expression used by P. Moreover, the P sections also contain vividly anthropomorphic descriptions (e.g., Exod. 12:12–13; 13:17). For that matter, an expression such as "God went up" (Gen. 17:22; 35:13 [P]) can hardly be regarded as being less anthropomorphic than the phrase "Yahweh came down" (11:5 [J]). It should not be overlooked that few narrative sections are attributed to P and that genealogies and laws are literary genres that typically contain few anthropomorphic descriptions.

As with the argument from language and style, also here there is the threat of circular reasoning. As I have indicated, nowadays it is assumed that the sources individually contain old and diverse material. It is thus possible that one source may include contradictory presentations, which renders it unnecessary to engage in a more refined splitting of the sources, as an earlier generation of Old Testament scholars did (see section 2.e.[2]). For example, Genesis 10:10 (J) mentions Babel, or Babylon, which receives its name only in 11:9 (J). It is obvious, however, that acceptance of the presuppositions of tradition-historical research renders the appeal to differences in presentation problematic. For now it is necessary to determine

where one encounters the views of the writer and where those of his sources. It has to be determined whether discrepancies in the texts are due to the intermeshing of the large literary layers (the sources) or whether they are due to the fact that the sources themselves contain a variety of material. Definitive answers are clearly difficult to reach. If the complex character of the tradition history of the material is consistently recognized, the question can be asked whether its allocation to the various sources is not to be regarded as arbitrary. The Pentateuch is unmistakably composed of traditions of various origins with diverse viewpoints, which in many cases cannot or only with difficulty can be harmonized. It is not easy, however, to find in the Pentateuch distinguishing features that would allow us to categorize the material uniquely into specific literary documents, each with its own coloring and viewpoint. In section (5) below I consider the discrepancies in the stipulations in the laws that have played an important role in the origin of the sources theory.

(4) THE APPEAL TO REPETITIONS

The presence of repetitions has always played a large role in defenses of the sources theory. It has been pointed out that there are two creation accounts (Gen. 1:1–2:4a and 2:4b–25), that Hagar's leaving Abraham is told twice (ch. 16; 21:8–21), that three times a patriarch passes off his wife as his sister (Abraham, in 12:10–20 and ch. 20; Isaac, in 26:1–11), that the Decalogue is found twice (Exodus 20; Deuteronomy 5), and many others.

A classic example of source splitting is the division made between Genesis 1:1–2:4a (P) and 2:4b–3:24 (J). Reference is made to the divine name that is used (Elohim in ch. 1; Yahweh Elohim in chs. 2–3), to the style (ch. 1 has a strict, schematic structure, in contrast to which chs. 2–3 give an anthropomorphic description of God, as in 2:7–8 and 3:8), and to material variations (water in 1:2 represents the power of chaos, and in 2:5 the lack of water means chaos; ch. 2 tells the creation of the man at the beginning [v. 7], after which his environment is created, whereas in ch. 1 the world in which humans are to live is first created in several stages, after which the man and woman come as the top of the pyramid [vv.

26–29]). Attempts to show that there are no tensions between Genesis 1 and Genesis 2–3 are unconvincing. Here two stories are combined. It is, however, important to note that, though chapters 1–3 are not a perfect unity, it appears that *they are intended as a unity*. In its context, Genesis 2:4 and following verses are not a second creation account but the story about what happened to human beings and the world when they had been created. Not to be overlooked is the fact that 2:8 begins the account of the formation of the garden and what happens in it.

Similar remarks could be made about other duplicate stories. Genesis, for example, intends to tell that Hagar left Abraham twice (Genesis 16; 21:8–21). For the issue of the origin of Genesis, the question is significant whether two such stories are versions of a common "basic story" (or at least derive from different authors or circles). For now, I defer discussion on whether an affirmative answer to this question must lead to the sources theory. First, I point out that adherents of the sources theory also appeal to the fact that, more than once in the Pentateuch, parallel traditions have been combined into one story. Familiar examples of such a combination are the story of the Flood (chs. 6–9) and the story about the selling of Joseph into Egypt (37:3–36; see esp. vv. 28–29).

The present text of the Genesis flood story is commonly regarded as a combination of a J version and a P version, with the elements divided and ordered as follows (see Eissfeldt):

J elements

- 6:5–8
- 7:1–5, 10, 7, 16b, 12, 17b, 22–23
- 8:6, 2b–3a, 7–12, 13b, 20, 22

P elements

- 6:9–22
- 7:6, 11, 13–16a, 17a, 18–21, 24
- 8:1–2a, 3b–5, 13a, 14–19
- 9:1–17.

In support of this division reference is made to the use of the divine names, to the many repetitions, to the anthropomorphic descriptions in J (7:16b; 8:21), to the attention to details in P (8:14–19), and to discrepancies: according to P only one pair of all the animals is taken into the ark (6:19–20; 7:14–16a), but according to J seven pairs of the clean animals and birds are taken and only one pair of the unclean animals (7:2–3); according to P the flood lasts 150 days and the entire event one year and ten days (7:6, 11, 13, 24; 8:3b–5); according to J the flood lasts 40 days (7:4, 10, 12, 17; 8:6, 10, 12).

The splitting and reordering results in two fairly continuous stories, although neither is complete by itself. It must be assumed that the redactor (R) did not include everything and, furthermore, considering the verses that had to be split and transposed (see the above list), that he introduced drastic alterations. Another significant contribution attributed to R is the name Elohim in Genesis 7:9 (J) and a rewriting of 6:7; 7:3, 7–9, 23; 8:7 to exhibit affinity with P. Because of the distinction made between clean and unclean (7:8), it is believed that these verses cannot be from P (according to the theory, such a distinction in P is possible only after the introduction of the Mosaic law). This supposition also has the consequence that verses that exhibit affinity with P (7:2; 8:20–22) are attributed to J. As regards the repetitions, some can be attributed to the need for variation or further elucidation (e.g., 7:11–12). In other instances such an explanation is more implausible (e.g., 6:13–22; 7:1–5, 7–8 next to 7:13–16). Considering such repetitions, discrepancies, and the often striking use of the divine name, it seems certain that the story of the Flood, despite its unity and coherence, is a composite. At the same time it is impossible to discern in detail the layers of which it is composed.

Do such data support the sources theory? The presence of repetitions certainly does not necessarily imply the existence of various layers. For one reason or another a writer may have included two or even three similar stories, or he may have augmented a story with which he was familiar with elements from another version of the story; quite simply, the repetitions may be due to considerations of style. The adherents of the sources theory recognize this factor, even pointing out that parallel traditions may already be interwoven into the material used by the writers of the sources, for which reason it is not necessary to distinguish between more than four main layers. The important question, however, is not so much whether, with respect to a few passages, one may suspect that the text is composed of or based upon a combination of elements from two or more parallel traditions but whether such a phenomenon occurs frequently enough for one to argue justifiably that large parts of the Pentateuch are composed of two or more continuous narrative strands. In my judgment such is not the case. The examples I have given here are among the showpieces cited in support of the sources theory. Other passages present great problems. It often happens that narratives that otherwise read very smoothly are pulled apart, on the grounds that the Pentateuch is constructed from parallel sources (e.g., Gen. 27:1–41; 28:10–22).

Because of the criticism raised against the arguments of the sources theory, its adherents have become more restrained and have emphasized the view that the theory is based on the cumulative impression of all the arguments (e.g., Bentzen; Kaiser; Westermann). At first sight such a position may seem strong. Its defenders do not wish to employ mechanically the criteria for dividing texts into sources but want to weigh individually the data that argue for or against attributing them to a particular source. Closer scrutiny reveals that this defense is not all that strong. The appeal to the cumulative effect of the arguments lends a considerable measure of flexibility to the argumentation. The fact that the criteria cannot be used mechanically implies a great measure of subjectivism in the evaluation of the passages and to that extent weakens the sources theory.

(5) THE DATING OF THE SOURCES

Fundamentally important for the dating of the sources in the Wellhausenian form of the newer documentary hypothesis are (1) the equation of the lawbook of Josiah with Deuteronomy and (2) the acceptance of the historical reliability of the story of Josiah's proclamation of the lawbook in 622/621 B.C. (2 Kings 22–23). Many have accepted these points, but critical voices have also been raised. Some have disputed the identification of Deuteronomy with the lawbook of Josiah and have given the former a later dating. The suggestion has been made that the so-called Holiness Code (Leviticus 17–26), not Deuteronomy, is the lawbook of Josiah, partly because the satyrs of 2 Kings 23:8 (corrected text) are not mentioned in Deuteronomy but do occur in Leviticus 17:7 and because Molech (2 Kgs. 23:10) is mentioned by name in Leviticus 18:21; 20:1–5 but not in Deuteronomy 18:10. Others use such data as an occasion to suggest that the lawbook of Josiah was larger than Deuteronomy. The problem is a difficult one. 2 Kings 22–23 has hardly any concrete points of contact that might make it possible to see a relationship with Deuteronomy, while its contents do not in all respects agree with those of Deuteronomy. Critics usually point to the incongruence between Deuteronomy 18:6–8 and 2 Kings 23:8–9. The major material similarity is that, according to verses 8, 19, 21–23, Josiah pursues the centralization of the cult and orders the Passover to be celebrated in one specific locality. This similarity leaves open the possibility that the lawbook of Josiah was larger than Deuteronomy or that it was another lawbook, possibly not known from the Old Testament. In favor of the latter possibility may be the report in 23:24, with a specific reference to the discovered lawbook, that Josiah put away the teraphim. The Pentateuch, however, contains no stipulation against the teraphim.

Other critical voices have not contested the connection between Deuteronomy and 2 Kings 22–23 but have raised doubts about the historical reliability of these last chapters, which was so highly praised by Wellhausen and his followers. The former believe that the description in these chapters is a literary fiction, created at a later time. In such a view the dating of Deuteronomy clearly loses its fixed reference point.

In addition, the manner in which the text of 2 Kings indicates the lawbook discovered at the time of Josiah (22:8, 13, 16; 23:2–3, 21, 24) resembles the manner in which the final chapters of Deuteronomy refer to this writing (28:58, 61, 69 [29:1]; 29:8, 20 [9, 21]; 30:10; 31:24, 26), so that it can be asked whether, at least for the writers of Kings, the lawbook was not identical with Deuteronomy. The possibility should not be excluded either (for a long time the common point of view among interpreters) that the authors of Kings had in mind the entire Pentateuch.

The above data make it clear that the *absolute*

dating of Deuteronomy by the supporters of the sources theory is problematic. In the following comments I suggest also that the customary *relative* dating of the sources can be disputed.

Exodus 20:24 and Deuteronomy 12. As described above in section 2.d, in Wellhausen's dating of the sources the demand of the centralization of the cult in Deuteronomy 12 played an important role. From the fact that the so-called altar law in the JE laws (Exod. 20:24) did allow several holy places, Wellhausen concluded that this law was older than Deuteronomy 12. Critics of the Wellhausenian conception have tried to demonstrate that the latter passage also allows more than one holy place. They contend that Deuteronomy seeks not the *oneness* of the cult but its *purity,* and they propose to translate 12:14, "at every place which the Lord will choose from whichever one of your tribes." Conservative Old Testament scholars have felt attracted to this idea (see, e.g., B. Holwerda, *De plaats, die de Heere verkiezen zal* [1949], in ". . . *Begonnen hebbende van Mozes* . . .*"* [Kampen, 1974²], pp. 7– 29). For—assuming it is correct— this translation removes the foundation of Wellhausen's conception, since it both eliminates the discrepancy between Exodus 20:24 and Deuteronomy 12 and solves the problem raised by the historical books if the Mosaic authorship of Deuteronomy is accepted—namely, that persons who are faithful to Yahweh, such as Samuel (1 Sam. 7:9–10, 17; 9:12), are not condemned for offering sacrifices away from Jerusalem, which is contrary to the requirements of Deuteronomy.

This approach, however, finds no support in the text of Deuteronomy. There the idea of the one God (Deut. 6:4) corresponds with the idea of the oneness of the cult. Other conservative authors have therefore rejected it and have tried to find other solutions to the problem. J. Ridderbos (*Deuteronomy* [Bible Student's Commentary; Grand Rapids, 1984]), for example, believes that Deuteronomy 12 does not embody an absolute prohibition but posits an ideal that must become reality when the people have been given rest from their enemies (see v. 10), a situation that became true at the time of David (see 2 Sam. 7:11). Before that time the stipulation in Exodus 20:24 had maintained validity to a certain extent.

Note that the problems discerned by Wellhausen are in the first place historical problems. The text of the Pentateuch and following books presents a fairly coherent picture. The laws in the Pentateuch are not mentioned in an arbitrary sequence but are presented in a historical framework, a fact that has consequences for the interpretation. The law of Exodus 20 is given before the construction of the tabernacle is related. Perhaps the editors of the Pentateuch intimated thereby that the law about altars functioned only prior to the time the tabernacle was made or only during the time in the desert. (For a journeying people such a law represents a meaningful stipulation.) After the settlement in Canaan the requirement in Deuteronomy 12 must be carried out when the people have been given rest from their enemies (v. 10). According to Joshua 21:43–45; 22:4; 23:1 (see also Deut. 3:20; 25:19; Josh. 1:13, 15), the rest had begun under Joshua, and the cult was concentrated at Shiloh (Josh. 18:1; 21:2; 22:12; Judg. 21:19; 1 Samuel 1–4; see esp. Jer. 7:12). After Joshua had died, the "rest" disappeared (Judg. 2:14) and the oneness in the cult was lost (thus justifying Samuel's conduct).

With the dawning of the "rest" under David and Solomon (2 Sam. 7:1, 11; 1 Kgs. 5:18–19 [4–5]; 8:56), the centralization of the cult becomes reality again. The ark is transported to Jerusalem (2 Samuel 6) and later placed in the temple (1 Kgs. 8:4). Jerusalem, specifically the temple, is the place where Yahweh has established his name (8:16, 44, 48; 9:3; etc.). From that time on the kings are evaluated in terms of their attitude toward the one sanctuary (1 Kgs. 15:14; 22:44 [43b]; 2 Kgs. 12:3; etc.). As indicated, the Bible itself presents a fairly coherent picture. A different kind of question is whether this picture agrees with Israel's real history or whether it was a redactional construction. Were the kings of Judah familiar with the stipulation of the centralization of the cult, or was that requirement formulated only at a later time, so that the editors of the books of the Kings evaluate the rulers in terms of norms with which the kings themselves were not familiar? There is no reason to assume that the picture of the centralization of the cult is of recent date. It can very well go back to the tribal league. The striving for centralization also appears integral to the monarchy (see, e.g., the remarks about Solomon in 1 Kgs. 8:65–66; note vv. 2, 5, 14, 22, 35, 62–63; Jeroboam pursues a countercentralization in 1 Kgs. 12:27, 32). These comments bring us to the question of the historical relationship of Exodus 20:24 and Deuteronomy 12.

The two passages clearly belong to collections of laws of diverse origin. Exodus 20:24 is part of the so-called Book of the Covenant (20:22–23:33), which to a great extent exhibits similarity with Deuteronomy (cf. Exod. 21:2–6 with Deut. 15:12–17; Exod. 21:12–13 with Deut. 19:1–13; etc.). Wellhausen and others presupposed familiarity of D with the Book of the Covenant (JE). However, in view of the differences in style, terminology, and specific contents between the parallel stipulations in both books, it is certainly plausible that the two writings are independent witnesses of the same tradition complex or that they trace back to two basically similar tradition complexes. We therefore do not need to assume that the legislation of Deuteronomy follows chronologically the Book of the Covenant. They perhaps initially existed side by side in various circles or were transmitted at various shrines. If other Old Testament data are also taken into account, the question arises whether we can simplistically force the data of the Old Testament into a straitjacket, as Wellhausen attempts to do.

The organization of cultic personnel. Wellhausen and others believed that the Old Testament presents the following development with respect to the organization of the cult personnel: Deuteronomy, the lawbook of Josiah, does not distinguish between priests and Levites and demands that, everywhere in the land, the priests serving at high places be recognized as priests at the central sanctuary in Jerusalem. 2 Kings 23:8–9, however, shows that this requirement of Deuteronomy 18:6–8 remains only a theory: the priests of the high places may not serve in the central sanctuary, but they may share in its income. Ezekiel 44:10–16 contains a compromise and offers a reason for this situation: on account of heathen practices the priests of the high places are demoted to Levites; only the sons of Zadok may be priests. Ezekiel thus differentiated between priest and Levite; the distinction is recorded in P, with the difference that the sons of Aaron may be priests.

For a number of reasons this picture is open to question. It is correct that Deuteronomy is not familiar with the distinction between priest and Levite as it is found in Exodus through Numbers (note Deut. 18:1). In these three books "Levite" is a sort of official title designating a lower functionary of the cult, one who is not a priest; both belong to the tribe of Levi. In Deuteronomy "Levite" is the same as "descendant of Levi"; the designation says nothing about the function of the person but characterizes him as one who is entitled to serve Yahweh cultically. In Deuteronomy there are two categories of these Levites: the priests at the one sanctuary (see 17:9, 18; 18:1; 21:5; 24:8) and the descendants of Levi living in the land who do not perform a cultic function (see 12:12, 18–19; 14:27, 29; 16:11, 14). Deuteronomy contains no indication at all that they were priests of the high places, with 18:6 allowing them to work at the one sanctuary. There is no connection between Deuteronomy 18:6–8 and 2 Kings 23:8–9 (there the concern is the priests of the high places in Judah; for the priests of the high places in northern Israel, see v. 20). The organizational structure of the cult is not worked out. Such a fact, however, need not mean that Deuteronomy does not presuppose an organizational structure. Because the picture in Deuteronomy is not elaborated, in the present text of the Pentateuch there is, on this point, little or no tension between Deuteronomy and Exodus through Numbers.

From the fact that Ezekiel 44:10–16 deals with no Levites other than demoted priests, it may not be concluded that there were no other kinds. Ezekiel 40:45–46 (see also 46:20, 24) shows that Ezekiel is aware of various classes of cultic personnel. The phenomenon of the hierarchically structured clericals is rooted in tradition (see, e.g., 2 Kgs. 12:10–11 [9–10]; 22:14; 23:4; 25:18). Nowhere in Ezekiel 44 is it intimated that the prophet was thinking of former priests of the high places. Perhaps he has in mind personnel from the temple in Jerusalem (see Ezek. 5:11; 8:16–18).

It must be concluded that the Old Testament clearly contains a variety of pictures with respect to the organization of the cultic personnel but that it is very difficult to connect them functionally and chronologically. The data in Deuteronomy and Ezekiel do not exclude the possibility that the elaboration of the hierarchy, as this occurs in the so-called P parts, is from an older period. The possibility of the existence of circles with diverse ideas ought to be considered.

Similar remarks could be made about the relationship of Deuteronomy to the prophetic writings. As mentioned earlier, Wellhausen and others contend that the authentic words of Amos, Hosea, and Isaiah betray no trace of familiarity with Deuteronomy but that Jeremiah displays clear evidence of Deuteronomic influence. My judgment is that the data of the Old Testament do not permit such a simplistic picture of the relationship of Deuteronomy and the prophetic writings.

Points of reference for dating. The above remarks will have made it evident that the absolute and relative dating of the sources is beset with questions. The adherents of the sources theory therefore speak nowadays in a more nuanced manner about the dating, while nevertheless maintaining the chief lines of Wellhausen's conception. Such a position is not strange. In order to obtain an insight into the developments within Israel's religion, it is necessary to try to date the varied Old Testament materials. Here I wish to look further at the important question of dating and to draw attention to some shifts in the argumentation since Wellhausen.

In arguments adduced for dating the sources, scholars today manifest somewhat less inclination to apply categories of development. Less quickly than used to be the case will they appeal to anthropomorphisms or presumed primitive ideas in a source to defend its antiquity. This shift is due partly to the conception, referred to above, that arose as the result of the studies of Gunkel and Gressmann—namely, that the sources themselves may contain old material, a conception that has in particular altered the picture of J and E. Wellhausen and his school regarded J and E as writers of unhistorical history, from whose writings one could learn about the religious and social ideas of their time, and whose work could thus be dated by comparing it with the words of the prophets Amos, Hosea, and Isaiah and with Deuteronomy. Form-critical and tradition-historical research has turned J and E into theologians who, by using old traditions, composed writings with a message for their own time. Scholars attempt to find points of

reference in their work in order to determine in which period of Israel's history these writings best fit, given their specific purport and character.

The current dating of J in the time of David and Solomon is defended with the argument that several passages in J reflect that period (cf. Gen. 12:2 and 2 Sam. 7:9; see, e.g., Soggin, pp. 101–102). Vriezen and van der Woude (*Literatuur,* pp. 161ff.) in their discussion of the dating of J, state that such a broad perspective on the relationship of Israel to the nations (see Gen. 12:3) could be expected only in the days of Solomon or later, when Israel had become part of the larger world of the nations, and they consider it likely that the promise to Abraham is really meant to refer to David. In several authors the dating of the sources becomes to a high degree the interpretative key. For example, there is a tendency to read every passage in J against the background of the tenth century. Thus, for example, Genesis 2–3 alludes to David's adultery with Bathsheba and the death of Uriah (2 Samuel 11–12); Genesis 4 has in mind the murder of Amnon by Absalom (2 Samuel 13–14). (See, e.g., W. Brueggemann, "Yahwist," *IDBS,* 973.)

This method of dating is far from objective, for the search for points of reference is done selectively. Vriezen and van der Woude (p. 164), for example, date E in the days of Jeroboam II (ca. 783–743 B.C.). They adduce that the opposition between Israel and Aram (cf. Jacob and Laban) is clearly evident in E. The source J, however, also speaks of the tense relationship between Jacob and Laban. Deuteronomy 17:14–20 offers a vivid illustration of the various interpretative possibilities that the search for a point of contact in history for dating can yield. Sometimes a premonarchical dating is argued, because the description of the king reflects so little the historical reality of kingship in Israel. Yet for that same reason it is also advocated that the description fits only the postexilic era. Most interpreters discern in the description a reaction to the kingship of Solomon. All these interpretative possibilities have a certain plausibility. It should be kept in mind that such uncertainty is due in part to our limited knowledge of Israel's religious history and in part to the material itself. For in the text we often encounter the fruits of pseudepigraphic writers whose aim it was to present the material as the work of Moses (see section 3.a). Illustrative in this connection is the so-called temple scroll from Qumran, a holiness law from the centuries before Christ, containing regulations concerning the monarchy based on Deuteronomy 17, which, according to the presentation in the scroll, were directly given by God in the wilderness (Y. Yadin, *Mgylt-hmqdsh*, I–IIIA [Jerusalem, 1977], col. 56, lines 12ff.).

For the sake of completeness I mention too that dating makes use of word usage and idiom (such as the presence of Aramaisms) and that the question in which period of a nation significant literary productions can be expected (in times of prosperity or in crisis situations?) can play a role. All these observations will have made it sufficiently clear that the dating of the material of the Pentateuch—whether absolute or relative dating—is beset with problems.

Having come to the end of this examination of the four-sources theory, I believe that, in the light of our findings, the question whether it offers the most acceptable solution to the problem of the origin of the Pentateuch is to be answered negatively. I offer now some final considerations concerning how we should view the Pentateuch.

4. FINAL CONSIDERATIONS

Research in the last few centuries has made it clear that the Pentateuch is a complex entity. The history of this research as it has been surveyed above has shown that biblical scholars have been unable to arrive at a consensus regarding how this complex totality attained its final shape. Hence at this point a detailed description of the process of how the Pentateuch came into being is simply an unattainable ideal. In my judgment it is impossible to trace satisfactorily the broad lines of this process using one of the existing theories. A combination of a fragmentary, supplementary, and crystallization hypothesis does perhaps the most justice to the material of the Pentateuch. For it does leave the impression that it has been composed from elements from smaller and larger narrative sections and collections of laws, each with its own history. The result is a *fairly integral unity* in which it is recounted why Israel was elected out of the nations for service to Yahweh in the land he

had given them and in which it is described how the people came into that land.

After centuries in which the emphasis has been on the heterogeneity of the material in the Pentateuch, it has gradually become time to pay more attention to the coherence in the Pentateuch and to the fact that, because of the creative manner in which stories and laws of diverse origin have been used as components (components often still recognizable and sometimes apparently not fully blended together), these books have been combined into a new integral unity. This integral unity—not, as is still so often the case, the reconstructed layers—should be the object of exegesis.

a. Composition, Purpose, Place, and Date of the Pentateuch

In the Pentateuch three larger units can be discerned: Genesis, Exodus through Numbers, and Deuteronomy. Each unit has its own character and, especially the second, contains varieties of material having its own prehistory.

Exodus is distinguished from Genesis not only through a chronological break (at Exod. 1:7-8) but also through structure and content. Genesis is a well-constructed and integral unity because the material has been compressed within the framework of *toledoth* formulas. Following the creation story (Gen. 1:1–2:3), these formulas introduce the following sections: 2:4–4:26; 5:1–6:8; 6:9–9:29; 10:1–11:9; 11:10–26; 11:27–25:11; 25:12–18; 25:19–35:29; 36:1, 9–37:1; 37:2–50:26. These parts consist sometimes of large narrative sections (e.g., 11:27–25:11; 37:2–50:26), sometimes of a genealogy (i.e., a compressed history; e.g., 11:10–26), sometimes of an enumeration of generations and narrative passages (e.g., 5:1–6:8). The meaning of *toledoth* (often translated as "history" or "descendants") is "what was begotten," "the outcome," "the result." Where the term is used, the writer does not present an entirely new theme but relates what happened further to the person whose name occurs in the genitive with *toledoth* and who in the preceding section has already been discussed. The passages introduced by this formula thus deal to a large extent with people who owe their existence to the person mentioned in the *toledoth* formula (e.g., 11:27–

25:11; 25:19–35:29; 37:2–50:26). Consequently, a phrase such as "these are the *toledoth* of Isaac" (25:19) does not mean "this is the history of Isaac" but "this is what happened further to Isaac" (who has been mentioned already), implying that the narrative deals to a large degree with Jacob and Esau.

In Exodus through Numbers the *toledoth* formula appears only in Numbers 3:1. A striking feature in this part is the fact that, unlike in Genesis (with the exception of Exod. 1:1–6; Numbers 1; 32; 34; and a few other references), the narrative typically deals continually with Israel as a unity, while the division of the people into tribes plays virtually no role. This part of the Pentateuch contains several of the law collections. Deuteronomy has its own character and stands by itself, but there are nevertheless clear linkages between Deuteronomy and the preceding books. As Moses' farewell address, Deuteronomy is situated in the fields of Moab, where, according to Numbers 22:1, Israel was encamped. Deuteronomy 31–34 harks back to themes in the concluding chapters of Numbers, and thus Deuteronomy is meaningfully integrated into the section Exodus through Numbers. Although Genesis clearly has its own character, after everything that has been told about the promises to the patriarchs (Gen. 12:2–3, 7; 13:15–17; 15:7; 17:2, 8; etc.), it demands a sequel, and the impression is unavoidable that the story of Joseph is intended to link the stories of the patriarchs with those of Israel in Egypt. The beginning of Exodus has evidently been written with such a purpose in mind. In brief, the various parts, though each having its own character, are integrally connected. Each becomes meaningful only in association with the other. Here we should note that, in the Pentateuch as a whole, the promise of a land to the patriarchs cannot be detached from the book of Joshua (and following books).

The various parts are related to each other through several connecting elements, including the following:

1. Josh. 24:32 harks back to Exod. 13:19; Gen. 50:25; 33:19.
2. In Gen. 50:24; Exod. 13:5, 11; 32:13; 33:1–3a; Num. 14:23; 32:11, the promises to the patriarchs are recalled.
3. In Exod. 3:6, 13, 15–16; 4:5, the God of the fathers known from Genesis is mentioned.
4. Exod. 2:23–25; 6:2–5 goes back to Genesis.
5. Josh. 2:1; 3:1 harks back to Num. 25:1, and Josh. 14:6 to Num. 14:24, 30.
6. Num. 27:18–23; Deut. 3:21–22; 31:7–8, 23; 34:9 speaks of Moses' succession by Joshua, which presupposes the conquest of the land; cf. also Num. 32:16–19; Deut. 3:18–20 and Josh. 1:12–15; 4:12–13; ch. 22.
7. The presentation of the twelve tribes links Genesis with Joshua.
8. Deuteronomy is entirely oriented to the entrance into the land (e.g., Deut. 1:8–9; 4:40).
9. In Joshua there are repeated allusions to things mentioned in the earlier books (e.g., Josh. 1:1–5; 2:10; 3:7; 4:23; 5:12).

In my opinion these connecting elements are to be regarded as the foundations upon which the Pentateuch is constructed. Moreover, on the basis of the coherence between the Pentateuch and Joshua and between Joshua and the other books, the likelihood is great that the books Genesis through 2 Kings in their present form are from the same author or group of writers. In the composition of these books, material of diverse provenance, character, and age has been used. It is not impossible or unlikely that use has been made of more extensive and coherent works, but it is not easy to reconstruct these works. At the most it can now and then be plausibly argued that certain passages originally belonged to a larger coherent work.

In my judgment it is not impossible that Genesis, characterized both by the *toledoth* formulas and by the typical promises to the patriarchs, belonged originally to a larger writing (with its own prehistory), of which the writer(s) of the work extending through 2 Kings included only the beginning (i.e., the present book of Genesis). Such a conclusion is reasonable because after Exodus the *toledoth* formula is no longer used and also because different terms are used for the land of promise than are used in Genesis (Exod. 13:5, 11; etc.). The fact that nothing further is said about numerous descendants is not strange, for this promise had been fulfilled (Exod. 1:7; Numbers 1–4). In view of the linkages with Genesis in Exodus 3:6, 13, 15–16; 4:5 and in 2:23–25; 6:2–5, it must be assumed that also elsewhere in Exodus through Numbers use is made of the material from which Genesis is derived, unless one assumes that these passages are from the writer(s) of the large work himself. It is possible that Deuteronomy never existed as an independent address of Moses but was composed by the writer(s) of the large work, though making use of a variety of material, in order to elucidate further their purpose in their composition: namely, to recount Israel's election out of the nations unto service to Yahweh in the land he had given them and to describe the settlement of the people in the land and its unfaithfulness to Yahweh, resulting in the Exile. As mentioned already, Deuteronomy is integrated in the material at hand.

Because the release of King Jehoiachin is the final event described in the great work (2 Kgs. 25:27–30), it is natural to assume that it was completed not long after this event, in the middle of the sixth century B.C. Where it was composed is difficult to determine. One could suggest Babylon, but perhaps there is more in favor of an origin in Palestine, which after the fall of Jerusalem was certainly not without people belonging to the intelligentsia.

To my comments regarding the purpose of the great work I would add here only that the work presents itself as a description of Israel's history from the perspective of its calling and its continual unfaithfulness. The work thus explains the catastrophe of Jerusalem's downfall in 586 and is also a continuous call to repentance, to faithfulness to Yahweh and his commandments.

b. The Pentateuch as Part of a Great Work, Genesis through 2 Kings

In the comments made above I have emphasized the unity of Genesis through 2 Kings. This conception must answer the question how it is possible that in the tradition the Pentateuch is regarded as an independent entity (the five books of Moses, the Torah) and how, at least in the Jewish tradition, which designates the books Joshua through 2 Kings the Former Prophets, these books are regarded as a set of writings having their own character, different from that of Genesis through

Deuteronomy. Elsewhere in this handbook attention is given to the origin and the division of the canon of the Old Testament. Here I can mention only that, in my judgment, the Talmudic and Massoretic tripartite division into the Law, the Former and Latter Prophets, and the Writings is not original but is of later date.

A case can be made for the statement that, in Judaism at the beginning of our era, the Pentateuch was not everywhere equally highly regarded. On the one hand these books were valued as Torah, as God's special gift, given by God to Moses at Sinai, to which the highest authority had to be accorded. This viewpoint, which is also at the basis of the Talmudic and Massoretic division, is accompanied by the idea that the other holy writings are elucidation and elaboration of the contents of the Torah. It is a likely assumption that this esteem of the Pentateuch gave rise to the notion of its Mosaic authorship. On the other hand there is the appreciation of the Pentateuch and following books as *historical* writings. It is thus possible that such appreciation, a view represented by the Septuagint and in the Christian tradition, may reach back to the centuries before Christ. All indications seem to point to the fact that the division between the Pentateuch and Joshua through Kings was brought about by the interpretation of the Pentateuch as Torah. In any case, seeing Genesis through 2 Kings as a historical work, without introducing a sharp break between Deuteronomy and Joshua, is in my judgment most in agreement with the material. Genesis through Deuteronomy taken by itself is a torso.

This position on the unity of Genesis through 2 Kings and on the dating of this great work makes it necessary to discuss a few other questions. The fact that the Samaritans recognize the Pentateuch (at least their version of it) as Holy Scripture but not Joshua through 2 Kings cannot be used as an argument against this position. It is often conjectured that the Samaritans adopted the Pentateuch after Ezra's arrival in Jerusalem. It is assumed that the schism between Samaritans and Jews arose at the time of Ezra, which is then taken as explanation for the fact that the Samaritans accord canonical authority only to the Pentateuch and not to the other books of the Old Testament. According to this reasoning, the other books became canonical only after the schism had become a fact. This conception goes along with the view, current after the introduction of the newer documentary hypothesis in Wellhausenian form, that P or the Pentateuch was the lawbook Ezra brought with him from Babylon and that the Pentateuch obtained its final form in his time or shortly afterward. For more than one reason this construction is disputable.

Both the question concerning the origin of the Samaritans and that concerning the origin of the rift between Jews and Samaritans pose problems (the latter maintain that the schism arose in the time of the judges and that they are the true heirs of the Mosaic religion; see R. J. Coggins, *Samaritans and Jews: The Origins of Samaritanism Reconsidered* [Oxford, 1975]). Here it will be sufficient to observe that the Samaritans are likely to be regarded as a Jewish sect and that the separation between them and the Jews was due to a process of gradual estrangement. In this process the tension between northern and southern Israel likely played a role. Recall only the Samaritans' choice of Shechem as the location of their central place of worship. The schism happened in the last centuries before Christ to the first century after Christ. Assuming that the large work comprising Genesis through 2 Kings arose in Palestine in the circles of those who did not go into captivity and that the Samaritans also came from the circles of the Yahweh worshipers living in Palestine, it may also be assumed that the Samaritans were familiar with the Pentateuch in the time prior to Ezra's arrival in Jerusalem. The fact that the Samaritans recognize only the Pentateuch is not strange. Because of the anti-Jewish and anti-Jerusalem feelings of the Samaritans, the section Joshua through 2 Kings was unacceptable to them on account of the large place it gave to the Davidic dynasty and to Jerusalem as the central place of worship. It ought not to be overlooked that the Samaritans do possess their own version of the events described in Joshua through Kings (see J. MacDonald, ed., *Samaritan Chronicle*, II [Berlin, 1969]).

Very often Ezra has been associated with the formation or promulgation of the Pentateuch or P. The arguments for this position are especially taken from Nehemiah 8 and 10. Closer scrutiny of these chapters renders this notion problematic. For example, the regulations with respect to the Feast of Tabernacles, in 8:14-18 explicitly derived from the law, are in that particular form not found in the Pentateuch (cf., in particular, Lev. 23:33-43). Several of the obligations mentioned in Nehemiah 10:30-40 (29-39) as being derived from the law of Moses do not occur in the Pentateuch, despite the phrase "as it is written in the law" (vv. 35, 37 [34, 36]). Also, several stipulations resembling or seemingly related to those found in the Pentateuch upon careful comparison exhibit considerable variation as regards substance, formulation, and terminology. These data and others suggest that the lawbook mentioned in Ezra and Nehemiah is not identical with the Pentateuch or a part of it but that the references in Ezra and Nehemiah point to a lawbook not referred to in the Pentateuch, one containing stipulations that agree with laws in the Pentateuch but also laws that deviate from it or are not found in it at all.

This supposition need not have consequences for our dating of the Pentateuch. For the possibility exists that, in the period following the Exile, not all Jewish circles had yet recognized the Pentateuch as canonical and that its existence did not yet rule out the composition of new books of law. The so-called temple scroll from Qumran (see section 3.b.[5]) contains stipulations familiar from the Pentateuch. It also has rules that deviate from it and not contained in it but that nevertheless are presented as given by God to Israel. This writing demonstrates that not only in ancient times but also later it was considered acceptable to compose new collections of law on the basis of familiar Mosaic laws (see the comments above on pseudepigraphy in section 3.a). The scroll is a clear witness of the variety existing in the Judaism of the first centuries after Christ, one that is revealed also in the existence of several cultic centers alongside of Jerusalem, such as the Samaritan temple on Mount Gerizim and Jewish sanctuaries in Elephantine and Leontopolis. Perhaps it is not too much to suggest that such sanctuaries possessed lawbooks, each of which in certain respects had its own character.

It should be obvious that, as a result of our increased knowledge of Judaism of the first centuries before Christ, the long-held notion that the composition and introduction of the Pentateuch at the time of Ezra marked the birth of Judaism is to be considered unlikely. This picture is too contrived, and the data of the Old Testament cannot be made to fit into it. Regularly it turns out that these data cannot be forced into a preconceived scheme. In this connection I note also that the common notion that P presupposes Chronicles or the Pentateuch is hard to prove on the basis of the content of Chronicles. One gets the impression that also in these books "the law of Moses" refers to a codex not mentioned in the Pentateuch. So in 2 Chronicles 30:16, in a reference to the law of Moses, mention is made of the position of the priests and Levites in the temple. No stipulation relating to such position, however, is found in the Pentateuch (see further 2 Chr. 8:13; 23:18; 25:4; 34:14; 35:12; cf. 1 Chr. 6:34 [49]; 2 Chr. 31:3 and see 1 Chr. 23:24–32 [cf. also 2 Chr. 30:17; Ezra 3:8] and Num. 4:35–49; 8:23–26 [cf. also 1 Chr. 23:3]). Earlier I pointed out that the identification of the lawbook of Josiah with Deuteronomy and the Pentateuch creates problems (see 3.b.[5]). In my judgment this complication and the above-mentioned data may be regarded as supporting the obvious conclusion that the legal passages known to us from the Pentateuch were not the only ones in circulation in Israel and in early Judaism. Rather there were several collections of laws. Only part of these rules found their way into the Pentateuch, and even then the process of formulating and expanding law codes continued.

LITERATURE

G. Ch. Aalders, *A Short Introduction to the Pentateuch* (London, 1949).

A. Bentzen, *Introduction to the Old Testament* I-II (Copenhagen, 1952²).

E. Blum, *Die Komposition der Vätergeschichte* (Neukirchen-Vluyn, 1984).

H. Cazelles, "La Torah ou Pentateuque," in *Introduction à la Bible*. Édition nouvelle (Paris, 1973), II: 95-244.

B. S. Childs, *Introduction to the Old Testament as Scripture* (Philadelphia, 1979).

J. L. Crenshaw, *Gerhard von Rad* (Waco, TX, 1978).

O. Eissfeldt, *Hexateuch-Synopse* (Leipzig, 1922).

———, *The Old Testament: An Introduction* (New York, 1965).

G. Fohrer, *Einleitung in das Alte Testament* (Heidelberg, 1979¹²).

W. H. Green, *The Higher Criticism of the Pentateuch* (New York, 1895; repr. Grand Rapids, 1978).

———, *The Unity of the Book of Genesis* (New York, 1895; repr. Grand Rapids, 1979).

A. H. J. Gunneweg, "Anmerkungen und Anfragen zur neueren Pentateuchforschung," *Theologische Rundschau* 48 (1983) 227-53; 50 (1985) 107-31.

M. Haran, *Temples and Temple-Service in Ancient Israel: An Inquiry into the Biblical Cult Phenomena and the Historical Setting of the Priestly School* (Oxford, 1978; repr. Winona Lake, IN, 1985).

R. K. Harrison, *Introduction to the Old Testament* (Grand Rapids, 1969).

C. Houtman, *Inleiding in de Pentateuch: Een beschrijving van de geschiedenis van het onderzoek naar het ontstaan en de compositie van de eerste vijf boeken van het Oude Testament met een terugblik en een evaluatie* (Kampen, 1980).

———, "Ezra and the Law: Observations on the Supposed Relation between Ezra and the Pentateuch," *OTS* 21 (1981) 91-115.

O. Kaiser, *Introduction to the Old Testament* (Minneapolis, 1975).

I. M. Kikawada and A. Quinn, *Before Abraham Was: The Unity of Genesis 1–11* (Nashville, 1985).

D. A. Knight, ed., *Julius Wellhausen and his Prolegomena to the History of Israel* (Chico, CA, 1983).

F. Kohata, *Jahwist und Priesterschrift in Exodus 3–14* (BZAW 166; Berlin/New York, 1986).

H.-J. Kraus, *Geschichte der historisch-kritischen Erforschung des Alten Testaments* (Neukirchen-Vluyn, 1969²).

C. J. Labuschagne, "Neue Wege und Perspektiven in der Pentateuchforschung," *VT* 36 (1986) 146-62.

W. Möller, *Grundriss für alttestamentliche Einleitung* (Berlin, 1958).

S. Mowinckel, *Erwägungen zur Pentateuch-Quellenfrage* (Oslo, 1964).

G. A. Rendsburg, *The Redaction of Genesis* (Winona Lake, IN, 1986).

R. Rendtorff, *The Old Testament: An Introduction* (Philadelphia, 1985).

J. Rogerson, *Old Testament Criticism in the Nineteenth Century: England and Germany* (London, 1984).

M. Rose, *Deuteronomist und Jahwist: Untersuchungen zu den Berührungspunkten beider Literaturwerke* (Zürich, 1981).

S. Sandmel, *The Hebrew Scriptures. An Introduction to their Literature and Religious Ideas* (New York, 1978).

H. Schmid, *Die Gestalt des Mose: Probleme alttestament-licher Forschung unter Berücksichtigung der Penta-teuchkrise* (Darmstadt, 1986) (good bibliography).

W. H. Schmidt, *The Faith of the Old Testament* (Philadelphia, 1983).

H. C. Schmitt, *Die nichtpriesterliche Josephsgeschichte: Ein Beitrag zur neuesten Pentateuchkritik* (BZAW 154; Berlin/New York, 1980).

M. H. Segal, *The Pentateuch. Its Composition and Its Authorship and Other Biblical Studies* (Jerusalem, 1967).

R. Smend, *Die Entstehung des Alten Testaments* (Stuttgart, 1981²).

J. A. Soggin, *Introduction to the Old Testament* (Philadelphia, 1976).

R. J. Thompson, *Moses and the Law in a Century of Criticism since Graf* (Leiden, 1970).

R. de Vaux, "A propos du second centenaire d'Astruc. Réflexions sur l'état actuel de la Critique du Penta-teuque," SVT 1 (1953) 182-98.

H. Vorländer, *Die Entstehungszeit des jehowistischen Geschichtswerkes* (Frankfurt am Main/Las Vegas, 1978).

Th. C. Vriezen and A. S. van der Woude, *De Literatuur van Oud-Israël* (Wassenaar, 1980⁶).

P. Weimar, *Untersuchungen zur Redaktionsgeschichte des Pentateuch* (BZAW 146; Berlin/New York, 1977).

———, *Die Berufung des Mose: Literaturwissenschaft-liche Analyse von Exodus 2,23–5,5* (Freiburg/Göttingen, 1980).

———, *Die Meerwundererzählung: Eine redaktionskri-tische Analyse von Ex 13,17–14,31* (Wiesbaden, 1985).

M. Weinfeld, *Deuteronomy and the Deuteronomic School* (Oxford, 1972).

R. N. Whybray, *The Making of the Pentateuch* (JSOT Supplement Series 53; Sheffield, 1987).

E. J. Young, *An Introduction to the Old Testament* (Grand Rapids, 1949).

E. Zenger, *Israel am Sinai: Analysen und Interpreta-tionen zu Exodus 17–34* (Altenberge, 1985²).

Recent Monographs:

A. G. Auld, *Joshua, Moses and the Land. Tetrateuch-Pentateuch-Hexateuch in a Generation since 1938* (Edinburgh, 1980).

W. Beyerlin, *Herkunft und Geschichte der ältesten Sinai-traditionen* (Tübingen, 1965).

U. Cassuto, *The Documentary Hypothesis and the Composition of the Pentateuch* (Jerusalem, 1972²).

R. E. Clements, *A Century of Old Testament Study* (Guildford-London, 1976).

———, "Pentateuchal Problems," in G. W. Anderson, ed., *Tradition and Interpretation* (Oxford, 1979), pp. 96-124.

D. J. A. Clines, *The Theme of the Pentateuch* (JSOT Supplement Series 10; Sheffield, 1978).

G. W. Coats, *Genesis, with an Introduction to Narrative Literature* (The Forms of the OT Literature 1; Grand Rapids, 1983).

P. F. Ellis, *The Yahwist. The Bible's First Theologian* (Collegeville, MN, 1968).

R. E. Friedman, *The Exile and Biblical Narrative. The Formation of the Deuteronomistic and Priestly Works* (Chico, CA, 1981).

A. Hurvitz, *A Linguistic Study of the Relationship between the Priestly Source and the Book of Ezekiel* (Paris, 1982).

A. W. Jenks, *The Elohist and North Israelite Traditions* (Missoula, MT, 1977).

Y. Kaufmann, *The Religion of Israel. From its Beginnings to the Babylonian Exile* (New York, 1960).

D. A. Knight, *Rediscovering the Traditions of Israel* (Missoula, MT, 1975).

———, "The Pentateuch," in D. A. Knight and G. M. Tucker, eds., *The Hebrew Bible and Its Modern Inter-preters* (Philadelphia/Chico, CA, 1985), pp. 263-96 (good bibliography).

N. Lohfink, ed., *Das Deuteronomium. Entstehung, Gestalt und Botschaft* (Leuven, 1985).

A. D. H. Mayes, *The Story of Israel between Settlement and Exile. A Redactional Study of the Deuteronomis-tic History* (London, 1983).

S. E. McEvenue, *The Narrative Style of the Priestly Writer* (Rome, 1971).

S. Mowinckel, *Tetrateuch-Pentateuch-Hexateuch. Die Berichte über die Landnahme in den drei altisraeli-tischen Geschichtswerken* (BZAW 90; Berlin, 1964).

E. W. Nicholson, *Deuteronomy and Tradition* (Oxford, 1967).

M. Noth, *A History of Pentateuchal Traditions* (Chico, CA, 1981).

———, *Überlieferungsgeschichtliche Studien. Die sam-melnden und bearbeitenden Geschichtswerke im Alten Testament* (Tübingen, 1967³).

H. D. Preuss, *Deuteronomium* (Darmstadt, 1982) (good bibliography).

G. von Rad, *The Problem of the Hexateuch and Other Essays* (New York, 1966).

———, *Studies in Deuteronomy* (London/Chicago, 1953).

R. Rendtorff, *Das überlieferungsgeschichtliche Problem des Pentateuch* (BZAW 147; Berlin, 1977).

H. H. Schmid, *Der sogenannte Jahwist. Beobachtungen und Fragen zur Pentateuchforschung* (Zürich, 1976).

L. Schmidt, "Überlegungen zum Jahwisten," *Evangelische Theologie* 37 (1977) 230-47.

F. V. Winnett, *The Mosaic Tradition* (Toronto, 1949).

———, "Re-examining the Foundations," *JBL* 84 (1965) 1-19.

H. W. Wolff, "The Kerygma of the Yahwist," *Interpretation* 20 (1966) 131-58 (repr. in W. Brueggemann and H. W. Wolff, *The Vitality of Old Testament Traditions* [Atlanta, 1975], pp. 41-66, 132-38).

Commentaries on Genesis:

G. Ch. Aalders, *Genesis* (Bible Student's Commentary; Grand Rapids, 1981).

F. M. Th. Böhl, *Genesis* (Tekst en Uitleg; Groningen/Den Haag; I, 1930²; II, 1925).

W. Brueggemann, *Genesis* (Interpretation: A Bible Commentary for Teaching and Preaching; Atlanta, 1982).

U. Cassuto, *A Commentary on the Book of Genesis. I: From Adam to Noah, Genesis I–VI 8* (Jerusalem, 1961); *II: From Noah to Abraham, Genesis VI 9–XI 32* (Jerusalem, 1964).

A. Clamer, *La Genèse traduite et commentée* (La Sainte Bible; Paris, 1953).

F. Delitzsch, *A New Commentary on Genesis* (Minneapolis, repr. 1978).

A. Dillmann, *Die Genesis* (KeH; Leipzig, 1892⁶).

S. R. Driver, *The Book of Genesis with Introduction and Notes* (Westminster Commentaries; London, 1904³).

W. H. Gispen, *Genesis vertaald en verklaard* (COT; Kampen; I [Gen. 1–11:26], 1974; II [Gen. 11:27–25:11], 1979; III [25:12–36:43], 1983).

H. Gunkel, *Genesis übersetzt und erklärt* (HKAT; Göttingen, 1910³).

B. Jacob, *Das erste Buch der Tora Genesis übersetzt und erklärt* (Berlin, 1934; repr. New York, 1974).

C. F. Keil and F. Delitzsch, *Commentary on the Old Testament, I: The Pentateuch* (Grand Rapids, repr. 1973).

D. Kidner, *Genesis* (TOTC; London/Downers Grove, IL, 1967).

O. Procksch, *Die Genesis übersetzt und erklärt* (KAT; Leipzig, 1924³).

G. von Rad, *Genesis* (OTL; Philadelphia, 1972²).

A. van Selms, *Genesis* (POT; Nijkerk, 1967).

J. Skinner, *A Critical and Exegetical Commentary on Genesis* (ICC; Edinburgh: 1930²).

E. A. Speiser, *Genesis* (AB; New York, 1964).

C. Westermann, *Genesis 1–11* (Minneapolis, 1984); *Genesis 12–36* (Minneapolis, 1985); *Genesis 37–50* (Minneapolis, 1986).

J. T. Willis, *Genesis* (The Living Word Commentary on the Old Testament; Austin, TX, 1979).

Commentaries on Exodus:

F. M. Th. Böhl, *Exodus* (Tekst en Uitleg; Groningen/Den Haag, 1928).

U. Cassuto, *A Commentary on the Book of Exodus* (Jerusalem, 1967).

B. S. Childs, *The Book of Exodus* (OTL; Philadelphia, 1974).

A. Clamer, *L'Exode traduit et commenté* (La Sainte Bible; Paris, 1956).

A. Cole, *Exodus* (TOTC; London/Downers Grove, IL, 1973).

A. Dillmann and V. Ryssel, *Die Bücher Exodus und Leviticus* (KeH; Leipzig, 1897³).

J. I. Durham, *Exodus* (Word Biblical Commentary; Waco, TX, 1987).

H. L. Ellison, *Exodus* (The Daily Study Bible; Philadelphia, 1982).

F. C. Fensham, *Exodus* (POT; Nijkerk, 1970).

W. H. Gispen, *Exodus* (Bible Student's Commentary; Grand Rapids, 1982).

C. Houtman, *Exodus vertaald en verklaard* (COT; Kampen, I [Ex. 1:1–7:13], 1986).

J. P. Hyatt, *Exodus* (New Century Bible; London/Grand Rapids, 1980²).

G. A. F. Knight, *Theology as Narration: A Commentary on the Book of Exodus* (Grand Rapids, 1976).

A. H. McNeile, *The Book of Exodus with Introduction and Notes* (Westminster Commentaries; London, 1931³).

M. Noth, *Exodus* (OTL; Philadelphia, 1962).

W. H. Schmidt, *Exodus* (BKAT; Neukirchen-Vluyn, 1974-1983 [Ex. 1:1–4:31]).

Commentaries on Leviticus:

A. Clamer, *Le Lévitique traduit et commenté* (La Sainte Bible; Paris, 1946).

K. Elliger, *Leviticus* (HAT; Tübingen, 1966).

W. H. Gispen, *Het Boek Leviticus verklaard* (COT; Kampen, 1950).

R. K. Harrison, *Leviticus: An Introduction and Commentary* (TOTC; Leicester/Downers Grove, IL, 1980).

G. A. F. Knight, *Leviticus* (Daily Study Bible; Philadelphia, 1981).

B. Maarsingh, *Leviticus* (POT; Nijkerk, 1974).

A. Noordtzij, *Leviticus* (Bible Student's Commentary; Grand Rapids, 1982).

M. Noth, *Leviticus* (OTL; Philadelphia, 1965).

R. Rendtorff, *Leviticus* (BKAT; Neukirchen-Vluyn; [Lev. 1:1-17], 1985).

N. H. Snaith, *Leviticus and Numbers* (New Century Bible; London, 1967).

G. J. Wenham, *The Book of Leviticus* (NICOT; Grand Rapids, 1979).

W. J. de Wilde, *Leviticus* (Tekst en Uitleg; Groningen/ Batavia, 1937).

Commentaries on Numbers:

L. Elliott Binns, *The Book of Numbers with Introduction and Notes* (Westminster Commentaries; London, 1927).

P. J. Budd, *Numbers* (Word Biblical Commentary; Waco, TX, 1984).

A. Clamer, *Les Nombres traduits et commentés* (La Sainte Bible; Paris, 1946).

A. Dillmann, *Die Bücher Numeri, Deuteronomium und Josua* (KeH; Leipzig, 1886²).

W. H. Gispen, *Het Boek Numeri verklaard* I-II (COT; Kampen, 1959-1964).

G. B. Gray, *A Critical and Exegetical Commentary on Numbers* (ICC; Edinburgh, 1912).

H. Jagersma, *Numeri* (POT; Nijkerk; I [Num. 1–15], 1983).

A. Noordtzij, *Numbers* (Bible Student's Commentary; Grand Rapids, 1984).

M. Noth, *Numbers* (OTL; Philadelphia, 1968).

G. J. Wenham, *Numbers: An Introduction and Commentary* (TOTC; Leicester/Downers Grove, IL, 1981).

Commentaries on Deuteronomy:

P. Buis and J. Leclercq, *Le Deutéronome* (Paris, 1963).

A. Clamer, *Le Deutéronome traduit et commenté* (La Sainte Bible; Paris, 1946).

P. C. Craigie, *The Book of Deuteronomy* (NICOT; Grand Rapids, 1976).

S. R. Driver, *A Critical and Exegetical Commentary on Deuteronomy* (ICC; Edinburgh, 1902³).

A. D. H. Mayes, *Deuteronomy* (New Century Bible; London/Grand Rapids, 1981²).

D. F. Payne, *Deuteronomy* (The Daily Study Bible; Philadelphia, 1985).

G. von Rad, *Deuteronomy* (OTL; Philadelphia, 1966).

J. Ridderbos, *Deuteronomy* (Bible Student's Commentary; Grand Rapids, 1984).

J. A. Thompson, *Deuteronomy* (TOTC; London/ Downers Grove, IL, 1974).

J. Wijngaards, *Deuteronomium uit de grondtekst vertaald en uitgelegd* (BOT; Roermond, 1971).

B. The Historical Books

by H. H. Grosheide

1. INTRODUCTION

In this chapter I will discuss the books that in the English Bible are called Joshua, Judges, 1 and 2 Samuel, 1 and 2 Kings, 1 and 2 Chronicles, Ezra, and Nehemiah. I wish to make the following three observations regarding these books. First, the two books of Samuel originally constituted a unity, which holds true also for Kings, Chronicles, and Ezra-Nehemiah. The division into two parts is found for the first time in the Septuagint or, in the case of Ezra and Nehemiah, at the time of Origen (A.D. 185–254). In the Septuagint the four books Samuel and Kings are called "royal rules." The Vulgate designates them as "the four books of the kings." In the Hebrew manuscripts the writings remained undivided for a long time. One indication is that the caption under each book in which the Massoretes mentioned the number of verses in the book is absent from 1 Samuel, 1 Kings, 1 Chronicles, and Ezra, while the ones under 2 Samuel, 2 Kings, 2 Chronicles, and Nehemiah refer respectively to these books and the preceding books. In the Hebrew manuscripts the division into two occurred for the first time in 1448 and in printed texts in 1517.

The usual assumption is that the books were divided because a scroll inscribed with both books would be too long and unwieldy. In the case of Ezra and Nehemiah, the reason must have been that Nehemiah 1:1 seems to make an entirely new beginning. The division was not in all cases made at the most appropriate point. In Kings, for example, the division comes right in the middle of the history of Ahaziah and Jehoshaphat.

Second, in the Hebrew canon as it is still used by the Jews, the books of Joshua, Judges, Samuel, and Kings constitute the category of the so-called Former Prophets, in the Hebrew Bible following immediately after the Torah, while the books of Chronicles, Ezra, and Nehemiah belong to the last group of books, the Writings. In most manuscripts these last-named books conclude the series of Old Testament books, usually in the order Ezra, Nehemiah, Chronicles. This order would be particularly striking if originally these books had constituted one great work, as until recently was almost generally assumed. In the Septuagint (also of Jewish origin) all these books belong to the second group, the so-called historical books. With it are included Ruth and Esther as well as various apocryphal books. The Vulgate does the same. The division followed in this handbook thus deviates from the one most commonly used. It is appropriate, however, in light of the fact that we are considering the contents of the books.

Third, many believe that these books were originally part of a much larger whole. Already in the past century the idea arose that the sources of the Pentateuch (see section A) could also be traced in Joshua, so that we should speak not of a Pentateuch but of a Hexateuch. Later this theory was extended to include other books. Some, for example, have maintained that originally there was a work of nine parts (Enneateuch), which comprised the Torah, Joshua, Judges, Samuel, and Kings, and that it came into being through a highly complex process. Even today prominent scholars such as Fohrer assume that a single work originally included the Pentateuch, Joshua, and the beginning of Judges (according to most, to Judg. 2:5). Some of the arguments for this view are that the sources of the Pentateuch can also be detected in Joshua and the beginning of Judges and that it is inconceivable that those sources would not have described the settlement in Canaan that is their primary focus. Fohrer believes that the attempt to discover the Pentateuchal sources in the rest of Judges and in Samuel and Kings is unsuccessful; others believe that such is also the case in Joshua. In these parts the peculiarities of the various sources are not clearly in evidence, something shown already by the lack of unanimity in the distribution of the material over the various sources. Other objections against the hypothesis of a Hexateuch include the observations that (1) the book of Joshua is an integral whole, (2) the Jewish canon makes a clear separation between the Torah and the Former Prophets, and (3) the Samaritans accept only the Torah, which implies that the division between the Pentateuch and Joshua occurred before the Samaritan schism (an event, however, that is very difficult to date).

Currently the hypothesis by Martin Noth that the books of Deuteronomy through Kings constituted originally one great historical corpus, containing very ancient and highly diverse traditions that were constructed into an integral whole and set in a specific scheme, has many adherents (as well as many opponents). According to Noth, this work was composed after the destruction of Jerusalem (586 B.C.) by those who had not been carried into exile. Presumably it was written about 550, for the end of 2 Kings describes the favor shown to Jehoiachin in 561 B.C. The writer (or group of writers) added Deuteronomy 1:1–4:43 as an introduction. Later the work was again reworked in the same spirit, and eventually it was augmented by yet other additions. Because of the spirit it breathes, it is called the Deuteronomistic work of history (abbreviated Dtr, to distinguish it from Deuteronomy—D or Dt). The chief theme of this work is that Israel is the people of God and has the law of God. By keeping that law, it walks the way that leads to life, whereas disobedience to the law leads to death and destruction— it is a matter of blessing or curse. The history follows a fixed pattern: apostasy of the people, judgment, crying to God in repentance, God's showing mercy, and so on until the point of no return.

Opinions differ on the question whether this work, with the account of the pardon given Jehoiachin at the end, intends to say that there may still be a future, that there is still room for hope. There are also other differences among those who follow Noth's hypothesis. For instance, some scholars maintain that the major editing of the book happened before the Exile (see section 5). In my judgment compelling grounds can be adduced in favor of this hypothesis, though it must be acknowledged that important objections have been brought against it: the hand of Dtr is not equally clearly discernible (in Judges and Kings it can be seen, but only barely in Samuel); the style, which is repetitive, rhetorical, and solemnly admonishing, cannot always be detected; and the book of Joshua evidences connections with what comes before and what comes after but also constitutes a fairly integral whole. Those who strongly oppose Noth's hypothesis acknowledge that the parts that he suggests belong to Dtr do exhibit somewhat of a Deuteronomistic influence, which may also be an editorial influence. It seems best therefore to discuss Joshua, Judges, Samuel, and Kings as separate compositions.

Third, I have noted already that until recently it was almost unanimously assumed that Chronicles and Ezra-Nehemiah were originally one large corpus. Recently, however, this idea has been contested by a number of scholars (T. Willi, P. Welten, and especially S. Japhet). In defense of the original unity of these writings, reference is made to the great similarity in language, style, and ideas in both books (the focus is everywhere on the temple, the cult, the Levites, and the Davidic dynasty). For some, the fact that the conclusion of Chronicles is virtually identical with the beginning of Ezra is convincing (2 Chr. 36:22–23 and Ezra 1:1–3a). Many also appeal to the third book of Ezra (see section 7), which in its present form is then regarded as an edition of the chronistic work of history that is older than the edition on which the books of Chronicles and Ezra-Nehemiah are based. In 3 Ezra, the beginning of Ezra immediately follows the end of Chronicles. There are, however, altogether different ideas about 3 Ezra (see the contribution of J. Nelis in vol. 3).

In my opinion Japhet's explorations have seriously challenged the view that Chronicles and Ezra-Nehemiah originally constituted a single work. It is at least questionable whether there is such a great similarity in language and style. The two works use sources quite differently. It is also striking that in Ezra-Nehemiah the house of David barely plays a role; Zerubbabel is not said to be a descendant of David (nor is Nehemiah, assuming, as some believe, that he too was from David's lineage); and the book seems to be devoid of any messianic expectation. On the other hand, there are also great resemblances between the two books. At any rate, one will have to speak with greater restraint about their original unity than used to be the case.

LITERATURE

Introductions to the Old Testament:

B. S. Childs, *Introduction to the Old Testament as Scripture* (Philadelphia, 1979).

O. Eissfeldt, *The Old Testament: An Introduction* (New York, 1965).

(E. Sellin and) G. Fohrer, *Introduction to the Old Testament* (Nashville, 1968).

R. Smend, *Die Entstehung des Alten Testaments* (Stuttgart, 1978).

Th. C. Vriezen and A. S. van der Woude, *De literatuur van Oud-Israël* (Wassenaar, 1980⁶).

Other Works:

J. Bright, *A History of Israel* (Philadelphia, 1981³).

F. M. Cross, "The Themes of the Book of Kings and the Structure of the Deuteronomistic History," in *Canaanite Myth and Hebrew Epic* (Cambridge, MA, 1973), pp. 274-89.

O. Eissfeldt, *Hexateuch-Synopse* (Darmstadt, 1962).

J. H. Hayes and J. Maxwell Miller, eds., *Israelite and Judaean History* (Philadelphia, 1977).

S. Herrmann, *A History of Israel in Old Testament Times* (Philadelphia, 1975).

H. Jagersma, *A History of Israel in the Old Testament Period* (Philadelphia, 1983).

R. D. Nelson, *The Double Redaction of the Deuteronomistic History* (JSOT Supplement Series 18; Sheffield, 1981).

M. Noth, *Überlieferungsgeschichtliche Studien* I (Halle [Saale], 1943; Darmstadt, 1957²).

———, *The History of Israel* (New York, 1960²).

R. Smend, "Das Gesetz und die Völker. Ein Beitrag zur deuteronomistischen Redaktionsgeschichte," in H. W. Wolff, ed., *Probleme biblischer Theologie. Gerhard von Rad zum 70. Geburtstag* (Munich, 1971), pp. 494-504.

On Chronicles:

D. N. Freedman, "The Chronicler's Purpose," *CBQ* 23 (1961) 436-42.

S. Japhet, "The Supposed Common Authorship of Chronicles and Ezra-Nehemiah Investigated Anew," *VT* 18 (1968) 330-71.

———, *The Ideology of the Book of Chronicles and its Place in Biblical Thought* (Hebrew; Jerusalem, 1973; repr. 1977; see the review by Th. Willi in *Theologische Zeitschrift* 31 [1975] 109ff.).

J. D. Newsome, "Towards a New Understanding of the Chronicler and his Purposes," *JBL* 94 (1975) 201-17.

J. R. Porter, "Old Testament Historiography," in G. W. Anderson, ed., *Tradition and Interpretation* (Oxford, 1979), pp. 152-62.

P. Welten, *Geschichte und Geschichtsdarstellung in den Chronikbüchern* (WMANT 42; Neukirchen-Vluyn, 1973).

Th. Willi, *Die Chronik als Auslegung* (FRLANT 106; Göttingen, 1972).

H. G. M. Williamson, *Israel in the Book of Chronicles* (Cambridge, 1977).

2. JOSHUA

In the Massoretic text this book bears the heading "Joshua." It has this name in the Septuagint as well (using the Greek form "Jesus"). The Talmud (*Baba Bathra* 14b) also calls it "Joshua" and notes that "Joshua wrote his book and the last eight verses of the Torah." The book, however, is anonymous, and Joshua himself could not be its author: the narrative recounts his death (24:29–31), the occasionally used expression "to this day" (4:9; 5:9; etc.) presupposes that what is narrated happened sometime previously, and a verse such as 4:14 can hardly have been written by Joshua. In 5:6 (perhaps also in 5:1), eyewitnesses appear to be speaking, using first-person plural pronouns. Such references may indicate that old material has been included in the book, but perhaps the writer also wants to say only that he and his contemporaries belong to the same people that once invaded the land. The book describes the fulfillment of the promise first made to Abram (Gen. 12:2–3) and regularly repeated afterward. It describes the conquest and partition of the Promised Land—at least its central part, the Cisjordan. (The conquest and partition of Transjordan are narrated largely in the Torah.) In that respect the book connects closely with the Pentateuch. But the book also describes the beginning of the new era of life in the Promised Land. In that regard it is an introduction to Judges, Samuel, and Kings. In itself it is also an integral unity. At the most, one could ask whether Judges 1:1–2:5 was originally part of Joshua. Is that passage a better ending to the book than Joshua 24:29–33?

The book can be divided as follows:

1. Chapters 1–12, THE CONQUEST OF THE LAND

1	Introduction
2	The spies of Jericho
3–4	Crossing of the Jordan
5:1–12	Circumcision and Passover at Gilgal
5:13–6:27	Capture of Jericho
7:1–8:29	Achan's theft and the two attacks on Ai
8:30–35	Construction of altar and reading of the law from Mount Ebal
9	The Gibeonites' deception
10	Conquest of the south
11	Conquest of the north
12	List of defeated kings

2. Chapters 13–22, THE DIVISION OF THE LAND

13:1–7	Parts not conquered
13:8–33	Division of Transjordan
14–19	Division of Cisjordan
20	The cities of refuge
21	The Levitical cities
22	The return of the Transjordan tribes

3. Chapters 23–24, JOSHUA'S FAREWELL

23	Joshua's farewell address
24:1–28	Making of the covenant at Shechem
24:29–33	Joshua's death

The book appears to be a well-arranged whole. Closer scrutiny, however, discloses numerous flaws, including repetitions, unmistakable additions, and contradictions. For example, the text twice reports that Ai was put to the torch (8:19, 28); twice it is reported that the Gibeonites were made woodcutters and water carriers (9:21, 27); we read two times of the conquests in Transjordan (12:1–6; 13:8–13); 13:2–6a is apparently an insertion in Yahweh's words to Joshua; in 6:22–23 Rahab and her family are spared because of the oath sworn to her, but in v. 25 she is spared because of her having hidden the spies; according to 10:38–39 Joshua took Debir, but according to 15:15–17 Othniel captured it; some cities seem to have been assigned to more than one tribe (see, e.g., Beth-hoglah in both 15:6 and 18:22); and it is particularly difficult to determine the relationship between what is recorded in chapter 23 and chapter 24.

It is generally assumed that the book has had a very complex compositional history, but there is no consensus about the course of that history. In section 1 above I mentioned two main views; however, there is much disagreement among the advocates of each view. For example, the adherents of the first view differ on the distribution of the material over the sources (the divine names cannot be used as a criterion). Generally the difficulty of recognizing the sources is attributed to the Dtr editing (or even two editings) of the book. Virtually all scholars are agreed that there are many traces of Dtr in Joshua (e.g., chs. 1, 12, and 23 as well as numerous separate verses or remarks). The second Dtr editing would have been very drastic (in ch. 24, for example).

There is also great disagreement about the historical value of the narratives in Joshua. As concerns chapters 1–12, particularly due to Alt's influence many have adopted the view that historically the rapid conquest of just about all of Canaan by all of Israel is impossible. Advocates of this position maintain that various groups slowly and for the most part peacefully invaded the land and settled there, initially in the less important areas, generally not in the plains or the fortified cities, of which perhaps some by a ruse fell into their hands (note the portrayal at the beginning of Judges). The stories in Joshua 2–9 were supposedly originally etiological tales, told to explain the origin of the Benjamite sanctuary in Gilgal and the origin of conspicuous things in Gilgal and surroundings, such as a heap of stones, a Canaanite house, or a ruin. Later, so the theory goes, these stories became connected with certain reports about military activities in the south and north and so became a conquest tale of all of Cisjordan by all of Israel; at that time the stories were also connected with the Ephraimite Joshua (24:29–30).

Albright and his pupils (esp. Bright) take a fairly skeptical stand toward this notion, including the idea of the etiological story in Joshua. They believe that excavations have demonstrated that many places in the Holy Land were destroyed at the end of the thirteenth century and later were rebuilt in a manner indicating a typically Israelite culture. In some cases the excavations have led to results that cast doubt on the historicity of the stories in Joshua (e.g., those at Jericho and Ai). In any case, Albright and his followers believe that there was a real conquest of the land, though perhaps at a slower pace than is intimated in Joshua.

It used to be generally assumed that chapters 13–22 were based on theoretical constructions of P. Following Alt, many today are of the opinion that these documents are based on especially two sources: a very incomplete system of tribal boundaries from the time of the judges and a list of places of the kingdom of Judah according to its division into twelve districts from the time of Josiah (according to some, of Jehoshaphat). Some hold that Joshua 24, though having had a Deuteronomistic editing, is based upon a much older document that told the story of the assembly in Shechem, where the twelve tribes entered into a covenant to serve Yahweh.

Possibly the compositional history of the book was not finished until shortly before or even during the Babylonian exile. As I have noted previously, though, Joshua clearly has preserved some old material (cf., e.g., the reference to Jerusalem in 15:63 with 2 Sam. 5:6–8 and the reference to Gezer in Josh. 16:10 with 1 Kgs. 9:16). In Joshua 10:13 reference is made to the "Book of the Upright" (cf. 2 Sam. 1:18; according to the Septuagint in 1 Kgs. 8:53, Solomon's prayer at the dedication of the temple was also included in this book). Perhaps the book was a collection of national songs.

In its present form the book of Joshua begins with a renewal of the promise of the land (1:1–4) and ends with the observation that the promise has been fulfilled (24:8–18). Heavy emphasis falls on the fact that the promise was God's grace to Israel and also that its fulfillment was the work of Yahweh (see vv. 12–13). Regularly the history also shows that it was not Israel that conquered the land but Yahweh (1:2; note the collapsing walls of Jericho, the sun that stood still, etc.). On the other hand it emphasizes that the fulfillment was not unconditional but conditional: Israel must be faithful to Yahweh (1:6–8; 8:30–35; 22:1–5; chs. 23–24). Such references indicate that the major editing of the book seems to have happened not long before or shortly after the demise of the kingdom of Judah, when, according to the history writers and the prophets, Israel was spiritually deeply corrupt and the great catastrophe was approaching or had just happened.

LITERATURE

Commentaries:

R. G. Boling, *Joshua* (AB; Garden City, NY, 1975).

J. Gray, *Joshua, Judges, Ruth* (New Century Bible; London/Grand Rapids, 1986²).

H. W. Hertzberg, *Die Bücher Josua, Richter, Ruth* (ATD 9; Göttingen, 1974⁵).

M. Noth, *Das Buch Josua* (HAT I/7; Tübingen, 1953²).

J. A. Soggin, *Joshua* (OTL; Philadelphia, 1972).

M. Woudstra, *The Book of Joshua* (NICOT; Grand Rapids, 1981).

Other Works:

A. Alt, *Schriften zur Geschichte des Volkes Israel* I-II (München, 1953) (see especially I: 89-125, 126-75, 176-92, 193-202; II: 276-88, 289-305).

A. G. Auld, *Joshua, Moses and the Land. Tetrateuch-Pentateuch-Hexateuch in a Generation since 1938* (Edinburgh, 1980).

J. Bright, *Early Israel in Recent History Writing* (London, 1956).

E. Jenni, "Zwei Jahrzehnte Forschung an den Büchern Josua bis Könige," *Theologische Rundschau* 27 (1961) 1-32, 97-146.

D. J. McCarthy, "The Theology of Leadership in Joshua 1–9," *Bibl* 52 (1971) 165-75.

M. Weippert, *The Settlement of the Israelite Tribes in Palestine* (Naperville, 1971).

S. Yeivin, *The Israelite Conquest of Canaan* (Leiden, 1971).

3. JUDGES

In the Massoretic text this book is called *shophe-tim.* The Septuagint renders this word as *kritai* and the Vulgate as *iudices,* both words meaning "judges." The Hebrew verb and noun *judge* can have a wider meaning than "(one to) administer justice." The noun can also designate a ruler, regent, helper, or deliverer.

The word *judge* is used generally only in 2:16–19 and in 11:27 (the latter in reference to God). In 3:9 Othniel is called a deliverer, and in verse 15 the same word is used for Ehud. The verb *judge* is not used for all "major" judges, though it is applied to all "minor" judges. The so-called major judges Othniel, Ehud, Shamgar (who actually stands somewhat apart; likely he was a non-Israelite from Beth-anath, house of [the goddess] Anath; see Josh. 19:38; Judg. 1:33), Deborah/Barak, Gideon, Jephthah, and Samson do not look much like holders of a fixed office; they are much more charismatic leaders who were instrumental in providing much-needed help in a certain area and who afterward likely enjoyed high esteem, perhaps even being acknowledged as leaders. It is different with the so-called minor judges, or Tolah, Jair, Ibzan, Elon, and Abdon. One gets the impression that they occupied a specific function that concerned all of Israel. Their residence, length of office, and funeral are mentioned. Actually Jephthah (see 12:7) and Samson (16:31) and perhaps also Gideon occur in both lists. Likely they had a fixed office, while in an emergency situation they also acted as charismatic leaders. This dual function may have been the reason that the detailed stories about the major judges have been combined with the more chronological information about the minor judges. The Talmud (*Baba Bathra* 14b) mentions that Samuel wrote "his own book, Judges and Ruth." Much of the evidence that we have argues against such an assertion.

The book of Judges is on the one hand closely associated with Joshua (cf. 1:1 with Josh. 24:29–30), while on the other hand it serves as a preparation for Samuel, which narrates the origin of the monarchy and the rule of the first kings. Judges describes the period between the settlement in the land and the origin of the actual state. The book is, however, also an integral whole, which in the framework of a particular thematic construction (apostasy, oppression, cry to Yahweh, raising up of a deliverer, deliverance, period of rest) describes a portion of Israel's history. The book consists of three parts: (1) the introduction (Judg. 1:1–3:6), with two distinct divisions—1:1–2:5 and 2:6–3:6; (2) the judges (3:7–16:31), containing stories and information about Othniel, Ehud, Shamgar, Barak and Deborah, Gideon, Abimelech, Tola, Jair, Jephthah, Ibzan, Elon, Abdon, and Samson; and (3) two appendixes (chs. 17–21), the first concerning the establishment of a sanctuary at Dan (chs. 17–18), the second concerning the outrageous act of the Benjamites and their punishment (chs. 19–21).

This survey makes it clear that the book is composed according to a particular outline. A cursory reading, however, reveals that the book is not a systematic, coherent, and logical whole and that it too must have had a complex compositional history. The stories about the major judges constitute the core of the present book. Those stories are placed in a certain setting or framework (see, e.g., 3:7–11; 4:1–3, 24; 5:31b; 6:1–2, 7–10; 8:28). In the second introduction (2:6–3:6) this framework is described; it can certainly be called Deuteronomistic. One of the final editions of Judges must thus have been a Dtr editing, made shortly before or not long after the great catastrophe of 586 B.C. The editor (or editors) must have had at his disposal a variety of material, perhaps even a preliminary version of the present book of Judges.

It is likely that the stories about the major judges, who were active on behalf of certain tribes or districts, were initially orally transmitted in their own environment and perhaps also recorded in writing there. Of certain stories it seems likely that there existed more than one tradition. In the Deborah and Barak story, for example, we have a song in chapter 5 (which must be very old) and also a prose story in chapter 4; in one Gideon story, the hero's name is Gideon and he defeats the Midianites, but in a second account his name is Jerubbaal and he defeats Zebah and Zalmunna. When the tribes who at first lived very much on their own became more of a unity, these histories became stories of all of Israel. The brief reports about the minor judges were likely derived from lists or annals. They are not placed in a specific framework.

The two appendixes contain no traces of a Dtr editing, but the first account incorporated into them—the story of the shrine at Dan—breathes very much the Deuteronomistic spirit (see the continuous protest in Kings against the cult on the high places of Jeroboam). The two stories contained in the appendixes constitute a particularly good conclusion to Judges. They aptly describe the time of the judges.

The favorable evaluation of the monarchy in both appendixes (17:6; 18:1; 19:1; 21:25) is remarkable. This feature suggests that the stories, which for other reasons must be ancient, were written down in the time of David or Solomon (or later, as in the case of 18:29–30). Elsewhere in Judges the monarchy is mentioned as well (8:22–27; ch. 9). The question can be asked whether various views about kingship are presented, as in Samuel, or whether the concern is the kingship and the king willed by Yahweh.

The first introduction to the book presents great problems (1:1–2:5). In part this piece has parallels in Joshua (see, e.g., 1:10–15 and Josh. 15:13–19; Judg. 1:21 and Josh. 15:63 [but note the difference!]; Judg. 1:28 and Josh. 17:13; Judg. 1:29 and Josh. 16:10) and in any case contains old material (cf. Judg. 1:21 with 2 Sam. 5:6–8 [see, however, Judg. 1:1–7] and 1:29 with 1 Kgs. 9:15–17). According to some scholars, this first introduction is the extract of the story of the settlement in Canaan from one of the sources of the Pentateuch (e.g., J), a story that would be more in agreement with the actual facts than that recorded in Joshua. There are, however, several arguments against such a view, such as the very beginning of 1:1 ("after the death of Joshua"). Others, therefore, have contested the antiquity and reliability of this first introduction (see Auld). The introduction does have a specific function in Judges. It explains why Israel was so easily seduced to apostasy, attributing it to the numerous heathen peoples that remained living in its midst.

The numbers in the book of Judges pose problems. They give the impression that the period of the judges lasted more than 400 years, whereas it was likely only half as long. It is often asserted that these figures are artificial and have been harmonized with the 480 years in 1 Kings 6:1, but this view can be maintained only by resorting to dubious interpretations. The problems may perhaps be partially solved by assuming that the activities of some of the judges in part or completely overlapped. So Judges 10:7 says that Yahweh gave the Israelites into the hands of the Philistines and of the Ammonites, whereas Jephthah acts alone against the Ammonites and Samson against the Philistines. It is thus possible that the period of oppression and the deeds of deliverance of both judges in part or completely overlapped.

In Judges the entire course of Israel's history is traced back to Yahweh. He uses other peoples to chastise Israel and to call it back to himself; he raises up deliverers and gives deliverance. Particularly this last element is frequently stressed: not Gideon with his army (a force eventually of only three hundred men), but Yahweh drives away the enemies. Furthermore, the specific interpretative accent follows the Dtr scheme. Perhaps it is significant that no period of rest is mentioned after Jephthah's ministry, while when Samson becomes judge under the Philistine domination, no crying of the people to Yahweh is recorded. Perhaps the editor intends to indicate a gradual worsening in Israel's spiritual condition. This observation in turn suggests that the book of Judges may have received its present form when the downfall of the people as an independent nation either was very close or had become a fact— that is, shortly before or during the time of the Babylonian captivity.

LITERATURE

Commentaries:

R. G. Boling, *Judges* (AB; Garden City, NY, 1975).

J. Gray, *Joshua, Judges, Ruth* (New Century Bible; London/Grand Rapids, 1986[2]).

H. W. Hertzberg, *Die Bücher Josua, Richter, Ruth* (ATD 9; Göttingen, 1974[5]).

G. F. Moore, *A Critical and Exegetical Commentary on Judges* (ICC; Edinburgh, 1895).

J. A. Soggin, *Judges* (OTL; Philadelphia, 1981).

Other Works:

A. G. Auld, "Judges 1 and History: A Reconsideration," *VT* 25 (1975) 261-85.

W. Beyerlin, "Gattung und Herkunft des Rahmens im Richterbuch," in E. Würthwein and O. Kaiser, eds.,

Tradition und Situation (Festschrift A. Weiser; Göttingen, 1963), pp. 1-30.

A. D. H. Mayes, *Judges* (OT Guides; Sheffield, 1985).

————, *The Story of Israel between Settlement and Exile* (London, 1983).

W. Richter, *Die Bearbeitungen des "Retterbuches" in der deuteronomischen Epoche* (BBB 21; Bonn, 1964).

————, *Traditionsgeschichtliche Untersuchungen zum Richterbuch* (BBB 18; Bonn, 1966²).

L. Schmidt, *Menschlicher Erfolg und Jahwes Initiative. Studien zu Tradition, Interpretation und Historie in Überlieferungen von Gideon, Saul und David* (WMANT 38; Neukirchen-Vluyn, 1970).

---

4. SAMUEL

In the Massoretic text as well as in the English this book is called Samuel. The Talmud (*Baba Bathra* 15a) mentions that Samuel wrote this book and that Gad and Nathan continued it. This comment likely alludes to 1 Chronicles 29:29, which as such need not be a reference to the book of Samuel. The final editing of the book must have been done considerably later than the events described in it (see, e.g., 1 Sam. 27:6, which presupposes a number of Judean kings).

The book fits in well both with Judges and with Kings. It describes the period between the events described in those books: the origin of the monarchy, the unification of the people, and the beginning of Israel's age of prosperity under David. Samuel can be divided as follows:

1. 1 Samuel 1:1–7:1, ELI AND SAMUEL

1–3	Samuel's youth
4:1–7:1	The ark in the land of the Philistines

2. 1 Samuel 7:2–15:35, SAMUEL AND SAUL

7:2–17	Samuel as judge
8–11	Saul becomes king
12	Samuel's farewell
13–14	Saul's wars
15	Saul rejected

3. 1 Samuel 16–31, SAUL AND DAVID

16	David anointed and at the court
17	David and Goliath
18–30	Saul's hatred of David and David's flight from Saul
31	Death of Saul and Jonathan

4. 2 Samuel 1–8, DAVID AS KING

1	David's lament over Saul and Jonathan
2:1–7	David established as king over Judah
2:8–4:12	David, Ishbosheth, and Abner
5	David king over all of Israel
6	The ark brought to Jerusalem
7	David, Nathan, and the building of the temple
8	David's victories

5. 2 Samuel 9:1–21:14, DAVID AND HIS SONS AND THE HOUSE OF SAUL

9	David and Mephibosheth
10–12	David and Bathsheba
13	Amnon, Absalom, and Tamar
14–19	David and Absalom
20	Sheba's rebellion
21:1–14	David and the Gibeonites

6. 2 Samuel 21:15–24:25, APPENDIXES

21:15–22	David's heroes in the war with the Philistines
22	David's song of thanksgiving
23:1–7	David's last words
23:8–39	David's heroes
24	David's census of the people

The observation made earlier with respect to Joshua and Judges is also appropriate here. On the one hand, the narrative seems to be continuous and the book more or less a unity; on the other hand, all sorts of duplications, contradictions, and variations in viewpoint can be noticed, especially in the history of Saul. Such is the case in the stories that narrate how he became king. At one time the institution of the monarchy appears as God's initiative; then again it seems to clash with the will of God (cf. 1 Samuel 9 and 10:1–16 with ch. 8 and 10:18–20). Saul is designated and anointed by Samuel (9:1–10:16), but at the same time he is chosen by lot (10:17–24). At one time Saul seems a tragic figure who perishes because God's Spirit leaves him; at another time his downfall is portrayed as the result of his own disobedience. His rejection is told twice (13:11–14; 15:24–29); twice David spares Saul's life (chs. 24 and 26). According to 16:14–23, David comes to Saul's court; in 17:55–58, however, Saul does not know him. Some are of the opinion that the author(s) of the book used two or three sets of stories or sources; others think of a collection of individual stories. The author(s) did not smooth out the seams between these narratives out of respect for the material he found.

It has rightly been pointed out that the apparently conflicting stories presuppose each other (cf., e.g., 1 Sam. 10:27 with 11:12–15). The notorious contradiction between 2 Samuel 21:19 and 1 Samuel 17 (see also 1 Chr. 20:5) over who killed Goliath is perhaps not as great a problem as is sometimes thought. There is good reason to suppose that the text of 2 Samuel 21:19 is corrupt and is to be changed in accordance with 1 Chronicles 20:5. Some lists and chroniclelike pieces of information, such as 2 Samuel 3:2–5; 5:13–16; 8:1–4, 15–18; 20:23–26; 23:8–39, and songs, such as in 1 Samuel 2:1–10 and 2 Samuel 22:3–51, must have been independent units. Likely the author of Samuel derived part of it from the national archive.

Especially since a study by L. Rost in 1926, many rightly maintain that 2 Samuel 9–1 Kings 2 (except for 2 Samuel 21–24 and some lists) has incorporated virtually unchanged a "history of throne succession," a lively and reliable narrative about David's succession to the throne, written by a contemporary. Presumably the intent of this story is to show that Solomon is David's legitimate successor. The sins of David and his house are certainly not swept under the rug, perhaps in an attempt to defend David's house against various objections to the effect that he and his house could not possibly be the lawful kings, willed by God, in view of the many great sins that were known of him. Others have defended the notion that the story is directed against David and Solomon. In any case, this history speaks almost exclusively about human activities (not always the best ones!), miracles do not happen, and human acts of expediency and deceit are central. Neverthe-

less, it is clearly evident that, for the writer, history is guided by Yahweh in spite of all human folly (2 Sam. 17:14; cf. 12:14). A variety of contemporaries of David, familiar from the Old Testament, have been mentioned as author of this history: Ahimaaz (15:27, 36; 17:17; etc.), Hushai (15:32–37; 16:16–19), and Nathan's son Zabud (1 Kgs. 4:5, in connection with 1 Chr. 29:29); but all such ideas are no more than conjecture.

According to some, 1 Samuel 16:14–2 Samuel 7:29 (with sizable exceptions, such as 1 Samuel 17) may have belonged to the above-mentioned writing. Not only do these chapters mention the same persons that appear beginning in 2 Samuel 9 (e.g., Joab and Abiathar), but this latter section also presupposes knowledge of 1 Samuel 16 and following. 2 Samuel 9, 16, and 19 assume familiarity with the history of David and Jonathan. If this conception is correct, it would make it very clear that the concern of this writing is the legitimacy of David's kingship and that of his house (see also 2 Samuel 7). David is no usurper. He and his house did not obtain the throne because they wrested it from Saul and his house; the guidance of Yahweh in the history of his people gave them the throne. Finally, it is possible that 1 Samuel 1–3 is derived from a writing in which Samuel's youth was related. Chapters 4–6 may have been derived from a "history of the ark," to which also 2 Samuel 6–7 may have belonged.

The present book of Samuel is thus based on a variety of writings, some of which may be from the time that is recounted in them. These writings were incorporated into the text without drastic changes. There are traces of a Dtr editing in Samuel (e.g., in 1 Samuel 7, 12, and 2 Samuel 7), but they are not numerous. The close coherence between 2 Samuel and 1 Kings 1–2 may indicate that originally Samuel and Kings belonged to one large book. As such it is possible that Samuel in its present form may have largely originated in the period of the kings. (A gloss such as 1 Sam. 9:9, for example, is a later insertion explaining the word *seer*, which had only recently come into use; cf. Isa. 29:10).

The text of Samuel has been badly transmitted. The Septuagint (esp. in codex B), deviates considerably from the Massoretic text. The Hebrew text of the fragments of Samuel discovered at Qumran is closer to the Septuagint than to the Massoretic text, but it is not identical with the sources on which the Septuagint must have been based. Scholars disagree about how to explain the differences.

LITERATURE

Commentaries:

S. R. Driver, *Notes on the Hebrew Text and Topography of the Books of Samuel* (Oxford, 1913).

H. W. Hertzberg, *I & II Samuel* (OTL; Philadelphia, 1964).

P. K. McCarter, *I Samuel* (AB; Garden City, NY, 1980).

————, *II Samuel* (AB; Garden City, NY, 1984).

H. J. Stoebe, *Das erste Buch Samuelis* (KAT VIII/1; Gütersloh, 1973).

Other Works:

B. C. Birch, *The Rise of the Israelite Monarchy. The Growth and Development of 1 Samuel 7–15* (Missoula, MT, 1976).

J. Blenkinsopp, "Theme and Motif in the Succession History (2 Sam. XI 2ff.) and the Yahwist Corpus," in SVT 15 (1965) 44-57.

H. J. Boecker, *Die Beurteilung der Anfänge des Königtums in den deuteronomistischen Abschnitten des 1. Samuelbuches. Ein Beitrag zum Problem des deuteronomistischen Geschichtswerks* (WMANT 31; Neukirchen-Vluyn, 1969).

A. F. Campbell, *The Ark Narrative (1 Sam 4–6; 2 Sam 6). A Form-Critical and Traditio-Historical Study* (Missoula, MT, 1975).

R. A. Carlson, *David, the Chosen King. A Traditio-Historical Approach to the Second Book of Samuel* (Stockholm, 1964).

C. Conroy, *Absalom, Absalom! Narrative and Language in 2 Sam. 13–20* (Rome, 1978).

F. Crüsemann, *Der Widerstand gegen das Königtum. Die antiköniglichen Texte des Alten Testaments und der Kampf um den frühen israelitischen Staat* (WMANT 49; Neukirchen-Vluyn, 1978).

O. Eissfeldt, *Die Komposition der Samuelisbücher* (Leipzig, 1931).

R. P. Gordon, *1 & 2 Samuel* (OT Guides; Sheffield, 1984).

J. H. Grønbaek, *Die Geschichte vom Aufstieg Davids* (Copenhagen, 1971).

D. M. Gunn, *The Fate of King Saul. An Interpretation of a Biblical Story* (JSOT Supplement Series 14; Sheffield, 1980).

————, *The Story of King David. Genre and Interpretation* (JSOT Supplement Series 6; Sheffield, 1978).

P. D. Miller and J. J. M. Roberts, *The Hand of the Lord. A Reassessment of the "Ark Narrative" of 1 Samuel* (Baltimore, 1977).

L. Rost, *Die Überlieferung von der Thronnachfolge Davids* (BWANT III/6; Stuttgart, 1926).

E. C. Ulrich, *The Qumran Text of Samuel and Josephus* (Missoula, MT, 1978).

J. Van Seters, "Problems in the Literary Analysis of the Court History," *JSOT* 1 (1976) 22-28.

T. Veijola, *Das Königtum in der Beurteilung der deuteronomistichen Historiographie. Eine redaktionsgeschichtliche Untersuchung* (Helsinki, 1977).

————, *Die ewige Dynastie. David und die Entstehung seiner Dynastie nach der deuteronomistischen Darstellung* (Helsinki, 1975).

A. Weiser, *Samuel. Seine geschichtliche Aufgabe und religiöse Bedeutung* (FRLANT 81; Göttingen, 1962).

————, "Die Legitimation des Königs David. Zur Eigenart und Entstehung der sogen. Geschichte von Davids Aufstieg," *VT* 16 (1966) 325-54.

R. N. Whybray, *The Succession History: A Study of II Samuel 9–20; 1 Kings 1 and 2* (London, 1968).

E. Würthwein, *Die Erzählung von der Thronnachfolge Davids: theologische oder politische Geschichtsschreibung?* (Zürich, 1974).

---

5. KINGS

In the Massoretic text the heading of these books is *melakim*, "kings." According to Jewish and Christian tradition, Jeremiah presumably wrote this book as well as Kings and Lamentations (*Baba Bathra* 15a). This tradition is devoid of historical value.

The book describes that part of Israel's history dealing with the reign of Solomon and the kings of Israel and Judah. The writer indeed intended to record history (at least in some sense), which is evident from the fact that generally he follows the chronological sequence. After dealing with the rule of a particular king in the one kingdom, he relates the reign of all the kings of the other kingdom who were contemporary with him. Even so, the author does not intend to offer "ordinary" history. Such an aim is shown, for instance, by the fact that he records very little about certain kings who, as we know from extrabiblical data, played an important role in the region (the clearest example is Omri of Israel). For other kings the author offers a rather one-sided picture (a good example is Ahab).

The author pictures the events from a particular viewpoint: the attitude of the kings (and thereby of the people) toward the service of Yahweh, particularly toward his commandments, his prophets, and the cult ordained by him. The writer deals extensively with these matters, to the extent that his sources provided the material. The book can be divided into three parts:

1. 1 Kings 1–11,
THE RULE OF SOLOMON

1–2	Solomon becomes king and removes his opponents
3–4	Prayer for wisdom, Solomon's wise judgment, ordering of the kingdom, Solomon's greatness
5–7	Building of temple and palace
8	Prayer at the dedication of the temple
9–10	Solomon's trade and wealth
11	His idolatry and his enemies

2. 1 Kings 12–2 Kings 17,
THE KINGS OF ISRAEL AND JUDAH

12:1–24	The schism of the realm
12:25–14:20	Institution of bull worship at Bethel and Dan, denouncement by the prophets
14:21–16:34	Kings Rehoboam, Abijah, and Asa (all of Judah); Nadab, Baasha, Elah, Zimri, Omri, and Ahab (all of Israel)
17:1–2 Kings 2:18	Elijah and Ahab, Elijah and Ahaziah (Israel), Elijah's ascension
2:19–8:15	Miracles of Elisha, Elisha and the campaign of Joram (Israel) and Jehoshaphat (Judah) against Moab, Elisha and the Shunammite woman, Elisha and Naaman, Elisha at the siege of Samaria
8:16–17:6	Kings Jehoram and Ahaziah (Judah); Jehu (Israel); Queen Athaliah (Judah); Kings Joash (Judah), Jehoahaz and Jehoash (Israel), Amaziah (Judah), Jeroboam II (Israel), Azariah/Uzziah (Judah), and Zechariah, Shallum, Menahem, Pekahiah, and Pekah (all Israel), Jotham (Judah), Hoshea (Israel); end of the northern kingdom
17:7–41	Retrospective look at Israel's history; the Samaritans

3. 2 Kings 18–25,
THE KINGS OF JUDAH

18–20	Hezekiah's reform, Hezekiah and Sennacherib, Hezekiah and Isaiah, Hezekiah's illness
21	Manasseh and Amon
22:1–23:30	Josiah's discovery of the book of the law, the great reform, the Passover celebration, Josiah's death at Megiddo
23:31–24:17	Kings Jehoahaz, Jehoiakim, and Jehoiachin
24:18–25:26	Zedekiah, the end of the kingdom of Judah, Gedaliah
25:27–30	Favor shown to Jehoiachin

Jepsen in particular has defended the view that Kings originated gradually. Most scholars, however, believe that the present book, with the exception of some later glosses, was partially or in toto written by one author (or a group of authors) at a specific time. (Some see the last part of Kings and some other sections arising from a later redactor.) One might also call the writer of the book a compiler, since he used many sources from which he copied large sections, leaving them virtually unchanged.

The unity of authorship is based on two facts in particular: (1) the same themes occur throughout the whole book, involving king and prophet, which are the themes of Deuteronomy (recall, for instance, the continuous protest in Kings against the cult on the high places), and (2) the formulas with which the reign of virtually every king is introduced and concluded constitute the grid of the book. The wording of all these formulas is identical or nearly so. Usually they contain: (a) a synchronism with the king of the other kingdom (in year such and such of X, king of Judah [Israel], Y became king of Israel [Judah]); (b) the length of reign; (c) the place of residence; and (d) an evaluation. The accounts of the kings of Judah also mention (e) age when ascending the throne and (f) name of the queen-mother and sometimes the place from which she came. In the evaluation, the writer always condemns the kings of Israel for their committing the sins of Jeroboam, the son of Nebat; only Joram (2 Kgs. 3:2) and Hoshea (17:2) receive a somewhat more favorable evaluation. Of the kings of Judah, only the judgment of Hezekiah and Josiah is totally favorable. Asa, Jehoshaphat, Joash, Amaziah, Azariah, and Jotham are judged positively with some reservations; all others are judged unfavorably.

The concluding formula (a) refers to a source, sometimes with a comment about the content of the source; (b) mentions death and burial; and (c) identifies the successor. In cases where the formula is absent, there is often a ready explanation, for example, with Hoshea (2 Kgs. 17:6), Jehoahaz (23:34), Jehoiachin (24:17), and Zedekiah (ch. 25). No concluding formula is found with the last two kings, because they were carried into exile. It is remarkable that 1 Kings 14:22 in the Septuagint reads Rehoboam instead of Judah, so that even Rehoboam is not left without an appraisal.

The final event recorded in the book is the favor shown to Jehoiachin (561 B.C.), a long time after the deportation in 586 (and that of 597, mentioned in 2 Kgs. 24:14–17). According to many scholars, this information cannot be used to date the book with certainty, because they regard 25:27–30 (according to some, also vv. 22–26) as a later addition or attribute it to the final redactor who augmented and continued the book. Some are of the opinion that Kings was written during the reign of one of the last kings of Judah, for example, under Josiah, who radically abolished the worship on the high places, or still later under Jehoiakim or Zedekiah. An additional argument in favor of a preexilic dating is the expression "to the present day" (1 Kgs. 8:8; 9:20–21; 12:19; 2 Kgs. 8:22), which presupposes the existence of the temple and the kingdom of Judah.

Others consider it possible that the author derived this expression from one of his sources. They believe that the purpose of Kings is to demonstrate that the downfall of the royal house and the nation was due to their continued disobedience to Yahweh. Therefore they date the book shortly after the catastrophe of 586 B.C. Much is to be said in favor of this view, but also in that case the last verses are to be regarded as a later addition. Proponents of this view assume that the book was written in Judah, thus by someone not carried off into captivity. Some maintain that the writer was from a northern Israelite family, noting his great interest in the kingdom of the ten tribes and in the prophets who labored there (see 1 Kings 13 as well as the accounts of Ahijah, Elijah, and Elisha).

The writer mentions three sources from which he drew: "the Book of the Acts of Solomon" (1 Kgs. 11:41); "the Book of the Chronicles of the Kings of Israel" (14:19; 15:31; etc.); and "the Book of the Chronicles of the Kings of Judah" (14:29; 15:23; etc.). He refers to his source for something he does not narrate, though sometimes briefly mentioning it (14:19; 15:23; 16:27; 2 Kgs. 20:20; etc.). Yet it seems certain that he made use of those sources. One gets the impression that they were a kind of annals, brief notations of the most important events during the king's reign, similar to the royal annals of the Assyrian and Babylonian kings. Perhaps the source about Solomon contained some more detail (1 Kgs. 11:41 mentions his wisdom). It seems doubtful that the author was able to use official national or court annals. He refers to his sources, which seems to indicate that his readers must have been able to consult them, scarcely a possibility with the national annals.

The author must also have used a variety of other sources, for his book contains much more than reports derived from annals. For various lists (such as 1 Kgs. 4:1–20) he was likely able to make use of official documents. Accounts such as the one about the division of the realm (ch. 12), Ahab's war against Ramoth-gilead (ch. 22), Jehu's kingship (2 Kings 9–10), and the like must have been derived from old historical sources. The description of the construction of the temple is probably based on a document preserved in the temple archives. The stories about the prophets, such as about Elijah and Elisha, have a character all their own. They are a separate kind of literature, the so-called prophetic legend. This designation is confusing, because it wrongly suggests that they contain no actual history whatever. The author used and sometimes edited all this material but in large part he incorporated it unchanged in his book. He mentions no sources with it, since he refers to sources only in the case of material he has not included in his book.

From the time of Omri (ca. 875 B.C.), we are fairly well able to fit the history of Israel into that of the surrounding world. Various kings of Israel and Judah are mentioned in extrabiblical texts, especially Assyrian and Babylonian. It thus is possible to calculate the approximate years of their reigns. Such can hardly be done on the basis of data in Kings and Chronicles, since these numbers often seem contradictory. Allowance must be made for errors in the transmission of the text (errors are particularly easy to make with dates). We know of a few coregencies (e.g., Azariah and Jotham [2 Kgs. 15:5]); in some cases—Hezekiah, for example—there may have been a regency, although we do not know how in such cases the length of a reign was calculated. It is also unknown from which moment the first year of a new king was calculated. Moreover, practices may have changed over time within Israel and also Judah, and there are other uncertainties. By using extrabiblical data, however, we can arrive at a fairly accurate chronology of the era of the kings, the more so because we know the exact date of certain events.

In general the Hebrew text of Kings has been accurately transmitted. One problem is that, in 1 Kings 3–12, the Septuagint deviates considerably from the Massoretic text. In chapter 2 (after vv. 35 and 46) and in chapter 12 (after v. 24), it has verses that in part are absent from the Massoretic text and in part are distributed over chapters 2–11, at which places they sometimes recur in the Septuagint. The text of the fragments of Kings that were discovered in Caves 5 and 6 of Qumran does not agree entirely with the Massoretic text. It is likely that various forms of the text were in circulation before a standard text was established.

I have mentioned briefly the theology of Kings. It is the typical Deuteronomistic theology (see section 1). The constant disobedience of Israel and its kings, including that of the Davidic dynasty, issues eventually in the destruction of both kingdoms. The king and his people share the blame for this catastrophe, for in Kings there is a close connection between the two; the sins of the king are also imputed to the people and vice versa. Yahweh shares no blame, for his words, spoken by his prophets, were fulfilled (1 Kgs. 8:56; 15:29; 16:12, 34; 2 Kgs. 1:17; 10:10; 23:16). The author's purpose with his book is to bring the people to their senses and to call them to repentance. Such an aim makes it likely that he still saw a place, and entertained hope, for his people; note the conclusion of the book and 1 Kings 8:46–53, and also the fact that, in the history of Solomon, Nathan's promise to David (2 Samuel 7) is quoted several times literally or more freely (1 Kgs. 2:4; 3:6; 8:25; 9:4–5). This theme might be called the messianic perspective of the book.

LITERATURE

Commentaries:

H. A. Brongers, *I Koningen* (POT; Nijkerk, 1979²).

———, *II Koningen* (POT; Nijkerk, 1982²).

J. Gray, *I & II Kings* (OTL; Philadelphia, 1980³).

G. H. Jones, *1 and 2 Kings* I-II (New Century Bible; London/Grand Rapids, 1984).

J. A. Montgomery and H. S. Gehman, *A Critical and Exegetical Commentary on the Books of Kings* (ICC; Edinburgh, 1951).

M. Noth, *Könige 1–16* (BKAT IX/1; Neukirchen-Vluyn, 1968).

A. Šanda, *Die Bücher der Könige übersetzt und erklärt* I-II (Münster, 1911-12).

E. Würthwein, *Die Bücher der Könige. 1 Könige 1–16* (ATD 11/1; Göttingen, 1985²).

———, *Die Bücher der Könige. 1. Kön. 17– 2. Kön. 25* (ATD 11/2; Göttingen, 1984).

Other Works:

W. Dietrich, *Prophetie und Geschichte. Eine redaktionsgeschichtliche Untersuchung zum deuteronomistischen Geschichtswerk* (FRLANT 108; Göttingen, 1972).

G. Fohrer, *Elia* (Zürich, 1968²).

V. Fritz, *Tempel und Zelt. Studien zum Tempelbau in Israel und zu dem Zeltheiligtum der Priesterschrift* (WMANT 47; Neukirchen, 1977).

A. Jepsen, *Die Quellen des Königsbuches* (Halle/Saale, 1956²).

A. Jepsen and R. Hanhart, *Untersuchungen zur israelitisch-jüdischen Chronologie* (BZAW 88; Berlin, 1964).

P. van der Meer, *The Chronology of Ancient Western Asia and Egypt* (Leiden, 1963²).

M. Noth, *Überlieferungsgeschichtliche Studien* I (Halle/Saale, 1943).

G. von Rad, "The Deuteronomic Theology of History in I and II Kings," in *The Problem of the Hexateuch and Other Essays* (New York, 1966), pp. 205-21.

H. C. Schmitt, *Elisa. Traditionsgeschichtliche Untersuchungen zur vorklassischen nordisraelitischen Prophetie* (Gütersloh, 1972).

O. H. Steck, *Überlieferung und Zeitgeschichte in den Elia-Erzählungen* (WMANT 26; Neukirchen, 1968).

T. Veijola, *Das Königtum in der Beurteilung der deuteronomistischen Historiographie. Eine redaktionsgeschichtliche Untersuchung* (Helsinki, 1977).

6. CHRONICLES

The name Chronicles became current likely by way of Luther's translation of the Bible. The Reformer probably derived the name from Jerome *(Prologus galateatus),* who wrote that the book can be called "chronicle of all of divine history." In the Vulgate the book is called *(liber) paralipomenon,* a latinization of *paraleipomenōn,* the name of the book in the Septuagint, which probably means "the things passed over, left out" (namely, in Samuel and Kings). Such a title does not properly characterize the book. Chronicles does contain much material not found in other Bible books, but it also has large sections that are virtually identical to Samuel and Kings. Large sections in these books are omitted in Chronicles (e.g., everything that deals with the northern kingdom that has no direct bearing on Judah's history, as well as almost everything about David's and Solomon's personal history), and smaller or larger portions from Samuel and Kings have been edited or reworked.

In the Massoretic text the book is called *dibre hayyamim,* which means something like "events of the days," or "annals." "Chronicles" (cf. Esth. 2:23; 6:1; 10:2, where in the Hebrew the same expression is found) is not a bad rendering of this name. According to Jewish tradition (*Baba Bathra* 14b), Ezra wrote Ezra-Nehemiah and Chronicles,

but it is a tradition without real historical foundation.

Like Kings, Chronicles purports to describe history, in this case from the very beginning of humankind to the return from Babylonian captivity. It has appropriately been noted, however, that the book offers more a *view* of history than a *description* of it. The author uses his material freely, supplements what he found in his sources, changes it, explains it, and so forth. Conspicuous are (1) the genealogies with which he describes the history from Adam to Saul; (2) the great interest in David and Solomon, primarily their association with the construction of the temple, the cult (the ark), and cultic persons; (3) the special interest in the Levites, where the author seems to have a predilection for the singers; (4) the exclusive attention to Judah and the Davidic dynasty ruling there; (5) the interest in the cult and cultic persons in general; (6) an accentuation of the retribution dogma; and (7) a delight in miraculous divine interventions (e.g., 2 Chr. 13:13–18; 14:8–13; 20:1–30). Even stronger than in the Deuteronomistic authors, the righteous are blessed and the wicked experience calamity and misery (see, e.g., 1 Chr. 10:13–14; 2 Chr. 12:1–8; 33:1–13 [cf. with 2 Kgs. 21:1–9; note how Chronicles explains the long reign of Manasseh]). The book bears a highly paraenetic character: the descriptions of the facts are often admonitions to remain faithful to Yahweh.

The work can be analyzed as follows: genealogical tables from Adam to Saul (1 Chronicles 1–9); the history of David (chs. 10–29); the history of Solomon (2 Chronicles 1–9); the history of Judah from the division of the kingdom to its destruction (10:1–36:21); and an appendix concerning permission to rebuild the temple and to return (36:22–23).

The genealogical material in 1 Chronicles 1–9 must largely have been taken from the Pentateuch. Other indications could also be mentioned that suggest that the author was acquainted with the Pentateuch in its entirety (though the Pentateuch may have been augmented here and there after the writing of Chronicles). The genealogies, however, also contain material not found in other Bible books. It would seem that the Chronicles writer was familiar with the books of Samuel and

Kings. Large parts of his work are verbatim identical to parts in these books. There are big differences, too, which raises the question whether the writer of Chronicles derived his material from Samuel and Kings as we have these books today or whether he used a source that was substantially similar to these books. An additional consideration is that the author refers to many books. These sources are usually divided into two categories.

The first category includes writings that involve records of kings:

1. The Books of the Kings of Israel and Judah (e.g., 2 Chr. 27:7; altogether three times)
2. The Books of the Kings of Judah and Israel (e.g., 16:11; altogether four times)
3. The Book of the Kings of Israel (20:34)
4. History of the Kings of Israel (33:18)
5. Interpretation (Heb. *midrash*) of the Book of Kings (24:27)

Much is to be said in favor of the idea that these five sources refer to one and the same book, which did not yet have a fixed title. It is also called *midrash,* although at this time the word did not yet have the meaning it acquired in later Judaism. In 24:27 it indeed means "interpretation" or, perhaps still better, "study." How did this book relate to Samuel and Kings? The question is unanswerable. Some think of an altogether different book than Samuel and Kings—in other words, a second source of Chronicles. Others think of a more extensive version of Samuel and Kings, which may be younger or older than our canonical writings. In the latter case the author would not have used our canonical books, at least not in the form in which we have them.

A second set of sources includes writings attributed to the prophets:

1. Samuel, Nathan, and Gad (1 Chr. 29:29)
2. Nathan, Ahijah, and Iddo (2 Chr. 9:29)
3. Shemaiah and Iddo (12:15)
4. Iddo (13:22)
5. Jehu (20:34)
6. Isaiah (26:22; 32:32)

The Chronicles of the Seers (33:19) may also be included with these. Two of these writings are said to be recorded in other books: the "Book of the Kings of Israel" (20:34) and the "Book of the Kings of Judah and Israel" (32:32). It is often assumed that this entire second category of prophetic writings refers not to separate books but to parts of books in the first list, in which various sections are attributed to the prophets who labored during the reign of the respective kings.

The Chronicler also likely made use of a variety of lists (see, e.g., 1 Chr. 27:24), many of which may have come from the temple archives. He inserted parts of psalms (16:7–36). Various parts may be from the Chronicler himself, such as certain speeches. In this way a highly variegated work came into being, but nevertheless one with a number of specific motifs that are found throughout the whole book.

Virtually all scholars are agreed that after Chronicles had been written, it was to some extent enlarged, but there is no unanimity about the nature of the additions. Some propose a systematic editing of Chronicles and therefore speak of a first and a second Chronicler. Most scholars assume that, in various times and by various persons, elements were added to the book. In my judgment the number and scope of the additions was not large.

The above comments are relevant also for determining the time of composition of Chronicles. The last recorded happening is the return from captivity (Cyrus's edict [2 Chr. 36:22–23] is from 538 B.C.). The genealogy of David's descendants likely recounts still another five generations after Zerubbabel and thus extends to about 400 B.C. (1 Chr. 3:17–24). The text of this list is very uncertain, however, and many scholars believe that chapter 3 was later added to 1 Chronicles. There is little ground for assuming that the book (not including a number of later additions) was written much later than about 400.

For a long time it was generally assumed that the material unique to Chronicles in the Old Testament was virtually devoid of historical value, except for its providing considerable information about the time in which the writer himself lived. Later this negative judgment was somewhat modified, so that many now hold that the material unique to Chronicles contains much that has historical value, particularly the reports about building activities, armies, and warfare (e.g., 2 Chr.

11:5–12; 27:5; 28:18; 32:30; 33:14a; 35:20–24). An altogether different opinion is held by Welten. Special difficulties are occasioned by the reports that contradict what is said in Samuel or Kings, such as 8:1–2 (Hiram gives cities) versus 1 Kings 9:10–14 (Hiram is given cities) or 1 Chronicles 14:12 (David orders the gods to be burned) versus 2 Samuel 5:21 (the gods are carried away). It is perhaps not possible or necessary to remove these difficulties by attempts at harmonization, which is often of a very artificial nature.

For a comparison of 1 Chronicles 20:5 and 2 Samuel 21:19, see section 4. Also problematic are the very large numbers in Chronicles, particularly when compared with the corresponding figures in Samuel and Kings (e.g., 1 Chr. 19:18 with 2 Sam. 10:18; 1 Chr. 21:5–6 with 2 Sam. 24:9 [v. 6 lacks a parallel in Samuel]). In other cases, Chronicles has a smaller number (cf. 2 Chr. 8:10 with 1 Kgs. 9:23). It is far from certain, however, that these figures are meant to be exact. Some of the figures that have come to us from the ancient Eastern world hide a particular mystical system; other large figures perhaps indicate no more than that Yahweh gave a tremendously great victory (as we might complain to someone, "You've told me that a hundred times!"). In some cases it is probably a case of textual corruption in the transmission of a number.

In recent years several studies have appeared regarding the manner in which the Chronicler recounts history and the related issue of his purposes and theology, studies that elaborate older viewpoints and also bring out new perspectives. These studies do not all come to identical conclusions. That the Chronicler was anti-Samaritan and that Chronicles was written after the temple had been built on Mount Gerizim (Josephus, *Antiquities* 11.8.4)—a fact difficult to date as it is—are nowadays rightly denied by several scholars. There is little ground for this view, especially if the books of Ezra and Nehemiah are left out of the picture. In former days scholars were also aware that the Chronicler was not a historian but a theologian (better yet, a preacher) who aimed at expounding the Scripture in order to admonish and exhort his people to be faithful to Yahweh and his service. Recently this view has properly been given even more emphasis.

It has often been said that the concern of Chronicles is the theocracy, but especially since Plöger's book *Theokratie und Eschatologie* (1959; English translation of 2nd edition: *Theocracy and Eschatology* [Richmond, 1968]) this view has received a great deal of attention. It is thought that after the Exile there were at least two movements in Judah, one theocratic and one eschatological. According to some the Chronicler and Ezra belonged to the former and Nehemiah to the latter group. The eschatological party expected a national restoration under a king from the house of David (a messianic expectation), whereas the theocratic movement believed that salvation was realized in the concrete community, especially as this community is portrayed in Nehemiah 12:44–13:3. It is present in the community gathered around the sanctuary under the leadership of the high priest. Even living under a foreign ruler (Persians, Ptolemies) does not nullify it, for that king is still the servant of Yahweh.

I will not address here the question whether there were indeed these parties in the days of Ezra and Nehemiah. It does seem highly unlikely, however, that Nehemiah belonged to an eschatological and the Chronicler to a theocratic party. The Chronicler has high hopes for David's house. Note the manner in which he describes Solomon and especially his view of David as the man who did so much for the organization of the cult and as the one who really built the temple. Note moreover that his exclusive interest is in the house of David (i.e., Judah and its kings). Furthermore, compared with the parallel passages in Samuel and Kings, a number of passages in Chronicles are particularly telling: 1 Chronicles 17:11–14 (2 Sam. 7:12–16); 1 Chronicles 28:5–7; 2 Chronicles 7:18 (1 Kgs. 9:5). The manner in which Kellermann and others try to dispute this argumentation lacks almost all cogency. The Chronicler's real concern is to create the expectation of a new king from the house of David, a great son of David, whose rule will be forever. The community must look forward to that ruler, must meanwhile remain loyal to the foreign rulers, but especially must be faithful to the commandments of Yahweh as these culminate in the worship service. In that service songs of praise become very important, as does increasingly the proclamation. Historically Chronicles is to be linked to the time of the Exile, when the sacrificial service was impossible. And if the synagogue worship arose not at that time but only some centuries later (which is more likely), at least at that earlier time its foundations were laid.

LITERATURE

Commentaries:

K. Galling, *Die Bücher der Chronik, Esra und Nehemia* (ATD 12; Göttingen, 1958²).

J. M. Myers, *I Chronicles* (AB; Garden City, NY, 1965).

———, *II Chronicles* (AB; Garden City, NY, 1965).

W. Rudolph, *Chronikbücher* (HAT I/21; Tübingen, 1955).

H. G. M. Williamson, *1 and 2 Chronicles* (New Century Bible; London/Grand Rapids, 1982).

Other Works:

R. L. Braun, "Solomon, the Chosen Temple Builder. The Significance of 1 Chronicles," *JBL* 95 (1976) 581-90.

———, "A Reconsideration of the Chronicler's Attitude to the North," *JBL* 96 (1977) 59-62.

A. M. Brunet, "Le Chroniste et ses sources," *RB* 60 (1953) 481-508; 61 (1954) 349-86.

D. N. Freedman, "The Chronicler's Purpose," *CBQ* 23 (1961) 436-42.

W. Th. In der Smitten, *Gottesherrschaft und Gemeinde* (Bern/Frankfurt am Main, 1974).

U. Kellermann, *Messias und Gesetz* (Neukirchen-Vluyn, 1971).

R. Mosis, *Untersuchungen zur Theologie des chronistischen Geschichtswerkes* (Freiburg/Basel/Wien, 1973).

M. Noth, *Überlieferungsgeschichtliche Studien* (Halle/Saale, 1943), pp. 110ff.

O. Plöger, *Theocracy and Eschatology* (Richmond, 1968).

G. von Rad, *Das Geschichtsbild des chronistischen Werkes* (BWANT IV/3; Stuttgart, 1930).

———, "The Levitical Sermon in I and II Chronicles," in *The Problem of the Hexateuch and Other Essays* (New York, 1966), pp. 267-80.

M. Smith, *Palestinian Parties and Politics that Shaped the Old Testament* (New York/London, 1971).

A. C. Welch, *The Work of the Chronicler. Its Purpose and its Date* (London, 1939).

P. Welten, *Geschichte und Geschichtsdarstellung in den Chronikbüchern* (WMANT 42; Neukirchen, 1973).

T. Willi, *Die Chronik als Auslegung. Untersuchungen zur literarischen Gestaltung der historischen Überlieferung Israels* (FRLANT 106; Göttingen, 1972).

H. G. M. Williamson, *Israel in the Book of Chronicles* (Cambridge, 1977).

7. EZRA AND NEHEMIAH

In the Septuagint the apocryphal book of Ezra (see section 1) was originally Ezra, and the book of Ezra-Nehemiah was 2 Ezra. In the division of the latter work, Ezra became 2 Ezra, and Nehemiah became 3 Ezra. In the Vulgate the canonical book Ezra is called 1 Ezra, Nehemiah is called 2 Ezra, and the apocryphal book 3 Ezra. After the division had been introduced into the Hebrew text, the books were called by their familiar names Ezra and Nehemiah. The name Nehemiah is fitting, for in much of the book named after him he is the chief figure. In the book of Ezra, however, Ezra is prominent only in chapters 7–10; in chapters 1–6, Zerubbabel and Jeshua (Joshua) are the chief figures. It is interesting that the Talmud (*Sanhedrin* 93b), in a passage that is not altogether clear, tries to explain why the book as a whole is not named as Nehemiah is.

The books of Ezra and Nehemiah offer segments from the history of the Jewish people after the Exile, mainly from the years 538–536, 520–515, 458, 445–432, and some years later (Neh. 5:14; 13:6). The author, whom, following general practice, I call the Chronicler (see, however, section 1), aims to describe how Israel as it returned from exile changed from a people (a national unity) to a community (a spiritual unity), an entity characterized not by political independence but by separateness from other nations and by living according to God's law. Or more precisely, the author aims to describe the attempts to become such a community. In my opinion he also indicates the difficulty of turning the ideal into reality (see Ezra 9–10; Nehemiah 13). The books appear to be for the most part a composite constructed from edited or unedited material the author had at his disposal. Ezra 4:8–6:18 and 7:12–26 are written in Aramaic. The first part is likely derived from an Aramaic source (or two such sources); the second is a decree written in Aramaic. At the time Aramaic was the official language in part of the Persian realm.

The books can be analyzed as follows:

1. Ezra 1–6, RETURN AND REBUILDING OF THE TEMPLE

1. Cyrus gives permission to return and rebuild the temple
2. List of returnees
3. Rebuilding of the altar and beginning to build the temple

4:1–5 Rebuilding of the temple stopped

4:6–23 Hostilities of the neighboring people during the reigns of Xerxes and Artaxerxes

4:24–6:18 Continuation of building and completion of the temple

6:19–22 Celebration of the Passover

2. Ezra 7–10, HISTORY OF EZRA

7. Ezra is given great power
8. Journey of Ezra and those with him: participants, preparations, and arrival

9–10 Ezra's fight against mixed marriages

3. Nehemiah 1–7, HISTORY OF NEHEMIAH, PART 1

1–2:10 Nehemiah asks and receives permission to go to Jerusalem

2:11–7:5 Successful rebuilding of the wall, despite opposition

7:6–73 List of returnees (= Ezra 2)

4. Nehemiah 8–10, RENEWAL OF THE COVENANT

8. Ezra reads from the law, the Feast of Tabernacles is celebrated
9. Day of repentance
10. Agreement to obey the law

5. Nehemiah 11–13, HISTORY OF NEHEMIAH, PART 2

11. Expansion of the Jerusalem population

12:1–26 List of priests and Levites

12:27–43 Dedication of the wall

12:44– Abuses and final reforms during Nehemiah's second stay in Jerusalem.

13:31

In writing Ezra 1–6, the Chronicler must have had available for his use a copy of the inventory to be signed by Sheshbazzar (1:8–11a), the list in chapter 2 (were these documents in the temple archives?), and one or two Aramaic sources. Whether he had still other sources for writing this section we do not know. Ezra 4:6–24 (largely written in Aramaic) poses great problems: verse 5 speaks of Darius I (522–486 B.C.), verse 6 of Xerxes (Ahasuerus, 485–465), verses 7–23 of Artaxerxes (Artahshashta, 465–424), but then verse 24 returns to Darius and ties in with verse 5. None of the solutions offered so far has found general acceptance.

The difficulties encountered in the history of Ezra (Ezra 7–10 and then again at least in Nehemiah 8, perhaps also chs. 9–10) are numerous, and many, greatly varying attempts have been made to solve them. All I can do here is state what I regard as the most likely (or the least unlikely) solutions. In my opinion, the Chronicler had in his possession a copy of Ezra, which was apologetic in character (i.e., it was a historical document, though of course it did not write history objectively). Of this copy he adopted certain sections, which in part he incorporated verbatim in his book (the parts in which Ezra speaks in the first person) and in part edited (the segments where Ezra speaks in the third person). There are indeed much more radical ideas; some scholars even hold that the whole figure of Ezra is a fantasy of the Chronicler.

Nehemiah 8–10 seem to be closely related but at the same time to differ considerably. Chapter 8 mentions Ezra, but apparently not Nehemiah (in 8:9 his name was likely inserted later), chapter 9 mentions neither Ezra nor Nehemiah, and chapter 10 only the latter. There seems to be a close coherence between Nehemiah 7:4–5, 72 and 11:1, which is interrupted by chapters 8–10. For these reasons many believe that Nehemiah 8 originally followed immediately upon Ezra 8 or 10. In my judgment, however, no one has given a satisfactory reason for the transposition of Nehemiah

8. It seems the least unlikely to assume that Ezra came to Jerusalem to exhort the people to live again according to the law (probably the Pentateuch, but not in its final redaction as we have it). He was shocked by the report about the many mixed marriages. He handled that problem first, but it also gave him many enemies (Ezra 9–10). In connection with that effort he also made an ill-fated attempt to restore the wall of Jerusalem (4:7–23; see, e.g., v. 12). Afterward, Ezra could do nothing more.

Thirteen years later, when Nehemiah had made an initial restoration of the wall, he saw his chance and first gave Ezra the opportunity to introduce the law again (Nehemiah 8). There followed the day of repentance that is described in 9:1–5, a section to which the Chronicler added a prayer (vv. 6–37), one that may have been used on that occasion but was likely composed in Judah shortly after the great catastrophe of 586 B.C. Next the covenant was renewed (ch. 10), the document of which was included by the Chronicler. Ezra did not sign this document, since he did not have an official function, but Nehemiah the governor did. Meanwhile measures were introduced to increase the population of Jerusalem, and only afterward was Nehemiah willing to dedicate the wall officially.

I thus believe that Ezra came to Jerusalem before Nehemiah and that there was cooperation between the two. It is certain that Nehemiah came to Jerusalem in 445 B.C. under Artaxerxes, the ruler in whose seventh year Ezra came to Jerusalem (Ezra 7:7). Many, however, consider this king to be Artaxerxes II (404–359), in which case Ezra would have come to Jerusalem in 398, or think that the date in Ezra 7:7 is wrong and put Ezra's arrival in, for example, 428 B.C.

Almost all scholars agree that the book of Nehemiah largely or in part contains a writing of Nehemiah himself, including 1:1–7:5 (perhaps with the exception of ch. 3, which may derive from the temple archives), parts of chapter 11, 12:27–43, and 13:4–31. Opinions differ regarding the literary genre of Nehemiah. It has been compared with many pieces from Old Testament and extrabiblical literature, but in my judgment a good parallel has not been found. Some believe that two chroniclers worked on Ezra and Nehemiah. The second

presumably made numerous additions to the original writing and reworked it. Others hold (correctly, I believe) that the original writing received only slight additions at a later time.

The last event recorded in this book is Nehemiah's second stay in Jerusalem (13:6), sometime after 432 B.C., the historical accuracy of which seems quite certain. It seems likely that the list of high priests (Neh. 12:10–11, 22) was updated to the time the book was written. According to the Elephantine Papyri the last official mentioned in the list, Jedaiah, must have become high priest after 408, which implies that the Darius mentioned in 12:22 must be Darius II, who died in 404. Jedaiah therefore assumed his office between 408 and 404. Many regard the list of high priests as an addition, but if so, it was probably incorporated into the text not much later than 400. There is thus good ground to suppose that the book Ezra-Nehemiah was written about 400 B.C.

If we should distinguish theocratic and eschatological groups, Ezra and Nehemiah as well as the writer of the book belonged to the theocrats (see section 6). They also regularly noticed that it was impossible to realize the theocratic ideal. They were thus at least instrumental in arousing eschatological expectations. In Ezra and Nehemiah, particularism, or the separation of the community, is strongly emphasized. In that sense Ezra and Nehemiah may be regarded as forerunners of Pharisaism. Their concern, however, was not some kind of racial purity (note Ezra 6:21 and Neh. 10:29 [28], which do not exclude proselytism) but the guarding of the pure worship of Yahweh. Considering their circumstances—a small group amid syncretists and pagans—we are not surprised that they pursue this goal by separation. Only in this way could the people be preserved till the coming of him who "has broken down the dividing wall of hostility" (Eph. 2:14) and who would gather for himself a congregation composed of Jews and Gentiles, from all nations.

The view of history in this work is remarkable. Miracles are not related, and the kindness of the pagan Persian rulers is emphasized (Ezra 1:2–4, 7; 3:7; 6:14, 22; 7:27–28; Neh. 2:8). In almost all these passages it is clear that ultimately Israel's God is in charge of history (note the remarkable apposition in Ezra 6:14). In this connection we should note the constant reference to "the (good) hand" of "our" (or "my") God (e.g., Ezra 7:6, 9; 8:18; Neh. 2:8; etc.).

LITERATURE

Commentaries:

L. H. Brockington, *Ezra, Nehemiah and Esther* (New Century Bible; London, 1969).

D. J. A. Clines, *Ezra, Nehemiah, Esther* (New Century Bible; London/Grand Rapids, 1984).

F. C. Fensham, *The Books of Ezra and Nehemiah* (NICOT; Grand Rapids, 1982).

A. H. J. Gunneweg, *Esra* (KAT XIX/1; Gütersloh, 1985).

J. M. Myers, *Ezra, Nehemiah* (AB; Garden City, NY, 1965).

W. Rudolph. *Esra und Nehemia mit 3. Esra* (HAT I/20; Tübingen, 1949).

Other Works:

H. H. Grosheide, *De terugkeer uit de ballingschap* (Exegetica II/4; Den Haag, 1957).

W. Th. In der Smitten, *Esra. Quellen, Überlieferung und Geschichte* (Assen, 1973).

S. Japhet, "The Supposed Common Authorship of Chronicles and Ezra-Nehemiah Investigated Anew," *VT* 18 (1968) 330-71.

A. S. Kapelrud, *The Question of Authorship in the Ezra-Narrative: A Lexical Investigation* (Oslo, 1944).

U. Kellermann, *Nehemia. Quellen, Überlieferung und Geschichte* (BZAW 102; Berlin, 1967).

R. W. Klein, "Ezra and Nehemiah in Recent Studies," in F. M. Cross, W. E. Lemke, and P. D. Miller, eds., *Magnalia Dei: The Mighty Acts of God. In Memoriam G. Ernest Wright* (Garden City, NY, 1976), pp. 361-76.

S. Mowinckel, *Studien zu dem Buche Ezra-Nehemia* I-II (Oslo, 1964); III (Oslo, 1965).

K. F. Pohlmann, *Studien zum dritten Esra* (FRLANT 104; Göttingen, 1970).

G. von Rad, "Die Nehemia-Denkschrift," *ZAW* 76 (1964) 176-87; repr. in *Gesammelte Studien zum Alten Testament* (TB 8; München, 1965[3]), pp. 297ff.

H. H. Rowley, "Nehemiah's Mission and its Background," *BJRL* 37 (1954) 528-61.

———, "The Chronological Order of Ezra and Nehemiah," in *The Servant of the Lord and Other Essays* (Oxford, 1952), pp. 129-60.

H. H. Schaeder, *Esra der Schreiber* (Tübingen, 1930).

C. The Prophets

by B. J. Oosterhoff

1. INTRODUCTION

In the Jewish canon the rabbis distinguished between the Former Prophets and the Latter Prophets. Included in the first category are the books of Joshua, Judges, Samuel, and Kings; in the second group are those of the writing prophets, so called because we have their writings. This latter category is a significant and unique part of the Old Testament. Though persons who announced a message from the gods to people (often while in a state of ecstasy) were also found among other nations—for instance, in Egypt, Mesopotamia, Canaan, and Greece—there is an essential difference between them and Israel's prophets. This difference is due to the God on whose behalf they spoke, as well as to their message and their function in Israel.

For many people, a prophet is someone who predicts the future. Yet prediction is only one aspect of the work of the prophets whom we encounter in the Bible. They were proclaimers of the Word of God that could relate to the future, but it could just as well be focused on the past and still more often on the present.

It is fairly generally assumed that there is affiliation between the Hebrew word *nabi,* "prophet," the Akkadian *nabu,* "call, name, speak, proclaim," and the Arabian *nabbaa,* "bring a message." A prophet is one who speaks and brings a message by order of God and on his behalf (see, e.g., Exod. 7:1–2; Jer. 1:6–7). God puts his words in the mouth of the prophet (Deut. 18:18; Jer. 1:9). The prophet is therefore also called "the mouth of God" (Exod. 4:16; Jer. 15:19). The people sometimes called a prophet "seer" because he saw things beyond the view of ordinary people

(1 Sam. 9:9, 11; Isa. 30:10). A prophet is also simply called "man of God" because of the unique manner in which he is related to God (1 Sam. 9:6–17; 2 Kgs. 1:10–17; 4:7, 9–37).

Ecstatic prophetism found among other nations was also known in Israel. Such prophecy occurred, for example, in the time of Samuel when Saul met a group of ecstatic prophets from Gibeah (1 Sam. 10:5–6, 10). They came down from a *bamah* (high place for sacrifices) in a state of ecstasy, led by players of a variety of musical instruments, such as harps, tambourines, flutes, and lyres. The music likely served to whip them into a state of ecstasy and keep them in that trance (see 2 Kgs. 3:15; 1 Chr. 25:1). Saul came under their influence and became ecstatic himself. Later the same thing happened again to him (1 Sam. 19:18–24) as well as to his messengers. Apparently such a state of ecstasy was contagious.

The Hebrew word used to express this state is a form of the verb *naba* (Niph. or Hith.), "act as a prophet," or "be ecstatic." Apparently such a trance was originally an essential characteristic of the prophet. The verb is also used for the Baal prophets at Mount Carmel, who likewise become ecstatic (1 Kgs. 18:29), and for Saul, who, when he was angry, acted like a possessed man (1 Sam. 18:10). To be a prophet is to be ecstatic, to act like a possessed person. The prophesying of the seventy elders and of Eldad and Medad in the desert (Num. 11:25–29) also consisted in a glorifying of God while being in a state of frenzy.

In the time of Elijah and Elisha there were prophets who lived together in groups (1 Kgs. 18:4; 2 Kgs. 2:5–18; 4:38; 6:1–7), the *bene hannebiim.* Later Amos refused to be regarded as one of them (Amos 7:14) because of the corruption that had entered those groups. They lived from gifts and therefore easily spoke words their benefactors liked to hear; they became "bread-eating prophets" (speaking words the person whose bread they ate liked to hear) and not real prophets. King Ahab employed a whole army of prophets from whom he expected to hear words favorable to him. Micaiah ben Imlah was a different sort of man and therefore ended up in prison (1 Kings 22).

Though the oldest prophetism was often marked by ecstasy, it is not found in the later prophets. Occasionally they do receive revelations from God while in a trance, but they deliver their messages in a fully rational condition. Often they receive God's revelation through visions in which they are lifted above the reality surrounding them and view another, visionary reality (see the calling visions of Isaiah, Jeremiah, and Ezekiel, or the visions of Amos and Zechariah). They see a vision (Num. 24:1–2; Isa. 1:1), an oracle (Isa. 13:1; Hab. 1:1), or the word they are to bring (Amos 1:1; Mic. 1:1; Isa. 2:1). The expression, "the hand of the Lord" came upon them (Isa. 8:11; Ezek. 1:3; 3:14; etc.), also points to a revelation from God in which the prophet was in an ecstatic condition. The emphasis, however, is always on the word that is to be proclaimed.

The periods in which the prophets proclaimed their message are different for every prophet. We get the impression that Amos, after his preaching at Bethel, returned to his farm at Tekoa. Isaiah was active when the political circumstances required speaking the Word of God. Jeremiah was called to be a lifetime prophet, though regularly he had to wait for new revelations.

The form and the style in which the prophets couched their message vary as well. This is due in part to their individual personalities. Amos speaks differently from Isaiah and differs from someone like Jeremiah. There are similarities too. The mode used by older prophets to deliver their messages is poetry, but from the time of Jeremiah, prose is also used. Furthermore, their style is derived from the current literary genres, for example, from wisdom literature (cf. Isa. 40:12–14 with Job 38:2, 5, 25, etc. and Prov. 30:4) or from the lament (cf. Amos 5:1–2 and Jer. 9:19–20 [20–21] with 2 Sam. 3:33–34).

The most prominent form is the so-called messenger saying, derived from the manner in which messengers or envoys announced a message from their lord, introduced with the words "thus says my lord," or something similar (see Gen. 32:4; Num. 22:16; Judg. 11:15; 1 Kgs. 20:3; 2 Kgs. 18:28–29). Prophets often introduce their message with "thus says the Lord" or "this is the word of the Lord" (neum yhwh). Sometimes without introduction they speak in the first-person singular, with "I" referring to God. In that case the messenger identifies himself with his sender, who speaks in the messenger (e.g., Zeph. 1:7, 12, 17). Often, however, prophets speak about God in the third person.

The prophets distinguish clearly between their own thoughts and the Word of God (see, e.g., Nathan in 2 Sam. 7:3–4; Jonah 1:1–3). Jeremiah charges the false prophets with regarding their own thoughts as the Word of God (Jer. 14:14; 23:26). Therefore they prophesy what is false (5:3; 23:25) and make the people trust in a lie (28:15; 29:31).

In their proclamation the prophets call the people to obey God and to practice justice and love. They promise his blessings if the people trust in God and do his will, but they announce God's judgment upon apostasy, idolatry, and disobedience. They speak of the day of the Lord, the day of God's judgment (Isa. 2:12; Amos 5:18–20; Joel 1:15; Zeph. 1:15; etc.). They are likewise heralds of the coming kingdom of peace (e.g., Isa. 2:2–4) and of the coming of the Messiah (e.g., 8:23–9:6 [9:1–7]; 11:1–5; Mic. 5:1–4 [2–5]).

Sometimes the prophets add symbolic actions to their proclamation. Isaiah for three years walks the streets of Jerusalem stripped and barefoot (Isaiah 20). At one point Jeremiah links his proclamation to a spoiled waistcloth (Jer. 13:1–11). On another occasion he walks with a yoke on his shoulders (27:1–11). See also Jeremiah 16:1–6 and Ezekiel 4–5 and 12. These symbolic deeds serve to illustrate the preaching so as to make it more emphatic. Hosea's married life was a visible proclamation of the relationship of God to Israel and of Israel to God (Hosea 1–3).

In the writings of the prophets we can distinguish between divine oracles, stories about the prophet, and "confessions." The latter are personal expressions of the prophet in which he lays

227

bare his heart. They are especially found in Jeremiah (12:1–4; 14:17–18; 15:15–18; 20:7–18). Stories about a prophet stem likely from people in his own immediate environment, for instance, his disciples. Much of what is related about Jeremiah likely came from his friend Baruch (36:4–8). Sometimes the prophets themselves recorded their own oracles (see Isa. 30:8) or dictated them to others (Jeremiah 36). Others, such as pupils, may have written down their preaching as they gave it. In many cases prophetic deliverances must have been first orally transmitted and only later recorded in writing. At such times things may have been added to it, or the deliverances may have been updated in accordance with the demands of the new situation. It is, however, wrong to go as far as certain Scandinavian scholars who believe that the ipsissima verba are totally beyond recall. Finally compilers or editors collected the utterances of the prophets and the stories about them and made the books that we have today, a process in which presenting the material in pure historical sequence was often not the only guideline followed. Sometimes the compilation is done on the basis of key words (e.g., "sword, famine, and pestilence" in Jer. 14:12 and v. 13) or similarity in subject matter (e.g., the three symbolic acts about the collapse of Judah in 16:1–9, the series of pronouncements about the royal house in 21:11–23:8, and the series of symbolic acts by Ezekiel in chs. 4–5).

In the following survey I discuss the prophets and their writings in the order in which they are found in the Hebrew Bible, the order that has been retained in the English Bible. In each case I consider the person and time, the book, and the preaching of the prophet.

LITERATURE

E. Balla, *Die Botschaft der Propheten* (Tübingen, 1958).

K. Baltzer, *Die Biographie der Propheten* (Neukirchen, 1975).

W. Brueggemann, *The Prophetic Imagination* (Philadelphia, 1978).

M. Buber, *The Prophetic Faith* (New York, 1949).

R. Clements, *Prophecy and Tradition* (London/Atlanta, 1975).

———, *Prophecy and Covenant* (London, 1965).

R. Coggins, A. Phillips, and M. Knibb, eds., *Israel's Prophetic Tradition. Essays in Honour of Peter R. Ackroyd* (Cambridge, 1982) (good bibliography).

J. A. Crenshaw, *Prophetic Conflict: Its Effect upon Israelite Religion* (BZAW 124; Berlin, 1971).

F. Ellermeier, *Prophetie in Mari und Israel* (Herzberg/Harz, 1968).

G. Fohrer, *Die symbolischen Handlungen der Propheten* (Zürich, 1953/1968²).

———, *Studien zur alttestamentlichen Prophetie* (BZAW 99; Berlin, 1967).

———, "Neue Literatur zur alttestamentlichen Prophetie (1961-70)," *Theologische Rundschau* 40 (1975) 193-209, 337-77; 41 (1976) 1-12; 45 (1980) 1-39, 109-32, 193-225.

N. K. Gottwald, *All the Kingdoms of the Earth. Israelite Prophecy and International Relations in the Ancient Near East* (New York, 1964).

A. H. J. Gunneweg, *Mündliche und schriftliche Tradition der vorexilischen Prophetenbücher als Problem der neueren Prophetenforschung* (FRLANT 73; Göttingen, 1959).

E. Hammershaimb, *Some Aspects of Old Testament Prophecy from Isaiah to Malachi* (Copenhagen, 1966).

S. Herrmann, *Die prophetischen Heilserwartungen im Alten Testament. Ursprung und Gestaltwandel* (BWANT 5; Stuttgart, 1965).

A. Heschel, *The Prophets* (New York, 1962).

D. R. Hillers, *Treaty Curses and the Old Testament Prophets* (Rome, 1964).

A. R. Johnson, *The Cultic Prophet in Ancient Israel* (Cardiff, 1962²).

K. Koch, *The Prophets, I: The Assyrian Period* (Philadelphia, 1983).

———, *The Prophets, II: The Babylonian and Persian Periods* (Philadelphia, 1984).

J. Lindblom, *Prophecy in Ancient Israel* (Philadelphia, 1963²) (good bibliography).

W. McKane, "Prophecy and Prophetic Literature," in G. W. Anderson, ed., *Tradition and Interpretation* (Oxford, 1979), pp. 163-88.

———, *Prophets and Wise Men* (London, 1965).

A. Neher, *The Prophetic Existence* (New York, 1969).

P. H. A. Neumann, ed., *Das Prophetenverständnis in der deutschsprachigen Forschung seit Heinrich Ewald* (Darmstadt, 1979).

E. Noort, *Untersuchungen zum Gottesbescheid in Mari. Die "Mariprophetie" in der alttestamentlichen Forschung* (AOAT 202; Kevelaer-Neukirchen/Vluyn, 1977).

G. Quell, *Wahre und falsche Propheten* (Gütersloh, 1952).

G. von Rad, *The Message of the Prophets* (New York, 1972).

R. B. Y. Scott, *The Relevance of the Prophets* (New York/London, 1968²).

C. Westermann, *Basic Forms of Prophetic Speech* (Philadelphia, 1967).

C. F. Whitley, *The Prophetic Achievement* (Leiden, 1963).

R. Wilson, *Prophecy and Society in Ancient Israel* (Philadelphia, 1980).

W. Zimmerli, *The Law and the Prophets* (New York, 1967).

2. THE MAJOR PROPHETS

a. Isaiah

(1) PERSON AND TIME

Isaiah ("Yahweh is salvation" or "Yahweh gives salvation") was called to be a prophet in the year that King Uzziah died (746 B.C.). The vision of his calling is described in Isaiah 6. He is called the son of Amoz (1:1). According to a rabbinic tradition this Amoz was a brother of King Amaziah, the father of Uzziah. In that case Isaiah was of royal blood.

His prophetic activities occurred during the reigns of Kings Jotham, Ahaz, and Hezekiah (1:1). According to the pseudepigraphical writing *Martyrdom of Isaiah,* he died a martyr's death under Manasseh, supposedly having been sawed in two (cf. Heb. 11:37). We are not certain of this event; the Bible does not mention labors by Isaiah under Manasseh, though such is not impossible. The prophet was married, perhaps to a prophetess (Isa. 8:3), and had at least two sons, Shear-jashub and Maher-shalal-hash-baz (7:3; 8:3). As far as we know he always lived in Jerusalem and prophesied only there.

In the ministry of Isaiah, whose preaching was closely connected with the politics of his day, four periods can be distinguished. The first is after the death of Uzziah during the reign of Jotham (746–743 B.C.). According to 2 Kings 15:33, Jotham ruled sixteen years, but that period includes the time when he was coregent with his father, who, due to leprosy, was unable to fulfill the kingly office (v. 5). The regnal period of Jotham was marked both by great prosperity and by bitter poverty. There was much social injustice. Chapters 2–5 of the book of Isaiah may be from this period.

The second period was during the reign of Ahaz (743–727). According to 2 Kings 18:1, 9, Samaria fell in the sixth year of the reign of Ahaz's son Hezekiah (722). According to this information he thus became king in 727. However, according to v. 13, Sennacherib's campaign against Judah (701) happened in the fourteenth year of Hezekiah. In that case Hezekiah did not become king until 714. It may be assumed that, at the death of his father in 727, he was still very young and remained under guardianship until 714. After 701 Hezekiah lived another fifteen years (20:6); he was thus king until 686. From 714, then, his reign thus lasted exactly twenty-nine years (18:2). The Syro-Ephraimite war took place during Ahaz's reign. Pekah of Israel and Rezin of Damascus attacked Ahaz of Judah, who refused to join a coalition against Assyria. During this war (734–732) Isaiah delivered the prophecies that are recorded in Isaiah 7:1–9:6. Perhaps chapter 1 is also from this time, as well as 17:1–6 and 28:1–4.

The third period of Isaiah's ministry was in the time of Hezekiah (727/714–686 B.C.), namely, about 711. In 713 there was a rebellion against Assyria led by the Philistine city of Ashdod, a rebellion with which Hezekiah sympathized. Sargon II (722–705) undertook a campaign against Palestine and destroyed Ashdod (711). From this period are Isaiah's prophecies in chapters 18–20. Egypt also participated in the coalition, creating great hopes in Palestine. In Egypt at the time the "Ethiopian dynasty" (712–663) was on the throne, beginning with the reign of Sabakah and ending with that of Tirhakah (see 2 Kgs. 19:9; Isa. 37:9).

The fourth period of Isaiah's activities as prophet coincides with the first regnal years of the Assyrian king Sennacherib (705–681). After the death of Sargon in 705, Babylon under Merodak-Baladan (Mardukapaliddina) rebels and also manages to get Philistia, Edom, Moab, Judah, and Phoenicia involved. The rebellion is put down by Sennacherib (recounted in detail on the prism of Sennacherib), and Jerusalem is besieged (701 B.C.) but not captured. Chapters 30–39 relate to that period, and perhaps also 10:5–19, 28–34;

14:24–27. It is, however, impossible to date all of Isaiah's prophecies exactly. Differences of opinion remain regarding many details.

(2) THE BOOK OF ISAIAH

The book of Isaiah has two main parts, chapters 1–39 and 40–66. The first part contains mainly prophecies from the time of Isaiah himself. The second puts us in the period of the Babylonian captivity or later (Deutero-Isaiah). The first part in turn is a compilation of various collections, a "small library in itself" (Vriezen). Only gradually were prophecies of diverse intent and background collected in separate units and later put together in larger collections, which eventually became the present chapters 1–39. In this collection we can distinguish a number of smaller units, which in turn are composed of various prophecies or collections of prophecies. I thus divide this part of Isaiah into seven sections, the contents of which I summarize below.

Chapter 1. This general introduction includes a collation of various prophecies, in part from the time of the Syro-Ephraimite war or of Sennacherib's campaign (701); see verses 7–9.

Chapters 2–5. According to the heading these chapters constitute a new collection. The subdivisions are 2:1–5, salvation for the nations and the coming kingdom of peace (cf. Mic. 4:1–5); 2:6–22, the day of judgment against all that is exalted; 3:1–15, judgment upon the godless leaders of the people; 3:16–4:1, announcement of judgment upon the wanton women of Jerusalem; 4:2–6, a remnant will be saved; 5:1–7, song of the vineyard; 5:8–24, the sixfold woe against the wicked; and 5:25–30, announcement of God's judgment. The prophecies are especially against luxury and social injustice. Likely they are from the time of Jotham.

Chapters 6–12. This collection begins with the vision of Isaiah's calling (ch. 6) and ends with a hymn of praise (ch. 12). It was not written during a single period. The first part is probably 6:1–8:22. In this section the use of the first-person singular is remarkable. The prophecies beginning in chapter 7 are from the time of the Syro-Ephraimite war. The Immanuel prophecy (7:14) was given during that time. Judah trusts in Assyria but some day will be punished by that nation (8:5–10). The people are exhorted to put their trust in God (8:11–22). The sections that follow tie in with it: 8:23–9:6 (9:1–7), the birth of the Messiah (the word *darkness* in v. 22 as well as in v. 23 is the connecting link); 9:7–10:4 (9:8–10:4), God's hand against Israel, likewise from the time of the Syro-Ephraimite war, shortly before the invasion of Tiglath-pileser III; 10:1–4 likely concerns Judah and ties in with 5:8–24, the prophecies of woe, but on account of the recurring refrain in 9:11, 16, 20 (vv. 12, 17, 21), and 10:4 is placed here; 10:5–19, woe over Assyria, dating from the time of Sennacherib's campaign in 701 B.C. (cf. vv. 8–11 and 36:18–20, placed here in connection with Assyria's acts in 9:7ff.; Assyria, which was used as a rod in God's hand, will be struck itself); 10:20–23, a remnant of Israel is saved and repents (the word *remnant* ties in with the same word in v. 19); 10:24–27, Zion is liberated from Assyria (a prophecy from 701); 10:28–34, advance and destruction of Assyria (also from 701); 11:1–10, announcement of the Messiah and the kingdom of peace (after the mention of the violence of war, it has a fitting place here; the linking element is the cut down tree in 10:33–34 and 11:1). The whole is concluded with a song of thanksgiving, 12:1–6, a liturgical song reminiscent of Psalm 118 and Exodus 15 and perhaps used on various occasions. Regularly God repeats for his people the exodus out of Egypt.

Chapters 13–23. Prophecies against the nations: 13:1–14:23, against Babylon (from the time of Merodak-Baladan in 705 B.C., perhaps based on a prophecy against Assyria but through reinterpretation and additions later made relevant for the time of the Babylonian captivity); 14:24–27, against Assyria (from 701?); 14:28–32, against the Philistines (at the death of Tiglath-pileser III in 727, likewise the year Ahaz died); 15:1–16:14, against Moab (dating and historical background are uncertain, perhaps a collection of prophecies, later updated to fit a new event, 16:13–14); 17:1–6, against Damascus and Ephraim (from the time of the Syro-Ephraimite war, before the fall of Damascus in 732); 17:7–11, Ephraim's sin, punishment, and conversion; 17:12–14, judgment upon the plunderers, the Assyrians (perhaps from 701, but here inserted at a suitable location); 18:1–7, against Ethiopia (from the time of the

Ethiopian dynasty, ca. 713). There is a prophecy against Egypt from the same time, 19:1–15, as well as a prophecy of salvation for Egypt, 19:16–25. Also from the same time is 20:1–6, a judgment upon Egypt (v. 1 speaks of Ashdod, which fell in 711 B.C.), which was carried out by Esarhaddon (681–669). Next is 21:1–10, another prophecy against Babylon, in its present form from the time of Cyrus's march against Babylon (v. 2), but it may have been based on a older prophecy. 21:11–12 contains a prophecy concerning Edom, 21:13–17 one against Arabia (time of origination uncertain). 22:1–13 offers an oracle against Jerusalem because it celebrates the victory without acknowledging God (from 711 or 701), followed by an oracle against Shebna, 22:15–19, scribe of Hezekiah (36:3), and about Eliakim, 22:20–25, who is appointed to take Shebna's place (see ill. 44). The collection is concluded with a prophecy concerning Tyre and Sidon, 23:1–18, from the time of Sennacherib's campaign in 701, which may have been repeated in a later time and applied to a new event (i.e., the capture of Tyre by Nebuchadrezzar; cf. Ezekiel 26–28).

Chapters 24–27. This section is the so-called Apocalypse of Isaiah, a collection of eschatological oracles concerning God's judgment of the world and the establishment of the kingdom of God upon Mount Zion. The dating is uncertain. Many assume a postexilic origin, for instance, from the time of the capture of Babylon by Alexander the Great in 331 (Rudolph) or by Xerxes in 485 (Lindblom). Duhm thought of the Maccabean period. The question concerns what is meant by the destroyed city in chapter 25. Some think of the destruction of Moab's capital by an earthquake in the time of Isaiah (Beek, Snijders). The destruction is the occasion for an eschatological message. The term *eschatological* is more fitting here than *apocalyptic*. The following parts can be distinguished: 24:1–23, God's judgment brings desolations on earth; 25:1–5, song of thanksgiving for the liberation of God's oppressed people; 25:6–12, God's kingship over Zion and salvation for the nations; 26:1–21, song of praise and of expectation by faith of God's redeemed people; 27:1–13, destruction of the world powers and Israel's liberation from captivity.

Chapters 28–35. In this section, chapters 28–32 are a collection of prophecies from the time of Sargon's and Sennacherib's threat (711–701 B.C.), and chapters 33–35 are an addition from a later time. The section 28:1–7 speaks of the fall of Samaria and is perhaps to be dated before 722. Chapters 30–31 are against Hezekiah's covenant with Egypt in 705. The final section contains prophecies about the deliverance of Jerusalem (ch. 33), the judgment upon Edom (ch. 34), and the messianic future (ch. 35).

Chapters 36–39. The final chapters constitute a historical appendix, derived from 2 Kings 18:13–20:19, to which the prayer of Hezekiah is added (Isa. 38:9–20) and from which the report of Hezekiah's payment of tribute to Sennacherib is omitted (2 Kgs. 18:14–16).

(3) ISAIAH'S PREACHING

The preaching of Isaiah is strongly intertwined with the political events of his day. Whether it be the Syro-Ephraimite war (chs. 7–8), the campaigns of the Assyrians under Sargon and Sennacherib (10:5–19; ch. 20), or the alliances of Hezekiah with Egypt (chs. 18–20; 30–31) and Babylon (ch. 39), nothing remains untouched in his preaching. All these events he addresses with the Word of God. The prophecies concerning the nations (chs. 13–23) are for the most part connected with events from the same time. For Yahweh is not only the God of Israel; he rules over the whole world. He guides the nations as he wills. He uses them as instruments in his hand (10:15), and they can go no further than he permits them to go (7:4; 10:24–34). His judgment is upon all.

In his preaching Isaiah denounces all sorts of social abuses that were current in his day in Jerusalem and Judah: oppression of the poor, widows, and orphans; bribery and injustice in the legal process; accumulation of capital; and large land ownership and a luxurious life, while exploiting others (chs. 3–4; 10:1–4). All this injustice is not redeemed by outward piety, accompanied by many sacrifices to God, long prayers, and innumerable feasts and gatherings. The crucial element is conversion and total renewal of life (1:10–17).

Central in Isaiah's preaching is the holiness of God. In the vision in which he was called, he saw God as the Holy One (6:1–7). By contrast he came to know himself as sinful and mortal. No one can exist before God except by God's forgiveness. In Isaiah God is frequently called "the Holy One of Israel" (1:4; 5:19, 24; 10:20; 12:6; 17:7; 29:19; etc.). Accordingly, his judgment strikes all that is exalted and sinful (2:6–22) and whatever opposes him (8:12–13), but there is also salvation for all who turn to him and trust in him (12:6; 17:7; 29:19). The proper attitude before God is one of reverence, faith, and acknowledgment of his blessings (7:9; 30:15).

In God's judgment only a remnant will escape. This conviction emphasizes the severity of the judgment (1:9; 6:13a; 14:30; 16:14; 17:3, 5; 21:17). That a remnant will be saved is, however, also a sign of grace. For that remnant a new future will dawn (4:3–6; 6:13b; 10:20; 11:11, 16). According to several exegetes, including von Rad, Isaiah spoke only of the judgment aspect of the remnant. The salvation aspect would presumably be of later date, and the passages in which it occurs would not be from Isaiah. Yet in the name of Isaiah's son Shear-jashub (7:3), that is, "a remnant returns" or "a remnant is converted," the salvation aspect of the remnant that will escape is already present.

A special place in Isaiah's preaching is occupied by Zion, the city of the temple and of God's dwelling. Enemies assail it but are thrown back (10:24–34; 29:8). As a lion growls over its prey, so God watches over Zion; he protects it as a bird does her young (31:4–5). Those who try to approach the city with hostile intentions meet in him a consuming fire (v. 9). Zion will escape the threat of enemies (37:32). Established by Yahweh, the city is inviolable, needing no help from strangers for its protection. On the contrary, she herself is a safe refuge for all the oppressed and afflicted (14:32). This proclamation of the safety and inviolability of Zion, because God protects her, agrees with what is said in Psalms 46, 48, and 76. Yet this truth may not lull the inhabitants of Zion into a false sense of security. The attacks of the enemies are meant to purify Zion's residents (Isa. 10:12; 29:1–10). In the measure that the inhabitants perpetrate injustice and put their trust in powers other than God, his judgment will smite them. Justice is the measure with which they will be measured; only trust in God will save Zion

(28:14–19). No sinner in Zion will be able to exist before God (33:14). Zion, too, must be cleansed from iniquity (4:3–6). She can be saved only through conversion and practicing righteousness (1:27). Someday Zion will be the center of the messianic kingdom, to which the dispersed people will return (35:8–10). Also the nations will go up to learn the service of Israel's God (2:2–4). Even if some scholars are correct that not all statements about Zion are Isaianic, still they are based upon Zion messages from Isaiah.

Finally I note the place of the Messiah in Isaiah's preaching. Mention can be made of 8:23–9:6 (9:1–7), describing the birth of the Messiah, and 11:1–10, portraying the messianic kingdom (see also ch. 35). The rule of the Messiah brings justice and peace. Not everyone agrees that these chapters are from Isaiah or that they contain a messianic prophecy. Some contend that originally they referred to the birth and the reign of an ordinary earthly king, perhaps Hezekiah, and that later they were designated messianic. Originally the Immanuel prophecy in 7:14 was not messianic. The birth of Immanuel is a sign of the redemption God gives, but later it was messianically interpreted (see Matt. 1:23).

(4) DEUTERO-ISAIAH

Chapters 40–66 of Isaiah transport us to a different time than that of Isaiah. Whereas many prophecies in 1–39 go back to Isaiah and relate to his time, the subsequent chapters relate to situations and events more than 150 years later, namely, the time of the Babylonian captivity (586–538). Jerusalem and the temple are destroyed (44:26, 28; 51:3; 52:9), and the people are in exile in Babylon (42:22; 47:5–6; 48:20; 52:2). The collapse of Babylon is imminent (chs. 46–47), and the people are at the point of being delivered from captivity (40:2). The Persian king Cyrus, who conquered the Babylonian empire, is mentioned by name. God will use him to save Israel from captivity (45:1–7). He will give orders to rebuild the temple (44:28). Though not mentioned by name in other passages, Cyrus is also referred to in 41:2–6, 25; 46:10–11; 48:14–15. He has already had his first victory, and the world trembles (41:2–4). One may think of Cyrus's conquest of Sardis from the Lydian king Croesus (547 B.C.). In that case these prophecies can be dated between 546 and 538 (the fall of Babylon and Cyrus's decree granting freedom to the Jews). These prophecies are often attributed to an unknown prophet in the time of the Babylonian exile, who is called Deutero-Isaiah (second Isaiah). Most think that he was active in Babylonia among the exiles, although Mowinckel and a few others have located him in Palestine. The fact that his prophecies are classed with those of Isaiah is attributed to a variety of reasons, such as that the prophet may have had a name similar to Isaiah's or issued his prophecies under the name of that prophet, or perhaps there was a relationship between the two prophets. Like the first Isaiah he regularly used the divine name "Holy One of Israel" (41:14, 16, 20; 43:3, 14; 45:11; etc.).

Yet not all prophecies in 40–66 are from one source. Particularly chapters 56–66 are attributed to another prophet, usually designated Trito-Isaiah (third Isaiah). This section itself, however, is varied and seems to be a collection from different prophets. Usually 40–66 is subdivided into three main parts: 40–48, 49–55, and 56–66. Because Cyrus is no longer mentioned after chapter 48, some contend that the prophecies in 40–48 are from the time before the fall of Babylon and those in 49–55 from the time afterward (Vriezen). Kuenen even places the prophecies in 49–55 in the time when the people had already returned from exile to their own land.

It is questionable whether 40–48 and 49–55 can be separated in this manner. Both parts concern the same situation and come with the same message concerning the Exile, the destruction of the temple and Jerusalem, and the promise of return and a new future. There is no break between chapter 48 and chapter 49. That the Cyrus prophecies are found only in 40–48 may be due to the fact that prophecies that were similar in theme were often put together. Chapters 40–55 are a collection of prophecies from the time of the Captivity, all dealing with the deliverance from captivity.

The following parts can be distinguished, all of which may also have been constructed from still smaller parts: 40:1–11, calling of the prophet and mandate to comfort the people with the message of deliverance; 40:12–31, exhortation to trust in God, who, as the Creator, will use his power to deliver his people; 41:1–5, the conqueror who will throw down Babylon's power is already coming; 41:6–7, likely placed here from chapter 40 after verse 20; 41:8–20, promises of deliverance; 41:21–29, the coming of the conqueror again announced; 42:1–7, first prophecy concerning the servant of the Lord; 42:8–17, promises of salvation; 42:18–25, the sins of the people were the cause of the affliction; 43:1–8, deliverance from captivity; 43:9–21, God prepares a new exodus; 43:22–28, there is forgiveness for sin; 44:1–5, God's Spirit brings forth a new people; 44:6–20, taunt of the idols; 44:21–28, God the Creator is also the Redeemer, he makes his word come true (Cyrus is mentioned by name for the first time); 45:1–8, God uses Cyrus as a Messiah to save Israel, his chosen; 45:9–25, Gentiles, too, will turn to the God of Israel; chapters 46–47, destruction of Babylon; 48:1–11, the fulfillment of the promise is near; 48:12–19, imminent fall of Babylon, and the people are urged to serve God; 48:20–22, the people flee from Babylon; 49:1–7, second prophecy concerning the servant of the Lord; 49:8–50:3, promises of return and restoration of the land; 50:4–11, third prophecy concerning the servant of the Lord; 51:1–16, collection of promises of blessings; 51:17–52:12, the end of Jerusalem's suffering is near; 52:13–53:12, fourth prophecy concerning the servant of the Lord; chapter 54, new future for Zion; and chapter 55, invitation to the exiles to come and take God's salvation.

Particularly prominent are the prophecies concerning the servant of the Lord (ebed Yahweh) in 42:1–7; 49:1–7; 50:4–11; 52:13–53:12. Though interspersed with the other prophecies, they are different from them. Duhm (1892) was the first to point out this difference and the independence of these passages. Since then it has been customary to speak of separate Ebed-Yahweh prophecies or songs. There is no consensus about the scope of the songs. Most scholars include in the specific prophecies 42:1–4; 49:1–6; 50:4–9; and 52:13–53:12. The remaining verses may be later additions or extensions.

There is also considerable difference of opinion concerning the identity of the ebed Yahweh. The collective interpretation understands the servant of the Lord to refer to Israel—the ideal Israel or the godly part of Israel or even the prophets.

Others point out that the servant has so many personal features that he must be a particular individual. But those who favor such an explanation also differ among themselves. Are we to think of a concrete historical figure—Moses, Isaiah, Jeremiah, Josiah, Jehoiakim, Zerubbabel, and others are mentioned—or of a future eschatological personality, the Messiah? In the New Testament Jesus Christ is seen as the *ebed Yahweh* (Matt. 8:17; 12:15–21; Luke 22:37; Acts 8:32–33). Nowadays many prefer to see in the servant of the Lord Deutero-Isaiah, but what is said of him may have been repeated and deepened in a later person. The *ebed Yahweh* is portrayed as a prophetic figure but also as a man with royal features who brings about redemption for Israel and the other nations. His task caused him much suffering. In a substitutionary act, he suffered on account of the sins of the people.

Chapters 56–66 are sometimes attributed to a Trito-Isaiah, a prophet who arose among the Jewish people after they had returned from the Babylonian captivity. Duhm first suggested such a prophet, placing the prophecy in the time of Malachi, when the temple had been rebuilt but not yet the wall of Jerusalem. Others prefer to think of the time of Zechariah and Zerubbabel, that is, shortly after the return (ca. 520 B.C.), when both temple and wall still had to be rebuilt (cf. 66:1). An occasional scholar thinks of a much later era, for instance, that of the Maccabees. Because the style and content of certain parts (e.g., chs. 60–65) show affinity with Deutero-Isaiah, he too is sometimes regarded as the author; he presumably still ministered among the people after the return (so Eissfeldt). Still others propose that it was a student of Deutero-Isaiah.

Some parts may relate to the end of the Exile or the beginning of the return (56:8; 57:14–19; 59:20–21; chs. 60–64; 65:21–25), but most cannot be dated. They may have been composed in the Exile, but also afterward. In some cases it is equally plausible to think of a pre- *and* a postexilic origin.

It is wrong to view these chapters as all being from one author. We have here a collection of prophecies of diverse style, with a variety of background and time of origin. They do have certain common traits: salvation is for all nations (56:1–8; 60:3–14; 66:18–19, 21); Israel remains the religious center (60:4–7, 10–14; 66:10–13); God's judgment extends to all nations (59:18; 60:12; 63:3–6; 64:1–3; 66:15–16) but also concerns Israel, from which only the true believers will be saved (57:13, 20–21; 58:13–14; 60:21; 65:13–16; 66:2, 17). Included in the sins of the people are idolatrous practices (57:5–9; 65:3–4; 66:3, 17) and social injustice (56:11; 57:1; 58:3–4; 59:3–9). Much store is set by the purity of the worship of God, the practice of fasting, and the keeping of the Sabbath (ch. 58; 66:3–6). Many of these thoughts, however, appear also in the prophets before the Captivity.

The following subparts can be distinguished: 56:1–8, admonition to admit strangers and eunuchs to the community; 56:9–57:13, the people are denounced on account of injustice and idolatry (this section fits well in the preexilic era, ca. 586 B.C.); 57:14–21, promise of deliverance; chapter 58, admonition to practice fasting and keep the Sabbath, likely postexilic (cf. v. 12); chapter 59, there is no redemption without conversion; chapter 60, future glory of Zion; chapter 61, the prophet as messenger of salvation; chapter 62, the salvation of Zion is imminent; 63:1–6, vengeance upon the nations; 63:7–64:12, prayer of repentance for God's compassion upon destroyed Jerusalem; 65:1–16, judgment for the wicked, and salvation only for the faithful (the people sacrifice to Gad and Meni, the gods Fortune and Chance, regarded by some as belonging to the Greek period [cf. Greek *Tuchē*], but the worship of these gods may also be much older); 65:17–25, promise of salvation for Jerusalem in cosmic perspective; 66:1–4, the people bring godless sacrifices, a passage reminiscent of the prophecies of Malachi; 66:5–24, last judgment and new future.

LITERATURE

Commentaries:

W. A. M. Beuken, *Jesaja deel IIB (= Jes. 49–55)* (POT; Nijkerk, 1983).

P. E. Bonnard, *Le second Isaïe, son disciple et leur éditerus* (Paris, 1972).

R. E. Clements, *Isaiah 1–39* (New Century Bible; London/Grand Rapids, 1980).

F. Delitzsch, *Isaiah* (Grand Rapids, repr. 1973).

B. Duhm, *Das Buch Jesaja* (HKAT III/1; Göttingen, 1892, 1968[5]).

K. Elliger, *Deutero-Jesaja 1* (= Isa. 40:1–45:7) (BKAT XI/1; Neukirchen, 1978).

G. B. Gray, *A Critical and Exegetical Commentary on Isaiah* (= Isa. 1–27) (ICC; Edinburgh, 1913).

O. Kaiser, *Isaiah 1–12* (OTL; Philadelphia, 1983[2]).

——, *Isaiah 13–39* (OTL; Philadelphia, 1974).

G. A. F. Knight, *Servant Theology: A Commentary on the Book of Isaiah 40–55* (International Theological Commentary; Grand Rapids/Edinburgh, 1984).

——, *The New Israel: A Commentary on the Book of Isaiah 56–66* (International Theological Commentary; Grand Rapids/Edinburgh, 1985).

J. L. Koole, *Jesaja II/1* (= Isa. 40–48) (COT; Kampen, 1985).

C. R. North, *The Second Isaiah. Introduction, Translation and Commentary to Chapters XL-LV* (Oxford, 1964).

J. Oswalt, *The Book of Isaiah, Chapters 1–39* (NICOT; Grand Rapids, 1986).

J. Ridderbos, *Isaiah* (Bible Student's Commentary; Grand Rapids, 1985).

J. D. Smart, *History and Theology in Second Isaiah. A Commentary on Isaiah 35, 40–66* (Philadelphia, 1965).

L. A. Snijders, *Jesaja I* (= Isa. 1–39) (POT; Nijkerk, 1979[2]).

C. Westermann, *Isaiah 40–66* (OTL; Philadelphia, 1969).

R. N. Whybray, *Isaiah 40–66* (New Century Bible; London/Grand Rapids, 1981).

H. Wildberger, *Jesaja 1–39* I-III (BKAT X; Neukirchen-Vluyn, 1972-82).

Other Works:

P. R. Ackroyd, "Isaiah I-XIII: Presentation of a Prophet," in SVT 29 (1978) 16-48.

O. T. Allis, *The Unity of Isaiah* (Philadelphia, 1950).

H. Barth, *Die Jesaja-Worte in der Josiazeit* (WMANT 48; Neukirchen-Vluyn, 1977).

M. A. Beek, "Ein Erdbeben wird zum prophetischen Erleben," *Archiv orientální* (1949) 31-40.

P. A. H. de Boer, *Second Isaiah's Message* (OTS 11; Leiden, 1956).

J. H. Eaton, *Festal Drama in Deutero-Isaiah* (London, 1979).

O. Eissfeldt, *Der Gottesknecht bei Deuterojesaja* (Halle/Saale, 1933).

K. Elliger, *Deuterojesaja in seinem Verhältnis zu Tritojesaja* (Stuttgart, 1933).

I. Engnell, *The Call of Isaiah* (Uppsala, 1949).

P. Grelot, *Les poèmes du Serviteur. De la lecture critique à l'herméneutique* (Paris, 1981).

H. Haag, *Der Gottesknecht bei Deuterojesaja* (Darmstadt, 1985).

W. L. Holladay, *Isaiah. Scroll of a Prophetic Heritage* (Grand Rapids, 1978).

Y. Kaufmann, *The Babylonian Captivity and Deutero-Isaiah* (New York, 1970).

R. Kilian, *Jesaja 1–39* (Darmstadt, 1983) (good bibliography).

De Knecht. Studies rondom Deutero-Jesaja aangeboden aan prof. dr. J. L. Koole (Kampen, 1978).

A. van der Kooij, *Die alten Textzeugen des Jesajabuches. Ein Beitrag zur Textgeschichte des Alten Testaments* (Freiburg-Göttingen, 1981).

R. Lack, *La symbolisme du livre d'Isaïe* (Rome, 1973).

J. Lindblom, *Die Jesaja-Apokalypse* (Lunds universitets årsskrift NF Band 34, no. 3; Lund, 1938).

——, *The Servant Songs in Deutero-Isaiah. A New Attempt to Solve an Old Problem* (Lund, 1951).

R. F. Melugin, *The Formation of Isaiah 40–55* (BZAW 141; Berlin/New York, 1976).

R. P. Merendino, *Der Erste und der Letzte: Eine Untersuchung von Jes. 40–48* (SVT 31; Leiden, 1981).

C. R. North, *The Suffering Servant in Deutero-Isaiah. An Historical and Critical Study* (Oxford, 1948).

H. M. Orlinsky and N. H. Snaith, *Studies in the Second Part of the Book of Isaiah* (SVT 14; Leiden, 1967).

G. von Rad, *Theology of the Old Testament* (New York, 1965[4]), II: 172.

W. Rudolph, *Jesaja 24–27* (Stuttgart, 1933).

A. Schoors, *I am God Your Saviour. A Form-Critical Study on the Main Genres in Is. XL-LV* (SVT 24; Leiden, 1973).

H. C. Spykerboer, *The Structure and Composition of Deutero-Isaiah With Special Reference to the Polemics Against Idolatry* (Meppel, 1976).

C. Stuhlmueller, *Creative Redemption in Deutero-Isaiah* (Rome, 1970).

J. Vermeylen, *Du prophète Isaïe à l'apocalyptique: Isaïe l-xxx, miroir d'un demi-milenaire d'expérience religieuse en Israël* I-II (Paris, 1977-78).

W. Vischer, *Die Immanuel-Botschaft im Rahmen des königlichen Zionsfestes* (1955).

Th. C. Vriezen and A. S. van der Woude, *De literatuur van oud-Israël* (Wassenaar, 1980[6]), p. 211.

C. Westermann, *Sprache und Struktur der Prophetie Deuterojesajas* (Stuttgart, 1981).

R. N. Whybray, *The Second Isaiah* (OT Guides; Sheffield, 1983).

——, *Thanksgivings for a Liberated Prophet. An Interpretation of Isaiah Chapter 53* (JSOT Supplement Series 4; Sheffield, 1978).

b. Jeremiah

(1) PERSON AND TIME

Jeremiah was called to be a prophet in the thirteenth year of the reign of King Josiah (640–609 B.C.; Jer. 1:2; 25:3)—that is, in 627. Since he was still very young at the time (1:6), the year of his birth is usually assumed to be about 650 B.C., which is during the reign of Manasseh (686–642) when the Assyrian king Ashurbanipal still was at the height of his power. Jeremiah was of priestly descent and was born in the priestly town of Anathoth (cf. Josh. 21:18), about 7 kilometers (4 mi.) northeast of Jerusalem, as a son of a certain Hilkiah (Jer. 1:1). It has been conjectured that Jeremiah belonged to the family of Abiathar, who was banished by Solomon to Anathoth (1 Kgs. 2:26) and who with his family was excluded from priestly service. It seems more likely, however, that Hilkiah was a functioning priest. Of a priestly function on the part of Jeremiah we know nothing. The prophet, who remained unmarried all his life (Jer. 16:2), brought the Word of God mainly to the people of Judah in Jerusalem but never forgot northern Israel, which had been carried off into captivity. Because of the faithfulness and the love of God, that Israel still has a new future as well (chs. 30–31).

The first period of Jeremiah's ministry fell between the years 627 (the year of his calling) and 622 (the year when the well-known lawbook was discovered that sparked Josiah's reform, 2 Kings 22–23). From this period are primarily the prophecies in Jeremiah 1–6 (see 3:6); from 2:18 it is shown that the Assyrian empire was still in existence, while nowhere is there an allusion to Josiah's reform. Among the people there is only deviation, idolatry, and the refusal to mend their ways. After 622 B.C. Jeremiah appears to have withdrawn himself for a little while (perhaps to await the outcome of the reform?).

A following prophecy dates from 609 B.C., the year of Josiah's death. Josiah is killed in action at Megiddo in a battle against Pharaoh Neco. He is succeeded by his son Jehoahaz (Shallum), who after only three months is deported by Pharaoh Neco to Egypt, where he dies in exile (2 Kgs. 23:34). Jeremiah 22:10–12 is a prophecy from that time.

The prophet was particularly active during the reign of Jehoiakim (608–597), who had succeeded his brother as king. The king and the people are denounced on account of their idolatry, immorality, and injustice. God's Word and his covenant are ignored. God's judgment upon these evil deeds is bound to come. From this time are especially the prophecies in chapters 7–19; 25–26; 35–36. The prophecy in 22:20–30 dates from the period of the next king, Jehoiachin, who ruled only three months and then was deported to Babylon by Nebuchadrezzar.

The prophecies in 21:1–10 and in chapters 24, 27–29, 32–34, and 37–39 are from the time of Zedekiah (597–586). It is not clear in which period chapters 30–31 are to be placed. They deal with the restoration of Israel. Messages of that nature may have been spoken by the prophet in connection with the fall of Nineveh and of the Assyrian empire (612), but also afterward he may have returned to that subject. These chapters are a collection of a variety of prophecies uttered at various times.

After the fall of Jerusalem in 586 B.C., Jeremiah remained in the country. Following the murder of Governor Gedaliah (580), however, who had been appointed by the Babylonians over the land, he was forcefully taken to Egypt by fleeing Jews and also there continued to bring God's message (43:8–44:30). According to an old tradition found in some of the church fathers, the prophet met his death there by stoning. Jeremiah lived to be over seventy and, perhaps with a brief interruption between 622 and 608, was active for about fifty years.

There is no prophet about whom we have as many biographical data as Jeremiah or into whose soul we can look as deeply. Likely we owe these data to Jeremiah's friend Baruch (32:12–15; 36:4–8; 43:3; ch. 45). Jeremiah did not have an easy life. He experienced much opposition from the people, from the priests, from false prophets, and from government officials. His fellow citizens once tried to kill him (12:18–23). More than once he was jailed on account of his preaching (32:1–2; 38:6). In his confessions he expresses his deepest feelings—his love for his people, the difficulty he finds in announcing God's judgments to the people, and his wrestling about it with God (12:1–

4; 15:10–18; 17:12–18; 18:19–23; 20:7–18). According to some scholars, the voice of the people is heard in the prophetic "I" of the prophet (see Henning Graf Reventlow, *Liturgie und prophetisches Ich bei Jeremiah* [Gütersloh, 1963]). It is also possible that later the Jewish community appropriated the words of the prophet.

Important events in the time of Jeremiah are the reform of Josiah (622 B.C.), the fall of Nineveh (612), the death of Josiah (609), the battle at Carchemish (605), Babylon's rule over Judah (604), the partial deportation of the people and Jehoiakim to Babylon (597), the fall of Jerusalem and the beginning of the Babylonian captivity (586), and the murder of Gedaliah (580).

(2) THE BOOK OF JEREMIAH

The book of Jeremiah can be divided into five main sections.

Chapters 1–25. After the heading in 1:1–3 and the account of the calling of the prophet in vv. 4–10; 11–19 and some prophecies about Israel in 2:1–4:2 from the time of Josiah, there follows in 6:30 a series of prophecies of judgment against Judah and Jerusalem, mainly from the time of Jehoiakim. This section is followed in chapters 7–20 by prophecies, also from the time of Jehoiakim, and in 21–25 by a series of oracles from the same time (21:11–22:9) and from the years following.

Chapters 26–36. These chapters contain primarily stories about words and deeds of the prophet, sometimes in the first person (27:12, 16; 28:1; 31:26), sometimes in the third person (26:1–9; 27:1; 28:12; etc.). Most chapters are dated in the time of Jehoiakim (chs. 26 and 36) and Zedekiah. Chapters 30–33 contain promises of restoration, for northern Israel as well as for Judah.

Chapters 37–45. These chapters contain stories about Jeremiah's work and suffering during the siege of Jerusalem and after the fall of the city, including his forceful emigration to Egypt and his preaching there. They are concluded with a prophecy of Jeremiah concerning his friend Baruch, who may also have been the composer of these chapters; out of humility he puts a prophecy concerning himself last, thereby still conveying the truth of what happened. All stories are written in the third person. 39:1–10 is derived in abbreviated form from chapter 52.

Chapters 46–51. This section is made up of prophecies against the nations (Egypt, Philistia, Moab, Ammon, Edom, Damascus, Arabia, Elam, and Babylon). The prophecies may have been uttered at different times, but are combined here because of their common subject matter. Likely there were later additions.

Chapter 52. This historical appendix, with few exceptions, is similar to 2 Kings 24:18–25:30.

Perhaps chapter 36 can shed some light on the question of the origin of the book of Jeremiah. There it is related that the prophet, through the services of his friend Baruch, had recorded on a scroll all the prophecies he had delivered up to that time, that is, before 605 B.C. As three or four columns were read to the king, he cut them off and threw them into the fire. Afterward Jeremiah instructed Baruch once again to record his prophecies while he himself dictated them and even added many similar words to them (v. 32). The document read to Jehoiakim is sometimes called the "ur scroll" of Jeremiah. It contained only prophecies, no stories, and, moreover, only oracles from before 605. The scroll was much smaller than our book of Jeremiah, which is also shown by the fact that in one day it was read twice or perhaps even three times. We can thus infer that Jeremiah himself took care of the recording of his prophecies. To the original writing, other prophecies from a later time were subsequently added. The narrative parts in the book may also be the work of Baruch. He followed the life of Jeremiah closely, certainly from 605. In this way the book of Jeremiah gradually grew into its present form.

A variety of literary styles can be discerned in the book. Many prophecies are in poetry, that is, in metric form. Often the prophet employs the qinah meter (3-2 accentual schema), the style form of the lament. Remarkable are his confessions, in which he pours out before God his personal problems and agonizing inner struggles (12:1–6; 15:10–21; 17:12–18; 18:18–23; 20:7–18). Beside it are large sections in prose, to which belong both narrative parts and many prophecies.

These data raise the question why some prophecies are in poetry and others in prose, and what the relationship between the two is. Opinions vary. Duhm, in his commentary *Das Buch Jeremia* (1901), was the first to ask the question. He attributed only sixty of the poetic sections to Jeremiah. The narrative parts in prose he regarded as from Baruch, while he viewed the remainder as later additions. Because of affinity in language and style with the Deuteronomistic history books (especially Kings), an affinity that he also detected with Deutero-Isaiah and even Trito-Isaiah, Duhm dated these pieces far after the Babylonian captivity, in the fourth or the third century B.C. Also before Duhm, exegetes such as Keil and Driver had noticed the affinity in language, style, and theology between Jeremiah and the Deuteronomistic literature (e.g., Judah perishes on account of its sin). However, this similarity was explained as due to the fact that Jeremiah consciously imitated the language, style, and ideas of Deuteronomy.

Mowinckel in *Zur Komposition des Buches Jeremias,* which appeared in 1914, originally accepted Duhm's idea. He distinguished four sources in the book of Jeremiah: (1) the poetic proverbs of Jeremiah, chiefly in chapters 1–25, composed in Egypt between 580 and 480 B.C.; (2) the narrative sections about Jeremiah (chs. 26–45, of which we are unsure whether they are from Baruch), likewise composed in Egypt; (3) speeches in prose composed about 400 B.C. in Babylonia or Palestine, whose affinity with Deuteronomy is due to their arising from a circle of adherents of the Deuteronomistic reform, who projected their ideas and terminology back onto Jeremiah; and (4) a collection of anonymous prophecies of salvation (including chs. 30–31) from the postexilic era. Chapters 46–52 are a still later appendix.

In 1946 Mowinckel published his *Prophecy and Tradition,* in which he adopts the view of Harris Birkeland that the prose parts are the precipitate of a long oral tradition in the circle of Jeremiah's students, in which the words of the prophet were transmitted and received their present form. Mowinckel explains the affinity with Deuteronomy by saying that this "circle of tradition" sided with Josiah's reform and, in line with the motifs of that reform, shaped the word of Jeremiah. This conception was defended by E. W. Nicholson in his *Preaching to the Exiles* (Oxford,

1970). Volz in his commentary sees the book of Jeremiah as mainly the work of Baruch. The book contains poetic proverbs as well as speeches in prose because, as he sees it, Jeremiah was not only a poet but also an orator and writer. The prophet used various styles. The similarity with Deuteronomy must be explained by the fact that Jeremiah favored Josiah's reform and followed it in his style and ideas. Deuteronomy is identified with the code of Josiah.

Eissfeldt also ascribes both the poetic and the prosaic parts to Jeremiah. In his opinion the prose style arose during the time of Jeremiah and is therefore also used in Deuteronomy and the Deuteronomistic history books, but particularly in Ezekiel. Both prophets and priests began using this style. Bright also holds that the prose parts received their basic form during the lifetime of Jeremiah. Presumably the affinity with Deuteronomy would be not an indication of literary dependency but of a unique style that emerged in Judah at the end of the seventh century and was used both in Deuteronomy and by Jeremiah. Weiser explains the prose style as cultic in origin. According to him it was first used by priests in cultic preaching, and Jeremiah would have taken over this form. Graf Reventlow agrees with Weiser to the extent that the prose style was cultic in origin, but according to him Jeremiah made use of it because he himself also ministered in the temple. Thiel, in *Die deuteronomistische Redaktion von Jer. 1–25* (1973), explains the prose style in the book of Jeremiah as well as the affinity with Deuteronomy by assuming that the words of Jeremiah received their form in a circle of Deuteronomists who rewrote them in prose style and in accordance with their own terminology and ideas.

The various ideas concerning the prose style of Jeremiah and its affinity with Deuteronomy can be characterized as follows, though with different nuances: the *redactional* explanation (Duhm, Thiel), the *tradition-historical* explanation (Mowinckel, Birkeland, Nicholson), and the *form-critical* explanation (Eissfeldt, Bright, Weiser, Graf Reventlow).

Finally, the striking differences between the text of the book of Jeremiah in the Hebrew (and English) Bible and in the Septuagint must be considered. That difference concerns not only the place of the prophecies against the foreign nations (which in the Hebrew Bible are in chs. 46–51 and in the LXX follow after 25:13 [v. 14 is lacking in the LXX]) but also the order in which the nations occur. Furthermore, the Greek text is one-eighth, that is, about 2,700 words, shorter. Sometimes the omission involves large sections, such as 33:14–26; 39:4–13; 51:44b–49a; 52:27b–30, but mostly a single verse or even part of a verse is missing. From these facts it cannot be simply deduced that the text used by the Greek translators was shorter and closer to the original and that the surplus in the Hebrew text demonstrates later additions. In part the shorter form of the Septuagint must be explained as due to deliberate omissions either because the passages caused difficulties to the translator or because they had occurred earlier and he wanted to avoid repetition. In part the differences must also be due to unintentional omissions, such as the case of homoeoteleuton in 39:4–13 and 51:44b–49a. It is also possible that in one or two instances (e.g., 33:14–26) the Hebrew manuscript used by the Greek translators was missing part of the Hebrew text known to us. The Greek text gives insufficient ground to assert that at one time two entirely different recensions of the book of Jeremiah were in circulation.

(3) JEREMIAH'S PREACHING

The preaching of Jeremiah and that of Hosea are quite similar. Both portray the relationship of God to Israel as a love relationship, for example, that of a father to his child (3:4, 19; 31:9, 20) or that between husband and wife (2:3; 12:7). Out of love God entered into covenant with the people in the Exodus (3:19; 31:3; 32:18–22). The covenant involves the arrangement in which, if the people keep God's commandments and walk in his ways, they will be his people and he will be their God, and they will experience blessing and protection (7:23; 11:4). This relation prevailed during the honeymoon period in the desert, immediately after the Exodus (2:2). Afterward, however, the people turned unfaithful, like a woman who becomes unfaithful to her husband (3:20). The prophet sees this unfaithfulness in every area of life—religious, political, social, and personal. The people serve the Baals, the gods of the Canaanites (2:8, 23; 9:13; 11:13); the Molech (7:25–31;

32:35); the Babylonian Ishtar as the queen of heaven (7:18; 44:17–19); and the son, moon, and stars (8:2). To Jeremiah these gods are all no gods; they can do nothing (2:28; 11:12) and are worthless (2:5; 14:22). By this unfaithfulness the people have broken the covenant with Yahweh (11:8). Yet they still offer him an elaborate cultic worship with many sacrifices and prayers. But these efforts are all worthless to the prophet. God has given no commandments that would require such an elaborate sacrificial worship. God wants obedience (7:21–23). Jeremiah here (contra Volz and others) does not reject all cultic worship. To Jeremiah all these sacrifices are meaningless if they are not accompanied by obedience and a genuine love toward Yahweh.

Politically the prophet sees Israel's apostasy from God in his days in the fact that, when faced with the threatening power of Babylon, they look to Egypt and other alliances for help (27:3; 37:6–10), while God is not being served. The prophet urges surrender to the king of Babylon because God has given this ruler the power to chastise Israel (21:1–10; chs. 27–28; 34:1–3). Jeremiah also addresses other nations. In chapters 46–51 he announces judgment upon the foreign nations of Egypt (46), Philistia (47), Moab (48), Ammon, Edom, Damascus, Arabia, Elam (49), and Babylon (50–51).

In the social area the prophet denounces the sins of lawlessness, perversion of justice, oppression, and extortion, both in his first period before and after the reform of Josiah (5:28; 6:7; 9:3 [4]) and later under Jehoiakim and Zedekiah (22:3, 13; 34:8–11). Unfaithfulness to each other, adultery, immorality, deception, perjury, stealing, and killing are the order of the day, all done in a disguise of piety (3:9; 5:2, 8, 26; 6:6, 13; 7:9; etc.).

God's judgments come upon all such behavior. The vision of the prophet's calling speaks of the enemy from the north who is sent by God to punish the people (1:13). Later this theme is repeatedly mentioned (4:6; 6:22; 8:16; 10:22; 13:20). At first this enemy from the north is not further specified, but in 25:9 it is identified as Babylon. The people will not escape this enemy. They have served foreign gods. Now they will also have to serve foreigners in a foreign land (5:19; 16:13).

This judgment preaching of Jeremiah is

countered by the words of other prophets. They tell the people that nothing will happen to them, that they will enjoy undisturbed peace, and that no sword, hunger, or pestilence will strike them (4:10; 6:14; 8:11; 14:13–16; 23:17). Without calling for repentance, they announce to the people that there is nothing to fear (23:17). At this point they differ radically from Jeremiah, who preaches salvation only in the way of repentance. It has been said that Jeremiah was a prophet of doom and that others were prophets of blessings. The real difference, however, is that Jeremiah preaches salvation on condition of conversion, whereas the other prophets preach salvation unconditionally. Precisely therein they reveal themselves as false prophets (23:21–22). They prophesy lies from their own heart; God has not sent them (5:31; 14:14; 32:21). Therefore they will be put to shame (4:9; 8:12). They will be punished because of their prophecies (23:30) and perish with the people they have misled (6:15; 14:15; 20:6; 27:15).

Jeremiah continually emphasizes the teaching that, unless the people repent, they cannot expect to receive blessings (2:19; 3:14; 4:1–2; 6:8; 13:15–17; 18:11; 26:3). External religion or circumcision by itself can be of no avail to the people; spiritual circumcision is necessary (4:4; 7:21–26; 9:25 [26]). Only in that way will there be blessings for the nation and will they be able to remain in the land (25:5; 26:13). Without that repentance no prayer or petition will avail the people (7:16; 11:14; 14:11; 15:1).

Yet God's judgment on the people is not final. He remains a gracious God. Therefore he will not totally destroy the people (4:27; 5:10, 18). The exile that will come as God's judgment over the sins of the people will last seventy years (25:11; 29:10). Then the judgment will come upon Babylon on account of its iniquity (25:12). Chapters 50–51 describe that judgment in detail. Israel will return from captivity (12:15; 16:15; 23:8; 29:10; ch. 31; 32:1, 36–41; 33:16). This return will be for the kingdom of the ten tribes, carried off into Assyrian captivity, as well as for Judah (30:1–3; 31:1–6). God's mercy is for all the people. So Jeremiah, in accordance with the vision of his calling, was not only a preacher of judgment but also a preacher of good tidings (1:10).

God will make a new covenant with his people. He will give them a heart that will make them live according to the covenant, and then they will acknowledge Yahweh as their God. Then the covenant promise will be fulfilled that Yahweh will be their God and they will be his people (24:7; 31:31–34). Instead of the sinful shepherds, the leaders of the people, there will come the great Branch from the house of David, the great son of David. He will reign like a wise king, and there will be peace in the land (23:5–6; 33:15–22). God will thus fulfill the prophecy of Nathan (2 Sam. 7:12–16).

LITERATURE

Commentaries:

J. Bright, *Jeremiah* (AB; Garden City, NY, 1965).

R. P. Carroll, *Jeremiah* (OTL; Philadelphia, 1986).

B. Duhm, *Das Buch Jeremia* (KHAT 9; Tübingen, 1901).

W. Holladay, *Jeremiah 1* (= Jer. 1–25) (Hermeneia; Philadelphia, 1986).

C. F. Keil, *Jeremiah, Lamentations* (Grand Rapids, repr. 1973).

W. McKane, *Jeremiah I* (= Jer. 1–25) (ICC; Edinburgh, 1986).

W. Rudolph, *Jeremia* (HAT I/12; Tübingen, 1947/1967³).

J. A. Thompson, *The Book of Jeremiah* (NICOT; Grand Rapids, 1980).

P. Volz, *Der Prophet Jeremia* (KAT 10; Leipzig, 1928²).

A. Weiser, *Das Buch Jeremia übersetzt und erklärt* (ATD 20/21; Göttingen, 1966⁵).

Other Works:

H. Bardtke, "Jeremia der Fremdvölkerprophet," *ZAW* 53 (1935) 209-39; idem, *ZAW* 54 (1936) 240-62.

J. M. Berridge, *Prophet, People and the Word of Yahweh. An Examination of Form and Content in the Proclamation of the Prophet Jeremiah* (Zürich, 1970).

P. M. Bogaert, ed., *Le livre de Jérémie. Le prophète et son milieu, les oracles et leur transmission* (Louvain, 1981).

R. P. Carroll, *From Chaos to Covenant. Uses of Prophecy in the Book of Jeremiah* (London, 1981).

T. K. Cheyne, *Jeremiah, His Life and Times* (London, 1888).

J. G. Janzen, *Studies in the Text of Jeremiah* (Cambridge, MA, 1973).

C. de Jong, *De volken bij Jeremia. Hun plaats in zijn prediking en in het boek Jeremia* ([Kampen], 1978).

I. Meyer, *Jeremia und die falschen Propheten* (Freiburg-Göttingen, 1977).

J. W. Miller, *Das Verhältnis Jeremias und Hesekiels sprachlich und theologisch untersucht. Mit besonderer Berücksichtigung der Prosareden Jeremias* (Assen, 1955).

S. Mowinckel, *Zur Komposition des Buches Jeremias* (Kristiania, 1914).

————, *Prophecy and Tradition* (Oslo, 1946).

E. W. Nicholson, *Preaching to the Exiles. A Study of the Prose Tradition in the Book of Jeremiah* (Oxford, 1970).

T. W. Overholt, *The Threat of Falsehood. A Study in the Theology of the Book of Jeremiah* (London/Naperville, IL, 1970).

H. Graf Reventlow, *Liturgie und prophetisches Ich bei Jeremia* (Gütersloh, 1963).

J. Skinner, *Prophecy and Religion. Studies in the Life of Jeremiah* (Cambridge, 1936³).

S. Soderlund, *The Greek Text of Jeremiah* (*JSOT* Supplement Series 47; Sheffield, 1985).

W. Thiel, *Die deuteronomistische Redaktion von Jeremia 1–25* (WMANT 41; Neukirchen-Vluyn, 1972).

————, *Die deuteronomistische Redaktion von Jeremia 26–45* (WMANT 52; Neukirchen-Vluyn, 1981).

H. Weippert, *Die Prosareden des Jeremiabuches* (BZAW 132; Berlin/New York, 1973).

A. C. Welch, *Jeremiah, His Time and his Work* (Oxford, 1928; repr. 1955).

H. Wildberger, *Jahwewort und prophetische Rede bei Jeremia* (Zürich, 1942).

C. Wolff, *Jeremia im Frühjudentum und Urchristentum* (Berlin, 1976).

c. Ezekiel

(1) PERSON AND TIME

Ezekiel, priest in Jerusalem, was the son of a certain Buzi (1:3). His wife died just prior to the collapse of Jerusalem in 586 B.C. (24:18), and he was apparently childless. Along with Jehoiachin and other Jewish notables, Ezekiel was deported by Nebuchadrezzar to Babylon (2 Kgs. 24:8–17). There together with many other captives he lived in Tel-abib (Ezek. 3:15; Akkadian *till abubi*, "flood hill"), apparently an area that had long been un-inhabited and that was assigned as residence to the exiles, located near the Chebar (1:1), one of the canals of Babylonia, not far from Nippur. There Ezekiel lived in a house of his own (3:24; 8:1; 12:3), in agreement with the counsel of Jeremiah (Jer. 29:5).

In 593 B.C., five years after his deportation, Ezekiel was called to be a prophet in the land of Babylon (1:2; as a rule the dates in Ezekiel are based on the year of his deportation; see 24:1 [2 Kgs. 25:1]; Ezek. 33:21; 40:1). According to some (e.g., Origen) the statement that the calling happened in the thirtieth year (1:1) refers to his age. Though this interpretation is not certain, the prophet may have been that age when he was called. He was not so young, for according to 4:14 he was past the time of his youth. The fact that he belonged to those deported may indicate that he had an influential position before his deportation. His prophetic labors lasted for over twenty years. The last date in his book is the twenty-seventh year of his deportation (29:17), or 571 B.C.

Ezekiel labored in Tel-abib. There he admonished his fellow captives, instructing and comforting them (3:11; 11:14–15; 14:1–11; 18:25; 33:2, 12, 17). His prophecies were also addressed to Judah and Jerusalem (chs. 6; 16; 21–22; 23:22–49). Before the fall of Jerusalem these prophecies were predominantly announcements of judgment (chs. 1–24); afterward, they were announcements of blessings (chs. 33–48). In his preaching the prophet also addressed other nations (chs. 25–32).

Some have denied that the scene of Ezekiel's labor was Babylon, or exclusively so. According to James Smith, *The Book of the Prophet Ezekiel* (London, 1931), Ezekiel was not from Judah but from the kingdom of the ten tribes and was included in those whom Tiglath-pileser III deported from the northern kingdom to Assyria in 734 B.C. There the prophet would at first have labored among his fellow exiles and then, in the thirtieth year after the fall of Samaria (Smith's explanation of 1:1), that is, 691, would have returned to Palestine, where, under the reign of Manasseh, he would have opposed the apostate priesthood and idol worship. Volkmar Herntrich, *Ezechielprobleme* (Giessen, 1932), while placing Ezekiel in the time of Jehoiachin, believes that the scene of his labors was not

Babylon but Jerusalem. There Ezekiel would have prophesied from 593 to 586 B.C. An exilic redactor would then have forced the work of Ezekiel into an exilic (i.e., Babylonian) framework and would have placed the prophet with the exiles of 597. The same conception is found in R. H. Pfeiffer, *Introduction to the Old Testament* (New York, 1941).

Robinson (see lit. under Oesterley and Robinson, 1934), Bertholet (1936), and van den Born (1954) believe that there were two scenes of activity: before 597 (Robinson) or before 586 (Bertholet, van den Born) in Jerusalem, and later in Babylon. Aage Bentzen (1948) believes that the prophet was indeed called to be a prophet in 593 in Babylonia but that he later returned to Jerusalem. Nils Messel, *Ezechielfragen* (Oslo, 1945), defends the view that Ezekiel did not prophesy in Babylon but toward the end of the fifth century, shortly after Nehemiah, labored among the returned captives in Jerusalem. About half a century later a redactor, while adding various other sections, would have reissued the book of Ezekiel and in the process would have projected his ministry back into the captivity. Torrey, following Smith, thinks of a prophet active during the reign of Manasseh, in the thirtieth year of his reign (1:1!), who prophesied against his atrocities. Later, about 230 B.C., someone would have issued the book pseudonymously as Ezekiel, under the pretext that Ezekiel was active during the captivity in Babylon.

All these notions in one way or another try to account for the fact that in the book of Ezekiel several prophecies are addressed to Judah and Jerusalem and that therefore presumably they presuppose a different scene of labor than Babylon. Eissfeldt observes, however, (1) that no cogent arguments have been adduced against the view that Ezekiel was called to be a prophet while in Babylon and labored there from 593 to 571 or perhaps even a little longer, and (2) that all hypotheses proposed to take its place have little foundation and are burdened with numerous objections. It is not so incredible that in Babylon Ezekiel addressed prophecies against Judah and Jerusalem, for he also addressed Egypt and other nations, without personally having been there. Zimmerli in his commentary accepts this

view, which has been defended by Eissfeldt and others.

Ezekiel is usually characterized as a highly complex personality and has been variously evaluated. Hölscher regarded him as a great poet, but Duhm denied to him all poetic inspiration. Fohrer calls him one of the greatest among the prophets, but according to Wellhausen he was an epigone who had nothing in common with prophets such as Isaiah and Jeremiah. Wellhausen's view is based in particular on the priestly traits exhibited by Ezekiel, as he represents a transition from the priestly morality religion to the Jewish law religion. Ezekiel does indeed exhibit priestly traits and did not deny his priestly background. One might point to his punctuality in keeping the cultic laws (4:14), though with him the cultic laws can never be detached from the moral laws (18:5–9; 20:19–20; 22:8–12, 26–29; 23:38–39; 33:25). His interest in temple and liturgical service is also demonstrated by his design of the new temple in chapters 40–48. But it would be unfair for that reason to mark him as a prophet of lesser significance. Ezekiel is still very much a prophet of the old dispensation.

He has also been regarded as an ecstatic, someone with paranormal gifts, or even as mentally ill. Visions are indeed very prominent in his book (note the visions of his calling in chs. 1–3, of the temple in chs. 8–11, of the valley of dry bones in ch. 37, and of the new temple in chs. 40–48). But visions are also found in other prophets. It seems certain that Ezekiel was a man with visionary ability. Clairvoyance is attributed to him on the basis of chapter 8, where from Babylon he sees what is happening in the temple in Jerusalem. Also from Babylon he witnesses the death of Pelatiah in Jerusalem (11:13). This phenomenon, however, also occurs in other prophets (e.g., 2 Kgs. 5:26). Mental illness has been attributed to the prophet because he fell on his face (Ezek. 1:28; 3:23) and for a time was unable to speak (3:26; 24:27). According to Klostermann, this condition would point to paralysis or catalepsy. In 4:4–6 it is said that the prophet for many days lay first on his left side and then on his right side. It has correctly been pointed out, both by the medical profession (Dieckhoff) and by theologians, that such behavior has nothing to do with mental aberration.

His bewilderment may have been related to a certain supersensitivity on his part, while his inability to speak may relate to the fact that he did not receive a divine revelation, so that he could not speak the Word of God. The prophet's poetic gifts are evident from his beautiful allegories (e.g., of the two eagles and the vine in ch. 17, of the lioness and her cub in ch. 19, of the ship Tyre in ch. 27), though the one of unfaithful Jerusalem and of the prostitutes Oholah and Oholibah (chs. 16 and 23) appear rather realistic.

(2) THE BOOK OF EZEKIEL

The chapters of Ezekiel can be divided into three main sections: 1–24, words of judgment about Jerusalem and Judah (before 586 B.C.); 25–32, words of judgment about the foreign nations; and 33–48, announcement of blessings (after 586). The first section contains the following subdivisions: 1:1–3:15, vision of Ezekiel's calling; 3:16–27, second calling and appearance of the glory of the Lord; 4–5, symbolic acts in connection with the siege of Jerusalem; 6–7, announcement of judgment over Judah; 8–11, temple vision in which the prophet is shown the sins in the temple and the judgment upon people and rulers; 12, a symbolic act that portrays the Exile; 13, prophecy against the false prophets; 14, prophecy against the idol worshipers; 15, Jerusalem and the useless vine; 16, Jerusalem allegorically depicted as a prostitute; 17, the allegory of the eagles; 18, Ezekiel's preaching concerning personal human responsibility; 19, allegory of the lioness and her cub; 20, Ezekiel's warning from history; 21, the sword drawn against Jerusalem; 22, Jerusalem's sins; 23, allegory of Oholah and Oholibah; and 24, Jerusalem a rusty pot and the death of Ezekiel's wife.

The second section (chs. 25–32) includes prophecies against several foreign nations: 25:1–7, Ammon; 25:8–11, Moab; 25:12–14, Edom; 25:15–17, Philistia; 26:1–28:19, Tyre; 28:20–26, Sidon; and chapters 29–32, Egypt. In the third section (chs. 33–48), we distinguish the following parts: 33, as a watchman Ezekiel must sound his warnings to the people—a righteous person who sins is not saved by his or her righteousness, and a godless person who repents does not perish on account of his or her godlessness; 34, God himself is the good shepherd of his people; 35, God's vengeance upon Edom; 36, Israel purified and restored; 37:1–14, the vision of the valley of dry bones; 37:15–28, Israel and Judah reunited; 38–39, prophecies over Gog and Magog; and 40–48, restoration of city and temple.

The book of Ezekiel has a fairly coherent structure. Chapters 1–24 contain prophecies uttered by the prophet before the fall of Jerusalem (see 24:25–27), and 33:21–33 also connects with that event. Various prophecies in this section have a specific date. The calling vision (1:1–3:15) was on the fifth day of the fourth month in the fifth year after the deportation in 597. The second calling and appearance of the Lord happened a week later (3:16–27). The temple vision was on the fifth day of the sixth month in the sixth year (8:1). Ezekiel's warning from history was given on the tenth day of the fifth month in the seventh year (20:1). The Word of God came to Ezekiel on the tenth day of the tenth month in the ninth year, the exact day on which Nebuchadrezzar began his siege of Jerusalem (24:1–2; 2 Kgs. 25:1).

The space between the siege of Jerusalem and the report of the capture of the city, which the prophet receives on the fifth day of the tenth month in the twelfth year (33:21), is filled up by the prophecies against the foreign nations and a prophecy about Ezekiel's office as watchman (vv. 1-20). The vision of the new temple he receives in the twenty-fifth year (573 B.C.), on the tenth day of the first month (40:1). The final dated prophecy is in 571 (29:17). We do not know when precisely the undated prophecies in chapters 34–39 were given, but certainly after 586.

The question whether the prophet himself organized his book in this fashion or whether it was the work of a redactor cannot be answered with certainty, although perhaps the latter is the case. The hand of the redactor is clearly recognizable at least in 1:2–3, where the prophet is mentioned in the third person, whereas everywhere else the first person is used. Apparently the redactor deemed it necessary to make this addition, because in 1:1 the first person is immediately used without any indication of who is doing the speaking. Zimmerli and others think of a school of Ezekiel's students who collected their teacher's prophecies, augmented them here and there, and organized them into the present book. In any case it should be assumed that a redactor or group of redactors brought together in the book notes from the prophet himself.

Ezekiel's first-person style and the frequent datings indicate that he himself recorded his prophecies. (Some have mistakenly asserted that these datings are purely fictional.) Even in the datings something of the priest Ezekiel can be seen. Priests were accustomed to take a census and to record data, which does not mean that the undated prophecies are not from Ezekiel. It is likewise wrong, as Hölscher has done, to ascribe only the poetic parts of the book to Ezekiel and to deny him the prose parts. The prophet wrote prose as well as poetry. Normally he spoke prose, but in certain poems and allegories he showed his poetic gifts.

In general his book gives a proper chronological sequence. Occasionally the material has determined the sequence. The prophecy against Tyre (ch. 26) was given in the eleventh year, after the fall of Jerusalem, and is followed by a series of other prophecies against Tyre (chs. 27–28). Then follows in 29:1–16 a prophecy against Egypt from the tenth year, and another one from the twenty-seventh year (29:17–21). This latter prophecy is placed here because the content fits in with the previously recorded prophecy. Next there are five additional prophecies against Egypt (30:1–19, 20–26; ch. 31; 32:1–16, 17–32), from the eleventh and the twelfth years. We can legitimately assume that a number of prophecies relating Tyre and Egypt, even before they were incorporated into the present book of Ezekiel, had already been collected in small separate volumes. It may likewise be assumed that chapters 40–48 were a separate writing from Ezekiel, one from the last period of his prophetic ministry (573 B.C.).

The text of Ezekiel is in many respects corrupt and sometimes difficult or almost impossible to translate. It also deviates in many respects from the Septuagint. Yet there is no reason to prefer the text of the latter to that of the Hebrew, because it is not certain whether the Septuagint version goes back to a better Hebrew text than the one we possess.

(3) EZEKIEL'S PREACHING

In chapters 1–24 Ezekiel's preaching is primarily a message of judgment. In his calling vision (chs. 1–3), in which he marvelously experienced the exaltedness and majesty of Yahweh and by contrast his own insignificance (something also forcefully expressed in the phrase "son of man," with which he is regularly addressed and which expresses the infinite distance between God and humankind), the prophet is appointed as a preacher of judgment. That task will not be pleasant, because he will have to face a stubborn and rebellious people who will express their hostility openly. However, unconditionally and fearlessly the prophet must be obedient to God and perform his mandate. It may be difficult to be faithful, but it will always be good and pleasant to do God's will. Therefore the scroll that he has to eat, inscribed on both sides with judgments and laments, is sweet as honey in his mouth (2:9–3:3).

God comes to Israel with judgment because of the sin of the people. It is pictured as disobedience, consisting in the people's disregard of God's ordinances and statutes and their rebellion against them (5:6–7; 11:12). Israel is a rebellious house (2:5, 8; 12:2). The people would not listen (20:8). Ezekiel depicts the cultic sins of the people: they polluted the temple with idolatrous practices (5:11); images of idols are erected in it (8:5); Tammuz is given homage there (v. 14) and the sun is worshiped (v. 16). Everywhere else as well images and altars abound, especially, in accordance with Canaanite custom, on heights and under green trees, and idols are worshiped (6:4, 6, 13; 7:20). The heart of Israel, including the exiles in Babylon, goes out to them (14:3; 20:16). Children are sacrificed to idols, though they were destined for the service of Yahweh (16:20; 20:31).

Morally the situation was equally deplorable. Justice was corrupted (18:10–13). Immorality, incest, robbery, social abuse, oppression, gain from usury, and the like were the order of the day. Strangers, widows, and orphans were oppressed (vv. 5–8; 22:7–12, 29). Even the leaders of the people participated in these practices. The priests trifled with the law, desecrated the holy things, disregarded the distinction between holy and unholy, and shut their eyes to the keeping of the sabbath (22:26). As a result the people desecrated the sabbath (20:16, 24; 22:8), which had been given as a sign between God and the people and which was to mark Israel as the special people of

43. *Part of an ivory ornament from a fortress near a northern border post of Aram (Syria). The inscription in Palaeo-Hebrew includes the name of Hazael, king of Aram ca. 842-798 B.C., who regularly fought King Joram and King Jehu of Israel and King Joash of Judah during the time of the prophets Elijah and Elisha (see pp. 54f.). (Musée du Louvre, Paris)*

44. *An early Hebrew inscription from the 7th century B.C., part of the doorpost of a tomb of a high court official during the reign of Hezekiah. The beautifully decorated tomb is cut out of the rock at Siloam near Jerusalem. The inscription mentions a "[. . .]-yahu, who is in charge of the palace." Some hold that this grave belonged to the chief steward Shebna (an abbreviation of Shebanyahu), who was denounced by Isaiah for his extravagant mode of living (Isa. 22:15) and after some time was replaced as steward by Eliakim (see p. 231). (Trustees of the British Museum)*

45. *The Siloam tunnel inscription (see p. 66). (Israel Department of Antiquities and Museums)*

46. *Ostracon with a message to Joash, commander of Lachish (part of Lachish ostracon no. 11; ca. 586 B.C.). (Trustees of the British Museum)*

47. *The hexagonal clay prism of Sennacherib (36.5 cm. [14 in.] high). The monarch tells of his successful campaign against Syria, Tyre, and Judah. He writes that he "locked up Hezekiah of Judah like a bird in its cage in Jerusalem." The prism dates from ca. 691 B.C. and is also called the Taylor Cylinder after its discoverer (see p. 65). (Trustees of the British Museum)*

48. *King Jehu of Israel bowing before Shalmaneser III: the black obelisk of Shalmaneser (see p. 55). (Trustees of the British Museum)*

50. *After the fall of Lachish a number of captives from the city, probably prominent men, are skinned alive. Relief from the palace of Sennacherib near Nineveh (Küyünjik; ca. 700 B.C.). (Trustees of the British Museum)*

51. *Prisoners from Judah are transported by wagon to Nineveh (see p. 69). Relief from the palace of Ashurbanipal in Nineveh (Küyünjik; ca. 600 B.C.). (Musée du Louvre, Paris)*

49. *The siege of Lachish in southern Judah depicted in a relief from the palace of Sennacherib of Assyria near Nineveh (Küyünjik; ca. 700 B.C.). (Trustees of the British Museum)*

52. *Tiglath-pileser III in his chariot: a relief from Nimrud (see pp. 56, 64). (Trustees of the British Museum)*

53. The part of the Babylonian Chronicle which tells of the fall of the Assyrian capital of Nineveh (see p. 68). (Trustees of the British Museum)

54. A clay tablet, part of the Babylonian Chronicle telling of events in 605–594 B.C., including Zedekiah's appointment as vassal king of Judah in 597 by Nebuchadrezzar and the deportation of King Jehoiachin and other prominent persons from Jerusalem (see p. 69). Height about 8 cm. (3 in.). (Trustees of the British Museum)

55. Remnants of fortifications in Samaria from the time of the Exile and of an amphitheater from Herod the Great's rebuilding of the city (under the name Sebaste) in Hellenistic fashion. (Dr. E. Noort, 't Harde, the Netherlands)

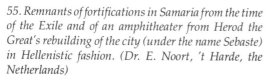

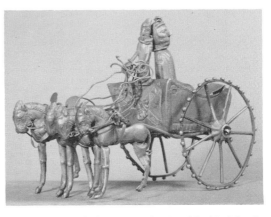

57. *A gold model of a Persian chariot of the kind developed by the Assyrian ruler Sennacherib. (Trustees of the British Museum)*

56. *Persian soldiers depicted in a relief at Persepolis. (Staatliche Museen zu Berlin, DDR, Vorderasiatisches Museum 2987)*

58. *Part of a relief from the palace of Darius I of Persia in Persepolis, Iran, about 2.5 meters (8 ft.) high, dating from ca. 500 B.C. Behind Darius, who is seated on his throne, stands Xerxes (Ahasuerus) his son, who in 485 B.C. became his successor (see pp. 82f., 84). (Oriental Institute, University of Chicago)*

59. *Persepolis, one of the principal royal residences of the Persian Empire. (Oriental Institute, University of Chicago)*

60. *An Assyrian monarch (probably Adad-nirari III), praying to his gods, who are represented by their symbols: the sun with rays (Shamash), the moon (Sin), seven stars (Sibitti), a stylus (Nabu), a spade (Marduk), lightning (Adad), a sacred headdress (Enlil), and a winged disk (Ashur). Part of a stele discovered at Tell Rimah in Iraq, on which presentation of tribute by King Joash is recorded (ca. 796 B.C.). (British School of Archaeology in Iraq)*

61. *A copy of a letter from the priest Jedoniah in the Jewish colony at Elephantine (see pp. 92f.) to Governor Bagoas of Judah requesting help in securing permission for the rebuilding of the temple at Elephantine. This papyrus also contains the names of Sanballat, the governor of Samaria, and of his sons Delaiah and Selemiah. (Staatliche Museen zu Berlin, DDR, Aegyptisches Museum)*

62. *Part of the Teaching of Amenemope, written on papyrus and dating from the Egyptian 22nd Dynasty (ca. 950–730 B.C.), earlier according to some. In some respects this document can be compared with the wisdom literature of Israel (see p. 157). (Trustees of the British Museum)*

63. *Musicians at a banquet depicted in an Egyptian tomb painting of the 15th century B.C. (Oriental Institute, University of Chicago)*

64. *Two columns from a commentary* (pesher) *on Habakkuk (1QpHab) from Cave 1 at Qumran* (see p. 262). *(Photo archive Kok, Kampen)*

65. *Column 37 of the Job targum from Cave 11 of Qumran. The column contains the text of a paraphrasing Aramaic translation of Job 41:25–42:6* (see p. 277). *(Koninklijke Akademie van Wetenschappen, Amsterdam)*

God (20:12, 20). The rulers were rapacious wolves who shed blood and killed people to acquire unjust gain (22:27). Instead of being good shepherds who pastured the sheep, they were bad shepherds and took care only of themselves (34:2–6). The prophets deceived the people, speaking in the name of Yahweh although he had not sent them, proclaiming peace when there was no peace (13:8–10; 22:28).

Through all these sins the people manifested their unfaithfulness to God, who from the beginning had entered into covenant with them to be their God and so had shown his love to them (16:8). Israel is pictured as a newborn girl who was thrown out into the open field. God took pity on her, clothed her, reared her, and entered into marriage with her (vv. 1–8). This portrayal of God's covenant with his people as a marriage is also found in Hosea and Jeremiah. As for Hosea, so also for Ezekiel the sin of the people was adultery and immorality (6:9; 16:15, 20; 23:5, 11–12). The people flirted with the foreign nations and their idols to gain their favor (23:5–21), but not for a moment did they remember the love God had once shown to them (16:22). The people had faithlessly violated and broken God's covenant (v. 59; 17:19; 44:7). All of Israel's history is a history of unfaithfulness toward God, who by giving them his statutes wanted to bind them close to himself (20:1–6). But Israel did not keep those statutes and forgot Yahweh (22:12). God had not destroyed his people sooner because he did not want his name to be profaned before the nations (20:9, 14, 22). But now his judgment will irrevocably strike the people (5:8–9).

Sword, hunger, and pestilence will come upon the people (5:12, 16–17; 6:12; 7:15; 14:21). They will be scattered in all directions (5:10, 12; 12:15; 22:15). Jerusalem is besieged and destroyed (21:23–28 [18–23]; 22:1–5; 24:1–14), thrown away like a useless vine (ch. 15). The other cities are also destroyed (6:6), and the land is turned into a desolate waste (33:28). Prophets and priests are not spared (14:9–11; 22:31). King Zedekiah is carried off to Babylon and will die there (12:13; 17:16, 20; 19:9). The prophet underscores his preaching by symbolic acts, in which he himself in advance experiences the misery that will come upon the people (chs. 4–5; 12). So Israel

will come to an end (ch. 7), and the people will learn from experience that Yahweh is a God who is not to be mocked (5:13; 6:7, 10, 13–14; 7:27; 11:12; etc.). Neither prayer nor cry will avert the judgment (8:18). Only conversion will still be able to save the people; therefore Ezekiel puts all the emphasis on each one's personal responsibility (ch. 18; 33:12–16). He is thus appointed as a watchman to warn the people to turn from their sinful ways, for God has no pleasure in the death of the sinner but only in the sinner's repenting and living (3:17–21; 33:1–20). The people, however, did not repent.

The preaching of judgment is not the prophet's final word. After the fall of Jerusalem he comforts the people with God's promises of salvation, found especially in chapters 34–37, though such promises are not absent in the earlier chapters either. Perhaps the prophet comforted the faithful even before the fall of Jerusalem with these promises; otherwise it must be assumed that later they were interspersed with the messages of judgment. In the judgment a remnant is spared (6:8–9). The people will be gathered from the countries to which they have been scattered (11:17; 20:34, 41; 36:24). They will again live in their own land (34:27; 36:28; 37:25). A new future will dawn as cities will again be inhabited and ruins rebuilt (34:25; 36:10–12, 33–38; 37:1–14).

Ezekiel pictures especially the spiritual renewal of the people. The adulterous heart is broken (6:9). The heart of stone is removed, and a heart of flesh is put in its place. The people receive a new heart and a new spirit to keep God's laws (11:19; 36:26). It is purified from sins (vv. 25, 33; 37:23). God's covenant made with the people in the time of their youth is renewed (16:60). God and people are reunited (14:11; 36:28; 37:23, 27), all of which will happen under the rule of a new David, the Messiah, who will be their shepherd (34:24; 37:24). Israel and Judah are also reunited (vv. 15–28). All the people will serve God (20:40). God acts as he does not because the people have merited it but only for the sake of his name, that is, his honor (v. 44; 36:21–22, 32). He thus reveals himself as the Holy One in the midst of his people and the other nations (28:25). His sanctuary will again be in the midst of his people (37:27). Everything is renewed: the temple buildings (chs. 40–43), the cult and the cultic personnel (chs. 44–46), and the land and the city of Jerusalem (chs. 47–48). The glory of the Lord that had departed from the old temple (11:23) returns in the new (43:4–5).

In chapters 25–32 the judgments of God are announced against the other nations. It is noteworthy that Babylon is not mentioned. It serves to carry out God's punishments upon the nations (26:7–14; 29:17–20; 30:10, 24–25).

LITERATURE

Commentaries:

A. Bertholet, *Das Buch Hesekiel* (KHAT; Freiburg/Leipzig/Tübingen, 1897).

A. Bertholet and K. Galling, *Hesekiel* (HAT I/13; Tübingen, 1936).

A. van den Born, *Ezechiël uit de grondtekst vertaald en uitgelegd* (BOT; Roermond-Maaseik, 1954).

G. A. Cooke, *A Critical and Exegetical Commentary on the Book of Ezekiel* (ICC; Edinburgh, 1936).

W. Eichrodt, *Ezekiel* (OTL; Philadelphia, 1970).

G. Fohrer and K. Galling, *Ezechiel* (HAT; Tübingen, 1955).

C. F. Keil, *Ezekiel, Daniel* (Grand Rapids, repr. 1973).

J. W. Wevers, *Ezekiel* (New Century Bible; London/Grand Rapids, repr. 1980).

W. Zimmerli, *Ezekiel* I-II (Hermeneia; Philadelphia, 1979-83).

Other Works:

A. Bentzen, *Introduction to the Old Testament* II (Copenhagen, 1948).

A. van den Born, *De historische situatie van Ezechiëls prophetie* (Leuven, 1947).

E. C. Broome, "Ezekiel's Abnormal Personality," *JBL* 65 (1946) 277-92.

D. Dieckhoff, "Der Prophet Ezechiel," *Zeitschrift für Religionspsychologie: Grenzfragen der Theologie und Medizin* (1908) 193-206.

G. Fohrer, *Die Hauptprobleme des Buches Ezechiel* (BZAW 72; Berlin, 1952).

V. Herntrich, *Ezechielprobleme* (BZAW 61; Giessen, 1932).

G. Hölscher, *Hesekiel, der Dichter und das Buch* (BZAW 39; Giessen, 1924).

C. G. Howie, *The Date and Composition of Ezekiel* (Philadelphia, 1950).

W. A. Irwin, *The Problem of Ezekiel* (Chicago, 1943).

A. Klostermann, "Ezechiel. Ein Beitrag zu besserer Würdigung seiner Person und seiner Schrift," *Theologische Studien und Kritiken* 50 (1877) 391-439.

N. Messel, *Ezechielfragen* (Oslo, 1945).

W. O. E. Oesterley and T. H. Robinson, *An Introduction to the Books of the Old Testament* (London, 1934).

H. Wheeler Robinson, *Two Hebrew Prophets* (London, 1948).

H. H. Rowley, "The Book of Ezekiel in Modern Study," in *Men of God* (London, 1963), pp. 169ff.

J. Smith, *The Book of the Prophet Ezekiel* (London, 1931).

C. C. Torrey, *Pseudo-Ezekiel and the Original Prophecy* (New Haven, 1930).

3. THE MINOR PROPHETS

Hosea is the first of the so-called minor prophets, the twelve of which constitute the *Dodekapropheton*, the "book of the twelve prophets." The name *Dodekapropheton* is from Jesus Sirach. The designation *minor* goes back to the church father Augustine, who adds that the term refers to the relatively shorter length of their sermons (*De civitate Dei* 18.29). It would be absolutely wrong to understand the designation as implying that the significance of the minor prophets is less than that of the other prophets. Men such as Amos and Hosea were certainly no less forceful and significant than such spokespersons for God as Isaiah and Jeremiah.

In the Hebrew Bible the minor prophets follow Ezekiel. In the Septuagint they come before Isaiah, reflecting the fact that Hosea and Amos preceded Isaiah and Jeremiah. Chronology also played a role in the Septuagint's arrangement of the minor prophets. The order there is Hosea, Amos, Micah, Joel, Obadiah, Jonah, Nahum, and then as in the Hebrew and English Bibles. The Hebrew Bible, besides arranging books on the basis of chronology (the oldest prophets first, the postexilic last), takes account of a book's length (Hosea thus precedes Amos) and its themes (Joel and Amos stand together, because both mention the day of the Lord [Joel 1:15; Amos 5:18] and a locust plague [Joel 1–2; Amos 7:1–3]). Joel precedes Amos because the theme of the judgment upon the nations at the end of Joel ties in with the beginning of Amos (see Joel 4:16 [3:16] and Amos 1:2).

LITERATURE

Commentaries on the Minor Prophets:

G. Ch. Aalders, *Obadja en Jona* (COT; Kampen, 1958).

L. Allen, *The Books of Joel, Obadiah, Jonah and Micah* (NICOT; Grand Rapids, 1976).

F. I. Andersen and D. N. Freedman, *Hosea* (AB; Garden City, NY, 1980).

J. Baldwin, *Haggai, Zechariah, Malachi* (TOTC; London/Downers Grove, IL, 1972).

Th. Chary, *Aggée–Zacharie–Malachie* (Sources Bibliques; Paris, 1969).

P. C. Craigie, *Twelve Prophets* I-II (Daily Study Bible; Philadelphia, 1984-85).

D. Deden, *De kleine profeten* (BOT; Roermond-Maaseik, 1953/1956).

A. Deissler and M. Delcor, *Les petits prophètes* (La Sainte Bible; Paris, 1961-64).

S. R. Driver, *The Books of Joel and Amos* (Cambridge Bible for Schools and Colleges; Cambridge, 1915).

J. H. Eaton, *Obadiah, Nahum, Habakkuk and Zephaniah* (Torch Bible Commentaries; London, 1961).

C. van Gelderen and W. H. Gispen, *Het boek Hosea* (COT; Kampen, 1953).

———, *Het boek Amos* (COT; Kampen, 1933).

W. R. Harper, *A Critical and Exegetical Commentary on Amos and Hosea* (ICC; Edinburgh, 1905).

D. R. Hillers, *Micah* (Hermeneia; Philadelphia, 1984).

A. van Hoonacker, *Les douze petits prophètes* (Études bibliques; Paris, 1908).

J. Jeremias, *Der Prophet Hosea übersetzt und erklart* (ATD 24/1; Göttingen, 1983).

C. F. Keil, *Minor Prophets* (Grand Rapids, repr. 1978).

G. A. F. Knight, *Hosea: God's Love* (Torch Bible Commentaries; London, 1960).

J. L. Koole, *Haggaï* (COT; Kampen, 1967).

C. van Leeuwen, *Amos* (POT; Nijkerk, 1985).

———, *Hosea* (POT; Nijkerk, 1968).

J. L. Mays, *Hosea* (OTL; Philadelphia, 1975[2]).

———, *Amos* (OTL; Philadelphia, 1976[3]).

———, *Micah* (OTL; Philadelphia, 1976).

H. G. Mitchell, J. M. P. Smith, and J. A. Bewer, *A Critical and Exegetical Commentary on Haggai, Zechariah, Malachi and Jonah* (ICC; Edinburgh, 1912).

D. L. Petersen, *Haggai and Zechariah 1–8* (OTL; Philadelphia, 1985).

J. Ridderbos, *De kleine profeten* I-III (Korte Verklaring; Kampen, 1976[4]).

W. Rudolph, *Hosea* (KAT XIII/1; Gütersloh, 1966).

———, *Joel. Amos. Obadja. Jona* (KAT XIII/2; Gütersloh, 1971).

———, *Micah. Nahum. Habakuk. Zephanja* (KAT XIII/3; Gütersloh, 1975).

———, *Haggai. Sacharja 1–8. Sacharja 9–14. Maleachi* (KAT XIII/4; Gütersloh, 1976).

E. Sellin, *Das Zwölfprophetenbuch* I-II (KAT 12; Leipzig, 1922, 1929[2], 1930[3]).

J. M. P. Smith, W. H. Ward, and J. A. Bewer, *A Critical and Exegetical Commentary on Micah, Zephaniah, Nahum, Habakkuk, Obadiah and Joel* (ICC; Edinburgh, 1911).

R. L. Smith, *Micah–Malachi* (Word Biblical Commentary; Waco, TX, 1984).

P. A. Verhoef, *The Books of Haggai and Malachi* (NICOT; Grand Rapids, 1987).

———, *Maleachi* (COT; Kampen, 1972).

A. Weiser and K. Elliger, *Das Buch der Zwölf Kleinen Propheten* (ATD 24-25; Göttingen, 1949-50/ 1967[5-6]).

J. Wellhausen, *Die Kleinen Propheten übersetzt und erklärt* (Berlin, 1963[4]).

H. W. Wolff, *Hosea* (Hermeneia; Philadelphia, 1974).

———, *Joel and Amos* (Hermeneia; Philadelphia, 1977).

———, *Obadiah and Jonah* (Minneapolis, 1986).

———, *Dodekapropheton 4. Micha* (BKAT XIV/4; Neukirchen, 1982).

———, *Dodekapropheton 6. Haggai* (BKAT XIV/6; Neukirchen, 1986).

A. S. van der Woude, *Micha* (POT; Nijkerk, 1985[3]).

———, *Jona. Nahum* (POT; Nijkerk, 1985[2]).

———, *Habakuk. Zefanja* (POT; Nijkerk, 1985[2]).

———, *Zacharia* (POT; Nijkerk, 1984).

———, *Haggai-Maleachi* (POT; Nijkerk, 1982).

Other Works:

K. Budde, "Eine folgenschwere Redaktion des Zwölfprophetenbuchs," *ZAW* 39 (1921) 218-29.

B. Duhm, *Anmerkungen zu den Zwölf Propheten* (Giessen, 1911).

R. E. Wolfe, "The Editing of the Book of the Twelve," *ZAW* 53 (1935) 90-130.

---

a. Hosea

(1) PERSON AND TIME

Hosea lived and worked in northern Israel during the reigns of Jeroboam II (ca. 786–746 B.C.) and the Judean kings Uzziah, Jotham, Ahaz, and Hezekiah (1:1). The prophet must have begun his labors in the final years of Jeroboam's reign. The destruction of Jehu's house is imminent (v. 4):

Jeroboam's son and successor Zechariah had been king only a half year when he was assassinated and succeeded by Shallum (2 Kgs. 15:8–10). Hosea thus began his labors about 750 B.C. At the time Uzziah was king over Judah. Shallum ruled only one month and was in turn murdered and succeeded by Menahem (745–738). Then came Pekahiah (738–737), who was murdered and succeeded by Pekah (737–732), and he again by Hoshea (732–722). When Samaria fell in 722, Hezekiah was king in Judah. It is not clear whether the prophet Hosea experienced the fall of Samaria and the deportation to Assyria (2 Kgs. 17:6). He does allude to the Syro-Ephraimite war (Hos. 5:8–11), the conquest of parts of Israel by Tiglath-pileser (v. 14; 7:8; cf. 2 Kgs. 15:19), the quick change in rulers in Israel and the intrigues and assassinations (Hos. 7:7; 8:4), and the vacillation in policy between seeking help from Egypt and paying tribute to Assyria (5:13; 7:11; 12:2 [1]), even while exile is imminent (9:3; 11:5). The prophet may have labored between 750 and 725, and so was an older contemporary of Isaiah in Judah.

The era of Jeroboam II was marked by great prosperity and wealth (2:7 [5]), while the period that followed was one of great confusion. Assyria stood at the zenith of its power under its rulers Tiglath-pileser, Shalmaneser, and Sargon. Religion was a mixture of Yahweh worship and Canaanite Baal worship, accompanied by immorality, murder, lovelessness, and unfaithfulness to the true service of God (4:1–2; 6:4–10). Hosea himself was from the north (note "our king" in 7:5). Places where he preached included Samaria (7:1; 8:5; 10:5, 7; 14:1 [13:16]), Bethel (which he called Beth-aven, "house of iniquity"; 4:15; 5:8; 10:5; 12:5 [4]), and Gilgal (4:15; 9:15; 12:12 [11]), places where there were sanctuaries and where the syncretistic, corrupted Yahweh worship was performed.

Of Hosea's personal life we know only that he was married to an immoral woman, perhaps a temple prostitute, who became unfaithful to him. Probably Hosea was not the father of the children she bore him. Yet he loved her. His marriage was thus a picture of the unfaithfulness of the people toward God, who continued to show his love to the people, though they did not remain un-

punished. The children bore symbolic names: Jezreel (the massacre by Jehu in *Jezreel* [2 Kgs. 9:30–10:11] would not go unpunished), Lo-Ruhamah (God will *no longer be merciful* to the people), and Lo-Ammi (the people will *no longer be God's people*). Yet God will again have pity on his people (ch. 1). In chapter 3 the prophet is again told to love a woman. Three interpretations have been proposed: (1) chapters 1 and 3 are parallel, although they are in the third person and the first person respectively; (2) the woman in chapter 3 is someone besides Gomer; or (3) the woman in chapter 3 is Gomer, but at a later time; she has ended up in slavery and must be redeemed by the prophet. The last suggestion is the most plausible. The woman is said to be adulterous, that is, she is a married woman; it would be hard to believe that the prophet would be told to marry a woman not his own. Moreover, Hosea's love is meant to illustrate God's love, who again loves his people and redeems them from captivity.

(2) THE BOOK OF HOSEA

The first-person report in chapter 3 shows that Hosea wrote prophecies himself and also recorded his life story insofar as it related to his preaching. Chapter 1, however, is clearly from a different hand. The editing of the book in its present form was apparently done by someone other than the prophet, perhaps by his students. From northern Israel the prophecies of Hosea also made their way into Judah, and likely his preaching was then also applied to Judah. The presence of the name Judah (1:11; 5:12–14; 8:14; 12:1 [11:12]) may indicate that Hosea also involved Judah in his preaching, but it may also be due to a Judean editing and interpretation and an actualization of Hosea's prophecies with a view to the situation in Judah. In addition, the fact that the superscription of the book (1:1) mentions not only Jeroboam but also Judean kings may suggest such a Judean editing. The postscript in 14:10 (9), which reminds us of the wisdom literature, may indicate that Hosea's prophecies were accepted in the wisdom schools.

The text of the book of Hosea is usually regarded as fairly corrupt. The difficulty in reading many of the passages, however, may also be due to the fact that the prophet employed a northern Israelite dialect that deviated from the regular Hebrew. Even the early translators had great difficulty with the text. The following parts can be distinguished in the book: 1:1, superscription; 1:2–2:3 (1:2–2:1), marriage of the prophet and birth of his children; 2:4–25 (2–23), preaching of judgment and salvation, and in the background the illustration of Hosea's marriage; chapter 3, even as the prophet again loves and redeems his wife, so God again loves his people and delivers them from captivity; chapter 4, sins of people and priests; 5:1–7, God's judgment upon priests, kings, and people; 5:8–15, Israel's leaning on other nations and the requirement of repentance for healing; 6:1–3, song of repentance; 6:4–11, God desires love, not sacrifices; chapter 7, Ephraim's persistence in sin; chapter 8, Ephraim's approaching destruction; 9:1–9, further announcement of judgment; 9:10–17, Israel becomes childless; chapter 10, sins in Bethel; chapter 11, preaching of God's love; 12:1–15 (11:12–12:14), Jacob's sin returns in his children; 13:1–14:1 (13:1–16), Israel will not escape judgment; 14:2–9 (1–8), call to conversion and promise of restoration; and 14:10 (9), postscript.

(3) HOSEA'S PREACHING

The central theme of Hosea's preaching is love. The love of God to his people Israel is symbolized in the marriage of the prophet. Even as Hosea's wife becomes unfaithful to the prophet, so Israel forsakes its God. From the very beginning of Israel's existence as a people, God showed his love to them. He delivered them from Egypt (12:10 [9]), led them through the wilderness, and cared for them there (13:5) through Moses, his prophet (12:14 [13]). Hosea views Israel's history as a history of God's salvation of his people, but at the same time as a history of Israel's sin.

From the very beginning Israel manifested its unfaithfulness toward God (9:10). The more God showed his love to them, the more the people apostatized and turned to the Baals (11:1–4). They attributed to the Baals the blessings God gave them (2:3, 6 [5, 8]). They expected more from Canaanite nature religion than from the service of Yahweh. The prophet characterizes this apostasy as immorality (1:2; 2:4 [2]; 4:13–15; 5:4). This image is derived from marriage, which pictures the intimate relationship between Yahweh and his people, to which Israel became unfaithful by going after other lovers (2:14–15 [12–13]). This term also depicts the temple prostitution, which the Canaanites expected would increase fertility. Idolatry was rampant (4:12–13). Fidelity, love, and knowledge of God were no longer to be found anywhere in the land (vv. 1, 6). These traits are worth more to God than all the sacrifices (6:6). Priests and prophets lead the people in their wickedness (4:4, 9; 5:1; 6:9; 9:7). Nor do the kings seek their help from God. Their life consists in festivities, deception, and murder (7:2–7; 13:10). Instead of turning to God (7:7), they go to Egypt or Assyria (5:13; 7:11; 8:9) for help. Therefore God's punishment comes upon the people. He will devour his people like a moth or a lion (5:12–14). Israel will go into exile (3:4).

This exile, however, not only is punishment but is intended to bring the people to repentance (2:9 [7]; 4:5; 5:15). In a sense, God begins anew his history with Israel. He carries them back to Egypt (8:13; 9:6). Egypt is the picture of the Assyrian captivity that will be brought upon the people (9:3; 11:5) and from which God will someday deliver them, as he delivered them once from Egypt. He will lead them through the wilderness, where he will again bind himself in love to his people and so again bring them into the Promised Land (2:16–17 [14–15]). God's activities will be accompanied by a conversion of the people, who then in love will turn to their God (3:5; 5:15). All such prophecies reveal the incomparable love of God, a love that is holy and not like that of human beings (11:9–11). Therefore Hosea must again love his unfaithful wife, even as God keeps loving his unfaithful people despite all that they do (3:1). The Messiah emerges in Hosea's preaching when he says that converted Israel, besides seeking God, will also seek David, its king (v. 5).

LITERATURE

W. Brueggemann, *Tradition for Crisis. A Study of Hosea* (Richmond, 1968).

M. J. Buss, *The Prophetic Word of Hosea. A Morphological Study* (BZAW 111; Berlin, 1969).

G. I. Emmerson, *Hosea. An Israelite Prophet in Judean*

Perspective (JSOT Supplement Series 28; Sheffield, 1984).

I. H. Eybers, et al., *Studies on Hosea and Amos* (Die Ou Testamentiese Werkgemeenskap in Suid-Afrika; Potchefstroom, 1964-65).

A. Gelston, *Kingship in the Book of Hosea* (OTS 19; Leiden, 1974), pp. 71-85.

G. Oestborn, *Yahwe and Baal. Studies in the Book of Hosea* (Lund, 1956).

H. H. Rowley, "The Marriage of Hosea," in *Men of God* (London, 1963), pp. 66-97.

H. Utzschneider, *Hosea. Prophet vor dem Ende* (Freiburg-Göttingen, 1980).

H. W. Wolff, "Wissen um Gott bei Hosea als Urform von Theologie," in *Gesammelte Studien* (TB 22; München, 1964), pp. 182-205.

———, "Hoseas geistige Heimat," *ibid.*, pp. 232-50.

b. Joel

(1) PERSON AND TIME

As for Joel himself, we know only that he was the son of a certain Pethuel (1:1). He labored in Judah, particularly in Jerusalem (2:1; 4:1, 16–21 [3:1, 16–21]), but the text tells us nothing concerning the time of his ministry. The dominant view used to be that he was a preexilic prophet. Reference was made to the position of the book between Hosea and Amos. Since the books of the prophets are not ordered strictly chronologically, this argument is not strong. Suggested times include the time of Joash (Keil) or Josiah (König). A. S. Kapelrud, *Joel Studies* (Uppsala, 1948), mentions the time of Jeremiah as a possibility.

Nowadays it is generally assumed that Joel was a postexilic prophet. The book mentions Israel's dispersion among the nations (4:2 [3:2]); the kingdom of the ten tribes is not mentioned; there is talk of elders but not of a king (1:2, 14; 2:16); and various expressions in Joel are found in the other prophets (2:6b = Nah. 2:11b [10b]; Joel 2:10a = Isa. 13:13a; Joel 2:10b = Isa. 13:10; Joel 2:13b = Jonah 4:2; Joel 2:20 = Jer. 1:14; etc.). Language and style are supposedly also from a later time (H. Holzinger, "Sprachcharakter und Abfassungszeit des Buches Joel," *ZAW* 9 [1889] 89ff.). Since the temple and temple worship are in existence (1:9, 13; 2:17), one would have to think of the time after Haggai and Zechariah—for instance, the time of Nehemiah. The mention of the Greeks (4:6 [3:6]) might even point to the third century B.C. Furthermore, there is supposedly affinity with apocalyptic literature (e.g., the judgment upon the nations in the valley of Jehoshaphat, mentioned in v. 12), though it is emphatically denied that Joel is an apocalyptic (Eissfeldt, Vriezen).

Counterarguments to this late dating are that nothing is said of the destruction of Jerusalem and that Israel's dispersion among the nations was also something that happened before the Captivity. The judgment upon Egypt in 4:19 (3:19) is said to agree more with the preexilic period. The silence about the king is not a cogent argument for a postexilic date, for language is a difficult criterion. The preaching is not apocalyptic but eschatological, a kind of preaching also found in preexilic prophets.

It is not easy to make a definite decision. Moreover, such arguments presuppose the unity of the book. Rothstein, however, believed that chapters 1 and 2 are preexilic and that Joel lived at that time. Later, after the Exile, chapters 3 and 4 were presumably added (Sellin). Yet some modern scholars have strongly defended the unity of the book of Joel (Wolff, Kapelrud, Weiser).

(2) THE BOOK OF JOEL

In the English translation the book of Joel has three chapters, one less than in the Hebrew Bible. In the latter the pericope 2:28–32 constitutes a separate chapter 3, while chapter 3 of our Bible translations is chapter 4 in the Hebrew. The English division comes from the chapter division that Stephan Langton made in the Vulgate text in about the year 1205. In the Bombergiana, issued by Daniel Bomberg in Venice in 1524 or 1525, Jacob ben Chayim split chapter 2, thus introducing the division into four in the Hebrew editions.

The following parts can be distinguished in the book of Joel: 1:1, superscription; 1:2–18, description of a locust plague that devastates the land and threatens the people with famine, along with a call to repentance and conversion; 1:19–20, prayer of lament to God; 2:1–11, another call to repentance and conversion and a description of the plague (the locust plague prefigures the day of the Lord, the day of judgment); 2:12–17, a third call to repentance; 2:18–27, the Lord's promise of relief; 3:1–5 (2:28–32), description of the day of the Lord, the outpouring of the Holy Spirit (a prophecy cited by Peter on the Day of Pentecost [Acts 2:17–21]), and of the judgment of God, from which there is escape in Zion; 4:1–8 (3:1–8), God's judgment of the nations for what they have done to Israel; and 4:9–21 (3:9–21), God's blessings to Israel.

Because chapters 3 and 4 make no further mention of the locust plague but deal with God's judgment against the nations and because they also differ stylistically from the preceding prophecies, it is sometimes assumed that they are a later addition. They speak of the day of the Lord as a day of judgment not against Israel but against the nations. The connecting link between 1:2–2:27 and the following sections is clearly this reference to the day of the Lord, which both in the first part (1:15; 2:1, 11) and in the second part (3:4 [2:31]; 4:14 [3:14]) constitutes the theme.

(3) JOEL'S PREACHING

The occasion for Joel's preaching was a locust plague (chs. 1–2). In this plague the day of the Lord, the day of judgment, comes near (1:15; 2:11). The people are called to keep a day of fasting; they must mourn and repent (1:13–14; 2:12–17). The prophet does not tell from what the people are to repent, other than from external religion: "Rend your hearts and not your garments" (2:13). Then God will be gracious (vv. 13–14). To the repentant people a new future is opened up. The locusts are driven out, and the land will again give its fruits. So God discloses himself as a gracious and merciful God (vv. 18–27).

The book of the prophet elaborates on the theme of the day of the Lord. That day is pictured as a day of judgment in which all of nature is involved (3:3–4 [2:30–31]), but also as a day of blessing. God will pour out his Spirit on "all flesh," without distinction regarding age, sex, or position (in the Septuagint this is somewhat minimized because it speaks only of "my" menservants and maidservants; cf. Acts 2:18). All become prophets, fulfilling the wish of Moses (Num. 11:29). On Mount Zion there will be deliverance for all who call upon the name of the Lord, all who are called by him. Here a door is opened even for the nations

(ch. 3 [2:28–32]), though it is a salvation that comes through judgment. The day of the Lord means blessing for Israel to the extent that it repents, but judgment for the nations that oppressed Israel (4:1–8 [3:1–8]). Like a farmer who puts his sickle into the grain, so God will harvest the nations (vv. 12–13). For Israel, however, he is a refuge (vv. 16–17). Joel's prophecy concludes with a proclamation of salvation for Israel (vv. 18–21).

LITERATURE

G. W. Ahlström, *Joel and the Temple Cult of Jerusalem* (SVT 21; Leiden, 1971).

O. Eissfeldt, *The Old Testament: An Introduction* (New York, 1965).

A. S. Kapelrud, *Joel Studies* (Uppsala-Leipzig, 1948).

C. F. Keil, *The Twelve Minor Prophets* (repr. Grand Rapids, 1973).

E. König, *Einleitung in das A.T.* (n.p., 1893), pp. 343-48.

C. van Leeuwen, "De mōrè liṣdāqā in Joël 2:23," in *Profeten en profetische geschriften, aangeboden aan A. S. van der Woude* (Kampen/Nijkerk, 1987), pp. 86-99.

————, *Ik zal mijn geest uitstorten* (Nijkerk, 1977).

L. H. van der Meiden, "De vertaling van het woord Môrèh in Joël 2:23," *GTT* 51 (1951) 136-39.

O. Plöger, *Theocracy and Eschatology* (Richmond, 1968), pp. 96-105.

J. W. Rothstein and S. R. Driver, *Einleitung in die Literatur des AT, übersetzt und mit Anmerkungen herausgegeben* (n.p., 1896), p. 333.

W. Rudolph, "Wann wirkte Joel?" in F. Maass, ed., *Das ferne und nahe Wort* (Festschrift L. Rost; BZAW 105; Berlin, 1967), pp. 193-98.

E. Sellin, *Das Zwölfprophetenbuch* (KAT XII; Leipzig, 1929[3]).

Th. C. Vriezen and A. S. van der Woude, *De literatuur van oud-Israël* (Wassenaar, 1980[6]).

A. Weiser, *Das Buch der zwölf Kleinen Propheten* I (A-D; Göttingen, 1949).

H. W. Wolff, *Die Botschaft des Buches Joel* (München, 1963).

---

c. Amos

(1) PERSON AND TIME

Amos was from Tekoa, 20 kilometers (12 mi.) south of Jerusalem. According to 1:1, he was a *noqed,* "sheep breeder." Because in Ugaritic texts the word *nqd* occurs as a title of a cultic functionary, it has been suggested that Amos may have had some function in the cult, perhaps being in charge of the temple animals. I find this suggestion highly unlikely. The Moabite king Mesha was also a *noqed* (2 Kgs. 3:4); here the word definitely means sheep breeder, though it may be assumed that Amos's operation was much smaller than that of the king of Moab. In 7:14 Amos calls himself "a herdsman and a dresser of sycamore trees." Because these trees are not grown in Tekoa but are found in the vicinity of the Dead Sea and because Amos's customers (both for wool and for figs) may have lived in a widespread area, it is thought that he traveled a lot and so also came to northern Israel, where he uttered his oracles. His prophecies mention Bethel (3:14; 5:5; 7:10), Gilgal near Shechem (4:4; 5:5), and Samaria (4:1), as well as Judah (2:4; 6:1). He is very familiar with the situation in northern Israel; he denounces the luxury and social abuse in the cities (5:10–12; 6:3–7; 8:4–6) and is acquainted with what is going on outside Israel (1:3–2:3).

That he was from Judah is also shown by the angry remark of the high priest Amaziah to him in the temple at Bethel: "Flee away to the land of Judah, and eat bread there, and prophesy there" (7:12), words that infuriated Amos, as if he were proclaiming the Word of God in order to make a living. Bread he can earn himself—he knows that he is called and sent by God (v. 15)! Many images in his proclamation are derived from nature and agricultural life, and they portray Amos as a rural type. He is familiar with the squeaking of a loaded cart (2:13), he knows from experience the fear that the roar of a lion strikes into a shepherd's heart (3:4, 8), he knows how a bird catcher goes about his work (v. 5), and with his own eyes he has seen the fat cows of Bashan with which he compares the well-favored ladies of Samaria (4:1).

Amos is said to have been active as a prophet during the reign of Uzziah, king of Judah (died 746 B.C.) and Uzziah's contemporary, Jeroboam II of Israel, a time designation further specified by the addition, "two years before the earthquake" (1:1). This earthquake must be the one that took place during the reign of Uzziah, which is also mentioned in Zechariah 14:5. Excavations in Hazor have demonstrated that about 760 there must have been an earthquake, which places the calling and labors of the prophet about this date. Amos's preaching seems to have covered only a brief span of time. Shortly after him, Hosea, a younger contemporary of Amos, assumed his prophetic activities.

(2) THE BOOK OF AMOS

Like other prophetic books, Amos includes three literary styles: (1) biographies in the first person—Amos relates five visions that he received and likely recorded himself (the vision of the locusts [7:1–3], of the consuming fire [vv. 4–6], of the plumb line [vv. 7–9], of the basket with fruit [8:1–3], and of the destructive judgment [9:1–6]); (2) biographies in the third person (1:1; 7:10–17), perhaps written by a student or follower of Amos, who also collated the prophecies of the prophet; and (3) brief oracles, recorded by the prophet himself. Amos is thus the first prophet we know of who recorded his prophecies.

His book can be divided as follows: 1:1, superscription; 1:2–2:3, prophecies against the nations (all starting with the formula "for three transgressions of *X,* and for four," the so-called number proverb, also known from wisdom literature [Prov. 30:18–31]), spoken against Syria, Philistia, Tyre, Edom, Ammon, and Moab; they are geographically arranged from the north via the west to the east, thus including Judah and Israel, against whom prophecies in the same style are directed in 2:4–5 and 2:6–16. Chapters 3 and 4 contain various prophecies with the introduction "hear this word," "hear," or "proclaim." Following sections are 5:1–3, a lament over Israel in the form of a funeral dirge (cf. 2 Sam. 1:27); 5:4–6, rejection of the pilgrimages to Bethel, Gilgal, and Beersheba; 5:7–13, prophecy against turning justice into injustice; 5:14–17, salvation only in the way of practicing justice; 5:18–20, on the day of the Lord; and 5:21–27, prophecy against Israel's worship and call for justice. Chapter 6 contains prophecies against the wealth and abuse in Samaria and an announcement of coming judgment.

In 7:1–9:6 a personal report by Amos concerning his visions is interrupted by the account of his expulsion from Bethel (7:10–17) and by prophecies against the trade in Israel, with the announcement of God's judgment on these practices in 8:4–14. The account is likely positioned as it is because of the similarity between 7:9 and 7:11. In 9:7–10 follows a prophecy against Israel's misguided confidence in God's election, and the book concludes with two prophecies of blessing in 9:11–12 and 9:13–15. The last prophecies have sometimes been denied to Amos on the ground that preexilic prophets were supposedly only prophets of doom, a notion that now is correctly rejected by many. Furthermore, some have believed that for Amos to preach blessings would blunt the thrust of his preaching of judgment, another argument that is not convincing because the prophets did not speak their prophecies at the same time nor always to the same audience.

(3) AMOS'S PREACHING

Amos is especially a prophet of judgment. God's judgment is directed against the nations (1:2–2:3) but also against Judah and Israel (2:4–16). The judgment upon Israel is even more severe than that upon the nations, because they are God's covenant nation, the people to whom God gave so many blessings, for which reason something better might have been expected from them (2:9–11; 3:1–2). The people are wrong in simply assuming that the God who led them out of Egypt will be on their side. God had also been concerned with the other nations (9:7). Therefore the day of the Lord, the real day of judgment, will strike not only the other nations, as Israel believed and its prophets proclaimed, but also Israel (5:18–27). The prophet denounces the sinful practices of idolatry, social injustice, extortion, and exploitation of the poor (2:4–8; 3:10; 5:7, 10–11); the sumptuous, exorbitant, and self-complacent life of the rich (4:1; 6:1–7); external religion (4:4–5; 5:21–27); and unrepentance (4:6–11). God's judgment will come upon all these sins, and Israel will fall (2:13) and go into exile (5:5). The judgment is irrevocable and will be so effective that only a small remnant will remain (3:12; 5:3). Unlike the message of other prophets, that of Amos concerning the remnant is not a proclamation of blessing but a demonstration of the effectiveness of the judgment. God demands righteousness from his people. Only then will he bless them (5:24). Yet there is perspective for the decimated (v. 3) people. The book concludes with a prophecy about the restoration of the Davidic royal house and the dawning of the time of salvation that will be characterized by abundant fruitfulness (9:11–15).

LITERATURE

H. M. Barstad, *The Religious Polemic in Amos* (SVT 34; Leiden, 1984).

J. Barton, *Amos' Oracles against the Nations: A Study of Amos 1:3–2:5* (Cambridge, 1980).

R. B. Coote, *Amos among the Prophets. Composition and Theology* (Philadelphia, 1981).

J. L. Crenshaw, "The Influence of the Wise upon Amos," *ZAW* 79 (1967) 42-51.

———, "Amos and the Theophanic Tradition," *ZAW* 80 (1968) 203-15.

———, *Hymnic Affirmation of Divine Justice: The Doxologies of Amos and Related Texts in the Old Testament* (Missoula, MT, 1975).

R. Fey, *Amos und Jesaja. Abhängigkeit und Eigenständigkeit des Jesaja* (Neukirchen-Vluyn, 1963).

E. Hammershaimb, *The Book of Amos. A Commentary* (Oxford, 1970).

A. S. Kapelrud, *Central Ideas in Amos* (Oslo, 1961²).

A. Neher, *Amos: Contribution à l'étude du prophétisme* (Paris, 1981²).

H. Graf Reventlow, *Das Amt des Propheten bei Amos* (FRLANT 80; Göttingen, 1962).

H. H. Schmid, "Amos. Die Frage nach der 'geistigen Heimat' des Propheten," *Wort und Dienst* 10 (1969) 85-103.

R. Smend, "Das Nein des Amos," *Evangelische Theologie* 23 (1963) 404-23.

J. D. W. Watts, *Vision and Prophecy in Amos* (Leiden, 1958).

A. Weiser, *Die Prophetie des Amos* (BZAW 53; Giessen, 1929).

H. W. Wolff, *Amos' geistige Heimat* (WMANT 18; Neukirchen, 1964).

E. Würthwein, "Amos Studien," *ZAW* 62 (1950) 10-52 (= *Wort und Existenz. Studien zum Alten Testament* [Göttingen, 1970], pp. 68-110).

d. Obadiah

(1) PERSON AND TIME

Nothing can be said about the person of Obadiah, for the small book is silent about him. Some even ask whether the name Obadiah, which means "servant of Yahweh," is to be regarded as a personal name or as an honorary title for an anonymous prophet, or whether the name Obadiah is derived from the well-known Obadiah from the time of King Ahab (1 Kgs. 18:3-16). The name Obadiah, however, was common in Israel (1 Chr. 7:3; 8:38; 12:9; 27:19; 2 Chr. 17:7; 34:12; cf. also the name Obed in Ruth 4:17). From his emotional involvement in the downfall of Judah and Jerusalem (Obad. 11-12), it can be inferred that he experienced this event himself and that he was thus himself a Judean (note "my people" in v. 13). The scene of his labors was Judah, likely Jerusalem.

Opinions differ as to the time of the prophet. Some date him about 850 B.C. in the time of the Judean king Jehoram, on account of his prophecy against Edom, which at the time of Jehoram revolted against Judah (2 Kgs. 8:20-22; on account of his prophecy against Edom, the book of Obadiah follows Amos in the Bible [cf. Amos 9:12]). In that case Obadiah lived about a hundred years before Amos and would be the first prophet of whom we have something in writing. Most scholars place him about 586 B.C., when Jerusalem was destroyed by Nebuchadrezzar and the people carried off into exile. Edom's gloating about the destruction of Jerusalem, mentioned by Obadiah (v. 12), was great at that time and is mentioned elsewhere (Ezek. 25:12-14; ch. 35; Ps. 137:7; Lam. 4:21). In this view Obadiah was a contemporary of Jeremiah, but he uttered his prophecy shortly after 586. He may have belonged to those who remained behind in Jerusalem after the destruction of the city and the deportation into exile of much of its population (2 Kgs. 25:12, 22).

(2) THE BOOK OF OBADIAH

One should speak of a booklet rather than a book. It contains only one chapter of twenty-one verses, a prophecy against Edom. God's judgment is announced upon this proud and arrogant nation. It will be cast down and plundered (vv. 1-9) because of its gloating over the destruction of Judah and Jerusalem and because it killed or delivered into the hands of the enemy the Judean fugitives who tried to find safety in the mountains of Edom (vv. 10-14). Connected with that theme is a prophecy about the day of the Lord, when judgment will strike not only Edom but all nations for what they have done to God's people. Their fate will correspond to what they did to God's people (vv. 15-16). The booklet ends with two prophecies of blessing: one in poetry, which speaks of deliverance on Mount Zion and mentions once again the judgment of Edom, or the house of Esau (vv. 17-18), and one in prose, which announces that Israel will again occupy its land. It is said once more that Zion will be delivered and that God's judgment will strike Edom, or Mount Esau, all of which will indicate that Yahweh is king (vv. 19-21).

There is a wide difference of opinion about the composition and time of origin of the booklet. "The booklet is as small as the literary-critical questions are large" (Vriezen). Scholars regard the book either as a unity or as a composite of various prophecies from different times. Rudolph and Weiser think of two prophecies that go back to Obadiah: (1) 1-14, 15b and (2) 15a, 16-18, to which later were added 19-21, verses that, however, may also very well be from Obadiah himself. The prophecies would presumably be from about 586 B.C. Vriezen for the most part concurs. Eissfeldt (*Introduction*) has about the same view: 1-14 and 15b form a unity and are from about 586; the remainder may be a later addition. Fohrer distinguishes five proverbs and an appendix: 1b-4; 5-7; 8-11; 12-14, 15b; 15a, 16-18; 19-21, all from about 586.

Sellin has defended another view, suggesting that verses 1-10 are from the time of King Jehoram (about 850 B.C.), on the ground of 2 Kings 8:20-24, which mentions Edom's revolt. Edom's gloating would supposedly date from that time. Verses 11-14, which relate to the situation in 586, would have been added to it somewhat later, about 500. Even in the time of Malachi the disgrace of Edom would have been remembered (Mal. 1:3). The prophecies in 15-21 would be from a still later period (about 400 B.C.). J. Ridderbos adopted that standpoint, but since he regards the book as a unity, he dates it in its totality in the time of Jehoram. The objection that 2 Kings 8 speaks of a defeat of Judah by Edom but does not mention a capture of Jerusalem (Obad. 11) or a destruction of Judah (vv. 12–13) is resolved with a reference to 2 Chronicles 21:16–17, which mentions a capture of Jerusalem by Philistines and Arabs in the days of Jehoram. This interpretation is quite unacceptable, however, in view of the fact that 2 Kings 8 mentions Edomites but not a plundering of Jerusalem, while 2 Chronicles 21 refers to a plundering of Jerusalem but does not mention Edomites. It is preferable to date the prophecies of Obadiah about 586.

A special problem is the relationship of the book of Obadiah to Jeremiah. Some passages in Jeremiah's prophecy concerning Edom (Jer. 49:7–22) agree almost verbatim with those in Obadiah (Jer. 49:9a = Obad. 5b; Jer. 49:9b = Obad. 5a; Jer. 49:14–16a ≈ Obad. 1–3a; Jer. 49:16b = Obad. 4). Four different explanations have been defended: (1) Jeremiah borrowed from Obadiah (Sellin, Ridderbos); (2) Obadiah borrowed from Jeremiah (Aalders); (3) both drew from a common preexilic source (Deden); and (4) the parts in Obadiah were later inserted in the prophecy of Jeremiah (Eissfeldt, Fohrer). It is difficult to choose with certainty one view or the other. It is very well possible that older utterances against Edom lie behind statements in Obadiah and Jeremiah (cf. Amos 1:11). The text of the book is not in the best of condition, making it often difficult to determine the exact meaning.

(3) OBADIAH'S PREACHING

Obadiah announces God's judgment upon proud Edom, which rejoiced in Judah's destruction. He combines with it a prophecy about the day of the Lord, when God will punish all nations that were hostile to Judah and did evil to it. For Zion, however, there will be deliverance. Israel will again live in its land, and God will be king. Because of the difference between Amos's message about the day of Lord, when God's judgment will also strike Israel (Amos 5:18–20), and that of Obadiah, who limits the judgment to the other nations, Fohrer believes that Obadiah was one of the prophets prophesying bliss whom Amos and Jeremiah attacked in their preaching. Fohrer is certainly mistaken in this view. The different cir-

cumstances ought to be taken into account. Amos and Jeremiah were confronted by prophets who instilled in the people a false sense of confidence and security. Obadiah lived in days when Judah was overrun by enemies. He announces judgment upon the invading nations (cf. Isa. 10:5–19) and opens up new perspectives for conquered Judah.

Vriezen believes that Obadiah was one of the men who prepared the way for the religious nationalistic feelings of the later Jewish community. That view, however, can be maintained only if Obadiah's preaching is detached from the totality of the preaching of the Old Testament prophets. Obadiah's ultimate concern is not vengeance for personal or nationalistic reasons. His concern is the manifestation of God's righteousness, which does not allow the destruction of God's people and the ultimate triumph of God's enemies.

LITERATURE

M. Bič, "Zur Problematik des Buches Obadjah," SVT 1 (1953) 11-25.

B. C. Cresson, "The Condemnation of Edom in Post-Exilic Judaism," in J. M. Efird, ed., *The Use of the Old Testament in the New and Other Essays* (Festschrift W. F. Stinespring; Durham, NC, 1972), pp. 125-48.

G. Fohrer, "Die Sprüche Obadjas," in *Studia biblica et semitica* (Festschrift Th. C. Vriezen; Wageningen, 1966), pp. 81-93.

W. Rudolph, "Obadja," ZAW 49 (1931) 222-31.

J. Wehrle, *Prophetie und Textanalyse. Die Komposition Obadja 1-21 interpretiert auf der Basis textlinguistischer und semiotischer Konzeptionen* (Freiburg, 1980).

H. W. Wolff, "Obadja—ein Kultprophet als Interpret," *Evangelische Theologie* 37 (1977) 273-84.

---

e. Jonah

(1) PERSON AND TIME

Jonah, further designated as the son of Amittai (1:1), is the chief figure in this book. Except for his father's name and the story that is told about him, we know nothing about Jonah's person or about the time in which he lived, other than that he lived at the time when Nineveh was still the capital of the Assyrian empire. A prophet by the name of Jonah, also son of Amittai, is mentioned in 2 Kings 14:25 as well, and there is good reason to assume that he is the same as the prophet in the book by that name. There it is reported that Jonah was from Gath-hepher, a town in Zebulun (Josh. 19:13), just north of Nazareth. Moreover, like Amos and Hosea, Jonah lived at the time of King Jeroboam II (8th century B.C.), for he told the king that he would recover the territory of Israel from Hamath in the north to the Dead Sea in the south, which was the territory east of the Jordan that had been relinquished to the Syrians. In what must be a later message, Amos prophesies that this territory will be lost (Amos 6:14), a reference to the conquest of the area by the Assyrians. Jonah thus lived and prophesied before Amos during the reign of Jeroboam, likewise in northern Israel. We possess no other prophecies of Jonah.

(2) THE BOOK OF JONAH

Unlike the other prophetic writings, the book of Jonah is not a collection of prophetic messages but a story about a prophet. Ordered to do so by Yahweh, Jonah must announce God's judgment upon Nineveh for its many sins. The prophet refuses. In an attempt to get away from God's commission, he flees from Joppa on a ship bound for Tarshish in Spain. A severe storm arises at sea, threatening to sink the ship. At the request of Jonah, who knows that he is the guilty one, the sailors cast him overboard into the sea, where he is swallowed by a great fish (1:1–2:1 [1:1–17]). Inside the belly of the fish Jonah prays to the Lord, after which the fish vomits Jonah out upon the dry land (2:2–11 [1–10]). Now for the second time Jonah receives the commission from Yahweh. This time he obeys, though with great reluctance. Nineveh repents, and God changes his plan to punish the city (ch. 3), which angers Jonah. While he is outside the city, awaiting God's judgment upon Nineveh, a tree miraculously grows up over him, enabling him to sit in its shade. This provision greatly pleases Jonah. The next day, however, the tree is attacked by a worm and withers, which angers Jonah. Then follows God's lesson to Jonah: while Jonah wanted to spare a miraculous tree for

his own pleasure, would it not be much more important for God to spare a large city such as Nineveh with so many people (more than 120,000) and many cattle besides (ch. 4)?

The writer of the story is not Jonah himself but someone from a much later time. It has been pointed out that there are many Aramaisms in the book (1:4–6, 12; 2:1 [1:17]; 3:7; etc.), a fact that is not too important for dating, since Aramaisms entered the Hebrew language very early. Reference has also been made to the universalistic outlook in the book, which portrays God's compassion as extending also to the nations outside Israel. Yet such an outlook does not necessarily require a late date. In Isaiah, for example, we read that the nations outside Israel will share in God's salvation (Isa. 2:2; 11:10). Such passages are not always late and postexilic. In preexilic times, however, many, Jonah included, found it difficult to accept such an unlimited love of God. In the case of Jonah one might even think of a nationalistic prophet who needs conversion. Nevertheless, it seems likely that the book may be of fairly late date. Nineveh *was* a great city (3:3), which would point to a distant past. For that reason the book is often dated in the fifth or fourth century before Christ.

The book is clearly a unity. The prayer in 2:3–10 (2–9) is more a prayer of thanks after deliverance than a prayer for deliverance in need. The prayer for deliverance is included in the prayer of thanks (cf. Isa. 38:9–20). It may have been an existing psalm, placed here by the author, because the words in verses 3 and 5 (2 and 4) were regarded as highly applicable to Jonah. Similar words are found in other psalms (Ps. 18:5–7 [4–6]; 42:8 [7]), where they are pictures of dire need. It is not necessary to think that they were inserted later. It is altogether possible that the composer of the book included the psalm at this point.

The alternate use of the names Yahweh and Elohim in the book is noteworthy. In part the explanation may be that the God of Jonah is designated as Yahweh (1:1, 3–4, 9, etc.) and the gods of non-Israelites as Elohim (1:5; 3:5–9). Yet it does not explain everything (see 4:7–9). The idea that this phenomenon points to two sources is totally unfounded.

(3) THE MESSAGE OF THE BOOK OF JONAH

The message is given in the form of a story, the intent of which is generally assumed to be a statement of God's mercy, not only for Israel but also for other nations. The difference in opinion concerns the nature of the story. Four viewpoints have been or are still being defended. First, the story is an *allegory*. Jonah represents the people of Israel, who forsook their calling. The fish stands for the Babylonian captivity, which has swallowed them and from which they are delivered. The people expect God's judgment upon the hostile nations and dislike it if those judgments are averted. Israel must learn that God's mercy extends even to foreign nations. Second, the book of Jonah has been considered a *parable*. As with the parables of Jesus, the main concern is not whether what is related actually happened; the important thing is the moral, the lesson. The third viewpoint is that Jonah is a historically reliable reproduction of an *actual event*. Finally, Jonah is considered a *legendary story* that may have some basis in fact but that incorporates a variety of motifs (e.g., the fish and the miraculous tree). The story may have been derived from oral tradition or from a collection of prophetic stories. Budde's contention that it is derived from a midrash on the book of Kings (see 2 Chr. 24:27) cannot be proven. The book contrasts the narrow-minded, nationalistic faith of Jonah and many others in Israel with the greatness of God's mercy that compasses not only Israel but all people and even animals (4:11). This message was altogether appropriate in the time after the Exile, when there was a strong surge of nationalism. There is no ground for the assumption that the book is a protest against Ezra's strict particularistic measures (Ezra 10:2–4).

Van der Woude suggests that the writer was a representative of the earliest scribes, who combined universalistic ideas and wisdom traditions with a careful study of Israel's holy writings. He regards as the chief themes of the book the relationship between God and his prophet, the reflection on the prophetic call, and the nature of the proclamation of judgment. The first main part (chs. 1–2) is about the senselessness of fleeing from the divine call; the second part (chs. 3–4)

about Yahweh's freedom in carrying out or in withdrawing the message of judgment. (Besides van der Woude's commentary, see also his article in *Kerk en Theologie* 29 [1978] 285–98.)

LITERATURE

G. Ch. Aalders, *The Problem of the Book of Jonah* (London, 1948).

R. E. Clements, "The Purpose of the Book of Jonah," SVT 28 (1974) 16-28.

T. E. Fretheim, *The Message of Jonah* (Minneapolis, 1977).

O. Kaiser, "Wirklichkeit, Möglichkeit und Vorurteil. Ein Beitrag zum Verständnis des Buches Jona," *Evangelische Theologie* 33 (1973) 91-103.

J. Magonet, *Form and Meaning: Studies in the Literary Techniques in the Book of Jonah* (Bern–Frankfurt am Main, 1976).

G. von Rad, *Der Prophet Jona* (Nürnberg, 1950).

L. Schmidt, *De Deo. Studien zur Literarkritik und Theologie des Buches Jona, des Gesprächs zwischen Abraham und Jahwe in Gen 18, 22ff. und von Hi 1* (BZAW 143; Berlin/New York, 1976).

G. Vanoni, *Das Buch Jona. Literar- und formkritische Untersuchung* (St. Ottilien, 1978).

H. Witzenrath, *Das Buch Jona. Eine literaturwissenschaftliche Untersuchung* (St. Ottilien, 1978).

H. W. Wolff, *Studien zum Jonabuch* (Köln, 1965).

A. S. van der Woude, "Compositie, strekking en plaats van het boek Jona," *Kerk en Theologie* 29 (1978) 285-98.

---

f. Micah

(1) PERSON AND TIME

Micah was from Moresheth (1:1), a town in the vicinity of Gath (v. 14) in the Shephelah, southwest of Jerusalem. He appears to be well acquainted with the towns in that area (vv. 13–15). Like Amos he was a man from the country, but unlike Amos he prophesied in the southern kingdom of Judah, in his own town and surroundings and also in Jerusalem (3:9–12). His preaching made a deep impression on the rural population, for a hundred years later, in the time of the prophet Jeremiah, "the elders of the land" (apparently from tradition) still refer to his preaching (Jer. 26:17–18). We read nothing about Micah's call to be a prophet, but in his struggle with the false prophets he shows that he was well aware of his divine calling (Mic. 3:8).

In 1:1 he is reported to have been active during the reigns of Jotham (746–743 B.C.), Ahaz (743–727), and Hezekiah (727–686). That Micah prophesied during Hezekiah's reign agrees with Jeremiah 26:18. His prophecies against Samaria (1:1, 6–7) must have been given just before Samaria's capture in 722. Prophecies that mention the threat from Assyria (5:4–5 [5–6]) may be from the time either of Sargon's expedition against Judah (711) or, less likely, of Sennacherib's campaign (701). If Micah was active not only during the reign of Hezekiah but also under Jotham and Ahaz, his prophetic activity must have extended over a period of at least twenty years. It is not possible, however, to give a closer dating to his prophecies. It can be said that Micah was a contemporary of Isaiah. There is even a remarkable similarity between Isaiah's prophecies and those of Micah. He was also a contemporary of Hosea in the northern kingdom. Amos's labors were some years earlier.

(2) THE BOOK OF MICAH

Three main parts can be distinguished in the book of Micah: chapters 1–3 (prophecies of judgment, except for 2:12–13); chapters 4–5 (prophecies of blessings); and chapters 6–7 (prophecies of judgment as well as of blessing). Each main part is constructed of smaller parts. The first main part contains a superscription (1:1) and then, in verses 2–16, either a single message or a composite of separate parts. Van der Woude considers the verses a sermon given by Micah at an autumnal feast in Lachish ("De prediking van het O.T.," *Micha* [Nijkerk, 1977²]). Other scholars view it as a composite of separate parts: verses 2–7, announcement of the judgment upon Samaria (shortly before 722); verses 8–9, a lament over Jerusalem; and verses 10–16, the march of the enemy (Assyria) from the southwest against Jerusalem (probably Sargon in 711, perhaps Sennacherib in 701). Chapter 2 then consists of 2:1–5, woe upon the violent rulers (cf. Isa. 5:8–10); 2:6–11, prophecy against the false prophets and those listening to them; and 2:12–13, prophecy of blessing concerning the reunion of the scattered

people. According to some, this final section is from the time of the Babylonian captivity. Others believe that it deals with the dispersed from northern Israel after 732 (the expedition of Tiglath-pileser III) or 722 (the fall of Samaria and Assyrian captivity). According to van der Woude (see also G. C. Aalders, *De valsche profetie in Israel* [1911], pp. 105–107), the section is a rejoinder against Micah by false prophets. The first part concludes with chapter 3, a prophecy against the leaders of the people because of their antisocial acts, concluding with a word about the fall of Jerusalem (v. 12).

The second main part begins with 4:1–5, a prophecy of the coming kingdom of peace (cf. Isa. 2:2–4). Here Micah borrows from Isaiah or vice versa, or both draw from a third source. According to van der Woude there is also a rejoinder here from the false prophets: he reads chapters 4 and 5 as a dispute between Micah and his opponents that started in the previous chapters. The second part continues with 4:6–14 (4:6–5:1), distress and redemption of Zion, and 5:1–14 (2–15), prediction of the Messiah and his kingdom (cf. Isa. 9:5 [6]).

The third main part can be divided as follows: 6:1–8, God's controversy with Israel (he desires not sacrifices but justice; Sellin places this section in the time of Manasseh, others date it during the reign of Ahaz or Hezekiah, and Eissfeldt and Weiser, while attributing the words to Micah, regard dating impossible); 6:9–16, judgment upon the city (most scholars think of Jerusalem, but Samaria is also possible); 7:1–6, prophecy against Israel's injustice; 7:7–10, oracle concerning trust in Yahweh; 7:11–13, promise of rebuilding of the walls and return from captivity; and 7:14–20, prayer for Israel and hymn of praise for God's mercy. Several exegetes regard 7:7–14 as additions from the time of the Captivity. Yet placing them in the time of Micah is not impossible. Van der Woude believes that Micah 6–7 is from a northern Israelite prophet who labored a decade or so before Micah of Moresheth and whose name was possibly also Micah. His prophecies would be from the time of Tiglath-pileser III from the years 732 to 727 B.C.

The book of Micah in its present form is not from Micah but from a redactor, who collected Micah's prophecies and gave them their present format. He put them in the following sequence: prophecies of judgment, prophecies of blessings, further prophecies of judgment, and prophecy of blessing. The text of the book is uncertain in several places. There is considerable variation between the Massoretic text and the Septuagint.

(3) MICAH'S PREACHING

Micah proclaims God's punishment upon the sins of the nation. Hostile powers—specifically, Assyria—will turn both Samaria (1:6) and Jerusalem (vv. 8–9; 3:12) into ruins. Their actions represent God's punishment of his people for their sins of idolatry (1:7) and especially social injustice. The rich increase their possessions at the expense of the poor, but their wealth will be taken from them (2:1–5). The prophet directs himself especially against the false prophets who mislead the people with their words and confirm the leaders in their evil (vv. 6–11; ch. 3). Judges allow themselves to be bribed, and for money prophets proclaim what the people like to hear. They tell the people that God is in their midst and that nothing can happen to them (3:11). Micah's message is altogether different (v. 12).

Yet Micah is not only a prophet of judgment. He too announces the coming kingdom of peace of the Messiah (4:1–5; 5:1–4 [2–5]). Participation in this kingdom, however, is not automatic. God comes with his promises, but he also requires that people repent and obey his Word. The words of 6:8 are beautiful: God requires that a person do justice and love kindness and, like a child with his father, walk humbly with his God. The book ends with one of the most marvelous hymns in the Old Testament, extolling God's incomparable faithfulness and forgiveness (7:18–20). Micah teaches his hearers to expect everything from God, but without reducing religion to formalism. Acts of injustice may not be covered with pious words. Only in a life lived according to God's Word may great things be expected from that Word.

LITERATURE

W. Beyerlin, *Die Kulttraditionen in der Verkündigung des Propheten Micha* (FRLANT 54; Göttingen, 1959).

K. Jeppesen, "New Aspects of Micah Research," *JSOT* 8 (1978) 3-32.

J. Jeremias, "Die Deutung der Gerichtsworte Michas in der Exilszeit," *ZAW* 83 (1971) 330-54.

B. Renaud, *La formation du livre de Michée* (Études Bibliques; Paris, 1977).

I. Willi-Plein, *Vorformen der Schriftexegese innerhalb des Alten Testaments. Untersuchungen zum literarischen Werden der auf Amos, Hosea und Micha zurückgehenden Bücher* (BZAW 123; Berlin, 1971).

J. T. Willis, "The Structure of the Book of Micah," *Svensk Exegetisk Årsbok* 34 (1969) 5-42.

————, "A Reapplied Prophetic Hope Oracle," in *Studies on Prophecy* (SVT 26; Leiden, 1978), pp. 64-76.

H. W. Wolff, "Wie verstand Micha von Moreschet sein prophetisches Amt?" SVT 29 (1978) 403-17.

————, *Micah the Prophet* (Philadelphia, 1981).

A. S. van der Woude, "Deutero-Micha: ein Prophet aus Nord-Israel?" *NTT* 25 (1971) 365-78.

---

g. Nahum

(1) PERSON AND TIME

Nothing is known about Nahum personally, other than his being called an Elkoshite, signifying that he was from a place called Elkosh. Its location, however, is unknown. It has been said to be in Galilee (Jerome), in Judah (Epiphanius), or in the vicinity of the earlier Nineveh. In that case it could be identified with Alkus, north of Mosul.

Neither can anything certain be said about the time of his ministry. In 1:1 his prophecies are announced as an oracle concerning Nineveh. The contention by Sellin, Humbert ("Essai d'analyse de Nahoum 1,2–2,3," *ZAW* 44 [1926] 266–80) and Haldar (*Studies in the Book of Nahum* [Uppsala, 1947]) that Nahum's book is to be regarded as a prophetic liturgy held in the temple on the Israelite new-year festival after the fall of Nineveh is disputed by many (including Eissfeldt, Elliger, Schulz). It seems certain that Nahum's prophecies concerning the fall of Nineveh were uttered prior to that event. Since 3:8 alludes to the fall of No-amon, the ancient capital of Upper Egypt (called Thebes by the Greeks), which was destroyed in 663 B.C. by the Assyrian king Ashurbanipal, the prophecies of Nahum are to be dated between 663 (fall of Thebes) and 612 (fall of Nineveh). The question is whether Nahum spoke his prophecies closer to 663 or closer to 612. Both views have been defended.

The latter view has in its favor the graphic portrayal in chapters 2 and 3 of the march of the enemy against Nineveh and the imminent destruction of the city. The scene is described so vividly that one gets the impression that the capture of the city is either in progress or just about to happen. Against this argument it can be pointed out that the mention of the destruction of No-amon by the Assyrians is best explained if this happening was still fresh in the memory. Moreover, soon after the fall of No-amon the Egyptians under Psammetichus I (664–610) regained their independence from the Assyrians, so that a reference to the fall of this city as an example of what would happen to Nineveh makes sense only shortly after this event. Furthermore, 1:12 and 3:15–17 show that, at the time of Nahum, Nineveh's power was still unbroken. Wealth and power mark Nineveh and its king (2:14 [13]; 3:1–4). The yoke of the Assyrians lies heavily also upon Judah (1:13). That fact points in the direction of the earlier date, particularly since, after the death of Ashurbanipal (ca. 630 B.C.), the Assyrian empire quickly disintegrated and Judah under Josiah (640–609) became more and more independent of Assyria.

I thus would date Nahum between 663 and 630, and likely closer to 663. C. J. Goslinga (*Nahums godsspraak tegen Ninevé* [Zutphen, 1923]) has suggested that Nahum spoke his prophecies concerning the fall of Nineveh under the influence of the revolt of the Babylonian king Shamashshumukin against his brother Ashurbanipal in 652. In that case Nahum is to be located not in the time of the Judean king Josiah (640–609) but during the reign of his grandfather Manasseh (686–642). At that time Assyria was still all-powerful, while Judah, in contrast to the time of Josiah, was still completely a vassal of this mighty empire.

According to 2:1 (1:15), Judah seems to be the locale of Nahum's labors. Consideration should, however, be given to van der Woude's suggestion that Nahum was an exile from northern Israel in Assyria and that the book is meant as an encouraging letter sent by Nahum from there to threatened and oppressed Judah.

(2) THE BOOK OF NAHUM

After the superscription (1:1), Nahum's prophecies are introduced by a hymn, an acrostic depicting the appearance of Yahweh, who judges his enemies and delivers his people (vv. 2–8). The acrostic is incomplete. Proceeding irregularly it runs from aleph to kaph, and it has induced many an exegete to transpose some verses. Likely Nahum himself composed this song, using an existing psalm, and made it the introduction to his prophecies. According to van der Woude, Nahum himself is also responsible for the present sequence of the verses, so that the first letters constitute a sentence that serves as the theme of the whole book. It so happens that in the Hebrew the first letters can be made into a sentence that reads, "I (Yahweh) am exalted, and before my eyes are those who abuse you."

In the following verses (1:9–2:3 [1:9–2:2]) the downfall of Assyria and the deliverance of Judah are proclaimed. Then follows a highly visual description of the capture of Nineveh (2:4–11 [3–10]), as the prophet himself may very well have seen it in a vision. Next there is a taunt of Assyria and its king (2:12–14 [11–13]), who is likened to a lion constantly on the prowl for food but who now is captured himself.

Chapter 3 contains another poem about the downfall of Nineveh. Three parts can be distinguished: verses 1–7, a woe over Nineveh (the city is punished for its murder and immorality); verses 8–17, Nineveh is no better than No-amon and will experience the same fate; and verses 18–19, a taunt of the king of Assyria in the form of a lament.

(3) NAHUM'S PREACHING

Because Nahum's preaching contains only judgment for Nineveh and promised blessings for Judah, he has been wrongly included among the so-called prophets of hope. Isaiah and Jeremiah, who did not ignore Judah, also proclaimed God's judgment upon the nations that oppressed Israel. The focus of Nahum's preaching is God's justice, with which he will someday judge all hostile nations and deliver his people. This theme can be nationalistically understood and applied, as we know from both the Old and New Testaments. A man such as Amos vehemently denounced this nationalism, as Jesus did later. The fact remains, however, that God judges the hostile nations to save his people. Such a truth is the abiding comfort that, along with the fall of Nineveh, is heard in the prophecy of Nahum. The fact that Nahum does not point out the sins of Judah need not be, as has been suggested, because he slighted them. His book has only one theme—God's judgment upon Nineveh—and the occasion was concrete historical situations. His proclamation also reaches far beyond this context. It receives an eschatological accent in the final judgment upon all nations and the ultimate manifestation of God's faithfulness for all his people.

LITERATURE

K. J. Cathcart, *Nahum in the Light of Northwest Semitic* (Rome, 1973).

A. Haldar, *Studies in the Book of Nahum* (Uppsala, 1947).

P. Humbert, "Essai d'analyse de Nahoum 1,2–2,3," *ZAW* 44 (1926) 266-80.

J. Jeremias, *Kultprophetie und Gerichtsverkündigung in der späten Königszeit Israels* (WMANT 35; Neukirchen-Vluyn, 1970).

C. A. Keller, "Die theologische Bewältigung der geschichtlichen Wirklichkeit in der Prophetie Nahums," *VT* 22 (1972) 399-419.

H. Schulz, *Das Buch Nahum* (BZAW 129; Berlin/New York, 1973).

A. S. van der Woude, "The Book of Nahum: A Letter Written in Exile," *OTS* 20 (1977) 108-26.

---

h. Habakkuk

(1) PERSON AND TIME

Nothing is known with certainty about Habakkuk personally, whose name occurs twice in the book named after him (1:1; 3:1), nor about the time in which he lived. The name Habakkuk is associated with an Assyrian-Babylonian word indicating a kind of plant. Whatever can be known about him must be inferred from his prophecies, a limitation that has led to much disagreement. The question is whom the prophet has in mind in 1:2–4 when he mentions oppressors who act violently and perpetrate injustice. He calls them the wicked who surround the righteous. He also speaks of them in 1:12–17 and 2:5–17. Habakkuk complains to God because God does nothing about it and so allows injustice and oppression to continue to exist (1:2–4). A reply from God follows in verses 5–11, where mention is made of the Chaldeans and their conquests. This datum points to the military exploits of the Chaldean king Nabopolassar (626–605 B.C.), the founder of the neo-Babylonian empire that defeated the Assyrian empire in 612, and his son Nebuchadrezzar (605–562), who defeated Pharaoh Neco of Egypt in 605 at the battle of Carchemish and then annexed Judah. But who are meant by the oppressors? Are they domestic or foreign opponents? Both views have been defended.

Rothstein (1896) thought of domestic oppressors, their chief representative being Jehoiakim (cf. Jer. 22:13–19). In the reference to the Chaldeans, he thought of the period around 605 B.C., the time in which he placed Habakkuk. Humbert (1944) and Nielsen (1953) think along the same lines.

Most scholars, however, regard the oppressors as foreign enemies, because it is said of them that they conquer nations (2:5), plunder (v. 8), and kill (1:17), and even bring about destruction on Lebanon (2:17). These things can hardly be said of Jehoiakim and his followers. But who are these foreign enemies? At 1:2–4 Elliger (ATD) thinks of the Egyptians, who in 609 killed Josiah in battle and who in 605 were punished by the Chaldeans. In 2:5–17 the oppressors are supposedly the Chaldeans, who also later harass Judah. In this view the prophet is to be dated between 609 and 597. Many agree that the Chaldeans are the oppressors (e.g., Wellhausen, Sellin, Smit, and Deden). Sellin views the entire book of Habakkuk as a prophetic liturgy relating to the oppression by the Chaldeans between 600 (2 Kgs. 24:2) and 586. Van Katwijk, Ridderbos, Aalders, and Vriezen believe that in Habakkuk 1:2–4 the oppressors are Jehoiakim and his followers, and in 2:5–17 the Chaldeans.

Budde, Eissfeldt, and Fohrer think of the Assyrians as the oppressors, who were punished by the Chaldeans. They place Habakkuk's prophecy sometime before 612.

Duhm dates the prophet much later, in the time of Alexander the Great, and he regards the Greeks as the oppressors. In 1:6 he reads *kasdim* (Chaldeans) as *kittim*, by which are meant the Greeks. The prophecy would have originated between the battle at Issus (333) and that at Arbela (331). Alexander the Great took Palestine in 332. This view must be rejected. The Qumran commentary on Habakkuk, discovered in 1947, also reads *kasdim,* though the commentary mentions the Kittim as well (see ill. 64). Sometimes the word refers to the Seleucids, but it seems certain that in this document the name refers to the Romans, so that it is a case of a later actualization of the text.

The lament of Habakkuk in 1:2–4 and his description of the wicked are similar to that in Jeremiah 22:13–17. There it concerns the wicked deeds of Jehoiakim and his group. Habakkuk perhaps was thinking of the same deeds, in which case he must have been active alongside of Jeremiah in the time of Jehoiakim. The use of the Chaldeans (1:5–11) to punish the wicked and godless Judeans is a message also found in Jeremiah. God calls the nation from the north to punish wicked Judah (Jer. 1:14; 4:6; 6:1). These people are the Chaldeans, led by the king of Babylon (21:4, 9; 32:3–5). In 1:12–13 Habakkuk again asks why God allows the wicked to swallow the righteous. This question, too, points to the domestic situations mentioned earlier. The wicked are also mentioned in 2:6b, 9, 11–12, 15–16, 19. By contrast in 1:14–17; 2:5, 8, 10, 17, the wicked oppressor is a nation, which must refer to the Chaldeans. It is possible to regard these verses as later additions to the book of Habakkuk. Possibly in the Babylonian captivity Habakkuk's prophecies were applied to the Chaldeans, and the "O Yahweh, how long" in 1:2 was uttered with a view to them. In that case the prophecies of Habakkuk were augmented with words relating to the Chaldeans and made to apply totally to them.

Habakkuk is generally regarded as a temple prophet, which the designation *nabi* in 1:1 may indicate. In that case he uttered his laments (1:2–4, 12–13) in the temple, which is also where he received the answer to his cries (1:5–11; 2:1–4). That he was a visionary may be inferred from 2:1 and 3:1. The words "with stringed instruments" in 3:19 may indicate that he received his visions

while such instruments were played (see 2 Kgs. 3:15). The name Habakkuk is associated with an Assyrian-Babylonian word indicating a kind of plant.

(2) THE BOOK OF HABAKKUK

According to several prominent scholars (Sellin, Mowinckel, Humbert), the book cannot be regarded as a continuous liturgy that was recited in the temple. Though from the same time, the various messages of the prophet (1:2–4, 5–11, 12–13; 2:1–4, 5–20) were uttered at different moments.

The contents of the book may be divided as follows: 1:1, superscription; 1:2–4, complaint of the prophet concerning oppression and injustice; 1:5–11, God's reply that the Chaldeans and the punishment they will bring are on the way; 1:12–13, a further complaint of the prophet about injustice and oppression, followed by a later elaboration in vv. 14–17 applied to the Chaldeans; 2:1–4, another reply from God, containing the familiar statement that the just shall live by his faith, a statement quoted a few times in the New Testament (Rom. 1:17; Gal. 3:11; Heb. 10:38). In the end God will vindicate the righteous who trusts in him. Then come five (or six) declarations of woe concerning the oppressor: 2:5–6a, 6b–8, 9–11, 12–14, 15–18, 19–20. In the Hebrew text 2:5–6a does not begin with "woe" and therefore according to others is to be taken with the answer in verse 4 (see A. S. van der Woude, "Der Gerechte . . . tot en met," *ZAW* 82 [1970] 281–82).

Chapter 3 is a prayer having as its contents the destruction of the oppressor. The prophet depicts God's coming for judgment and ends with an asseveration of faith and confidence. Some have incorrectly denied this section to the prophet, regarding it as a later addition of a postexilic psalm. Nowadays the passage is commonly accepted as from Habakkuk. Its contents fit what precedes entirely, justifying the remark by Eissfeldt, "There are no compelling arguments against ascribing this song to Habakkuk." That the Dead Sea scroll of Habakkuk contains only the first two chapters says nothing about the origin of chapter 3 and does not prove that at that time chapter 3 was not yet part of the book of Habakkuk. The commentator of this Dead Sea scroll may have regarded the last chapter less suitable for his purpose. In the book it is an impressive song, entirely agreeing with the theme in 2:4.

(3) HABAKKUK'S PREACHING

Experiencing the suffering of his people as they are oppressed by godless enemies, Habakkuk cries to God and prays that he will intervene. From God he receives the answer that oppression and injustice in this world will be punished and that only the righteous who steadfastly trusts in God (a trust also exercised by the prophet himself in 3:17–19) shall live. The prophecy is given an eschatological accent. Someday the whole earth will have to be silent before God (2:20), and all enemies will perish. Then "the earth will be filled with the knowledge of the glory of Yahweh, as the waters cover the sea" (v. 14).

LITERATURE

W. H. Brownlee, *The Text of Habakkuk in the Ancient Commentary of Qumran* (Philadelphia, 1959).

K. Elliger, *Studien zum Habakuk-Kommentar vom Toten Meer* (Tübingen, 1953).

P. Humbert, *Problèmes du livre d'Habacuc* (Neuchâtel, 1944).

J. Jeremias, *Kultprophetie und Gerichtsverkündigung in der späten Königszeit Israels* (WMANT 35; Neukirchen-Vluyn, 1970).

P. Jöcken, *Das Buch Habakuk. Darstellung der Geschichte seiner kritischen Erforschung mit einer einigen Beurteilung* (BBB 48; Köln/Bonn, 1977).

C. A. Keller, "Die Eigenart der Prophetie Habakuks," *ZAW* 85 (1973) 156-67.

E. Nielsen, "The Righteous and the Wicked in Habaqquq," *ST* 6 (1953) 54-78.

E. Otto, "Die Stellung der Wehe-Worte in der Verkündigung des Propheten Habakuk," *ZAW* 89 (1977) 73-107.

J. W. Rothstein, "Über Habakkuk, Kap. 1 und 2," *Theologische Studien und Kritiken* 67 (1894) 51-85.

H. Schmidt, "Ein Psalm im Buche Habakuk," *ZAW* 62 (1950) 52-63.

G. Smit, *Habakuk-Maleachi* (Tekst en Uitleg—De Kleine Profeten II; Groningen/Den Haag, 1926).

W. Vischer, *Der Prophet Habakuk* (Neukirchen, 1958) (= *Le Prophète Habaquq* [Geneva, 1959]).

A. S. van der Woude, "Der gerechte wird durch seine treue leben," in *Studia Biblica et Semitica. Th. C. Vriezen dedicata* (Wageningen, 1966), pp. 367-75.

---

i. Zephaniah

(1) PERSON AND TIME

According to the superscription of the book that bears his name, Zephaniah was the great-great-grandson of a certain Hezekiah. Many believe that this name refers to the well-known king by that name, which might explain the highly unusual fact that the genealogy of the prophet is carried back to the fourth generation. Others assume that the Hezekiah mentioned was someone other than the ruler because the word *king* is not used, whereas in other cases it is (cf. Mic. 1:1). It is also suggested that three ancestors of Zephaniah with genuine Israelite names are mentioned because otherwise, given the Ethiopian name of Zephaniah's father Cushi, he might have been thought to be of pagan extraction. The superscription also mentions that Zephaniah was active during the reign of Josiah (640–609 B.C.). The contents of the prophecy, which include a denunciation of idolatry (1:4–6), of the injustice perpetrated by princes and rulers, and of the faithlessness of prophets and priests (3:3–4), suggest the period before Josiah's reform (622), in particular the time when regents were in charge of the government, since Josiah was only eight years of age when he became king (2 Kgs. 22:1). The period of Zephaniah's activity as a prophet falls therefore between 639 and approximately 625. According to 2:13 Nineveh was still in existence, and the invasion of the Chaldeans (626) was still to come.

The scene of Zephaniah's activity was Jerusalem (see 1:4–5, 10–12; 3:1–4, 14–17). It is unlikely that Zephaniah is the same as the priest by that same name in 2 Kings 25:18 and Zechariah 6:10, 14, as D. L. Williams points out ("The Date of Zephaniah," *JBL* 82 [1963] 77ff.).

(2) THE BOOK OF ZEPHANIAH

The original text of the book is well preserved. The contents can be divided as follows: 1:1, superscription; 1:2–6, 10–13, announcement of God's judgment upon Jerusalem and Judah for their idolatry and wickedness; 1:7–9, 14–18, announcement of the Day of the Lord (cf. Amos 5:18–20); 2:1–3, call to confession of sin and repentance, before the Day of the Lord comes. The poor of the land are here exhorted to persist in their righteousness and humility; by so doing they "perhaps" will be saved on that day, a qualification that implies the severity of the judgment (cf. Amos 5:15; 1 Pet. 4:18). The book continues with 2:4–15, announcement of God's judgment upon the other nations—Philistia (vv. 4–7), Moab and Ammon (vv. 8–11), Ethiopia (v. 12), and Assyria (vv. 13–15, with the coming destruction of Nineveh announced in v. 13); 3:1–4, pronouncement of woe upon godless, unrepentant Jerusalem, namely, upon its covetous rulers, corrupt judges, and faithless prophets and priests who profane what is sacred and set an example of wickedness to the people; 3:5–8, God's punishments have not induced the city to repent and therefore the divine judgment will also strike the population of this city. The book ends with a series of positive messages: 3:9–13, a promise of blessing for the nations and for the oppressed people who trust in the Lord; 3:14–15, a song of joy for Zion when the Lord gives deliverance; and 3:16–20, another word of comfort for Zion. Verses 14–20 bear a strong resemblance to Deutero-Isaiah, for which reason these parts have often been regarded as exilic or postexilic additions to the prophecies of Zephaniah.

(3) ZEPHANIAH'S PREACHING

With his message concerning the Day of the Lord, Zephaniah reminds us very much of the prophet Amos. God's judgment strikes the nations (2:4–15; 3:8), but also Judah and Jerusalem (1:2–13; 3:11). This judgment has been linked to the raids of the Scythians, who, according to Herodotus (I, 103–106), between 630 and 625 B.C. lived scattered throughout the entire Middle East. This assumption, however, is doubtful. The Chaldeans have also been mentioned (cf. 2:13). Though they are in the picture, in Zephaniah God's judgment is especially eschatologically focused, referring to his final judgment upon all nations. Through judgment, however, a remnant is being saved (2:3; 3:12). This part of Zephaniah's message reminds us of Isaiah. The sins mentioned by the prophet include idolatry (1:4–6), the imitation of other na-

tions, culturally and morally (v. 8), injustice and greed on the part of judges and rulers and arrogance on the part of prophets and priests (3:1–4), incorrigibility (v. 2), and pride (2:10; 3:11). Like Isaiah (see Isa. 2), Zephaniah views pride as the basic sin. God requires of people humility, trust, and righteousness (Zeph. 2:3; 3:2, 12–13). The prophecy concludes with a promise of blessing for the nations (3:9–11) as well as for Israel (vv. 12–13). Judgment as well as salvation is universal in Zephaniah.

LITERATURE

H. Cazelles, "Sophonie, Jérémie et les Scythes," *RB* 74 (1967) 22-44.

K. Elliger, "Das Ende der 'Abendwölfe' Zeph. 3,3, Hab. 1,8," in *Festschrift Alfred Bertholet* (Tübingen, 1950), pp. 158-75.

H. Irsigler, *Gottesgericht und Jahwetag. Die Komposition Zef 1,1–2,3 untersucht auf der Grundlage der Literarkritik des Zefanjabuches* (St. Ottilien, 1977).

A. S. Kapelrud, *The Message of the Prophet Zephaniah* (Oslo-Bergen-Tromsø, 1975).

G. Langohr, "Le livre de Sophonie et la critique d'authenticité," *Ephemerides Theologicae Lovanienses* 52 (1976) 1-27.

A. S. van der Woude, "Predikte Zefanja een wereldgericht?" *NTT* 20 (1965) 1-16.

---

j. Haggai

(1) PERSON AND TIME

We are fairly accurately informed about the time of the prophet Haggai. His prophecies are dated in the second year of the Persian king Darius (1:1), or Darius I Hystaspes, who was king from 522 to 486 B.C. He was preceded by Cambyses (530–522) and Cambyses by Cyrus, the founder of the Persian empire, who in 539 had defeated Babylon and had permitted the Jews in Babylon to return to their own land. Initially Darius had to contend with several rebellions in his realm, but by 520 peace had been restored. In that year Haggai began preaching in Judah, between the first day of the sixth month (August 29) and the twenty-fourth day of the ninth month (December 18), thus a little over three months (1:1; 2:10, 20).

Haggai exhorted the people to resume the rebuilding of the temple, for which Cyrus had given permission as well as active support (Ezra 1). That rebuilding of the temple had started sixteen years earlier, when Zerubbabel was governor and Joshua was high priest (Ezra 3:8). These leaders of the people had returned with the people from Babylon. Zerubbabel, a descendant of King Jehoiachin (1 Chr. 3:17-19), was the Persian governor (Hag. 1:1). Joshua, the high priest, the son of Jozadak (Ezra 3:2), was a grandson of Seraiah (1 Chr. 6:14), who had been executed by order of Nebuchadrezzar (2 Kgs. 25:18-21). The rebuilding of the temple had come to an abrupt halt because of opposition by the Samaritans (Ezra 4:1-5) and because of poor economic conditions in the land (Hag. 1:6, 11). Haggai and the prophet Zechariah exhorted the people to resume the construction of the temple, and while the work was in progress they encouraged the people (Ezra 5:2; 6:14). The rebuilding took five years (Ezra 6:15).

It is not known how long Haggai accompanied the reconstruction of the temple with his messages. The prophecies found in his book deal only with the resumption of the rebuilding. Did Haggai die shortly afterward, or does the book contain only part of his preaching? It has been said on the basis of 2:3 that Haggai was already an old man when he began to preach and that he had seen the first temple. This verse, however, does not require such an interpretation. Nowadays most scholars assume that Haggai did not belong to the returned exiles but that he was from the Jews who in 586 had remained behind in Judah. The name Haggai may indicate that he was born on a feast day (cf. the name Shabbethai in Ezra 10:15).

(2) THE BOOK OF HAGGAI

The book of Haggai contains four dated prophecies in prose, chronologically arranged and all relating to the rebuilding of the temple. The first, 1:1-15a, is a call on the first day of the sixth month (feast of the new moon) to become active and faithful and to resume the building of the temple (vv. 1-11), with a report that the people heeded the prophet's message (vv. 12-14). The construction activities are resumed on the twenty-fourth day of the month. In the second prophecy, 1:15b-2:9, given on the twenty-first day of the seventh month (the last day of the Feast of Tabernacles), Haggai proclaims that, contrary to outward appearance, the glory of the second temple will be greater than that of the first. The third section, 2:10-19, is a proclamation on the twenty-fourth day of the ninth month (exactly three months after the resumption of the rebuilding) in which the prophet announces God's promise of prosperity and blessing after the rebuilding of the temple. According to Rothstein, *Juden und Samaritaner* (1908), and later other scholars, verses 10-14 refer to the Samaritans' offer to help with the rebuilding of the temple, an offer rejected on account of their uncleanness, and verses 15-19 are to be placed after 1:15a (see BHK³). Others such as J. L. Koole reject this suggestion. The final prophecy, 2:20-23, has wrongly been regarded as inauthentic. It is likewise dated on the twenty-fourth day of the ninth month and contains a specific promise in messianic language concerning Zerubbabel, a descendant of David. Under his leadership the temple was built. When all royal thrones and kingdoms collapse, Yahweh will make Zerubbabel his signet ring. Unlike his ancestor Jehoiachin (see Jer. 22:24), Zerubbabel will be a blessing to his people.

(3) HAGGAI'S PREACHING

With his call to rebuild the temple, Haggai directs all the attention to the cultic service of Yahweh and the place he ought to have in the life of his people. The Jews may therefore not live solely for themselves, being interested only in building their own houses and looking after their own interests, at the expense of the service of God. The relationship and obligations to God should be central in their life, which accounts for Haggai's interest in the temple. His concern is not the temple as such. It is therefore wrong to accuse the prophet of ritualism and thereby of departing from the proclamations of earlier prophets. Haggai views the temple especially in relation to the coming messianic kingdom, which he clearly expects, as did the prophets before him. Haggai's preaching is thus clearly eschatologically accented. As in Isaiah (Isa. 2), so in Haggai the temple has a central position in the salvation that the nations will likewise share in. They will come to the temple in Jerusalem and bring their treasures into it, to the glory of Israel's God (2:6–7).

All power and all the kingdoms of the nations will be destroyed, but Zerubbabel will stand in a special relationship to God, and thus he will be a blessing to the people (2:23). In him, a descendant of David's royal family, the prophecy of Nathan (2 Samuel 7) is continued, and someday in the coming of the Messiah this prophecy will be completely fulfilled. Zerubbabel himself is not the Messiah, but he foreshadows and points to the coming anointed one.

LITERATURE

P. R. Ackroyd, *Exile and Restoration* (Philadelphia, 1972²).

W. A. M. Beuken, *Haggai-Sacharja 1–8. Studien zur Überlieferungsgeschichte der frühnachexilischen Prophetie* (Assen, 1967).

K. M. Beyse, *Serubbabel und die Königserwartungen der Propheten Haggai und Sacharja* (Stuttgart, 1972).

K. Galling, *Studien zur Geschichte Israels im persischen Zeitalter* (Tübingen, 1964).

J. L. Koole, *Haggaï* (COT; Kampen, 1967).

J. W. Rothstein, *Juden und Samaritaner* (BWANT 3; Leipzig, 1908).

H. W. Wolff, *Haggai* (Neukirchen, 1951).

k. Zechariah

(1) PERSON AND TIME

In 1:1, 7 the prophet is called Zechariah, the son of Berechiah, the son of Iddo. In Ezra 5:1; 6:14, he is called only the son of Iddo. According to some, "the son of Berechiah" was erroneously inserted from Isaiah 8:2, which also mentions a Zechariah the son of Jeberechiah. It is also possible that in Ezra only the name of Zechariah's grandfather is mentioned, because he was a better-known figure than his father. So Laban is called the son of Nahor (Gen. 29:5), though he was his grandson (see 24:24, 29), and Jehu is identified as the son of Nimshi (2 Kgs. 9:20), though Nimshi was his grandfather (v. 14).

According to Nehemiah 12:4, 16, Zechariah was of priestly descent, and his grandfather was among those who had returned from Babylon. As a child he may have belonged to these returnees, having been born just before the end of the Exile. Under the high priest Joiakim, the son of Jeshua/Joshua (v. 10), Zechariah was one of the heads of the priestly families (v. 16). Ezra 5:1 and 6:14 show that he was a contemporary of Haggai, although he must have been much younger than Haggai. According to Zechariah 1:1, the prophet was first active in the eighth month of the second year of Darius (the day has dropped out), that is, October/November 520 B.C. For a little less than two months, then, he worked together with Haggai (see Hag. 2:10), at least according to the datings known to us. The last dating of Zechariah's prophecies is found in 7:1 (the fourth day of the ninth month of the fourth year of Darius), but the prophetic labors of the prophet may have extended over more than two years. It would be remarkable, though, if his later prophecies were undated. Like Haggai, Zechariah exhorted the returned exiles to rebuild the temple, and he accompanied the work of reconstruction with his oracles (Ezra 5:1; 6:14). Though the building of the temple occupies an important place in his preaching (Zech. 1:16; 4:9; 6:12–13), it is not limited to it. Zechariah is especially known for his so-called night visions (1:7–6:8).

(2) THE BOOK OF ZECHARIAH

It is generally the custom to distinguish between chapters 1–8 and 9–14. Though the majority of scholars assign chapters 9–14 to a prophet other than Zechariah or to more than one prophet, those scholars who wish to maintain the unity of the book also recognize a clear difference between these two sections. The latter explain the difference by dating the second part of Zechariah's prophecies in a later period of his life.

The superscription in 1:1 is followed in 1:2–6 by a call to repentance, with the promise that God will not withhold his grace. It is noteworthy that this appeal is made by referring to the messages of the earlier prophets. It is not stated what the people are to repent of. Zechariah's preaching was possibly along the same lines as Haggai's (see Hag. 1:3–11). In the section 1:7–6:8 follow the night visions of the prophet, received in the night of the twenty-fourth day of the eleventh month of the second year of Darius's reign (1:7). They are written in the first person and belong to an original writing from the prophet himself. Zechariah reports eight night visions: the vision of the horsemen and of the rider on the red horse (1:8–15), the four horns and the four smiths (2:1–4 [1:18–21]), the man with the measuring line (2:5–9 [1–5]), the cleansing of the high priest Joshua (3:1–7), the golden lampstand and the two olive trees (ch. 4), the flying scroll (5:1–4), the woman in the basket (5:5–11), and the four chariots (6:1–8). A number of separate proverbs have been interspersed, namely, 1:16, 17; 2:10–13 (6–9), 14–17 (10–13); 3:8–10. This section is followed in 6:9–15 by the symbolic act of the crowning of Joshua and the announcement of the Branch, the messianic figure. According to some this section was later reworked and originally had Zerubbabel as the person who was crowned. A prophecy about fasting (7:1–6; 8:18–19) is augmented by an oracle about the destruction of the people (7:7–14), with an allusion to the preaching of the former prophets. Chapter 8 contains promises of blessings for the returned people.

Chapters 9–14 are altogether different from the preceding. There are no dates, nothing is said about the building of the temple or about Joshua or Zerubbabel, and the prophet's name is not mentioned. We do read of Greece, or "the sons of Javan" (9:13); as in preexilic days, a distinction is made between Ephraim and Judah (v. 13) or Israel and Judah (11:14) and between the house of Judah and the house of Joseph (10:6); mention is made of the worship of the teraphim (10:2) and idolatry (13:2); and false prophecy is denounced (vv. 3–6). Furthermore, the people are promised that they will return from exile (10:8–10); as in Hosea (11:11), Egypt and Assyria are mentioned as the countries to which the people had been deported (Zech. 10:10).

For the above reasons many are of the opinion that chapters 9–14 are not from Zechariah but from one or more other prophets. Mede (1655) believed, on the basis of Matthew 27:9, where a quotation from Zechariah 11:12–13 is attributed to Jeremiah, that at least chapters 9–11 are from the prophet Jeremiah. According to Bertholet (1814), chapters 9–11 were spoken by the Zecha-riah ben Jeberechiah mentioned in Isaiah 8:2 and, because of the similarity in name, the prophecies were placed after those of Zechariah ben Iddo, after which the names were conjoined into one (Zechariah ben Berechiah ben Iddo). The prophecies in chapters 9–11 (and 13:7–9) would thus have been composed before 722, the chapters 12–14 about 586.

Kuenen and Baudissin assumed a preexilic original document in chapters 9–14. An indication would be the names of the Philistine cities (9:1–7), the juxtaposition of Israel and Judah (9:13; 10:6; 11:14), and the reference to the Exile and to Assyria (10:8–11). This preexilic material would have been reworked and supplemented with postexilic material in the Greek period. Hugo de Groot, followed among others by Eichhorn and Stade, placed the origin of chapters 9–14 in the period of the diadochi, while Duhm and Marti thought of the time of the Maccabees. Sellin also adopted this latter position, regarding the chapters as a pseudepigraphal apocalypse, to which was assigned the name of Zechariah ben Jeberechiah from Isaiah 8:2, since apocalyptic material has a preference for old material with a new meaning. Names such as Assyria and Egypt would thus refer to the Syria of the Seleucids and to the Egypt of the Ptolemies (as in the book of Revelation, Babylon represents Rome). Eissfeldt dated chapters 9–11 (Deutero-Zechariah) about 330, or the period of the diadochi, and 12–14 (Trito-Zechariah) some decades later, although he did not consider it impossible that older material had been used. Vriezen also holds that chapters 9–11 and 12–14 are two separate collections. Both have their own superscription: "Oracle, the word of the Lord." According to Vriezen, chapters 9–11 are written in a prophetic-messianic spirit, while 12–14 betray a more apocalyptic style. In the first collection some prophecies from Zechariah's time may have been included, but other prophecies are likely from the third century (9:11–17, in which the Greeks are mentioned) or are still younger (11:4–17 and 13:7–9, from the second century just before the time of the Maccabees). Because of their apocalyptic and theocratic character, chapters 12–14 are perhaps from the third century.

Others, such as Aalders, Ridderbos, Smit,

C. Brouwer *(Wachter en herder)*, and A. H. Edel-koort *(De Christusverwachting in het Oude Testament* [1941], p. 461; *De profeet Zacharia)*, maintain the unity of the book and place the prophecies in chapters 9–14 in a much later period in the life of the prophet. According to them the mention of Greece (9:13) need not be an allusion to the Hellenistic period, since the Greeks had already made their influence felt in Zechariah's time. The defeats of the Persians by the Greeks in the battle at Marathon (490) and at Salamis (480) must have made a deep impression on the world of that time. Damascus and the Philistine cities (9:1–7) were still in existence at the time. Israel and Judah are also mentioned together in 8:13. The name Assyria was not unusual in that period (see Ezra 6:22).

It is virtually impossible to date chapters 9–14 with certainty, because they allude to all kinds of events and conditions that are unknown to us. Moreover, they are often written in a cryptic, apocalyptic style. The possibility that they are based on old prophecies should always be taken into consideration.

If it is assumed that chapters 9–14 contain two main parts (9–11 and 12–14), the following pericopes can be discerned in the first part: 9:1–8, announcement of judgment against Damascus, Hamath, Tyre and Sidon, and the Philistine cities, with a promise that God will help Judah; 9:9–10, promise to Jerusalem of the king of peace; 9:11–17, promise of return from exile and victory of Ephraim and Judah over their enemies; 10:1–2, fruitfulness and rain are only from God; 10:3–12, God's mercy upon his people that he brings back from captivity; 11:1–3, end of the world powers and their leaders; and 11:4–17, a shepherd's allegory about the wicked shepherds and the breaking of the two staffs Grace and Union.

The second main part contains the following prophecies: 12:1–9, announcement of Jerusalem's siege and deliverance; 12:10–14, dirge about the one violently slain; 13:1–6, extermination of idolatry and false prophecy; 13:7–9, the shepherd struck and the flock scattered, with a remnant being spared; 14:1–7, God's appearance as judge and savior on the Mount of Olives; and 14:8–21, God's kingship recognized and his kingdom come to the whole world.

(3) ZECHARIAH'S PREACHING

The starting point for Zechariah's preaching is the building of the new temple (Ezra 6:14; Zech. 1:16; 4:9; 6:12, 15), but Zechariah's vision goes much further. He sees the temple as the center of a new Jerusalem (1:16–17; 2:5–9, 14–17 [1–5, 10–13]; 8:1–3) and of a new world in which, after God's judgment (2:1–4 [1:18–21]), the nations will share in God's salvation (6:15; 8:20–23). God punished Israel on account of its sins (7:11–14), but his electing love did not end (1:16–17)—a new future will dawn. That fact implies a spiritual renewal of the people. Zechariah speaks of a cleansing from sin (note the fourth, sixth, and seventh night visions). Spiritual and moral renewal is more important than fasting (7:1–7, 9–10; 8:16–17). The building of the temple involves more than just the work of human hands; it is the fruit of God's Spirit. The work must be a spiritual work (4:6). For Zechariah, all these themes are connected with his messianic expectation. He builds upon Jeremiah's prophecy concerning the Branch (6:12; Jer. 23:5; 33:15). In the Messiah, king and priest are united in one person (Zech. 6:13). In other respects as well Zechariah continues in the train of the earlier prophets (1:4–6; 7:7). Several statements from Zechariah recall what was said by these prophets (Zech. 8:3 = Isa. 1:26 and Jer. 31:23; Zech. 8:8 = Hos. 2:25 [23] and Jer. 31:33; Zech. 8:21 = Isa. 2:3 and Mic. 4:2). Words once spoken by earlier prophets retain their significance.

The main theme of Zechariah 9–14 is God's victory over the nations and his everlasting kingship. Jerusalem is the center of the new kingdom over which God rules, but all nations share in the salvation. The central position is occupied by the figure of the king of peace (9:9–10). The blessings begin when Israel returns from captivity (10:3–12) and repents (vv. 1–2). There will be mourning for "him whom they have pierced" (12:10–14). Idolatry and false prophecy are done away with (13:1–6). Then God will reveal himself, and he will reign over the whole world. The chapters thus clearly have a strong eschatological emphasis.

LITERATURE

P. Ackroyd, *Exile and Restoration* (Philadelphia, 1972²).

A. H. Edelkoort, *De profeet Zacharia* (Baarn, 1945).

Proto-Zechariah (Zech. 1–8):

C. Jeremias, *Die Nachtgesichte des Sacharja* (FRLANT 117; Göttingen, 1977).

A. Petitjean, *Les oracles du Proto-Zacharie* (Paris, 1969).

Deutero-Zechariah (Zech. 9–14):

C. Brouwer, *Wachter en herder. Een exegetische studie over de herder-figuur in het Oude Testament* (Wageningen, 1949).

C. R. North, "Prophecy to Apocalyptic via Zechariah," *SVT* 22 (1972) 47–71.

P. Lamarche, *Zacharie IX–XIV. Structure littéraire et messianisme* (Études Bibliques; Paris, 1961).

O. Plöger, *Theocracy and Eschatology* (Richmond, 1968), pp. 78–96.

M. Saebø, *Sacharja 9–14. Untersuchungen von Text und Form* (WMANT 34; Neukirchen, 1969).

———, "Die deuterosacharjanische Frage. Eine forschungsgeschichtliche Studie," *ST* 23 (1969) 115–40.

I. Willi-Plein, *Prophetie am Ende. Untersuchungen zu Sacharja 9–14* (BBB 42; Köln, 1974).

l. Malachi

(1) PERSON AND TIME

Many think of Malachi not as a proper name but as a title or insertion from 3:1. Presumably the book was originally anonymous. Like the heading of Zechariah 9 and 12, the superscription would originally have been, "the oracle of the word of Yahweh to Israel." Later there would have been added, "by my messenger" *(malaki)*. The Septuagint has "through his messenger," but there the name of the book is Malachias. Others regard Malachi as a proper name. The name would be an abbreviation and mean "messenger of Yahweh."

Nothing personal is known about the prophet. It is certain that his ministry was after the Exile (1:8 refers to a Persian governor) and considerably later than that of Haggai and Zechariah. The temple stands in Jerusalem and the temple service is in full swing (1:7, 10; 3:1, 10). There-fore the prophet must have lived after 515. These passages also indicate that the cultic worship was marred by much negligence and carelessness. Inferior sacrifices were brought, the priests neglected their duties, and the people were unfaithful in paying the tithes. All such activities indicate that considerable time had elapsed since the completion of the temple. The evils that are censored by Malachi are similar to those denounced by Ezra and Nehemiah in their days, such as divorces, followed by marriages with pagan women (Mal. 2:10–16; see Ezra 9–10; Neh. 10:29–31 [28–30]; 13:23–31), failure to pay the tithes (Mal. 3:8–12; see Neh. 10:33–40 [32–39]; 13:12), and exploitation of the poor (Mal. 3:5; see Neh. 5:1–13).

Eissfeldt, Fohrer, and Vriezen, for example, place Malachi just before Ezra's arrival in Jerusalem in the seventh year of Artaxerxes I (465–424 B.C.), which would date Malachi's ministry at about 470 or 460. Ridderbos, Verhoef, and, before them, Keil and Kuenen think of the time between Nehemiah's first and second visits to Jerusalem, thus after 433 (see Neh. 13:6). It is not known when Nehemiah returned to Jerusalem, perhaps between five and twenty years later, in which case Malachi's ministry fell between 433 and about 420 (see the situation described in Neh. 13:11–13, 23–28). Deden places Malachi at about the first visit of Nehemiah to Jerusalem, that is, 445 B.C. (see Neh. 2:1).

Mention should also be made of Malachi's discussion or dispute style (1:2, 6, 13, etc.). Such a presentation is also found elsewhere in the Old Testament (Mic. 2:6–7; Isa. 28:23–25; 40:12–14, 27–31) and is often used in later rabbinic teaching.

(2) THE BOOK OF MALACHI

Six addresses or dialogues can be distinguished in the book of Malachi: 1:2–5, God's electing love for Israel; 1:6–2:9, denunciation of the priests for bringing unworthy offerings; 2:10–16, condemnation of the Jews who divorce their wives to marry heathen women; 2:17–3:5, reply to those who doubt God's justice and the speedy coming of his judgment; 3:6–12, call to the people to repent and to pay the tithes, after which they will surely be blessed; 3:13–21 (3:13–4:3), the Day of the Lord manifests the difference between the devout and the wicked, for the former will not fail to receive their reward and the latter will surely be punished. The final three verses—3:22 (4:4), an admonition to keep the law of Moses, and 3:23–24 (4:5–6), a prediction that Elisha will appear before the coming of the Day of the Lord— are usually regarded as later additions, either from the prophet himself or from someone else. The New Testament sees the coming of Elijah fulfilled in the ministry of John the Baptist, who preceded the Christ (Matt. 11:14; 17:11–13; Luke 1:17). There is also some question about the authenticity of Malachi 1:11 and 2:11–12.

(3) MALACHI'S PREACHING

Malachi points to God's love for Israel (1:2–5) and for that reason denounces the people all the more for their ingratitude. Israel is like an ungrateful son (v. 6). This attitude is evident in priests who bring inferior sacrifices (vv. 6–9) and in people who bring these sacrifices and do not pay the tithes (3:6–10). Ingratitude is also manifest in the moral and social life of the people. The prophet mentions divorces (2:10–16), injustice, and oppression of the poor (3:5). Because of these evils God will soon come with his judgments, though some doubt it (2:17–3:1). That judgment will strike both priests and people (3:2–5). The day of judgment comes like a fiery furnace (3:19 [4:1]), and the fire will have a purifying effect, in this way making evident the distinction between the righteous and the wicked. The wicked will be destroyed, but God's righteousness will shine like the sun upon those who revere his name. It brings light, life, and deliverance (3:20 [4:2]). Before God comes in judgment himself, he will send his messenger to prepare the way (3:1). In 3:23 (4:5) this messenger is called Elijah. Afterward the Lord himself comes as Messenger of the Covenant (3:1), not to be confused with Elijah. In this mode of appearance (cf. the Angel of the Lord in the Old Testament; e.g., Gen. 16:7; Exod. 3:2), God, through judgment, upholds and renews his covenant with his people.

Malachi's preaching ends with an expectation, a kind of open window on what will come, namely, the one who is Judge and Deliverer. The New Testament links up with that expectation and seeks to provide the answer. Malachi's preaching thus fits at the end of the Old Testament, for with its expectation it demands a sequel. It is likewise appropriate just before the New Testament, for the latter intends to be this sequel and therefore not just coincidentally but deliberately links up with Malachi's proclamation (Matt. 11:14).

LITERATURE

K. Elliger, "Maleachi und die kirchliche Tradition," *Tradition und Situation: Studien zur alttestamentlichen Prophetie* (Festschrift A. Weiser; Göttingen, 1963), pp. 43-48.

E. Pfeiffer, "Die Disputationsworte im Buche Maleachi," *Evangelische Theologie* 19 (1959) 546ff.

G. Wallis, "Wesen und Struktur der Botschaft Maleachis," in F. Maass, ed., *Das ferne und nahe Wort* (Festschrift L. Rost; BZAW 105; Berlin, 1967), pp. 229-37.

A. S. van der Woude, *Der Engel des Bundes* (Festschrift H. W. Wolff; Neukirchen, 1981), pp. 209-300.

D. The Writings

by J. P. M. van der Ploeg

The *ketubim,* "Writings," constitute the third section of the Jewish canon of the Old Testament. The sequence in which they are found in the manuscripts is not everywhere the same; important variations can be noted (see C. D. Ginsburg, *Introduction to the Masoretico-Critical Edition of the Hebrew Bible* [London, 1897; New York, 1966], pp. 6–8). The Psalms, Job, and Proverbs usually come first (the last two not always in the same order). Sometimes these three are preceded by Ruth or Chronicles. Then follow as a rule the five *megilloth,* or (small) Scrolls. The last books in the collection are Daniel, Ezra-Nehemiah, and Chronicles. Variations in the sequence can also be seen in present editions of the Bible; not even those of Kittel and Snaith agree. The sequence is somewhat but not wholly due to the time of origin of the books or their gaining canonical status. I discuss here the various books of this part with the exception of Chronicles and Ezra-Nehemiah (which are considered above in section B.6–7), following the sequence in Kittel's *Biblia Hebraica.*

1. PSALMS

The Psalms are undoubtedly the most important book of the Writings. (Note Luke 24:44, where the term "Psalms" perhaps refers to all the Writings.) In Hebrew the book is called *tehillim,* "praises," after their main use, that of praising and honoring God in the worship services. All editions of the Bible count 150 psalms, though in the old translations they are not always identically numbered. The major deviations are those between the Massoretic text (MT) and the Septuagint (LXX) and the translations based on the latter, such as the Vulgate. The following listing shows the correspondence of psalms in the two versions.

MT	LXX
9–10	9
11–113	10–112
114–15	113
116	114–15
117–46	116–45
147	146–47

At some point in the editorial process, the psalms were divided into five books: Psalms 1–41; 42–72; 73–89; 90–106; 107–50. It should be noted, too, that in English translations the superscriptions of the psalms are often omitted and not included in the numbering of the verses. As a result there is often a difference of one or two verses between the Hebrew and the English.

The book of Psalms came into existence gradually. Some very old psalms are likely from King David or from his time. The eighth century B.C. appears to have been a golden age of psalmody. Many psalms were composed after the Exile, as late as the third century B.C. Some of these psalms were early combined in small collections. These units were combined into larger collections, until finally the whole book of Psalms was complete, not later than the third century B.C.

In the Massoretic text a great number of psalms are supplied with a superscription, partly musical in nature, partly historical. Some of the superscriptions indicate the nature of the psalm. Most of these headings seem to have been added later. The Septuagint contains more headings than the former text, and Syrian manuscripts have their own system of headings. Many psalms are attributed to David without being from his hand or having come from his mouth. Psalm 72 is attributed to Solomon, Psalm 90 to Moses, others to "the sons of Korah," still others to "the sons of Asaph," and many lack a superscription altogether.

Scholars are not agreed on the purpose for which the psalms were composed. Because ultimately all the psalms found their way into the liturgy of synagogue and church, some believe that they were *all* composed for the cult, initially for worship in the temple. This conclusion cannot be demonstrated, certainly not for all the psalms. Likely a number of psalms were from the outset meant for public worship, whereas others, especially postexilic psalms, are the expression of personal piety.

Claus Westermann has emphasized the fact that devout individuals who approach God usually do so for two main reasons: they desire something from him, and they seek to praise and honor him. In the relationship to God both attitudes almost always go together. The psalms have rightly been called "the clearest mirror of the piety of the most devout people in the Old Covenant" (Peters, *Psalmen*, p. 9). For the same reason the psalms have always been held in high esteem in Christianity, though perhaps not in as great esteem as in Israel and among the Jews. It is no longer possible to determine exactly how the psalms functioned in the old cult. The idea that they were used as in the Christian church today, verse by verse, must be abandoned. The ancients preferred solo singing, which, particularly in later times, could be interrupted by refrains that were sung by all. An example of this structure is Psalm 136 (see also Psalm 145 in Qumran). Likely there were professional singers, in the second temple especially belonging to the Levites, who sang the psalms in public, on behalf of others or on behalf of the community.

S. Mowinckel has contended that about half of the psalms were cultic in nature and belonged to what he called an "enthronement festival of Yahweh." His theory nowadays is unacceptable. He also maintained that just about all the psalms were composed either for or in the cult. Gunkel has disputed this claim, maintaining that only the origin of the various *types* of psalms lies in the cult, but that later most of the psalms were no longer specifically composed for the cult. A brief but stimulating description of the cult in the first quarter of the second century before Christ can be found in the Wisdom of Sirach 50:5–24 (note the reference in v. 18 to the hymns of the singers). It is difficult to determine for each psalm whether it was originally composed for the worship services and what function it occupied in these services.

Nowadays scholars usually classify psalms according to their literary types (Ger. *Gattungen*). Such a focus is not new, but it was carried out most consistently by Gunkel in his program of *Gattungsforschung* ("investigation of types") with respect to the book of Psalms. (See especially his large commentary on the Psalms [1926] and the introduction to it by J. Begrich [1933].) In every psalm Gunkel looked for what he called the *Sitz im Leben*, an untranslatable expression that has become common currency in other languages. He assumed that the psalmists composed their psalms on the basis of a specific life situation, whereby they used fixed schemes and modes of expression that were common to each *Gattung*, or genre. Many psalms do not have a specific *Gattung*, in which case Gunkel speaks of *Mischgattungen*, meaning that style and modes of expression are mixed.

Whereas Gunkel was flexible in his application of *Gattungsforschung*, others later carried the method to extremes, apparently assuming that the ancient Israelite and Jewish poets could use only rigidly defined forms. Many disagreed with such an assumption. Claus Westermann, for example, pointed out that praise is often followed by prayer, and prayer by praise; for the devout believer in God these two naturally go together. Hence it is wrong to attribute psalms with these two elements to two different *Gattungen*. It would also seem preferable to speak of *types* rather than of *Gattungen* (W. Richter, "Text typus," in *Exegese als Literaturwissenschaft* [Göttingen, 1971], p. 74; earlier, J. van der Ploeg, *De Psalmen* [Roermond, 1963], p. 21). This latter volume (see also J. van der Ploeg, *De Psalmen*, I [Roermond, 1971], p. 30) makes the following general classification of psalms according to types: (1) *lyric poems*—hymns or songs about Zion or Jerusalem, laments (of the people and by individuals, with penitential psalms as a special type), certain royal psalms; and (2) *nonlyric poems*—didactic poems (discussing wisdom problems, the law, virtues, and obligations), narrating poems (nonepic, but didactic in intent and shape), certain royal psalms.

These divergent types are not combined in groups in the book of Psalms but are scattered throughout the whole book. Some commentators (e.g., König, Castellino, Leslie) attempt to alleviate this problem by grouping the psalms according to contents, but this practice cannot be recommended. The question has been asked why the psalms are arranged as they are. C. T. Niemeyer ("Het probleem van de rangschikking der Psalmen" [diss., Leiden, 1950]) has explored this question, without finding a solution. The smaller and larger collections that gradually grew into the present book of Psalms appear generally to have retained their ancient ordering, and it is not possible now to devise one or more guidelines that would enable us to explain the sequence of all the psalms.

Cave 11 of Qumran has yielded a severely damaged, incomplete scroll of the Psalms in which they are arranged in a different order than the traditional one. Some fragments from the same cave indicate that there must have been a second copy of this text. Because the text of this scroll (11QPs^a) is as a rule secondary to that of the transmitted Massoretic text, it seems safe to assume that the sequence is also secondary and likely is from the Qumran sect. Moreover, the text contains a number of apocryphal psalms, including some that were already known (such as Psalm 151 in the LXX). The idea that the order of the psalms in 11QPs^a comes from a time when they did not yet have their fixed location in the book of Psalms has little to commend it.

All psalms are written in poetic form. Some authors were excellent poets, having a good command of their language and style, and were not afraid to demonstrate their ability by the use of rare, strange, or archaic words. Some psalms lack this last characteristic, being written in a more popular style. In the older psalms, parallelism and form are more strictly adhered to than in psalms of more recent date. The psalms in the last part of the book of Psalms are, as a rule, of more recent date than those earlier in the book; in some cases

they are as recent as the third century B.C., but here, too, there are exceptions (e.g., Psalm 110).

In the context of this essay not much can be said about the theology of Psalms. The psalms were composed over a period of six hundred to seven hundred years and deal with many subjects. The most outstanding characteristic is the piety of the individual, a piety exhibiting such universally human traits that the Jewish book of Psalms could without any conscious difficulty be adopted by the Christian church as its hymnbook from the earliest days. Many psalms are petitions, often expressing grief, in which righteous individuals pour out their needs before God, asking him for help. The righteous person may be a representative of the people or of the whole nation. The modern conception that all petitions that express grief were composed by people who experienced need is unfounded, since these petitions are often prayers on behalf of people in need. In the hymns God's greatness is praised, above all the truth that he is the creator God and, furthermore, that he is the savior and protector of his people. Some superscriptions ascribe psalms to David as being composed in particular circumstances in his life; this practice points out what at a later time was regarded as a possible setting for the psalm.

Some psalms deal with problems also discussed in wisdom literature, although doing so in a different way, for the psalms remain *songs*. The law, a privileged and precious possession of Israel, also plays a role in some psalms, particularly in the longest one of all, Psalm 119. Other psalms draw instruction from the history of the people, in particular from the deliverance from Egypt and the later suffering. Some psalms relate particularly to the king; in most cases they contain prayers on behalf of a king (e.g., Psalms 20–21), sometimes prayers by a king (Psalm 19). Some of these royal psalms present such an ideal picture of the king that the New Testament applies them to the Messiah. According to most expositors, a life in the presence of God after death is certainly taught in Psalm 49:16 (15). On the analogy of this psalm, some (but not all) Old Testament scholars have seen the same teaching in other verses in certain psalms (Pss. 16:11; 17:15; 73:24).

LITERATURE

Commentaries:

A. A. Anderson, *Psalms* I-II (New Century Bible; repr. London/Grand Rapids, 1981).

C. A. and E. G. Briggs, *A Critical and Exegetical Commentary on the Book of Psalms* I-II (ICC; Edinburgh, 1906-1907).

G. Castellino, *Libro dei Salmi* (Torino, 1955).

P. C. Craigie, *Psalms 1–50* (Word Biblical Commentary; Waco, TX, 1983).

M. Dahood, *Psalms* I-III (AB; Garden City, NY, 1965, 1968, 1970).

B. D. Eerdmans, *Psalms* (OTS IV; Leiden, 1947).

B. Gemser, *Die Psalmen* (= Pss. 90–150) (Tekst en Uitleg; Groningen, 1949).

H. Gunkel, *Die Psalmen* (HKAT IV/2; Göttingen, 1926).

F. M. Th. de Liagre Böhl, *De Psalmen* I-II (= Pss. 1–89) (Tekst en Uitleg; Groningen, 1946, 1947) (repr. with Gemser [see above], Nijkerk, 1968).

E. J. Kissane, *The Book of Psalms* I-II (Dublin, 1953/1964).

G. A. F. Knight, *Psalms* I-II (Daily Study Bible; Philadelphia, 1982-83).

H.-J. Kraus, *Psalmen* I-II (BKAT XV; Neukirchen, 1960).

E. Leslie, *The Psalms* (New York/Nashville, 1959).

S. Mowinckel, *The Psalms in Israel's Worship* I-II (Oxford, 1962).

N. Peters, *Das Buch der Psalmen* (Paderborn, 1930).

J. van der Ploeg, *De Psalmen* (Roermond-Maaseik, 1963).

——, *Psalmen* I-II (BOT; Roermond-Maaseik, 1971-75).

E. Podechard, *Le Psautier* I-III (= Pss. 1–100 + 110) (Louvain, 1949).

R. Tournay, *Les Psaumes* (La Sainte Bible de Jérusalem; Paris, 1964³).

A. Weiser, *Psalms* (OTL; Philadelphia, 1962).

Other Works:

Chr. Barth, *Einführung in die Psalmen* (Neukirchen, 1961).

F. M. Cross, Jr., and D. N. Freedman, *Studies in Ancient Yahwistic Poetry* (Missoula, MT, 1975).

R. C. Culley, *Oral Formulaic Language in the Biblical Psalms* (Toronto, 1967).

G. B. Gray, *The Forms of Hebrew Poetry* (New York, repr. 1972).

H. Gunkel and J. Begrich, *Einleitung in die Psalmen* (Göttingen, 1933).

A. R. Johnson, *The Cultic Prophet and Israel's Psalmody* (Cardiff, 1979).

H.-J. Kraus, *Theology of the Psalms* (Minneapolis, 1986).

L. G. Perdue, *Wisdom and Cult* (Missoula, MT, 1977).

L. Sabourin, *The Psalms, Their Origin and Meaning* I-II (Staten Island, 1969).

J. A. Sanders, *The Dead Sea Psalms Scroll* (Ithaca, 1967).

P. W. Skehan, *Studies in Israelite Poetry and Wisdom* (Washington, D.C., 1971).

C. Westermann, *The Psalms. Structure, Content and Message* (Minneapolis, 1980).

——, *The Praise of God in the Psalms* (Richmond, 1965).

——, *Der Psalter* (Stuttgart, 1967).

G. H. Wilson, *The Editing of the Hebrew Psalter* (Chico, CA, 1985).

2. JOB

The book of Job belongs to the wisdom literature and thus has affinity with non-Israelite wisdom literature. Yet it is a typically Israelite book, unequaled elsewhere in the ancient Near East, even though comparisons have been made. The problem poetically discussed in the book is that of the suffering of an innocent or righteous man. The book treats this subject in a unique manner. It begins and concludes with a prologue and epilogue in prose (chs. 1–2; 42:7–17), which serve as the framework containing the long speeches in poetic form by Job, by his friends Eliphaz, Bildad, and Zophar, later also by Elihu, and finally by Yahweh. These speeches are the heart of the book, though the prologue (and to some extent the epilogue) cannot be ignored, for it informs the reader about the chief actor.

Yahweh is righteous, an attribute that belongs inherently to his being. The life that people live on earth, however, is brief; afterward the same fate awaits all, the existence as shades in the world of the dead, called *sheol*, in which, according to the general belief in Israel, there is no retribution for good and evil. The idea of retribution after this life—punishment for the wicked and reward for the righteous—arose fairly late in Israel's history. This hope is found in the form of a belief in a physical resurrection and also in the hope to be with God in the hereafter (Ps. 49:16 [15]). The author of Job did not yet know of this idea and therefore faced several questions: Why is so much injustice on earth never punished? Why do numerous righteous people have to suffer? Why are sinners often so prosperous? Could it be that God does not reward the righteous?

This question was asked before the Exile (Jer. 12:1–4) and afterward (Mal. 3:14–15). Echoes of it are also heard in the Psalms (see Psalm 73; also Psalms 37 and 49). The book of Job does not give a complete answer to this question that has occupied the minds of God-fearing people of all times, regardless of their faith in a retribution in the hereafter. The book does offer partial solutions to the problem of the suffering of the righteous, such as that God tests them or warns them. But it does not get much further. It climaxes in the responses given by Yahweh (Job 38–41), in which God points to the infinite wisdom with which he created the world and all creatures, doing so in a manner Job cannot possibly comprehend. In the face of such wisdom, a puny individual such as Job must be silent. He is not allowed to ask questions of that great God, and God in any case is certainly under no obligation to answer them. Job may definitely not accuse God. God knows why the righteous suffer, even though Job does not know. Yahweh is humankind's sovereign Lord, who may deal with people as he pleases, and the individual must believe that what God does is right. The problem of the meaning of suffering remains thus an open question. Not until the New Testament did it receive a more satisfactory answer than that in the book of Job.

The prologue introduces Job, the chief figure in the book, and the situation in which he finds himself. With the permission of God and through the instrumentality of Satan, Job is stripped of everything and in utter misery ends up sitting on a heap of ashes. Satan afflicted him in this way to cause him to despair and to curse God; Yahweh allowed it to happen to test this righteous man, knowing that, having stood the test, his possessions and much more would be returned to him (see the epilogue). This setting permits the author to show Job's highly virtuous life. The prologue gives one explanation why there is suffering: it may be the work of a nonearthly, eerie power that is hostile to human beings, the Antagonist whom God al-

lows to do his dark deeds, thereby giving the godly an opportunity to manifest love and faithfulness to God. The prologue is, however, no more than the indispensable introduction to what follows.

Job is then approached by three friends: Eliphaz, Bildad, and Zophar. With these friends he carries on a lengthy dialogue in poetry, consisting of three parallel cycles. In the first and second cycles, Job speaks, then the first friend, then again Job, then the second friend, and so on. The third cycle begins similarly, with Job and Eliphaz and then Job and Bildad, but the expected speeches of Job and Zophar are missing, while the length of Bildad's words is only a fraction of that of all the preceding monologues. This irregularity poses a problem that some Old Testament scholars try to solve by reconstructing from the text a complete answer both from Bildad and from Zophar. It is possible that the Hebrew text here has become corrupt and that all three cyles were originally very much identical in composition. With the present condition of the text, however, one can only guess how it might have to be restored.

In any case, in the dialogue with his friends Job has the final word. Throughout he asserts his innocence. In the first cycle his friends point out to him the standard doctrine that no one suffers without personal guilt. In the second cycle they go further, stressing that Job's suffering proves that he is guilty of some sin. In the third cycle Eliphaz even goes so far as to accuse Job of all kinds of concrete sins that he must have committed. The reader knows, from the prologue, that these accusations are false. And so the accusations of the friends are shown to be absurd.

In his responses to his friends Job does not always observe proper bounds. He draws conclusions from the sufferings that have come upon him and from the injustice he sees happening in the world, and he accuses God not a little. In the book of Job these accusations are not intended as actual accusations. Using this literary device, the author of the book contrasts the contention of the three friends and the opposite view that he puts in the mouth of Job. He agrees neither with the friends nor with some extremely bold statements from Job, such as his accusation that God is indifferent, is unconcerned about what is happening, and is even unjust (see, e.g., Job 9). Job remains aware throughout that he may not call God to account and that no human is in the right before him (see 9:2–4). Job's posture before God is ambivalent. On the one hand he holds on to God and continues to trust in him (see the noted 19:25, not to be regarded as speaking of the resurrection). On the other hand he reproaches God with accusations that are to be understood as human (but erroneous) conclusions from his own observations. Such accusations are to be understood as antithesis and as simple observations. The author, however, wishes to dig deeper.

At the end of the dialogue with his friends, Job makes a long speech in which, with an oath, he totally rejects all the accusations leveled against him (ch. 31). With that Job has won the dispute with his friends. It also gives the dialogue the character of a kind of trial. The entire event takes place before the bar of the invisible but highest judge: God. According to the present text, chapters 26–27 and 29–30 contain only words of Job (the text appears to be corrupt). Chapter 28 is a wisdom poem, inserted here, in which it is declared that wisdom can be found only in God and that for human beings wisdom consists in true reverence before him.

In chapters 32–37 suddenly an unknown person begins to speak, the young Elihu, who gives four speeches. The intent of these speeches is undoubtedly to disabuse the reader of the idea that there might possibly be some truth in Job's charges against God. Job's allegations may not remain uncontradicted. The friends are also rebuked because they were unable to refute Job (32:3). Elihu declares that God sometimes brings suffering upon people in order to warn them about worse things in case they are doing wrong (ch. 32). Then he takes issue with a number of charges Job had brought against God (without refuting these charges) and in great detail points to God's wisdom, power, might, justice, omniscience, and the like. He concludes by stating that people should fear God, that is, reverence and serve him; human wisdom is as nothing before him (37:24).

Finally Yahweh himself enters the scene. He makes his voice heard and in two speeches admonishes Job (chs. 38–39; 40:1–41:26 [40:1–41:34]). Yahweh points out to Job his divine wisdom and almighty power, as these attributes are seen in his creation, specifically, the sun, the moon and stars, the elements, the earth, the animals, Behemoth (the hippopotamus), and Leviathan (the crocodile). Job is compelled to acknowledge that these mighty works confront him with an impenetrable mystery. Stupidly he spoke about God and his providence; he will no longer do so.

In his book *The Idea of the Holy,* Rudolph Otto has pointed out that Yahweh's answer to Job "relies in the last resort on something quite different from anything that can be exhaustively rendered in rational concepts, namely, on the sheer absolute wondrousness that transcends thought, on the *mysterium,* presented in its pure non-rational form, namely the miraculous as paradox" (p. 105). God points out the mystery in his creation and his work, a mystery that an individual must not try to penetrate. This answer can satisfy only the person who is content to stand in awe at the tremendous mystery of the divine, not the person who insists on rational explanations. Therefore the problem of suffering continued to occupy the thinkers in Israel. Only the Christian is aware of an acceptable resolution, though it has not entirely lost its mysterious character.

The book of Job was apparently not composed originally in exactly the format it has today, but it has expanded. The prologue and epilogue are often viewed as a popular story that was used by the author as a framework. In that connection it is pointed out that there is a difference between the virtuous statements made by Job in 1:21 (see also the assessment of Job in v. 22) and the rebellious language he employs in the poetic sections. I discussed above the possibility that something may have happened to the third cycle of speeches. It also seems, however, that a later redactor tried to make corrections, making it forever impossible to recover the original text. The speeches of Elihu are apparently not part of the original composition but were added later. It is not impossible that such was done by the author himself at a later time, since he may have been concerned that he could be misunderstood by his God-fearing readers. The chief concern of authors like those of the book of Job was to edify people, not to cause difficulties or to raise doubts, certainly not about God. The wisdom poem in chapter 28 may also have been a later insertion, by the same author or someone else. Its purpose is to set the stage for what is to come, especially Yahweh's speeches. It is hardly defensible to argue that the speeches by Yahweh were added later. The stage for Yahweh's intervention is already set in 19:25-27. Job expected Yahweh's replies. But because God's ways are not those of humankind, Yahweh speaks in an altogether different manner than Job could have imagined. Some hold that the fantastic descriptions of Behemoth and Leviathan in the Yahweh speeches were added later. There is no compelling evidence for this assumption, however; like poets over the centuries, ancient poets exercised poetic freedom.

Despite the history of its origin, the book of Job in its present form is an integral whole. To remove parts from it would be to impoverish the book. It has come to us as a unity, which is how it must be read.

We know very little about the time of composition of the book. It would seem best to date it between 500 and 300 B.C. In that time Job was a legendary or familiar figure from antiquity, as is evident from Ezekiel 14:14, where he is mentioned together with Noah and Daniel. In Wisdom of Sirach 49:9 (Heb. and Syr. text), Job is mentioned in connection with the passage in Ezekiel; in Tobit 2:12, 15 (Vulgate) and James 5:11, he is adduced as an example of patience. The author places him in the land of Uz, to be located somewhere in Arabia, more particularly in the ancient land of Edom (see Gen. 36:28), which was famous for its wise men (Obad. 8).

The three friends were not Israelites. Eliphaz was from Teman, a place that, according to Baruch 3:22-23, was the residence of wise men. It is located in Arabia and, in Genesis 36:11, is the name of an Edomite tribe. Bildad was from Shuah, which is the name of one of Abraham's sons by Keturah (Gen. 25:2). Zophar was from Naama, an unknown location (Dhorme thinks of it as lying in the Arabian desert, east of Tebuch). The young man with the significant name of Elihu ("he is God") was from Buz, a place often located in northern Syria, the land of the Arameans, on account of the personal name Buz in Genesis 22:21. All these identifications are unsure and disputed (see esp. the commentaries by Dhorme and

Fohrer). It is certain, however, that the author does not present his dramatis personae as Israelites, for which reason they never use the name Yahweh (the poetic part uses the names *el, eloah, elohim,* and *shadday*). The writer thus had the advantage that, as the story progresses and as he develops his thesis and antithesis, many of the ideas did not have to be said by Israelites. In the prose parts where the author himself speaks, the name of Yahweh does occur. The concern of the book is Yahweh and his mysterious government of the world.

The language of the book of Job contains numerous rare expressions. The reason is partly that it was composed by a poet who wished to demonstrate his skill and linguistic ability. Another reason appears to be that the three persons in the first cycles are non-Israelites, so that it is not surprising that they speak a somewhat colored language. J. L. Palache used to say paradoxically that the language of the book of Job is Arabic, not Hebrew. Arabic is no doubt helpful in the interpretation of Job, as are other Semitic languages.

In the transmission of the text many words and passages suffered corruption, perhaps because of the general difficulty in understanding the text. This difficulty may also be the reason that the Septuagint often gives a very free rendering of the Hebrew text, sometimes omitting a sizable part of it (see the calculation or estimate in Dhorme, pp. cxcix-cc). In later Greek texts the missing parts are supplied. It is proper to ask whether the author of the oldest Greek translation intended to give a proper translation of Job or whether he wanted to provide a free rendering so that the book could also be read by non-Jews.

Cave 11 of Qumran has yielded fragments of a targum of Job (see ill. 65). The manuscript seems to be from the first century B.C., and the text from the second century B.C. The fragments contain especially the last part of the book of Job. The translation is fairly literal, with even the speeches by Yahweh being woodenly literal; in the prose parts the translation is freer. The text used by the translator was in the main the Massoretic text, with here and there some variants, some of which agree with the Septuagint. A few times the familiar targumic inclination to give an interpretation (according to the ideas of the translator) is noticeable.

LITERATURE

Commentaries:

F. I. Andersen, *Job* (TOTC; London/Downers Grove, IL, 1976).

L. H. K. Bleeker, *Job* (Tekst en Uitleg; Groningen, 1926).

E. Dhorme, *A Commentary on the Book of Job* (Nashville, repr. 1984).

S. R. Driver and G. B. Gray, *The Book of Job* (ICC; Edinburgh, 1921).

G. Fohrer, *Das Buch Hiob* (KAT XVI; Gütersloh, 1963).

R. Gordis, *The Book of Job* (New York, 1978).

N. C. Habel, *The Book of Job* (OTL; Philadelphia, 1985).

E. J. Kissane, *The Book of Job* (Dublin, 1939; New York, 1946).

E. König, *Das Buch Hiob* (Gütersloh, 1929).

M. H. Pope, *Job* (AB; Garden City, NY, 1965).

H. H. Rowley, *Job* (New Century Bible; repr. London/Grand Rapids, 1980).

P. Szcygiel, *Das Buch Job* (Bonn, 1931).

A. Weiser, *Das Buch Hiob* (ATD 13; Göttingen, 1956²).

A. de Wilde, *Das Buch Hiob* (OTS 22; Leiden, 1981).

Other Works:

J. Barr, "The Book of Job and its Modern Interpreters," *BJRL* 54 (1971) 28-46.

D. Cox, *The Triumph of Impotence. Job and the Tradition of the Absurd* (Rome, 1978).

J. L. Crenshaw, *Old Testament Wisdom. An Introduction* (Atlanta, 1981).

————, ed., *Theodicy in the Old Testament* (Philadelphia, 1983).

J. H. Eaton, *Job* (OT Guides; Sheffield, 1985).

H. Gese, *Lehre und Wirklichkeit in der alten Weisheit* (Tübingen, 1958).

N. N. Glatzer, *The Dimensions of Job* (New York, 1969).

O. Keel, *Jahwes Entgegnung an Hiob* (FRLANT 121; Göttingen, 1978).

J. Lévêque, *Job et son Dieu* I-II (Paris, 1970).

H. P. Müller, *Das Hiobproblem* (Darmstadt, 1978) (good bibliography).

————, *Hiob und seine Freunde* (Zürich, 1970).

J. P. M. van der Ploeg and A. S. van der Woude, *Le targum de Job de la grotte XI de Qumrân* (Leiden, 1971).

G. von Rad, *Wisdom in Israel* (New York/Nashville, 1972).

J. A. Sanders, *Suffering as Divine Discipline in the Old Testament and Post-Biblical Judaism* (Rochester, 1955).

P. S. Sanders, *Twentieth Century Interpretations of the Book of Job* (Englewood Cliffs, 1955).

S. Terrien, *Job: Poet of Existence* (New York, 1957).

C. Westermann, *The Structure of the Book of Job* (Philadelphia, 1981).

3. PROVERBS

Like Job the book of Proverbs belongs to the wisdom literature. It can even be said that in Israel this type of literature started with proverbs. These proverbs are not ordinary popular proverbs such as are found all over the world and of which large collections have been made in many different languages. Instead, Proverbs contains maxims specially composed by wise men. As found in the book of Proverbs, they follow the familiar form of a Hebrew verse: two or three brief, for the most part parallel, segments of a verse, divided by a caesura. Most of the proverbs in the book belong to this genre. There are also parts in which the concise maxim, retaining the traditional form of the verse, has been expanded into longer sections of admonitions. Such units can be found in Proverbs 1–9, where the hearer or reader is instructed in the nature of true wisdom and the mode of conduct that becomes a student of the wise (e.g., in relationship to seductive women). The author sings the praise of wisdom (ch. 8, climaxing in vv. 22–36). The anticlimax in chapter 9 is the invitation to those who are foolish to become wise and the description of the "woman Folly" (vv. 13–18).

This introduction is followed by several collections of simple and, for the most part, double proverbs. The first collection is in 10:1–22:16. It is a large collection, attributed to Solomon, and consists of loose proverbs that do not have much inner coherence, though the meaning of the one proverb often suggested a following proverb to the collector. Next is the first appendix, 22:17–24:22, consisting in "words of the wise" (22:17), comprising longer admonitions (perhaps thirty; see 22:20, corrected text), always in the same poetic form. To this appendix a second is added, 24:23–27, having the heading "these are also sayings of the wise" (v. 23).

The next major section is chapters 25–29. It is attributed to Solomon and was compiled, according to the heading, by "the men of Hezekiah king of Judah" (25:1). In the first half the proverbs are somewhat more topically arranged; some of these sayings obviously belong together. In a few cases, proverbs from the first collection are later mentioned again (e.g., 25:24 = 21:9). The second large collection of "Solomonic" proverbs is concluded by four appendixes: 30:1–14, "words of Agur" (a wise man unknown to us), brief and connected sayings of wisdom; 30:15–33, a collection of number proverbs, at best only loosely related to each other (see, e.g., v. 18, which begins, "Three things are too wonderful for me; four I do not understand"), proverbs not meant to indicate a climax, but whose introductory verse exhibits a verse parallelism also known from Ugarit (see C. H. Gordon, *Ugaritic Literature,* Text 75, pp. 45ff., where seven . . . eight and seventy-seven . . . eighty-eight are found); 31:1–9, "words of Lemuel, king of Massa, which his mother taught him" (v. 1), a brief series of admonitions for a king; and 31:10–31, the famous song in praise of the energetic woman, consisting of twenty-two verses (intentionally equal to the number of letters in the Hebrew alphabet), extolling the virtues and diligence of a well-to-do, Yahweh-fearing wife in managing the affairs of her household.

Like the book of Psalms, Proverbs was composed and collected in the course of a few centuries. Tradition viewed Solomon as a wise man, whose wisdom excelled that of all Oriental wise men, even those of Egypt, and who had composed no less than three thousand proverbs (1 Kgs. 5:9–12 [4:29–32]). Proverbs 10:1 and 25:1 undoubtedly echo this tradition. It is, however, impossible to determine how many genuinely Solomonic proverbs are included in the two large collections of Proverbs; even if we could, it would be of little value. Almost all the sayings are timeless, having a constant meaning; in Solomon's time they would have had the same meaning that they did later in the time of Hezekiah or after the Exile. There is no reason to doubt the authenticity of the statement in Proverbs 25:1 that a collection was formed under Hezekiah. Therefore it is an entirely reasonable assumption that the first large Solomonic collection was made before the Captivity, even before Hezekiah. No one is able to say how many and which proverbs were later added. That some were added is certain, as is evi-

dent for instance from the Septuagint. A parallel example of a book that was greatly expanded is the collection of proverbs of Jesus Sirach, as is evident from its text and translations. It can no longer be determined when the two large Solomonic collections were made, nor is it really important for the exegesis of these two parts. In the case of Proverbs 1–9, however, the style of these chapters and the contents of some parts (e.g., 8:22–31) have generally led scholars to regard them as postexilic. The author who issued the entire book used these chapters as a general introduction to his proverbs. Perhaps he was also the one who added the song in praise of the virtuous woman, of which the next to the last verse (31:30) agrees beautifully with Proverbs 1:7.

The wisdom of Israel and other nations of the ancient Near East was of a practical bent, not the speculative philosophy of the Greeks. Its aim was to provide sound advice on how to act sensibly, how to succeed in life, and how to avoid difficulties and also to give instructions concerning proper modes of behavior toward other people, in particular toward high officials. On account of this last feature, some have held that wisdom was especially practiced at royal courts, by and for officials (see, e.g., the detailed study by Duesberg). Ancient Eastern wisdom was cosmopolitan in character, not restricted to one nation, nor to special gods, though occasionally names of deities are mentioned. Egyptian proverbs often simply speak of "the deity." General non-Israelite ancient wisdom is of a nonreligious character.

In Israel, however, the chief principle, regularly repeated, was "the fear of Yahweh is the beginning of wisdom (knowledge)" (see Ps. 111:10; Prov. 1:7; Sir. 1:14, 18, 20). This perspective is typically Yahwistic: Yahweh created the world, he ordered it, and he elected Israel. He gave her the law as a privileged possession. To regulate and conduct one's life as sensibly as possible it is necessary to heed God's law and observe his order. Such a foundation provides the surest guarantee for success in life. It is likewise a duty: as the courtier is obliged to obey his king and faithfully serve him in everything, so the Israelite is to serve and fear Yahweh before all else. In the course of the centuries this aspect of wisdom grew in prominence. Wisdom was more and more identified with the law. In Baruch 3:9–38 wisdom is extolled first, but then it is said of her in 4:1, "She [i.e., wisdom] is the book of God's commandments, the Law that exists for ever." Thomas Aquinas selected this last text as the theme of his inaugural address when he assumed the office of *magister sacrae paginae*.

It has been asked whether parts of Proverbs are literarily dependent on non-Israelite wisdom literature. A frequent question concerns the relationship of Proverbs 22:17– 24:22 to the Egyptian wisdom book Amenemope (a translation of which can be found in Pritchard, *ANET,* 421ff., and Gressmann, *Altorientalische Texte zum AT²,* 38ff.). Both views, the dependence of the Hebrew text upon the Egyptian and of the Egyptian upon the Hebrew, have been argued. It seems likely, however, that there is no direct literary dependence of the one upon the other.

The book of Proverbs contains cosmopolitan, universally valid wisdom, interspersed with typically Yahwistic wisdom. This Yahwistic wisdom has set its stamp upon the whole book and has been the reason for its inclusion in the canon. The book obtained its present form likely between 500 and 300 B.C. It is difficult to determine any more accurate dating. Comparison with the text of the Septuagint shows that in the course of the centuries several proverbs were added and others were dropped.

LITERATURE

Commentaries:

A. Barucq, *Le livre des Proverbes* (Sources Bibliques; Paris, 1964).

H. Duesberg, *Les scribes inspirés* I-II (Paris, 1938/1939).

B. Gemser, *Sprüche Salomos* (HAT I/16; Tübingen, 1963²).

W. H. Gispen, *Spreuken* I-II (Korte Verklaring; Kampen, 1975²).

W. McKane, *Proverbs* (OTL; Philadelphia, 1977²).

J. van der Ploeg, *Spreuken* (BOT; Roermond-Maaseik, 1952).

O. Plöger, *Sprüche Salomos* (BKAT 17; Neukirchen-Vluyn, 1981-84).

R. B. Y. Scott, *Proverbs, Ecclesiastes* (AB; Garden City, NY, 1965).

U. Skladny, *Die ältesten Spruchsammlungen in Israel* (Göttingen, 1962).

C. H. Toy, *A Critical and Exegetical Commentary on the Book of Proverbs* (ICC; Edinburgh, 1899).

Other Works:

G. Boström, *Proverbiastudien. Die Weisheit und das fremde Weiss in Spr. 1–9* (Lund, 1935).

W. Bühlmann, *Vom rechten Reden und Schweigen* (Göttingen, 1976).

J. L. Crenshaw, *Old Testament Wisdom. An Introduction* (Atlanta, 1981).

O. Eissfeldt, *Der Maschal im Alten Testament* (BZAW 24; Berlin, 1923).

J. Fichtner, *Gottes Weisheit* (Stuttgart, 1949).

J. Gammie, et al., eds., *Israelite Wisdom* (Festschrift S. Terrien; Missoula, MT, 1978).

H. J. Hermisson, *Studien zur israelitischen Spruchweisheit* (WMANT 28; Neukirchen, 1968).

C. Kayatz, *Studien zu Proverbien 1–9* (WMANT 22; Neukirchen, 1966).

B. Lang, *Frau Weisheit. Deutung einer biblischen Gestalt* (Düsseldorf, 1975).

R. E. Murphy, *Wisdom Literature: Job, Proverbs, Ruth, Canticles, Ecclesiastes, and Esther* (The Forms of the Old Testament Literature 13; Grand Rapids, 1981).

P. J. Nel, *The Structure and Ethos of the Wisdom Admonitions in Proverbs* (BZAW 158; Berlin/New York, 1982).

M. Noth and D. Winton Thomas, eds., *Wisdom in Israel and in the Ancient Near East* (Festschrift H. H. Rowley; SVT 3; Leiden, 1955).

G. von Rad, *Wisdom in Israel* (New York/Nashville, 1972).

W. Richter, *Recht und Ethos. Versuch einer Ortung des weisheitlichen Mahnspruches* (Munich, 1966).

H. H. Schmid, *Wesen und Geschichte der Weisheit* (BZAW 101; Berlin, 1966).

R. B. Y. Scott, *The Way of Wisdom in the Old Testament* (New York, 1971).

G. T. Sheppard, *Wisdom as a Hermeneutical Construct* (BZAW 151; Berlin/New York, 1980).

P. W. Skehan, *Studies in Israelite Poetry and Wisdom* (Washington, D.C., 1971).

F. Wendel, *Les sagesses du Proche-Orient ancien* (Paris, 1963).

R. N. Whybray, *Wisdom in Proverbs* (London, 1965).

———, *The Intellectual Tradition in the Old Testament* (BZAW 135; Berlin/New York, 1974).

J. G. Williams, *Those who Ponder Proverbs. Aphoristic Thinking and Biblical Literature* (Sheffield, 1981).

4. THE FIVE "SCROLLS"

The five scrolls are the books of Ruth, Canticles (or Song of Songs, or Song of Solomon), Ecclesiastes, Lamentations, and Esther. The last book was called *megillah*, "scroll," especially because at the feast of Purim it was read in its entirety from a single scroll. In later years, on other feast days or commemorative occasions, the other scrolls were added, a practice that, except for Esther and Lamentations, has largely fallen into disuse.

a. Ruth

This booklet of only four chapters contains an idyllic story about the ancestors of David. Driven by famine, a Judean couple with its two sons leaves the town of Bethlehem and settles in Moab. There the husband and the two sons die, after which Naomi, the wife, returns accompanied by Ruth, her Moabite daughter-in-law. Naomi still has rights to a piece of land in Israel. Ruth manages to persuade the Bethlehemite Boaz to redeem this land, after which she marries him. The son born from this union was David's grandfather (Ruth 4:17). This last bit of information occurs at the end of the book and is followed by five more verses containing a brief genealogy of David. Many exegetes regard the conclusion (vv. 17 and 18–22) as nonauthentic. They are wrong, I believe, concerning verse 17. It is unlikely that the author, who lived many years after David (see below), would have ascribed a Moabite ancestor to the great king if such was not actually known from history. Furthermore, it would have made little sense for a later editor to point out such an ancestry if the book had been totally silent about it.

Ruth is written in beautiful, almost classical language. Some Aramaisms and the rather late inclusion in the canon make it virtually certain that it is postexilic. This conclusion raises the difficult question concerning the meaning of the book or the purpose for which it was written. Although expositors are far from agreed among themselves, we may say generally that the book of Ruth was written for edification and instruction. The book thus lays great stress on the virtuous character of the chief figures: Naomi's unselfishness toward her daughters-in-law, the unusual faithfulness of

Ruth toward her mother-in-law and family, and the nobility and family awareness of Boaz. What is said of Boaz articulates the duty of a family member toward the family property. Boaz fulfills this duty in exemplary fashion, doing even more than the law required from him. That a marriage between an Israelite and a foreign woman was not necessarily evil, and that even king David had such a union in his ancestry, is a lesson that recalls an altogether different view in Ezra (see Ezra 9–10). Furthermore, the story indicates clearly how the God of Israel rewards the faithfulness of those who believe in him; particularly the faithfulness of Naomi in observing her family duties is striking.

It is best not to single out one of these motifs as the chief purpose of the author. Edification in the most general sense of the term was what he had in mind. He achieved that goal in various ways, since the reader can learn a variety of lessons from the book. The book of Ruth was read in the synagogue during the Feast of Pentecost (I. Elbogen, *Der jüdische Gottesdienst* [Frankfurt am Main, 1931³], p. 185).

LITERATURE

Commentaries:

E. F. Campbell, Jr., *Ruth* (AB; Garden City, NY, 1975).

G. Gerleman, *Ruth. Das Hohelied* (BKAT XVIII; Neukirchen-Vluyn, 1965).

J. Gray, *Joshua, Judges, Ruth* (New Century Bible; London/Grand Rapids, 1986²).

P. Joüon, *Ruth* (Rome, 1953²).

W. Rudolph, *Das Buch Ruth–Das Hohe Lied–Die Klagelieder* (KAT XVII/1-3; Gütersloh, 1962).

J. M. Sasson, *Ruth. A New Translation with a Philological Commentary and a Formalist Interpretation* (Baltimore, 1979).

G. Smit, *Ruth, Esther en Klaagliederen* (Tekst en Uitleg; Groningen, 1930).

E. Würthwein, K. Galling, and O. Plöger, *Die Fünf Megilloth* (HAT I/18; Tübingen, 1969²).

Other Works:

D. R. G. Beattie, "The Book of Ruth as Evidence for Israelite Legal Practice," *VT* 24 (1974) 251-67.

M. David, "The Date of the Book of Ruth," *OTS* 1 (1942) 55-63.

G. S. Glanzman, "The Origin and Date of the Book of Ruth," *CBQ* 21 (1959) 201-207.

R. Gordis, "Love, Marriage, and Business in the Book of Ruth. A Chapter in Hebrew Customary Law," in H. N. Bream, et al., eds., *A Light unto my Path. Studies in Honor of Jacob M. Myers* (Philadelphia, 1974), pp. 241-64.

R. M. Hals, *The Theology of the Book of Ruth* (Philadelphia, 1969).

A. Lacocque, "Date et milieu du livre de Ruth," *Revue d'Histoire et de Philosophie religieuses* 59 (1979) 583-93.

D. A. Leggett, *The Levirate and Goel Institutions in the Old Testament with Special Attention to the Book of Ruth* (Cherry Hill, NJ, 1974).

J. M. Myers, *The Linguistic and Literary Form of the Book of Ruth* (Leiden, 1955).

D. Thompson, "Some Legal Problems in the Book of Ruth," *VT* 18 (1968) 79-99.

H. H. Witzenrath, *Das Buch Ruth* (Munich, 1975).

b. Canticles

This book has always fascinated Jewish and Christian exegetes. They tried to discover an intentional allegorical meaning to it, with the result that no two interpreters agreed with each other. Jewish expositors regarded the love relationship described in the Canticles especially as an allegory of Yahweh's love for his people, whereas Christians thought particularly of the love between Christ and the church or God and the church. Origen also saw pictured the relationship between the Logos and the soul.

In its present form the book consists of several nuptial or love songs, describing the love of a young man and a young woman. No fixed structure can be detected in it without violating the text, despite attempts to find such a structure. The love poetry in the Canticles is related to love poems of the ancient and modern Near East. Parts of it read like songs sung at wedding parties. Wedding customs, particularly some observed in Damascus, in which bridegroom and bride were crowned or addressed as king and queen or as sultan and sultana, have also contributed to the interpretation of the work. While there is dancing and feasting, physical attributes of the bride and bridegroom are described. All these customs appear to have parallels in the Canticles. I say only "appear," because there is a great time gap between these modern and ancient customs, which is why parallels should be drawn only with great caution.

Very early in ancient Israel love was already a symbol of the relationship between Yahweh and his people (see, e.g., Hosea 1–3). Early interpreters attempted to read the Canticles in this light. It cannot be demonstrated, however, that the original composers had such in mind. Neither can it be proved that the book was accepted into the canon on account of its supposedly deeper or higher meaning. The pure love between a man and woman, established by a covenant that in Proverbs 2:17 is called a "covenant of God" (cf. Eccl. 9:9, which regards the life "with the wife whom you love" as a gift from God), can be the subject of a biblical book. Note also the praise of the virtuous woman (the exemplary housewife) in Proverbs 31:10–31.

Characteristic of the Canticles is its alternation of the voices. This feature exists elsewhere in the Old Testament, but nowhere as much as here. The various sections tend to blend, making it difficult to distinguish between parts.

LITERATURE

Commentaries:

G. Ch. Aalders, *Het Hooglied* (COT; Kampen, 1952).

———, *Het Hooglied* (Korte Verklaring; Kampen, 1977[3]).

A. Feuillet, *Le Cantique des Cantiques* (Paris, 1953).

G. Gerleman, *Ruth. Das Hohelied* (BKAT XVIII; Neukirchen-Vluyn, 1965).

R. Gordis, *The Song of Songs* (New York, 1954).

M. H. Pope, *Song of Songs* (AB; Garden City, NY, 1977).

H. Ringgren, A. Weiser, and W. Zimmerli, *Sprüche. Prediger. Das Hohe Lied. Klagelieder. Das Buch Esther* (ATD 16; Göttingen, 1967[2]).

A. Robert, R. Tournay, and A. Feuillet, *Le Cantique des Cantiques* (Paris, 1963).

W. Rudolph, *Das Buch Ruth–Das Hohe Lied–Die Klagelieder* (KAT XVII/1-3; Gütersloh, 1962).

E. Würthwein, K. Galling, and O. Plöger, *Die Fünf Megilloth* (HAT I/18; Tübingen, 1969[2]).

Other Works:

J. P. Audet, "Le sens du cantique des cantiques," *RB* 62 (1955) 197-221.

J. C. Exum, "A Literary and Structural Analysis of the Song of Songs," *ZAW* 85 (1973) 47-49.

S. Grill, *Die Symbolsprache des Hohenliedes* (Heiligenkreuz, 1970²).

A. Hermann, *Altägyptische Liebesdichtung* (Wiesbaden, 1959).

O. Loretz, *Studien zur althebräischen Poesie I. Das althebräische Liebeslied* (Neukirchen-Vluyn, 1971).

R. E. Murphy, "The Structure of the Canticle of Canticles," *CBQ* 11 (1949) 381-91.

————, "Recent Literature on the Canticle of Canticles," *CBQ* 16 (1954) 1-11.

H. H. Rowley, "The Interpretation of the Song of Songs," in *The Servant of the Lord and Other Essays on the Old Testament* (London, 1952), pp. 189-234.

J. B. White, *A Study of the Language of Love in the Song of Songs and Ancient Egyptian Poetry* (Missoula, MT, 1978).

E. Würthwein, "Zum Verständnis des Hohenliedes," *Theologische Rundschau* 32 (1967) 177-212.

---

c. Ecclesiastes

This booklet is called *qoheleth* in Hebrew. It is an interesting term, designating someone convening or conducting a meeting. In the Septuagint and the Vulgate the book is called *Ecclesiastes,* an attempt at a literal translation of *qoheleth.* This term is better than "Preacher" (note the title *Prediger* in German or *Prediker* in Dutch), for the author of the book was not a preacher and what he presents are not sermons. The Old Testament does contain some sermons (e.g., in Deuteronomy 1–11). The book of Ecclesiastes, however, is part of wisdom literature. It contains wise admonitions and reflections written in prose, together with proverbs or series of proverbs. Using literary fiction, the author presents himself as the wise king Solomon (2:4–9).

The language the author uses indicates that he cannot have lived earlier than the third century B.C., likely not much later either. He was a Jewish sage who pondered the meaning of human existence. His most familiar statement is "vanity of vanities [i.e., the utmost in vanity], all is vanity" (1:2). The word *vanity* here means futility, emptiness, insignificance (concretely, a puff of air or a gust of wind), something of short duration, without much content, and quickly vanishing. The author viewed short-lived human existence

in this manner, with all its misery and suffering and its happiness and possessions (often acquired through hard toil) that quickly vanish. Sometimes it seems as if the author has pondered the words of Job, although he reaches his own conclusion. Any good that life offers must be viewed as a gift of God, from whose hands it must be accepted. For the rest, one must accept life as it is, convinced as the writer is that what happens now has always happened and that there is nothing new under the sun (1:9). One cannot be certain that there will be reward for righteous deeds in this life, nor does the author know whether there is something after this life, though he does raise the question (3:21).

Because Ecclesiastes contains contradictions, particularly in respect to retribution for good and evil (e.g., cf. 2:21 with v. 26; 3:16 with v. 17; etc.), it used to be thought that different voices were heard in the book. In more recent times others have tried to show that the composer of the book had a variety of sources at his disposal from which he cited. The most reasonable supposition seems to be that a student of the "Preacher" issued a collection of his words (he refers to the master in 1:2 and 12:10, thus showing that he is not the Preacher himself). Because the book had to have an edifying character, the collector made sure that the bad impression some of the words of his master could create (see, e.g., 2:24a; 3:16, 19; 5:17; 6:2, 8; 7:15; etc.) were balanced by others; these "good" proverbs stress the advantages of wisdom and of proper conduct.

The combination of apparently contradictory elements is a special problem in Ecclesiastes. It is best solved by holding that the author/sage does not demand absolute validity for all his pronouncements. He is partial to expressing himself paradoxically, and he knows that human life, including that of the pious Israelite, is full of unresolvable paradoxes. But he remains a pious Jew, who acknowledges God as his creator and who remains convinced that he is to be served and that all good can come only from him. Sometimes he seems to be very pessimistic (not "revolutionary," as some would say), even as the author of Job, but later he acquiesces in all the evil, vanity, and foolishness there seems to be in life and turns his thoughts toward God.

LITERATURE

Commentaries:

G. Ch. Aalders, *Het boek De Prediker* (COT; Kampen, 1948).

G. A. Barton, *A Critical and Exegetical Commentary on the Book of Ecclesiastes* (ICC; Edinburgh, 1908).

L. Di Fonzo, *Ecclesiaste* (La Sacra Bibbia; Torino/Rome, 1967).

B. Gemser, *Prediker* (Tekst en Uitleg; Groningen, 1931).

H. W. Hertzberg and H. Bardtke, *Der Prediger. Das Buch Esther* (KAT XVII/4-5; Gütersloh, 1963).

A. Lauha, *Kohelet* (BKAT XIX; Neukirchen, 1978).

J. A. Loader, *Ecclesiastes* (Text and Interpretation; Grand Rapids, 1986).

J. van der Ploeg, *Prediker* (BOT; Roermond-Maaseik, 1953).

H. Ringgren, A. Weiser, and W. Zimmerli, *Sprüche. Prediger. Das Hohe Lied. Klagelieder. Das Buch Esther* (ATD 16; Göttingen, 1967²).

R. B. Y. Scott, *Proverbs, Ecclesiastes* (AB; Garden City, NY, 1965).

E. Würthwein, K. Galling, and O. Plöger, *Die Fünf Megilloth* (HAT I/18; Tübingen, 1969²).

Other Works:

R. Braun, *Kohelet und die frühhellenistische Popularphilosophie* (BZAW 130; Berlin/New York, 1973).

H. L. Ginsberg, *Studies in Koheleth* (New York, 1950).

R. Gordis, *Kohelet—The Man and his World* (New York, 1963³).

————, *The Wisdom of Ecclesiastes* (New York, 1945).

D. A. Hubbard, *Beyond Futility. Messages of Hope from the Book of Ecclesiastes* (Grand Rapids, 1976).

O. Loretz, *Qohelet und der Alte Orient. Untersuchungen zu Stil und theologischer Thematik des Buches Qohelet* (Freiburg, 1964).

J. A. Loader, *Polar Structures in the Book of Qohelet* (BZAW 152; Berlin/New York, 1979).

C. F. Whitley, *Koheleth. His Language and Thought* (BZAW 148; Berlin/New York, 1979).

J. G. Williams, "What Does It Profit a Man? The Wisdom of Koheleth," *Judaism* 20 (1971) 179-93.

W. Zimmerli, "Das Buch Kohelet—Traktat oder Sentenzensammlung?" *VT* 24 (1974) 221-30.

d. Lamentations

This booklet, which some scholars, on account of its style and contents, used to ascribe to Jeremiah, consists of five laments, composed to commemorate the destruction of Jerusalem in 586 B.C., or to commemorate the razed city that had not yet been rebuilt. The first four are acrostic poems. In the second, third, and fourth poems, the letter *pe* (incorrectly) comes before *ayin* (as is done elsewhere), which seems to indicate that at least the first lament is from an author different from the one who wrote the second, third, and fourth. The first three songs consist of strophes of three verses, the fourth of strophes of two; the fifth song simply has twenty-two single verses. The form is that of a dirge for a deceased person, beginning with *ekah*, "how." The third begins with "I am the man who has seen affliction," which reminds us of Jeremiah. A few verses suggest that Jeremiah was not the author, something nowhere even intimated in the book.

Lamentations seems to have been composed during the Exile, though it became part of the canon much later. It should be noted, however, that only the first, second, and fourth songs relate to the devastated city; the third is an individual lament, and the fifth a lament of the people, so that at least these last two might be from a later time.

Lamentations is still sung in synagogues on the ninth of Ab (August), the day when the destruction of Jerusalem in 586 is commemorated. In the Latin liturgy of the Roman Catholic church, the five laments, with a special melody, have been included in the matins of the last three days of the week of Good Friday, to sing of the misery of Jerusalem that came as a result of the death of Christ.

LITERATURE

Commentaries:

D. Hillers, *Lamentations* (AB; Garden City, NY, 1972).

H.-J. Kraus, *Klagelieder* (BKAT 20; Neukirchen-Vluyn, 1956).

T. Paffrath, *Die Klagelieder* (Bonner Bibel; Bonn, 1932).

H. Ringgren, A. Weiser, and W. Zimmerli, *Sprüche. Prediger. Das Hohe Lied. Klagelieder. Das Buch Esther* (ATD 16; Göttingen, 1967²).

W. Rudolph, *Das Buch Ruth—Das Hohe Lied—Die Klagelieder* (KAT XVII/1-3; Gütersloh, 1962).

G. Smit, *Ruth, Esther en Klaagliederen* (Tekst en Uitleg; Groningen, 1930).

E. Würthwein, K. Galling, and O. Plöger, *Die Fünf Megilloth* (HAT I/18; Tübingen, 1969[2]).

Other Works:

B. Albrektson, *Studies in the Text and Theology of the Book of Lamentations* (Lund, 1963).

G. Brunet, *Les lamentations contre Jérémie. Réinterprétation des quatre premières lamentations* (Paris, 1968).

H. Gottlieb, *A Study on the Text of Lamentations* (Aarhus, 1978).

N. K. Gottwald, *Studies in the Book of Lamentations* (London, 1962[2]).

---

e. Esther

In Judaism the book of Esther in particular is called the scroll. The Hebrew text relates how the Persian king Ahasuerus (= Xerxes I, 485–465 B.C.) rejected his wife Queen Vashti because she refused to exhibit herself before him and his male courtiers when the king commanded her to do so at the end of a banquet. A diligent search was then made throughout the empire for a new wife for the king. The extremely beautiful Esther, foster daughter of the Jew Mordecai, became the king's choice. This Mordecai refused to bow down to Haman the Persian, a man whom the king had promoted to a chief administrative position in the land. Mordecai apparently was willing to bow down only to God. Furious, Haman resolved to avenge himself by liquidating by royal decree all the Jews in the Persian empire. Esther became instrumental in having Haman put on the gallows he had erected for Mordecai; he and his sons were put to death, and all the Jews were by royal edict allowed to arm and defend themselves when their enemies tried to put into effect the unalterable decree to exterminate them. So it happened that, on the thirteenth and fourteenth days of the month of Adar (March), the Jews, supported by Persian nobles and soldiers, killed seventy-five thousand of their enemies. The Persian government provided this support as a result of the influence of Mordecai, who had become very powerful at the court of Xerxes. On the fifteenth day of Adar the Jews held a large victory celebration, called Purim, a feast Jews still celebrate with great enthusiasm every year.

The name of God does not occur in the book of Esther. On the surface it hardly seems to be a religious book, though 4:4 alludes to appealing to divine help. There are indications that ancient Judaism was unsure about the canonical character of the book. It has not been found among the literature discovered at Qumran. To compensate for its lack in religious emphasis, a lack for which there must have been a special reason, an elaborate Greek text of Esther was made. This much longer edition of Esther can be found in various recensions in the Greek manuscripts, and it gives the whole book a decidedly religious flavor. The additions consist of several longer and shorter passages that were interspersed at various points in the story. First there is a dream of Mordecai and its interpretation, which are made the framework of the book. In the dream God reveals that two dragons will fight each other, which is explained as referring to the struggle between Mordecai and Haman. Then there is the text of the decree of Xerxes, in which orders are given to kill all the Jews in the kingdom. There is further a brief augmentation between 4:8 and 4:9, the text of the prayers with which Esther and Mordecai in their need come before God, a religiously colored story detailing Esther's unsolicited audience with the king, and finally the text of the decree in which the Jews are given permission to defend themselves. The addition of all these pieces, probably by one author, has turned Esther into a distinctly religious book. In the Vulgate the additions, not considered canonical by Jerome, are put at the end. They are part of the canon of Trent.

The difference between the Hebrew and Greek texts underscores once more the problematic nature of the book of Esther. As a biblical book it needs a religious purpose, yet in the Hebrew such a purpose is not immediately obvious. The most important purpose of the book is certainly to provide an exciting account of the origin of the celebration of Purim. This holiday is not a typically religious observance but a secular feast; nowadays a variety of explanations for the name are given. As we have noted, the book at least alludes to God, and no pious Jew would attribute the Jewish success described in the book exclusively to the cleverness of Esther and Mordecai or to a happy coincidence of circumstances. Moreover, Mordecai's refusal to give homage to Haman seems religiously motivated. The devout reader observes Israel's God at work, even though it is not stated expressly.

The question to what extent the book relates actual history is not easily answered. It would be wrong to say that the book is totally without basis in history. Purim is a historical feast, referred to in 2 Maccabees 15:36 (where it is called Mordecai's day). Josephus mentions it in detail in his *Antiquities* (11.6). The Esther scroll is also the subject of a separate Mishna and Talmud tract *(megillah)*. The most plausible assumption is that the book arose in the Jewish Diaspora because of a historical happening, of which echoes are heard in this book. Tradition and likely also the imagination of the author elaborated on this event, turning it into the present book, which each year is read in the synagogue at the feast of Purim and, according to many, also written for that purpose. The Greek editor who augmented the book must have been aware that what he had before him was not a purely historical work. Many others have also noticed that the book presents a mixture of truth and fiction. Jews have always heard in it the message of God's protection of his people. Its literary genre is comparable to that of a historical novel. It can also be compared with a *midrash haggada* with a historical core. The time of origin of the book is likely late in the third century B.C.

A. Meinhold, *Das Buch Esther* (Zürcher Bibelkommentare 13; Zürich, 1983).

C. A. Moore, *Esther* (AB; Garden City, NY, 1971).

L. B. Paton, *A Critical and Exegetical Commentary on the Book of Esther* (ICC; Edinburgh, 1908).

H. Ringgren, A. Weiser, and W. Zimmerli, *Sprüche. Prediger. Das Hohe Lied. Klagelieder. Das Buch Esther* (ATD 16; Göttingen, 1967²).

J. Schildenberger, *Das Buch Esther* (Bonner Bibel; Bonn, 1941).

E. Würthwein, K. Galling, and O. Plöger, *Die Fünf Megilloth* (HAT I/18; Tübingen, 1969²).

Other Works:

S. B. Berg, *The Book of Esther. Motifs, Themes and Structure* (Missoula, MT, 1979).

W. H. Brownlee, "Le livre grec d'esther et la royauté divine, Corrections orthodoxes au livre de'Esther," *RB* 73 (1966) 161-85.

D. J. Clines, *The Esther Scroll. The Story of the Story* (JSOT Supplement Series 30; Sheffield, 1984).

W. Dommershausen, *Die Estherrolle. Stil und Ziel einer alttestamentlichen Schrift* (Stuttgart, 1968).

G. Gerleman, *Studien zu Esther. Stoff-Struktur-Stil-Sinn* (Neukirchen-Vluyn, 1966).

R. Gordis, "Religion, Wisdom and History in the Book of Esther. A New Solution to an Ancient Crux," *JBL* 200 (1981) 359-88.

A. Meinhold, "Die Gattung der Josephgeschichte und des Estherbuches—Diasporanovelle," *ZAW* 87 (1975) 306-24; 88 (1976) 72-93.

C. A. Moore, *Daniel, Esther, and Jeremiah. The Additions* (AB; Garden City, NY, 1977).

———, ed., *Studies in the Book of Esther* (New York, 1982).

LITERATURE

Commentaries:

G. Ch. Aalders, *Esther* (Korte Verklaring; Kampen, 1976⁴).

L. H. Brockington, *Ezra, Nehemiah and Esther* (New Century Bible; London, 1969).

D. J. Clines, *Ezra, Nehemiah and Esther* (New Century Bible; London/Grand Rapids, 1984).

G. Gerleman, *Esther* (BKAT XXI; Neukirchen-Vluyn, 1973).

H. Gunkel, *Esther* (Tübingen, 1916).

H. W. Hertzberg and H. Bardtke, *Der Prediger. Das Buch Esther* (KAT XVII/4-5; Gütersloh, 1963).

J. A. Loader, *Esther* (POT; Nijkerk, 1980).

5. DANIEL

The book of Daniel presents serious difficulties to the exegete. The Massoretic text is partly in Hebrew, partly in Aramaic. The Greek text contains additions: the song of the three young men in the fiery oven (inserted between 3:23 and 24), a story of Bel and the dragon, and the story of Susanna (in the Greek texts this story comes before Daniel).

Following the sequence of the chapters, I summarize the contents as follows: Daniel and other Jewish exiles are trained to serve at the court of King Nebuchadrezzar (ch. 1). The king has a dream that his wise men are unable to interpret. Daniel then interprets the dream, explaining that it deals with world history, summed up in the history of four kingdoms (ch. 2). Next comes the story of Daniel's three friends who are thrown into a fiery oven because they refuse to do homage to an image of the king; they escape harm (ch. 3). Nebuchadrezzar has another dream, this one about a tall tree. Daniel explains that the dream concerns the king himself, who for seven times will be cast out of society (ch. 4). In a banquet given by Belshazzar, writing appears on the wall: *mene, tekel, peres* (ch. 5). Darius the Mede is tricked into being forced to throw Daniel into the den of lions, because in defiance of the king's orders he had prayed to his God. The lions do not harm Daniel (ch. 6). Daniel has a vision of four beasts and a Son of Man (ch. 7). Next he has a vision of a ram attacking a he-goat. The he-goat becomes very powerful; it sprouts four horns, the last of which sprouts another horn. A voice explains the historical meaning of the vision to the seer (ch. 8). Daniel prays and then hears a prophecy about the seventy-year weeks (ch. 9). Daniel receives new revelations, all relating to the Syrian-Egyptian wars in the third and second centuries B.C., following which there will be a resurrection and the establishment of God's kingdom (chs. 10–12).

The book of Daniel belongs to apocalyptic literature. Its time of composition, or, more accurately, the time when it received the form in which it occurs in the Jewish Bible, can be fairly precisely determined. It must have happened shortly before the restoration of the cult in Jerusalem by Judas Maccabeus, that is, approximately 165 B.C. It is exegetically important to remember, however, that the whole book was likely not written at that time.

It is best to make a distinction between the apocalyptic sections (chs. 6–12) and the other parts. The latter belong to a cycle of stories that were told about a wise man, called Daniel, who in Babylon lived at the court of several kings. An aged sage by that name is mentioned in Ezekiel 14:14, 20; 28:3. In the last passage it is asked of the ruler of Tyre, "Are you wiser than Dan(i)el?" (NIV), a name that recalls the wise man Danel in Ugarit. In Cave 4 of Qumran the remains of an Aramaic prayer by Nabonidus have been dis-

covered, of which it is assumed that it belonged to the cycle of Daniel stories. The name Daniel does not occur in it, but some scholars conjecture that originally it was part of it. For a long time it had been suspected that in the transmission the name Nebuchadrezzar in Daniel 5:18 (and likely also in other passages) has been substituted for that of Nabonidus (= Nabunaid, king of Babylon 556–539). The discovery at Qumran has strengthened this conjecture.

The stories in the book of Daniel are clearly folktales that had been told for many years before they were recorded to extol the name of Israel's God, the sole ruler of the world. It would be wrong in a priori fashion to declare them totally unhistorical, but it can no longer be determined to what extent they may have had a basis in actual history. The stories of Daniel and his friends belong to the genre of edifying heroic tales from a bygone time. If we read Nabonidus (who, according to a Babylonian inscription known since 1958, was forced to spend ten years in Tema in the Arabian desert, after which he returned to Babylon in triumph) instead of Nebuchadrezzar in 4:28–30, we can detect in this passage the echo of a historical event. His son is the Belshazzar of Daniel 5, who was coruler, and therefore appropriately is called king (5:1; 8:1).

The visions and revelations in chapters 7–12 are of a different nature. They are apocalyptic—that is, revelations with respect to the distant future, eschatologically focused, given by a famous person from the more distant or nearer past, preferably through the mediation of an angel. In that sense apocalyptic was a form of literature, as such readily intelligible to initiates and those familiar with this type of literature. It was not an attempt to mislead those for whom it was intended (namely, devout Jews in time of need), but it could be used to deceive their enemies. In the time of Antiochus IV Epiphanes (175–164 B.C.), devout Jews could learn from the apocalypse of Daniel that with the help of God they should resist this persecutor of the Jews, while it would escape the henchmen and soldiers of Antiochus that these exhortations were given by a contemporary Jew. The book of Daniel (at least the last six chapters) is the first genuine apocalypse known to us. This type of literature created by the author, likely with the use of elements in the Prophets, was so successful that for more than three centuries it was used as a literary form, even in early Christianity.

In Daniel the history of the world is viewed as that of four kingdoms, or of their kings (2:37–43; 7:17), nowadays usually identified as the Babylonian, Median, Persian, and Greek (Seleucid) kingdoms. The last ruler of the fourth kingdom is Antiochus Epiphanes, a terrible ruler and the notorious persecutor of the Jews. After him will come a kingdom that "shall stand forever" (2:44), the kingdom of the "Son of Man" (7:13–14), the messianic realm of peace promised to Israel by the prophets (2:44; 7:18, 27). The struggle of the ram and the he-goat symbolizes Alexander's war against the Medo-Persian kingdom, a struggle in which Alexander is victorious. Alexander is the horn of the he-goat. The four horns stand for the four generals and their successors, who took control of the empire after Alexander's death. From one of these, the Seleucids, came Antiochus Epiphanes, of whom it is said that he will be destroyed (8:25). The famous prophecy of the seventy weeks (or years) in chapter 9 reaches a climax in the announcement of the war of Antiochus Epiphanes against the people of the Jews and their religion. He will even put an end to the service in the temple, but his end is near (9:27). The last three chapters contain a history, cast in the form of a revelation, of the war between the Egyptian Ptolemies and the Syrian Seleucids. This story also culminates in the actions of the great persecutor of the Jews, Antiochus Epiphanes. His wickedness is described, and his end is predicted. Then Michael will protect the Israelites, and the resurrection of the Jews will take place (12:2).

There is good reason to assume that the fairly accurate description of the actions of Antiochus Epiphanes, which must have been written toward the end of his rule, is from a time later than the narrative parts of Daniel. But in that case it is also natural to assume that a passage such as 2:41–43 (see also v. 33) was later added to the story of the metal image, meaning that older passages in the book of Daniel, which received its present shape about 165 B.C., were subjected to a later reworking.

An attractive hypothesis is, moreover, that chapters 1–7 (at least chs. 2–7) were originally written in Aramaic. In that case the author, living in Maccabean times, translated chapter 1 into Hebrew (unless he wrote it himself), which he had precede 2:1–4a (translated or not) in the Hebrew. Then he left the Aramaic text of chapters 2–7 more or less as it was, but did add verses such as 2:42–44 and 7:8, 11a, 20–22, 24–25. These additions gave a unity to the book, and the wicked rule of Antiochus Epiphanes became the conclusion of the outline of the four kingdoms. This scheme is older than the time of composition of the book of Daniel. It may be, as has been argued by H. Junker, that originally it was intended to refer not to four *historical* kingdoms but to a period of increasingly greater decline and corruption in the history of humankind, as is shown in the composition of the image in Nebuchadrezzar's dream (gold, silver, bronze, iron/clay). Junker explains the horns in 7:7 not as ten rulers but as a general number, corresponding to that of the ten toes (a figure is not mentioned) of the image in 2:42.

In summary it can be said, on the basis of the above-mentioned hypothesis, that the Maccabean author of Daniel reworked the material in the stories of chapters 1–7 (or chs. 2–7), which already contained apocalyptic features (four world empires, replaced by the yet much more powerful and altogether different kingdom of the God of Israel), to focus the predictions on the godless rule and devastating end of Antiochus Epiphanes and then added chapters 8–12 to lend even greater relief to Antiochus's defeat. The book that was the result must have been an immense support to the devout Jews, who suffered greatly under the persecutions by the Syrian king, and it must have been an exhortation to them to continue trusting in the almighty God of Israel, who does not forsake his own, who destroys their enemies when he deems the time for it has come, and who will establish his kingdom on earth.

Not everyone agrees with this interpretation of the book of Daniel, which is understandable because much of Daniel is not clear, largely because of its being an apocalyptic book. Formerly, virtually all Christian expositors regarded the fourth kingdom as the Roman empire, partly because they applied the prophecy of the seventy weeks of years exclusively to Jesus Christ and saw in him the anointed one who was killed (9:26). History does not know of a Median empire coming between the Babylonian and the Persian, and if Babylonia is regarded as the first kingdom, *historically* Rome becomes the fourth. Junker holds that the four kingdoms are not intended to be a historical scheme but are presented as a totality, implying that the author did not intend to identify the second kingdom as the Median. This view perhaps has its merits. It is clear, however, that the main concern of the Maccabean author was the final kingdom (of which Antiochus Epiphanes was the last wicked king) and the kingdom of God that followed. The identification of the fourth kingdom with that of the Romans must be rejected on the combined grounds of the apocalyptic nature, the date of the book, and the interpretation of the text.

The parts interpolated in the Greek texts and the Vulgate demonstrate the popularity of the cycle of Daniel stories. Some of these added parts are also found in the Hebrew-Aramaic book of Daniel. It is clear that in the present book of Daniel, the Jew Daniel is not identified with the sage of Ugarit, also mentioned by Ezekiel. It is possible that the latter may have served as an example. For a long time the Septuagint text was lost. The Greek church used a translation of Theodotion. The former was first published in Rome in 1772.

LITERATURE

Commentaries:

R. A. Anderson, *Signs and Wonders: A Commentary on the Book of Daniel* (International Theological Commentary; London/Grand Rapids, 1984).

A. Bentzen, *Daniel* (HAT I/19; Tübingen, 1952).

M. Delcor, *Le livre de Daniel* (Sources Bibliques; Paris, 1971).

S. R. Driver, *The Book of Daniel* (Cambridge Bible for Schools and Colleges; Cambridge, 1905).

L. Hartman and A. di Lella, *The Book of Daniel* (AB; Garden City, NY, 1978).

A. Lacocque, *The Book of Daniel* (Atlanta, 1979).

J. Lebram, *Das Buch Daniel* (Zürcher Bibelkommentare 23; Zürich, 1984).

P. J. de Ménasce, *Daniel* (La Sainte Bible de Jérusalem; Paris, 1958[2]).

J. A. Montgomery, *A Critical and Exegetical Commentary on the Book of Daniel* (ICC; Edinburgh, 1927).

C. A. Moore, *Daniel, Esther and Jeremiah: The Additions* (AB; Garden City, NY, 1977).

O. Plöger, *Das Buch Daniel* (KAT XVIII; Gütersloh, 1965).

N. W. Porteous, *Daniel* (OTL; Philadelphia, 1979[2]).

G. Rinaldi, *Daniele* (La Sacra Bibbia; Torino/Roma, 1952).

E. J. Young, *The Prophecy of Daniel* (Grand Rapids, 1949).

Other Works:

W. Baumgartner, "Ein Vierteljahrhundert Danielforschung," *Theologische Rundschau* 11 (1939) 59-83, 125-44, 201-28.

M. Casey, *Son of Man. The Interpretation and Influence of Daniel 7* (London, 1979).

J. J. Collins, *The Apocalyptic Vision of the Book of Daniel* (Missoula, MT, 1977).

———, *Daniel with an Introduction to Apocalyptic Literature* (The Forms of the Old Testament Literature 20; Grand Rapids, 1984).

F. Dexinger, *Das Buch Daniel und seine Probleme* (Stuttgart, 1969).

W. Dommershausen, *Nabonid im Buche Daniel* (Mainz, 1964).

J. Gammie, "The Classification, Stages of Growth, and Changing Intentions in the Book of Daniel," *JBL* 95 (1976) 191-204.

H. L. Ginsberg, *Studies in Daniel* (New York, 1948).

K. A. Kitchen, D. J. Wiseman, et al., *Notes on Some Problems in the Book of Daniel* (London, 1965).

K. Koch, et al., *Daniel* (Darmstadt, 1980) (good bibliography).

A. Lenglet, "La structure littéraire de Daniël 2–7," *Bibl* 53 (1972) 169-90.

A. Mertens, *Das Buch Daniel im Lichte der Texte vom Toten Meer* (Würzburg-Stuttgart, 1971).

M. Noth, "Zur Komposition des Buches Daniel," *Theologische Studien und Kritiken* 98/99 (1926) 143-63.

H. H. Rowley, *Darius the Mede and the Four Empires in the Book of Daniel* (Cardiff, 1959[2]).

———, *The Aramaic of the Old Testament* (London, 1929).

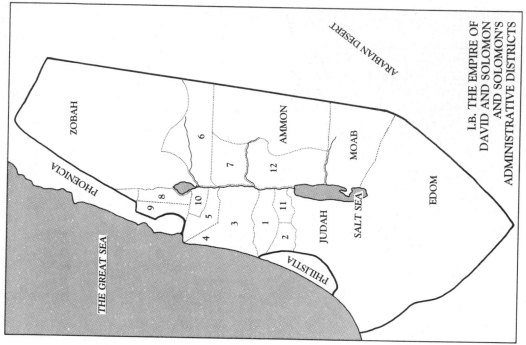

I.B. THE EMPIRE OF
DAVID AND SOLOMON
AND SOLOMON'S
ADMINISTRATIVE DISTRICTS

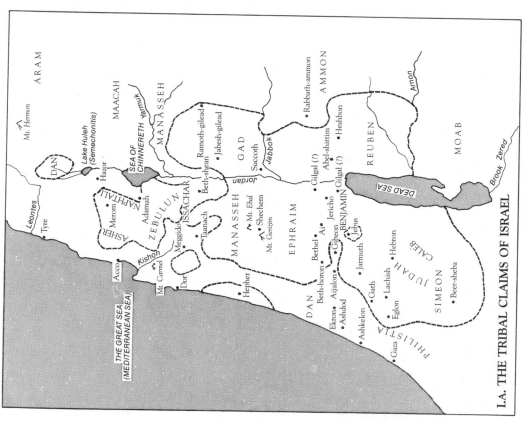

I.A. THE TRIBAL CLAIMS OF ISRAEL

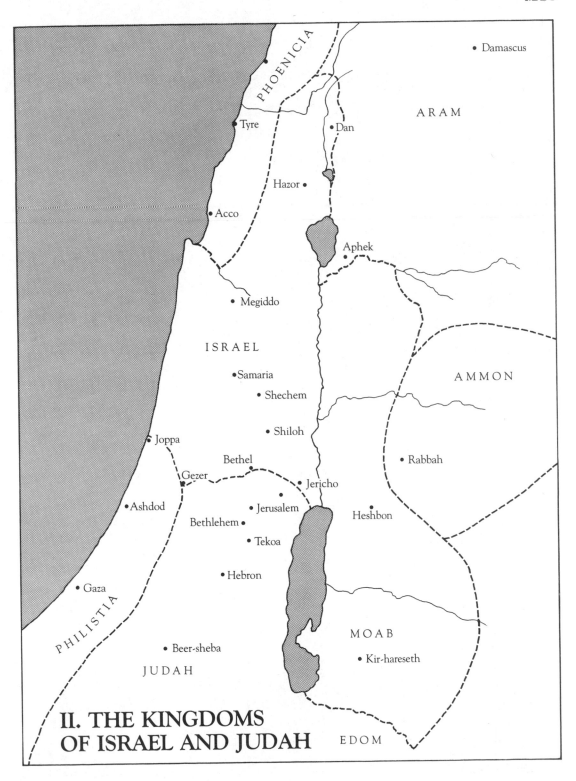

II. THE KINGDOMS
OF ISRAEL AND JUDAH

III. THE ANCIENT NEAR EAST

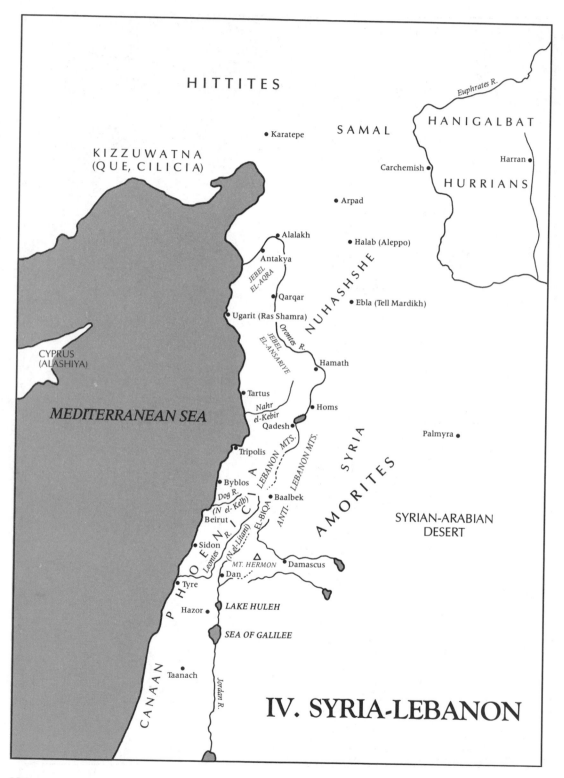

HITTITES

• Karatepe

SAMAL

Euphrates R.

HANIGALBAT

KIZZUWATNA
(QUE, CILICIA)

Carchemish •

Harran •

HURRIANS

• Arpad

• Alalakh

• Halab (Aleppo)

Antakya

JEBEL EL-AQRA

• Qarqar

NUHASHSHE

• Ebla (Tell Mardikh)

Ugarit (Ras Shamra) •

Orontes R.

JEBEL EL-ANSARIYE

CYPRUS
(ALASHIYA)

• Hamath

MEDITERRANEAN SEA

• Tartus

Nahr el-Kebir

• Homs

Qadesh

SYRIA

• Palmyra

• Tripolis

LEBANON MTS.

ANTI-LEBANON MTS.

AMORITES

• Byblos

Dog R.
(N el-Kelb)

P
H
O
E
N
I
C
I
A

• Baalbek

EL-BIQA

SYRIAN-ARABIAN
DESERT

Beirut

(N el-Litani)
R.

Leontes

• Sidon

△
MT. HERMON

• Damascus

• Dan

• Tyre

Hazor •

LAKE HULEH

SEA OF GALILEE

C
A
N
A
A
N

• Taanach

Jordan R.

IV. SYRIA-LEBANON

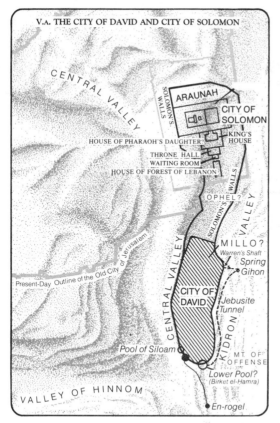

V.a. THE CITY OF DAVID AND CITY OF SOLOMON

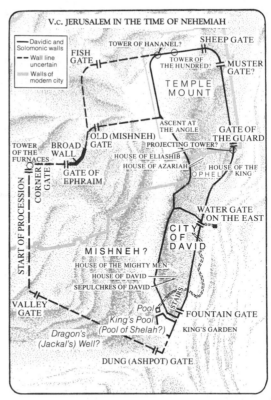

V.c. JERUSALEM IN THE TIME OF NEHEMIAH

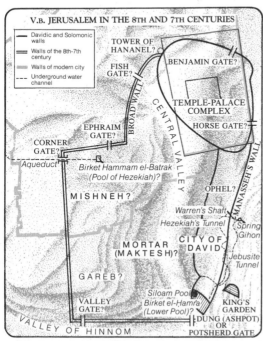

V.b. JERUSALEM IN THE 8TH AND 7TH CENTURIES

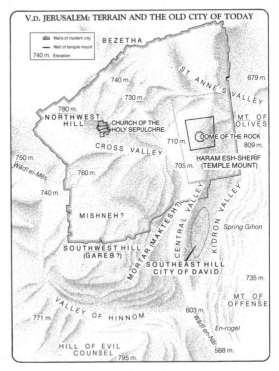

V.d. JERUSALEM: TERRAIN AND THE OLD CITY OF TODAY

Index

Aaron, 18
Abednego, 134-35
Abiathar, 37, 41, 43, 45, 236
Abijah, 50, 60
Abimelech, 30, 34, 136
Abner, 38, 39
Abraham, 9-12, 122
Absalom, 42
Achaemenes, 8
Achish, 33
acrostic, 260, 284
Acts of Solomon, book of, 98
Adad-nirari III, 56
addresses, 142-44
Adonijah, 43
Adoniram, 46
Ahab, 51-55, 129, 133, 134
Ahasuerus, 285
Ahaz, 57
Ahaziah, 54, 55, 61, 62, 130
Ahijah, 49, 50, 51, 220
Ahikar, wisdom book, 58
Ahithophel, 42
Aijalon, 24
allegory, 257
alphabet, 39
Amalekites, 36
Amarna letters, 9, 23, 24
Amasa, 42
Amaziah, 55, 62-63
Amenemope, 138, 280
Amenhotep III, 23
Amenhotep IV, 23
Amman, 31
Amminadab, 31
Ammonites, 30-31, 35, 36, 41, 61, 121
Amon, 66
Amorites, 31, 32
Amos, 56, 154; book of, 252-53; person and time, 252; preaching of, 253
amphictyony, 5, 12, 25-27
Anat, 28
anecdote, 136-37
Angel of the Lord, 270
Antiochus IV Epiphanes, 287
Apiru, 14
apocalyptic literature, 287

apocryphal psalms, 273
Apries, Pharaoh, 70
Arabia, 277
Arabians, 61
Aram, 55
Aram-Naharaim, 9
Aramaic, 223
Aramaisms, 256, 281
Arameans, 53, 61
Araunah, 31, 40, 42, 124
ark, 26, 40, 125
Artachsasta, 86
Artaxerxes I, 84
Artaxerxes II, 85
Artaxerxes III, 86
Asa, 51, 60
Asahel, 38
Ashdod, 65, 89
Asher, 24
Asherat, 27
Ashurbanipal, 66, 149
Ashuruballit II, 68
Assyrians, 61
Astarte(s), 28, 33
Athaliah, 52, 54, 61, 62
Atra-hasis Epic, 117
Avaris, 14
Avva, 57
Azekah, 70

Baal, 19, 28, 37, 40, 51, 53, 57
Baalism, 57-58
Baal-Peor, 19, 28
Baal-Shamem, 53
Baal-Zebub, 33, 54, 130
Baal-Zephon, 15
Baasha, 51, 60
Babylonian captivity, 34, 237
Bagoas, 92
Balaam, 136
bamah, 226
baru (priest), 148, 149
Baruch, 71, 228, 236, 237
Bathsheba, 39, 41, 43, 136
Beer-sheba, 12, 122
Behemoth, 276, 277
Belshazzar, 287

Benaiah, 43
bene hannebiim, 226
Benhadad, 53, 55, 60
Benjamin, 49
Bethel, 23, 26, 50, 56, 124
Beth-horon, 48
Beth-shean, 23
Beth-shemesh, 55
Betin, 23, 37
Bildad, 274, 277
birth stories, 126, 127
Blessing of Jacob, 24
Boaz, 281
Boghazköy, 8
book of the covenant, 67, 161-63
Bostra, 63
Branch, 240, 267, 268
brook of Egypt, 56
bulls, 50, 51
Buz, 277
Buzi, 241

Cain, 18
Calah, 57
Caleb, 22
Cambyses, 80
Canaanite religion, 43
Canaanites, 29, 32
Canon of Ptolemy, 44
Canticles, 100, 101, 282
Caphtor, 32
Carchemish, 68, 237
Carmel, Mount, 53, 131
census, 42
Chaldeans, 9
Chemosh, 33, 52
child sacrifice, 161-62, 244
Chronicles, book of, 39, 59, 98, 206-7, 219-22
chronicles of Gad the seer, 98; of Nathan the prophet, 98; of Samuel the seer, 98; of Shemaiah, 98; of the Seers, 220
chronology, 43-45, 72-76, 95
circumcision, 33, 240
city lists, 23
city-states, 23

clairvoyance, 242
confessions, 153-55, 227
conquest, 13-21
conversion, 240, 245
court annals, 140
covenant, 16, 26, 239; new, 240
criticism, historical and literary, 168-70
Cush, 60
Cuthah, 57
Cyrus, 79-81, 135
Cyrus Cylinder, 80, 81

D (Deuteronomic code), 173-202 (passim)
dabdu ("defeat"), 39
Dagon, 33
Damascus, 57
Dan, 25, 50
Danaoi, 25
Daniel, 134, 277, 286-89
Darius I, 80
Darius III Codomannus, 93
Darius the Mede, 134
David, 32, 36, 37, 38-43, 141, 271
dawidum, 39
day of the Lord, 227, 251, 254, 264
Debir, 23, 24
Deborah, song of, 25, 28, 29-30
Decalogue(s), 18, 159-61; cultic, 160-61; ethical, 159-60
Delaiah, 92, 93
Denyen, 25
Deutero-Isaiah, 77, 79, 80, 230, 232-34
deuteronomic code, 162-63
deuteronomist(ic), 22, 34, 218
Deuteronomistic history, 78, 142, 207
dibre hayyamim, 219
dimorphic society, 10
documentary hypothesis, newer, 172-75; newest, 177-79; older, 170-72
Dodekapropheton, 246
Dtr. *See* Deuteronomistic history

E (Elohist code), 173-202 (passim)
earthquake, 63, 252
Ebla, 8, 17
ebed Yahweh, 233-34
Ecclesiastes, 158, 283
ecstatic prophetism, 226, 242
ecstasy, 226, 227
Edom, 57, 254
Edomites, 32, 41
Eglon, 30
Ehud, 30, 136
ek, ekah, 103, 284
El, 27, 40, 47
El Bethel, 11
el elyon, 11
el olam, 11

el shadday 11
El worshipers, 11
Elah, 51
Elath, 63, 64
Eldad, 226
eleph, 16
Elephantine, 80, 92, 201
Elephantine Papyri, 224
Eliakim, 68
Eliashib, 86, 89
Elihu, 274, 277
Elijah, 28, 53, 61, 129, 130, 131
elim, 11
Eliphaz, 274, 277
Elisha, 54, 55, 129, 131, 132
Elkoshite, 259
elohim, 18
Enlil, 117
Enneateuch, 206
Enuma elish, 105, 115
Ephraim, 26, 28
epic, 115
Esarhaddon, 66, 82, 148
Esau, 10
Eshbaal, 38, 39
Esther, book of, 138, 285-86
et-Tell, 23
etiology, 118, 120, 121, 125, 139, 177, 209, 210
execration texts, Egyptian, 9, 23, 30
exodus, 13-21
Ezekiel, 70, 79, 80, 154, 156; book of, 243-44; person and time, 241-43; preaching of, 244-46
Ezion-geber, 61
Ezra (also book of), 78, 81, 84, 85-91, 206-8, 222-25
Ezra (apocryphal book), 222

fable, 119
fairy tale, 118
farewell address, elements, 143
fasting, 234
Fear of Isaac, 11, 12
Feast of the Firstfruits, 162
Feast of Tabernacles (of Ingathering), 87, 162
Feast of Unleavened Bread, 162
Five "Scrolls," 281-86
Flood, 117
form criticism, 176-77
Formgeschichte, 177
four-sources theory, 170-75, 188-98
Fundamentalism, 4

Gad, 78, 220
Gadatas, 80
Gattungen, 176, 272
Gattungsforschung, 177, 272
Geba, 60
Gedaliah, 71, 78, 79, 236, 237

genealogies, 10
Genesis, book of, 8, 9, 198-99
Gerizim, Mount, 90, 93, 201
Geschichte, 3
Gezer, 24, 45, 48
Gibbethon, 51
Gibeah, 36
Gibeon, 47
Gibeonites, 42
Gideon, 28, 30, 123, 211
Gihon spring, 66
Gilboa, 37
Gilgal, 36
Gilgamesh Epic, 105, 117
glory of the Lord, 246
Gog and Magog, 243
Goliath, 33
Goshen, 14
Grundschrift, 189

Habakkuk, 78, 116; book of, 262-63; person and time, 261-62; preaching of, 263
habiru. See Apiru
Habur River, 57
Hadad, 28, 45
Haggai, 79, 82; book of, 265; person and time, 264-65; preaching of, 265-66
hagiology, 131
Haman, 285
Hammurabi, 8, 31, 147
Hanani, 88
Hananiah, 70
Hannah (also song of), 102, 126
Hanun, 56
Haran, 9, 68
Hatti, 65, 69
Hazael, 54
Hazor, 23, 25, 48, 252
Hebrew canon, 206
Hebrew Old Testament, tripartite division, 200-202
Hebrew(s), 7, 8
Hebron, 40
Helel, 117
henotheism, 18
Herod, 32
heroic tales, 287
Hexateuch, 177, 206, 207
Hezekiah, 64-66
high places, 37
Hilkiah, 67
Hiram of Tyre, 45-46, 56
Hishai, 42
historical books, 206-25
historical-critical study of the Bible, 3
Historie, 3
historiography, 140-42
history, secular, 2
history, writing of, 4, 14

Hittites, 31
Hobab, 18-20
hokmah, 158. *See also* wisdom
Holiness Code, 162
holiness of God, 231
Holy Spirit, outpouring of, 251
holy wars of YHWH, 27, 29
Hophra, pharaoh, 70, 107
Horeb, 131
Hosea, 56, 153, 155; book of, 248-49; person and time, 247-48; preaching of, 249
Hoshea, 57
Huldah, 67
Hyksos, 14, 23
hyperbole, 132

Iddo, 220
Immanuel prophecy, 230
Inaros, 86
Ipu-Wer, admonitions of, 145-46
Isaac, 10-12, 123, 126
Isaiah, 64, 154, 155, 220; apocalypse of, 231; book of, 230-31; person and time, 229-30; preaching of, 231-32
Ishmael, 10, 123
Israel, name of, 4, 7, 15, 123
Issachar, 24

J (Yahwist), 173-202 *(passim)*
Jabesh, 35, 37
Jacob, 10-12, 123
Jael, 136
Jashar, book of, 22, 98
Jebel Barkal, stele of, 23
Jebus, 24, 31, 40
Jehoahaz, 55, 68
Jehoash, 55, 63
Jehoiachin, 69, 78
Jehoiada, 62
Jehoiakim, 68, 69
Jehoram, 52, 54, 61, 62
Jehoshaphat, 54, 61, 133, 134
Jehu, 51, 52, 54, 55, 62, 220
Jephthah, 19
Jeremiah, 68, 71, 77, 78, 126, 127, 154, 156, 255; book of, 237-39; confessions of, 237; person and time, 236-37; preaching of, 239-40
Jericho, 4
Jeroboam I, 48, 49, 50, 57, 217
Jeroboam II, 56
Jerubbaal, 211
Jerusalem, 40, 46, 77, 237
Jesse, 39
Jethro, 16, 18-19
Jezebel, 52, 53, 55
Jezreel, 54, 248
Joab, 39, 40, 43, 45
Joash, 55
Job, 158, 274-77

Joel, book of, 250-51; person and time, 250; preaching of, 251
Jonadab, 55
Jonah, book of, 138, 256; message of, 257; person and time, 255-56
Jonathan, 37, 39, 137
Joram, 54, 55, 62, 132
Joseph, 12-13, 26, 137-38
Joshua, book of, 22, 23, 208-10
Joshua, high priest, 81, 92
Joshua, judge, 25, 29, 142
Josiah, 67, 162, 237
Jotham, 63, 64, 136
Judah (and Tamar), 138-39
Judah, 24; after division of kingdom, 59-71; under Babylonian domination, 77-79; under Persian domination, 79-83; in period between Zerubbabel and Ezra, 84-85; during final century of Persian domination, 91-93
Judas Maccabeus, 134
judges, 26, 27, 29-30, 211; major, 211; minor, 211
Judges, book of, 22, 23, 30, 211-12

Kadesh, 16, 19-20
Kadesh-barnea, 19, 187
Kalhu, 7
kasdim, 262
Kebra Nagast, 46
kemarim, 67
Kenite hypothesis, 17
Kenites, 18, 121
Keret Text, 43
ketubim, 271
kingdom of peace, 227
Kings, interpretation (Heb. *midrash*) of the book of, 220
Kings, book of, 98, 206-7, 215-18
Kings of Israel, Book of the Chronicles of, 217
Kings of Israel, Book of, 220
Kings of Israel and Judah, Books of, 220
Kings of Judah, Book of the Chronicles of, 217
Kings of Judah and Israel, Books of, 220
Kings of Israel, history of, 220
Kiriath-jearim, 40
Kiriath-sepher, 23, 24
kittim, 262
Kue, 46

L *(Laienquelle),* 178
Labaya, 24
Lachish (Tell ed-Duweir), 23, 63, 70
Laish, 25
Lament(s), 103-7, 154-55

Lamentations, book of, 77, 78, 104, 284
language of Canaan, 8
law of Ezra, 90
laws, 159-63
Leah group, 26
legend, 123-35, 217-18, 257
Leontopolis, 201
letters, 144
Levi, 24, 26
Leviathan, 116, 117, 276, 277
levirate marriage, 138-39
Levites, 24, 39, 51
Libnah, 61
lions' den, 135
literary-functional approach, 185-86
literature, apocalyptic, 287; historical, 140-44; prophetic, 145-58; wisdom, 157-58
Lo-Ammi, 248
Lo-Ruhamah, 248
Lot, 10, 11
ludlul bel nemeqi, 158
Luz, 23

Maacah, 60
Maccabean war, 134
Mahanaim, 38
Malachi, 84, 90; book of, 269-70; person and time, 269; preaching of, 270
malaki, 269
Manasseh, 26
Manasseh, king, 66, 219
Manat, 78
Marah, 20
Marduk, 116
Mari, 8, 10, 29, 39, 42
Mari texts, 147-48
Martyrdom of Isaiah, 229
Massoretes, 206
Mattaniah, 69
Medad, 226
Medes, 67
medinah, 81
Megabyzus, 86-87
Megiddo, 23, 48, 68
megillah, 281
megilloth, 271
melakim, 215
Melchizedek, 11, 31
Melqart, 53
Menahem, 56
mene, tekel, peres, 287
Meni, 78
Merneptah Stele, 14-15
Merodak-Baladan, 66
Mesha Stone, 30, 31, 33, 52, 54
Meshach, 134-35
Messenger of the Covenant, 270
messenger saying, 227
Messiah, 227, 230, 245, 259, 268

Meunites, 63
Micah, 52; book of, 258-59; person and time, 257-58; preaching of, 259
Micaiah, son of Imlah, 134
Middle Bronze Age, 8
Midian, 16
Midianites, 30
midrash, 220
Migdol, 15
Mighty One of Jacob, 11, 12
Milcom, 33
minor (prophets), 246
miracle (including miraculous signs), 127, 129, 131, 214
Miriam, 20
Mischgattungen, 272
mishpatim, 161
Mizpah, 60
Mizraim, 46
Moabites, 30, 36, 55, 61, 121
Moabite stone. *See* Mesha Stone
Moloch, 33
monarchy, 212
monolatry, 18, 159
monotheism, 17
Mons Casius, 15
Mordecai, 285, 286
Moresheth, 257
morning star, 117
Moses, 5, 16-17, 29, 126, 127
Mot, 28
movement, eschatological, 221, 224; theocratic, 221, 224
muhhum, 148
Murashu Documents, 93
mysterium, 276
myth, 115

Naamah, 49, 277
Nabateans, 32
nabbaa, 226
nabi, 226
Nabopolassar, 67, 68, 69
nabu, 226
Nadab, 51
Nahash, 116, 117
Nahum, book of, 260; person and time, 259-60; preaching of, 261-62
Naomi, 281
Naphtali, 25
Nathan, 43, 77, 136, 220
Nazirite, 126, 128
Nebo, Mount, 16
Nebuchadrezzar, 32, 68, 69, 79, 134
Neco, Pharaoh, 68
Negeb, 11
Nehemiah (also book of), 81, 85, 85-91, 206-8, 222-25
Nehushtan, 66, 125
Nefer-Rohu, prophecy of, 146
neum yhwh, 227

new year, 44
Nikaso, 93
Nineveh, 68, 237, 256, 259, 260, 264
Noah, 277
noqed, 252
novelette, 137
Numbers, book of, 22
numbers, use of, 10, 16, 212, 221
Nuzi tablets, 9

Obadiah, 78; book of, 254-55; person and time, 254; preaching of, 255
Odes of Solomon, 47
Og of Bashan, 22
Oholah, 243
Oholibah, 243
Omri, 51, 52
Onomasticon of Amenemope, 47
Ophir, 46, 54, 61
Ophrah, 124
oracles, 148-49, 227
oral tradition, 183

P (Priestly code), 173-202 *(passim)*
Paddan-Aram, 9
Papyrus Anastasi I, 9
Papyrus Anastasi III, 9
Papyrus Anastasi V, 15
Papyrus Sanballat, 86
parable, 136, 257
parallelism, 113-14, 273
paralipomenon. See Chronicles, book of
Paran, Mount, 20
Passover, 15
Passover Papyrus, 80, 92
patriarchs, 7-13
Peha, 81
Pekah, 56, 57, 63
Pekahiah, 56
Peniel, 12, 50
pentapolis, 33
Pentateuch, 166-205, 206; Mosaic authorship of, 166-70; Mosaic material in, evaluation of, 186-202
Pentecost, 251, 281
Perez-uzzah, 122, 126
Persians, 67
Petra, 63
Pharisaism, 224
Philistines, 11, 23-25, 32-33, 35, 36, 40, 61
Phoenicians, 39, 48, 52
phw, 81
Pihahiroth, 15
Pithom, 15
plagues, ten, 15, 127
poetry, religious, 110-14; secular, 100-109
predictions of blessings, 150-51; concerning hostile neighbors, 152; of woe, 151-53

priestly laws, 162
priests, 39
prophecies, 150-53
prophecy of Ahijah, 98
prophecy, true and false, 134
prophet, 226
prophetic literature, of Israel, 149-58; outside Israel, 145-49
prophets, 49, 141; false, 240, 245, 258; historical stories about, 158; stories about, 227
Prophets, 226-70; Former, 206, 226; Latter, 226; Minor, 246-70
Proverbs, 158, 278-80; Egyptian collections, 157-58
Psalms, 110, 271-73; apocryphal, 273; categories, 110; dating, 112; superscriptions, 112
Psalms of Solomon, 47
Psammetichus I, 67, 260
Psammetichus II, 70
pseudepigraphy, 187
Purim, 281, 285, 286

Qarqar, 55
qinah, 103, 104, 105, 107
qoheleth, 283
queen of Sheba, 46
Qumran, 218, 262, 273, 277

Raamses, 14-15
Rabbath-ammon, 31
Rachel tribes, 16, 22
Rahab, 116, 117
Ramah, 60
Ramoth-gilead, 54, 62, 133, 134
Ramses II, 14-15
Ramses III, 25
Ras Shamra, 8, 27
Rechabites, 18, 55, 58, 121
Red Sea, 15
Rehoboam, 45, 49
Rehum, 84
remnant, 230, 232, 245
renewal, spiritual, 245
repentance, 240, 264
retribution, 274
Reuben, 24
Rezin, 56, 57
rhetorical criticism, 185
Rizpah, 38
roeh, 148
royal rules, 206
Ruth, book of, 138, 281

Saba, 46
sabbath, 90, 159, 160, 234
sabbatical year, 162
sacral league, 26
saga, 10, 119-23
salvation history, 2, 13

Samaria, 52, 57
Samaria Papyri, 92-93
Samaritans, 57, 82, 90, 200-201, 207
Samson, 25, 33, 126, 128
Samuel, 35, 37, 126, 129, 143, 220
Samuel, book of, 206-7, 213-15
Sanballat, 89
Sarah, 122-23
Sargon I, 16, 52
Sargon II, 57, 64, 65
Saul, 29, 34-38, 39
"Scrolls." See Five "Scrolls"
Sea Peoples. See Philistines
Seir, 18
Sela, 63
Sennacherib, 64, 65, 143-44, 229
Septuagint, 206, 215, 218, 219, 222, 238-39, 271
serpent, 120
servant of the Lord, 233-34
Seti, 65
seventy years, 240
Shaalbim, 24
Shabako, 65
Shadrach, 134-35
Shallum, 56, 68
Shalmaneser III, 52, 55, 64
Shalmaneser V, 57
Shamash, 111, 112
shapitu, 29
Shapitu Nahari, 28
Sheba, 42
Shechem, 24, 26, 49, 50, 201
Shelemaiah, 92
shema, 17
Shemaiah, 49, 220
sheol, 274
Shephelah, 24
Sheshbazzar, 79, 81, 82
Shield of Abraham, 11, 12
Shiloh, 26, 35, 36
Shimei, 45
Shishak, 59
shophetim. See judges
Shoshenq I, 50
shrines, 11, 12
Shuah, 277
Shunem, 24
Shur, wilderness of, 19
Sidon, 39
Sidonians, 25, 52
Sihon of Heshbon, 22
Simeon, 24
Sinai, 18, 19-20
Sinuhe, story of, 9
Sisera, 30, 136
Sitz im Buche, 185
Sitz im Leben, 176, 272

Sitz in der Literatur, 185
snake, bronze, 20
So, 57
Solomon, 32, 39, 43-44, 141, 278, 279
Solomon, Book of the Acts of, 217
Song, drinking, 100; harvest, 100; marriage and love, 100; mocking, 107; of the vineyard, 136; of victory, 102; of the watchmen, 102; work, 100
Song of Solomon. See Canticles, 282
Stoffgeschichte, 176
stories, poetic, 115-39
Succoth, 15
Sufeten, 29
suffering, 275, 276
Sumer, 9
Sumerians, 47
sun: stands still over Gibeon, 127
Syro-Ephraimite war, 57, 64

table of nations, 8
Taharqa, 65
Tammuz, 244
Tanis, 14-15
Tannin, 116, 117
tehillim, 271
tehom, 116
Tekoa, 252
Tel-abib, 241
Tell Beit Mirsim, 23
Tell ed-Duweir (Lachish), 23
Tell el-Hariri (Mari), 8
Tell el-Qedah (Hazor), 23
Tell el-Maskhuta, 15
Tell es-Sultan, 4, 23
Tell Mardikh (Ebla), 8, 17
Teman, 277
temple, 47, 80, 82, 265; new, 242, 243
temple scroll (Qumran), 201
Territorialordnung, 23
tetragrammaton, 11, 17
theocracy, 221
Thutmose III, 14, 107
Tiamat, 116
Tiglath-pileser II, 48
Tiglath-pileser III, 52, 56, 63
Timsah, Lake, 15
tirshata, 81
Tirzah, 50, 51
Tjeker, 25
Tjeku, 15
Tobiah, 89
toledoth formula, 198-99
torah, 166
tradition criticism, 180-83
transhumance, 10, 22
tribal league. See amphictyony

tribes, 24
Trito-Isaiah, 77, 233, 234
tunnel, of Hezekiah, 66
Tyre, 39

Überlieferungsgeschichtliche method, 180
Ugarit. See Ras Shamra
Upright, book of, 210
Ur of the Chaldeans, 9
Uriah, 39, 41
Ursagen, 177
Utnapishtim, 117
Uz, land of, 277
Uzziah, 63-64

valley of dry bones, 242
vanity. See Ecclesiastes
Vashti, 285
Vatersagen, 177
via maris, 15
visions, 242; of Iddo the seer, 98; of Zechariah, 266
Vulgate, 206, 222, 271

Wadi el-Arish, 56
Wadi Fara, 50
Wars of Yahweh, book of, 98
wasf, 101
Wen-Amon story, 25, 146-47
wilderness tradition, 21
wisdom, 279
Wisdom of Solomon, 47
Writings, 206, 271-89

Xerxes I, 84, 285

Yam, 28, 116, 117
Yahwism, 19, 28, 57-58
YHWH, 11, 12, 17-20, 27-28, 67

Zadok, 41, 43
Zarephath, 130
Zebulun, 24
Zechariah, king, 56
Zechariah, 62, 78, 83; book of, 266-68; person and time, 266; preaching of, 268
Zedekiah, 69-71
Zephaniah, 78; book of, 263-64; person and time, 263; preaching of, 264
Zera, 60
Zerubbabel, 79, 81, 82, 83
Zimri, 51
Zion, 232, 234
Zion, Mount, 47
Zoan, 14-15
Zophar, 274, 277